BEGINNING SOFTWARE ENGINEERING

Continues

BEGINNING

Software Engineering

BEGINNING

Software Engineering

Second Edition

Rod Stephens

WILEY

ABOUT THE AUTHOR

Rod Stephens started out as a mathematician, but while studying at MIT, he discovered how much fun programming is and he's been programming professionally ever since. He's a long-time developer, instructor, and author who has written more than 250 magazine articles and 35 books that have been translated into many different languages.

During his career, Rod has worked on an eclectic assortment of applications in such fields as telephone switching, billing, repair dispatching, tax processing, wastewater treatment, concert ticket sales, cartography, optometry, and training for professional football teams. (That's US football, not one of the kinds with the round ball. Or the kind with three downs. Or the kind with an oval field. Or the indoor kind. Let's just say NFL and leave it at that.)

Rod's popular C# Helper website (www.csharphelper.com) receives millions of hits per year and contains thousands of tips, tricks, and example programs for C# programmers. His VB Helper website (www.vb-helper.com) contains similar material for Visual Basic programmers.

You can contact Rod at RodStephens@csharphelper.com.

ABOUT THE TECHNICAL EDITOR

John Mueller is a freelance author and technical editor. He has writing in his blood, having produced 122 books and more than 600 articles to date. The topics range from networking to artificial intelligence and from database management to heads-down programming. Some of his current books include discussions of data science, machine learning, and algorithms. He also writes about computer languages such as C++, C#, and Python. His technical editing skills have helped more than 70 authors refine the content of their manuscripts. John has provided technical editing services to a variety of magazines, performed various kinds of consulting, and he writes certification exams. Be sure to read John's blog at http://blog.johnmuellerbooks.com. You can reach John on the Internet at John@JohnMuellerBooks.com. John also has a website at www.johnmuellerbooks.com.

ACKNOWLEDGMENTS

Thanks to David Clark, Christine O'Connor, Kenyon Brown, Judy Flynn, Barath Kumar Rajasekaran, and all of the others who worked so hard to make this book possible. David was this book's project manager. You'll learn what a project manager does in Chapter 4. It's a bit different for writing a book but not as different as you might think. Many thanks for your hard work, David!

Thanks also to technical editor and longtime friend John Mueller for giving me the benefit of his valuable experience. You can see what John's up to at www.johnmuellerbooks.com.

Special thanks to Mary Brodie at https://gearmark.blogs.com for letting me use her quote at the beginning of Chapter 18, "Iterative Models."

CONTENTS

PART III: ADVANCED TOPICS

INTRODUCTION

Programming today is a race between software engineers striving to build bigger and better idiot-proof programs, and the universe trying to build bigger and better idiots. So far the universe is winning.

—*Rick Cook*

With modern development tools, it's easy to sit down at the keyboard and bang out a working program with no previous design or planning, and that's fine under some circumstances. My VB Helper (www.vb-helper.com) and C# Helper (www.csharphelper.com) websites contain thousands of example programs written in Visual Basic and C#, respectively, and built using exactly that approach. I had an idea (or someone asked me a question) and I pounded out a quick example.

Those types of programs are fine if you're the only one using them and then for only a short while. They're also okay if, as on my websites, they're intended only to demonstrate a programming technique and they never leave the confines of the programming laboratory.

If this kind of slap-dash program escapes into the wild, however, the result can be disastrous. At best, nonprogrammers who use these programs quickly become confused. At worst, they can wreak havoc on their computers and even on those of their friends and coworkers.

Even experienced developers sometimes run afoul of these half-baked programs. I know someone (I won't give names, but I also won't say it wasn't me) who wrote a simple recursive script to delete the files in a directory hierarchy. Unfortunately, the script recursively climbed its way to the top of the directory tree and then started cheerfully deleting every file in the system. The script ran for only about five seconds before it was stopped, but it had already trashed enough files that the operating system had to be reinstalled from scratch. (Actually, some developers believe reinstalling the operating system every year or so is character-building. If you agree, then perhaps this approach isn't so bad.)

I know another experienced developer who, while experimenting with Windows system settings, managed to set every system color to black. The result was a black cursor over a black desktop, displaying black windows with black borders, menus, and text. This person (who wasn't me this time) eventually managed to fix things by rebooting and using another computer that wasn't color-impaired to walk through the process of fixing the settings using only keyboard accelerators. It was a triumph of cleverness, but I suspect she would have rather skipped the whole episode and had her two wasted days back.

For programs that are more than a few dozen lines long, or that will be given to unsuspecting end users, this kind of free-spirited development approach simply won't do. To produce applications that are effective, safe, and reliable, you can't just sit down and start typing. You need a plan. You need . . . <drumroll> . . . software engineering.

This book describes software engineering. It explains what software engineering is and how it helps produce applications that are effective, flexible, and robust enough for use in real-world situations.

This book won't make you an expert systems analyst, software architect, project manager, or programmer, but it explains what those people do and why they are necessary for producing high-quality software. It also gives you the tools that you need to start. You won't rush out and lead a 1,000-person effort to build a new air traffic control system for the FAA, but it can help you work effectively in small-scale and large-scale development projects. (It can also help you understand what a prospective employer means when he says, "Yeah, we mostly use scrum with a few extra XP techniques thrown in.")

WHAT IS SOFTWARE ENGINEERING?

A formal definition of software engineering might sound something like, "An organized, analytical approach to the design, development, use, and maintenance of software."

More intuitively, software engineering is everything that you need to do to produce successful software. It includes the steps that take a raw, possibly nebulous idea and turn it into a powerful and intuitive application that can be enhanced to meet changing customer needs for years to come.

You might be tempted to restrict software engineering to mean only the beginning of the process, when you perform the application's design. After all, an aerospace engineer designs planes but doesn't build them or tack on a second passenger cabin if the first one becomes full. (Although I guess a space shuttle riding piggyback on a 747 sort of achieved that goal.)

One of the big differences between software engineering and aerospace engineering (or most other kinds of engineering) is that software isn't physical. It exists only in the virtual world of the computer. That means it's easy to make changes to any part of a program even after it is completely written. In contrast, if you wait until a bridge is finished and then tell your structural engineer that you've decided to add two extra lanes and lift it three feet higher above the water, there's a good chance he'll cackle wildly and offer you all sorts of creative but impractical suggestions for exactly what you can do with your two extra lanes.

The flexibility granted to software by its virtual nature is both a blessing and a curse. It's a blessing because it lets you refine the program during development to better meet user needs, add new features to take advantage of opportunities discovered during implementation, and make modifications to meet evolving business requirements. Some applications even allow users to write scripts to perform new tasks never envisioned by the developers. That type of flexibility isn't possible in other types of engineering.

Unfortunately, the flexibility that allows you to make changes throughout a software project's life cycle also lets you mess things up at any point during development. Adding a new feature can break existing code or turn a simple, elegant design into a confusing mess. Constantly adding, removing, and modifying features during development can make it impossible for different parts of the system to work together. In some cases, it can even make it impossible to tell when the project is finished.

Because software is so malleable, design decisions can be made at any point up to the end of the project. Actually, successful applications often continue to evolve long after the initial release. Microsoft Word, for example, has been evolving for roughly 40 years, sometimes for the better, sometimes for the worse. (If you don't remember Clippy, search online to learn the tragic tale.)

The fact that changes can come at any time means that you need to consider the whole development process as a single, long, complex task. You can't simply "engineer" a great design, turn the programmers loose on it, and ride off into the sunset wrapped in the warm glow of a job well done. The biggest design decisions may come early, and software development certainly has stages, but those stages are linked, so you need to consider them all together.

WHY IS SOFTWARE ENGINEERING IMPORTANT?

Producing a software application is relatively simple in concept: Take an idea and turn it into a useful program. Unfortunately for projects of any real scope, there are countless ways that a simple concept can go wrong. Programmers may not understand what users want or need (which may be two separate things), so they build the wrong application. The program might be so full of bugs that it's frustrating to use, impossible to fix, and can't be enhanced over time. The program could be completely effective but so confusing that you need a PhD in puzzle-solving to use it. An absolutely perfect application could even be killed by internal business politics or market forces.

Software engineering includes techniques for avoiding the many pitfalls that otherwise might send your project down the road to failure. It ensures that the final application is effective, usable, and maintainable. It helps you meet milestones on schedule and produce a finished project on time and within budget. Perhaps most importantly, software engineering gives you the flexibility to make changes to meet unexpected demands without completely obliterating your schedule and budget constraints.

In short, software engineering lets you control what otherwise might seem like a random whirlwind of chaos.

WHO SHOULD READ THIS BOOK?

Everyone involved in any software development effort should have a basic understanding of software engineering. Whether you're an executive customer specifying the software's purpose and features, an end user who will eventually spend time working with (and reporting bugs in) the finished application, a lead developer who keeps other programmers on track (and not playing too much *Minecraft*), or the guy who fetches donuts for the weekly meeting, you need to understand how all of the pieces of the process fit together. A failure by any of these people (particularly the donut wallah) affects everyone else, so it's essential that everyone knows the warning signs that indicate the project may be veering toward disaster.

This book is mainly intended for people with limited experience in software engineering. It doesn't expect you to have any previous experience with software development, project management, or programming. (I suspect most readers will have some experience with donuts, but that's not necessary either.)

Even if you have some familiarity with those topics, particularly programming, you may still find this book informative. Most software developers focus primarily on one piece of the puzzle and don't really understand the rest of the process. It's worth learning how the pieces interact to help guide the project toward success.

This book does not explain how to program. It does explain some techniques programmers can use to produce code that is flexible enough to handle the inevitable change requests, is easy to debug (at least your code will be), and is easy to enhance and maintain in the future (more change requests), but they are described in general terms and don't require you to know how to program.

If you don't work in a programming role—for example, if you're an end user or a project manager—you'll hopefully find that material interesting even if you don't use it directly. You may also find some techniques that are surprisingly applicable to nonprogramming problems. For example, techniques for generating problem-solving approaches apply to all sorts of problems, not just programming decisions. (You can also ask developers, "Are you using assertions and gray-box testing methods before unit testing?" just to see if they understand what you're talking about. Basically, you're using gray-box testing to see if the developers know what gray-box testing is. You'll learn more about that in Chapter 13, "Testing.")

APPROACH

This book is divided into three parts. The first part describes the basic tasks that you need to complete and deliver useful software, things such as design, programming, and testing. The book's second part describes some common software process models that use different techniques to perform those tasks.

The third and final part of the book contains two bonus chapters, "Software Ethics" and "Future Trends," that provide useful information for any software developer but that didn't fit in well with the earlier parts of the book. After those come the Appendix, which contains the answers to the chapters' exercises, and the Glossary.

Before you can begin to work on a software development project, however, you need to do some preparation. You need to set up tools and techniques that help you track your progress throughout the project. If you don't keep track of your progress, it's shockingly easy to fall hopelessly far behind. Chapter 1, "Software Engineering from 20,000 Feet," provides a high-level overview. Chapter 2, "Before the Beginning," and Chapter 3, "The Team," describe some of the other setup tasks that you need to start before the more concrete development can really get rolling.

After you have the preliminaries in place, there are many approaches that you can take to produce software. All of those approaches have the same goal (making useful software), so they must handle roughly the same tasks. These are things such as gathering requirements, building a plan, and actually writing the code. The first part of this book describes these tasks. Chapter 1 explains those tasks at a high level. Chapters 4 through 16 provide additional details about what these tasks are and how you can accomplish them effectively.

The second part of the book describes some of the more popular software development approaches. All of these models address the same issues described in the earlier chapters but in different ways.

Some focus on predictability so that you know exactly what features will be provided and when. Others focus on creating the most features as quickly as possible, even if that means straying from the original design. Chapters 17 through 19 describe some of the most popular of these development models.

Chapter 20 discusses software ethics. Software presents some unique ethical dilemmas and artificial intelligence (AI) provides a framework for some situations that are interesting if somewhat unlikely. Finally, in Chapter 21, I make some (probably foolish) predictions about software engineering trends.

That's the basic path this book gives you for learning software engineering. First learn the tasks that you need to complete to deliver useful software. Next, learn how different models handle those tasks. Then finish with some more thoughtful material.

However, many people have trouble learning by slogging through a tedious enumeration of facts. (I certainly do!) To make the information a bit easier to absorb, this book includes a few other elements.

Each chapter ends with exercises that you can use to see if you were paying attention while you read the chapter. I don't like exercises that merely ask you to repeat what is in the chapter. (Quick, what are some advantages and disadvantages of the ethereal nature of software?) Most of the exercises ask you to expand on the chapter's main ideas. Hopefully, they'll make you think about new ways to use what's explained in the chapters.

Sometimes, the exercises are the only way I could sneak some more information into the chapter that didn't quite fit in any of its sections. In those cases, the questions and the answers provided in the Appendix are more like extended digressions and thought experiments than quiz questions.

I strongly recommend that you at least skim the exercises and think about them. Then ask yourself if you understand the solutions. All of the solutions are included in the Appendix.

WHAT THIS BOOK COVERS (AND WHAT IT DOESN'T)

This book describes software engineering, the tasks that you must perform to successfully complete a software project, and some of the most popular developer models that you can use to try to achieve your goals. It doesn't cover every last detail, but it does explain the overall process so that you can figure out how you fit into the process.

This book does not explain every possible development model. Actually, it barely scratches the surface of the dozens (possibly hundreds) of models that are in use in the software industry. This book describes only some of the most popular development approaches and then only relatively briefly.

If you decide that you want to learn more about a particular approach, you can turn to the hundreds of books and thousands of web pages written about specific models. Many development models also have their own organizations with websites dedicated to their promotion. For example, see www .extremeprogramming.org, https://agilemanifesto.org, and www.scrum.org.

This book also isn't an exhaustive encyclopedia of software development tricks and tips. It describes some general ideas and concepts that make it easier to build robust software, but its focus is on higher-level software engineering issues, so it doesn't have room to cover all of the clever techniques that developers use to make programs better. This book also doesn't focus on a specific programming language, so it can't take advantage of language-specific tools or techniques.

WHAT TOOLS DO YOU NEED?

You don't need any tools to read this book. All you need is the ability to read the book. (And perhaps reading glasses. Or perhaps a text-to-speech tool if you have an electronic version that you want to "read" while driving. Or perhaps a friend to read it to you. Okay, I guess you have several options.)

To actually participate in a development effort, you may need a lot of tools. If you're working on a small, one-person project, you might need only a programming environment such as Jupyter Notebook, Visual Studio, Eclipse, RAD Studio, or whatever. For larger team efforts, you'll also need tools for project management, documentation (word processors), change tracking, software revision tracking, and more. And, of course, you'll need other developers to help you. This book describes these tools, but you certainly don't need them to read the book.

> **NOTE** For anyone who's adopted the book as part of teaching a software engineering course, I've provided instructor supplemental materials (ISM) that you can use. Go to the book details page. Click the "Related Resources" link (or scroll down the page) to navigate to the "View Instructor Companion Site" link. Click the link to open the Instructor Companion Site page. To access and download the ISM, you'll need to sign in to request them. If you don't have a Wiley account, you'll need to sign up to create one.

CONVENTIONS

To help you get the most from the text and keep track of what's happening, I've used several conventions throughout the book.

> ### SPLENDID SIDEBARS
>
> Sidebars such as this one contain additional information and side topics.

> **WARNING** Boxes like this one hold important information that is directly relevant to the surrounding text. There are a lot of ways a software project can fail, so these warn you about "worst practices" that you should avoid.

> **NOTE** *These boxes indicate notes, tips, hints, tricks, and asides to the current discussion. They look like this.*

As for styles in the text:

➤ Important words are *highlighted* when they are introduced.

➤ Keyboard strokes are shown like this: Ctrl+A. This one means you should hold down the Ctrl key (or Control or CTL or whatever it's labeled on your keyboard) and press the A key.

➤ This book includes little actual program code because I don't know what programming languages you use (if any). When there is code, it is formatted like the following:

```
// Return true if a and b are relatively prime.
private bool AreRelativelyPrime(int a, int b)
{
    // Only 1 and -1 are relatively prime to 0.
    if (a == 0) return ((b == 1) || (b == -1));
    if (b == 0) return ((a == 1) || (a == -1));
    int gcd = GCD(a, b);
    return ((gcd == 1) || (gcd == -1));
}
```

(Don't worry if you can't understand a particular piece of code. The text explains what it does.)

➤ Filenames, URLs, and the occasional piece of code within the text are shown like this: www .csharphelper.com.

ERRATA

I've done my best to avoid errors in this book, and this book has passed through the word processors of a small army of editors and technical reviewers. However, no nontrivial project is ever completely without mistakes. (That's one of the more important lessons in this book.) The best I can hope for is that any remaining errors are small enough that they don't distract you from the meaning of the text.

If you find an error in one of my books (like a spelling mistake, broken piece of code, or something that just doesn't make sense), I would be grateful for your feedback. Sending in errata may save other readers hours of frustration. At the same time, you'll be helping me provide even higher quality information.

To find the errata page for this book, go to www.wiley.com and search for the book. Then, on the book details page, click the Errata link. On this page you can view all of the errata submitted for this book.

If you don't spot "your" error on the Book Errata page, please email it to our Customer Service Team at wileysupport@wiley.com with the subject line "Possible Book Errata Submission."

IMPORTANT URLs

Here's a summary of important URLs related to this book:

➤ RodStephens@CSharpHelper.com—My email address. I hope to hear from you!

➤ www.CSharpHelper.com—My C# website, which contains thousands of tips, tricks, and examples for C# developers.

➤ www.vb-helper.com—My Visual Basic website, which contains thousands of tips, tricks, and examples for Visual Basic developers.

CONTACTING THE AUTHOR

If you have questions, suggestions, comments, just want to say hi, want to exchange cookie recipes, or whatever, email me at RodStephens@CSharpHelper.com. I can't promise that I'll be able to help you with every problem, but I do promise to try. (And I have some pretty good cookie recipes.)

DISCLAIMER

Software engineering isn't always the most exciting topic, so in an attempt to keep you awake, I picked some of the examples in this book for interest or humorous effect. (If you keep this book on your nightstand as a last-ditch insomnia remedy, then I've failed.)

I mean no disrespect to any of the many talented software engineers out there who work long weeks (despite the call for sustainable work levels) to produce top-quality applications for their customers. (As for the untalented software engineers out there, their work can speak for them better than I can.)

I also don't mean to discount any of the development models described in this book or the people who worked on or with them. Every one of them represents a huge amount of work and research, and all of them have their places in software engineering, past or present.

Because this book has limited space, I had to leave out many software development methodologies and programming best practices. Even the methodologies that *are* described are not covered in full detail because there just isn't room.

Finally, I mean no disrespect to people named Fred, or anyone else for that matter. (Except for one particular Fred, who I'm sure retired from software development long ago.)

So get out your reading glasses, grab your favorite caffeinated beverage, and prepare to enter the world of software engineering. Game on!

PART I
Software Engineering Step-by-Step

➤ **CHAPTER 15:** Metrics

➤ **CHAPTER 16:** Maintenance

Software and cathedrals are much the same. First we build them, then we pray.

—*Samuel Redwine*

In principle, software engineering is a simple two-step process: (1) Write a best-selling program, and then (2) buy expensive toys with the profits. Unfortunately, the first step can be rather difficult. Saying "write a best-selling program" is a bit like telling an author, "Write a best-selling book," or telling a baseball player "triple to left." It's a great idea, but knowing the goal doesn't actually help you achieve it.

To produce great software, you need to handle a huge number of complicated tasks, any one of which can fail and sink the entire project. Over the years people have developed a multitude of methodologies and techniques to help keep software projects on track. Some of these, such as the *waterfall* and *V-model* approaches, use detailed requirement specifications to exactly define the desired results before development begins. Others, such as *Scrum* and *agile techniques,* rely on fast-paced incremental development with frequent feedback to keep a project on track. Still other techniques, such as cowboy coding and extreme programming, sound more like action-adventure films than software development techniques. (I'll say more about these in Part II, "Process Models.")

Different development methodologies use different approaches, but they all perform roughly the same tasks. They all determine what the software should do and how it should do it. They generate the software, remove bugs from the code (some of the bugs, at least), make sure the software does more or less what it should, and deploy the finished result.

> **NOTE** I call these basic items "tasks" and not "stages" or "steps" because different software engineering approaches tackle them in different ways and at different times. Calling them "stages" or "steps" would probably be misleading because it would imply that all projects move through the stages in the same predictable order and that's not true.

The chapters in the first part of this book describe those basic tasks that any successful software project must handle in some way. They explain the main steps in software development and describe some of the myriad ways a project can fail to handle those tasks. (The second part of the book explains how different approaches such as waterfall and agile handle those tasks.)

The first chapter in this part of the book provides an overview of software development from a high level. The subsequent chapters explain the pieces of the development process in greater detail.

1

Software Engineering from 20,000 Feet

> If you fail to plan, you are planning to fail.
>
> —*Benjamin Franklin*

> There are two ways of constructing a software design. One way is to make it so simple that there are obviously no deficiencies. The other way is to make it so complicated that there are no obvious deficiencies. The first method is far more difficult.
>
> —*C.A.R. Hoare*

What You Will Learn in This Chapter:

➤ The basic steps required for successful software engineering

➤ Ways in which software engineering differs from other kinds of engineering

➤ How fixing one bug can lead to others

➤ Why it is important to detect mistakes as early as possible

In many ways, software engineering is a lot like other kinds of engineering. Whether you're building a bridge, an airplane, a nuclear power plant, or a new and improved version of Sudoku, you need to accomplish certain tasks. For example, you need to make a plan, follow that plan, heroically overcome unexpected obstacles, and hire a great band to play at the ribbon-cutting ceremony.

The following sections describe the steps you need to take to keep a software engineering project on track. These are more or less the same for any large project, although there are some important differences that are specific to software engineering. Later chapters in this book provide a lot more detail about these tasks.

REQUIREMENTS GATHERING

No big project can succeed without a plan. Sometimes a project doesn't follow the plan closely, but every big project must have a plan. The plan tells project members what they should be doing, when and how long they should be doing it, and most important, what the project's goals are. They give the project direction.

One of the first steps in a software project is figuring out the requirements. You need to find out what the customers want and what the customers need. Depending on how well-defined the user's needs are, this chore can be time-consuming.

WHO'S THE CUSTOMER?

Sometimes, it's easy to tell who the customer is. If you're writing software for another part of your own company, it may be obvious who the customers are. In that case, you can sit down with them and talk about what the software should do.

In other cases, you may have only a vague notion of who will use the finished software. For example, if you're creating a new online card game, it may be hard to identify the customers until after you start marketing the game.

Sometimes, *you* may even be the customer. I write software for myself all the time. This has a lot of advantages. For example, I know exactly what I want (usually) and I know more or less how hard it will be to provide different features. (Unfortunately, I also sometimes have a hard time saying no to myself, so projects can drag on for a lot longer than they should.)

In any project, you should try to identify your customers and interact with them as much as possible so that you can design the most useful application possible.

After you determine the customers' wants and needs (which are not always the same), you can turn them into requirements documents. Those documents tell the customers what they will be getting, and they tell the project members what they will be building.

> **NOTE** *I refer to requirements a lot in this book. In general, when I say require-ments, I mean the officially sanctioned requirements as recorded in the requirements documents and later carved in marble on the project's memorial. Anything else (such as customer suggestions, developer complaints, and management wishful thinking) are not part of the requirements until they are approved by the powers that be.*

Throughout the project, both customers and team members can refer to the requirements to see if the project is heading in the right direction. If someone suggests that the project should include a video tutorial, you can see if that was included in the requirements. If this is a new feature, you might allow that change if it would be useful and wouldn't mess up the rest of the schedule. If that request doesn't make sense, either because it wouldn't add value to the project or you can't do it with the time you have, then you may need to defer it for a later release.

CHANGE HAPPENS

Although there are some similarities between software and other kinds of engineering, the fact that software doesn't exist in any physical way means there are some major differences as well. Because software is so malleable, users frequently ask for new features up to the day before the release party. They ask developers to shorten schedules and request last-minute changes such as switching database platforms or even hardware platforms. (Yes, both of those have happened to me.) "The program is just 0s and 1s," they reason. "The 0s and 1s don't care whether they run on an Android tablet or an iPhone, do they?"

In contrast, a company wouldn't ask an architectural firm to move a new convention center across the street at the last minute; a city transportation authority wouldn't ask the builder to add an extra lane to a freeway bridge right after it opens; and no one would try to insert an atrium level at the bottom of a newly completed 90-story building.

HIGH-LEVEL DESIGN

After you know the project's requirements, you can start working on the high-level design. The high-level design includes such things as decisions about what platform to use (such as desktop, laptop, tablet, or phone), what data design to use (such as direct access, 2-tier, or 3-tier), and what interfaces with other systems to use (such as external purchasing systems or a payroll system hosted in the cloud).

The high-level design should also include information about the project architecture at a relatively high level. You should break the project into the large chunks that handle the project's major areas of functionality. Depending on your approach, this may include a list of the modules that you need to build or a list of families of classes.

For example, suppose you're building a system to manage the results of ostrich races. You might decide the project needs the following major pieces:

➤ Database (to hold the data)

➤ Classes (for example, Race, Ostrich, Jockey, and Wager classes)

➤ User interfaces (to enter Ostrich and Jockey data, enter race results, calculate odds, produce result reports, and create new races)

➤ External interfaces (to send information and spam to participants and fans via email, text message, voicemail, pager, carrier pigeon, and anything else we can think of)

You should make sure the high-level design covers every aspect of the requirements. It should specify what the pieces do and how they should interact, but it should include as few details as possible about *how* the pieces do their jobs.

TO DESIGN OR NOT TO DESIGN, THAT IS THE QUESTION

At this point, fans of extreme programming, Scrum, and other incremental development approaches may be rolling their eyes, snorting in derision, and muttering about how they don't need high-level designs.

Let's defer this argument until Chapter 6, "High-Level Design," which talks about high-level design in greater detail. For now, I'll just claim that every design methodology needs design, even if it doesn't come in the form of a giant written design specification carved into a block of marble.

LOW-LEVEL DESIGN

After your high-level design breaks the project into pieces, you can assign those pieces to groups within the project so they can work on low-level designs. The low-level design includes information about *how* that piece of the project should work. The design doesn't need to give every last nitpicky detail necessary to implement the project's major pieces, but it should give enough guidance to the developers who will implement those pieces.

For example, the ostrich racing application's database piece would include an initial design for the database. It should sketch out the tables that will hold the race, ostrich, and jockey information using proper first, second, and third normal forms. (You can argue about whether it needs higher levels of normalization.)

At this point you will also discover interactions between the different pieces of the project that may require changes here and there. For example, while working on the ostrich project's external interfaces, you may decide to add a new table to hold email, text messaging, and other information for fans. Or you may find that the printing module will be easier if you add a new stored procedure to the database design.

DEVELOPMENT

After you've created the high- and low-level designs, it's time for the programmers to get to work. (Actually, the programmers should have been hard at work gathering requirements, creating the high-level designs, and refining them into low-level designs, but development is the part that many programmers enjoy the most, so that's often where they think the "real" work begins.) The programmers continue refining the low-level designs until they know how to implement those designs in code.

(In fact, in one of my favorite development techniques, you basically just keep refining the design to give more and more detail until it would be easier to just write the code instead. Then you do exactly that.)

As the programmers write the code, they test it to make sure it doesn't contain any bugs.

At this point, any experienced developers should be snickering if not actually laughing out loud. It's a programming axiom that no nontrivial program is completely bug-free. So let me rephrase the previous paragraph.

As the programmers write the code, they test it to find and remove as many bugs as they reasonably can.

TESTING

Effectively testing your own code is extremely hard. If you just wrote the code, you obviously didn't insert bugs intentionally. If you knew there was a bug in the code, you would have fixed it before you wrote it. That idea often leads programmers to assume their code is correct (I guess they're just naturally optimistic), so they don't always test it as thoroughly as they should.

Even if a particular piece of code is thoroughly tested and contains no (or few) bugs, there's no guarantee that it will work properly with the other parts of the system.

One way to address both of these problems (developers don't test their own code well and the pieces may not work together) is to perform different kinds of tests. First developers test their own code. Then testers who didn't write the code test it. After a piece of code seems to work properly, it is integrated into the rest of the project, and the whole thing is tested to see if the new code broke anything.

Any time a test fails, the programmers dive back into the code to figure out what's going wrong and how to fix it. After any repairs, the code goes back into the queue for retesting.

A SWARM OF BUGS

At this point you may wonder why you need to retest the code. After all, you just fixed it, right?

Unfortunately, fixing a bug often creates a new bug. Sometimes the bug fix is incorrect. Other times it breaks another piece of code that depended on the original buggy behavior. In that case, the known bug hides an unknown bug.

Still other times the programmer might change some correct behavior to a different correct behavior without realizing that some other code depended on the original correct behavior. (Imagine if someone switched the arrangement of your hot- and cold-water faucets. Either arrangement would work just fine, but you may get a nasty surprise the next time you take a shower.)

Anytime you change the code, whether by adding new code or fixing old code, you need to test it to make sure everything works as it should.

Unfortunately, you can never be certain that you've caught every bug. If you run your tests and don't find anything wrong, that doesn't mean there are no bugs; it just means you haven't found them. As programming pioneer Edsger W. Dijkstra said, "Testing shows the presence, not the absence of bugs." (This issue can become philosophical. If a bug is never detected, is it still a bug?)

The best you can do is test and fix bugs until they occur at an acceptably low rate. If bugs don't bother users too frequently or too severely when they do occur, then you're ready to move on to deployment.

COUNTING BUGS

Suppose requirements gathering, high-level design, low-level design, and development works like this: Every time you make a decision, the next task in the sequence includes two more decisions that depend on the first one. For example, when you make a requirements decision, the high-level design includes two decisions that depend on it. (This isn't exactly the way it works, but it's not as ridiculous as you might wish.)

Now suppose you made a mistake during requirements gathering. (The customer said the application had to support 30 users with a 5-second response time, but you heard 5 users with a 30-second response time.)

If you detect the error during the requirements gathering phase, you need to fix only that one error. But how many incorrect decisions could depend on that one mistake if you don't discover the problem until after development is complete?

The one mistake in requirements gathering leads to two decisions in high-level design that could be incorrect.

Each of the two possible mistakes in high-level design leads to two new decisions in low-level design that could also be wrong, giving a total of 2 × 2 = 4 possible mistakes in low-level design.

Each of the four suspicious low-level design decisions lead to two more decisions during development, giving a total of 4 × 2 = 8 possible mistakes during development.

Adding up all the mistakes in requirements gathering, high-level design, low-level design, and development gives a total of 1 + 2 + 4 + 8 = 15 possible mistakes. Figure 1.1 shows how the potential mistakes propagate.

Requirements
High-level Design
Low-level Design
Development

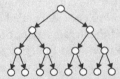

FIGURE 1.1: The circles represent possible mistakes at different stages of development. One early mistake can lead to many later mistakes.

To make matters worse, you usually won't know that all of these decisions were related. Just because you find some of the 15 bugs doesn't mean you'll know that the others exist.

In this example, you have 15 times as many decisions to track down, examine, and possibly fix than you would have if you had discovered the mistake right away during requirements gathering. That leads to one of the most important rules of software engineering:

The longer a bug remains undetected, the harder it is to fix.

Some people think of testing as something you do after the fact to verify that the code you wrote is correct. Actually, testing is critical at every stage of development to ensure the resulting application is usable.

DEPLOYMENT

Ideally, you roll out your software, the users are overjoyed, and everyone lives happily ever after. If you've built a new variant of Tetris and you release it on the Internet, your deployment may actually be that simple.

Often, however, things don't go so smoothly. Deployment can be difficult, time-consuming, and expensive. For example, suppose you've written a new billing system to track payments from your company's millions of customers. Deployment might involve any or all of the following:

➤ New computers for the backend database

➤ A new network

➤ New computers for the users

➤ User training

➤ On-site support while the users get to know the new system

➤ Parallel operations while some users get to know the new system and other users keep using the old system

➤ Special data maintenance chores to keep the old and new databases synchronized

➤ Massive bug fixing when the 250 users discover dozens or hundreds of bugs that testing didn't uncover

➤ Other nonsense that no one could possibly predict

WHO COULD HAVE PREDICTED?

I worked on one project that assigned repair people to fix customer problems for a phone company. Twice during live testing, the system assigned someone to work at his ex-wife's house. Fortunately, the repair people involved recognized the address and asked their supervisors to override the assignments.

If psychics were more consistent, it would be worth adding one to every software project to anticipate these sorts of bizarre problems. Failing that or a working crystal ball, you should allow some extra time in the project schedule to handle these sorts of completely unexpected complications.

MAINTENANCE

As soon as the users start pounding away on your software, they'll find bugs. (This is another software axiom. Bugs that were completely hidden from testers appear the instant users touch the application.)

Of course, when the users find bugs, you need to fix them. As mentioned earlier, fixing a bug sometimes leads to another bug, so now you get to fix that one as well.

If your application is successful, users will use it a lot. More than one billion people use Microsoft Office products. Imagine the amount of involuntary testing they perform! Even if you spend thousands of hours testing, users are likely to find bugs that you missed.

Users also think up a slew of enhancements, improvements, and new features that they want added immediately. This is the kind of problem every software developer wants to have: customers that like an application so much, they're clamoring for more. It's the goal of every software engineering project, but it does mean more work.

WRAP-UP

At this point in the process, you're probably ready for a break. You've put in long hours of planning, design, development, and testing. You've found bugs you didn't expect, and the users are keeping you busy with bug reports and change requests. You want nothing more than a nice, long vacation.

There's one more important thing you should do before you jet off to Cancún: You need to perform a postmortem. You need to evaluate the project and decide what went right and what went wrong. You need to figure out how to make the things that went well occur more often in the future. Conversely, you need to determine how to prevent the things that went badly in the future.

Right after the project's completion, many developers don't feel like going through this exercise, but it's important to do right away before everyone forgets any lessons that you can learn from the project.

EVERYTHING ALL AT ONCE

Several famous people have said, "Time is nature's way to keep everything from happening all at once." Unfortunately, time doesn't work that way in software engineering. Depending on how big the project is and how the tasks are distributed, many of the basic tasks overlap—and sometimes in big ways.

Suppose you're building a huge application that's vital to national security interests. For example, suppose you want to optimize national energy drink ordering, distribution, and consumption. This is a big problem. (Really, it is.) You might have some ideas about how to start, but there are a lot of details that you'll need to work out to build the best possible solution. You'll probably need to spend quite a while studying existing operations to develop the user requirements.

You could spend several weeks peppering the customers with questions while the rest of the development team plays *Mario Kart* and consumes the drinks you're studying, but that would be inefficient.

A better use of everyone's time would be to put people to work with as much of the project that is ready to roll at any given moment. Several people can work with the customers to define the requirements. This takes more coordination than having a single person gather requirements, but on big projects it can still save you a lot of time.

After you think you understand some of the requirements, other team members can start working on high-level designs to satisfy them. They'll probably make more mistakes than they would if you waited until the requirements are finished, but you'll get things done sooner.

As the project progresses, the focus of work moves down through the basic project tasks. For example, as requirements gathering nears completion, you should finalize the high-level designs so team members can move on to low-level designs and possibly even some programming.

Meanwhile, throughout the entire project, testers can try to shoot holes in things. As parts of the application are finished, they can try different scenarios to make sure the application can handle them.

Depending on the testers' skills, they can even test things such as the designs and the requirements. Of course, they can't run the requirements through a compiler to see if the computer can make sense of them. They can, however, look for situations that aren't covered by the requirements. ("What if a shipment of Quickstart Energy Drink is delayed, but the customer is on a cruise ship and just crossed the international date line? Is the shipment still considered late?")

Sometimes tasks also flow backward. For example, problems during development may result from a problem with the design or even the requirements. The farther back a correction needs to flow, the greater its impact. Remember the earlier example where every problem caused two more? The requirements problem you discovered during development could lead to a whole assortment of other undiscovered bugs. In the worst case, testing of "finished" code may reveal fundamental flaws in the early designs and even the requirements.

REQUIREMENT REPAIRS

The first project I worked on was an inventory system for NAVSPECWARGRU. (That stands for Navy Special Warfare Group, basically the Navy SEALs. SEALs stands for SEa, Air, and Land. The military sure does love its acronyms!) The application lets you define equipment packages for various activities and then lets team members check out whatever was necessary. (Sort of the way a Boy Scouts quartermaster does this. For this campout, you'll need a tent, bedroll, canteen, cooking gear, and M79 grenade launcher.)

Anyway, while I was building one of the screens, I realized that the requirements specifications and high-level design didn't include any method for team members to return equipment when they were done with it. In a matter of weeks, the quartermaster's warehouse would be empty and the barracks would be packed to the rafters with ghillie suits and snorkels!

This was a fairly small project, so it was easy to fix. I told the project manager, he whipped up a design for an inventory return screen, and I built it. That kind of quick correction isn't possible for every project, particularly not for large ones, but in this case the whole fix took approximately an hour.

In addition to overlapping and flowing backward, the basic tasks are also sometimes handled in very different ways. Some development models rely on a specification that's extremely detailed and rigid. Others use specifications that change so fluidly it's hard to know whether they use any specification at all. Iterative approaches even repeat the same basic tasks many times to build ever-improving versions of the final application. The chapters in the second part of this book discuss some of the most popular of those sorts of development approaches.

SUMMARY

All software engineering projects must handle the same basic tasks. Different development models may handle them in different ways, but they're all hidden in there somewhere.

In fact, the strengths and weaknesses of various development models depend in a large part on how they handle these tasks. For example, agile methods and test-driven development use frequent builds to force developers to perform a lot of tests early on so that they can catch bugs as quickly as possible. (For a preview of why that's important, see the "Counting Bugs" example earlier in this chapter and Exercise 4.)

The chapters in Part II, "Process Models," describe some of the most common development models. Meanwhile, the following chapters describe the basic software engineering tasks in greater detail. Before you delve into the complexities of requirements gathering, however, there are a few things you should consider.

The next chapter explains some basic tools that you should have in place before you consider a new project. Chapter 3 talks about how to assemble a project team, and Chapter 4 discusses project management tools and techniques that can help you keep your project on track.

EXERCISES

1. What are the basic tasks that all software engineering projects must handle?

2. Give a one-sentence description of each of the tasks you listed for Exercise 1.

3. I have a few customers who do their own programming, but they occasionally get stuck and need a few pointers or a quick example program. A typical project runs through the following stages:

    a. The customer sends me an email describing the problem.

    b. I reply telling what I think the customer wants (and sometimes asking for clarification).

    c. The customer confirms my guesses or gives me more detail.

    d. I crank out a quick example program.

    e. I email the example to the customer.

    f. The customer examines the example and asks more questions if necessary.

    g. I answer the new questions.

    Earlier in this chapter, I said that every project runs through the same basic tasks. Explain where those tasks are performed in this kind of interaction. (For example, which of those steps includes testing?)

4. List three ways fixing one bug can cause others.

5. List five tasks that might be part of deployment.

6. If customers spend more time using a program than testers do, does that mean they are more likely to find bugs?

7. Earlier, this chapter described a "one bug leads to two in the next phase" problem. How many bugs in total would you have at the start of testing if each bug leads to *three* others instead of just two?

WHAT YOU LEARNED IN THIS CHAPTER

➤ All projects perform the same basic tasks:

1. Requirements gathering

2. High-level design

3. Low-level design

4. Development

5. Testing

6. Deployment

7. Maintenance

8. Wrap-up

➤ Different development models handle the basic tasks in different ways, such as making some less formal or repeating tasks many times.

➤ The basic tasks often occur at the same time, with some developers working on one task while other developers work on other tasks.

➤ Work sometimes flows backward with later tasks requiring changes to earlier tasks.

➤ Fixing a bug can lead to other bugs.

➤ The longer a mistake remains undetected, the harder it is to fix.

➤ Surprises are inevitable, so you should allow some extra time to handle them.

Before the Beginning

> Every project is an opportunity to learn, to figure out problems and challenges, to invent and reinvent.
>
> —*David Rockwell*

> It's not whether you win or lose, it's how you place the blame.
>
> —*Oscar Wilde*

What You Will Learn in This Chapter:

- ➤ The features that a document management system provides
- ➤ Why documentation is important
- ➤ How you can easily archive emails for later use
- ➤ Typical types of documentation

Before you start working on a software project, even before you dig into the details of what the project is about, there are preparations you should make. In fact, some of these can be useful even if you're not considering a software project.

These tools improve your chances for success in any complicated endeavor. They raise the odds that you'll produce something that will satisfy the application's customers. They'll also help you survive the process so that you'll still be working on the project when the accolades start rolling in.

Typically, you'll use these tools and techniques throughout all of a project's tasks. You'll use them while you're gathering requirements from the customer, during the design and programming phases, and as you roll out the final result to the users. You'll even use them after you've finished releasing an application and you're considering enhancements for the next version.

The following sections describe some beginning-to-end tools that you can use to help keep team members focused and the project on track.

DOCUMENT MANAGEMENT

A software engineering project uses a lot of documents. It uses requirements documents, use cases, design documents, test plans, user training material, lunch menus for team-building exercises, resumes if the project doesn't go well, and much more. (I'll describe some of these kinds of documentation in later chapters.) Even a relatively modest project could have hundreds or even thousands of pages of documentation.

To make matters more confusing, many of those are "living" documents that evolve over time. In some projects, the requirements are allowed to change as the project progresses. As developers get a better sense for which tasks will be hard and which will be easy, the customers may want to revise the requirements to include new, simple features and eliminate old, complicated features.

As the project advances, the customers will also get a better understanding of what the system will eventually do and they may want to make changes. They may see some partially implemented feature and decide that it isn't that useful. They may even come up with new features that they just plain forgot about at the beginning of the project. ("I know we didn't *explicitly* say you need a way to log into the system, but I'm quite sure that's going to be necessary at some point.")

CHANGE CONTROL

If you let everyone make changes to the requirements, how can you meet them? Just when you satisfy one requirement, someone can change it, so you're not done after all. (Imagine running after the bus in the rain while the driver cackles evilly and checks the side mirror to make sure he's going just a little faster than you're running.) Eventually, the requirements need to settle down so that you can achieve them.

Allowing everyone to change the requirements can also result in muddled, conflicting, and confusing goals and designs. This is more or less how laws and government spending bills are written, so it shouldn't be a surprise that the results aren't always perfect. ("Yes, you can have a $3,000 study to decide whether people should carry umbrellas in the rain if I can have my $103,000 to study the effects of tequila and gin on sunfish." Someone really should spend a few dollars to study whether that kind of budget process is efficient.)

To keep changes from proliferating wildly and becoming hopelessly convoluted, many projects (particularly large ones) create a *change control board* that reviews and approves (or rejects) change requests. The board should include people who represent the customers ("We really *need* to log in telepathically from home") and the development team ("The best we can do is let you log in on your smartphone").

Even on small projects, it's usually worthwhile to assign someone as the final arbiter. Often that person is either a high-ranking customer (such as the executive champion) or a high-ranking member of the development team (such as the project lead).

During development, it's important to check the documentation to see what you're supposed to be doing. You need to easily find the most recent version of the requirements to see what the application should do. Similarly, you need to find the most recent high-level and low-level designs to see if you're following the plan correctly.

Sometimes, you'll also need to find older versions of the documentation, to find out what changes were made, why they were made, and who to blame for them.

FONT FIASCO

To understand the importance of historical documentation, suppose your application produces quarterly reports showing projected root beer demand. At some point the requirements were changed to require that the report be printed in landscape mode with a 16-point Arial font.

Now suppose you're working on the report to add new columns that group customers by age, weight, ethnic background, car model, and hat size. That's easy enough, but now the report won't fit on the page. If you could bump the font size down to 14-point, everything would fit just fine, but the 16-point Arial requirement is killing you.

At this point, you should go back to the requirements documents and find out why the font requirement was added. If the requirement was added to make it easier to include reports in PowerPoint slides, you may be able to reduce the font size and your boss can live with slightly more crowded slides during his presentations to the VP of strategic soft drink engineering.

Another option might be to continue producing the original report for presentations and create a new expanded report that includes the new columns for research purposes.

It's even possible that the original issue was that some developers were printing reports with the Comic Sans font. Management didn't think that looked professional enough so made a font requirement. They never actually cared about the font size, just the typeface. In that case, you could probably ask to change the requirement again to let you use a smaller font, as long as you stick with Arial.

Unless you have a good document history, you may never know why and when the requirement was changed, so you won't know whether it's okay to change it again.

Meanwhile, as you're changing the font requirement to allow 14-point Arial, one of your coworkers might be changing some other part of the same requirements document (perhaps requiring that all reports must be printed in renewable soy ink on 100 percent post-consumer recycled paper). If you both open the document at the same time, whichever change is saved second will overwrite the other change, and the first change will be lost. (In programming terms, this is called a *race condition* in which the second person wins.)

To handle all of these issues, you need a good document management system. Ideally, the system should support at least the following operations:

➤ People can share documents so that they can all view and edit them.

➤ Only one person can edit a document at a given time.

➤ You can fetch the most recent version of a document.

➤ You can fetch a previous version of a document by specifying either a date or version number.

➤ You can search documents for tags, keywords, and anything else in the documents.

➤ You can compare two versions of a document to see what changed, who changed it, and when the change occurred. (Ideally, you should also see notes indicating why a change was made, although, that's a less common feature.)

➤ You should have the ability to access documents over the Internet or on mobile devices.

Following are some other features that are less common but still useful:

➤ The ability for multiple people to collaborate on documents so they can see each other making changes to a shared document.

➤ Integration into other tools such as Microsoft Office, Google Workspace, or project management software.

➤ Document branches so that you can split a document into two paths for future changes. (This is more useful with program code where you might need to create two parallel versions of the program. Even then it can lead to a lot of confusion.)

➤ User roles and restricted access lists.

➤ Email change notification.

➤ Workflow support and document routing.

Some document management systems don't include all these features, and some of these aren't necessary for smaller projects, but they can be nice to have.

INDUSTRIAL AGE DOCUMENT MANAGEMENT

Document management is far from new. In precomputer times, you could achieve many document management features by simply keeping a book in your office. You could write the requirements, cross out and rewrite sections, and add your initials to the changes so you and others would later know who made them. You could even allow others to edit the book, although multiple people couldn't edit the book at the same time. (Well, I suppose they could, but it would be awkward.) The first Wheel Working Group probably recorded its early designs in cuneiform on clay tablets. Those systems might work today for very small projects, but they don't provide much in the way of keyword searches.

The following sections describe some special features of different kinds of documentation you should save.

HISTORICAL DOCUMENTS

After you've installed some sort of document management system, you may wonder what documents you should put in it. The answer is *everything*. Every little tidbit and scrap of intelligence dealing with the project should be recorded for posterity. Every design decision, requirements change, and memo should be tucked away for later reference.

If you don't have all this information, it's too easy for project meetings to devolve into finger-pointing sessions and blame-game tournaments. Let's face it: people forget things. (I'm writing Chapter 2 and I've already forgotten what Chapter 1 was about.) Not every disagreement has the vehemence of a blood feud between vampires and werewolves, but some can grow that bad if you let them. If you have a good, searchable document database, you can simply find the memo where your customer said that all the monitors had to be pink, pick the specific shade, and move on to discuss more important matters.

Collecting every scrap of relevant information isn't quite as big a chore as you might think. Most of the information is already available in an electronic form, so you just need to save it. Whenever someone sends an email about the project, save it. Whenever someone makes a change request, save it. If someone creates a new document and doesn't put it in the document repository, put it there yourself or at least email it to yourself so there's a record.

The only types of project activity that aren't usually easy to record electronically are meetings and phone calls. You can record meetings and phone calls if you want a record of everything (subject to local law), but on most projects you can just type up a quick summary and email it to all the participants. Anyone who disagrees about what was covered in the meeting can send a follow-up email that can also go into the historical documents.

It's also well worth your effort to thrash through any disagreements as soon as possible, and sending out a meeting summary can help speed that process along. The biggest purpose of documentation is to ensure that everyone is headed in the same direction, so it's good to make sure everyone agrees on what that direction is.

EMAIL

Memos, discussions about possible change requests, meeting notes, and lunch orders are all easy to distribute via email. Storing those emails for historical purposes is also easy: Simply create an email address for the project and CC it for every project email. For example, you could create an email address named after the project and copy every project message to that account.

Suppose you're working on project CLASP (CLeverly Acronymed Software Project). Then you would create an email account named CLASP and send copies of any project email to that account.

> **TIP** I've had project managers who extracted every project email into text files and tucked them away in a folder for later use. That lets you perform all sorts of other manipulations that are tricky inside an email system. For example, you could write a program to search the files for messages from the user Terry that include the words "sick" and "Friday." I've even had project managers who printed out every email, although that seems a bit excessive. Usually just having the emails saved in a project account is good enough.

Sometimes, it's hard for team members to easily find project-related emails in the daily spamalanche of offers for cheap Canadian prescriptions, low interest rates guaranteed by the "US National Bank," letters from your long-lost Nigerian uncle, and evacuation notices from your Building Services department.

To make finding project emails easier, you can prefix their subjects with an identifier. The following text might show the subject line for an email about the CLASP project.

```
[CLASP] This week's meeting canceled because all tasks are ahead of schedule
```

Of course, if you receive an email with this subject, you should suspect it's a hoax because all tasks have never been ahead of schedule in the entire history of software engineering. I think the day the term "software engineering" was coined, its definition was already a week overdue.

You can further refine the subject identifier by adding classes of messages. For example, [CLASP .Design] might indicate a message about design for the CLASP project. You can invent any message classes you think would be useful. Following is a list of a few that may come in handy:

➤ Admin—Administration

➤ Rqts—Requirements

➤ HLDesign—High-level design

➤ LLDesign—Low-level design

➤ Dvt—Development

➤ Test—Testing

➤ Deploy—Deployment

➤ Doc—Documentation

➤ Train—Training

➤ Maint—Maintenance

➤ Wrap—Wrap-up

> **TIP** It doesn't matter what subject line tags you use, as long as you're consistent. Make a list at the beginning of the project and make sure everyone uses them consistently.

You could even break the identifier further to indicate tasks within a message class. For example, the string [CLASP.LLDesign.1001] might indicate a message regarding low-level design task 1001.

> **ROUTING RULES** *Some email systems can even use rules to route particular messages to different folders. For example, the system might be able to copy messages with the word "CLASP" in the title into a project email folder. (Just don't spend more time programming your email system than you spend on the actual project.)*

If team members use those conventions consistently, any decent email system should make it easy to find messages that deal with a particular part of the project. To find the test messages, you can search for [CLASP.Test. To find every CLASP email, search for [CLASP.

An alternative strategy is to include keywords inside the message body. You can use a naming convention similar to the one described here, or you can use something more elaborate if you need to. For example, a message might begin with the following text to flag it as involving the testing, bug reports, and login screen.

```
Key: Test
Key: Bugs
Key: Login
```

Now you can search for strings like Key: Bugs to find the relevant messages.

Another trick is to include Unicode emojis in message titles to indicate things such as the group to which it applies, messages that are suggestions, and messages that should remain private to the development team and should not be shared with customers. Your email system may not be able to filter and search for emojis, but they can make it easier to quickly scan a list of messages and pick out specific categories.

Some email systems also let you assign icons to specific people so you can easily spot emails from them.

In addition to making emails easy to find, you should take steps to make them easy to distribute. Create some email groups so that you can distribute messages to the appropriate people. For example, you may want groups for managers, user interface designers, customers, developers, testers, and trainers—and, of course, a group for everyone.

Then be sure you use the groups correctly! Customers don't want to hear the developers argue over whether a b+tree is better than an AVL-tree, and user interface designers don't want to hear the testers dispute the fine points of white-box versus beige-box testing. (In one project I was on, a developer accidentally included customers in an email that described the customers in less than flattering terms. Basically, he said they didn't really know what they needed. It was true, but they sure didn't like hearing it!)

As you design your email strategy, try not to overwhelm your team members with 172 different project-related mailing lists. I worked on one project that had more Slack channels than team members. (I wish I was exaggerating!)

CODE

Program source code is different from a project's other kinds of documents. Normally, you expect requirements and design documents to eventually stabilize and remain mostly unchanged. In contrast, code changes continually, up to and sometimes well beyond the project's official ending date.

That gives source code control systems a slightly different flavor than other kinds of document control systems. A requirements document might go through a dozen or so versions, but a code module might include hundreds or even thousands of changes. That means the tools you use to store code often don't work particularly well with other kinds of documents and vice versa.

Source code is also generally line-oriented. Even in curly bracket languages such as C#, Kotlin, and Java, which are technically not line-oriented, programmers insert line breaks to make the code easier to read. If you change a line of source code, that change probably doesn't affect the lines around it. Because of that, if you use a source code control system to compare two versions of a code file, it flags only that one line as changed.

In contrast, suppose you added the word "incontrovertibly" to the beginning of the preceding paragraph. That would probably make every line in the paragraph wrap to the following line, so every line in the paragraph would seem to have been changed. A document revision system, such as those provided by Microsoft Word or Google Docs, correctly realizes that you added only a single word. A source code control system might decide that you had modified every line in the paragraph.

What this means is that you should use separate tools to manage source code and other kinds of documents. This usually isn't a big deal, and it's easy to find a lot of choices online. (In fact, picking one that every developer can agree on may be the hardest part of using a source code control system.)

Ideally, a source code control system enables all the developers to use the code. If a developer needs to modify a module, the system checks out that module to that developer. Other developers can still use the most recently saved version of the code, but they can't edit that module until the first developer releases it. (This avoids the race condition described earlier in this chapter.)

Some source code control systems are integrated into the development environment. They make code management so easy even the most advanced programmers don't mess it up too often.

CODE DOCUMENTATION

Something that most nonprogrammers (and quite a few programmers) don't understand is that code is written for people, not for the computer. In fact, the computer doesn't execute the source code. The code must be compiled, interpreted, and otherwise translated into a sequence of 0s and 1s that the computer can understand.

The computer also doesn't care what the code does. If you tell it to erase its hard disk (something I don't recommend), the computer will merrily try to do just that.

The reason I say source code is written for people is that it's people who must write, understand, and debug the code. The single most important requirement for a program's code is that it be understandable to the people who write and maintain it.

Now I know I'm going to get a lot of argument over that statement. Programmers have all sorts of favorite goals like optimizing speed, minimizing bugs, and including witty puns in the comments. Those are all important, but if you can't understand the code, you can't safely modify it and fix it when it breaks.

Without good documentation, including both design documents and comments inside the code, the poor fool assigned to fix your code will stand little or no chance. This is even more important when you realize that the poor fool may be you. The code you find so obvious and clever today may make no sense at all to you in a year or even a few months. In some cases, it may not make sense a few hours later. You owe it to posterity to ensure that your genius is properly understood throughout the ages.

To that end, you need to write code documentation. You don't need to write enormous tomes explaining that the statement `numInvoicesLost = numInvoicesLost + 1` means you are adding 1 to the value `numInvoicesLost`. You can probably figure that out even if you've never seen a line of code before. However, you do need to give yourself and others a trail of breadcrumbs to follow on their quest to figure out why invoices are being sent to employees instead of customers.

Code documentation should include high- and low-level design documents that you can store in the document repository with other kinds of documentation. These provide an overview of the methods the code is using to do whatever it's supposed to do.

Code documentation should also include comments in the code to help you understand what the code is actually doing and how it works. You don't need to comment every line of code (see the `numInvoicesLost` example again), but it should provide a fairly detailed explanation that even the summer intern who was hired only because he's the boss's nephew can understand. Debugging code should be an exercise in understanding the code and figuring out why it isn't doing what it's supposed to do. It shouldn't be an IQ test.

JBGE

There's a school of thought in software engineering that says you should provide code documentation and comments that are "just barely good enough" (*JBGE*). The idea is that if you provide too much documentation, you end up wasting a lot of time updating it as you make changes to the code.

This philosophy can reduce the amount of documentation you produce, but it's an idea that's easy to take too far. Most programmers like to program (that's why they're not lawyers or doctors; that and the whole malpractice thing) and writing and updating documentation and comments doesn't feel like writing code, so sometimes they skip it entirely.

A software engineering joke says, "Real programmers don't comment their code. If it was hard to write, it should be hard to understand and harder to modify." Unfortunately, I've seen plenty of code that proves the connection between poor documentation and difficult modification.

continues

(continued)

I worked on one project that included more than 55,000 lines of code and fewer than 300 comments. (I wrote a program to count them.) And if there were design documents, I never heard about them. I'm sure the code made sense when it was written, but modifying it was next to impossible. I sometimes spent four or five days studying the code, trying to figure out how it worked before changing one or two lines. Even after all that time, there was a decent chance I misunderstood something and the change added a new bug. Then I got to remove the change and start over.

I worked on another project that included tons of comments. Probably more than 80 percent of the lines of code included a comment. They were easy to ignore most of the time, but they were always there if you needed them.

After we transferred the project to the company's maintenance organization, the folks in the organization went on a JBGE bender and removed every comment that they felt wasn't *absolutely* necessary to understand the code. A few months later, they admitted that they couldn't maintain the code because . . .drumroll. . . they couldn't understand it. In the end, they put all of the comments back and just ignored them when they didn't need them.

Some integrated development environments (IDEs) even let you hide comments, so you only see them when you want them.

Yes, excessive code documentation and comments are a hassle and slow you down, so you can't rush off to the next task, but suck it up and write it down while it's still fresh in your mind. You don't need to constantly update your comments every time you change a line of code. Wait until you finish writing and testing a chunk of code. Then write it up and move on with a clear conscience. Comments may slow you down a bit, but I've never seen a project fail because it contained too many comments.

JBGE, REDUX

JBGE is mostly applied to code documentation and comments, but you could apply the same rule to any kind of documentation. For example, you could write barely enough documentation to explain the requirements. That's probably an even bigger mistake than skimping on code comments.

Documentation helps keep the whole project team working toward the same goals. If you don't spell things out unambiguously, developers will start working at cross-purposes. At best you'll lose a lot of time arguing about what the requirements mean. At worst you'll face a civil war that will destroy your team.

As is the case with code documentation and comments, you don't need to turn the requirements into a 1,200-page novel. However, if the requirements are ambiguous or confusing, pull out your thesaurus and clarify them.

JBGE is okay as long as you make sure your documentation actually is GE. Remember that JBGE is just barely better than "not good enough."

You can extend the JBGE idea even further and create designs that are just barely good enough, write code that's just barely good enough, and perform tests that are just barely good enough. I'm a big fan of avoiding unnecessary work, but if everything you do is just barely good enough, the result probably won't be anywhere near good enough. (Not surprisingly, no one advocates that approach. The JBGE philosophy seems to be reserved only for code comments.)

Some programming languages provide a special kind of comment that is intended to be pulled out automatically and used in text documentation. For example, the following shows a snippet of C# code with XML comments:

```
/// <summary>
/// Deny something bad we did to the media.
/// </summary>
/// <param name="type">What we did (Bug, Virus,
/// PromisedBadFeature, etc.)</param>
/// <param name="urgency">High, Medium, or Low</param>
/// <param name="media">One or more of Blog, Facebook,
/// Friendster, etc.</param>
private void PostDenial(DenialType type, UrgencyType urgency,
    MediaType media)
{
...
}
```

The comment's summary token explains the method's purpose. The param tokens describe the method's parameters. The Visual Studio development environment can automatically extract these comments into an XML file that you can then process to produce documentation. The result doesn't explain how the code works, but if you do a good job writing the comments, it does explain the interface that the method displays to other pieces of code. (Visual Studio also uses these comments to provide useful help pop-ups called IntelliCode, formerly called IntelliSense, to other developers who call this code.)

As is the case when you write code documentation and other comments, you don't need to constantly update this kind of information as you work on a method. Finish the method, test it, and then write the comments once.

APPLICATION DOCUMENTATION

All the documentation described so far deals with building the application. It includes such items as requirements and design documents, code documentation and comments, meeting and phone call notes, and memos.

At some point you also need to prepare documentation that describes the application. Depending on the eventual number and kinds of users, you may need to write user manuals (for end users, managers, database administrators, and more), quick start guides, cheat sheets, user interface maps, training materials, and marketing materials. You may even need to write meta-training materials to teach the trainers how to train the end users. (No kidding, I've done it.)

In addition to basic printed versions, you may need to produce Internet, screencast, video, Power-Point, audiobook, and other multimedia versions of some of those documents. Producing this kind of documentation isn't all that different from producing requirements documents. You can still store documents in an archive. (Although you may not be able to search for keywords in a video.)

Although creating this material is just another task, don't start too late in the project schedule. If you wait until the last minute to start writing training materials, then the users won't be able to use the application when it's ready. (I remember one project where the requirements and user interface kept changing right up until the last minute. It was somewhat annoying to the developers, but it practically drove our lead trainer insane.)

SUMMARY

Documentation is produced throughout a project's life span, starting with early discussions of the project's requirements, extending through design and programming, continuing into training materials, and lasting even beyond the project's release in the form of comments, bug reports, and change requests. To get the most out of your documentation, you need to set up a document tracking system before you start the project. Then you can effectively use the project documents to determine what you need to do and how you should do it. You can also figure out what was decided in the past so that you don't need to constantly rehash old decisions.

Document control is one of the first tools you should set up when you're considering a new project. You can use it to archive ideas before you know what the project will be about or whether there will even be a project.

There's one other thing you need before you unleash your team on the project: a team. The next chapter discusses teams. It explains features of good teams and symptoms of bad ones. It talks about ways to build a good team and discusses care and feeding practices that keep a team healthy.

EXERCISES

1. List seven features that a document management system should provide.

2. Microsoft Word provides a simple change tracking tool. It's not a full-featured document management system, but it's good enough for small projects. For this exercise, follow these steps:

   a. Create a short document in Word and save it.

   b. Turn on change tracking. (In recent versions of Word, go to the Review tab's Tracking group and click Track Changes.)

   c. Modify the document and save it with a new name. (You should see the changes flagged in the document. If you don't, go to the Review tab's Tracking group and use the drop-down to select Final: Show Markup.)

d. On the Review tab's Tracking group, click the Reviewing Pane button to display the reviewing pane. You should see your changes there.

e. In the Review tab's Tracking group, open the Track Changes drop-down and select Change User Name. Change your user name and initials.

f. Make another change, save the file again, and see how Word indicates the changes.

3. Microsoft Word also provides a document comparison tool. If you followed the instructions in Exercise 2 carefully, you should have two versions of your sample document. In the Review tab's Compare group, open the Compare drop-down and select Compare. (When Microsoft finds a name they like, they really go with it!) Select the two versions of the file and compare them. How similar is the result to the changes shown by change tracking? Why would you use this tool instead of change tracking?

4. Like Microsoft Word, Google Docs provides some simple change tracking tools. Go to www.google.com/docs/about to learn about Google Docs and to sign up. Then create a document, open the File menu's Version History submenu, select Name Current Version, and name the file Version 1. Make some changes and repeat the preceding steps to name the revised document Version 2. Now open the File menu's Version History submenu again but this time select See Version History. Click the versions listed on the right to see what changed between versions.

5. What does JBGE stand for and what does it mean?

6. Why do you think the CLASP example puts brackets around keywords such as [CLASP] and [CLASP.Design]?

7. End-user documentation, training materials, and the like must reflect the final project. Does that mean you can't start creating the documentation until after the project is finished?

WHAT YOU LEARNED IN THIS CHAPTER

➤ Documentation is important at every step of the development process.

➤ Good documentation keeps team members on track, provides a clear direction for work, and prevents arguments over issues that were previously settled.

➤ Document management systems enable you to do the following:

  ➤ Share documents with other team members.

  ➤ Fetch a document's most recent version.

  ➤ Fetch an earlier version of a document.

  ➤ Search documents for keywords.

  ➤ Show changes made to a document.

> ➤ Compare two documents to show their differences.

> ➤ Prevent two people from editing the same document at the same time.

➤ A simple way to store project history is to create an email account named after the project and then send copies of all project correspondence to that account.

➤ You can use email subject tags such as [CLASP.Rqts] to make finding different types of project emails easy.

➤ Your project may include the following types of documentation:

> ➤ Requirements

> ➤ Project emails and memos

> ➤ Meeting notes

> ➤ Phone call notes

> ➤ Use cases

> ➤ High-level design documents

> ➤ Low-level design documents

> ➤ Test plans

> ➤ Code documentation

> ➤ Code comments

> ➤ Extractable code comments

> ➤ User manuals

> ➤ Quick start guides

> ➤ Cheat sheets

> ➤ User interface maps

> ➤ Training materials

> ➤ Meta-training materials

> ➤ Marketing materials

➤ JBGE (just barely good enough) states that you should provide only the absolute minimum number of comments necessary to understand the code.

3

The Team

Alone we can do little; together we can do so much.

—Helen Keller

No member of a crew is praised for the rugged individuality of his rowing.

—Ralph Waldo Emerson

What You Will Learn in This Chapter:

➤ Features of an effective team

➤ Team roles

➤ Team culture

➤ Physical environment

➤ Collaboration software

A team is a group of people working together to achieve a common goal. In practice, the effectiveness of teams can vary widely for many reasons. Some members may not understand the goals, the work environment may not support the team, or the team may not have the skills and equipment it needs to be productive. Some teams sink under the weight of too much management, while others drift aimlessly because of too little. Sometimes outsiders or even team members actively work against the team for their own personal ends.

Because different teams contain different sets of people, have different goals, and live in different environments, every team is unique. That means you shouldn't treat them all in exactly the same way, and therefore you should take any advice about the care and feeding of a team with a grain of salt. What works well with one team (or one team member) may not work well with another.

Rather than trying to cover every possible situation (which would take volumes and is probably impossible anyway), this chapter covers some issues and techniques that seem to apply particularly well to software development teams. (No guarantees that they'll work equally well for your Formula One, curling, or quidditch teams.)

TEAM FEATURES

Every team is different, but effective teams tend to have several features in common. The following sections describe some of those features, features that you should encourage in your teams.

Some of the development approaches described in Chapter 19, "RAD," place a strong emphasis on teams. For example, the Lean and Crystal approaches include sets of values or guiding principles, many of which are team-oriented.

Clear Roles

This isn't only about who the leader is. It's about knowing who should make which decisions and work on what tasks. If it's not clear who has what responsibilities, then team members will waste time trying to figure that out when decisions are necessary.

If you need to change the database design, it should be obvious who will do that. If you need to pick among several user interface designs, you should know whose decision that will be.

Usually, particularly on smaller teams, the people involved in a decision can come to an agreement. Sometimes, however, someone needs to cast the tiebreaking vote. At times like that, it's nice to have an official leader (team lead, project lead, executive champion) with the power to make decisions. After a decision is made, the interested parties should gracefully accept the verdict and move on. (Next week's meeting will feature bagels, not croissants. Get over it!)

Effective Leadership

Very small teams may be able to get by making decisions by consensus, but any team with more than a few members will probably need some form of leadership. Let's face it, sometimes a team needs a border collie to keep the flock pointed in the correct direction.

Note that the term "effective" here doesn't mean "powerful," "in control," or "in charge." The leadership should do whatever is necessary to make the team as effective as possible and not break the team spirit by micromanaging every decision. If the team is headed in the right direction, keep an eye on things but stay out of the way.

This is one place where what works for a software development team may not work for other kinds of teams. A good software team can self-organize and come up with reasonable designs. A hockey team can only go so far without a coach to design drills, run practices, refine the players' techniques, and pull Matt out of the game when he keeps shooting at his own goal. It's hard to imagine a goalie practicing alone, shooting at the goal, and then racing around to block the shot. (Although there are "batting cages" for hockey, passing practice tools, and portable puck cannons, so maybe you can do a lot on your own. You still need a coach to pull Matt out, though.)

Notice also that "leadership" does not necessarily mean "management." An effective leader may just be a project member who can also provide guidance as needed. (To recycle the sports metaphor, many sports teams have a leader who isn't necessarily a coach.)

The official team leader should track the project, arbitrate (but not necessarily make) decisions, and generally keep the team focused on the project goals. Sometimes the leader will also advocate for the team to obtain important resources such as equipment, software, staffing, office space, and a donut budget.

As a project grows larger and more formal, the leader may become a primary interface between the team and outsiders such as high-level customers and upper management. (In one project I worked on, the customers asked team members for updates so often that the developers couldn't get anything done. Our project leader made a rule that customers could ask only him for updates and only after 5 p.m.. This worked extremely well. The developers had more time to work, and the customers got the information they needed.)

WORKING PROJECT MANAGERS

On some projects, a project manager does exactly what the title says: manage the project. In other situations, the project manager is also expected to provide technical guidance and possibly even code. That tends to work best with small projects. Large, high-profile projects tend to make management a full-time (or more than full-time) job.

As the project progresses, a working manager may need to offload some technical chores. Don't be afraid to delegate if possible.

One of the most important characteristics of good management is trustworthiness. If the team members don't trust the leader, they won't follow and may not end up headed in the right direction. (Or even the same direction.)

Finally, a good leader works to ensure that the team has all of the other good features described in this chapter.

Unfortunately, ineffective leadership is one of the hardest team problems to fix. It's hard enough to tell someone that they aren't doing a good job. It's even harder if that person is your boss (at least for that project).

Clear Goals

The team must have clear, common goals. If the goals are fuzzy, the team will waste time on decisions that should be obvious. In the best case, someone will spend time trying to decide what to do. If things are slightly worse, multiple team members will spend time arguing and may even need some-one higher up, like the team leader or possibly even a customer sponsor, to clarify the situation. In the worst case, team members may come to blows with recriminations, name calling, and removal from holiday card lists.

Sometimes achieving clear goals is easy and everyone intuitively knows what the final application needs to do. For example, if you're building something similar to an existing program, you can point to it and say, "It should work like that."

You don't need to model your entire project on one existing program either. You can say, "We'll store data in the cloud the way *this* program does, print reports like *that* program, build a user interface similar to *that other* one (with the following exceptions)." (Try not to turn this into a plagiarism smorgasbord, however. You can be *inspired* by commercial products, but don't steal their designs outright unless you're willing to add time into the schedule to defend against lawsuits.)

If you don't have existing models for what the program should do, you should spend some extra time "testing" the high-level design. Try to think of as many issues as you can and make sure the design can handle them. If necessary, go to the customers (if you can) and ask them to clarify anything that's hazy.

Finally, make the necessary decisions, go over them in team meetings, write them down, email them to everyone on the team, and otherwise make sure everyone has the same notion of what the application should do. Decisions don't count unless everyone knows what they are.

Consensus

I mentioned earlier that sometimes it's useful to have some sort of authority like a team or project lead to cast a tiebreaking vote. Usually it's better if team members can reach a consensus on their own. That helps reduce the feeling that there is a winner and a loser and makes it more likely that members will work together in the future.

If a consensus isn't reached easily, you can resort to classic decision-making exercises such as making lists of pros and cons, giving the interested parties time to speak without interruption, and drawing straws. Then at least everyone will feel that their viewpoint has been heard and given a chance. (Okay, I was kidding about drawing straws. You should only do that if the decision is so unimportant that no one cares.)

Open Communication

Communication among team members must be free, easy, safe, and secure.

By "safe" I mean that no one should be punished for voicing concerns, delivering bad news, requesting help, or admitting failure. If there's even a hint that someone might get in trouble for communicating openly, then no one will do so and you'll be left to find your worst bugs during testing or even after deployment.

By "secure" I mean that communications should be protected against loss or theft. You can decide on the level of security you need. If the project is small and politically neutral in your company, then simple emails stored on company servers may suffice. If there are competitors or other parts of the company actively trying to undermine you or steal your designs, then you may want to take extra precautions such as encrypting messages and storing backups in a separate location.

> **CAUTIOUS COMMUNICATION** *If you really want communication to be secure, you also need to define what types of communication are allowed. For example, it would be easy for someone to send pictures, screenshots, documents, and other confidential information from their phones via text message, Facebook Messenger, Microsoft Teams, Skype, or any number of other chat applications. Not only does that allow a team member to send information outside of the team, but it's also fairly easy for a spy to intercept text messages and possibly chat data (depending on the app).*
>
> *If your project doesn't rise to that level of paranoia, great! If you're worried about corporate espionage, you're dealing with sensitive data (such as financial or medical records), or you work for MI6, then you may want to prohibit cellphone use (and any other form of unsecured communication).*

The team should foster communication but not force it unnecessarily. Many teams have regular meetings, perhaps weekly or less often, just to make sure everyone is still headed in the right direction, that any foreseeable problems are foreseen, and that everyone is caught up on the latest gossip. Those meetings should be short.

Team members will also need to communicate with peers on a regular basis just to get things done, with those working most closely together needing more frequent communication. Make that as easy as possible. (The section "Collaboration Software" later in this chapter talks a bit about tools that you can use for communication.)

Support for Risk-Taking

The team (particularly the leadership) should support risk-taking and change, particularly early in the project. If you don't encourage people to try new things, then you won't be able to build anything new.

If you don't provide support, or worse, if you punish those who make bad decisions, then team members will be less creative and may miss opportunities that might otherwise improve the project.

Team members should have enough independence to make decisions and try new things within their pieces of the project to further the team's goals. This is the concept of *collaborative independence*: members working independently to help the team achieve its goals.

Shared Accountability

Here "shared accountability" means individuals aren't blamed; the team takes responsibility. Yes, one developer might have written some bad code, but the team should catch and fix it. Pointing fingers will lead to hostility, fear of trying new things, and a less effective team.

This isn't the same as "no accountability." If someone does something irredeemably stupid, their performance review may include some choice words. However, if someone makes a bad decision based on the best information available at the time, then finger-pointing serves no purpose.

This also doesn't mean you need to be willfully reckless and assign the most complicated tasks to a novice programmer who heard about some intricate algorithm in school and wants to give it a try. You should still assign the best people for each task, but don't take it out on someone who has trouble with their assignment. After all, the team made that assignment, so in some sense it's the team's fault that they failed.

Everyone should make the best decisions possible but not make it personal when things don't work out as expected.

On a related note, criticism should be based on issues, not people. Rather than saying, "Prometheus told the customers about project FIRE and now they want changes," you can say, "The customers want changes based on project FIRE." Everyone will know who let the secret out, but there's no need to make the problem personal.

Informal Atmosphere

Some level of formality may occasionally be required (my boss used to keep an emergency jacket and tie on a hook behind his door in case a corporate executive wandered by), but many teams benefit from an informal atmosphere. A lack of formality encourages many of the good practices described earlier in this chapter. It promotes open communication and makes it easier to come to consensus. If one or more team members are having trouble working something out, it makes it easier for them to ask for help from each other, the team leader, and possibly the customer.

Trust

Hopefully most of the features of good teams covered in the previous sections should seem obvious, but this may be the most obvious of all. Team members must trust each other. If they don't, then they can't communicate openly, reach consensus, share accountability, or maintain an informal atmosphere. If they don't trust leadership (which is part of the team after all), then they cannot rely on common goals.

Basically, if the team members don't trust each other, then they really aren't a team.

TEAM ROLES

Any effective software development team should have members that play certain roles. For example, at some point someone needs to write some code. Otherwise the project is just a bunch of talking that doesn't produce anything useful. (Kind of like Congress.)

Some development methodologies have very specific names for their roles. In Scrum, for example, the *scrum master* is similar to a *project manager* in other methodologies. Other approaches have someone who performs the same function, just with a different name. (It would be weird to call the project manager a scrum master in a waterfall or kanban project.)

The following sections briefly summarize the roles that seem most useful in most development approaches. You'll see some of these described again in Chapter 19, which talks about different rapid development methodologies.

Common Roles

These roles are present in most projects. On smaller projects, one person may play many roles. For example, on many of my projects, I play every role including customer (like when I'm goofing off drawing fractals, prime factoring my Social Security number, or writing a program that can build its own source code as a string).

- ➤ Project manager/tracker—Tracks schedules, monitors progress, and generally makes sure the project stays on track. Sometimes this may be a nontechnical person trained in project management. Other times this is a technical developer with other roles, such as team lead or mentor.

- ➤ Technical lead—The highest-ranking technical person. Ideally this person has experience with similar past projects so they can work on all levels of the project and make decisions when necessary.

- ➤ Team leader/chief programmer—Leads one of the development teams when a large project is broken into teams. Basically the team's technical lead.

- ➤ Developer/programmer—The people who write the actual code in some programming language. Because of the idiosyncrasies of programming languages, these people can often type really fast while using only a few fingers.

- ➤ Customer/client—The people for whom the application is being built. They could be consumers or people in another part of the same company.

- ➤ Analyst/business analyst/domain expert—The customers' representatives, particularly when the customers are within the company. (Normally mass consumers don't have business analysts.) These are the people that the team members pump for information about the customers' needs.

- ➤ System administrator/sys admin—Ensures that the team's tools work properly. That includes installing and maintaining hardware and software, performing frequent backups, restoring files when someone accidentally deletes the database, and nagging people about using good passwords and not clicking suspicious links. (At least not on work computers. What you do at home is your business.)

- ➤ Database administrator/DBA—Maintains the team's databases, possibly including the documentation and source code databases.

Sometimes it's hard to decide exactly who the customer is. It might be the end users who play your *Mushroom Bounce* game on their phone, someone in management who is running the project, your boss, or whoever signs your paycheck. Sometimes you may have multiple customers, such as the project manager, your boss, your boss's boss, and so on up to the VP of app development.

I'm going to keep this term a little vague, and I won't expand it to cover all stakeholders. Basically, I consider a customer to be someone who can make your life miserable if you mess up too badly.

More-Specialized Roles

The roles described in the preceding section are fairly general and most projects have them, even if some people play multiple roles. The following list summarizes a few roles that are more specialized, so they are usually only formally defined on larger projects.

➤ Database designer—A specialist at designing databases who will design and build the application's databases.

➤ Change manager—Studies and approves or rejects changes requested by the customers, analysts, developers, and others.

➤ Chief architect/architect/software architect—Works at a relatively high level on the project's architecture and high-level design.

➤ Tester/test engineer/test designer—Earns a salary by breaking your code.

➤ User interface designer/human factors engineer—Studies human-computer interactions to help design user interfaces, workflow, and other issues that can improve end-user effectiveness. (Many programmers prefer to design user interfaces themselves, but if you have these sorts of people available, make use of them!)

➤ Technical writer—Writes user documentation, code documentation, executive summaries, press releases, possibly advertising, and so on. (And an updated resume if they do a bad job.)

➤ Trainer—Trains the application's end users.

➤ Interested internal party—People who are interested in the project and may need to interact with it in some way later. For example, sales, marketing, and legal people may want to be kept in the loop so they can shout out in panic if they see you doing something that will make their jobs harder.

For example, you might need a data scientist, subject matter expert (SME), AI designer, algorithm specialist, radar technician, master carpenter, and caterer. Basically, whatever your specific project requires. (I'm not kidding about the last three. If you're building software to analyze radar signals, design kitchen remodels, or price catering events, then you may need those people.)

You can often shoehorn these people into existing categories if you like (for example, an algorithm specialist is a kind of developer and a master carpenter is an SME), or you can give them special titles if that would make them feel more appreciated.

Informal Roles

In addition to the roles described in the previous sections, many projects have certain informal roles that are typically played by someone who has another official title. For example, few companies explicitly list "language lawyer" as a position, but anyone who has worked on a large project has seen them.

➤ Language lawyer—Knows the intricate details of the project's programming language and can answer elaborate questions about it. (Programmer: What happens if I use
`i < 100 ? --j / 5 * 5 : j++ / 10 * 10, j`? Language lawyer: Don't do that, it's confusing!)

➤ Toolsmith—Builds small tools and utilities for other developers. Some care may be needed to avoid turning a small parsing tool into a doctoral thesis.

➤ Facilitator—Generally makes everyone else's life easier and makes the team work more smoothly. Can sometimes calm tempers and help others reach consensus.

➤ Coach/mentor—Works with less experienced team members to help them learn and be more effective.

➤ Scribe—Records things such as meeting notes, call transcripts, and team bowling league schedules.

Roles Wrap-Up

If you're building a new team, try to first decide how many people you will need. If you're building a small tool that will only take a few weeks to develop, you won't need a big team. If you're building a new air traffic control system, you'll need a much larger team, hopefully including several members who have previous experience on large projects.

After you know roughly how large the team must be, start thinking about who can cover which roles and make sure you have the most important roles covered. Remember, if the project is large, you will need extra people to manage different parts of the team.

Smaller projects may not need coaches or a dedicated technical writer, and you may not be able to afford a trained DBA or a human resources department, but you should know who will handle those roles when they arise. If you don't assign a sys admin, then you have only yourself to blame when your hard disk crashes and you have no backups.

After you've selected a good fraction of the team, let them self-assemble if possible. That will allow people to gravitate into the roles where they fit best. That may require some compromise, but the more the team builds itself, the more likely it will be to grow a strong, productive culture.

TEAM CULTURE

Team culture is one of those fuzzy intangibles that seems like no big deal but can destroy a team. Because culture is so ethereal, it's hard to define, much less provide, steps for building a positive culture. To make matters even more confusing, different groups may have very different cultures but still be effective.

For example, a group of middle-aged NASA developers who have used the waterfall model for decades will have a very different culture than a startup e-commerce company filled with young agile developers (that is, developers who use the agile method, not necessarily developers who are particularly frisky). Nevertheless, the two groups may both be very productive.

In a nutshell, a good culture is one that makes the team effective. (And an effective team must have a good culture, so yes, it's circular reasoning.)

Team members should feel comfortable working together and confident working alone on their individual assignments. They should feel at ease discussing the project's design and making group decisions. Everyone should be a team player with a positive can-do attitude who can work together synergistically, pull in the same direction, and have each other's backs (to bust out some execuspeak).

Ideally the team should feel a bit like a family, although not one like the Simpsons or the Sopranos.

The best tips I know of for building a team culture are group activities that let the team members get to know each other while not working on the project. The following list shows some possible activities:

➤ Lunch

➤ Party

➤ Picnic

➤ Escape room

➤ Amusement park

➤ Ski/beach trip (depending on where you live)

➤ Hike

➤ Community service activities (blood drive, charity work, etc.)

➤ Professional conferences

➤ Lunch talks/lectures

➤ Any activity where team members can socialize

Some people don't like these sorts of activities, so you can encourage them but should probably not make them mandatory. One great way to encourage people to participate is to have the company pay for the event. Buying lunch or even ski tickets is a small price to pay if it helps the team bond.

Swag like shirts, hats, jackets, coffee mugs, or sports cars (for *really* high-priced projects) can help build a team identity if used appropriately. For example, in a more formal workplace, you might embroider team golf shirts but probably not screen-printed T-shirts. Again, some people may not feel comfortable wearing a team propeller beanie, so you should probably make those optional.

While it may be hard to identify what makes a good team culture, it's easier to identify features that make a toxic work culture. Here's a Top Ten list of ways to ruin a team's performance:

➤ Sexual harassment

➤ Discrimination based on race, age, sexual orientation, or pretty much anything other than ability

➤ Playing favorites

➤ Cliques and gossip

➤ Bad, weak, or no leadership

➤ Ignoring team member feedback and concerns

➤ Different rules for different people (for example, different rules for managers)

➤ No work-life balance, long hours, burnout

➤ Frequent employee turnover

➤ Bullying (it's not just for the playground anymore)

WEAK LEADERSHIP

At one job, my boss's boss was a great guy and very likeable, but not very assertive. (Let's call my boss Able and his boss Baker for convenience.) If we needed something critical like a bigger hard drive for our project, Able would ask Baker, and Baker would promise to pass the request along to his boss. (Let's call him Charlie).

In the next week or so, when Baker happened to bump into Charlie in the hallway, they would be a brief conversation something like this:

Baker: By the way, we could use a new hard drive.

Charlie: Not right now, it's not in the budget.

Baker: Okay.

And that would be the end of it. After the project suffered for a while, Able would pester Baker again and the whole cycle would repeat.

After about five repetitions (you have to respect the chain of command, even if it doesn't always work), Able would go directly to Charlie and they would have this conversation:

Able: Hey, we really need a new disk drive.

Charlie: Not right now, there's no budget.

Able: It's starting to hurt the team. We're wasting a ton of time moving files to and from long-term storage. We're working less effectively, so it's costing us time. If we don't do something soon, we'll start to miss deadlines.

Charlie: Well why didn't you say so? Fill out the req. and I'll sign it.

At the time, a 300 MB hard drive cost about $5,000, so this wasn't a trivial matter. Now you could buy a 1 TB external hard drive on Amazon and have it delivered the next day for the price of dinner for two, but hopefully you get the idea. A good leader ensures that the team gets what it needs to function efficiently. Sometimes that takes extraordinary measures, but often it just requires explaining things properly to the powers that be.

(As an aside to this aside, Able, Baker, and Charlie were all great guys who sincerely wanted the team to succeed, so no one hated Baker even though he did cause some amount of annoyance.)

When in doubt, treat people the way you would like to be treated. If you're building a team, try to pick people who seem comfortable with the team so far. If you're considering joining a team, ask yourself whether you would enjoy working with this team.

INTERVIEWS

You can read online and in books all about how to be a good interviewer or interviewee. You definitely should read some of those resources, particularly if you've never played that part in an interview before.

I won't go into all of the details about what to bring, what kinds of questions to ask a candidate, and how to dress. (No, shorts and flip-flops are not okay, unless you're interviewing to become a lifeguard or sand volleyball coach.) I do, however, want to mention two topics: interview puzzles and the bottom line.

Interview Puzzles

In a word, don't.

Way back in days of yore when programmers worked on treadle-powered computers by candlelight, computers cost millions of dollars. This was during the 1950s and 1960s when a million dollars was a lot of money.

In those days, there were no university degrees in software engineering, web design, or making *Candy Crush* clones, so companies like UNIVAC, Logicon, and IBM had a problem: they didn't know how to determine whether someone would make a good programmer. Reasoning that it took clever people to write clever programs, companies decided to use interview puzzles to identify clever people and then train them to program.

Since then, it's been shown that interview puzzles don't predict programming ability very well, but because big companies like IBM used them, interview puzzles became part of the programming interview meta-culture and they stuck around for a very long time. Today big companies like Microsoft, Google, and Amazon no longer use programming puzzles (although they used to), but many smaller companies still use them, figuring that the big companies must have done so for a reason.

So skip the programming puzzle part of the interview and buy the candidate lunch instead.

> **POINTLESS PUZZLES**
>
> What a programming puzzle *does* do is test whether you've seen that particular puzzle before. I've only been given a puzzle in an interview once. I just happened to have written a book about programming puzzles a few weeks earlier (*Programming Puzzles Dissected*, Rod Stephens, 2016), so I was able to rattle off the solution immediately. The interviewer didn't learn much from it, but I found it mildly amusing.

The Bottom Line

There's really only one important question that an interview should resolve for both the interviewer and the candidate: "Should the candidate take the job?"

If you are the candidate, ask yourself whether you think it would be enjoyable to work with this group. There are a myriad other questions that go into that answer such as, "What is the salary and benefits package?" "What are the prospects for advancement?" and "Can I wear my bunny slippers on Casual Friday?" However, I humbly submit that the single most important question is, "Will I get along with these people?"

If you work with the right people, almost any job can be fun and rewarding. If you work with the wrong people, almost no job is worth the effort. I've worked on many projects with wonderful people where we had a great time building programs that solved customer problems effectively. I worked on one project that had no team spirit and a leader who didn't believe in the project, and that one was a miserable death march that everyone could see was doomed to failure.

Try to meet as many team members as possible during the interview and imagine sharing an office with each of them. You'll probably be spending more time with those people than you spend with anyone else outside of your immediate family, so think long and hard.

If you're the interviewer, the question is pretty much the same: "Will the team get along with this person?" It doesn't matter how brilliant a candidate is if they won't fit in with the team's culture.

To help make that decision, let the candidate interact with as many team members as possible. Take the team to lunch or something so the team members can get to know the candidate and vice versa.

Try to make things casual enough so the terrified candidate can work through any nervousness and bad first impressions and you can learn who they really are. You may need to make some allowances for introverts, the socially awkward, technophiles, manga fans, and others who are often attracted to software engineering. Yes, I'm being a bit glib here, but you should try not to penalize someone who doesn't do well in an interview setting. That person may be a perfect fit once they get settled in. Work and character references may be able to help. (This is sometimes the hardest part of the interview process.)

When the interview is over, ask the team members whether they could work with this person.

PHYSICAL ENVIRONMENT

The physical environment is as important as the cultural one. Developers can't do good work if they are uncomfortable, constantly distracted, or not distracted enough.

The following sections are far from complete, but they do highlight some of the key issues of a good physical work environment.

Creativity

As much as some managers might like to think that developers are interchangeable and you can buy them shrink-wrapped by the dozen, software engineering is a creative process. The best developers use their creativity to find the best solutions to their customers' problems. (In execuspeak, they synergize outside the box to shift paradigms and redefine core competencies.)

One of the keys to creativity seems to be a balance between two opposing forces: intense focus and distraction. When you know what you need to create (a high-level design, user interface, normalized database, or algorithm to calculate satellite transfer orbits), you need to focus on it so you can build it correctly. Sometimes this kind of work takes many hours of intense focus (the real kind, not the kind printed on an energy drink can).

During a long period of uninterrupted concentration, you can enter what psychologists call a *flow state* and the rest of us call *the zone*. Here everything just seems to fall into place (sometimes with a few nudges and harsh language). It's the programmer equivalent of a runner's high. In extreme cases I've awakened from the zone to realize that many hours have passed, the sun has set, and I really, *really* need to use the bathroom.

However, if you stay continually focused on a single problem, you may develop tunnel vision, where you only see one possible approach to a problem. If you already know that the approach will work, that's fine, but if you're still searching for a solution or you have reached a dead end, you can waste hours trying to force the wrong solution on the problem. At that point, some distraction is in order. Have lunch with your team, get coffee, take a walk, or do something else to distract yourself and let your subconscious wander through other possible solutions while you're not holding it back with intense focus. (Don't use the Internet for distraction, however, or you might get sucked into the endless vortices of social media and cat pictures.)

After you've cleared your head, you can go back to the problem you've been working on and perhaps you'll see a new approach.

Different people work best with different amounts of distraction. Some work effectively in a disciplined way with very little distraction. Others are more intuitive and need frequent interruptions for maximum effect. Let team members find their own balances. (And try to keep the super distractible people from interfering with the more disciplined team members too often.)

The COVID-19 pandemic provided an interesting and serendipitous experiment when tens of millions of people started working from home. Most people showed an increase in productivity due to fewer interruptions. It turns out that the workplace is even more distracting than a cat and close proximity to a refrigerator. Who knew?

At least they were more productive initially. After a few weeks, many were much less happy working remotely. They needed the distraction of the workplace and interaction with coworkers. You can get some interaction via Zoom and other online conferencing tools, and you can try to remember to give yourself appropriate distractions as needed, but humans are social creatures, and they need some interaction with other members of the software developer species to stay healthy.

Again, this applies differently to different people. Some would be perfectly happy to work remotely forever without seeing anyone from work for weeks at a time. For others remote work seems like the Hole in Shawshank State Prison.

Some companies view remote work as a way to save on office costs. Occasional remote work may be helpful, but too much might break your team.

Office Space

Over the decades, companies have experimented with many physical arrangements ranging from closed door offices and cube farms to enormous open spaces containing dozens of developers.

One of the key features of a good working environment seems to be balance. Developers must be able to easily collaborate (so open spaces are good), but they also sometimes need peace and quiet to work alone (so open spaces are bad). They work best without distraction (so closed-door offices are good), but sometimes they need to clear their minds with a little distraction (so closed door offices are bad).

The two most productive environments that I've worked in were openish. There was both privacy and distraction as needed.

The first had individual offices, but pieces of the team met very frequently and informally. We would work for a few hours in the morning, and then a small group would go get coffee. A few more hours of work, and another group (not always the same people) would get lunch. If you wanted privacy, you closed your door and everyone knew not to knock unless the building was on fire.

The second had offices surrounding a central meeting area called the Pit. (It seems like developers always give such areas cute names like the Pit, the Bullpen, or the Command Center. Naturally, true code warriors will call it the Thunderdome.) The Pit was broken up into semiprivate work areas by plastic plants and other dividers to give the illusion of privacy when needed, and everyone respected that illusion. Anyone who needed extra concentration wore headphones, and removing headphones was a sign that you were open to distraction.

I've also worked in cube farms (we affectionately called one with brightly colored partitions the Crayola Factory), chemistry labs, closed offices with officemates (who were working on other projects), and closed offices without frequent team interaction. I survived them all, but none of those were as productive because they didn't give the right privacy/distraction balance that I needed.

Ergonomics

The word "ergonomics" comes from the Greek root *ergon*, meaning work, so ergonomics is the study of work. In its broad sense, it's everything that goes into an effective workplace, so it covers everything in this chapter and more. In this section, I want to mention just a few ergonometric safety ideas that apply to software developments.

If you've worked in software engineering for any length of time, you've probably met someone with severe eyestrain, carpal tunnel syndrome, computer back, trigger finger, mouse shoulder, tech neck, BlackBerry thumb, iPad hand, Wiiitis, or Nintendinitis. (No, I didn't make up any of those.) They may have silly names (they have more medical-sounding names too), but if you've had any of them, you know how terrible they can be.

PAINFUL ENCOUNTERS

My editor tells me that he got a bad case of tendonitis and some weird Ctrl-key-itis while writing a book on an IBM XT clone. I remember a former teammate who had a case of carpal tunnel that was so bad it kept her in wrist braces for months. I've occasionally had weird Ctrl- and mouse-induced injuries too. I wouldn't be surprised if most developers have a brush with at least one of these at some point in their careers.

You don't know pain until you've had a back or neck injury so bad that you can only get two or three hours of sleep per night. Obviously, these sorts of injuries can ruin your ability to develop software.

This topic is worth a chapter on its own and there isn't room for that here, so here's a list of rules that you can follow to help prevent these sorts of injury.

➤ Use an adjustable ergonomic chair that lets you use good posture. Don't hunch over your computer. Ideally, also use an adjustable desk so you can get everything just right.

➤ Note that you may need to make adjustments if you're used to working in an office and are now working remotely. You may not have the same kind of chair and desk at home, and you may need to adjust the spacing if you're now typing with a cat on your lap.

➤ Place your monitor at or slightly below eye level. Adjust your chair and desk so your elbows are a bit above the desk so they are unsupported and your forearms are parallel to the floor. (If you're using a laptop, you probably can't put the screen at eye level and keep the keyboard low enough for proper elbow positioning. A docking station with a separate keyboard can help.)

➤ Position your mouse at the same height as the keyboard and close to the keyboard so you don't have to reach far for it.

➤ Makes sure your main light source doesn't shine in your face or directly on the screen. Use an anti-glare shield if that helps. (I once worked in an office where, for about three months of the year, the sun shone through the window at a low angle in the afternoon so I couldn't see anything. Building maintenance wouldn't let me install heavier curtains to block the light because they thought it would mess up the building's exterior esthetics, so I stapled some sheets of paper between the curtains and their inner lining. It looked terrible, but no one noticed because no one looked at the building's exterior. It's not like it was the Louvre or anything.)

➤ Most importantly, take frequent breaks and move around. Many of these injuries are caused by holding the same position or repeating the same fine motor motions without a break. Walk around, stretch, visit the watercooler, or go bug a coworker.

➤ Most importantly (okay, there are two most importantlies), if you start feeling symptoms of any of these problems (pain in the wrist, thumb, neck, shoulder, back, legs; frequent headaches; eyestrain or watering eyes; muscle spasms or referred pain), seek help. At least do an online search to figure out what's causing the problem and fix it. Left unchecked, some of these injuries can require surgery and extensive rehab.

As is often the case when you're working with people, individuals may have different styles of working comfortably. Some like a hard chair with arm rests while others like ball chairs or standing desks. Some like a monitor inset into a desk while others like a giant screen on the wall. Some like to listen to death metal in a dim room while others prefer a brightly lit environment filled with bubblegum pop. Try to let team members figure out what works best for them. And if the death metal rocker and the bubblegum popper must share an office, buy the former some sunglasses, the latter a desk lamp, and both of them nice headphones.

Work-Life Balance

Reasoning that happy, healthy employees are productive employees, many companies provide some pretty useful benefits like healthcare, profit sharing, conference travel budgets, unlimited vacation, and season passes to local attractions.

Some companies provide features to encourage developers to stay on-site. I worked with one company that had an official "company mom" whose job was to ensure that developers had the snacks, drinks, and other basic comforts. I've worked with several companies that provided free snacks, coffee, and soft drinks, and just about any company can have pizza delivered for late night design sessions. And I've heard of companies that offer on-site childcare, foot massages, ping-pong tables, and gourmet cafeteria food.

Some of the larger software juggernauts provide similar benefits in a grandiose attempt to duplicate the atmosphere of a university campus. They try to create an environment where you can work, play, eat, sleep, and practically live.

Apple Park in Cupertino, California, is surrounded by parkland and includes a 100,000 square foot fitness center, two miles of walking and running trails, and a store where employees can presumably get the latest iPhone without waiting in line overnight.

Salesforce Tower in San Francisco has social lounges, meditation rooms stocked with pillows and books about mindfulness, and kitchen islands stocked with snacks and drinks. (Probably not the hard stuff, except perhaps on the executive floors.)

Facebook's campus in Menlo Park, California, has a nine-acre green roof with a half-mile walk that winds through gardens, cafes, gathering spaces, and work cabanas.

Microsoft's complex in Redmond, Washington, has outdoor meeting spaces grouped into "villages" or "team neighborhoods," walking and running trails, soccer and cricket pitches, and retail space.

Finally, Google's Googleplex in Mountain View, California, in addition to having a cool name, boasts free gBikes to help employees get around, outdoor seating with colorful umbrellas, an organic fruit and vegetable garden, a sculptures garden featuring various androids, sports fields, tennis courts, sand volleyball courts, 24/7 gym, on-site doctor, dry cleaning, cafeterias, micro kitchens, lawnmower goats, nap pods, slides from floor to floor, and even temperature-controlled toilet seats.

Recently some have questioned the long-term benefits of these arrangements. Fitness centers, slides, and gourmet cafeterias are nice (or so I would imagine), but they skew the work-life balance toward work. There's nothing wrong with occasionally distracting yourself by playing table tennis at work, but is it better to stay on campus than to go home and walk the dog or go out with nonwork friends?

You should try to maintain a reasonable work-life balance, and you should encourage your teammates to do the same. Sometimes team members can put in a few extra hours to meet a tight deadline, but working 80-hour weeks isn't sustainable, even if a few of those hours are spent in a meditation room. You'll either reduce the team's capabilities or lose your best people to your competitors. (Or they may quit to open a bookstore, bakery, or organic taqueria cart.)

Spending time with the team to build a good work culture is important, but it's also important to visit friends and relatives. After all, your company isn't a secret society that makes you abandon all outside contact like the Freemasons, Illuminati, or Cub Scouts.

COLLABORATION SOFTWARE

Collaboration software from A to Z: Airtable, Basecamp, ClearMeeting, Drupal, Elluminate, Figma, Gliffy, HumHub, InLoox, JotSpot, Kahootz, Liferay, Mikogo, Nefsis, OpenProject, PlayCanvas, (IBM Lotus) QuickPlace, RelateIQ, Slack, Telligent, ubiDesktop, Vignette, Workamajig, XaitPorter, Yammer, Zulip. Those are just a few of the vast throng of available collaboration tools. (I was planning to invent names for any missing letters, but that turned out to be unnecessary.)

These sorts of tools became much more popular when the COVID-19 pandemic really got rolling in 2020 and millions of people suddenly started working at home (often using the Zoom online collaboration tool, hence the term "zoom boom"). Tools like these sit in the programmer's sweet spot, combining shiny technology, working from home in your pajamas, and the ability to make your Zoom background look like the bridge of the *Millennium Falcon*.

Some people have even used MMOs (massively multiplayer online games) to host meetings. Everyone creates an avatar and interacts in a virtual environment that could look like a boardroom, beach, or sidewalk café (or a monster-infested castle allowing you to say things like, "Look out! Here comes a troll!" without anyone knowing whether you're talking about the game or a coworker). These sorts of environments may become even more common if Mark Zuckerberg's vision of the metaverse comes true.

Many people who might otherwise never have discovered remote collaboration have given these programs a try, so they are probably here to stay. Even as the pandemic fades into a minor annoyance, it will still be convenient (and cheaper) to do at least some work and have at least some meetings remotely.

These tools provide various levels of all sorts of collaboration and have different features, prices, platforms (some are web-based and others are local programs), email integration, telephony support, web conferencing, file sharing, project management, faxing, and more. Some can probably even host meetings over telegraph and record conference calls on eight-track tape. There are so many options that I can't cover them all here.

However, I do want to mention two items that you might consider when trying to pick and use one of the hundreds (perhaps thousands) of programs available: searching and overload.

Searching

Video and audio meetings are convenient and easy (although many people can't seem to get their cameras working, particularly if they just woke up and haven't combed their hair yet), but those kinds of meetings are hard to search. If you have a five-hour weekly meeting (my friend Mark did), it's going to be hard to search through the archives to find exactly who suggested that everyone should wear propeller beanies to build team spirit. (Actually, that idea is so weird that everyone would probably remember exactly who said it, but you get the idea.)

If some important decision was made during a video or audio conference call, pinpointing where it happened and getting details will probably be hard, even if you record the call. (If you do record the call, then you could probably use a speech-to-text application to make a transcript, although that will add more work to your schedule. For example, see `threads.cloud/5-call-transcription-software-tools-to-record-transcribe-meetings`.)

Some video call services can provide automatic close captioning, which is surprisingly good, but the ones I've seen don't save the captioning even if you save a record of the call, so you can't search the captions. Some, like Zoom, may allow you to create captions for saved video, so you could create a transcript that way, but it'll probably take a few extra steps.

If you don't have that option, you may want to appoint a scribe to type minutes and record any important decisions. The minutes can then be saved in an email archive or some other location for later searching.

Overload

The second point I want to make about these sorts of tools is that you should try to avoid overloading the team members with a huge library of tools, no matter how dazzling they are. It seems like everyone has their favorite application that they are convinced is the communication and management holy grail.

I've worked on projects that used two or three different tools for different purposes. Sometimes I've worked on multiple projects at the same time, and of course, they used different tools. And of course my kids' school projects and other activities used still more tools. My defense mechanism was to ignore most of the tools and just check the others occasionally.

If you want to prevent team members from becoming Slack slackers as I did, try to use just one or two of the simplest tools possible and only a few broad information channels. If you throw too may tools or too much information at people, they will either ignore most of it or waste a huge amount of time trying to keep track of everything.

OUTSOURCING

I want to briefly touch on one last topic before this chapter ends: outsourcing. Some companies think outsourcing is a magical formula that will let them save costs on office space, equipment (such as chairs, desks, and computers), salary, benefits, and other overhead. If the project needs more people, you just hire more outsourced workers. If the project is going smoothly, you let some go.

Some of that is true to an extent, but outsourcing isn't always as simple as management might wish, particularly for something as complicated as software development. Some of the issues that can cause problems when outsourcing include things like working across multiple time zones, language and cultural differences, decreased security, and different tax and legal systems. Some of the most difficult problems, however, revolve around the team concepts described in this chapter.

If parts of the team are located in multiple places, it's harder to develop a common culture, harder to communicate, and harder to stay pointed in the same direction.

The "add or remove developers as needed" strategy rarely works well in practice because it takes a relatively long time to bring new people up to speed. On the other side of the equation, however, I've known outsourcing agencies to move someone from project A to project B because project B was in trouble, thus leaving project A to train someone new.

It's also harder for the project manager to keep control of the remote pieces. I worked on one project where a large reporting subsystem was outsourced, complete with its own project management to track progress. They remained on track (at least officially) right up until their due date, when they were suddenly only half done. They hadn't really been on track the whole time, but the main project manager only knew what the outsourcing agency told us. Had the remote team been local, we probably would have had better communication and might have realized there was a problem in time to take action. After working with the outsourced members for a while, the project manager could also have developed a better sense of how accurate their time estimates were.

Outsourcing isn't always a total disaster, however, and I know of one project that used outsourcing extremely well. The main development team (in the United States) would make changes during their workday and then send their changes to a test team in India. The test team would do their best to break the code during *their* workday while the Americans slept and post the results for the American team to review in the morning. This arrangement worked well because the test team had very clear goals and that let it work independently. Their testing also wasn't on the critical path, so some tests could be delayed, if necessary, without seriously hurting the rest of the project's schedule. The fact that new development and testing did not need to occur at the same time let the team take advantage of the different time zones. (Although video meetings between the two groups were terribly early or terribly late for one group or the other.)

Outsourcing (and to a lesser extent remote work) works best if the remote team has very clearly defined goals that don't affect the project's schedule too heavily and you make extra effort to communicate and track progress.

SUMMARY

The construction, care, and feeding of an effective team is as much art as science. Different software development teams generally have different people, goals, schedules, environments, and other factors that make the team behave differently as a whole. You may be able to build the perfect house-painting team and run things pretty much the same way for every project, but that isn't usually the case with software development teams.

When you're building your team, think about desirable features such as well-defined roles, clear goals, shared accountability, and trust. Create a pleasant physical environment that uses good ergonomics. Then let people modify it to suit their needs.

As the team comes together, keep an eye on its growing culture to ensure that team members bond and aren't torn apart by cliques, gossip, or toxic workplace syndrome.

Throughout it all use effective collaboration tools but try not to overload the team members. A few authoritative channels bolstered by individual communication will generally be more effective than dozens of subchannels covering increasingly specialized topics.

After you do build a successful team, try to preserve what worked and change what didn't. If some of the team members work well together, try to keep them together in the future. If the Thunderdome was too distracting for some people, you might try upgrading to cubes or offices, or at least add more barriers to create some extra privacy.

Building an effective team is an enormous topic. Ergonomics alone can fill a book or two. If you search online (and I encourage you to do so), you can find team-building books, DVDs, games, and activities all designed to help you build a team and foster teamwork.

Effective leadership is one of the more important features of a productive team. The next chapter talks about one facet of effective leadership: project management. It describes project management in general and mentions some of the tools that you can use to help keep a project moving in the right direction.

EXERCISES

1. List nine features of an effective project team.

2. List eight common software development team roles.

3. Match the following situations with the person who should handle them.

TASK	PERSON
Writing up notes listing decisions made during a video conference call	Language lawyer
Figuring out why the compiler doesn't like the statement ++i++	Toolsmith
Helping a new developer learn how to use the project's arcane document tracking system	Facilitator
Building a tool to format and display customized reports	Mentor
Helping the dispatch team and the email team agree on an interface	Scribe

4. List six activities that promote team culture.

5. List 10 team culture killers that can create a toxic workplace.

6. What is the most important question for a job candidate to answer while meeting the team during an interview?

7. To promote creativity, you need a balance between what two things?

8. What is ergonomics?

9. Which of the following are real injuries: BlackBerry thumb, computer back, iPad hand, mouse shoulder, Nintendinitis, tech neck, trigger finger, Wiiitis?

10. Do you agree or disagree with this statement: "The best way to get the proper information to the right people is to create many specialized communication channels." Why?

WHAT YOU LEARNED IN THIS CHAPTER

➤ Features of an effective team:
  ➤ Clear roles
  ➤ Effective leadership
  ➤ Clear goals
  ➤ Consensus
  ➤ Open communication
  ➤ Support for risk-taking
  ➤ Shared accountability
  ➤ Informal atmosphere
  ➤ Trust
➤ Common team roles:
  ➤ Project manager
  ➤ Technical lead
  ➤ Team leader
  ➤ Developer
  ➤ Customer
  ➤ Analyst
  ➤ Sys admin
  ➤ DBA
➤ Anything that lets team members socialize (get together without working on the project) can build team culture.
➤ Toxic workplace practices destroy team culture.

➤ The main question in an interview is, "Can this candidate work with this team?"

➤ Interview puzzles are fun but not very useful in interviews.

➤ Physical environment is important for an effective team.

➤ Creativity is fostered by a balance of concentration and distraction.

➤ Improper posture, poor equipment, and bad equipment arrangement can lead to severe, painful injuries.

➤ Team members can work extra-hard for short periods, but they need a work-life balance for the process to be sustainable.

➤ Ideally, collaboration tools should be searchable. If a tool is not searchable (for example, phone conferencing or videoconferencing), consider writing up notes that are searchable.

➤ Don't overload team members with too many information channels.

4

Project Management

Effective leadership is putting first things first. Effective management is discipline, carrying it out.

—Stephen Covey

No man goes before his time—unless the boss leaves early.

—Groucho Marx

What You Will Learn in This Chapter:

➤ What project management is and why you should care

➤ How to use PERT charts, critical path methods, and Gantt charts to create project schedules and estimate project duration

➤ How you can improve time estimates

➤ How risk management lets you respond quickly and effectively to problems

Part of the reason you implemented all the change tracking described in Chapter 2, "Before the Beginning," is so that you have historical information when you're writing your memoirs. It's so you know what happened, when, and why.

In addition to this peek into the past, you also need to keep track of what's going on in real time. Someone needs to track what's happening, what should be happening, and why the two don't match. That's where project management comes in.

Many software developers view management with suspicion, if not downright fear or loathing. They feel that managers were created to set unrealistic goals, punish employees when those goals aren't met, and take credit if something accidentally goes right. There are certainly managers like that, and Scott Adams has made a career out of making fun of them in his *Dilbert* comic strip, but some management is actually helpful for producing good software.

Management is necessary to ensure that goals are set, tracked, and eventually met. It's necessary to keep team members on track and focused on the problems at hand, without becoming distracted by inconsequential side issues such as new unrelated technology, impending layoffs, and *Angry Birds* tournaments.

On smaller projects, a single person might play multiple management roles. For example, a single technical manager might also handle project management tasks. On a really small project, a single person might perform every role, including manager, developer, tester, and end user. (Those are my favorite kinds of projects because the meetings and arguments are usually, but not always, short.)

No matter how big the project is, however, management tasks must be performed. The following sections describe some of the key management responsibilities that must be handled by someone for any successful software development project.

EXECUTIVE SUPPORT

Lack of executive management support is often cited as one of the top reasons why software projects fail. This is so important, it deserves its own note.

> **NOTE** To be successful, a software project must have consistent executive management support.

The highest-ranking executive who supports your project is often known as an *executive champion* or an *executive sponsor*.

Robust executive support ensures that a project can get the budget, personnel, hardware, software, office space, executive washroom keys, and other resources it needs to be successful. It lets the project team specify a realistic schedule even when middle management or customers want to arbitrarily shorten the timeline. Managers with limited software development experience often don't understand that writing quality software takes time. The end result isn't physical, so they may assume that you can compress the schedule or make do with fewer resources if you're properly motivated by pithy motivational posters.

Unfortunately, that usually doesn't work well with software development. When developers work long hours for weeks at a time, they burn out and write sloppy code. That leads to more bugs, which slows development, resulting in a delayed schedule, greater expense, and a low-quality result. Not only do you fail to achieve the desired time and cost savings, but you also get to take the blame for missing the impossible deadlines.

Executive support is also critical for allowing a project to continue when it encounters unexpected setbacks such as missed deadlines or uncooperative software tools. In fact, unexpected setbacks are so common that you should expect some to occur, even if you don't know what they will be. (Donald Rumsfeld would probably consider them "known unknowns." Some of us have been around long enough to remember him.)

Overall, the executive champion provides the gravitas needed for the project to survive in the rough-and-tumble world of corporate politics. It's a sad truth that different parts of a company don't always have the same goals. (In execuspeak, you might say the oars aren't all pulling in the same direction.) The executive champion can head off attempts to cancel a project and transfer its resources to some other part of the company.

In cases like those, work can be somewhat unnerving, even if you do have strong executive support. I once worked on a project where both our executive champion and our arch nemesis were corporate vice presidents directing thousands of employees. At times I felt like a movie extra hoping Godzilla and Mothra wouldn't step on us while they slugged it out over Tokyo. After two years of unflagging support by our champion, we finished the project and transferred it to another part of the company where it was quite successful for many years.

The executive champion is responsible for the following duties:

➤ Providing necessary resources such as budgets, hardware, and personnel
➤ Making "go/no-go" decisions and deciding when to cancel the project
➤ Giving guidance on high-level issues such as how the project fits into the company's overall business strategy
➤ Helping navigate any administrative hurdles required by the company
➤ Defining the business case
➤ Working with analysts, users, and other stakeholders to get buy-in
➤ Providing high-level feedback to developers about implemented features
➤ Buffering the project from external distractions (such as the rest of the company)
➤ Refereeing between managers, analysts, users, developers, and others interested in the project
➤ Supporting the project team
➤ Staying out of the way

The last point deserves a little extra attention. Most executives are too busy to micromanage each of the projects they control, but this can sometimes be an issue, particularly if the executive champion is near the bottom of the corporate ladder. If you are an executive champion, monitor the project to make sure it's headed in the right direction and that it's meeting its deadlines and other goals, but try not to add extra work. As Tina Fey says in her book *Bossypants*, "In most cases being a good boss means hiring talented people and then getting out of their way."

However, studies have shown that more engaged executives result in more successful projects, so don't just get things started and then walk away.

PROJECT MANAGEMENT

A *project manager* is often the highest-ranking member of the project team. Ideally, this person works with the team through all stages of development, starting with requirements gathering, moving through development and testing, and continuing until application rollout (and sometimes even beyond into future versions).

The project manager monitors the project's progress to ensure that work is heading in the right direction at an acceptable pace. This person meets with customers and other stakeholders to verify that the finished product meets their requirements. If the development model allows changes, the project manager ensures that changes are made and tracked in an organized manner so that they don't get lost and don't overwhelm the rest of the team.

A project manager doesn't necessarily need to be an expert in the users' field or in programming. However, both of those skills can be extremely helpful because the project manager is often the main interface between the customers and the rest of the project team.

Project manager duties are as follows:

- ➤ Helping define the project requirements
- ➤ Tracking project tasks
- ➤ Anticipating and responding to problems
- ➤ Managing risk
- ➤ Keeping users (and the executive champion) up-to-date on the project's progress
- ➤ Providing an interface between customers and developers
- ➤ Managing resources such as time, people, budget, hardware, software tools, and office space
- ➤ Managing delivery

MYRIAD MANAGERS

There are a lot of different kinds of project managers in addition to software project managers. Construction, architecture, engineering, and other fields have project managers. Just about any activity that involves more than a few people needs someone to perform project management duties, even if that person isn't called a project manager.

This book even has a project manager extraordinaire, David Clark. He makes sure I'm turning chapters in on time, passes chapters to various technical editors and copyeditors, and generally guides the book through the development process.

In practice, some project managers are promoted from the developer ranks, so they often have good development skills but weak project management skills. They can give useful advice to other programmers about how a particular piece of code should be written or how one subsystem should interact with another. They can provide technical leadership, but they're not always good at recognizing and handling scheduling problems when something goes wrong.

For that reason, some larger projects divide the project manager's duties among two or more people. One project I worked on had a person dedicated to task tracking and making sure we kept to the schedule. She had training in project management but no programming experience. If something started to slip, she immediately jumped all over the issue, figured out how much delay was required, asked about contingencies in case the task couldn't be finished, determined whether the delay would affect other tasks, and did all the nontechnical things a project manager must handle.

That person was called the "project manager," in contrast with the other project manager who was called the "project manager." It got a little confusing at times. Perhaps we should have called the task-tracking person the "developer babysitter" or the "border collie" because she gently guided us toward our goals by nipping at our heels. Often people call the other manager the "technical project manager," although that person may also handle nontechnical tasks such as interaction with customers and executives.

Meanwhile the "main" project manager was freed up to attack the problem from the development side. He could work with the developers to figure out what was wrong and how to fix it.

When I first encountered this setup, I thought it was kind of silly. Couldn't a single project manager handle both technical and tracking tasks? In our project, the separation actually made things easier. This may not be the right approach for every project, particularly small ones, but it was useful in our case.

If you are a project manager or want to become one, you should do a lot more reading about specific tools and techniques that are useful for keeping a project on track.

Before moving on to other topics, however, I want to cover a few more project management issues in greater detail. The next three sections describe PERT charts, the critical path method (CPM), and Gantt charts. PERT charts and CPM are generally used together but are separated here so that you can digest them in smaller pieces. Together these three tools can help you study the project's total duration, look for potential bottlenecks, and schedule the project's tasks.

However, you can't understand how tasks fit into a schedule unless you know how long those tasks will take, so the last sections about project management deal with predicting task lengths and with risk management.

PERT Charts

A *PERT chart* (PERT stands for Program Evaluation and Review Technique) is a graph that uses nodes (circles or boxes) and links (arrows) to show the precedence relationships among the tasks in a project. For example, if you're building a bunker for use during the upcoming zombie apocalypse, you need to build the outer defense walls before you can top them with razor wire.

PERT charts were invented in the 1950s by the United States Navy. The fact that they are still in use shows how useful they are. They come in two flavors: activity on arrow (AOA), where arrows represent tasks and nodes represent milestones, and activity on node (AON), where nodes represent tasks and arrows represent precedence relations. Activity on node diagrams are usually easier to build and interpret, so that's the kind described here.

To build an AON PERT chart, start by listing the tasks that must be performed, the tasks they must follow (their predecessors), and the time you expect each task to take. (You can also add best-case and worst-case times to each task if you want to perform more extensive analysis of the tasks and what happens when things go wrong.)

Note that you don't need to include every possible combination of predecessors. For example, suppose task C must come after task B, which must come after task A. In that case, task C must come after task A, but you don't need to include that relationship in the table if you don't want to. The fact that task C must come after task B is enough to represent that relationship. However, you also don't need to remove every unnecessary relationship. Those extra relationships won't hurt anything.

If you like, you can add a Start task as a predecessor for any other tasks that don't have predecessors. Similarly, you can add a Finish task for any other tasks that don't have successors.

To make rearranging tasks easy, make an index card or sticky note for each task. (You can draw the chart on a piece of paper or with a drawing tool, but index cards and sticky notes make it easy to shuffle tasks around if necessary.) Include each task's name, predecessors, and expected time.

Then to build the chart, follow these steps:

1. Place the Start task in a Ready pile. Place the other tasks in a Pending pile.

2. Position the tasks in the Ready pile in a column to the right of any previously positioned tasks. (The first time through, the Ready pile only contains the Start task, so position it on the left side of your desk.)

3. Look through the tasks in the Pending pile and cross out the predecessors that you just positioned. (Initially that means you'll be crossing out the Start task.) If you cross out a card's last predecessor, move it to a new Ready pile.

4. Repeat steps 2 and 3 until you have positioned the Finish task.

PUZZLING PREDECESSORS

If you don't move any tasks into the Ready pile during step 3, that means the tasks have a predecessor loop. In this case, task A is task B's predecessor and task B is task A's predecessor.

For example, at my college, you needed to pay registration fees before you could get your student ID; you needed a student ID to get financial aid checks; and you needed financial aid checks to pay registration fees. (At least, you probably did if you needed financial aid.) You needed to fill out extra paperwork to break out of the predecessor loop.

After you finish positioning all of the cards, draw arrows representing the predecessor relationships. (You may want to use a dry-erase marker so that you can get the arrows off your desk later.)

At this point, you have a chart showing the possible paths of execution for the tasks in the project.

BUILDING A PERT CHART

The steps for building a PERT chart are a bit confusing, so let's walk through an example that creates a PERT chart for a project that builds a bunker to protect you and your video games in case of a zombie apocalypse. (The U.S. Strategic Command actually developed a plan for fighting off a zombie apocalypse as part of a training exercise. You can read it at i2.cdn.turner .com/cnn/2014/images/05/16/dod.zombie.apocalypse.plan.pdf.)

Start by building a table that lists the tasks, their predecessors, and the times you expect them to take. Table 4.1 shows some of the tasks you would need to perform to build the bunker. To keep things simple, I've omitted a lot of details such as installing sewer lines, building forms for pouring concrete, and obtaining permits (assuming the planning officials haven't been eaten yet).

After you've built the task table, create index cards for the tasks (or be prepared to draw them with a drawing tool). Figure 4.1 shows what the card for task I might look like.

Next, start working through the four steps described earlier to arrange the cards. This is a lot easier to understand if you go to the trouble of creating index cards or sticky notes instead of trying to imagine what they would look like. Trust me. If you found the steps confusing, make the cards.

1. Place the Start task in a Ready pile. Place the other tasks in a Pending pile.

    Figure 4.2 shows the initial positions of the cards. (I've omitted the task names and abbreviated a bit to save space.)

2. Position the tasks in the Ready pile in a column to the right of any previously positioned tasks. (The first time through, the Ready pile contains only the Start task. Just position it on the left side of your desk.)

3. Look through the tasks in the Pending pile and cross out the predecessors that you just positioned. (Initially, that means you'll be crossing out the Start task.) If you cross out a card's last predecessor, move it to the new Ready pile.

    Referring to Figure 4.2, you see that tasks A, F, and H have the Start task as predecessors. In fact, the Start task is the only predecessor for those tasks, so when you cross out the Start task, you move tasks A, F, and H into the Ready pile. Figure 4.3 shows the new arrangement.

4. Repeat steps 2 and 3 until you have positioned the Finish task.

    During the first repetition, position tasks A, F, and H because they're in the Ready pile. Then cross them out for any tasks that are still in the Pending pile. When you cross out those tasks, task B loses its last predecessor so move it into the Ready pile. Figure 4.4 shows the new arrangement.

    During the second repetition of steps 2 and 3, position task B and remove it from the remaining tasks' predecessor lists. After you cross task B off, tasks C and I have no more predecessors so move them to the Ready pile. Figure 4.5 shows the new arrangement.

    By now you probably have the hang of it. Position tasks C and I, and remove them from the Pending tasks' predecessor lists. That removes the last predecessors from tasks D, E, and G, so move them to the ready pile, as shown in Figure 4.6.

In the next round, position tasks D, E, and G, and move the Finish task to the Ready pile. Then one final round positions the Finish task.

Now draw arrows showing the predecessor relationships between the tasks. You may need to adjust the spacing and vertical alignment of the tasks to make the arrows look nice. Figure 4.7 shows the final result.

To check your work, you can verify that each task has one arrow entering it for each of its predecessors. For example, task G has two predecessors, so it should have two arrows entering it.

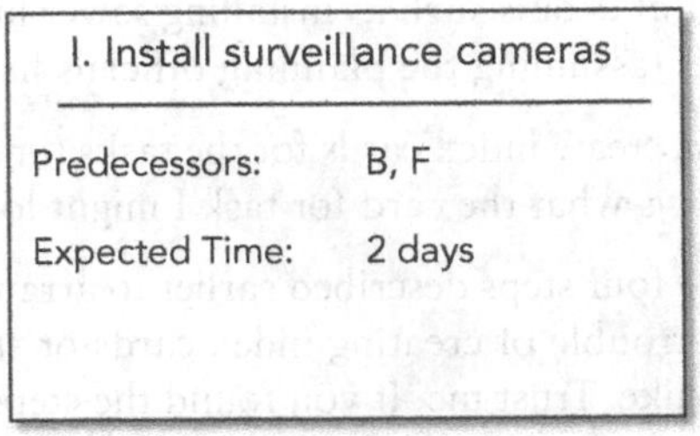

I. Install surveillance cameras

Predecessors: B, F

Expected Time: 2 days

FIGURE 4.1: Each task's card should hold its name, duration, and predecessors. You'll fill in the total time later.

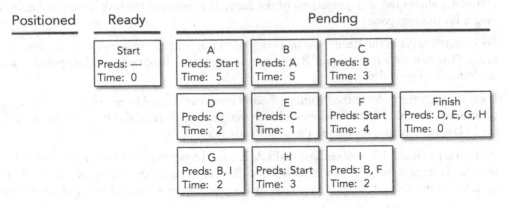

FIGURE 4.2: Initially only the Start task is in the Ready pile.

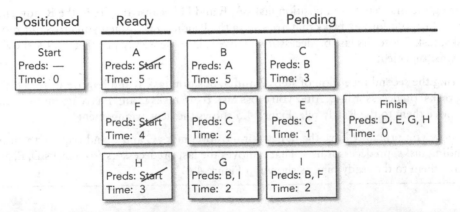

FIGURE 4.3: After one round, the Start task is positioned and tasks A, F, and H are in the Ready pile.

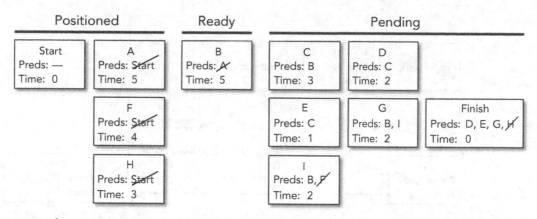

FIGURE 4.4: After two rounds, the Start task and tasks A, F, and H are positioned. Task B is in the Ready pile.

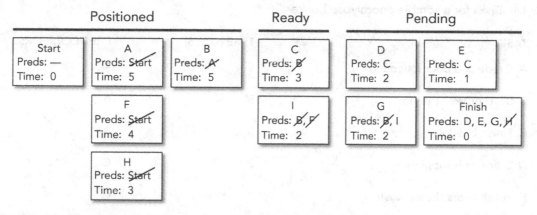

FIGURE 4.5: After three rounds, the Start task and tasks A, F, H, and B are positioned. Tasks C and I are in the Ready pile.

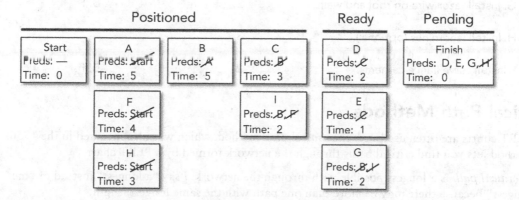

FIGURE 4.6: After four rounds, only the Finish task is still in the Pending pile.

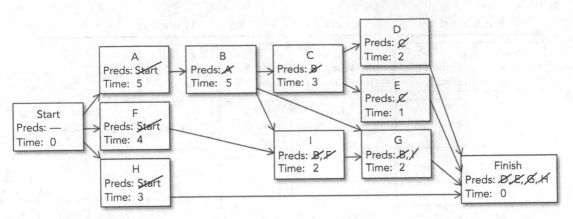

FIGURE 4.7: This PERT chart shows the paths of execution of the project's tasks.

TABLE 4.1: Tasks for a zombie apocalypse bunker

TASK	TIME (DAYS)	PREDECESSORS
A. Grade and pour foundation.	5	—
B. Build bunker exterior.	5	A
C. Finish interior.	3	B
D. Stock with supplies.	2	C
E. Install home theater system.	1	C
F. Build outer defense walls.	4	—
G. Install razor wire on roof and walls.	2	B, F
H. Install landmines (optional).	3	—
I. Install surveillance cameras.	2	B, F

Critical Path Methods

PERT charts are often used with the critical path method, which was also invented in the 1950s. That method lets you find critical paths through the network formed by a PERT chart.

A *critical path* is a longest possible path through the network. I say "a longest" instead of "the longest" because there may be more than one path with the same longest length.

For example, refer to the PERT network shown in Figure 4.7. The path Start ⇨ H ⇨ Finish has a total time of 3 days. (No charge for the Start and Finish, plus 3 days for task H.)

Similarly, the path Start ⇨ F ⇨ I ⇨ G ⇨ Finish has a total time of 0 + 4 + 2 + 2 + 0 = 8 days.

With a little study of Figure 4.7 and some trial and error, you can determine that this network has a single longest path: Start ⇨ A ⇨ B ⇨ C ⇨ D ⇨ Finish with a total length of 0 + 5 + 5 + 3 + 2 + 0 = 15 days. Because that's the longest path, it is also the critical path.

The critical path is called critical because, if any task along the path is delayed, the project's final completion is also delayed. For example, if task C "Finish the interior" takes 5 days instead of 3 (perhaps you decided to add a nice bar with beer and root beer taps), then the whole project will take 17 days instead of 15.

For a simple project like this one, it's fairly easy to find the critical path. For projects containing hundreds or even thousands of tasks, this could be a lot harder. Fortunately, there's a relatively easy way to find critical paths.

Start at the left with the Start task. It takes no time to start, so label that task with the total time 0.

Now move to the right, one column at a time. For each task in the current column, set its total time equal to that task's time plus the largest total time for its predecessor tasks.

While you're at it, highlight the link that came from the predecessor with the greatest total time. If more than one predecessor is tied for the largest total time, highlight them both.

When you're done, the Finish task will be labeled with the total time to complete the project (assuming nothing goes wrong, of course). You can follow the highlighted links back through the network to find the critical paths.

CRITICAL PATHS

In this example, let's walk through the steps for adding total time and critical path information to the zombie apocalypse bunker project PERT chart shown in Figure 4.7.

Start by setting the total time for the Start task to 0.

Referring to Figure 4.7, you can see that the next column of tasks holds tasks A, F, and H, which have expected times 5, 4, and 3, respectively. Each has only Start as a predecessor, and that task has a total time 0 (we just labeled it), so each of these tasks' total time is the same as its own expected time. (So far, not too interesting.)

The next column holds only task B. It has an expected time of 5 and a single predecessor with time 5, so its total time is 5 + 5 = 10. Figure 4.8 shows the network at this point. The new total times and the critical links are highlighted in bold. (You could also make them red, but that wouldn't show up well in this book.)

Now things get a bit more interesting. The next column holds tasks C and I. Task C has an expected time of 3 and a single predecessor with a total time of 10, so C's total time is 3 + 10 = 13.

Task I has an expected time of 2. It has two predecessors with total times of 10 and 4, so its total time is 2 plus the larger of 10 and 4, which is 2 + 10 = 12. Figure 4.9 shows the updated network.

The next column holds tasks D, E, and G.

Task D has an expected time of 2. Its single predecessor, C, has a total time of 13, so task D's total time is 2 + 13 = 15.

Task E has an expected time of 1. It also has the predecessor C with the total time 13, so task E's total time is 1 + 13 = 14.

Task G has an expected time of 2. It has two predecessors: B with a total time of 10 and I with a total time of 12. That means task G's total time is 2 + 12 = 14.

The final column holds the Finish task. It has an expected time of 0, so its total time is the same as its predecessor with the largest total time. That's task D with a total time of 15. Figure 4.10 shows the final network.

You can trace the bold arrows backward from the Finish to the Start in Figure 4.10 to find the critical path. Those tasks are (in their forward order) Start ⇨ A ⇨ B ⇨ C ⇨ D ⇨ Finish (as we found earlier).

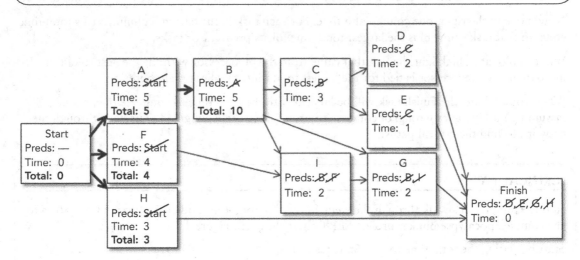

FIGURE 4.8: The total time for each task is its expected time plus the largest of its predecessors' total times.

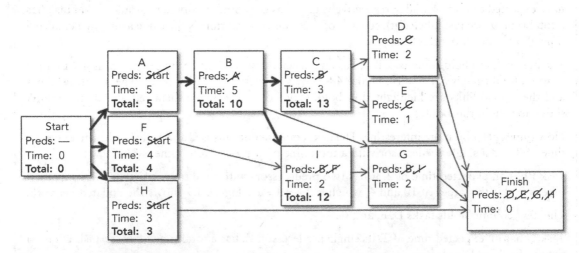

FIGURE 4.9: Task I's largest time predecessor is task B, so task I has a total time of 2 + 10 = 12.

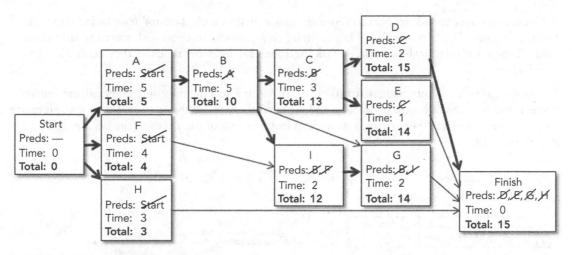

FIGURE 4.10: The complete zombie apocalypse bunker project has a total time of 15 days.

In addition to showing you the critical path, the PERT network with total times can help you study the project for other possible problems. For example, the critical path network shows you *task critical paths*. These are paths that are critical for some tasks but not for the project as a whole. For example, suppose task I is delayed because your electrical contractor dropped all of the cameras. If you follow the critical links out of task I, you can see that the delay will also push back task G. That's good to know as early as possible because it lets you call the razor wire contractors from Bob's Carpet, Tile, and Razor Wire to reschedule.

On a larger project, a delay on one task might ripple through the network and cause delays in many later tasks.

Figure 4.10 also shows two "almost critical paths." The paths through tasks E and G to the Finish task have total times of 14 days, which is only 1 day less than the project critical path. That means if any tasks along those paths are delayed by more than 1 day, the project's completion will be delayed.

The finished network also shows that tasks F and H don't play a major role in the project's final completion time. Task F could stretch out for up to 10 days without changing the critical path. Task H could run even longer, lasting up to 15 days without impacting the finish date.

To look at this another way, that means you have some flexibility with tasks F and H. You can delay their start a bit if you like without changing the critical path. Sometimes, delaying a task can be useful to balance staffing levels. (After they finish building the bunker walls in task B, you may want to use the same masons to build the outer defense walls in task F.)

There may also be some reason to rearrange tasks slightly. For example, task H is landmine installation. The whole project will probably be a lot safer if you delay that as long as possible so that people working on the project don't need to worry about stepping in the wrong places.

Gantt Charts

A *Gantt chart* is a kind of bar chart invented by Henry Gantt in the 1910s to show a schedule for a collection of related tasks. The fact that we're still using them more than 100 years later shows how useful they are for project scheduling.

A Gantt chart uses horizontal bars to represent task activities with the bars' lengths indicating the tasks' durations. The bars are placed horizontally on a calendar to show task start and stop times. Arrows show the relationships between tasks and their predecessors much as they do in a PERT chart.

Figure 4.11 shows a Gantt chart that I drew in Microsoft Excel for the zombie apocalypse bunker project. I've followed a common practice and repeated the task names on the right to make it easier to see which tasks start the arrows. Arrows lead from the end of each task to the beginning of successor tasks.

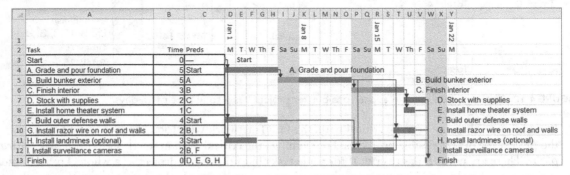

FIGURE 4.11: A Gantt chart shows task durations, start times, end times, and dependencies.

Notice that some of the tasks have been extended to cover the gaps created by weekends. (Figure 4.11 ignores holidays such as New Year's Day for simplicity, but in a real project you would need to account for them as well.) Also notice that the weekends have extended the project's total duration from 15 working days to 19 calendar days. (In case of a real zombie emergency, you might want to work through the weekends and holidays. I'm sure the zombies will!)

To build a Gantt chart, list the tasks, their durations, and their predecessors on the left, as shown in Figure 4.11.

Next, cut out a thin rectangle for each task. Give each rectangle a width that represents its duration. (For example, you could make each rectangle 1-inch wide per day.) Write the tasks' names on their rectangles.

Next, move from left to right through the columns in the PERT chart, placing each rectangle so that its left edge lines up with the right edge of its rightmost predecessor rectangle. For example, in Figure 4.11, the left edge of task G lines up with the right edge of task I.

If a rectangle includes a weekend, lengthen it so that it gets its required number of working days.

Finally, after you've positioned all the rectangles, add arrows to show the predecessor relationships.

A Gantt chart has a couple of advantages over a PERT chart. Instead of displaying tasks in somewhat arbitrary columns, it graphically shows each task's start and end time. Because the tasks are aligned with a calendar instead of in columns, you can see which tasks will span weekends and holidays.

A Gantt chart also shows task *slack time*, the time by which a task can be delayed without delaying successor tasks. For example, you can slide tasks F and H to the right until their right edges line up with their closest successor tasks (I and Finish, respectively).

Scheduling Software

The preceding sections explained how you can build PERT charts, find critical paths, and draw Gantt charts by hand. The process isn't too difficult, but the result isn't very flexible. For example, suppose you decide to add a gas-powered generator and you want to run underground cables between it and the bunker before you pour the foundation.

Or suppose you start work and building the bunker takes longer than expected. In both of those cases, you need to shift some of the tasks farther to the right. Because I drew the schedule by hand, rearranging those tasks can be a hassle. The problem would be much worse for larger projects.

Fortunately, there are lots of project scheduling tools available for your computer. They make building schedules relatively easy and provide lots of extra features. For example, some enable you to click and drag to connect two tasks or to change a task's duration.

Some of those tools also enable you to define other kinds of relationships between tasks. For example, you might indicate that two tasks should start at the same time or that one task should start five days after another task starts.

I hesitate to recommend any particular application because I've only tried a handful and there are so many that, as a percentage, I've tried roughly 0.0 percent of them. In fact, there are so many project management tools out there that it's even hard to count the sites that review them. Here are just a few articles that review project management tools.

➤ www.consumervoice.org/top-project-management-software

➤ www.capterra.com/project-management-software

➤ www.softwareadvice.com/project-management

➤ thedigitalprojectmanager.com/tools/best-project-management-software

➤ www.proofhub.com/articles/project-management-app-comparison

➤ www.top10.com/project-management/comparison

➤ mopinion.com/top-20-best-project-management-software-an-overview

Some of those articles give ratings and detailed tips about what you should look for in project management applications. Some of the application names that pop up on several of these lists include (in alphabetical order):

➤ Asana

➤ ClickUp

➤ Jira

➤ Kintone

➤ Monday.com

> ➤ Trello
>
> ➤ Wrike

If you need to manage a lot of project schedules or schedules with many tasks, you should test-drive some of these tools to find one you like.

Predicting Times

PERT charts, critical path methods, and Gantt charts are great tools for figuring out how long a project will take, but they depend on your time estimates being accurate. If the times you assign for the tasks aren't reasonable, then those carefully built charts are nothing more than elaborate examples of GIGO (garbage in, garbage out).

One of the hardest parts of software engineering is predicting how long each task will take. One reason for this difficulty is that you rarely need to do *exactly* the same thing on multiple projects. You may need to do something similar to something you did earlier, but the details are different enough to add some uncertainty. If a project includes a task that is *exactly* the same as one you've performed before, you can just copy the code you used before, pop the champagne, and take credit for a job well done. High fives all around!

For example, suppose you're building an inventory application for a unicycle store and you want to include screens that let the employees record daily timesheets. If you've built timesheet forms in a previous application, you can probably copy most or all the forms and code you wrote for the previous application and save a huge amount of time on that task.

Even if you need to make some fairly major changes, you can probably still skip a lot of the database design, form layout, and other pieces of this task that took up a lot of time when you built your first timesheet system.

Sometimes, you can take this idea even further and avoid building an entire project, either by reusing a previous project or by purchasing a commercial off-the-shelf (*COTS*) application.

COTS

CUSTOMER: I need to perform a lot of calculations, but they may change over time. Can you build something where I can enter values and equations in some sort of grid and make the program perform the calculations for me?

CONSULTANT: I could, but it would probably take a month or so and cost $20,000. What you should probably do is buy a COTS spreadsheet. It'll save you time and money and will probably be better in the long run.

CUSTOMER: Hmm. Okay. How about a program that helps me track task assignments for a long project? You know, to keep track of who's falling behind and how that will impact the final schedule?

> CONSULTANT: Well, a basic program wouldn't be too hard. Maybe three weeks and $10,000 or $15,000. But you could just download some project management software. There are even free versions available if you don't need all the bells and whistles.
>
> CUSTOMER: I see. Is there anything you *can* do for me?
>
> CONSULTANT: I just saved you $30,000, didn't I? Ha ha.
>
> CUSTOMER: Yes you did! Ha ha. You're fired.

The fact that you can reuse code (to some extent anyway) if you've performed the same task before means many software engineering tasks either have fairly short well-defined times or you have little notion about how long they will take. In contrast, jobs that don't live inside cyberspace often include tasks that have well-defined durations even if they take a long time.

For example, suppose your company builds bee fences to keep elephants away from villages. You know from years of experience that it takes one person one day to build 50 feet of fence. If you have four employees and a customer wants a 400-foot fence, you can do some simple math to figure out how long it will take: $400 \div 50 \div 4 = 2$ days.

If a new customer wants another 400-foot fence, you still know with reasonable certainty that it will take two days.

In contrast, suppose you want to build a bee fence design program. It will enable the user to enter some specifications and draw the fence on a map. The program will create a bill of materials, create purchase orders for the materials, and either print them or transmit them to suppliers electronically, create a work schedule based on expected delivery dates, print (or transmit) an invoice for upfront costs, and generate a final invoice.

If you've never built this kind of application before, you probably don't know how long it will take to build. After you've built it, however, you won't need to build it again.

So if you assume a task's time estimate is either (1) short and well known or (2) long and highly uncertain, how can you create usable time estimates? Or are you doomed to rely on uninformed guesses and a Ouija board? Fortunately, there are a few things you can do to minimize your risk even when you step into the great unknown.

Get Experience

One way to improve time estimates is to make the unknown known. If you can find someone who has done something similar to what you need to do, get that person to help. In smaller projects, you may be unable to pull people from other parts of your company to bring much needed experience to your team, but sometimes you can get them to help part time. They may give you time estimates that are better than random guesses, and they may give your team members some guidance about how to do the work.

Experience is even more important for long and difficult tasks. In a large project, it may be worthwhile to hire new, experienced team members to tackle tricky tasks. I worked on one algorithmic project where we hired an algorithms specialist to help with maintenance. It was a good thing we did because he was the only one on the maintenance team who could understand how that part of the program worked.

Having people with previous experience can make or break a project. In fact, it's a software engineering best practice.

> **TIP** *Create a team that includes people who have done something similar before. This is particularly important for the project lead, who will give guidance to the other team members.*

Using experienced team members is the single best way to make time estimates more reliable.

Break Unknown Tasks into Simpler Pieces

Sometimes, you can break a complicated task into simple pieces that are easier to understand. In fact, that's basically what high-level and low-level designs are all about—breaking complicated tasks into simpler pieces.

For example, suppose the bee fence application needs an inventory component to track the materials your company has on hand and to order more material as needed. You may not know exactly how hard this is because you haven't done it before, but with some work (and possibly some advice from someone with previous experience), you can break the tasks into smaller pieces. The following list includes some of the things you'll need to do to build the inventory system:

➤ Design an Inventory database table to store information about inventory items.

➤ Build a screen to let the user add and remove items from the Inventory table.

➤ Build an interface to let the program add and remove items from inventory as they are ordered and used in projects.

➤ Create an alert system to let someone know when you're running out of bees.

You may not know *exactly* how much time you'll need for each of these subtasks, but you can probably make better guesses than you could for the inventory subsystem as a whole.

> **TIP** *If you have access to people experienced with the task, have them review your breakdown before you finalize your time estimates. They may know from experience that you'll need to add a* LeadTime *field to the Inventory table or that creating an alert system takes a lot longer than you might expect. You'd probably discover those things as the project continued anyway, but learning this at the start will make your time estimates more accurate and may save you a lot of time and frustration trying to overcome problems that have been solved before.*

Breaking a complex task lets you convert a large unknown into several smaller pieces, which may individually be a bit more predictable.

Look for Similarities

Sometimes, tasks that you don't understand are at least somewhat similar to tasks that you have performed before. You may not have ordered live bees before, but you have ordered wire and fence posts, so you know at least a little about how to order supplies from distributors.

Obviously, there are some differences between bees and spools of wire, so you should expect to do some extra research before making your time estimates: Should you buy packaged bees, nucs, or established colonies? How early should you order the bees? They probably won't last as long in the warehouse as a pile of fence posts will.

As is the case in which you break large tasks into smaller ones, you should run your ideas past someone with experience if you can. They can tell you the things you missed and tell you where you may find unexpected problems.

Expect the Unexpected

Obviously, you can't predict every problem that comes along, but there are some delays that are reasonably predictable. For example, in any large project, some team members will become ill and miss some work time. They'll go on vacation and need time off for personal emergencies.

One way to handle this sort of lost time is to expand each task's time estimate by some amount. For example, adding 5 percent to each task's time allows for 2.6 weeks per year for vacation and sick leave.

One drawback to this approach is that people tend to use up any extra time scheduled for a task. For example, suppose a task should take 20 working days and you add an extra day to allow for lost time. If there are no problems with the task, you should finish it in 20 days and save the extra day for later in the project when you catch the plague and need to use that day as sick leave. Unfortunately, most people will use up all 21 days and save nothing for later. Instead of allowing a 5 percent margin, you've basically just extended the project timeline by 5 percent.

Another approach is to add specific tasks to the project to represent lost time. If team members schedule their vacations in advance, you can include those explicitly. (Be sure not to let one team member volunteer for every "vacation time" task.)

You can also add tasks to represent sick time. Of course, you can't predict when people will get sick (with a few exceptions such as the days before and after long weekends), but you can add "sick time" tasks to the end of the schedule. Then when someone contracts a bad case of Sunny Friday-itis, you can move the time from the "sick time" tasks to the tasks that are delayed.

Another kind of lost time problem occurs when your team is all geared up and raring to go but can't get anything done because of some other scheduling problem. The classic example is trying to get management approval during the holiday season. You have your project schedule worked out to the millisecond, but progress grinds to a halt because you need approval from the VP of Pens and Pencils to order more highlighters and he's in Jamaica for two weeks. And don't expect your developers to be productive on August 20 if you order their computers on August 19. It's going to take some time to receive the computers, get the network running, test the email system, and install *Call of Duty*.

You can avoid these kinds of problems by carefully planning for approvals, holidays, order lead times, and setup. In fact, while you're at it, you may as well make them tasks and put them in the schedule.

A fairly new form of lost time that has become common during the COVID-19 pandemic is supply chain delays. Supply chain issues are complicated, but two of the biggest issues are (1) too little production to meet demand and (2) no excess capacity in the supply chain (no extra ships, port space, warehouse space, truck drivers, and so on). This made the supply chain a lean, mean, car part delivery machine, but when demand shifted, the system failed catastrophically. Now a delivery that used to take days or weeks may take months or years.

JUST-IN-TIME DISASTER

In the mid-1900s, Japanese industrial engineer Taiichi Ohno pioneered an inventory technique called kanban that allowed Toyota to reorder parts only when they were needed. That allowed the company to avoid a buildup of inventory. Imagine an ever-growing pile of tires on the manufacturing floor because you order too many each week. Or worse, if you order too few vanity mirrors each week, the entire assembly line comes to a halt until you can FedEx a pallet load from Monaco (I'm assuming).

The kanban system formed the basis of modern *lean manufacturing*, which is also called *just-in-time manufacturing* or *JIT*. (The term "JIT" has also been applied to JIT compilers, which compile code just before it is executed. When used alone, "JIT" usually refers to the inventory and manufacturing process.) (In Chapter 19, "RAD," you'll see how kanban is applied to a software development model that is appropriately named kanban.)

Fast-forward to 2020. Imagine a long supply chain of parts, each depending on the one before and all fine-tuned with the latest JIT principles. Chips go onto boards that go into subassemblies that make up assemblies that get duct-taped to a car (again, I'm assuming), and the finished cars are shipped to your local Lexus dealer. Now imagine a shock to the system where the people who make the chips can't go to work for some hypothetical reason (*cough* pandemic *cough*). This reverberates up the chain causing massive disruption all the way to the Lexus dealer.

When the chips stop flowing, good JIT principles stop the flow of all of the other parts too. For example, the manufacturer sees that they can't make any new boards, so they stop the flow of other board components such as wires, transistors, heat sinks, fans, and whatnot. Not only are the chip people out of work, but so are the people who make the board components. These problems make the supply chain vibrate like a guitar string struck by a sledgehammer and everything grinds to a halt.

To make matters worse, once those processes have stopped, many of them take a while to get back up and running. The chip manufacturers may be ready to roll again, but the heat sink company may not be. It may take a few years to get back to finely tuned JIT production. Meanwhile, customer demand may have changed, and people may decide to buy bicycles instead of Lexi, but that's another story.

Long and fragile supply chains shouldn't be a problem for software resources (I don't think there's a huge shortage of sorting algorithms), but it may be an issue when you're trying to build a call center with hundreds of workstations, printers, ergonomic chairs, backlit split keyboards, *Dilbert* calendars, and amusing desk toys. Try to get estimates of shipping times (people are learning to track the new, slower delivery pipeline) and allow some slack for delays. For nonperishable items (like keyboards, not bees), order early so your equipment is handy when you need it.

Track Progress

Even if you have previous experience with a type of task, break the task into smaller pieces, plan for lost time, and allow a buffer for unexpected problems, sometimes things just take longer than you expect. It's extremely important to keep track of tasks as they progress and take action if one is not going according to plan.

For example, suppose a task was scheduled to take 20 days. After 5 days, you ask the developer assigned to that task how much is done, and he says he's 25 percent complete and has 15 days of work remaining. In another week, the developer says he's 50 percent done and has 10 days of work remaining. So far so good, but after another week, the developer says he's 60 percent done (when he should be 75 percent finished).

Initially, it seemed like he was making good progress, but as the task's completion date draws near, the developer realizes how much work is left to do. This is normal and not necessarily a cause for panic, but it does require attention. You need to dig deeper and find out if the developer can actually finish the task on time or if you need to adjust the schedule.

In reality the developer is just making the best guesses he can. If he hasn't performed a task like this one before, those guesses may not be perfect. In this example, the developer's first two estimates were probably off, so he had actually completed only 20 percent of the task after one week and 40 percent after two weeks. If that's the case, he probably needs another two weeks to finish the task instead of the one week that's scheduled. (Of course, that assumes the third estimate of 60 percent is correct, and it may not be.)

Many developers are naturally optimistic and assume they can make up lost time, but they're often wrong. Or they can make up the time but only by working ridiculously long hours or skimping on unit tests. Working extra hours once in a while is okay, but developers who work extra hours too often eventually burn out. (Keeping a sustainable pace is one of the core principles behind agile development, which is discussed in Chapter 19, "RAD.")

At this point, you may want to add the extra week to the task and see what happens to the rest of the project's schedule.

> ### 80 PERCENT RIGHT 50 PERCENT OF THE TIME
>
> The whole schedule depends on time estimates that are uncertain at best. You make estimates for each task, and during development, the developers make estimates about how much work they have finished and how much work they have left to do.
>
> *continues*

(continued)

It's hard to make estimates more accurate (that requires experience), but it's easy to make estimates worse. All you need to do is to yell at the developers, draw lines in the sand, talk about red lines and points of no return, brag about how you *don't* miss deadlines, and generally throw execuspeak at the developers. If you make it clear that developers have to stay on track *at all costs*, their estimates will show that they *are* on track. . . right up to the point at which they miss their deadlines.

A much better approach is to encourage developers to give you estimates that are as truthful and accurate as possible. Over time you'll figure out who can make good estimates and who's always low by 15 percent. That improves your ability to plan and that greatly increases your chances of success.

If the developer can get the task back on schedule, that's great, but you should pay extra attention to that task to see if the latest 60 percent estimate is correct or if the task is really in even more trouble than the developer thinks. The biggest mistake you can make is to ignore the problem and hope you can make up the time later. Unless you have a reason to believe you can catch up, you need to assume you'll fall farther behind. Working on a task that continues to slip week after week feels like trying to bail out a sinking lifeboat with a colander.

Possibly the second biggest mistake you can make is to pile extra developers on the task and assume they can reduce the time needed to finish it. As Fred Brooks said in his famous book *The Mythical Man-Month*, "Adding manpower to a late software project makes it later." Adding someone with appropriate expertise to a task can sometimes help, but it takes time for new people to get up to speed on any task, so you shouldn't just throw more bodies at a task and hope that'll help. This feels like someone's thrown more people with colanders into the sinking lifeboat. You may like the company, but unless they have a working pump, their weight will just make you sink faster.

Risk Management

The preceding section talks about task-tracking and how you can react if a task starts to slip. Often you need to add extra time to the schedule and keep a close watch on that task. Sometimes, you can add extra people to the task, although bringing them up to speed may actually slow the task down if they don't bring particularly useful expertise to the job.

Risk management is more proactive. Instead of responding to problems after they occur, risk management identifies possible risks, determines their potential impacts, and studies possible workarounds ahead of time.

For each task, you should determine the following:

➤ Likelihood—Do you know more or less how to perform this task? Or is this something you've never done before so it might hold unknown problems?

➤ Severity—Can the users live without this feature if the task proves difficult? Can you cancel this feature or push it into a future release?

➤ Consequences—Will problems with this task affect other tasks? If this task fails, will that cause other tasks to fail or make other tasks unnecessary?

➤ Workarounds—Are there workarounds? What other approaches could you take to solve this problem? For each workaround, consider the following:

   ➤ Difficulty—How hard will it be to implement this workaround? How long will it take? What are the chances that this workaround will work?

   ➤ Impact—What effects do the workarounds have on the project's usability? Is this going to make a lot of extra work for the users?

   ➤ Pros—What are the workarounds' advantages?

   ➤ Cons—What are the workarounds' disadvantages?

Occasionally when you're studying workarounds, you may find a better approach than the one in the original plan.

You can use your analysis to study how different kinds of problems will affect the schedule. For example, suppose a task is harder than you originally planned. You've used 5 of the 10 days allocated to the task but you haven't really made any progress. If that task's risk analysis includes a surefire workaround that provides an acceptable alternative and you're fairly certain it would take 8 days to implement, you might want to switch to the workaround and take the 3-day schedule slip rather than following the original approach with its unknown duration.

RISKY REORDERS

In this example, let's perform risk analysis on a reordering feature for the bee fence design application.

Suppose you want the application to automatically place orders for staples, envelopes, fence posts, and other supplies whenever inventory runs low. Unfortunately, you've never written code to do that before. This is a possible point of risk because you don't know how to do it, and it may be much harder to do than you think it is.

In this case, you might use the following notes to describe this task's risk:

➤ Task—Reorder inventory. (Reorder when inventory is low.)

➤ Likelihood—Medium. (We don't really know whether this will be a problem, but the likelihood is definitely not low.)

➤ Severity—High. (We need some way to reorder supplies, or we'll be out of business!)

➤ Consequences—None. (Except, obviously, for the company going bankrupt and all the employees ending up on the street begging for spare change. By none I mean there are no other tasks that depend on this one working as originally planned.)

Having described the task's risk, we can now think of some workarounds.

➤ Workaround 1—Send an email to an administrator who then places the order manually.

   ➤ Difficulty—Easy. I've done this before and it's not too hard. Estimated time: 3 days.

> ➤ Impact—This change would make about 1 hour more work for the administrator per month.
>
> ➤ Pros—Simple. Keeps a person in the loop. (A programming bug can't make the administrator accidentally order 1 million fence posts or 12,000 miles of wire.) Keeps an email record of the process. (Assuming you save the emails.)
>
> ➤ Cons—Not automatic. The administrator needs to follow through. Will need some sort of backup when the administrator is out of the office.
>
> ➤ Workaround 2—Send a text message to an administrator who then places the order manually.
>
> ➤ Difficulty—Easy. (Similar to Workaround 1).
>
> ➤ Impact—Similar to Workaround 1.
>
> ➤ Pros—Similar to Workaround 1. The administrator receives notification even if not at work. Could be added in addition to Workaround 1 for little extra work. Faster than email.
>
> ➤ Cons—The administrator might forget to place the order, particularly if he receives the message while away from work.

After you've performed the risk analysis on the reorder inventory task, you can use it in your project planning. For example, you could allow five days to do this task. If you haven't made good progress in the first day days, you can drop back to Workaround 1 and push automatic reordering to the second release.

SUMMARY

As much as some programmers might like to deny it, management is an important part of software engineering. It's like eating your vegetables: you may prefer dessert, but management will help make your project grow up healthy and strong.

Executive management is essential for the project to succeed. Project management is critical for scheduling and tracking tasks to make sure the project moves toward completion instead of into a morass of side issues and never-ending tasks.

PERT charts, critical path methods, and Gantt charts can help a project manager keep things on track, but they won't do any good unless you have reasonable time estimates. Techniques such as using experienced team members, breaking large tasks into smaller pieces, and allowing for unexpected lost time can make time estimates more accurate and adaptable in the face of unexpected delays.

Even if you use every conceivable time estimation trick, unexpected surprises can throw a monkey wrench into the works. Risk management lets you handle those sorts of unpredictable disasters quickly and efficiently. If a task looks like it will be impossible or greatly delayed, you can switch to a workaround to stay on track and still produce something usable.

This chapter and the previous ones provide background that you need before you move on to actually starting a new software project. The next chapter describes the first step in building a new application: requirements gathering.

Okay, I admit the zombie apocalypse bunker project isn't software-related. . .*unless* you decide to write a 3-D computer game based on that concept! Sort of *World of Warcraft* meets *World War Z*. You could call it *World of Z-Craft*.

Table 4.2 summarizes some of the classes and modules you might need (and their unreasonably optimistic expected times) to develop players and zombies for the game. (The program would also need lots of other pieces not listed here to handle other parts of the game.)

TABLE 4.2: Classes and modules for *World of Z-Craft*

TASK	TIME (DAYS)	PREDECESSORS
A. Robotic control module	5	—
B. Texture library	5	C
C. Texture editor	4	—
D. Character editor	6	A, G, I
E. Character animator	7	D
F. Artificial intelligence (for zombies)	7	—
G. Rendering engine	6	—
H. Humanoid base classes	3	—
I. Character classes	3	H
J. Zombie classes	3	H
K. Test environment	5	L
L. Test environment editor	6	C, G
M. Character library	9	B, E, I
N. Zombie library	15	B, J, O

TASK	TIME (DAYS)	PREDECESSORS
O. Zombie editor	5	A, G, J
P. Zombie animator	6	O
Q. Character testing	4	K, M
R. Zombie testing	4	K, N

1. Draw a PERT chart for these tasks. Include the tasks' letters, predecessors, and expected times.

2. Use critical path methods to find the total expected time from the project's start for each task's completion. Find the critical path(s). What are the tasks on the critical path(s)? What is the total expected duration of the project in working days?

3. How long is the second-longest path in the PERT network you built for Exercise 2? What tasks lie along a second-longest path? By how much could the tasks on that path slip before impacting the project's total time?

4. Build a Gantt chart for the network you drew in Exercise 3. Start on Wednesday, January 1, 2031, and don't work on weekends or these holidays:

HOLIDAY	DATE
New Year's Day	Wednesday January 1
Martin Luther King Jr. Day	Monday January 20
President's Day	Monday February 17
Alien Overlord Appreciation Day	Tuesday February 18

(These are US holidays. If you live somewhere else, feel free to use your own holidays. Except for Alien Overlord Appreciation Day, which will be an international holiday.)

On what date do you expect the project to be finished?

5. Find a free or trial version of the project management tool of your choice (either in the cloud or as a download) and use it to enter the zombie apocalypse tasks. Does it agree with the end date you found in Exercise 4? (The Internet is crawling with useful project management tools, so you have lots of choices. The solution shown in the Appendix, "Solutions to Exercises,"

uses GanttProject. It's simple and you can download it for free at `www.ganttproject.biz`, at least as I write this.) What are the advantages and disadvantages of using the tool you selected over building a Gantt chart manually?

6. In addition to losing time from vacation and sick leave, projects can suffer from problems that just strike out of nowhere. Sort of a bad version of *deus ex machina*. For example, senior management could decide to switch your target platform from Windows desktop PCs to the latest smartwatch technology. Or a pandemic, hurricane, trade war, earthquake, alien invasion, and so on could delay the shipment of your new servers. (Not that anything as far-fetched as a pandemic might occur.) Or one of your developers might move to Iceland. How can you handle these sorts of completely unpredictable problems?

7. What techniques can you use to make accurate time estimates?

8. What are the two biggest mistakes you can make while tracking tasks?

WHAT YOU LEARNED IN THIS CHAPTER

➤ Executive support is critical for project success.

➤ A project manager schedules and tracks tasks and keeps developers moving forward.

➤ PERT charts show precedence relationships among tasks.

➤ While building a PERT chart, if you can't find a task with no unsatisfied predecessors, the tasks contain a precedence loop and no schedule is possible.

➤ Critical path methods show the longest paths through a PERT network. If a task on one of those paths is delayed, the project's final completion is delayed.

➤ Gantt charts show task durations, start time, and end times.

➤ You can improve time estimates by using experience, breaking complex tasks into smaller tasks, and looking for similarities to previous tasks.

➤ You should plan for delays such as illness, vacation, and unexpected problems.

➤ Risk management lets you anticipate problems and plan workarounds so that you can react quickly when problems occur.

5

Requirements Gathering

> The hardest single part of a software system is deciding precisely what to build.
>
> —*Fred Brooks*

> If you don't know where you are going, you'll end up someplace else.
>
> —*Yogi Berra*

What You Will Learn in This Chapter:

➤ Why requirements are important

➤ The characteristics of good requirements

➤ The MOSCOW method for prioritizing requirements

➤ Audience-oriented, FURPS, and FURPS+ methods for categorizing requirements

➤ Methods for gathering customer goals and turning them into requirements

➤ Brainstorming techniques

➤ Methods for recording requirements such as formal specifications, user stories, and prototypes

It's tempting to say that requirements gathering is the most important part of a software project. After all, if you get the requirements wrong, the resulting application won't solve the users' problems. You'll be like a tourist in Boston with a broken GPS. You may get somewhere interesting, but you probably won't get where you want to go.

Even though requirements are important for setting a project's direction, a project can fail at any other stage too. If you build a flawed design, write bad code, fail to test properly, or even provide incorrect training materials, the project can still fail. If any one of the links in the development chain fails, the project will fail.

Let's just say that requirements gathering is the first link in the chain, so it's the first place where you can screw things up badly. Requirements *do* set the stage for everything that follows, so while you can argue over whether this is the most important step, it's definitely *an* important step.

This chapter explains what requirements gathering is and lists some typical requirements that are useful in many projects. It also describes some techniques you can use to gather requirements effectively.

REQUIREMENTS DEFINED

Requirements are the features that your application must provide. At the beginning of the project, you gather requirements from the customers to figure out what you need to build. Throughout development, you use the requirements to guide development and ensure that you're heading in the right direction. At the end of the project, you use the requirements to verify that the finished application actually does what it's supposed to do.

Depending on the project's scope and complexity, you might need only a few requirements, or you might need hundreds of pages of requirements. The number and type of requirements can also depend on the level of formality the customers want.

For example, if you're working on a casual in-house project, your boss may be satisfied with a few blanket requirements such as "find ways to improve order processing" or "write a tool to send spam to customers." As long as you create something vaguely useful, your project will probably be viewed as a success. (If not, you'll find out at your performance review.) As you'll see shortly, these sorts of vague requirements have some problems.

Large projects with higher stakes typically have far more requirements that are spelled out much more formally and in great detail. For example, if you're building an autopilot system for Boeing 747s or you're writing software to control pacemakers, your requirements must be unambiguous. You can't wait until the final weeks of testing to start thinking about whether "easy installation" means patients should change their own pacemaker parameters from a cell phone.

The following sections describe some of the properties that requirements should have to be useful.

Clear

Good requirements are clear, concise, and easy to understand. That means they can't be pumped full of execuspeak, florid prose, and confusing jargon.

It is okay to use technical terms and abbreviations if they are defined somewhere or they are common knowledge in the project's domain. For example, when I worked at a phone company research lab, we often used terms like POTS (plain old telephone service), PBX (public branch exchange), NPA (numbering plan area, known to nontelephone people as an area code), and ISDN (integrated services digital network, or as some of us used to call it, "I still don't know"). The customers and development team members all knew those terms, so they were safe to use in the requirements.

To be clear, requirements cannot be vague or ill-defined. Each requirement must state in concrete, no-nonsense terms exactly what it requires.

For example, suppose you're working on a program to schedule appointments for utility repair people. (Those appointments that typically say, "We'll be there sometime between 6:00 a.m. and midnight during the next two weeks.") A requirement such as "Improve appointment scheduling" is too vague to be useful. Does this mean you should tighten the appointment windows even if it means missing more appointments? Does it mean repair people should leave and make a new appointment if they can't finish a job within one hour? Or does it mean something crazy like letting customers tell you what times they can actually be home and then fitting appointments to those times?

A better requirement would be "Reduce appointment start windows to no more than two hours while meeting 90 percent of the scheduled appointments."

Unambiguous

In addition to being clear and concrete, a requirement must be unambiguous. If the requirement is worded so that you can't tell what it requires, then you can't build a system to satisfy it. Although this may seem like an obvious feature of any good requirement, it's sometimes harder to guarantee than you might think.

For example, suppose you're building a street map application for inline skaters and you have a requirement that says the program will "find the best route from a start location to a destination location." This can't be all that hard. After all, Google Maps, Apple Maps, MapQuest, Bing Maps, and other sites and phone apps all do something like this.

But how do you define the "best" route? The shortest route? The route that uses only physically separated bike paths so that the user doesn't have to skate in the street? Or maybe the route that passes the most Starbucks locations?

Even if you decide the "best" route means the shortest one, what does that mean? The route that's the shortest in distance? Or the shortest in time? What if the route of least distance goes up a steep hill or down a set of stairs and that increases its time? (In this example, you might change the requirements to let the users decide how to pick the "best" route at runtime.)

As you write requirements, do your best to make them unambiguous. Read them carefully to make sure you can't think of any way to interpret them other than the way you intend.

Then run them past some other people (particularly customers, analysts, and other end-user representatives) to see if they agree with you.

A TIMELY JOKE

Executive: I need you to write a program to find customers that haven't paid their bills within 5 seconds.

Developer: Harsh! Most companies give their customers 30 days to pay their bills.

Consistent

A project's requirements must be consistent with each other. That means that they not only cannot contradict each other but that they also don't provide so many constraints that the problem is unsolvable. Each requirement must also be self-consistent. (In other words, it must be possible to achieve.)

Consider again the earlier example of utility repair appointments. You might like to include the following two requirements:

➤ Reduce appointment start windows to no more than two hours.

➤ Meet 90 percent of the scheduled appointments.

It may be that you cannot satisfy these two requirements at the same time. (At least using only software. You might do it if you hire more repair people.)

In a complex project, it's not always obvious if a set of requirements is mutually consistent. Sometimes, any pair of requirements is satisfiable but larger combinations of requirements are not.

A common software engineering expression is "Fast, good, cheap. Pick two." The idea is you can trade development speed, development quality, and cost, but you can't win in all three dimensions. Only three possible combinations work:

➤ Build something quickly with high quality and high cost.

➤ Build something quickly and inexpensively but with low quality.

➤ Build with high quality and low cost but over a long time.

Try to keep new requirements consistent with existing requirements. Or rewrite older requirements as necessary. When you finish gathering all the requirements, go through them again and look for inconsistencies.

Prioritized

When you start working on the project's schedule, it's likely you'll need to cut a few nice-to-haves from the design. You might like to include every feature, but you don't have the time or budget, so something's got to go.

At this point, you need to prioritize the requirements. If you've assigned costs (usually in terms of time to implement) and priorities to the requirements, then you can defer the high-cost, low-priority requirements until a later release.

Customers sometimes have trouble deciding which requirements they can live without. They'll argue, complain, and generally act like you're asking which of their children they want to feed to the dingoes. Unfortunately, unless they can come up with a big enough budget and timescale, they're going to need to make some sort of decision.

The exception occurs when you work on life-critical applications such as nuclear reactor cooling, air traffic control, and space shuttle flight software. In those types of applications, the customer may have a lot of "must have" requirements that you can't remove without compromising the applications' safety. They may also have legal requirements that you can't remove even if they don't make much sense. You may remove cosmetic requirements like a space shuttle's automatic turn-signal cancellation feature, but you're probably going to need to keep the fuel monitor and flight path calculator.

THE MOSCOW METHOD

MOSCOW is an acronym to help you remember a common system for prioritizing application features. The consonants in MOSCOW stand for the following:

M—Must. These are *required* features that must be included. They are necessary for the project to be considered a success.

S—Should. These are *important* features that should be included if possible. If there's a workaround and there's no room in the release 1 schedule, these may be deferred until release 2.

C—Could. These are *desirable* features that can be omitted if they won't fit in the schedule. They can be pushed back into release 2, but they're not as important as the "should" features, so they may not make it into release 2 either.

W—Won't. These are *completely optional* features that the customers have agreed will not be included in the current release. They may be included in a future release if time permits. (Or they may just be included in the requirements list to make a particularly loud and politically connected customer happy, and you have no intention of ever including these features.)

Let's face it. If a feature isn't a "must" or "should," then its chances of ever being implemented are slim. After this release has been used for a while, you'll probably receive tons of bug reports, requests for changes, and pleas for new features, so in the next release you still won't have time for the "could" and "won't" features.

(Unless you're one of these big software companies, who shall remain nameless, that thinks it needs to push a new version of its products out every two years to make customers buy something. Sometimes those products reach deep into the "could" and "won't" categories, and perhaps even the "why?" and "you must be joking!" categories.)

CLASSYDRAW

For an example of using the MOSCOW method, consider a fictional drawing program named ClassyDraw. It's somewhat similar to MS Paint and allows you to draw line segments, ellipses, polygons, text, and other shapes. The big difference is that ClassyDraw represents each shape you draw as an object that you can later select, move, resize, modify, and delete.

Here's an initial requirement list:

1. Draw: line segments, sequences of line segments, splines, polygons, ellipses, circles, rectangles, rounded rectangles, stars, images, and other shapes.

2. Save and load files.

3. Protect the current drawing. For example, if the user tries to close the program while there are unsaved changes, warn the user.

4. Let the user specify the line style and colors used to draw shapes.

5. Let the user specify the fill style and colors used for shapes.

6. Click to select an object.

7. Click and drag to select multiple objects.

8. Click or click and drag with the Shift key down to add objects to the current selection.

9. Click or click and drag with the Ctrl key down to toggle objects in and out of the current selection.

10. Click and drag the selected objects to move them.

11. Edit the selected objects' line and fill styles.

12. Delete the selected objects.

13. Select colors from a palette.

14. Place custom colors in a custom palette.

15. Support transparency.

16. Cut, copy, and paste the entire drawing, a rectangular selection, or an irregular selection as a bitmapped image.

17. Copy, cut, and paste the currently selected objects.

18. Allow the user to write scripts to add shapes to a drawing.

19. Let the user rearrange the palettes and toolbars.

20. Auto-save the current drawing periodically. If the program crashes, allow the user to reload the most recently saved version.

21. Auto-save the current drawing every time a change is made. If the program crashes, allow the user to reload the most recently saved version.

22. Provide online help.

23. Provide online tutorials.

Now you can use the MOSCOW method to prioritize these requirements.

Must. To identify the "must" requirements, examine each requirement and ask yourself the following questions: Could that requirement be omitted? Would the program be usable without that feature? Will users give the product 1-star reviews and say they wish they could give 0 stars? Will users say the product would be overpriced if it were freeware?

The ClassyDraw application *must* be able to save and load files (2). You could build early test versions that don't, but it would be unacceptable to users.

Similarly, the program must ensure the safety of the current drawing (3). The users would never forgive the program if it discarded a complicated drawing without any warning.

The program wouldn't be useful if it didn't draw, so the program must draw at least a few shapes (1). For starters, it could draw line segments, rectangles, and ellipses. You could add more shapes in later releases. (I've written programs like this before, and it's relatively easy to add many shapes after you get the first few working.)

The program should probably allow the user to click objects to select them. Otherwise, the user may as well use MS Paint, so requirement 6 is a must. Of course, there's little point in selecting an object if you can't do anything with it, so the program must let the user at least move (10) and delete (12) the selected objects.

The "must" requirements include 1 (partial), 2, 3, 6, 10, and 12.

Should. To identify the "should" requirements, examine each of the remaining requirements and ask yourself the following questions: Does that feature significantly enhance the product? If it were omitted, would users be constantly asking why it wasn't included? Is the feature common in other, similar applications? Will users give the product 2-star and 3-star reviews?

Several requirements that are fairly standard for drawing applications didn't make the cut for the "must" category. (You could say they didn't pass muster.)

Most (if not all) of the other shapes in requirement 1 should be included in this group. When drawing new shapes, the user should also indicate the line and fill styles the new shapes should have (4, 5). That will require specifying colors, at least from a palette (13).

The click-and-drag selection technique (7) should be included, as should the ability to hold down the Shift or Ctrl key while making selections (8, 9).

Any decent application should have help (22) and documentation (23), so those should also be included.

The "should" requirements include 1 (remaining), 4, 5, 7, 8, 9, 13, 22, and 23.

Could. To identify the "could" requirements, examine each of the remaining requirements and ask yourself these questions: Would that requirement be useful to the users? Is it something special that other similar applications don't have? Will this help bump reviews up to 4 or 5 stars? Is this a feature that we should include at some point, just not in the first release?

Another way to approach this category is to ask the following questions: Which features will we need in the long term? Which of the remaining features shouldn't be dumped in the trash heap labeled "won't?"

Most of the remaining requirements should probably not go in the "won't" pile. If they were that bad, they probably wouldn't have made it into the requirements list in the first place.

The "could" category should definitely include the ability to edit selected objects (11). This is another of the main reasons for allowing the user to select objects and it sets this program apart.

Support for custom colors (14) and transparency (15) would also be nice, if time permits. Cut, copy, and paste for images (16) and selected objects (17) would be useful, so they could be included.

The "could" requirements include 11, 14, 15, 16, and 17.

Won't. To identify the "won't" requirements, examine the remaining requirements and ask yourself these question: Is this unnecessary, confusing, or just plain stupid? Will it be used only rarely? Does it add nothing useful to the application? If you can't answer yes to those questions for a particular requirement, then you should think about moving that requirement into one of the other categories.

For this application, allowing users to write scripts (18) would be cool but probably rarely used and isn't something most other drawing programs do. Letting the user rearrange palettes and tool-bars (19) would be a nice touch, but isn't important.

Auto-saving (20, 21) is also a nice touch, but probably unnecessary. We can look at user requests and conduct surveys to see if this feature would be worth adding to a future release. This is mostly necessary if the program crashes frequently, and if that's the case, then we have serious problems.

The "won't" requirements include 18, 19, 20, and 21.

After you've assigned each requirement to a category, go back through them and make sure you're happy with their assignments. If a requirement in the "could" category seems more important than one in the "should" category, switch them.

Also make sure every requirement is in some category and that every category contains some requirement. If every requirement is in the "must" category, then you may need to rethink your priorities (or your customer's priorities) or be sure you'll have enough time to get everything done.

Verifiable

Requirements must be verifiable. If you can't verify a requirement, how do you know whether you've met it? More importantly, how can you prove to your customers that you've met it?

Being verifiable means the requirements must be limited and precisely defined. They can't be open-ended statements such as, "Process more work orders per hour than are currently being processed." How many work orders is "more"? Technically, processing one more work order per hour is "more," but that probably won't satisfy your customer. What about 100? Or 1,000?

A better requirement would say, "Process at least 100 work orders per hour." It should be relatively easy to determine whether your program meets this requirement.

Even with this improved requirement, verification might be tricky because it relies on some assumptions that it doesn't define. For example, the requirement probably assumes you're processing work orders in the middle of a typical workday, not during a big clearance event, during peak ordering hours, or during a power outage.

An even better requirement might be, "Process at least 100 work orders per hour on average during a typical work day." You may want to refine the requirement a bit to try to say what a "typical work day" is, but this version should be good enough for most reasonable customers.

Words to Avoid

Some words are ambiguous or subjective, and adding them to a requirement can make the whole thing fuzzy and imprecise. The following list gives examples of words that may make requirements less exact.

- ➤ Comparatives—Words like faster, better, more, and shinier. How much faster? Define "better." How much more? These need to be quantified.

- ➤ Imprecise adjectives—Words like fast, robust, user-friendly, efficient, flexible, and glorious. These are just other forms of the comparatives. They look great in executive summaries, business cases, and marketing material, but they're too imprecise to use in requirements.

- ➤ Vague commands—Words like minimize, maximize, improve, and optimize. Unless you use these in a technical algorithmic sense (for example, if you optimize flow through a network), these are just fancy ways to say, "Do your best." Even in an algorithmic sense, these sorts of words are often applied to hard problems where exact solutions may not be possible. In any case, you need to make the goals more concrete. Provide some numbers or other criteria you can use to determine whether a requirement has been met.

REQUIREMENT CATEGORIES

In general, requirements tell what an application is supposed to do. Good requirements share certain characteristics (they're clear, unambiguous, consistent, prioritized, and verifiable), but there are several kinds of requirements that are aimed at different audiences or that focus on different aspects of the application. For example, business requirements focus on a project's high-level objectives and functional requirements give the developers more detailed lists of goals to accomplish.

Assigning categories to your requirements isn't the point here. (Although there are two kinds of people in the world: those who like to group things into categories and those who don't. If you're one of the former, then you may need to do this for your own peace of mind.) The real point here is that you can use the categories as a checklist to make sure you've created requirements for the most important parts of the project. For example, if you look through the requirements and the reliability category is empty, you might consider adding some new requirements.

You can categorize requirements in several ways. The following sections describe four ways to categorize requirements.

Audience-Oriented Requirements

These categories focus on different audiences and the different points of view that each audience has. They use a somewhat business-oriented perspective to classify requirements according to the people who care the most about them.

For example, the corporate vice president of Plausible Deniability probably doesn't care too much about which button a call center clerk needs to press to launch a customer into a never-ending call tree as long as it works. In contrast, the clerk needs to know which button to press.

The following sections describe some of the more common business-oriented categories.

Business Requirements

Business requirements lay out the project's high-level goals. They explain what the customer hopes to achieve with the project.

Notice the word "hopes." Customers sometimes try to include all their hopes and dreams in the business requirements in addition to verifiable objectives. For example, they might say the project will "Increase profits by 25 percent" or "Increase demand and gain 10,000 new customers." Although those goals have numbers in them, they're probably outside the scope of what you can achieve through software engineering alone. They're more like marketing targets than project requirements. You can craft the best application ever put together, but someone still needs to use it properly to realize the new profits and customers.

Sometimes, those vague goals are unavoidable in business requirements, but if possible you should try to push them into the business case. The business case is a more marketing-style document that attempts to justify the project. Those often include graphs and charts showing projected costs, demand, sales figures, and other values that aren't known exactly in advance. (In other words, made up by an executive trying to justify the project.)

To think of this another way, I have no qualms about promising to write a system that can pull up a customer's records in less than three seconds or find the closest donut shop that's open at 2 a.m. (if you give me the data). But I wouldn't want to promise to improve morale in the customer complaints department by 15 percent. (What would that even mean?)

User Requirements

User requirements (*stakeholder requirements* in execuspeak), describe how the project will be used by the eventual end users. They often include things like sketches of forms, scripts that show the steps users will perform to accomplish specific tasks, use cases, and prototypes. (The sections "Use Cases" and "Prototypes" later in this chapter say more about the last two.)

Sometimes these requirements are very detailed, spelling out exactly what an application must do under different circumstances. Other times they specify *what* the user needs to accomplish but not necessarily *how* the application must accomplish it.

OVERLY SPECIFIC SELECTIONS

In this example, you see how you can turn an overly specific requirement into one that's flexible without making it vague.

Suppose you're building a phone application that lets customers place orders at a sandwich and bagel shop called the Loxsmith. The program should let customers select the toppings they want on their bagels. They include lox (naturally), butter, cream cheese, gummy bears, and so on. Here's one way you could word this requirement:

> The toppings form will display a list of toppings. The user can check boxes next to the toppings to add them to the bagel.

That's a fine requirement. Clear, concise, verifiable. Everything you could want in a requirement. Unfortunately, it's also unnecessarily specific. It forces the designers and developers to use a specific technique (check boxes) to achieve the higher-level goal of letting the customer select toppings.

During testing, you might discover that the Loxsmith provides more than 200 toppings. In that case, the program won't be able to display a list of every topping at the same time. The user will need to scroll through the list, and that will make it hard for the customer to see what toppings are selected.

Here's a different version of the same requirement that doesn't restrict the developers as much.

> The toppings form will allow the user to select the toppings to put on the bagel.

The difference is small but important. With this version, the developers can explore different methods for selecting toppings. If you have user-interface specialists on your team, they may create a variety of possible solutions. For example, customers might drag and drop selections from a big scrollable list on the left onto a shorter list of selected items on the right. Then they could always see what toppings were selected. You might even display a cartoon picture of a bagel holding the user's four dozen selected toppings piled up like the Leaning Tower of Pisa.

Vague requirements are bad, but flexible requirements let you explore different options before you start writing code. To keep requirements as flexible as possible, try to make the requirements spell out the project's *needs* without mandating a particular approach.

Functional Requirements

Functional requirements are detailed statements of the project's desired capabilities. They're similar to the user requirements but they may also include things that the users won't see directly. For example, they might describe reports that the application produces, interfaces to other applications, and workflows that route orders from one user to another during processing.

These are things the application should do.

Note that some requirements could fall into multiple categories. For example, you could consider most user requirements to be functional requirements. They not only describe a task that will be performed by the user, but they also describe something that the application will do.

Nonfunctional Requirements

Nonfunctional requirements are statements about the quality of the application's behavior or constraints on how it produces a desired result. They specify things such as the application's performance, reliability, and security characteristics.

For example, a functional requirement would be, "Allow users to reserve a hovercraft online." A nonfunctional requirement would be, "The application must support 20 users simultaneously making reservations at any hour of the day."

Implementation Requirements

Implementation requirements are temporary features that are needed to transition to using the new system but that will be later discarded. For example, suppose you're designing an invoice-tracking system to replace an existing system. After you finish testing the system and are ready to use it full-time, you need a method to copy any pending invoices from the old database into the new one. That method is an implementation requirement.

The tasks described in implementation requirements don't always involve programming. For example, you could hire a bunch of teenagers on summer break to retype the old invoices into the new system. (Although you'll probably get a quicker and more consistent result if you write a program to convert the data into the new format. The program won't get bored and stop coming to work when the next release of *Grand Theft Auto* comes out.)

Other implementation requirements include hiring new staff, buying new hardware, preparing training materials, and actually training the users to use the new system.

FURPS

The previous sections described audience-oriented requirements. Another way to categorize requirements is the FURPS system. FURPS is an acronym for the system's requirement categories: functionality, usability, reliability, performance, and scalability. It was developed by Hewlett-Packard (and later extended by adding a + at the end to get FURPS+).

The following list summarizes the FURPS categories:

➤ Functionality—What the application should do. These requirements describe the system's general features including what it does, interfaces with other systems, security, and so forth.

➤ Usability—What the program should look like. These requirements describe user-oriented features such as the application's general appearance, ease of use, navigation methods, and responsiveness.

➤ Reliability—How reliable the system should be. These requirements indicate such things as when the system should be available (12 hours per day from 7:00 a.m. to 8:00 p.m.), how often it can fail (3 times per year for no more than 1 hour each time), and how accurate the system is (80 percent of the service calls must start within their predicted delivery windows).

➤ Performance—How efficient the system should be. These requirements describe such things as the application's speed, memory usage, disk usage, and database capacity.

➤ Supportability—How easy it is to support the application. These requirements include such things as how easy it will be to maintain the application, how easy it is to test the code, and how flexible the application is. (For example, the application might let users set parameters to determine how it behaves.)

Recent advances in cloud computing have given developers new options for some of these. For example, storing your database in the cloud may affect the application's reliability and performance. Different cloud vendors may provide varying levels of those (for a fee, of course). They can also provide backup services, which may save you some effort.

The cloud may also affect scalability, which fits in the supportability category. For example, if you build your database on a single host computer, then you need to figure out what to do if the application becomes wildly popular (a problem we all hope to have) and the database grows to 20 times its original size. If the database is hosted in the cloud, then you may be able to just pour a little money on the cloud service provider and you're good to go.

Similarly, if you build a desktop application, then troubleshooting installations can be a problem when your 100 users balloon into 10,000 users. If you build your program as a browser app, then you can just tell everyone to stop using Netscape Navigator and install a newer browser.

FURPS+

FURPS was extended into FURPS+ to add a few requirements categories that software engineers thought were missing. (I guess they added the + because they thought that FURPSDIIP would be too hard to pronounce.) The following list summarizes the new categories:

➤ Design constraints—These are constraints on the design that are driven by other factors such as the hardware platform, software platform, network characteristics, or database. For example, suppose you're building a financial application and you want an extremely reliable backup system. In that case, you might require the project to use a shadowed or mirrored database in case the main database crashes. You might even require the shadow database to be stored off-site in case the main site is hit by an asteroid or something. (I've worked on a couple of projects with that requirement.)

➤ Implementation requirements—These are constraints on the way the software is built. For example, you might require developers to meet the Capability Maturity Model Integration (CMMI) or ISO 9001 standards. (For more information on those, see www.cmmifaq.info and www.iso.org/iso-9001-quality-management.html, respectively.)

➤ Interface requirements—These are constraints on the system's interfaces with other systems. They tell what other systems will exchange data with the one you're building. They describe things like the kinds of interactions that will take place, when they will occur, and the format of the data that will be exchanged.

➤ Physical requirements—These are constraints on the hardware and physical devices that the system will use. For example, they might require a minimum amount of processing power, a maximum amount of electrical power, easy portability (such as a tablet or smartphone), touch screens, or environmental features (must work in boiling acid).

As with FURPS, the cloud can change the way you approach some of these categories. For example, design constraints such as mirroring a database off-site takes on a whole new meaning if (1) the database is in the cloud and (2) the cloud provider normally shuffles databases back and forth across multiple servers as needed. For another example, you might need to guarantee that your data never leaves your home country for legal reasons.

FURPS+ CHECKLIST

In this example, we'll use FURPS+ to see if any requirements are missing for the Loxsmith ordering application. Consider the following abbreviated list of requirements. The program should allow the user to do the following:

➤ Start an order that might include multiple items.

➤ Select bagel type.

➤ Select toppings.

➤ Select sandwich bread.

➤ Select sandwich toppings.

➤ Select drinks.

➤ Select pickup time.

➤ Pay now or decide to pay at pickup.

I've left out a lot of details from this list such as the specific bagel, bread, and topping types that are available, but at first glance, this seems like a reasonable set of requirements. It describes what the application should do but doesn't impose unnecessary constraints on how the developers should build it. It's a bit vaguer than I would like (how do you *verify* that the user can select toppings?), but you can flesh that out. (In fact, I'll talk a bit about ways you can do that later in this chapter, particularly when I talk about use cases in the section "Use Cases.")

For this example, assume the requirements are spelled out in specific (but flexible) detail. Then use FURPS+ to see if there's anything important missing from this list. Spend a few minutes to decide in which FURPS+ category each of the requirements belongs.

Although the initial requirements all seem reasonable, they're all functionality requirements. They tell what the application should do but don't give much information about usability, reliability, performance, and other requirements that should belong to the other FURPS+ categories.

You might think that a requirements list containing only functionality requirements would be an unusual situation. However, left to their own devices, many programmers come up with exactly this sort of list. They focus on the work they are going to do and how it will look to the users. That's a good place to start the design, but in the background, they're making a huge number of assumptions about things they take for granted.

For example, suppose you're a developer who writes Java applications running on Android tablets. In that case, you may think the previous list of requirements is just fine. Your version of the Eclipse

Java development environment is up-to-date, you've installed the Android software development kit (SDK), and you have "Eye of the Tiger" blasting on your headphones. You're ready to start cranking out code.

Unfortunately you're also making a ton of assumptions that may or may not sit well with the customer. In this example, you're assuming the application will be written in Java to run on Android tablets. What if the customer wants the application written in Kotlin to run on an iPhone, desktop system, mobile-oriented web page, augmented reality glasses, or some sort of smart wearable ankle bangle device? Or maybe all of the above?

Sometimes, you may not want any requirements in a particular category, but the fact that the preceding list contains *only* functionality requirements is a strong hint that we're doing something wrong. You should at least think about every category and either (1) come up with some new requirements that belong there or (2) write down why you don't think you need any requirements for that category.

So now look at the FURPS+ requirement categories:

➤ Functionality—(What the program should do.) The initial list of requirements covers this category.

➤ Usability—(What the program should look like.) You could add some requirements indicating how the user navigates from starting an order to picking sandwich and bagel ingredients. You could also provide details about login (should we create customer accounts?) and the checkout method. You should also specify that each form will display the Loxsmith logo.

➤ Reliability—(How reliable the system should be.) Should the application be available only while the Loxsmith is open? Or should customers be able to preorder a morning jalapeno popper bagel and double kopi luwak to pick up on the way in to work?

➤ Performance—(How efficient the system should be.) How quickly should the application respond to customers (assuming they have a fast Internet connection)?

➤ Supportability—(How easy should the system be to support?) The requirements should indicate that the Loxsmith employees or at least managers can edit the information about the types of breads, bagels, toppings, and other items that are available. You might also want to add automated testing requirements, information about help available to customers, and any plans for future versions of the project.

➤ Design—(Design constraints.) Here's where you would specify the target hardware and software platforms. For example, you might want the program to run on iPhones (code written with Xcode) and Android devices (code written in Kotlin).

➤ Implementation—(Constraints on the way the software is built.) You can specify software standards. For example, you might require pair programming or agile methods. (Those are described in Chapter 19, "RAD.")

➤ Interface—(Interfaces with other systems.) Perhaps you want the application to interact with food delivery services such as Grubhub, DoorDash, Uber Eats, and Youbuyillfly (You Buy I'll Fly). Or perhaps this category will be intentionally left blank.

> ➤ Physical—(Hardware requirements.) For this application, the customers provide their own hardware (such as phones and tablets) so you don't need to specify those. You might want to specify the server hardware. Or you might want to use the cloud so that you don't need to buy your own hardware, and you can reconfigure if needed. (You should probably still study the available options so that you know how powerful they are and how much they cost.)
>
> Using requirements categories as a checklist can help you notice if you are missing certain kinds of requirements. In this example, it helped identify a lot of requirements that might have been missed or hidden inside developer assumptions.

Common Requirements

The following list summarizes some specific requirements that arise in many applications.

➤ Screens—What screens or forms are needed?

➤ Menus—What menus will the screens have?

➤ Navigation—How will the users navigate through different parts of the system? Will they click buttons, use menus, or tap forward and backward arrows? Or some combination of those methods?

➤ Workflow—How does data (work orders, purchase requests, invoices, and other data) move through the system?

➤ Login—How is login information stored and validated? What are the password formats (such as, must require at least one letter, number, special character, and emoji) and rules (as in, passwords must be changed monthly)?

➤ User types—Are there different kinds of users such as order entry clerk, shipping clerk, supervisor, and admin? Do they need different privileges?

➤ Audit tracking and history—Does the system need to keep track of who made changes to the data? (For example, so you can see who changed a customer to premier status or gave a 99 percent discount.)

➤ Archiving—Does the system need to archive older data to free up space in the live database? Does it need to copy data into a data warehouse for analysis?

➤ Configuration—Should the application provide configuration screens that let the system administrators change the way the program works? For example, those screens might let system administrators edit product data, set shipping and handling prices, and set algorithm parameters. (If you don't build these sorts of screens, you'll have to make those changes for the customers later.)

GATHERING REQUIREMENTS

At this point you know what makes a good requirement (clear, unambiguous, consistent, prioritized, and verifiable). You also know how to categorize requirements using audience-oriented, FURPS, or

FURPS+ methods. But how do you actually pry the requirements out of the customers? Are a polygraph and sodium pentothal required?

The following sections describe several techniques you can use to gather and refine requirements.

Listen to Customers (and Users)

Sometimes, customers come equipped with fully developed requirements spelling out exactly what the application should do, how it should work, and what it should look like. More often they just have a problem that they want solved and a vague notion that a computer might somehow help.

Start by listening to the customers. Learn as much as you can about the problem they are trying to address and any ideas they may have about how the application might solve that problem. Initially, focus as much as possible on the problem, not on the customers' suggested solutions, so you can keep the requirements flexible.

If the customers insist on a particular feature that you think is unimportant, or if they request something that just seems strange, ask them why they want it. Sometimes, the requirement may be a random thought that isn't actually important, but sometimes the customers have a good reason that you just don't understand. Often the reason is so obvious to them that it doesn't occur to them to explain it until you ask. The customers probably know a lot more about their business than you do, and they may make assumptions about facts that are common knowledge to them but mysterious to you.

> ### AN OFFER YOU CAN'T REFUSE
>
> Suppose the Don's Waste Removal Service asks you to write an application that lets users plot out routes for garbage trucks. You're working through the list of requirements with the owner, Don, and he says, "A route that contains lots of left turns should be given no respect."
>
> To most people, that may seem like a strange requirement. What does Don have against left turns?
>
> Don's been working with garbage trucks for a long time so, like many people who do a lot of vehicle routing, he knows that trucks turning left spend more time waiting for cross traffic, so they burn more fuel. They are also more likely to be involved in traffic accidents. (It always amazes me that people can fail to notice a 20-ton garbage truck stopped in front of them, but it happened in my neighborhood not long ago.) Penalizing routes that contain left turns (and U-turns) will save the company money.

Take lots of notes while you're listening to the customers. They sometimes mention these important but puzzling tidbits in passing. If a customer requirement seems odd, dig a bit deeper to find out what, if anything, is behind the request.

Use the Five *W*s (and One *H*)

Sometimes customers have trouble articulating their needs. You can help by using the five *W*s (who, what, when, where, and why) and one *H* (how).

Who

Ask who will be using the software and get to know as much as you can about those people. Find out if the users and the customers are the same.

For example, if you're writing medical billing software, the users might be data entry operators who type in patient data all day. In contrast, your customers may be corporate executives. They may have worked their way up through the ranks (in which case they probably know everything about medical data entry down to the last billing code) or they may have followed a more business-school-oriented career path (in which case they may not know a W59.22 from a V95.43). (It's worth the time to look these up in your favorite browser. Seriously, this is a must.)

What

Figure out what the customers need the application to do. Focus on the goals as much as possible rather than the customers' ideas about how the solution should work. Sometimes, the customers have good ideas about what the application should look like, but you should try to keep your options open. Often the project members have a better idea than the customers of the kinds of things an application can do, so they may come up with better solutions if they focus on the goals.

(Of course, the customer is always right, at least until your paycheck clears the bank, so if the customer absolutely insists that the application must include a graphical slide rule instead of a calculator, chalk it up as an interesting exercise in graphics programming and make it happen.)

When

Find out when the application is needed. If the application will be rolled out in phases, find out which features are needed when.

When you have a good idea about what the project requires, use Gantt charts and the other techniques described in Chapter 4, "Project Management," to figure out how much time is *actually* needed. Then compare the customers' desired timeline to the required work schedule. If the two don't match, you may need to talk to the customers about deferring some features to a later release.

Don't let the customers (and your management, by the way) assume they can get everything on their schedule just by "motivating you harder." In *Star Trek*, Scotty can squeeze eight weeks' worth of work into just two, but that rarely works in real-world software engineering. You're far more likely to watch helplessly as your best programmers jump ship before your project hits the rocky shoals of impossible deadlines.

Where

Find out where the application will be used. Will it be used on desktop computers in an air-conditioned office? On phones in a noisy subway? On a tablet while clinging to the underside of an oil platform in the North Sea?

Why

Ask why the customers need the application. Note that you don't need to be unnecessarily stupid. If the customers say, "We want to automate our parts ordering system so that we can build custom scooters more quickly," you don't need to respond with, "Why?" The customers just told you why.

Instead, use the "why" question to help clarify the customers' needs and see if they are real. Sometimes, customers don't have a well-thought-out reason for building a new system. They just think it will help but don't actually know why. (Or customers may have just received a new copy of *Management Buzzwords Monthly* and they're convinced they can crowdsource custom scooter design.)

Find out if there is a real reason to believe a new application will help. Is the problem really that ordering parts is inefficient? Or is the problem that each order requires a different set of parts that have a long shipping time? If streamlining the ordering process will cut the ordering time from 2 days to 1.5 days, while still leaving 4–6 weeks of shipping delay, then a new software application may not be the best place to spend your resources. (It might be better to maintain an inventory of slow-to-order parts such as wheel spinners and spoilers.)

How

The "What" section earlier in this chapter said you should focus on the goals rather than the customers' ideas about the solution. That's true, but you shouldn't completely ignore the customers' ideas. Sometimes, customers have good ideas, particularly if they relate to existing practices. If the users are used to doing something a certain way, you may reduce training time by making the application mimic that approach. Be sure to look outside the box for other solutions, but don't automatically think that software developers always make better decisions than the customers. Sometimes the best solution is already sitting there inside the box.

Study Users

Interviewing customers (and users) can get you a lot of information, but often customers (and users) won't tell you everything they do or need to do. They often take for granted details that they consider trivial but that may be important to the development team. (Here's where the polygraph and sodium pentothal come in handy.)

For example, suppose the users grind through long, tedious reports every day. The reports are so long, they often end the day in the middle of a report and need to continue working on it the next day. This may seem so obvious to the users that you don't discuss the issue.

A typical reporting application might require the users to log in every day, search for a particular report, and double-click it to open it. That could take a while (particularly if the user forgets which report it is). Fortunately, you know that users often start the day by reopening the last report of the previous day, so you can streamline the process. Instead of making users remember what report they last had open, the program can remember. You can then provide a button or menu item to immediately jump to that report.

By studying users as they work, you can learn more about what they need to do, how they currently do it, and how frequently they do it. Then with your software-engineering perspective, you can look for solutions that might not occur to the users.

PRINTING PUZZLE

Watching users in their natural habitat often pays off. Many years ago, I was visiting a telephone company billing center in preparation for a project that automatically identified customers who hadn't paid their bills so it could disconnect their service. We spent a week there studying the existing software systems and the users. It was interesting, but the reason I'm mentioning it now is a small comment made by one of the managers. In passing, she said something like, "I sure wish you could do something about the *Overdue Accounts* report. Ha, ha."

That's the sort of comment that should make you dig deeper. What was this report and why was it a problem? It turned out that the existing software system printed out a list of every customer with an outstanding balance for every billing cycle. This was a *big* billing center serving approximately 15 million customers, so every two days (there were 15 billing cycles per month) the printer spit out a three-foot tall pile of paper listing every customer in the cycle with an outstanding balance!

Balances ranged from a few cents to tens of thousands of dollars, and the big-balance customers were costing the company truckloads of money. Unfortunately, the printout listed the customers in some weird arrangement (sorted by customer ID or zodiac sign or something), so the billing people couldn't find the customers with the big balances.

What the customers didn't know (but we did) is that it's relatively easy to build a printer emulation program. It took approximately one week (mostly spent getting management approval) to write a program that pretended to be a printer, sucked up all the overdue account information, and sorted it by balance. It turned out that of the thousands of pages of data produced every two days, the customers only needed the first two.

The moral of the story is, you need to pay close attention to the customers' comments. They don't know what you can do with the computer, and you don't know their needs.

As you study the users, pay attention to how they do things. Look at the forms they fill out (paper or online). Figure out where they spend most of their time. Look for the tasks that go smoothly and those that don't. You can use that information to identify areas in which your project can help.

REFINING REQUIREMENTS

After you've talked to the customers and users, watched the users at work, and asked pesky questions until they're thoroughly sick of you, you should have a good understanding about the users' current operations and needs. (If you don't, ask more questions and watch the users some more until you do.)

Next, you need to use what you've learned to develop ideas for solving the user's problems. You need to distill the goals (what the customers need to do) into approaches (how the application will do it).

At a high level, the requirement "Process customer records" is fine. It's also nice and flexible, so it allows you to explore many options for achieving that goal.

At some point, however, you need to turn the goals into something that you can actually build. You need to figure out how the users will select records to edit, what screens they will use, and how they will navigate between the screens. Those decisions will lead to requirements describing the forms, navigation techniques, and other features that the application must provide to let the users do their jobs.

> **NOTE** *Moving from goals to requirements often forces you to make some design decisions. For example, you may need to specify form layouts (at least roughly) and the way work flows through the system.*
>
> *You might think of those as design tasks, but they're really part of requirements gathering. The next three chapters, which talk about design, deal with program design (how you structure the code), not the sorts of design described here. The chapter after those three talks about user experience design.*

The following sections describe three approaches for converting goals into requirements.

Copy Existing Systems

If you're building a system to replace an existing system or a manual process, you can often use many of the behaviors of the existing system as requirements for the new one. If the old system sends customers emails on their birthdays, you can require the new system to do that too. If the users currently fill out a long paper form, you can require the new system to have a computerized form that looks similar—possibly with some tabs, scrolled windows, and other format changes to make the form look a bit better on a computer.

This approach has a few advantages. First, it's reasonably straightforward. It doesn't take an enormous amount of software engineering experience to dig through an existing application and write down what it does. (If you're lucky, you might even get the customers to do at least some of it for you so that you can focus on software design issues.)

This approach also makes it more likely that the requirements can actually be satisfied, at least to the extent the current system works. If an existing system does something, then you at least know it's possible.

Finally, this approach provides an unambiguous example of what you need to do. In the specification, you don't need to write out in excruciating detail exactly how the "Lazy Backup" screen works. Instead you can just say, "The Lazy Backup screen will work as it does in the existing system with the following changes: . . ."

Even though this approach is straightforward, it has some disadvantages. First, you probably wouldn't be building a new version of an existing system unless you planned to make some changes. Those changes aren't part of the original system, so there's no guarantee that they're even possible.

They may also be incompatible with the original system. (Not all pieces of software play nicely together.)

A second problem with this approach is that users are often reluctant to give up even the tiniest features in an existing program. In the projects I've worked on, I've found that no matter how obscure, difficult, and downright worthless a feature is, there's at least one user willing to fight to the death to preserve it. If the software has been in use for a long time, it may contain all sorts of odd quirks and peccadillos. You might like to streamline the new system by removing the feature that changes the program's background color to match the weather each day, but that's not always possible.

FOREVER FEATURES

I was once asked to help port part of an application to a new platform. The key piece of the application that the customer wanted to keep was fairly small, and the project manager estimated it would take a few hundred hours of work to get the job done.

When I dug through the original application, however, I found that it included more than 100 forms, each of which was moderately complicated. The system also included interfaces to a number of external databases and automated systems.

At this point, we went back to the customer and asked if they were willing to give up most of those 100+ forms and just keep the key tools we were trying to port.

By now you've probably guessed the punchline. The customer wouldn't give up any of the existing application's features. The project's estimated time jumped from a few hundred hours to several thousand hours, and the whole thing was scrapped.

There is some good news in this tale, however. We discovered the problem quickly during initial requirements gathering, so we hadn't wasted too much time before the project was canceled. It would have been much worse if we had started work only to have the requirements gradually expand to include everything in the original application. Then we would have wasted hundreds of hours of work before the project was canceled.

Using an existing system to generate requirements can be a big time-saver, as long as the development team and the customers all agree on which parts of the existing system will be included in the new one.

Clairvoyance

A lot more often than you might think, one or more people simply look at the project's goals, visualize a finished result, and start cranking out requirements. For example, the project lead might use gut feelings, common sense, tea leaves, tarot cards, and other arcane techniques to cobble together something they think will work. If the project is large, pieces might be doled out to team leads so that they can work on their own pieces of the system, but the basic approach is the same: someone sits down and starts churning out form designs, workflow models, login procedures, and descriptions of reports.

I'm actually being a bit unfair characterizing this approach as clairvoyance because it's really an educated guess based on experience, and it can be quite effective in practice. Assuming the people writing the requirements understand the customers' needs and have previous experience, they often produce a good result. Ideally, team leads are chosen for their experience and technical expertise (not because they're the boss's cousin), so they know what the computer can do, and they can design a system that works.

This technique is particularly effective if the project lead has previously built a similar system. In that case, the lead already knows more or less what the application needs to do, which things will be easy and which will be hard, how much time everything requires, and which kinds of donuts motivate the programmers the best.

Having an experienced project lead greatly increases the chances that the requirements will include everything you need to make the project succeed. It also greatly increases the chances the team will anticipate problems and handle them easily as development continues. In fact, this is such an important point, it's a best practice.

BEST PRACTICE: EXPERIENCED PROJECT LEADS

A project's chances for success are greatly improved if the project lead has previous experience with the same kind of project.

The same holds true for the other project members. Programmers with previous experience with the same kind of project will encounter fewer problems and meet their scheduled milestones more often. Documenters who have written user manuals for similar applications will find writing manuals for the new project easier. Project managers with similar experience will know what tasks are likely to be difficult. Even customers with previous experience specifying software requirements will be better at creating good requirements.

If you have access to design specialists such as user interface designers or human factors experts, get them to help. Any programmer can build forms, menus, and colorful labels in the same way anyone can cook. It's true that anyone can put a pot on a stove, but that doesn't mean the result will be edible.

A good user interface makes users productive. A bad one, if it even works, is frustrating and ineffective. (It's like trying to empty a bathtub with a teaspoon. You'll eventually succeed, but you'll spend the whole time thinking, "This is stupid. There has to be a better way!")

Brainstorm

Copying an existing application and clairvoyance are good techniques for generating requirements, but they share a common disadvantage: they are unlikely to lead you to new innovative solutions that might be better than the old ones. To find truly revolutionary solutions, you need to be more creative.

One way to look for creative solutions is the group creativity exercise known as *brainstorming*.

You're probably somewhat familiar with brainstorming, at least in an informal setting, but there are several approaches that you can use under different circumstances.

The basic approach that most people think of as brainstorming is called the *Osborn method* because it was developed by Alex Faickney Osborn, an advertising executive who tried to develop new, creative problem-solving methods starting in 1939. Basically, he was tired of his employees failing to come up with new and innovative advertising campaigns. (As is the case with the Gantt charts described in Chapter 4, the fact that we're still using Osborn's techniques after all these years shows how useful they are.) Osborn's key observation is summed up nicely in his own words.

It is easier to tone down a wild idea than to think up a new one.

—*Alex Faickney Osborn*

Basically, the gist of the method is to gather as many ideas as possible, not worrying about their quality or practicality. After you assemble a large list of possible ideas, you examine them more closely to see which deserve further work.

To allow as many approaches as possible, you should try to get a diverse group of participants. In software engineering, that means the group should include customers, users, user interface designers, system architects, team leads, programmers, trainers, and anyone else who has an interest in the project. Get as many different viewpoints as you can. (Although in practice, brainstorming becomes less effective if the group becomes larger than 10 or 12 people.)

To keep the ideas flowing, don't judge or critique any of the ideas. If you criticize someone's ideas, that person may shut down and stop contributing. Even a truly crazy idea can spark other ideas that may lead somewhere promising. Just write down every idea no matter how impractical it may seem. Even if an idea is impossible to implement using today's technology, it may be simple by next Wednesday.

(It wasn't that long ago that portable phones had the size, weight, and functionality of a brick. Now they're small enough to lose in the sofa cushions and have more computing power than NASA had when Neil Armstrong flubbed his "one small step" line on the moon.)

Osborn's method uses the following four rules:

➤ Focus on quantity—Do everything you can to keep the ideas flowing. The more ideas you collect, the greater your chances of finding a really creative and revolutionary solution.

➤ Withhold criticism—Criticism can make people stop contributing. Early criticism can also eliminate seemingly bad ideas that lead to better ideas.

➤ Encourage unusual ideas—You can always "tone down a wild idea," but you may need to think way outside of the box to find really creative solutions.

➤ Combine and improve ideas—Form new ideas by combining other ideas or using one idea to modify another.

Only after the flow of ideas is slowing to a trickle or has morphed into knock-knock jokes should you start evaluating the ideas to see what you've got. At that point, you can pick out the most promising ideas to develop further (possibly with more brainstorming).

Many people are familiar with Osborn's method (although they may not know its name), but there are also several other brainstorming techniques, some of which can be even more effective. The following list describes some of those techniques.

- ➤ Popcorn—(I think of this as the Mob technique.) People just speak out as ideas occur to them. This works fairly well with small groups of people who are comfortable with each other. It works less well if there are so many people that you can't write the ideas down.

- ➤ Subgroups—Break the group into smaller subgroups (possibly in corners of the same room) and have each group brainstorm. When the subgroups are finished, have the larger group discuss their best ideas. This works well if the main group is very large, if some people feel uncomfortable speaking in the larger group (the new developer in shorts and sandals may be afraid to speak out in front of the corporate vice president in a thousand dollar suit), or if one or two people are monopolizing the discussion.

- ➤ Sticky notes—Also called the nominal group technique (NGT). Participants write down their ideas on sticky notes, index cards, papyrus, or whatever. The ideas are collected and read to the group, and the group discusses and votes on each idea. The best ideas are developed further, possibly with other rounds of brainstorming.

- ➤ Idea passing—Participants sit in a circle. (I suppose you could use some other arrangement such as an ellipse, rectangle, or nonagon. As long as you have an ordering for the participants.) Each person writes down an idea and passes it to the next person. The participants add thoughts to the ideas they receive and pass them on to the next person. The ideas continue moving around the circle until everyone gets their original idea back. At this point, each idea should have been examined in great detail by the group. (Instead of a circle, nonagon, or whatever, you can also swap ideas randomly.)

- ➤ Circulation list—This is similar to idea passing except the ideas are passed via email, envelope, or some other method outside of a single meeting. This can take a lot longer than idea passing but may be more convenient for busy participants.

- ➤ Rule breaking—List the rules that govern the way you achieve a task or goal. Then everyone tries to think of ways to break or circumvent those rules while still achieving the goal.

- ➤ Individual—Participants perform their own solitary brainstorming sessions. They can write (or speak) their trains of thought, use word association, draw mind maps (diagrams relating thoughts and ideas—search online for details), and any other technique they find useful. Some studies have shown that individual brainstorming may be more effective than group brainstorming.

The following list describes some tips that can make brainstorming even more productive.

- ➤ Work in a comfortable room where everyone can feel at ease.
- ➤ Provide food and drinks. (I'll let you decide what kinds of drinks.)

➤ Start by recapping the users' current processes and the problems you are trying to solve.

➤ Use a clock to keep sessions short and lively. If you're using an iterative approach such as idea passing, keep the rounds brief.

➤ Allow the group's attention to wander a bit, but keep the discussion more or less on topic. If you're designing a remote mining rig control system, then you probably don't need to be discussing Ouija boards or Monty Python quotes.

➤ However, a few jokes can keep people relaxed and help ideas flow, so a *few* Monty Python quotes may be okay. (Remember what I said about creativity coming from a combination of focus and distraction? A few jokes can provide some distraction.)

➤ If you get stuck, restate the problem.

➤ Allow silent periods so that people have time to think about the problem and their ideas.

➤ Reverse the problem. For example, instead of trying to think of ways to build better blogging software, think of ways to build worse blogging software. (Obviously, don't actually do them.)

➤ Write ideas in slightly ambiguous ways and let people give their interpretations.

➤ At the end, summarize the best ideas and give everyone copies so they can think about them later. Sometimes, a great idea pops into someone's head after the official brainstorming sessions are over.

Brainstorming is useful anytime you want to find creative solutions to complex problems, not just during requirements gathering. You can use it to pick problems in your company that you might solve with a new software project. You can use it to design user interfaces, explore possible system architectures, create high-level designs, and plan interesting exercises for training classes. (You can even use brainstorming techniques outside of software engineering to decide where to go on your next vacation, reduce pollution in your city, or pick a school science fair project.)

Keep brainstorming in mind throughout the project as a technique you can use to attack difficult problems.

RECORDING REQUIREMENTS

After you decide what should be in the requirements, you need to write them down so that everyone can read them (and argue about whether they're correct). There are several ways you can record requirements so team members can refer to them throughout the project's lifetime.

Obviously, you can just write the requirements down as a sequence of commandments as in, "Thou shalt make the user change passwords on every full moon." There's a lot to be said for writing down requirements in simple English (or whatever your team's native language is). For starters, the team members already know that language and have been using it for many years.

You can still mess things up by writing requirements ambiguously or in hard-to-understand formats (such as limericks or haiku), but if you're reasonably careful, requirements written in ordinary language can be very effective.

The following sections describe some other methods for recording requirements.

UML

The Unified Modeling Language (UML) lets you specify how parts of the system should work. Despite its name, UML isn't a single unified language. Instead, it uses several kinds of diagrams to represent different pieces of the system. Some of those represent program items such as classes. Others represent behaviors, such as the way objects interact with each other and the way data flows through the system.

I won't bash UML (it's too popular and I'm not famous enough to get away with it), but it does have some drawbacks. Most notably it's complicated. UML includes two main categories of diagrams that are divided into more than a dozen specific types, each with its own complex set of rules.

Specifying complex requirements with UML is only useful if everyone understands the UML. Unfortunately, many customers and users don't want to learn it. It's not that they couldn't. They just usually have better things to do with their time, like helping you understand their needs. (I did actually work on one project where the customers taught themselves how to use some types of UML diagrams so that they could specify parts of the system. It worked reasonably well, but it took a long time.)

I'll talk more about UML in the next chapter. For now, during requirements gathering, you probably shouldn't rely heavily on UML unless your customers are already reasonably familiar with it (for example, if you're writing a library for use by other programmers who already use UML).

User Stories

Storytelling strikes me as a more powerful tool than quantification or measurement for what we do.

—Alan Cooper

A *user story* is exactly what you might think: a short story explaining how the system will let the user do something. For example, the following text is a story about a user searching a checkers database to find opponents:

The user enters his Harkness rating (optional), whether moves should be timed or untimed, and the variant (such as traditional, three-dimensional, upside-down, or Gliński). When the user clicks Search, the application displays a list of possible opponents that have compatible selections.

Many developers write stories on index cards to encourage brevity. The scope of each story should also be limited so that no story should take too long to implement (no more than a week or two).

Notice that the story doesn't contain a lot of detail about things like whether the game variants are given in a list or set of radio buttons. The story lets you defer those decisions until later during design.

User stories should come with acceptance testing procedures that you can use at the end of development to decide whether the application satisfied the story.

User stories may seem low-tech, but they have some big advantages, not least of which is that people are already familiar with them. They are easy to write, easy to understand, and can cover just about any situation you can imagine. They can be simple or complex depending on the situation. Unlike with UML, your customers, developers, managers, and other team members already know how to understand stories without any new training.

User stories give you a lot of expressiveness and flexibility without a lot of extra work. (In execuspeak, user stories allow you to leverage existing competencies to empower stakeholders.)

User stories do have some drawbacks. For example, you can easily write stories that are confusing, ambiguous, inconsistent with other stories, and unverifiable. (Like Jasper Fforde's book *Shades of Grey*. One of my favorites, but pretty confusing.) Of course, that's true of any method of recording requirements.

Use Cases

A *use case* is a description of a series of interactions between actors. The actors can be users or parts of the application.

Often a use case has a larger scope than a user story. For example, a use case might explain how the application will allow a user to examine cardiac ultrasound data for a patient. That user might need to use many different screens to examine different kinds of recordings and measurements. Each of those subtasks could be described by a user story, but the larger job of examining all the data would be too big to describe on a single index card and would take longer to implement than a week or two.

Use cases also follow a template more often than user stories. A simple template might require a use case to have the following fields:

➤ Title—The name of the goal, as in "User Examines Cardiac Data." Usually, the title includes the main actor (user) and an action (examines).

➤ Main success scenario—A numbered sequence of steps describing the most normal variation of the scenario.

➤ Extensions—Sequences of steps describing other variations of the scenario. This may include unusual cases such as when the user enters invalid data or the application can't handle a request. (For example, if the user searches for a nonexistent patient or if the patient is an octopus and therefore has three hearts.)

Other templates include a lot more fields such as lists of stakeholders interested in the scenario, preconditions that must be met before the scenario begins, and success and failure variations.

Prototypes

A *prototype* is a mockup of some or all of the application. The idea is to give the customers a more intuitive hands-on feel for what the finished application will look like and how it will behave than you can get from text descriptions such as user stories and use cases.

A simple user interface prototype might display forms that contain labels, text boxes, and buttons showing what the finished application will look like. In a *nonfunctional prototype*, the buttons, menus, and other controls on the forms wouldn't actually do anything. They would just sit there and look pretty.

A *functional prototype* (or *working prototype*) looks and acts much as the finished application will but it's allowed to cheat. It may do something that looks like it works, but it may be incomplete and it probably won't use the same methods that the final application will use. It might use less efficient algorithms, load data from a text file instead of a database, or display random messages instead of getting them from another system. It might even use hard-coded fake data.

For example, the prototype might let you enter search criteria on a form. When you clicked the Search button, the prototype would ignore your search criteria and display a prefilled form showing fake results. This gives the customers a good idea about how the final application will work but it doesn't require you to write all the code.

There are a couple of things you can do with a prototype after it's built. First, you can use it to define and refine the requirements. You can show it to the customers and, based on their feedback, modify it to better fit their needs.

After you've fine-tuned the prototype so that it represents the customers' requirements as closely as possible, you can leave it alone. You can continue to refer to it if there's a question about what the application should look like or how it should work, but you start over from scratch when building the application. This kind of prototype is called a *throwaway prototype*.

Alternatively, you can start replacing the prototype code and fake data with production-quality code and real data. Over time, you can evolve the prototype into increasingly functional versions until eventually it becomes the finished application. This kind of prototype is sometimes called an *evolutionary prototype*. This approach is used by some of the iterative approaches described in Chapter 18, "Iterative Models."

SURVIVAL OF THE LAZIEST

You need to be careful if you use an evolutionary prototype. While throwing together an initial version to show the customers what the final application will do, developers can (and should) take shortcuts to get things done as quickly as possible. That can result in code that's sloppy, riddled with bugs, and hard to maintain.

As long as the prototype works, that's fine. The prototype is only supposed to give you an idea about how the program will work, so it doesn't need to be as maintainable as the finished application must be.

That's good enough if you're using the prototype only to define requirements, but if you try to evolve the prototype into a production application, you need to be sure to go back and remove all of the shortcuts and rewrite the code properly. If you don't remove all of the prototype code, you'll certainly pay the price later in increased bug fixes and maintenance.

Requirements Specification

How formally you need to write up the requirements depends on your project. If you're building a simple tool to rename the files on your own computer in bulk, a simple description may be enough. If you're writing software to fill out legal forms for a law firm, you probably need to be much more formal. (And you might want to hire a different law firm to review your contract.)

If you search the Internet, you can find several templates for requirements specifications. These typically list major categories of requirements such as user documentation, user interface design, and interfaces with other systems.

Search online for "software requirements template" to find some templates that you can adapt for your projects. Add the keyword "IEEE" to your search to get templates based on IEEE standards. (IEEE is usually pronounced "eye-triple-ee" and stands for Institute of Electrical and Electronics Engineers.)

VALIDATION AND VERIFICATION

After you record the requirements (with whatever methods you prefer), you still need to validate them and later verify them. The two terms "validation" and "verification" are sometimes used interchangeably. Here are the definitions I use. (I think these are the most common interpretations.)

Requirements validation is the process of making sure that the requirements say the right things. Someone, often customers, analysts, or users, needs to work through all the requirements and make sure that they (1) describe things the application should do and (2) describe *everything* the application should do.

Requirements verification is the process of checking that the finished application actually satisfies the requirements.

> ### VALIDATION VERSUS VERIFICATION
>
> Here's another way to think of this:
>
> **Validation**—Are we doing the right things?
>
> **Verification**—Are we doing the things right?
>
> Those two statements are glib, but it's hard to remember which is which. Perhaps a better way to remember the difference is that "validation" comes before "verification" alphabetically and validation comes before verification in a software project.

CHANGING REQUIREMENTS

In many projects, requirements evolve over time. As work proceeds, you may discover that something you thought would be easy is hard. Or you may stumble across a technique that lets you add a high-value feature with little extra work.

Often changes are driven by the customers. After they start to see working pieces of the application, they may think of other items that they hadn't thought of before.

Depending on the kind of project, you may accommodate some changes, as long as they don't get out of hand. You can help control the number of changes by creating a *change control board*. Customers (and others) can submit change requests to this board (which might actually be a single person) for approval. The board decides whether a change should be implemented or deferred to a later release.

The development models described in Chapters 18 and 19 are particularly good at dealing with changing requirements because they tend to build an application in small steps with frequent opportunities for refinement. If you plan to add new features in a mini-project every two weeks, it's easy to add new requirements into the next phase. There's still a danger of never finishing the project, however, if the change requests keep trickling in.

DIGITAL TRANSFORMATION

Digitization is the process of converting some existing system into a digital form. For example, suppose you run a small mall kiosk called the Lace Place where you sell artisanal shoelaces. You take cash payments using an old-fashioned shiny brass cash register. If you switch to an online *point of sale (POS) system* that takes cash and perhaps credit cards, you've merely digitized an existing process, so that's digitization.

In contrast, *digital transformation* (*DT* or sometimes *DX*, because the *X* makes it sound cooler) is a more systemic, transformational change. For example, modern POS systems may come with all sorts of bells and whistles such as employee shift scheduling, inventory tracking, sales tax calculation and collection, item sales analysis, an online store, gift cards (electronic and IRL), online ordering for pickup or shipping, and the ability to send spam text messages to customers' phones. Implementing those features would transform the business from a small mall kiosk into a streamlined shoelace selling juggernaut. Add a shoelace-of-the-month club and you may want to close the brick-and-mortar kiosk and move entirely online!

In a sense, DX is like extreme digitization. If you digitize enough, particularly when you connect systems so they can accomplish something that you couldn't before, then you've transformed the business and crossed the line into DX.

That explains what digitization and transformation are. Two remaining topics are what to digitize and how to do it.

What to Digitize

Obviously, you can digitize anything that can benefit the business by making it more efficient, more profitable, or a generally better place to work. Automatically filing employment paperwork doesn't contribute much to the bottom line, but it removes one more headache from the business owner.

One way to look for opportunities for digitization is to study flows through the system. Sometimes these are suspiciously similar to use cases. For example, you could write up something like a use case that follows the flow of raw materials as they are converted into finished products and sold.

You buy ribbons and aglets, heat-seal the aglets onto the ends of pieces of ribbon, package the laces, and sell them. If you digitally track this flow, you can know at any moment roughly how many aglets, feet of ribbon, and finished laces you have on hand. You'll be able to predict how many shoelaces you're likely to sell in the next few weeks, so you'll know if you have to make more. You'll know how long it takes to order more ribbon and aglets, so you'll know when you need to reorder.

With a little work, you might be able to automate much of that (transformationally) so the sales system could automatically reorder ribbon periodically or when the ribbon and finished laces inventory reaches certain levels.

In addition to production flow, look closely at money flowing from customers, through the system, and into the bank. One of the fundamental rules of business is to make it easy for customers to give you money, so think about the tasks that a customer goes through during a transaction and see if you can find ways to streamline the process. Can they order online? Over the phone? Via a smartphone?

When you're looking for flows, it's useful to put yourself in the shoes of everyone associated with the business. That includes employees, managers, customers, and even vendors and suppliers. Look for ways that you can make a process smoother or connect it with other processes.

> **NONDIGITAL TRANSFORMATION** As long as you're studying the business's flows and processes, you may as well watch for opportunities to improve things nondigitally. For example, you probably cannot digitize moving aglets from the mailbox into storage bins, but you can track the process, and you might be able to find a better location for the storage bins.

Perhaps as important as deciding what to digitize is deciding what not to digitize. Custom software is expensive, so you should be sure the effort is worth it.

For example, I'm sure you *could* digitize moving aglets from the mailbox to storage bins with some bespoke robots, but that would cost far more money than it would save.

How to Digitize

This section isn't about how to build a software project. That's what the whole rest of the book is about. Yes, you'll need to gather requirements, create high-level and low-level designs, write code, test, and all of that, but there are also some less obvious issues to handle.

Chief among those issues is culture. If you own a small business and just want to build an online store, your main difficulty may be learning how to use the website builder. (And handling the 1000 percent increase in sales!)

However, if you work for a larger company, then you may face resistance. If your software is useful, it will require change, and people fear change. Some people will need to change the way they do things. They will probably take a while to learn the new system, and that will make them less productive in the short term. Your software may even replace some jobs and put people out of work. (Hopefully the company can move them into new jobs, but unfortunately that doesn't always happen.)

Perhaps the best way to reduce resistance is to include all interested parties in the planning. Keep those who will be affected in the loop so they know what is happening. Make them part of the team. They *will* talk about the project, so if you don't give them facts, they'll make up conspiracy theories.

Emphasize how the project will help the company. Most employees are okay with the idea of working for the good of the company, or at least they'll acknowledge that they're supposed to work for the good of the company.

One particularly useful technique is to draft one or two of the more vocal interested parties to be user representatives. You can even call them analysts to make them seem more official. Make sure they know what's going on and let them provide limited feedback. Take their suggestions seriously and act on some of them if you can. If something isn't too hard and won't do too much damage, add it to the project. You may not win these people over completely, but they may at least come to think of the project as a necessary evil rather than the end of all civilization.

SUMMARY

Requirements gathering may not be *the most* important stage of a project, but it certainly is *an* important stage. It sets the direction for future development. If you get the requirements wrong, you may develop something, but there's no guarantee that it will be useful.

Good requirements must satisfy some basic requirements of their own. For example, they must be clear and consistent. Having hundreds of requirements won't do you any good if no one can understand what they mean or if they contradict each other.

Some developers group requirements into categories. For example, you can use audience-oriented categories, FURPS, or FURPS+ to organize requirements. Categorizing requirements alone doesn't help you define the project, but you can use the categories as a checklist to make sure you haven't forgotten anything obvious. (They also make it easier to understand other software engineers at parties when they say, "This party has good functional requirements but the nonfunctionals could use some work!")

There are several ways you can gather requirements. Obviously, you should talk with the customers and, if possible, the users. You can use the five Ws and one H to help guide the conversation. Studying the users as they currently perform their jobs is often instructive. It can help clarify the project's goals, and occasionally you may discover simple things you can add to the project that will make the users' jobs a whole lot easier.

After you understand the customers' needs, you must refine those needs into requirements. Three techniques that can help include copying an existing system, using previous experience to just write down requirements, and brainstorming. Brainstorming is often more work but can sometimes lead to creative solutions that you might not have discovered otherwise.

Finally, after you know what the requirements are, you need to record them so everyone can refer to them as the project continues. Some ways you can record requirements are formal written specifications, UML diagrams, user stories, use cases, and prototypes.

Before you move on to the next phase of development, you should validate the requirements to ensure that they actually meet the customers' needs. (Later, near the end of the project, you'll also need to verify that the project has met the requirements.)

If you think this seems like a lot of work before the project "actually" begins, you're right. However, it's critical to the project's eventual success. Without sound requirements, how will you know what to build? Unless the requirements are clear and verifiable, how will you know if you've achieved your goals?

After you gather, record, and validate the requirements, you're ready to move on to the next stage of development: high-level design. You may have already incorporated some design decisions into the requirements. For example, you might have made some user interface decisions or picked a system architecture.

The next chapter explains some of the high-level design decisions you might need to make, whether in the requirements phase or during a separate high-level design step. It also provides some guidance on how to make those decisions.

EXERCISES

1. List five characteristics of good requirements.

2. What does MOSCOW stand for? (Other than a city in Russia.)

3. Suppose you want to build a program called TimeShifter to upload and download files at scheduled times while you're on vacation. The following list shows some of the application's requirements.

   a. Allow users to monitor uploads/downloads while away from the office.
   b. Let the user specify website login parameters such as an Internet address, a port, a username, and a password.
   c. Let the user specify upload/download parameters such as time-out and number of retries if there's a problem.
   d. Let the user select an Internet location, a local file, and a time to perform the upload/download.
   e. Let the user schedule uploads/downloads at any time.
   f. Allow uploads/downloads to run at any time.
   g. Make uploads/downloads transfer at least 8 Mbps.
   h. Run uploads/downloads sequentially. Two cannot run at the same time.
   i. If an upload/download is scheduled for a time when another is in progress, it waits until the other one finishes.
   j. Perform scheduled uploads/downloads.
   k. Keep a log of all attempted uploads/downloads and whether they succeeded.
   l. Let the user empty the log.
   m. Display reports of upload/download attempts.
   n. Let the user view the log reports on a remote device such as a phone.
   o. Send an email to an administrator if an upload/download fails its maximum number of retries.
   p. Send a text message to an administrator if an upload/download fails its maximum number of retries.

   For this exercise, list the audience-oriented categories for each requirement. Are there requirements in each category?

4. Repeat Exercise 3 using the FURPS requirement categories.

5. What are the five Ws and one H?

6. List three techniques for gathering requirements from customers and users.

7. Explain why brainstorming can be useful in defining requirements.

8. List the four rules of the Osborn method.

9. Figure 5.1 shows the design for a simple hangman game that will run on smartphones. When you click the New Game button, the program picks a random mystery word from a large list and starts a new game. Then if you click a letter, either the letter is filled in where it appears in the mystery word or a new piece of Mr. Bones's skeleton appears. In either case, the letter you clicked is grayed out so that you don't pick it again. If you guess all of the letters in the mystery word, the game displays a message that says, "Congratulations, you won!" If you build Mr. Bones's complete skeleton, a message says, "Sorry, you lost."

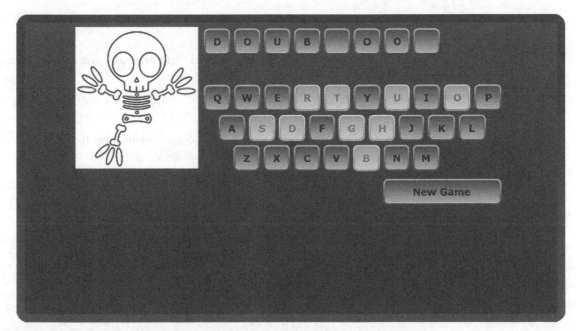

FIGURE 5.1: The Mr. Bones application is a hangman word game for smartphones.

Brainstorm this application and see if you can think of ways you might change it. Use the MOSCOW method to prioritize your changes.

10. (Instructors) Have the class brainstorm ideas to address a fairly difficult issue (such as reversing global warming, ending global hunger, or making politicians honor their campaign promises). If time permits, try a couple of different brainstorming variations such as popcorn, subgroups, and individual. Discuss what went well and what didn't.

WHAT YOU LEARNED IN THIS CHAPTER

➤ Requirements are important to a project because they set the project's goals and direction.

➤ Requirements must be clear, unambiguous, consistent, prioritized, and verifiable.

➤ The MOSCOW method provides one way to prioritize requirements.

➤ FURPS stands for functionality, usability, reliability, performance, and supportability.

➤ FURPS+ also adds design constraints, implementation requirements, interface requirements, and physical requirements.

➤ You can gather requirements by talking to customers and users, watching users at work, and studying existing systems.

➤ You can convert goals into requirements by copying existing systems and methods, using previous experience, and brainstorming.

➤ You can record requirements in written specifications, UML diagrams, user stories, use cases, and prototypes.

➤ Requirements may change over time. That's okay as long as it happens in a controlled manner.

➤ Requirement validation is the process of checking that the requirements meet the customers' needs.

➤ Requirement verification is the process of checking that the finished project satisfies the requirements.

6

High-Level Design

Design is not just what it looks like and feels like. Design is how it works.

—*Steve Jobs*

Design is easy. All you do is stare at the screen until drops of blood form on your forehead.

—*Marty Neumeier*

What You Will Learn in This Chapter:

➤ The purpose of high-level design

➤ How a good design lets you get more work done in less time

➤ Specific things you should include in a high-level design

➤ Common software architectures you can use to structure an application

➤ How UML lets you specify system objects and interactions

High-level design provides a view of the system at an abstract level. It shows how the major pieces of the finished application will fit together and interact with each other.

A high-level design should also specify assumptions about the environment in which the finished application will run. For example, it should describe the hardware and software you will use to develop the application and the hardware that will eventually run the program.

The high-level design does not focus on the details of how the pieces of the application will work. Those details can be worked out later during low-level design and implementation.

Before you start learning about specific items that should be part of the high-level design, you should understand the purpose of a high-level design and how it can help you build an application.

THE BIG PICTURE

You can view software development as a process that chops up the system into smaller and smaller pieces until the pieces are small enough to implement. Using that viewpoint, high-level design is the first step in the chopping-up process.

The goal is to divide the system into chunks that are self-contained enough that you could give them to separate teams to implement.

PARALLEL IMPLEMENTATION

Suppose you're building a relatively simple application to record the results of Twister games for a championship. It needs to store the names of the players in each match, the date and time they played, and the order in which they fell over during play.

You might break this application into two large pieces: the database and the user interface. You could then assign those two pieces to different groups of developers to implement in parallel.

(You'll see in the rest of this chapter that there are actually a lot of other pieces you might want to specify even for this simple application.)

There are a lot of variations on this basic theme. On a small project, for example, the pieces might be small enough that they can be handled by individual developers instead of teams.

In a large project, the initial pieces might be so big that the teams will want to create their own medium-level designs that break them into smaller chunks before trying to write any code. This can also happen if a piece of the project turns out to be harder than you had expected. In that case, you may want to break it into smaller pieces and assign them to different people.

ADDING PEOPLE

Breaking an existing task into smaller pieces is one of the few ways you can sometimes add people to a project and speed up development.

Adding new people to the same old tasks usually doesn't help and often actually slows development as the new people get up to speed and get in each other's way. (Like the Three Stooges trying to walk through a door at the same time.)

However, if you can break a large task into smaller pieces and assign them to different people, you may speed things up a bit. The new people still need time to come up to speed, so this won't always help, but at least people won't trip over each other trying to perform the same tasks.

In some projects, you may want to assign multiple pieces of the project to a single team, particularly if the pieces are closely related. For example, if the pieces pass a lot of data back and forth, it will be helpful if the people building those pieces work closely together. (Multitier architectures, which are described in the section "Client/Server" later in this chapter, can help minimize this sort of interaction.)

Another situation in which this kind of close cooperation is useful is when several pieces of the application all work with the same data structure or with the same database tables. Placing the data structure or tables under the control of a single team may make it easier to keep the related pieces synchronized.

WHAT TO SPECIFY

The stages of a software engineering project often blur together, and that's as true for high-level design as it is for any other part of development. For example, suppose you're building an application to run on the Android phone platform. In that case, the fact that your hardware platform is Android phones should probably be in the requirements. (You may also want to add extra details to the high-level design, such as the models of phones that you will test.)

Exactly what you should specify in the high-level design varies somewhat, but some things are constant for most projects. The following sections describe some of the most common items you might want to specify in the high-level design.

Security

The first thing you see when you start most applications is a login screen. That's the first *obvious* sign of the application's security, but it's actually not the first piece and definitely not the last.

The high-level design should at least sketch out the kinds of security that the project will need during development and after implementation. You should consider problems that are intentional attacks from outside, bugs, and random mistakes (like losing a laptop or a flash drive containing a backup) that might compromise data.

You should also at least briefly consider problems that could be caused by that discontented team member who's been passed up for promotion five times (although you've read Chapter 3, "The Team" so your team is presumably running like a happy, well-oiled machine). If you work for a large company, you may also face hostility from employees who are not part of your coding clan team. (On one project, someone from another part of the company tried to delete all of our source code.)

You can protect the project from many of these issues by backing up the project documentation, source code, data, and anything else you can think of.

In the high-level design, sketch out any weaknesses that you spot and start protecting the project's assets immediately. Then fill in more details in the low-level design.

Security in general, both physical and electronic, is a large topic, so I'll defer a more detailed discussion until Chapter 8, "Security Design."

Hardware

Back in the old days when programmers worked by candlelight on treadle-powered computers, hardware options were limited. You pretty much wrote programs for large mainframes, and your choice of operating system (and sometimes even programming language) was determined by your choice of hardware.

These days you have a lot more choices and you need to specify the ones that you'll be using. You can build systems to run on mainframes (yes, they still exist), desktops, laptops, tablets, and phones. A mini-computer acts sort of as a mini-mainframe that can serve a handful of users.

Wearable devices include such gadgets as computers strapped to the wearer's wrist (sort of like a cell phone with a wrist strap and possibly extra keys and buttons), wristbands, bracelets, watches, eyeglasses, monocles, headsets, rings, clothing, artificially intelligent hearing aids, and smart dog collars.

Appliances include refrigerators, doorbells, fire alarms, smart bicycles, door locks, toasters, medical sensors, voice-controlled devices, smart thermostats, lighting systems, printers, cameras, farm equipment, televisions, and who knows how many other kinds of devices form the *Internet of Things (IoT)*. These devices may communicate with each other or with your application.

Additional hardware that you need to specify might include the following:

- ➤ Printers
- ➤ Network components (cables, modems, gateways, and routers)
- ➤ Servers (database servers, web servers, and application servers)
- ➤ Specialized instruments (scales, microscopes, programmable signs, and GPS units)
- ➤ Audio and video hardware (webcams, headsets, and VOIP)
- ➤ IoT appliances

With all the available options (and undoubtedly many more on the way), you need to specify the hardware that will run your application. Sometimes, this will be relatively straightforward. For example, your application might run on a laptop or in a web page that could run on any web-enabled hardware. Other times the hardware specification might include multiple devices connected via the Internet, text messages, a custom network, the IoT, or by some other method.

SELECTING A HARDWARE PLATFORM

Suppose you're building an application to manage the fleet of dog washing vehicles run by the Pampered Poodle Emergency Dog Washing Service. When a customer calls to tell you Fifi ran afoul of a skunk, an emergency dog-washer rushes to the scene with lights flashing and siren blaring.

In this case, your drivers might access the system over cell phones. A desktop computer back at the office would hold the database and provide a user interface to let you do everything else the business needs such as logging customer calls, dispatching drivers, printing invoices, tracking payments, and ordering more doggy shampoo.

For this application, you would specify the kind of phones the drivers will use (such as Android or iOS), the model of the computer used to hold the database and business parts of the application, and the type of network connectivity the application will use. (Perhaps the database desktop serves data on the Internet and the phones download data from there.)

Another strategy would be to have the desktop serve information to the drivers as web pages. Then the drivers could use any web-enabled device (smartphone, tablet, augmented reality glasses) to view their assignments.

User Interface

During high-level design, you can sketch out the user interface, but only at a high level. Save the details for later. For example, you can indicate the main methods for navigating through the application, but don't specify any exact screen layouts.

Older-style desktop applications use forms with menus that display other forms. Often the user can display many forms at the same time and switch between them by clicking with the mouse, tapping if the hardware has a touch screen, or using key combinations such as Alt+Tab.

In contrast, some newer tablet-style applications tend to use a single window (that typically covers the entire tablet, or whatever hardware you're using) and buttons or arrows to navigate. When you click a button, a new window appears and fills the device. Sometimes a Back button lets you move back to the previous window.

Whichever navigational model you pick, you can specify the forms or windows that the application will include. You can then verify that they allow the user to perform the tasks defined in the requirements. In particular, you should walk through the user stories and use cases and make sure you've included forms to handle them all.

In addition to the application's basic navigational style, the high-level user interface design can describe special features such as clickable maps, important tables, or methods for specifying system settings (such as sliders, scroll bars, or text boxes).

This part of the design can also address general appearance issues such as color schemes, company logo placement, and form skins.

FOLLOW EXISTING PRACTICES

Most users have a lot of experience with other applications, and those applications follow certain standardized patterns. For example, desktop applications typically have menus that you access from a form's title bar. The menus drop down below and submenus cascade to the right and/or left. That's the way Windows applications have been handling menus for decades and users are familiar with how they work.

continues

(continued)

If your application sticks to a similar pattern, users will feel comfortable with the application with little extra training. They already know how to use menus, so they won't have any trouble using yours. Instead they can concentrate on learning how to use the more interesting pieces of your system. If you plan to use these sorts of standard interactions, say so in the high-level design.

In contrast, suppose your application changes this kind of standard interaction. Perhaps you access the menus by clicking a little icon on the right edge of the toolbar and then menus cascade out to the left instead of the right. Or perhaps there are no menus, just panels filled with icons that you can click to open new forms. In that case, users will need to learn how to use your new system. That will lead to at least some confusion, and it might create a lot of annoyance for the users.

Nonstandard behavior may also disqualify an app for inclusion in some online stores. For example, Google Play, Microsoft Store, and Apple's App Store all have basic requirements. I'm not saying that you can't be creative, but you might want to have a plan B ready in case your app fails the store's testability or usability requirements.

(I use one tool in particular, which I won't name, that for some reason thinks it knows a better way to handle menus, toolbars, and toolboxes. It's frustrating, incredibly annoying, and sometimes leads to outbreaks of Tourette syndrome.)

Unless you have a good reason to change the way most applications already work, stick with what the users already know.

You shouldn't specify every label and text box for every form during high-level design. You can handle that during low-level design and implementation (and after you've read Chapter 7, "Low-Level Design."). Often the controls you need follow from the database design anyway, so you can sometimes save some work if you do the database design first. Some tools can even use a database design to build the first version of the forms for you.

Internal Interfaces

When you chop the program into pieces, you should specify how the pieces will interact. Then the teams assigned to the pieces can work separately without needing constant coordination.

It's important that the high-level design specifies these internal interactions clearly and unambiguously so that the teams can work as independently as possible. If two teams that need to interact don't agree on how that interaction should occur, they can waste a huge amount of time. They'll waste time squabbling about which approach is better. They'll also waste time if one team needs to change the interface and that forces the other team to change its interface, too. The problem increases dramatically if more than two teams need to interact through the same interface.

It's worth spending some extra time to define these sorts of internal interfaces carefully before developers start writing code. Unfortunately, you may not be able to define the interfaces before writing at least some code. In that case, you may need to insulate two project teams by defining a temporary interface. Then, after the teams have written enough code to know what information they need to exchange, they can define the final interface.

DEFERRED INTERFACES

I worked on one project where two teams needed to pass a bunch of information back and forth. Of course, at the beginning of the project, neither team had written any code to work with the other team, so neither team could call the other. We also weren't sure what data the two teams would need to pass, so we couldn't specify the interface with certainty.

To get both teams working quickly, the high-level design specified an ASCII text file format that the teams could use to load test data. Instead of calling each other's code, the teams could write data into test files and then read data from those files. They were also free to modify the formats of their files as their needs evolved.

After several months of work, the two teams had written code to process the data and their needs were better defined. At that point, they agreed on a format for passing data and switched from moving data to and from files to actually calling each other's code.

It would have been more efficient to have defined the perfect interface at the beginning during high-level design, but that wasn't an option. Using text files to act as a temporary interface allowed both teams to work independently.

(The multitier design described in the section "Architecture" later in this chapter does something similar.)

External Interfaces

Many applications must interact with external systems. For example, suppose you're building a program that assigns crews for a large chartered fishing company called Fishspedition. The application needs to assign a captain, first mate, cook, and barnacle scraper for each trip. Your program needs to interact with the existing employee database to get information about crew members. (You don't want to assign a boat three cooks and no captain or three captains and no first mate.) You might also need to interact with a sales program that lets salespeople book fishing trips.

In a way, external interfaces are often easier to specify than internal ones because you usually don't have control over both ends of the interface. If your application needs to interact with an existing system, then that system already has interface requirements that you must meet.

Conversely, if you want future systems to interface with yours, you can probably specify whatever interface makes sense to you. Systems developed later need to meet your requirements. (Try to make your interface simple and flexible so that you don't get flooded with change requests.)

Architecture

An application's architecture describes how its pieces fit together at a high level. Developers use a lot of "standard" types of architectures. Many of these address particular characteristics of the problem being solved.

For example, rule-based systems are often used to handle complex situations in which solving a particular problem can be reduced to following a set of rules. Some troubleshooting systems use this approach. You call in because your computer can't connect to the Internet, and a customer rep asks you a sequence of hopefully relevant questions to try to diagnose the problem. The rep reads a question off a computer screen, you answer, and the rep clicks the corresponding button to get to the next question. Rules inside the rep's diagnostic system decide which question to give you next.

Other architectures attempt to simplify development by reducing the interactions among the pieces of the system. For example, a component-based architecture tries to make each piece of the system as separate as possible so that different teams of developers can work on them separately.

The following sections describe some common architectures that you might want to use.

Monolithic

In a *monolithic architecture*, a single program does everything. It displays the user interface, accesses data, processes customer orders, prints invoices, orders lunch, launches missiles, and does whatever else the application needs to do.

This architecture has some significant drawbacks. In particular, the pieces of the system are tied closely together, so it doesn't give you a lot of flexibility. For example, suppose the application stores customer address data and you later need to change the address format. (Perhaps you add a field to hold suite numbers.) Then you also need to change every piece of code that uses the address. This may not be too hard, but it means the programmers working on related pieces of code must stop what they're doing and deal with the change before they can get back to their current tasks. (The multitier architectures described in the next section handle this better, allowing the different teams of developers to work more independently.)

A monolithic architecture also requires that you understand how all the pieces of the system fit together from the beginning of the project. If you get any of the details wrong, the tight coupling between the pieces of the system makes fixing them later difficult.

Monolithic architectures do have some advantages. Because everything is built into a single program, there's no need for complicated communication across networks. That means you don't need to write and debug communication routines, you don't need to worry about the network going down, and you don't need to worry about network security. (Well, you still need to worry about some hacker sneaking in through your network and attacking your machines, but at least you don't need to encrypt messages sent between different parts of the application. Probably.)

Monolithic architectures are also useful for small applications where a single programmer or team is working on the code.

> **OS Monoliths** *Operating systems tend to be monolithic with a single (albeit large) set of programs managing local logins, desktop, file system, task management, user access control, program access, program priorities, etc. (It's a major source of contention whether certain other programs such as a browser should be allowed as part of the OS.)*
>
> *This has the advantage of improving performance but has the disadvantage of sometimes making one program too dependent on another unrelated application. For example, if the File Explorer in Windows 10 or 11 crashes, it can drag the taskbar, desktop, and Alt+Tab Task Switcher down with it. In one test, I had to reboot to get everything back.*
>
> *This problem has generally gotten better over the years (in the old days, many programs could summon the Blue Screen of Death), but these programs are still more tightly coupled than they would be had they been built by completely separate teams.*

Client/Server

A *client/server architecture* separates pieces of the system that need to use a particular function (clients) from parts of the system that provide those functions (servers). That decouples the client and server pieces of the system so that developers can work on them separately.

For example, many applications rely on a database to hold information about customers, products, orders, and employees. The application needs to display that information in some sort of user interface. One way to do that would be to integrate the database directly into the application. Figure 6.1 shows this situation schematically.

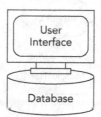

FIGURE 6.1: An application can directly hold its own data.

One problem with this design is that multiple users cannot use the same data. You can fix that problem by moving to a *two-tier architecture*, where a client (the user interface) is separated from the server (the database). Figure 6.2 shows this design. The clients and server communicate through some network such as a local area network (LAN), wide area network (WAN), or the Internet.

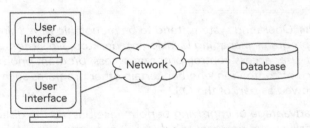

FIGURE 6.2: In a two-tier architecture, the client is separate from the server.

In this example, the client is the user interface (two instances of the same program) and the server is a database, but that need not be the case. For example, the client could be a program that makes automatic stock purchases, and the server could be a program that scours the Internet for information about companies and their stocks.

The two-tier architecture makes it easier to support multiple clients with the same server, but it ties clients and servers closely together. The clients must know what format the server uses, and if you change the way the server presents its data, you need to change the client to match. That may not always be a big problem, but it can mean a lot of extra work, particularly in the beginning of a project when the client's and server's needs aren't completely known.

You can help to increase the separation between the clients and server if you introduce another layer between the two to create the *three-tier architecture*, as shown in Figure 6.3.

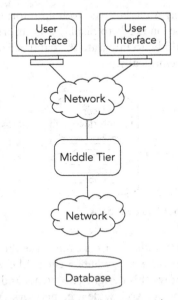

FIGURE 6.3: A three-tier architecture separates clients and servers with a middle tier.

In Figure 6.3, the middle tier is separated from the clients and the server by networks. The database runs on one computer, the middle tier runs on a second computer, and the instances of the client run on still other computers. This isn't the only way in which the pieces of the system can communicate. For example, in many applications the middle tier runs on the same computer as the database.

In a three-tier architecture, the middle tier provides insulation between the clients and server. In this example, it provides an interface that can map data between the format provided by the server and the format needed by the client. If you need to change the way the server stores data, you need to update only the middle tier so that it translates the new format into the version expected by the client. Similarly, if the client needs the data in a new format, the middle tier can translate the data to suit the client.

If the data format changes more drastically than just a formatting change (for example, if you need additional data that just isn't there), the middle tier can insert fake data until you have a chance to update the server to provide the actual data. That way development can continue on both the client and server while you straighten things out.

The separation provided by the middle tier lets different teams work on the client and server without interfering with each other too much.

In addition to providing separation, a middle tier can perform other actions that make the data easier to use by the client and server. For example, suppose the client needs to display some sort of aggregate data. Perhaps Martha's Musical Mechanisms needs to display the total number of carillons sold by each employee for each of the last 12 quarters. In that case, the server could store the raw sales data, and the middle tier could aggregate the data before sending it to the client.

> ### TIER TERMINOLOGY
>
> Sometimes, the client tier is called the *presentation tier* (because it presents information to the user), the middle tier is called the *logic tier* (because it contains business logic such as aggregating data for the presentation tier), and the server tier is called the *data tier* (particularly if all it does is provide data).

You can define other *multitier architectures* (or *N-tier architectures*) that use more than three tiers if that would be helpful. For example, a data tier might store the data, a second tier might calculate aggregates and perform other calculations on the data, a third tier might use artificial intelligence techniques to make recommendations based on the second tier's data, and a fourth tier would be a presentation tier that lets users see the results.

> ### BEST PRACTICE
>
> Multitier architectures are a best practice, largely because of the separation they provide between the client and server layers. Few applications use more than three tiers.

Component-Based

In *component-based software engineering (CBSE)*, you regard the system as a collection of loosely coupled components that provide services for each other. For example, suppose you're writing a system to schedule employee work shifts. The user interface could dig through the database to see what hours are available and what hours an employee can work, but that would tie the user interface closely to the database's structure.

An alternative would be to have the user interface ask components for that information, as shown in Figure 6.4. (Unified Modeling Language [UML] provides a more complex diagram for services that is described in the section "UML" later in this chapter.)

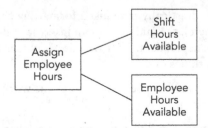

FIGURE 6.4: In a component-based architecture, components help decouple pieces of code.

The Assign Employee Hours user interface component would use the Shift Hours Available component to find out what hours were not yet assigned. It would also use the Employee Hours Available component to find out what hours an employee has available. After assigning new hours to the employee, it would update the other two components so that they know about the new assignment.

A component-based architecture decouples the pieces of code much as a multitier architecture does, but the pieces are all contained within the same executable program, so they communicate directly instead of across a network.

Service-Oriented

A *service-oriented architecture (SOA)* is similar to a component-based architecture except the pieces are implemented as services. A *service* is a self-contained program that runs on its own and provides some kind of service for its clients.

Sometimes, services are implemented as *web services*. Those are simply programs that satisfy certain standards, so they are easy to invoke over the Internet. Two common approaches for transmitting data across the web are SOAP and REST.

SOAP is a protocol that allows programs to invoke processes running on other computers, even computers that use a different operating system. In SOAP, requests are packaged in *Extensible Markup Language (XML)* where elements describe the function that the service should perform and any necessary parameters.

> **A SOAPY FUTURE** SOAP was originally a backronym for *Simple Object Access Protocol*, but in version 1.2 that was scrapped and now it's just called SOAP. (Perhaps because they thought the S no longer applied and OAP would make a weird name?) Since then, many SOAP features have been deprecated and most development is moving in other directions, such as REST.

> In general, the term *deprecate* means to disapprove of something and discourage its use. In programming terms, it means that a vendor such as Microsoft still supports something but does not recommend using it and may discontinue support in the future. (Basically, they're saying, "Yes, we know that two years ago we told you that this was the wave of the future, but now that the future is here, we've changed our minds.")

REST (representational state transfer) is an architectural style that was created to define how large-scale hypermedia systems such as the web should work. For example, a *RESTful* web service might send a request over the Internet via a specially formatted *URI (uniform resource locator)* and in response receive a *payload* containing data in XML, HTML, JSON, or some other data format.

In addition to the basic idea of a service, there are several variations with a service-oriented flavor.

Some big software vendors such as IBM and Oracle define *Service Component Architecture (SCA)*. This is basically a set of specifications for SOA defined by those companies.

Others define *microservices* as small services that you can glue together to build part or all of an application. As the name implies, the microservices are small, giving you benefits such as the ability to work on them separately, swap in new versions when necessary without disrupting the rest of the system, and use off-the-shelf microservices.

These ideas are also related to *aaS*, which stands for *as a service*. Broadly speaking, these include anything that is presented to the customer as a service. I suppose that includes pet-sitters and diaper services, but in this context it usually means some company wants to provide you some sort of software tool as a service. The term for talking about aaS when you don't know what service is being provided is *anything as a service (XaaS)*.

These services may be provided through methods such as libraries and programming interfaces, web-based control panels, or services in the SOAP and REST sense (in which case I suppose you could say that you had implemented "as a service" as a service).

There are many sub-genres of aaS that provide different types of service and that come with their own aaS acronyms. For example, artificial intelligence as a service (AIaaS), banking as a service (BaaS), database as a service (DBaaS), security as a service (SaaS), and so forth.

Two aaSs that are of particular interest to software development are infrastructure as a service and platform as a service.

Infrastructure as a service (IaaS) provides pieces of application infrastructure such as processors, network, storage, backups, security, recovery, firewalls, and so on.

Platform as a service (PaaS) provides everything that you need to develop software, such as compute power, compilers, tool libraries, and the ability to deploy applications to the cloud. This service may not include the ability to directly control the underlying cloud infrastructure, such as how the servers are arranged, where data is stored, or what operating system those servers use.

Microservices and XaaS are very popular with vendors eager to sell them to you. Search online for more details and to learn about more types of XaaS.

Data-Centric

Data-centric or *database-centric architectures* come in a variety of flavors that all use data in some central way. The following list summarizes some typical data-centric designs:

➤ Storing data in a relational database system. This is so common that it's easy to think of this as a simple technique for use in other architectures rather than an architecture of its own.

➤ Using tables instead of hard-wired code to control the application. Some artificial intelligence applications such as rule-based systems use this approach.

➤ Using stored procedures inside the database to perform calculations and implement business logic. This can be a lot like putting a middle tier inside the database.

Event-Driven

In an *event-driven architecture (EDA)*, various parts of the system respond to events as they occur. For example, as a customer order for robot parts moves through its life cycle, different pieces of the system might respond at different times. When the order is created, a fulfillment module might notice and print a list of the desired parts and an address label. When the order has been shipped, an invoicing module might notice and print an invoice. When the customer hasn't paid the invoice for 30 days, an enforcement module might notice and send RoboCop to investigate.

Rule-Based

A *rule-based architecture* uses a collection of rules to decide what to do next. These systems are sometimes called *expert systems* or *knowledge-based systems*.

The troubleshooting system described earlier in this chapter uses a rule-based approach.

Rule-based systems work well if you can identify the rules necessary to get the job done. Sometimes, you can build good rules even for complicated systems, although that can be a lot of work.

Rule-based systems don't work well if the problem is poorly defined so you can't figure out what rules to use. They also have trouble handling unexpected situations.

ROTTEN RULES

For several years I had a fairly odd network connection leading directly to my phone company's central office, so one wire provided both phone and Internet service. One day it didn't work, so I called tech support, and the service rep started working through his troubleshooting rules. Unfortunately, the phone company hadn't offered my type of service for several years, so the rules didn't cover it anymore.

Eventually, the rep reached a rule that asked me to unplug my modem and reconnect it. I explained that the modem was in the central office and that unplugging anything on my end would also disconnect my phone. The rules didn't give him any other options, so he insisted. I unplugged my cable and predictably the phone call dropped.

I called back, got a different rep who was a little better at thinking outside of the rules, and we discovered (as I had suspected) that the problem was at the central office.

Rule-based systems are great for handling common simple scenarios, but when they encounter anything unexpected, they're useless. For that reason, you should always give the user a way to handle special situations manually.

Distributed

In a *distributed architecture*, different parts of the application run on different processors and may run at the same time. The processors could be on different computers scattered across the network, or they could be different cores on a single computer. (Modern computers have multiple cores that can execute code at the same time.)

Service-oriented and multitier architectures are often distributed, with different parts of the system running on different computers. Component-oriented architectures may also be distributed, with different components running on different cores on the same computer.

In general, distributed applications can be extremely confusing to write and hard to debug. For example, suppose you're writing an application that sells office supplies such as staples, paper clips, and demotivational posters. You sell to companies that might have several authorized purchasers.

Now suppose your application uses the following steps to add the cost of a new purchase to a customer's outstanding balance:

1. Get customer balance from database.
2. Add new amount to balance.
3. Save new balance in database.

This seems straightforward until you think about what happens if two people make purchases at almost the same time with a distributed application. Suppose a customer has an outstanding balance of $100. One purchaser buys $50 worth of sticky notes while another purchaser is buying a $10 trash can labeled "suggestions." Now suppose the application executes the two purchasers' steps in the order shown in Table 6.1.

TABLE 6.1: Office supply purchasing sequence

PURCHASER 1	PURCHASER 2
Get balance. ($100)	
	Get balance. ($100)
Add to balance. ($150)	
	Add to balance. ($110)
Save new balance. ($150)	
	Save new balance. ($110)

In Table 6.1, time increases downward so Purchaser 1 gets the account balance first and then Purchaser 2 gets the account balance.

Next Purchaser 1 adds $50 to his copy of the balance to get $150, and then Purchaser 2 adds $10 to her copy of the balance to get $110.

Purchaser 1 then saves his new balance of $150 into the database. Finally, Purchaser 2 saves her balance of $110 into the database, writing over the $150-balance that Purchaser 1 just saved. In the end, instead of holding a balance of $160 ($100 + $50 + $10), the database holds a balance of $110.

In distributed computing, this is called a *race condition*. The two processes are racing to see which one saves its balance first. Whichever one saves its balance second "wins." (Although either way, you lose.)

A distributed architecture can improve performance as long as you don't run afoul of race conditions and a host of other confusing potential problems.

Mix and Match

An application doesn't need to stick with a single architecture. Different pieces of the application might use different design approaches. For example, you might create a distributed service-oriented application. Some of the larger services might use a component-based approach to break their code into decoupled pieces. Other services might use a multitier approach to separate their features from the data storage layer. (Combining different architectures can also sound impressive at cocktail parties. "Yes, we decided to go with an event-driven multitier approach using rule-based distributed components.")

CLASSYDRAW ARCHITECTURE

Suppose you want to pick an architecture for the ClassyDraw application described in Chapter 5, "Requirements Gathering." (Recall that this is a drawing program somewhat similar to MS Paint except it lets you select and manipulate drawing objects.) One way to do that is to think about each of the standard architectures and decide whether it would make sense to use while building the program.

➤   Monolithic—This is basically the default if none of the more elaborate architectures apply. We'll come back to this one later.

➤   Client/server, multitier—ClassyDraw stores drawings in files, not a database, so client/server and multitier architectures aren't needed. (You could store drawings in a database if you wanted to, perhaps for an architectural firm or some other use where there would be some benefit. For a simple drawing application, it would be overkill.)

➤ Component-based—You could think of different pieces of the application as components providing services to each other. For example, you could think of a "rectangle component" that draws a rectangle. For this simple application, it's probably just as easy to think of a `Rectangle` class that draws a rectangle, so I'm not going to think of this as a component-based approach.

➤ Service-oriented—This is even less applicable than the component-based approach. Spreading the application across multiple computers connected via web services (or some other kind of service) wouldn't help a simple drawing application.

➤ Data-centric—The user defines the drawings, so there's no data around which to organize the program. (Although a more specialized program, perhaps an aerospace design program, might interact with data in a meaningful way.)

➤ Event-driven—The user interface will be event-driven. For example, the user selects a tool and then clicks and drags to create a new shape. Or the user clicks to select a shape and then changes its properties or drags it to a new position.

➤ Rule-based—There are no rules that the user must follow to make a drawing, so this program isn't rule-based.

➤ Distributed—This program doesn't perform extensive calculations, so distributing pieces across multiple CPUs or cores probably wouldn't help.

Because none of the more exotic architectures apply (such as multitier or service-oriented), this application can have a simple monolithic architecture with an event-driven user interface.

Reports

Almost any nontrivial software project can use some kind of reports. Business applications might include reports that deal with customers (who's buying, who has unpaid bills, where customers live), products (inventory, pricing, what's selling well), and users (which employees are selling a lot, employee work schedules).

Even relatively simple applications can sometimes benefit from reports. For example, suppose you're writing a simple shareware game that users will download from the Internet and install on their phones. The users won't want reports (except perhaps a list of their high scores), but you may want to add some reporting. You could make the game upload information such as where the users are, when they use the game, how often they play, what parts of the game take a long time, and so forth. You can then use that data to generate reports to help you refine the game and improve your marketing.

AD HOC REPORTING

A large application might have dozens or even hundreds of reports. Often customers can give you lists of existing reports that they use now and that they want in the new system. They may also think of some new reports that take advantage of the new system's features.

However, as development progresses, customers inevitably think of more reports as they learn more about the system. They'll probably even think of extra reports after you've completely finished development.

Adding dozens of new reports throughout the development cycle can be a burden to the developers. One way to reduce report proliferation is to forbid it. Just don't allow the customers to request new reports. Or you could allow new reports but require that they go through some sort of approval process to stem the flood.

Another approach is to allow the users to create their own reports. If the application uses a SQL database, it's not too hard to buy or build a reporting tool that lets users type in queries and see the results. I've worked on projects where the customers used this capability to design dozens of new reports without creating any extra work for the developers.

If you use this technique, however, you may need to restrict access to it so the users don't see confidential data. For example, a typical order entry clerk probably shouldn't be able to generate a list of employee salaries.

Some SQL statements can also damage the database. For example, the SQL `DROP TABLE` statement can permanently remove a table from the database, destroying all its data. Make sure the ad hoc reporting tool is only usable by trusted users or that it won't allow those kinds of dangerous commands.

As is the case with high-level user interface design, you don't need to specify every detail for every report here. Try to decide which reports you'll need and leave the details for low-level design and implementation.

Other Outputs

In addition to normal reports, you should consider other kinds of outputs that the application might create. The application could generate printouts (of reports and other things), web pages, data files, image files, audio (to speakers or to audio files), video (to the screen or to video files), output to special devices (such as electronic signs, thermostats, and other IoT devices), email, or text messages (which is as easy as sending an email to the right address). It could even send messages to pagers, if you can find any that aren't in museums.

> **TIP** *Text messages (or pager messages if you're old school) are a good way to tell operators that something is going wrong with the application. For example, if an order processing application is stuck and jobs are piling up in a queue, the application can send a message to a manager, who can then try to figure out what's wrong. I also knew a sys admin who had a program send her messages if her computer lab grew too hot.*

Database

Database design is an important part of most applications. The first part of database design is to decide what kind of database the program will need. You need to specify whether the application will store data in text files, XML files, a full-fledged relational database, something more exotic such as a temporal database or object store, or a combination of those. Even a program that doesn't use databases still needs to store data, perhaps inside the program within arrays, lists, or some other data structure.

If you decide to use an external database (in other words, more than data that's built into the code), you should specify the database product that you will use. Many applications store their data in relational databases such as Access, SQL Server, Oracle, or MySQL. (There are dozens if not hundreds of others.)

If you use a relational database, you can sketch out the tables it contains and their relationships during high-level design. Later you can provide more details such as the specific fields in each table and the fields that make up the keys linking the tables.

DEFINING CLASSES

Often the tables in the database correspond to classes that you need to build in the code. At this point, it makes sense to write down any important classes you define. Those might include fairly obvious classes such as `Employee`, `Customer`, `Order`, `WorkAssignment`, and `Report`.

You'll have a chance to refine those classes and add others during low-level design and implementation. For example, you might create subclasses that add refinement to the basic high-level classes. You could create subclasses of the `Customer` class such as `PreferredCustomer`, `CorporateCustomer`, and `ImpulseBuyer`.

Use good database design practices to ensure that the database is properly normalized. Database design and normalization is too big a topic to cover in this book. (For an introduction to database design, see my book *Beginning Database Design Solutions, Second Edition*, Wiley, 2023.) Although I don't have room to cover those topics in depth, I'll say more about normalization in the next chapter.

Meanwhile, there are three common database-specific issues that you should address during high-level design: audit trails, user access, and database maintenance.

Audit Trails

An *audit trail* keeps track of each user who modifies (and in some applications, views) a specific record. Later, management can use the audit trails to see which employee gave a customer a 120-percent discount. Auditing can be as simple as creating a history table that records a user's name, a link to the record that was modified, and the date when the change occurred. Some database products can even create audit trails for you.

A fancier version might store copies of the original data in each table when its data is modified. For example, suppose a user changes a customer's billing data to show the customer paid in full. Instead of updating the customer's record, the program would mark the existing (unpaid) record as outdated. It would then copy the old record, update it to show the customer's new balance, and add the date of the change and the user's name. Some applications also provide space for the users to add a note explaining why they gave the customer a $12,000 credit on the purchase of a box of cereal.

Later, you can compare the customer's records over time to build an audit trail that re-creates the exact sequence of changes made for that customer. (Of course, that means you need to add a way for the application to display the audit trail, and that means more work.)

> **NOTE** Some businesses have rules or government regulations that require them to delete old data, including audit trails.

Many applications don't need auditing. If you write an online multiplayer rock-paper-scissors game, you probably don't need an extensive record of who picked paper in a match two months ago. You also may not need to add auditing to programs written for internal company use and to other programs that don't involve money, confidential records, or other data that might be tempting to misuse. In cases like those, you can simplify the application by skipping audit trails.

User Access

Many applications also need to provide different levels of access to different kinds of data. For example, a fulfillment clerk (who throws porcelain dishes into a crate for shipping) probably doesn't need to see the customer's billing information, and only managers need to see the other employees' salary information.

One way to handle user access is to build a table listing the users and the privileges they should be given. The program can then disable or remove the buttons and menu items that a particular user shouldn't be allowed to use.

Many databases can also restrict access to tables, views, or even specific columns in tables. For example, you might be able to allow all users to view the Name, Office, and PhoneNumber fields in the Employees table without letting them see the Salary field.

Database Maintenance

A database is like a hall closet: Over time it gets disorganized and full of random junk like incorrect zip codes, out-of-service phone numbers, records of customers who moved out of state years ago, string, and unmatched socks. Every now and then, you need to reorganize so that you can find things efficiently.

If you use audit trails and the records require a lot of changes, the database will start to fill up with old versions of records that have been modified. Even if you don't use audit trails, over time the database can become cluttered with outdated records or records that are no longer important. You probably don't need to keep the records of a customer's gum purchase three years ago.

In that case, you may want to move some of the older data to long-term storage to keep the main database lean and responsive. You'll also need to design a way to retrieve the old data if you decide you want it back later.

You can move the older data into a *data warehouse*, a secondary database that holds older data for analysis. In some applications, you may want to analyze the data and store modified or aggregated forms in the warehouse instead of keeping every outdated record.

You may even want to discard the old data if you're sure you'll never need it again.

Removing old data from a database can help keep it responsive, but a lot of changes to the data can make the database's indexes inefficient and that can hurt performance. For that reason, you may need to periodically *re-index* key tables or run database-tuning software to restore peak performance. In large, high-reliability applications, you might need to perform these sorts of tasks during off-peak hours such as between midnight and 2 a.m.

Finally, you should design a database backup and recovery scheme (which you should also do for the cybersecurity reasons described in Chapter 8). In a low-priority application, that might involve copying a data file to a DVD or flash drive every now and then. More typically, it means copying the database every night and saving the copy for a few days or a week. For high-reliability systems, it may mean buying a special-purpose database that automatically shadows (on multiple computers) every change made to any database record in real time. (One telephone company project I worked on even required the computers to be in widely separated locations so that they wouldn't all fail if a computer room was flooded or wiped out by an earthquake.)

These kinds of database maintenance activities don't necessarily require programming, but they're all part of the price you pay for using big databases, so you need to plan for them.

NoSQL

Relational databases are the workhorses of many applications, but there are other kinds of databases available that may be useful under some circumstances. NoSQL databases have become increasingly popular as computing power and data storage speed have improved.

Some people assume that *NoSQL* means "no SQL" (in other words, not a relational database), but others take it to mean "not only SQL." Either way, the interesting pieces are the things that NoSQL databases can do that relational databases do not. Typically a NoSQL database is assumed to be one of four types: a document database, a key-value store, a column-oriented database, or a graph database.

A *document database* is designed to store documents such as data stored in XML or JSON files. The data is relatively nonstructured so queries may have to search through much or all of the available data (hence the need for fast computers and speedy storage access).

A *key-value store* holds some sort of data that is fetchable by a key. For example, you might use a customer's name or ID to retrieve all of the information you have for that customer.

A *column-oriented database* (or *wide-column database*) stores data in columns much as a relational database does. The big difference is that a column-oriented database stores the columns separately. That makes it easy to distribute the data across many locations in the cloud. It also means you don't need to pull in all of the information for every row of data if you only need to study a few columns.

A *graph database* stores objects that are related to each other in interesting ways. For example, a social network map might contain nodes representing people with edges connecting people who know each other. You can store this sort of data in a relational database, but it's awkward and won't give you the same graph-oriented tools that a graph database can provide.

In general, NoSQL databases are flexible, work well with semi- and unstructured data, and can handle changes to requirements without the major reengineering that might be required with a relational database.

Of course, that lack of rigid structure is both a blessing and a curse. A relational database may contain more reliable data because it won't allow you to enter data that violates its rules and constraints.

If you're interested, look online for more information about NoSQL databases.

Cloud Databases

Cloud databases give you a new option for your database needs. Different cloud providers offer varying levels of backups, reliability, and expandability on demand, which can make scaling much easier. Some even offer data warehousing, audit trails, user access control, and more.

If you don't want to manage your databases personally, consider cloud data services. Make a list of your database needs and then shop around to see which vendors can meet those needs.

Configuration Data

I mentioned earlier that you can save yourself a lot of time if you let users define their own ad hoc queries. Similarly, you can reduce your workload if you provide configuration screens so that users can fine-tune the application without making you write new code. Store parameters to algorithms, key amounts, and important durations in the database or in configuration files.

For example, suppose your application generates late payment notices if a customer has owed at least $50 for more than 30 days. If you make the values $50 and 30 days part of the configuration, then you won't need to change the code when the company decides to allow a 5-day grace period and start pestering customers only after 35 days.

Make sure that users can only modify the appropriate parameters. In many applications, only managers should change values such as the amounts and days that trigger late payment notices, but all users might be able to change their personal icon and font sizes or background colors.

Data Flows and States

Many applications use data that flows among different processes. For example, a customer order might start in an Order Creation process, move to Order Assembly (where items are gathered for shipping), and then go to Shipping (for actual shipment). Data may flow from Shipping to a final Billing process that sends an invoice to the customer via email. Figure 6.5 shows one way you might diagram this data flow.

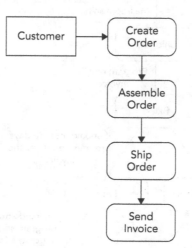

FIGURE 6.5: A data flow diagram shows how data such as a customer order flows through various processes.

You can also think of a piece of data such as a customer order as moving through a sequence of states. The states often correspond to the processes in the related data flow. For this example, a customer order might move through the states Created, Assembled, Shipped, and Billed.

Not all data flows and state transitions are as simple as this one. Sometimes events can make the data take different paths through the system. Figure 6.6 shows a state transition diagram for a customer order. The rounded rectangles represent states. Text next to the arrows indicates events that drive transitions. For example, if the customer hasn't paid an invoice 30 days after the order enters the Billed state, the system sends a second invoice to the customer and moves the order to the Late state.

These kinds of diagrams help describe the system and the way processes interact with the data.

Training

Although it may not be time to start writing training materials, it's never too early to think about them. The details of the system will probably change a lot between high-level design and final installation, but you can at least think about how you want training to work. You can decide whether you want users to attend courses taught by instructors, read printed manuals, watch instructional videos, or browse documentation online.

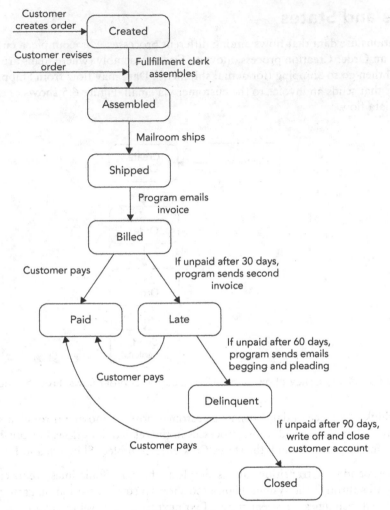

FIGURE 6.6: Complicated data flows may take different paths depending on circumstance.

Different people learn best in different ways, so you might want to provide several different kinds of training and either combine them or let the users pick those that are best for them. Supervised hands-on training is often effective because the users eventually need to use the application (that's why they're called users), and hands-on training is as close to actual use as possible.

During the high-level design, document the kinds of training that will be necessary. Trainers may be able to create content that discusses the application's high-level purpose now, but you'll have to fill in most of the details later as the project develops.

UML

As mentioned in Chapter 5, "Requirements Gathering," the *Unified Modeling Language (UML)* isn't actually a single unified language. Instead, it defines several kinds of diagrams that you can use to represent different pieces of the system.

The Object Management Group (OMG, yes, as in "OMG, how did they get such an awesome acronym before anyone else got it?") is an international not-for-profit organization that defines modeling standards, including UML. (You can learn more about OMG and UML at www.uml.org.)

UML 2.0 defines 14 diagram types divided into three categories as shown in the following list:

- ➤ Structure diagrams:
  - ➤ Class diagram
  - ➤ Component diagram
  - ➤ Composite structure diagram
  - ➤ Deployment diagram
  - ➤ Object diagram
  - ➤ Package diagram
  - ➤ Profile diagram
- ➤ Behavior diagrams:
  - ➤ Activity diagram
  - ➤ State machine diagram
  - ➤ Use case diagram
  - ➤ Interaction diagrams:
    - ➤ Communication diagram
    - ➤ Interaction overview diagram
    - ➤ Sequence diagram
    - ➤ Timing diagram

Many of these are rather complicated so I won't describe them all in excruciating detail here. Instead, the following sections give overviews of the types of diagrams in each category and provide a bit more detail about some of the most commonly used diagrams. Search online for "UML" to get more information.

Structure Diagrams

A *structure diagram* describes things that will be in the system you are designing. For example, a class diagram shows relationships among the classes that will represent objects in the system such as inventory items, vehicles, expense reports, and coffee requisition forms.

> **OBJECTS AND CLASSES**
>
> I'll say a bit more about classes and class diagrams shortly, but briefly a *class* defines a type (or class) of items, and an *object* is an instance of the class. Often classes and objects correspond closely to real-world objects.
>
> For example, a program might define a Student class to represent students. The class would define properties that all students share such as Name, Grade, and HomeRoom.
>
> A specific instance of the Student class would be an object that represents a particular student, such as Rufus T. Firefly. For that object, the Name property would be set to "Rufus T. Firefly," Grade might be 12, and HomeRoom might be "11-B."

The following list summarizes UML's structure diagrams:

- ➤ Class diagram—Describes the classes that make up the system, their properties and methods, and their relationships.

- ➤ Component diagram—Shows how components are combined to form larger parts of the system.

- ➤ Composite structure diagram—Shows a class's internal structure and the collaborations that the class allows.

- ➤ Deployment diagram—Describes the deployment of *artifacts* (files, scripts, executables, and the like) on *nodes* (hardware devices or execution environments that can execute artifacts).

- ➤ Object diagram—Focuses on a particular set of objects and their relationships at a specific time.

- ➤ Package diagram—Describes relationships among the packages that make up a system. For example, if one package in the system uses features provided by another package, then the diagram would show the first "importing" the second.

- ➤ Profile diagram—Allows you to extend the UML syntax.

The most basic of the structure diagrams is the class diagram. In a class diagram, a class is represented by a rectangle. The class's name goes at the top, is centered, and is in bold. Two sections below the name give the class's properties and methods. (A *method* is a routine that makes an object do something. For example, the Student class might have a DoAssignment method that makes the Student object work through a specific class assignment.) Figure 6.7 shows a simple diagram for the Student class.

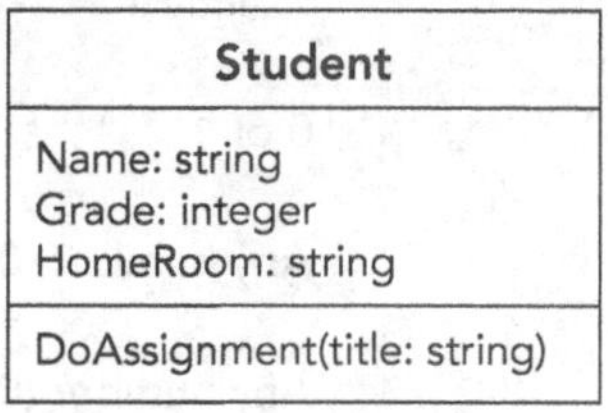

Student
Name: string Grade: integer HomeRoom: string
DoAssignment(title: string)

FIGURE 6.7: A class diagram describes the properties and methods of classes.

Some developers add annotations to class representations to give you more detail. Most class diagrams include the data types of properties and parameters passed into methods, as shown in Figure 6.7. You can also add the symbols shown in Table 6.2 to the left of a class member to show its visibility within the project.

TABLE 6.2: Class diagram visibility symbols

SYMBOL	MEANING	EXPLANATION
+	Public	The member is visible to all code in the application.
−	Private	The member is visible only to code inside the class.
#	Protected	The member is visible only to code inside the class and any derived classes.
~	Package	The member is visible only to code inside the same package.

Class diagrams also often show relationships among classes with lines connecting related classes. A variety of line styles, symbols, arrowheads, and annotations gives more information about the kinds of relationships.

The simplest way to use relationships is to draw an arrow indicating the direction of the relationship and label the arrow with the relationship's name. For example, in a school registration application, you might draw an arrow from the Student class to the Course class to indicate that a Student is associated with the Courses that student is taking. You could label that arrow "is taking."

At the line's endpoints, you can add symbols to indicate how many objects are involved in the relationship. Table 6.3 shows symbols you can add to the ends of a relationship.

TABLE 6.3: Class diagram multiplicity indicators

SYMBOLS	MEANING
1	Exactly 1
0..1	0 or 1
0..*	Any number (0 or more)
*	Any number (0 or more)
1..*	1 or more

The class diagram in Figure 6.8 shows the "is taking" relationship between the Student and Course classes. In that relationship, 1 Student object corresponds to 1 or more Course objects.

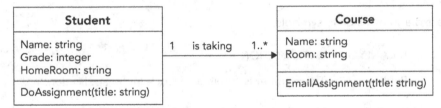

FIGURE 6.8: The relationship in this class diagram indicates that 1 student takes 1 or more courses.

Another important type of class diagram relationship is inheritance. In object-oriented programming, one class can inherit the properties and methods of another. For example, an honors student is a type of student. To model that in an object-oriented program, you could define an HonorsStudent class that inherits from the Student class. The HonorsStudent class automatically gets any properties and methods defined by the Student class (Name, Grade, HomeRoom, and DoAssignment). You can also add new properties and methods if you like. Perhaps you want to add a GPA property to the HonorsStudent class.

In a class diagram, you indicate inheritance by using a hollow arrowhead pointing from the child class to the parent class. Figure 6.9 shows that the HonorsStudent class inherits from the Student class.

Class diagrams for complicated applications can become cluttered and hard to read if you put everything in a single huge diagram. To reduce clutter, developers often draw multiple class diagrams showing parts of the system. In particular, they often make one set of diagrams to show inheritance and another set of diagrams to show relationships.

For information about more elaborate types of class diagrams, search the Internet in general or the OMG website, www.omg.org, in particular.

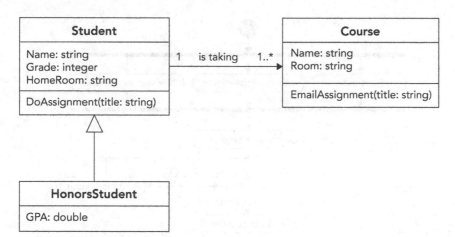

FIGURE 6.9: A class diagram indicates inheritance with a hollow arrowhead.

Behavior Diagrams

UML defines three kinds of basic *behavior diagrams*: activity diagrams, use case diagrams, and state machine diagrams. The following sections provide brief descriptions of these kinds of diagrams and give a few simple examples.

Activity Diagrams

An *activity diagram* represents workflows for activities. They include several kinds of symbols connected with arrows to show the direction of the workflow. Table 6.4 summarizes the symbols.

TABLE 6.4: Activity diagram symbols

SYMBOL	REPRESENTS
Rounded rectangle	An action or task
Diamond	A decision
Thick bar	The start or end of concurrent activities
Black circle	The start
Circled black circle	The end

Figure 6.10 shows a simple activity diagram for baking cookies.

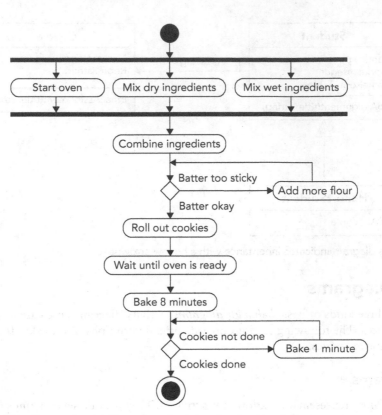

FIGURE 6.10: An activity diagram is a bit like a flowchart showing how work flows.

The first thick bar starts three parallel activities: Start oven, mix dry ingredients, and mix wet ingredients. If you have assistant cookie chefs (perhaps your children, if you have any), those steps can all proceed at the same time in parallel.

When the three parallel activities all are done, the workflow resumes after the second thick bar. The next step is to combine all the ingredients.

A test then checks the batter's consistency. If the batter is too sticky, you add more flour and recheck the consistency. You repeat that loop until the batter has the right consistency.

When the batter is just right, you roll out the cookies, wait until the oven is ready (if it isn't already), and bake the cookies for eight minutes.

After eight minutes, you check the cookies. If the cookies aren't done, you bake them for one more minute. You continue checking and baking for one more minute as long as the cookies are not done.

When the cookies are done, you enter the stopping state indicated by the circled black circle.

Use Case Diagram

A *use case diagram* represents a user's interaction with the system. Use case diagrams show stick figures representing actors (someone or something that performs a task) connected to tasks represented by ellipses.

To provide more detail, you can use arrows to join subtasks to tasks. Use the annotation <<include>> to mean the task includes the subtask. (It can't take place without the subtask.)

If a subtask might occur only under some circumstances, connect it to the main task and add the annotation <<extend>>. If you like, you can add a note indicating when the extension occurs. (Usually both <<include>> and <<extend>> arrows are dashed.)

Figure 6.11 shows a simple online shopping use case diagram. The Customer actor performs the "Search site for products" activity. If he finds something he likes, he also performs the "Buy products" extension. To buy products, the customer must log in to the site, so the "Buy products" activity includes the "Log on to site" activity.

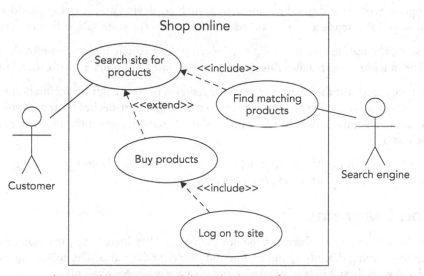

FIGURE 6.11: A use case diagram shows actors and the tasks they perform (possibly with subtasks and extensions).

The website's search engine also participates in the "Search site for products" activity. When the customer starts a search, the engine performs the "Find matching products" activity. The "Search" activity cannot work without the "Find" activity, so the "Find" activity is included in the "Search" activity.

State Machine Diagram

A *state machine diagram* shows the states through which an object passes in response to various events. States are represented by rounded rectangles. Arrows indicate transitions from one state to another. Sometimes annotations on the arrows indicate what causes a transition.

As in an activity diagram, a black circle represents the starting state and a circled black circle indicates the stopping state.

Figure 6.12 shows a simple state machine diagram for a program that reads a floating-point number (as in –17.32) followed by the Enter key.

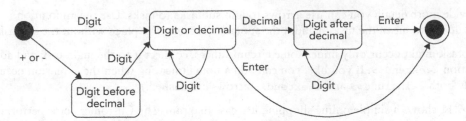

FIGURE 6.12: This state machine diagram represents reading a floating-point number.

When the program starts, it can read a digit, +, or –. (If it reads any other character, the machine fails and the program would need to take some action, such as playing an annoying sound and displaying an error message.) If it reads a + or –, the machine moves to the state "Digit before decimal."

From that state, the user must enter a digit, at which point the machine moves into the state "Digit or decimal." The machine also reaches this state if the user initially enters a digit instead of a + or –.

Now if the user enters another digit, the machine remains in the "Digit or decimal" state. When the user enters a decimal point, the machine moves to the "Digit after decimal" state. If the user presses the Enter key, the machine moves to its stopping state. (That happens if the user enters a whole number such as 37.)

The machine remains in the "Digit after decimal" state as long as the user types a digit. When the user presses the Enter key, the machine moves to its stopping state.

Interaction Diagrams

Interaction diagrams form a subset of behavior diagrams. They include sequence diagrams, communication diagrams, timing diagrams, and interaction overview diagrams. The following sections provide brief descriptions of these kinds of diagrams and give a few simple examples.

Sequence Diagram

A *sequence diagram* shows how objects collaborate in a particular scenario. It represents the collaboration as a sequence of messages.

Objects participating in the collaboration are represented as rectangles or sometimes as stick figures for actors. They are labeled with a name or class. If the label includes both a name and class, they are separated by a colon.

Below each of the participants is a vertical dashed line called a *lifeline*. The lifeline basically represents the participant sitting there waiting for something to happen.

An *execution specification* (called an *execution* or informally an *activation*) represents a participant doing something. In the diagram, these are represented as gray or white rectangles drawn on top of the lifeline. You can draw overlapping rectangles to represent overlapping executions.

Labeled arrows with solid arrowheads represent synchronous messages. Arrows with open arrowheads represent asynchronous messages. Finally, dashed arrows with open arrowheads represent return messages sent in reply to a calling message.

Figure 6.13 shows a customer, a clerk, and the `Movie` class interacting to print a ticket for a movie. The customer walks up to the ticket window and requests the movie from the clerk. The clerk uses a computer to ask the `Movie` class whether tickets are available for the desired show. The `Movie` class responds.

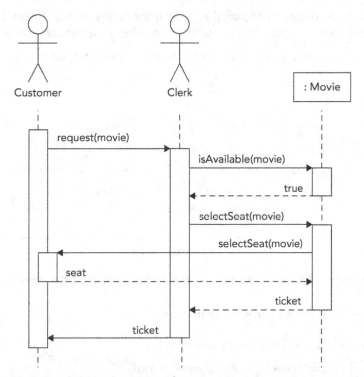

FIGURE 6.13: A sequence diagram shows the timing of messages between collaborating objects.

Notice that the `Movie` class's response is asynchronous. The class fires off a response and doesn't wait for any kind of reply. Instead it goes back to twiddling its electronic thumbs, waiting for some other request.

If the class's response is `false`, the interaction ends. (This scenario covers only the customer successfully buying a ticket.) If the response is `true`, control returns to the clerk, who uses the computer to ask the `Movie` class to select a seat. This causes another execution to run on the `Movie` class's lifeline.

The `Movie` class in turn asks the customer to pick a seat from those that are available. The customer is still waiting for the initial request to finish, so this is an overlapping execution for the customer.

After the customer picks a seat, the `Movie` class issues a ticket to the clerk. The clerk then prints the ticket and hands it to the customer.

The point of this diagram is to show the interactions that occur between the participants and the order in which they occur. If you think the diagram is confusing, feel free to add some text describing the process.

Communication Diagram

Like a sequence diagram, a *communication diagram* shows communication among objects during some sort of collaboration. The difference is the sequence diagram focuses on the sequence of messages, but the communication diagram focuses more on the objects involved in the collaboration.

The diagram uses lines to connect objects that collaborate during an interaction. Labeled arrows indicate messages between objects. The messages are numbered so you can follow the sequence.

Figure 6.14 shows a communication diagram for the movie ticket buying scenario that was shown in Figure 6.13.

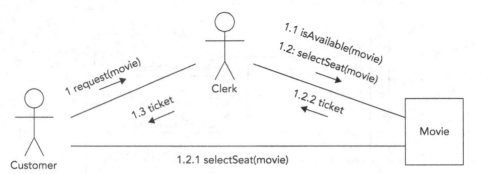

FIGURE 6.14: A communication diagram emphasizes the objects participating in a collaboration.

Following is the sequence of messages in Figure 6.14:

> 1: The customer asks the clerk for a movie ticket.
>> 1.1: The clerk asks the Movie class if a seat is available.
>> 1.2: The clerk asks the Movie class to select a seat.
>>> 1.2.1: The Movie class asks the user to pick a seat.
>>> 1.2.2: The Movie class sends the clerk a ticket for the selected seat.
>> 1.3: The clerk prints the ticket and hands it to the customer.

The exact timing of the messages and some of the details (such as return messages) are not represented well in the communication diagram. Those details are better represented by a sequence diagram.

Timing Diagram

A *timing diagram* shows the way one or more objects change state over time. A timing diagram looks a lot like a sequence diagram turned sideways, so time increases from left to right. These diagrams can be useful for giving a sense of how long different parts of a scenario will take.

More elaborate versions of the timing diagram show multiple participants stacked above each other with arrows showing how messages pass between the participants.

Interaction Overview Diagram

An *interaction overview diagram* is basically an activity diagram where the nodes can be frames that contain other kinds of diagrams. Those nodes can contain sequence, communication, timing, and other interaction overview diagrams. This lets you show more detail for nodes that represent complicated tasks.

UML Summary

You may not need to use all of the UML diagrams for a particular application. For simple applications, you might not need any. Often well-written user stories, scripts, and use cases can better explain interactions to users who don't know UML.

Use whichever UML diagrams you find useful and describe other parts of the system in good old prose.

SUMMARY

High-level design sets the stage for later software development. It deals with the grand decisions such as these:

- ➤ What hardware platform will you use?
- ➤ What type of database will you use?
- ➤ What other systems will interact with this one?
- ➤ What reports can you make the users define so you don't have to do all the work?

After you settle these and other high-level questions, the stage is set for development. However, you're still not quite ready to start slapping together code to implement the features described in the requirements. Before you start churning out code, you need to create low-level designs to flesh out the classes, modules, interfaces, and other pieces of the application that you identified during high-level design. The low-level design will give you a detailed picture of exactly what code you need to write so you can begin programming.

The next chapter covers low-level design. It explains how you can refine the database design to ensure the database is robust and flexible. It also describes the kinds of information you need to add to the high-level design before you can start putting 0s and 1s together to make the final program.

EXERCISES

1. What's the difference between a component-based architecture and a service-oriented architecture?

2. Suppose you're building a phone application that lets you play tic-tac-toe (noughts and crosses) against a simple computer opponent. It will display the user's high scores stored on the phone, not in an external database. Which architectures would be most appropriate and why?

3. Repeat Exercise 2 for a chess program running on a desktop, laptop, or tablet computer.

4. Repeat Exercise 3 assuming the chess program lets two users play against each other over an Internet connection.

5. What kinds of reports would the game programs described in Exercises 2, 3, and 4 require?

6. What kind of database structure and maintenance should the ClassyDraw application use?

7. What kind of configuration information should the ClassyDraw application use?

8. Which of the following inputs would be accepted by the state machine diagram shown in Figure 6.12?

    ➤ 1.23.45
    ➤ 8
    ➤ ++45
    ➤ 1337
    ➤ −1337
    ➤ 1.2e34
    ➤ (A blank string)
    ➤ 67. (Ends in a decimal point)

9. Draw a state machine diagram to let a program read floating-point numbers in scientific notation as in +37 or −12.3e + 17 (which means -12.3×10^{17}). Allow either E or e for the exponent symbol.

WHAT YOU LEARNED IN THIS CHAPTER

➤ High-level design is the first step in breaking an application into pieces that are small enough to implement.

➤ Decoupling tasks allows different teams to work on them simultaneously.

➤ These are some of the things you should specify in a high-level design:

  ➤ Important data that requires security

  ➤ General security needs

  ➤ Operating system (Windows, iOS, or Linux)

  ➤ Hardware platform (desktop, laptop, tablet, phone, mainframe)

  ➤ Other hardware (networks, printers, programmable signs, pagers, audio, video, IoT devices)

  ➤ User interface style (navigational techniques, menus, screens versus forms)

➤ Internal interfaces

➤ External interfaces

➤ Architecture (monolithic, client-server, multitier, component-based, service-oriented, data-centric, event driven, rule-based, distributed)

➤ Reports (application usage, customer purchases, inventory, work schedules, productivity, ad hoc)

➤ Other outputs (printouts, web pages, data files, images, audio, video, email, text messages)

➤ Database (database platform, major tables and their relationships, auditing, user access, maintenance, backup, data warehousing)

➤ Top-level classes (`Customer`, `Employee`, and `Order`)

➤ Configuration data (algorithm parameters, due dates, expiration dates, durations, cutoff values)

➤ Data flows

➤ Training

➤ UML diagrams let you specify the objects in the system (including external agents such as users and external systems) and how they interact.

➤ The main categories of UML diagrams are structure diagrams and behavior diagrams.

7

Low-Level Design

> We try to solve the problem by rushing through the design process so that enough time is left at the end of the project to uncover the errors that were made because we rushed through the design process.
>
> —*Glenford Myers*

> Premature optimization is the root of all evil in programming.
>
> —*Sir Tony Hoare*

What You Will Learn in This Chapter:

➤ Design approaches

➤ OO design

➤ Database design

➤ When to optimize

High-level design paints an application's structure in broad strokes. It identifies the system's general environment (hardware, operating system, network, and so on) and architecture (such as monolithic, client/server, and service-oriented). It identifies the system's major components such as reporting modules, databases, and top-level classes. It should also sketch out how the pieces of the system will interact.

Low-level design fills in some of the gaps to provide extra detail that's necessary before developers can start writing code. It gives more specific guidance for how the parts of the system will work and how they will work together. It refines the definitions of the database, the major classes, and the internal and external interfaces.

High-level design focuses on *what*. Low-level design begins to focus on *how*.

As an analogy, if you were building a highway system, high-level design would determine what cities (and perhaps what parts of those cities) would be connected by highways. The low-level design would indicate exactly where the highways would be placed, where the ramps would be, and what elementary schools would be surrounded by four-lane traffic circles.

The border between high-level and low-level design is often rather fuzzy. Typically, after a piece of the system is added to the high-level design, team members continue working on that piece to develop its low-level design. Particularly on a large project, some people will be working on high-level designs while others work on low-level designs. Developers may even start prototyping or implementing parts of the system that have been adequately defined.

In a way, you can describe low-level design as high-level design for micromanagers. You extend the high-level design by providing more and more detail until everything is specified precisely enough to start implementation.

However, refining a high-level design isn't necessarily easy. You may know generally what you need in the database (customer data and stuff), but unless you refine that knowledge into a good detailed database design, you may run into all sorts of problems later. The data may become inconsistent, the program might lose critical information, and finding data may be slow. Different database designs can make the difference between finding the data you need in seconds, hours, or not at all.

The following sections describe some of the most important concepts you should keep in mind during low-level design. They explain how to refine an object model to identify the application's classes, how to use stepwise refinement to provide additional detail for a task, and how to design a database that is flexible and robust.

DESIGN APPROACHES

Today two of the most important pieces of low-level design are object-oriented design and database design. Before we get to those, the following sections summarize a few overall design approaches that you can apply to just about any kind of design.

PLENTIFUL PARADIGMS

Currently object-oriented and procedural programming rule the programming paradigm roost, but there are many other paradigms out there vying for your attention. Different approaches focus on such things as style, code packaging (for example, object-oriented models package functional code with state information), and whether to allow side effects (when a method changes the program's state outside of its own local variables).

Two approaches that have become more popular lately are declarative programming in general and functional programming in particular.

In *declarative programming*, you do not specify the exact order in which operations are performed. Instead you describe *what* the program should accomplish and then the program uses rules about the situation to figure out *how* to achieve that result. A common example of a declarative language is SQL. It lets you write a database query such as the following:

```
SELECT * FROM Customers WHERE Status = 'Premier'
```

The database engine then figures out how to find that data.

In *functional programming*, which is a subcategory of declarative programming, you build a program by writing, calling, and composing functions. (I'm glossing over a lot of details with both of these definitions.)

These approaches are nothing new. The first functional programming language, Lisp, was invented in the late 1950s and has roots based in lambda calculus, which was invented in the 1930s.

Lately they have become more popular because they fit certain artificial intelligence and machine learning approaches nicely. They tend to be hard to learn, however, so they are mostly used by more experienced programmers.

I'll say a little bit more about declarative and functional programming in Chapter 12, "Programming Languages." Meanwhile you can learn more by searching online for "programming paradigms" or you can use https://en.wikipedia.org/wiki/Programming_paradigm as a starting point.

There are always multiple ways to solve any programming problem, and different methods come with trade-offs. Some are easy but produce a slower program. Others may be more efficient but harder to implement and debug. Still others may be easy to implement but provide only 80 percent of the features that you need.

The following sections describe ways you can view the project to gain perspective that will help you decide which direction your design should take.

Design-to-Schedule

In a *design-to-schedule* approach, you decide how to implement features based on your schedule and other resources. If your time and resources are limited, you should select simpler solutions even if it means giving up some performance or functionality.

If you have plenty of time, you might use a more sophisticated design that will take longer but produce a faster, more accurate, or generally shinier result. For example, you might spend extra time optimizing your vehicle routing or you might devise a robust incremental backup and restoration plan.

If you have early deadlines, then you might try to find an off-the-shelf tool to handle some of the less domain-specific parts of the system. You might use Microsoft Excel to solve dynamic programming problems instead of writing your own algorithms. Or you might back up the entire database every night instead of just the parts that have been modified, even though that will take six or seven hours rather than one or two.

Then you can improve the parts of the system that are most troublesome in the next release. (Or not, if the simpler solutions prove adequate.)

It's always a good idea to prioritize the parts of the system so you know which pieces should move to simpler, less perfect approaches.

In fact, it's useful to prioritize the parts of the system in any case and with any design approach in case you start to run out of time. If your Gantt chart shows slippage on critical paths, priorities will help you decide which tasks need rethinking.

Design-to-Tools

In a *design-to-tools* approach, you provide only those features that are supported by the tools that you have or can easily acquire. You don't write custom sorting routines; you use those that are available in your programming language or a library. You don't build a three-dimensional graphing system; you find a graphing package. Or perhaps you extract the 3D graphing feature from the project and do it in MATLAB.

The design-to-tools approach doesn't necessarily guarantee that the result will be simple. Some tools (such as MATLAB) can be quite complicated. However, you can generally find out the capabilities of an existing tool so you will know if it will do what you need. If you want to draw 3D surface plots, MATLAB can do that. If you try to use your own code to build 3D surface plots, you may or may not succeed, depending on your skill level and time constraints. (Three-dimensional graphics is actually really fun and interesting, so I encourage you to give it a try in your spare time. See my book *WPF 3d: Three-Dimensional Graphics with WPF and C#*, Stephens, 2018.)

In addition to having confidence that a tool will work, you may be able to find examples, user groups, and forums online. If it's a commercial product, you may also be able to access technical support.

Once in a while, you'll find a tool that does more than you need. In that case, you may be able to bring in some new features that you didn't originally plan with only a little extra effort.

Unfortunately, this approach may sometimes force you to compromise. A particular tool may not give you *exactly* the result you want, but it may be worth some concessions to make implementation and debugging easier.

Process-Oriented Design

A *process-oriented design* focuses on the processes that the system will perform. Some of those will be the processes that the users follow to do their jobs. Other processes, such as generating reports or analyzing historical sales data, will be more abstract.

To use this approach, focus on the processes and then figure out what data you need to support them. When you've figured that out, look at the data that you have available and see how it is used, what data is missing, and what data is present but unused.

If you can keep the processes separate from each other and from the data, then you may be able to run the processes in parallel, possibly on multiple computers. You'll still need to do some work to prevent problems that arise in distributed systems, such as race conditions and deadlocks, but the result may give you greatly increased scalability and performance.

Data-Oriented Design

A *data-oriented design* focuses on the data that you need to get the job done. (In a sense this is the flip side of the process-oriented design.) Instead of focusing on how a user creates a new customer order, you focus on the data needed to create the order.

As you consider the project's data needs, you think about what pieces of data will be used together so you can keep them together in the database. For high-performance applications, you may need to think about caching, preloading some values when others are loaded, and lazy initialization to load data only when it is necessary.

Object-Oriented Design

In *object-oriented design*, you concentrate on the object classes that the application needs to work properly. Often the system's key objects will represent actors (such as users, external system, and internal systems) and data entities (such as customers, employees, orders, and inventory items).

Database entities often map so naturally to classes that some programming environments can automatically build classes to represent database tables. Those classes may even be able to load data from the database and save changes back into the database.

The section "OO Design" a little later in this chapter says more about object-oriented design.

Hybrid Approaches

Each of these design approaches (and there are probably others) focuses on a particular aspect of the design, but that doesn't mean you need to use one approach to the exclusion of the others. It's often useful to use a data-oriented approach to understanding the data that you have and need, a process-oriented approach to understand how the users will do their jobs, and an object-oriented design to map the data and processes to classes and methods within the classes.

Each of the approaches can help refine the others and nudge you toward a better design. For example, while studying a user process, you may discover that you're missing some data from the database design.

There may be some software engineering paradise where you're given all of the time and resources you need to build the best possible solution, but it's far more common to have real deadlines and a limited budget. In that case, the design-to-schedule and design-to-tools approaches can help you control your schedule. Start with the easiest and fastest approaches. Then, after the application is working properly, you can consider replacing some pre-built packages with more customized code of your own.

Instead of thinking of these approaches as distinct choices, you can think of them as each shining light on the project from a different angle. By using them all, you can get the best understanding of the project's needs.

High, Low, and Iterative Design

I've presented these approaches as low-level design techniques for deciding how to implement parts of the system, but they also work well for deciding what to include in the requirements and high-level design. (Those chapters were getting pretty long, however, so I put that material here.)

Design-to-schedule and design-to-tools can definitely help you decide what features to include. Process-oriented, data-oriented, and object-oriented design have a low-level flavor, but they can still be useful during high-level design to sketch out the main pieces for at least some parts of the system. For example, after you've built a few invoice systems, you'll know from day one (or perhaps day two) many of the kinds of processes, data, and classes you'll need.

When you look at the agile programming methodologies described later in the book, some of these techniques will become even more useful. For example, if you work in one-week cycles, you need to keep design-to-schedule and design-to-tools in mind to decide what to include in each build. Otherwise, you may spend the whole week building something that you could have downloaded in a few hours, or you might rule out features that are easy to build with the right tool.

OO DESIGN

Somewhere between high-level design, low-level design, and various design approaches, you should have identified the major types of classes that the application will use. Now it's time to refine that design to identify the specific classes the program will need. The new classes should include definitions of the properties, methods, and events they will provide for the application to use.

A QUICK OO PRIMER

In object-oriented (OO) development, classes define the general properties and behaviors for a set of objects. An *instance* of a class is an object with the class's type.

For example, you could define an `Author` class to represent authors. An instance of the class might represent the specific author William Shakespeare. After you define the `Author` class, you could create any number of instances of that class to represent different authors such as Stephen King, J. K. Rowling, and John Lithgow.

Classes define three main items: properties, methods, and events.

➤ A *property* is something that helps define an object. For example, the `Author` class might have `FirstName` and `LastName` properties to identify the specific author that an instance represents. It might have other properties such as `DateOfBirth`, `DateOfDeath`, and `WrittenWorks`.

➤ A *method* is a piece of code that makes an object do something. The `Author` class might have a `Search` method that searches an object's `WrittenWorks` values for a work that contains a certain word or phrase. It might also have methods to print a formatted list of the author's works or to search online for places to buy one of the author's works.

> ➤ An *event* is something that occurs to tell the program that something interesting has happened. An object *raises* an event when appropriate to let the program take some action. For example, an `Author` object might raise a `BirthdayOccurred` event to tell the program when the author's birthday occurred. (That would be hard for Shakespeare because no one knows exactly when he was born.) The program could then respond by taking some action such as posting a message on social media or sending the author a "Happy Birthday" email.

Together, properties, methods, and events are called *members* of the class.

After you design a class, you can use it like a cookie cutter to make as many instances of the class as you like. Each instance has the same properties, methods, and events, although the properties can have different values in different instances. For example, different `Author` objects would have different `FirstName` and `LastName` properties.

Object-oriented development involves lots of other details, but this should be enough to get you through the following discussion. If you want more information about object-oriented programming, look for a book on the subject, either in general or for your favorite programming language.

Also look for books on design patterns. An object-oriented *design pattern* is an arrangement of classes that performs some common and useful task. For example, the model-view-controller (MVC) pattern breaks a user interface interaction into three pieces: a model object that represents some data, view objects that display a view of the data to the user, and controller objects that control the model, possibly allowing the user to manipulate the data. I'll say a bit more about design patterns in Chapter 11, "Algorithms" which talks about algorithms.

The following sections explain how you can define the classes that an application will use.

Identifying Classes

The previous chapter tells you that you should identify the main classes that the application will use, but it doesn't tell you how to do that. One way to pick classes is to look for nouns in a description of the application's features.

For example, suppose you're writing an application called FreeWheeler Automatic Driver (FAD) that automatically drives cars. Now consider the sentence "The program drives the car to the selected destination." That sentence contains three nouns: program, car, and destination.

The program probably doesn't need to directly manipulate itself, so it's unlikely that you'll need a `Program` class. (Although some languages automatically create such as class.) It will almost certainly need to work with cars and destinations, so you probably do need `Car` and `Destination` classes.

When you're studying possible classes, think about what sorts of information the class needs (properties), what sorts of things it needs to do (methods), and whether it needs to notify the program of changing circumstances (events). For this example, the `Car` class is going to be fully loaded, providing all sorts of properties (such as CurrentSpeed, CurrentDirection, and FuelLevel), methods (such as Accelerate, Decelerate, ActivateTurnSignal, and HonkHorn), and events (such as DriverPressedStart, FuelLevelLow, CollisionImminent, and EjectorSeatFired).

The Destination class is probably a lot simpler because it basically just represents a specific location. In fact, it may be that the application needs only a single instance of this class to record the current destination.

Making only a single instance of a class is a warning sign that perhaps the class isn't necessary. The fact that the Destination class doesn't do anything or change on its own (so it doesn't provide methods or events) is another indication that you might not need that class. In this example, you could store the destination information in a couple of variables holding latitude and longitude.

Note that the class definitions depend heavily on how you will use the objects. For example, you could define a Passenger class to represent people riding in the car. A passenger has all sorts of interesting information such as Name, Address, Age, HairStyle, and CreditScore. However, the FreeWheeler program doesn't need to know any of that information. It might not even need to know if the car contains any passengers. (Although it probably needs to have a driver, at least until self-driving cars become so good that they can travel on their own.)

Building Inheritance Hierarchies

After you define the application's main classes, you need to add more detail to represent variations on those classes. For example, FreeWheeler is going to need a Car class to represent the vehicle it's driving, but different vehicles have different characteristics. A 106-horsepower Toyota Yaris handles differently than a 460-horsepower Chevrolet Corvette. It would be bad if the program told the Yaris to pull out in front of a speeding tractor trailer, assuming it could go from 0 to 60 miles per hour in 3.7 seconds.

You can capture the differences between related classes by *deriving* a *child class* from a *parent class*. In this example, you might derive the Yaris and Corvette child classes from the Car parent class.

Child classes automatically inherit the properties, methods, and events defined by the parent class. For example, the Car class might define methods such as SetParkingBrake, TurnLeft, and DeployDragChute. Because Corvette inherits from the Car class, a Corvette object automatically knows how to perform those methods.

This is one important way object-oriented programming languages achieve code reuse. You write code once in the parent class and any child classes use that same code without you rewriting it.

The fact that Corvette inherits from Car also means that a Corvette *is a kind of* Car. Intuitively, that makes sense. In real life, a Corvette is a car, so it should be able to do anything that any other car can do. In a very real sense, a Corvette is a Car. (If this seems blindingly obvious, then you're getting it.)

Because an instance of a child class also belongs to the parent class, the program should be able to treat the object as if it were of the parent class if that would be helpful. In this example, that means a program should be able to treat a Corvette object as either a Corvette or as a more generic Car.

For instance, the program could create an array of Car objects and fill it with instances of the Corvette, Yaris, VolkswagenBeatle, or DeLorean classes. The program should be able to treat all of those objects as if they were Cars without knowing their true classes. The capability to treat objects as if they were actually from a different class is called *polymorphism*.

You can derive multiple classes from a single parent class. For example, you could derive Corvette, Edsel, and Pinto all from the Car class.

Conversely, most object-oriented programming languages do *not* allow *multiple inheritance*, so a class can have at most a single parent class. Because classes can have at most one parent but any number of children, the relationships among classes form a treelike *inheritance hierarchy*.

There are many ways you can modify basic inheritance relationships. For example, a child class can add properties, methods, and events that are not available in the parent class. A child class can also replace a parent class member with a new version.

In some languages, the child class can even define a new version of a member that applies when the program refers to an object by using the child class but not when it refers to it with a variable that has the parent class's type. For example, you might give the Car class a ParallelPark method that carefully backs the car into a parking space. The Corvette class might define a new version that locks up the brakes and slides the car into the space sideways as if James Bond were driving. Now if the program defines a variable of type Car that refers to a Corvette object and invokes its ParallelPark method, you get the first version. If the program defines a second variable of type Corvette that refers to the same object and invokes its ParallelPark method, you get the second version.

The details of how you define classes, build inheritance hierarchies, and add or modify their members depend on the language you use, so those things aren't covered in this book. Before moving on to other topics, however, you should know about the two main ways for building inheritance hierarchies: refinement and generalization.

Refinement

Refinement is the process of breaking a parent class into multiple subclasses to capture differences between objects in the class. When I derived the Corvette, Edsel, and Pinto classes from the Car class, that was refinement.

One danger to refinement is *overrefinement*, which happens when you refine a class hierarchy unnecessarily, making so many classes that programming becomes more complicated and confusing. People are naturally good at categorizing objects. It takes only a few seconds of thought to break cars into the classes shown in Figure 7.1. The open (unfilled) arrowheads point from child classes to their parent classes.

With a bit more work, you can grow this hierarchy until it is truly enormous. There are a couple hundred models of car on the roads in the United States alone. You could refine most of those models with different options such as different engine sizes, radios, speakers, cup holders, spoilers, wheel spinners, underglow, and seat warmers. You could add still more subclasses to represent different colors.

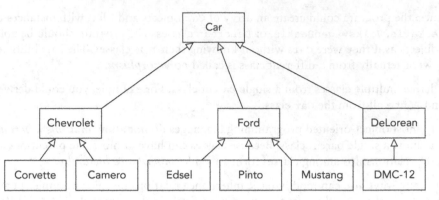

FIGURE 7.1: People are naturally good at building inheritance hierarchies.

The resulting hierarchy would contain many thousands (possibly millions) of classes. Obviously, a hierarchy that large wouldn't be useful. There's no way you could write enough code to actually use each of the classes, and if you're not going to use a class, why build it?

There are two main problems here. First, the classes are capturing data that isn't relevant to the application. The FreeWheeler application doesn't care what color a car is or whether it has a CD changer. It only cares about the car's driving characteristics: mileage, maximum acceleration, turn radius, and so forth. The hierarchy in Figure 7.1 doesn't capture any of that information.

RISKY REFINEMENT

Even if the program cares about certain differences between objects, that doesn't mean those differences would make a good inheritance hierarchy. For example, suppose you're writing a car sales application. Customers often want to shop for cars first by make, then by model, and then by option packages and other features. In that case, the customer's search strategy looks a lot like Figure 7.1.

Unfortunately, if you use those values to build the inheritance hierarchy, you get a monstrously huge hierarchy. Even though the program cares a lot about those differences, they're better handled as properties rather than subclassing. It's easy enough for a program to search a database for specific property values such as make or model without storing the data in a hierarchical format.

The second problem with this hierarchy is that the differences between cars could easily be represented by properties instead of by different classes. The differences identified so far are actually just different values for the same properties. For example, Chevrolet, Ford, and DeLorean are all just different values for a Make property. You could eliminate that whole level of the hierarchy by simply adding a Make property to the Car class.

Similarly, a car's model (Corvette, Edsel, and Mustang) is just a name for a specific type of car. You may have some expectations based on the name (you probably think a Corvette is faster than a Pinto), but to the FreeWheeler program, those are just labels.

You can avoid these kinds of hierarchy problems if you focus on behavioral differences between the different kinds of objects instead of looking at differences in properties.

For example, what are the behavioral differences between a Corvette and a Pinto? The Corvette accelerates quicker, but both cars *can* accelerate, just at different rates. They still have the same acceleration behavior, so you can represent that difference as an Acceleration property in the Car class.

For an example, where there is a behavioral difference, consider transmission type. To accelerate a car with automatic transmission to freeway speeds, you simply stomp on the gas pedal until the car is going fast enough. Bringing a manual transmission car up to speed is much more complicated, requiring you to use the gas pedal, the clutch, and the gear shift. Both kinds of vehicles accelerate, but the details about how they do it are different.

In object-oriented terms, the Car class might have an Accelerate method that makes the car accelerate. The Automatic and Manual subclasses would provide different implementations of the Accelerate method that handle the appropriate details.

Figure 7.2 shows a revised inheritance hierarchy. The first section under a class's name lists its properties (just Acceleration in this simplified example). A subclass does not repeat items that it inherits without modification from its parent class. In this example, the Automatic and Manual classes inherit the Acceleration property.

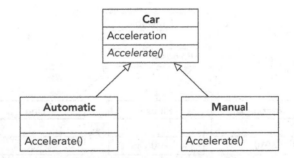

FIGURE 7.2: This hierarchy focuses on behavioral differences between classes.

The second section below a class's name shows methods (Accelerate in this example). The method is italicized in the Car class to indicate that it is not implemented there and must be overridden in the child classes.

Generalization

Refinement starts with a single class and creates child classes to represent differences between objects. Generalization does the opposite: It starts with several classes and creates a parent for them to represent common features.

For example, consider the ClassyDraw application in the examples in Chapter 5, "Requirements Gathering," and Chapter 6, "High-Level Design." This program is a drawing application somewhat similar to MS Paint, except it allows you to manipulate drawn objects. It enables you to select an object, drag it into a new position, stretch it, move it to the top or bottom of the stacking order, delete it, copy and paste it, change its color, and so forth.

The program represents drawn objects as (you guessed it) objects, so it needs classes such as Rectangle, Ellipse, Polygon, Text, Line, Star, and Hypotrochoid.

These classes draw different shapes, but they also have a lot in common. They all let you click their object to select it, move the object to the top or bottom of the drawing order, change the object's outline and fill colors, move the object, and so forth.

Because all of those objects share these features, it makes sense to create a parent class that defines those features. The program can build a big array or list to hold all of the drawing objects represented by the parent class and then use polymorphism to invoke the common methods as necessary.

For a concrete example, suppose the user clicks part of a drawing to select a drawn object. Classes such as Rectangle and Ellipse use different techniques to decide whether you clicked their objects, but they both need a method to do that. (For example, if you click on the corner of an ellipse's bounding rectangle, you'll miss the ellipse.) You could call this method ObjectIsAt and make it return true if the object is at a specific clicked location. The parent class, which I'll call Drawable, can define the ObjectIsAt method. The child classes would then provide their own implementations.

Figure 7.3 shows the drawing class inheritance hierarchy.

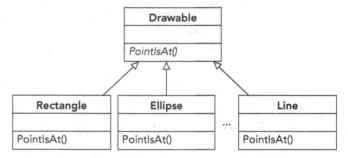

FIGURE 7.3: Generalization creates the Drawable parent class.

Just as you can go overboard with refinement to build an inheritance hierarchy containing thousands of car classes, you can also get carried away with generalization. For example, suppose you're building a pet store inventory application. You define a Customer class and an Employee class. They share some properties such as Name, Address, and ZodiacSign, so you generalize them by making a Person class to hold the common properties.

Next, you define various pet classes such as Dog, Cat, Gerbil, and Capybara. You generalize them to make a Pet class.

In a fit of inspiration (possibly assisted by whatever you were drinking), you realize that people and pets are all animals! So you make an Animal class to be a parent class for Person and Pet. They can even share some properties, such as Name.

Logically, this makes sense. People and pets really are animals (as long as your pet store doesn't sell pet rocks or stuffed toys). However, it's unlikely that the program will ever take advantage of this fact. It's hard to imagine the program building an array or list containing both employees and birds and then treating them in a uniform way. In all likelihood, the program will treat people and pets in different ways, so they don't need to be merged into a single inheritance hierarchy.

Hierarchy Warning Signs

The following list holds some questions that you can ask yourself when trying to decide if you have an effective inheritance hierarchy.

➤ Is it tall and thin? In general, tall, thin inheritance hierarchies are more confusing than shorter ones. Tall hierarchies make it hard for developers to remember which class to use under different circumstances. How tall an inheritance hierarchy can be depends on your application, but if it contains more than three or four levels, you should make sure you really need them all.

➤ Do you have a huge number of classes? Suppose your car sales application needs to track make, model, year, color, engine, wheel size, and motorized cup holders. If you try to use classes to represent every possible combination, you'll get a combinatorial explosion and thousands of classes. If you have more than a dozen or so classes, see if you can replace some with simple properties.

➤ Does a class have only a single subclass? If so, then you can probably remove it and move whatever it was trying to represent into the subclass.

➤ Is there a class at the bottom of the hierarchy that is never instantiated? If the Car hierarchy has a HalfTrack class and the program never makes an instance of that class, then you probably don't need the HalfTrack class.

➤ Do the classes all make common sense? If the Car hierarchy contains a Helicopter class, there's probably something wrong. Either the class doesn't belong there, or you should rename some classes so that things make sense. (Perhaps you need a Vehicle class?)

➤ Do classes represent differences in a property's value rather than in behavior or the presence of properties? A simple sales program might not need separate classes to represent notebooks and three-hole punches because they're both simple products that you sell one at a time. You might want a separate class for more expensive objects like computers because they might have a Warranty property that notebooks and hole punches probably don't have.

Object Composition

Inheritance is one way you can reuse code. A child class inherits all of the code defined by its parent class, so you don't need to write it again. Another way to reuse code is *object composition*, a technique that uses existing classes to build more complex classes.

For example, suppose you define a Person class that has FirstName, LastName, Address, and Phone properties. Now you want to make a Company class that should include information about a contact person.

You could make the `Company` class inherit from the `Person` class so it would inherit the `FirstName`, `LastName`, `Address`, and `Phone` properties. That would give you places to store the contact person's information, but it doesn't make intuitive sense. A company is not a kind of person (despite certain Supreme Court rulings), so `Company` should not inherit from `Person`.

A better approach is to give the `Company` class a new property of type `Person` called `ContactPerson`. Now the `Company` class gets the benefit of the code defined by the `Person` class without the illogic and possible confusion of inheriting from `Person`.

This approach also lets you place more than one `Person` object inside the `Company` class. For example, if you decide the `Company` class also needs to store information about a billing contact and a shipping contact, you can add more `Person` objects to the class. You couldn't do that with inheritance.

DATABASE DESIGN

There are many different kinds of databases that you can use to build an application. For example, specialized kinds of databases store hierarchical data, documents, graphs and networks, key/value pairs, and objects. However, the most popular kind of database is the relational database.

> **DATABASE RANKINGS**
>
> To see the top database engines ranked by popularity, go to `https://db-engines.com/en/ranking`. It's a pretty interesting (and very long) list.

Relational databases are simple and easy to use and provide a good set of tools for searching, combining data from different tables, sorting results, and otherwise rearranging data.

Like object-oriented design, database design is too big a topic to squeeze into a tiny portion of this book. However, there is room here to cover a few of the most important concepts of database design. You can find a book on database design for more complete information. (For example, see my book *Beginning Database Design Solutions, Second Edition*, Wiley, 2023.)

The following section briefly explains what a relational database is. The sections after that explain the first three forms of database normalization and why they are important.

Relational Databases

Before you learn about database normalization, you need to at least know the basics of relational databases.

A *relational database* stores related data in *tables*. Each table holds *records* that contain pieces of data that are related. Sometimes a record is called a *tuple* to emphasize that it contains a set of related values.

The pieces of data in each record are called *fields*. Each field has a name and a data type. All the values in different records for a particular field have that data type.

Figure 7.4 shows a small `Customer` table holding five records. The table's fields are `CustomerId`, `FirstName`, `LastName`, `Street`, `City`, `State`, and `Zip`. Because the representation shown in Figure 7.4 lays out the data in rows and columns, records are often called *rows* and fields are often called *columns*.

CustomerId	FirstName	LastName	Street	City	State	Zip
1028	Veronica	Jenson	176 Bradley Ave	Abend	AZ	87351
2918	Kirk	Wood	61 Beech St	Bugsville	CT	04514
7910	Lila	Rowe	8391 Cedar Ct	Cobblestone	SC	35245
3198	Deirdre	Lemon	2819 Dent Dr	Dove	DE	29183
5002	Alicia	Hayes	298 Elf Ln	Eagle	CO	83726

FIGURE 7.4: A table's records are often called rows, and its fields are often called columns.

The "relational" part of the term "relational database" comes from relationships defined between the database's tables. For example, consider the `Orders` table shown in Figure 7.5. The `Customers` table's `CustomerId` field and the `Orders` table's `CustomerId` field form a relationship between the two tables. To find a particular customer's orders, you can look up that customer's `CustomerId` in the `Customers` table in Figure 7.4 and then find the corresponding `Orders` records.

CustomerId	OrderId	DateOrdered	DateFilled	DateShipped
1028	1298	4/1/2015	4/4/2015	4/4/2015
2918	1982	4/1/2015	4/3/2015	4/4/2015
3198	2917	4/2/2015	4/7/2015	4/9/2015
1028	9201	4/5/2015	4/6/2015	4/9/2015
1028	3010	4/9/2015	4/13/2015	4/14/2015

FIGURE 7.5: The `Customers` table's `CustomerId` column provides a link to the `Orders` table's `CustomerID` column.

One particularly useful kind of relationship is a foreign key relationship. A *foreign key* is a set of one or more fields in one table with values that uniquely define a record in another table.

For example, in the `Orders` table shown in Figure 7.5, the `CustomerId` field uniquely identifies a record in the `Customers` table. In other words, it tells you which customer placed the order. There may be multiple records in the `Orders` table with the same `CustomerId` (a single customer can place multiple orders), but there can be only one record in the `Customers` table that has a particular `CustomerId` value.

The table containing the foreign key is often called the *child table*, and the table that contains the uniquely identified record is often called the *parent table*. In this example, the `Orders` table is the child table, and the `Customers` table is the parent table.

> **LOOKUP TABLES**
>
> A *lookup table* is a table that contains values just to use as foreign keys.
>
> For example, you could make a `States` table that lists the states that are allowed by the application. If your company has customers only in New England, the table might contain the values Maine, New Hampshire, Vermont, Massachusetts, Connecticut, and Rhode Island.
>
> The `Customers` table would be a child table connected to the `States` table with a foreign key. That would prevent a user from adding a new customer in a state that wasn't allowed.
>
> In addition to validating user inputs, lookup tables allow the users to configure the application. If you let users modify the `States` table, they can add new records when they decide to work with customers in new states.

Building a relational database is easy, but unless you design the database properly, you may encounter unexpected problems:

> ➤ Duplicate data can waste space and make updating values slow.

> ➤ You may be unable to delete one piece of data without also deleting another unrelated piece of data (because they are linked).

> ➤ An otherwise unnecessary piece of data may need to exist so that you can represent some other data.

> ➤ The database may not allow multiple values when you need them.

The database-speak euphemism for these kinds of problems is *anomalies*.

Database normalization is a process of rearranging a database to put it into a standard (normal) form that prevents these kinds of anomalies. There are seven levels of database normalization that deal with increasingly obscure kinds of anomalies. The following sections describe the first three levels of normalization, which handle the worst kinds of database problems.

First Normal Form

First normal form (1NF) basically says the table can be placed meaningfully in a relational database. It means the table has a sensible, down-to-earth structure like the kind your grandma used to make.

Relational database products tend to enforce most of the 1NF rules automatically, so if you don't do anything too weird, your database will be in 1NF with little extra work.

The official requirements for a table to be in 1NF are as follows:

1. Each column must have a unique name.
2. The order of the rows and columns doesn't matter.

3. Each column must have a single data type.

4. No two rows can contain identical values.

5. Each column must contain a single value.

6. Columns cannot contain repeating groups.

To see how you might be tricked into breaking these rules, suppose you're a weapons instructor at a fantasy adventure camp. You teach kids how to whack each other safely with foam swords and the like. Now consider the signup sheet shown in Table 7.1.

TABLE 7.1: Weapons training signup sheet

NAME	WEAPON	WEAPON
Shelly Silva	Broadsword	
Louis Christenson	Bow	
Lee Hall	Katana	
Sharon Simmons	Broadsword	Bow
Felipe Vega	Broadsword	Katana
Louis Christenson	Bow	
Kate Ballard	Everything	

Here campers list their names and the weapons for which they want training. You'll call them in for instruction on a first-come-first-served basis.

This signup sheet violates the 1NF rules in several ways.

It violates Rule 1 because it contains two columns named Weapon. The idea is that a camper might want help with more than one weapon. That makes sense on a paper signup sheet but won't work in a relational database.

It violates Rule 2 because the order of the rows indicates the order in which the campers signed up and the order in which you'll tutor them. In other words, the ordering of the rows is important. (The order of the columns might also be important if you assume the first Weapon column holds the camper's primary weapon.)

It violates Rule 3 because Kate Ballard didn't enter the name of a weapon in the first weapon column. Ideally, that column's data type would be Weapon and campers would just enter a weapon's name, not a general comment such as "Everything" or "Distance Weapons."

It violates Rule 4 because Louis Christenson signed up twice for tutoring with the bow. (I guess he wants to get *really* good with the bow.)

The signup sheet doesn't violate Rule 5, but that's mostly due to luck. There's nothing (except common sense) to stop campers from entering multiple weapons in each Weapon column, and that would violate Rule 5.

That's a lot of violations for a simple signup sheet that looks so innocent at first glance!

Here's how you can put this signup sheet into 1NF.

Rule 1—The signup sheet has two columns named Weapon. You can fix that by changing their names to Weapon1 and Weapon2. (That violates Rule 6, but we'll fix that later.)

Rule 2—The order of the rows in the signup sheet determines the order in which you'll call campers for their tutorials, so the ordering of rows is important. To fix this problem, add a new field that stores the ordering data explicitly. One way to do that would be to add an Order field, as shown in Table 7.2.

TABLE 7.2: Ordered signup sheet

ORDER	NAME	WEAPON1	WEAPON2
1	Shelly Silva	Broadsword	
2	Louis Christenson	Bow	
3	Lee Hall	Katana	
4	Sharon Simmons	Broadsword	Bow
5	Felipe Vega	Broadsword	Katana
6	Louis Christenson	Bow	
7	Kate Ballard	Everything	

An alternative that might be more useful would be to add a Time field instead of an Order field, as shown in Table 7.3. That preserves the original ordering and gives extra information that the campers can use to schedule their days.

TABLE 7.3: Signup sheet with times

TIME	NAME	WEAPON1	WEAPON2
9:00	Shelly Silva	Broadsword	
9:30	Louis Christenson	Bow	

TIME	NAME	WEAPON1	WEAPON2
10:00	Lee Hall	Katana	
10:30	Sharon Simmons	Broadsword	Bow
11:00	Felipe Vega	Broadsword	Katana
11:30	Louis Christenson	Bow	
12:00	Kate Ballard	Everything	

Rule 3—In Table 7.3, the `Weapon1` column holds two kinds of values: the name of a weapon and "Everything" (for Kate Ballard).

Depending on the application, there are several approaches you could take to fix this kind of problem. You could split a column into two columns, each containing a single data type. Alternatively, you could move the data into separate tables linked to the original record by a key.

In this example, I'll replace the value "Everything" with multiple records that list all the possible weapon values. The result is shown in Table 7.4.

TABLE 7.4: Signup sheet with explicitly listed weapons

TIME	NAME	WEAPON1	WEAPON2
9:00	Shelly Silva	Broadsword	
9:30	Louis Christenson	Bow	
10:00	Lee Hall	Katana	
10:30	Sharon Simmons	Broadsword	Bow
11:00	Felipe Vega	Broadsword	Katana
11:30	Louis Christenson	Bow	
12:00	Kate Ballard	Broadsword	
12:00	Kate Ballard	Bow	
12:00	Kate Ballard	Katana	

Rule 4—The current design doesn't contain any duplicate rows (where corresponding fields have the same values), so it satisfies Rule 4.

Rule 5—Right now each column contains a single value, so the current design satisfies Rule 5. (The original signup sheet would have broken this rule if it had used a single Weapons column instead of using two separate columns and people had written in lists of the weapons they wanted to study.)

Rule 6—This rule says a table cannot contain repeating groups. That means you can't have two columns that represent the same thing. This means a bit more than two columns don't have the same *data type*. Tables often have multiple columns with the same data types but with different meanings. For example, the Camper table might have HomePhone and CellPhone fields. Both of them would hold phone numbers, but they represent different *kinds* of phone numbers.

In the current design, the Weapon1 and Weapon2 columns hold the same type and kind of data, so they form a repeating group.

ROTTEN REPETITION

In general, adding a number to field names to differentiate them is a bad idea. If the program doesn't need to differentiate between the two values, then adding a number to their names just creates a repeating group.

The only time this makes sense is if the two fields contain similar items that truly have different meanings to the application. For example, suppose a space shuttle requires two pilots: one to be the primary pilot and one to be the backup in case the primary pilot falls asleep or is abducted by aliens. In that case, you could name the fields that store their names Pilot1 and Pilot2 because there really is a difference between them.

Usually in cases like this, you can give the fields more descriptive names such as Pilot and Copilot.

Another way to look at this is to ask yourself whether the record "Sharon Simmons, Broadsword, Bow" and the rearranged record "Sharon Simmons, Bow, Broadsword" would have the same meaning. If the two have the same meaning when you switch the values of the two fields, then those fields form a repeating group.

The way to fix this problem is to pull the repeated data out into a new table and use fields in the original table to link to the new one. Figure 7.6 shows the new design. Here the Tutorials and TutorialWeapons tables are linked by their Time fields.

Second Normal Form

A table is in *second normal form (2NF)* if it satisfies these rules:

1. It is in 1NF.
2. All non-key fields depend on all key fields.

Tutorials	
Time	**Name**
9:00	Shelly Silva
9:30	Louis Christenson
10:00	Lee Hall
10:30	Sharon Simmons
11:00	Felipe Vega
11:30	Louis Christenson
12:00	Kate Ballard

TutorialWeapns	
Time	**Weapon**
9:00	Broadsword
9:30	Bow
10:00	Katana
10:30	Broadsword
10:30	Bow
11:00	Broadsword
11:00	Katana
11:30	Bow
12:00	Broadsword
12:00	Bow
12:00	Katana

FIGURE 7.6: This design is in first normal form (1NF). Lines connect related records.

Without getting too technical, a *key* is a set of one or more fields that uniquely identifies a record. Any table in 1NF must have a key because 1NF Rule 4 says, "No two rows can contain identical values." That means there must be a way to pick fields to guarantee uniqueness, even if the key must include every field.

For an example of a table that is not in 2NF, suppose you want to schedule games for campers at the fantasy adventure camp. Table 7.5 lists the scheduled games.

TABLE 7.5: Camp games schedule

TIME	GAME	DURATION	MAXIMUMPLAYERS
1:00	*Goblin Launch*	60 mins	8
1:00	*Water Wizzards*	120 mins	6
2:00	*Panic at the Picnic*	90 mins	12
2:00	*Goblin Launch*	60 mins	8
3:00	*Capture the Castle*	120 mins	100
3:00	*Water Wizzards*	120 mins	6
4:00	*Middle Earth Hold'em Poker*	90 mins	10
5:00	*Capture the Castle*	120 mins	100

The table's primary key is Time+Game. It cannot have two instances of the same game at the same time (because you don't have enough equipment or counselors), so the combination of Time+Game uniquely identifies the rows.

You should quickly review the 1NF rules and convince yourself that this table is in 1NF. In case you haven't memorized them yet, the 1NF rules are as follows:

1. Each column must have a unique name.
2. The order of the rows and columns doesn't matter.
3. Each column must have a single data type.
4. No two rows can contain identical values.
5. Each column must contain a single value.
6. Columns cannot contain repeating groups.

Even though this table is in 1NF, it suffers from the following anomalies:

➤ Update anomalies—If you modify the Duration or MaximumPlayers value in one row, other rows containing the same game will be out of sync.

➤ Deletion anomalies—Suppose you want to cancel the *Middle Earth Hold'em Poker* game at 4:00, so you delete that record. Then you've lost all the information about that game. You no longer know that it takes 90 minutes and has a maximum of 10 players.

➤ Insertion anomalies—You cannot add information about a new game without scheduling it for play. For example, suppose *Banshee Bingo* takes 45 minutes and has a maximum of 30 players. You can't add that information to the database without scheduling a game.

The problem with this table is that it's trying to do too much. It's trying to store information about both games (duration and maximum players) and the schedule.

The reason it breaks the 2NF rules is that some non-key fields do not depend on *all* the key fields. Recall that this table's key fields are Time and Game. A game's duration and maximum number of players depends only on the Game value and not on the Time value. For example, *Water Wizzards* lasts for 120 minutes whether you play at 1:00, 4:00, or midnight.

To fix this table, move the data that doesn't depend on the *entire* key into a new table. Use the key fields that the data does depend on to link to the original table.

Figure 7.7 shows the new design. Here the ScheduledGames table holds schedule information, and the Games table holds information specific to the games.

Third Normal Form

A table is in *third normal form* (3NF) if the following is true:

1. It is in 2NF.
2. It contains no transitive dependencies.

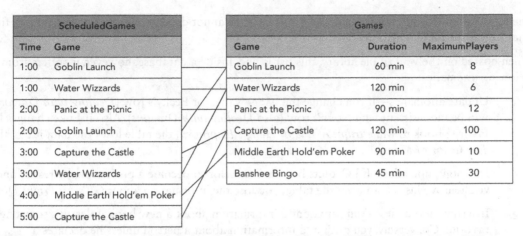

FIGURE 7.7: Moving the data that doesn't depend on *all* the table's key fields puts this table in 2NF.

A *transitive dependency* is when a non-key field's value depends on another non-key field's value.

For example, suppose the fantasy adventure camp has a library. (So campers have something to read after they get injured playing the games.) Posted in the library is a list of the counselors' favorite books, as shown in Table 7.6.

TABLE 7.6: Counselors' favorite books

COUNSELOR	FAVORITEBOOK	AUTHOR	PAGES
Becky	*Dealing with Dragons*	Patricia Wrede	240
Charlotte	*The Last Dragonslayer*	Jasper Fforde	306
J.C.	*Gil's All Fright Diner*	A. Lee Martinez	288
Jon	*The Last Dragonslayer*	Jasper Fforde	306
Luke	*The Color of Magic*	Terry Pratchett	288
Noah	*Dealing with Dragons*	Patricia Wrede	240
Rod	*Equal Rites*	Terry Pratchett	272
Wendy	*The Lord of the Rings Trilogy*	J. R. R. Tolkein	1178

This table's key is the Counselor field.

If you run through the 1NF rules, you'll see that this table is in 1NF.

The table has only a single key field, so a non-key field cannot depend on only *some* of the key fields. That means the table is also in 2NF.

When posted on the wall of the library, this list is fine. Inside a database, however, it suffers from the following anomalies:

➤ Update anomalies—If you change the `Pages` value for Becky's row (*Dealing with Dragons*), it will be inconsistent with Noah's row (also *Dealing with Dragons*). Also if Luke changes his favorite book to *Majestrum: A Tale of Hengis Hapthorn*, the table loses the data it has about *The Color of Magic*.

➤ Deletion anomalies—If J.C. quits being a counselor to become a professional wrestler and you remove his record from the table, you lose the information about *Gil's All Fright Diner*.

➤ Insertion anomalies—You cannot add information about a new book unless it's someone's favorite. Conversely, you can't add information about a person unless he declares a favorite book.

The problem is that some non-key fields depend on other non-key fields. In this example, the `Author` and `Pages` fields depend on the `FavoriteBook` field. For example, any record with `FavoriteBook` *The Last Dragonslayer* has `Author` Jasper Fforde and `Pages` 306 no matter whose favorite it is.

DIAGNOSING DEPENDENCIES

A major hint that there is a transitive dependency in Table 7.6 is that there are lots of duplicate values in different columns. Another way to think about this is that there are "tuples" of data (`FavoriteBook+Author+Pages`) that go together.

You can fix this problem by keeping only enough information to identify the dependent data and moving the rest of those fields into a new table. In this example, you would keep the `FavoriteBook` field in the original table and move its dependent values `Author` and `Pages` into a new table. Figure 7.8 shows the new design.

CounselorFavorites	
Counselor	**FavoriteBook**
Becky	Dealing with Dragons
Charlotte	The Last Dragonslayer
J.C.	Gil's All Fright Diner
Jon	The Last Dragonslayer
Luke	The Color of Magic
Noah	Dealing with Dragons
Rod	Equal Rites
Wendy	The Lord of the Rings Trilogy

BookInfo		
Book	**Author**	**Pages**
Dealing with Dragons	Patricia Wrede	240
The Last Dragonslayer	Jasper Fforde	306
Gil's All Fright Diner	A. Lee Martinez	288
The Color of Magic	Terry Pratchett	288
Equal Rites	Terry Pratchett	272
The Lord of the Rings Trilogy	J.R.R. Tolkien	1178

FIGURE 7.8: Moving non-key fields that depend on other non-key fields into a separate table puts this table in 3NF.

Higher Levels of Normalization

Higher levels of normalization include Boyce-Codd normal form (BCNF), fourth normal form (4NF), fifth normal form (5NF), and Domain/Key Normal Form (DKNF). Some of these later levels of normalization are fairly technical and confusing, so I won't cover them here. See a book on database design for details.

Many database designs stop at 3NF because it handles most kinds of database anomalies without a huge amount of effort. In fact, with a little practice, you can design database tables in 3NF from the beginning, so you don't need to spend several steps normalizing them.

More complete levels of normalization can also lead to confusing database designs that may make using the database harder and less intuitive, possibly giving rise to extra bugs and sometimes reduced performance.

One particular compromise that is often useful is to intentionally leave some data denormalized for performance reasons. A classic example is in zip codes. Zip codes and street addresses are related, so if you know a street address, you can look up the corresponding zip code. For example, the zip code for 1 Main St., Boston, MA is 02129-3786.

Ideally, normalization would tell you to store only the street address and then use it to look up the zip code as needed. Unfortunately, these relationships aren't as simple as, "All Main St. addresses in Boston have the zip code 02129-3786." Zip codes depend on which part of the street contains the address and sometimes even which side of the street the address is on. That means you can't build a table to perform a simple lookup.

You could build a much more complicated table to find an address's ZIP code, perhaps with some confusing code. Or you might use some sort of web service provided by the United States Postal Service such as www.usps.com/business/web-tools-apis/address-information-api .htm.

Usually, however, developers just include the zip code as a separate field in the address. That means there's a lot of "unnecessary" duplication, but it doesn't take up much extra room and it makes looking up addresses much easier.

> ## LOADS OF CODES
>
> Addresses and postal codes are also related outside of the United States. For example, the postal code for 1 Main St., Dungiven, Londonderry England is BT47 4PG, and the postal code for 1 Main St., Vancouver, BC, Canada is V6A 3Y5. You can use various postal websites to look up codes for different addresses in different countries.
>
> In theory, you could look up the postal codes for any address. In practice, it's a lot easier to just include them in the address data.

WHEN TO OPTIMIZE

Before we wrap up this chapter, I want to say a quick word about the second quote at the beginning of the chapter.

> Premature optimization is the root of all evil in programming.
>
> —*Sir Tony Hoare*

You may have noticed that I've repeatedly said that the requirements and high-level design should specify *what* and not *how* so you can keep your options open. During low-level design, you start to specify *how*, but you should still keep your options open to an extent. If you begin optimizing your code too soon, parts of the design will start to solidify and become harder to change later.

Just as importantly, you may spend a lot of time optimizing a part of the application that doesn't really need it. For example, you could spend weeks fine-tuning an inventory system that lets repair people know exactly what kinds of equipment they will need for practically any kind of job only to discover later that everyone always carries all of the equipment they will ever need for any job.

Programs usually obey the 80/20 rule: 80 percent of the time is spent by 20 percent of the code. If you start optimizing code too early, you risk spending long hours on the 80 percent of the code that isn't a problem and ignoring the 20 percent that is.

First, focus on getting the program working correctly. Then, after you can run the program and possibly use code profilers to see where the performance bottlenecks lie, optimize those and ignore the pieces that already work well enough. I've known several projects to fail because they didn't work but none that failed because they were underoptimized.

SUMMARY

Low-level design fills in some of the gaps left by high-level design to provide extra guidance to developers before they start writing code. It provides the level of detail necessary for programmers to write that code, or at least for them to start building classes and to finish defining interfaces. Low-level design moves the high-level focus from *what* to a lower level focus on *how*.

Like most of the topics covered in this book, low-level design is a huge subject. There's no way to cover every possible approach to low-level design in a single chapter. However, this chapter does at least describe several design approaches and provide an introduction to two important facets of low-level design: object-oriented design and database design.

Object-oriented design determines what classes the application uses. Database design determines what tables the database contains and how they are related. Object-oriented design and database design aren't all you need to do to ensure success, but poor designs almost always lead to failure.

Of course, those aren't the only places where low-level design is important. You should create designs for any complex part of the system. The following two chapters describe particularly important pieces of the application that deserve their own designs: security and the user interface.

EXERCISES

1. Consider the ClassyDraw classes `Line`, `Rectangle`, `Ellipse`, `Star`, and `Text`. What properties do these classes all share? What properties do they not share? Are there any properties shared by some classes and not others? Where should the shared and nonshared properties be implemented?

2. Draw an inheritance diagram showing the properties you identified for Exercise 1. (Create parent classes as needed, and don't forget the `Drawable` class at the top.)

3. The following list gives the properties of several business-oriented classes.

   ➤ Customer—Name, Phone, Address, BillingAddress, CustomerId
   ➤ Hourly—Name, Phone, Address, EmployeeId, HourlyRate
   ➤ Manager—Name, Phone, Address, EmployeeId, Office, Salary, Boss, Employees
   ➤ Salaried—Name, Phone, Address, EmployeeId, Office, Salary, Boss
   ➤ Supplier—Name, Phone, Address, Products, SupplierId
   ➤ VicePresident—Name, Phone, Address, EmployeeId, Office, Salary, Managers

   Assuming `Supplier` is someone who supplies products for your business, draw an inheritance diagram showing the relationships among these classes. (Hint: Add extra classes if necessary.)

4. How would the inheritance hierarchy you drew for Exercise 3 change if you decide to add the `Boss` property to the `Hourly` and `VicePresident` classes?

5. How would the inheritance hierarchy you drew for Exercise 3 change if `Supplier` represents a business instead of a person?

6. Suppose your company has many managerial types such as department manager, project manager, and division manager. You also have multiple levels of vice president, some of whom report to other manager types. How could you combine the `Salaried`, `Manager`, and `VicePresident` types you used in Exercise 3? Draw the new inheritance hierarchy.

7. If a table includes a zip code with every address, what 1NF, 2NF, and 3NF rules does the table break?

8. What data anomalies can result from including postal codes in address data? How bad are they? How can you mitigate the problems?

9. In the United States Postal Service's ZIP+4 system, zip codes can include 4 extra digits, as in 20500-0002. Suppose you store address data with a single `Zip` field that has room for 10 characters. Some addresses include only a 5-digit zip code and others include a ZIP+4 code. Does that violate any of the 1NF, 2NF, or 3NF rules? Should you do anything about it?

10. Do telephone area codes face issues similar to those involving zip codes?

11. Suppose you're writing an application to record times for dragon boat races and consider the table shown in Figure 7.9. Assume the table's key is Heat. What 1NF, 2NF, and 3NF rules does this design violate?

12. How could you fix the table shown in Figure 7.9 ?

Distance	Heat	Time	Team	Team	Winner	Time	Time
500	1	9:00	Buddhist Temple	Wicked Wind	Buddhist Temple	2:55.372	2:57.391
500	2	9:20	Rainbow Energy	Rising Typhoon	Rising Typhoon	3:10.201	3:01.791
1000	3	9:40	Math Dragons	Supermarines	Math Dragons	5:52.029	6:23.552
1000	4	10:00	Flux Lake Tritons	Elf Power	Elf Power	6:08.480	6:59.717

FIGURE 7.9: This table records dragon boat race results.

WHAT YOU LEARNED IN THIS CHAPTER

➤ A class defines the properties, methods, and events provided by instances of the class.

➤ Nouns in the project description make good candidates for classes.

➤ Inheritance provides code reuse.

➤ Polymorphism lets a program treat an object as if it had a parent class's type.

➤ In refinement, you add details to a general class to define subclasses.

➤ In generalization, you extract common features from two or more classes to define a parent class.

➤ The following are inheritance hierarchy warning signs:

   ➤ The hierarchy is tall and thin.

   ➤ The hierarchy contains a large number of classes.

   ➤ A class has a single subclass.

   ➤ A class at the bottom of the hierarchy is never instantiated.

   ➤ The classes don't make common sense.

   ➤ Classes represent differences in property values, not different properties themselves or different behaviors.

➤ Composition provides code reuse. It also lets you include multiple copies of a type of object inside a class, something inheritance doesn't do.

➤ Relational databases contain tables that hold records (or rows). The records in a table all have the same fields (or columns).

➤ A foreign key forms a relationship between the values in a parent table and the values in a child table. The child table's fields must contain values that are present in the parent table.

➤ A lookup table is a foreign key parent table that simply defines values that are allowed in other tables.

➤ Normalization protects a database from data anomalies.

➤ 1NF rules:

1. Each column must have a unique name.

2. The order of the rows and columns doesn't matter.

3. Each column must have a single data type.

4. No two rows can contain identical values.

5. Each column must contain a single value.

6. Columns cannot contain repeating groups.

➤ 2NF rules:

1. It is in 1NF.

2. All non-key fields depend on all key fields.

➤ 3NF rules:

1. It is in 2NF.

2. It contains no transitive dependencies. (No non-key fields depend on other non-key fields.)

8

Security Design

> The best way to get management excited about a disaster plan is to burn down the building across the street.
>
> —*Dan Erwin*

> Security is not a product, but a process.
>
> —*Bruce Schneier*

What You Will Learn in This Chapter:

- ➤ Cybersecurity terms such as shift-left security and DevSecOps
- ➤ Kinds of malware including phishing attacks, viruses, Trojans, spoofs, sploits, and ransomware
- ➤ Signs of social engineering attacks
- ➤ Malware countermeasures

Security has been a key issue in software engineering as long as there has been software. Early computers were huge behemoths with limited or no dial-up access, so security was mainly physical.

Today computers are small, portable, and massively interconnected, so the security landscape has changed dramatically. Physical security is still important (you don't want someone to steal a laptop, phone, or flash drive containing sensitive data), but attacks through a network are far more common. It's hard to calculate exact numbers because many cyberattacks go unreported or even unnoticed, but the estimates are frightening. For example, it's estimated that around 30 percent of the world's computers are currently infected with malware.

This chapter describes some of the security issues that you should consider and address during high-level and low-level design.

SECURITY GOALS

You can summarize basic security goals with the acronym CIA, also known as the *CIA triad*. Here the letters in CIA stand for confidentiality, integrity, and availability.

➤ Confidentiality—Your data should be kept secret. This is important for company secrets and for customer data such as financial information, phone numbers, medical information, student grades, etc.

➤ Integrity—Your data should be protected from unauthorized modification. You can't trust the data if an attacker can corrupt it.

➤ Availability—You should be able to use your data when you need to do so. An attacker should not be able to destroy your data or prevent you from accessing it, for example, with a DoS, DDoS, or ransomware attack. (These are described later in this chapter.)

(Presumably the CIA uses the CIA triad because the goals are the same whenever you have secrets to keep. I suppose the FBI has similar goals, although they may not call them the CIA triad out of a sense of professional rivalry.)

These probably aren't your only data goals. For example, you might also want to produce quarterly sales reports in less than five seconds, find delinquent customer accounts in under a minute, and check the cafeteria menu to see when you should bring your lunch next week. Those are all valid data goals, just not security goals.

Unfortunately, there are many ways your security design can fail to achieve the goals of the CIA triad. The rest of this chapter describes possible attacks and defenses that you can use in the security arms race.

SECURITY TYPES

The first thing you see when you start most applications is a login screen. That's the first *obvious* sign of the application's security, but it's actually not the first piece and definitely not the last. In addition to a password on your computer, you'll also need other types of security, such as network, computer, and physical security.

This section describes some different types of basic high-level security issues. Later sections focus on cybersecurity issues.

Your high-level design should sketch out all of the application's security needs. Those needs may include the following:

➤ Physical security—If you have some sort of operations center or central computer room (or even a small office in the back of your stationary store), you'll need physical security such as locks, alarms, cameras, and the like. If you have a larger facility, you may also need guards, keypads, and a moat filled with sharks. Your application won't do much good if the laptop it runs on is stolen from an unlocked office. Search the Internet for "stolen laptop costs millions" to see many stories of laptops containing sensitive data being lost and costing companies millions of dollars. Or take a look at www.eweek.com/security/lost-stolen-laptops-cost-companies-billions-in-2010.

➤ Remote physical security—People often think about physical security at a central location but forget security when people work remotely. You should outline policies for security during remote work. If team members will be logging in remotely on their own computers, you should make sure that they have solid security on their systems. Your data could be exposed if their computer is hacked.

➤ Portable device security—In addition to security on remote computers, you should devise a plan for small devices such as tablets, laptops, phones, and flash drives. If someone loses one of those devices, your data may be at risk.

➤ Network security—Even if your application and data are secure, cyber banditos might steal your data from the network or break into your computers over the network. (I'll say more about this shortly in the section about social engineering attacks.)

➤ Operating system security—This includes login procedures, password expiration policies, and password standards. (Password standards are those annoying rules that say your password must include at least one letter, one number, one special character like # or %, and three Egyptian hieroglyphs.)

➤ Application security—Some applications may rely on the operating system's security and not provide their own. Others may use the operating system's security to make the user reenter the same username and password. Still others may use a separate application username and password. Application security also means providing the right level of access to different users. For example, some users might not be allowed access to every part of the system. (I'll say more about this in the section "User Access" later in the chapter.)

➤ Online Application Security—When an application runs in the cloud, it has the same kinds of application security needs as desktop applications, but it also has some new options. For example, browsers commonly include password managers so they can fill in login information automatically. *Federated security* also allows you to log in to an *identity provider* and then other applications can use that to see if you are authorized. For example, you may have seen websites that allow you to log in either with a site-specific user name and password or by logging in to a Google, Facebook, Microsoft, or Apple identity provider. If you're building a more complicated application ecosystem, you can even define identities on your network to control access to different resources.

➤ Data security—You need to make sure your customers' credit card information doesn't fall into the hands of North Korean hackers. If your application holds sensitive data such as financial data or medical data, then you need to not only be sure that you can use it but also guarantee that no one else can. In that case, you may need to encrypt your data, either in your code or by using a cryptographically secure database.

➤ Cloud security—Bad guys might even compromise your cloud data security. It's tempting to place data on the cloud and assume that the cloud provider will keep everything backed up, safe, and secure. They may do that (if you pay them enough), but they probably still can't protect you if the attackers capture critical passwords from the computers on your local network and those passwords are used to safeguard your cloud data.

All of these forms of security interact with each other, sometimes in nonobvious ways. For example, physical security also applies to passwords. I've seen large customer service environments where almost every user had their username and password written down somewhere on their desk. I've also seen operations where users needed manager approval for certain kinds of common operations. Those overrides were so common that the manager didn't have time to handle them all and get any other work done. The solution they adopted was to write the manager's username and password on a whiteboard at the front of the room so that everyone could use it to perform their own overrides.

The password was insecure, so any hacker who got into the room could do just about anything with the system. (Fortunately, the room had no windows and was difficult to get into without the right badge and lock combinations.)

This also meant that any user could impersonate the manager and do just about anything. If users can become the manager at will, why bother having user permissions?

If you need to make 50 exceptions per day, then they're not really exceptions. A better solution would have been to not require manager approval for those kinds of common tasks. Then the manager could have kept her password private and used overrides only for truly important stuff.

Any one of these basic issues can compromise an application's security.

CYBERSECURITY

Since the first computer viruses were written in the 1970s, hackers have had plenty of time to experiment. Over the years they've gone from very specialized attacks that only work under specific circumstances to programs that use multiple methods and sophisticated social engineering principles to spread incredibly quickly and widely. (Despite their sophistication, however, many hackers seem to be unable to master simple grammar and punctuation.)

Today there are dozens of different categories of *malware* (short for *malicious software*), tens of thousands of different viruses have been written (that's just viruses and doesn't include adware, spamware, other spyware, worms, Trojans, and other forms of malware wildlife), and billions of programs are currently infected worldwide.

> **CYBER WHATSITS** *You may not have seen a formal definition of "cyber" before but don't worry, it means exactly what you think: something related to computers, computer culture, Internet technology, and the like. If you replace "cyber" with "computer" and it still makes sense, then you've found a valid cyberconcept.*

The following sections describe some of the more common cyberthreats, things you can do to mitigate them, and related software engineering topics.

SHIFT-LEFT SECURITY

The recent explosive growth of malware has encouraged software engineers to build security into the design process much earlier than was done in the past. Once upon a time, you would write a program and then add security around it almost as an afterthought. In some cases, a program would rely on the operating system's login procedure as its only real security.

Now it's much more common to build in security throughout the entire project. The operating system still provides a login, but after that an application may have its own logins or piggyback on the operating system's credential system. Programs may restrict user access to specific parts of the system (so clerks can't give their friends huge discounts), validate the user's rights to access parts of databases, pre-process database queries to prevent SQL injection attacks, restrict access to the hardware (for example, placing limits on the amount of memory a program can use), use encrypted databases, obfuscate code (so it's harder for an attacker to disassemble the program to search for vulnerabilities), and so forth.

Building security into the application earlier in the software engineering process is sometimes called *shift-left security*. The idea is, if you read a project timeline from left to right, then shifting something left moves it earlier in the schedule. (Apologies to readers of Arabic, Chinese, Hebrew, Japanese, and other languages that don't work left to right.)

You can also use the term "shift-left" with other developmental stages. For example, *shift-left testing* builds testing into earlier phases of development, a very hip, agile concept. (You can probably extend the concept even further. I like the idea of a shift-left lunch and shift-left weekend.)

Two other related terms are DevOps and DevSecOps. *DevOps* is a portmanteau (smooshing together of words) of "development" and "operations." Different people use different definitions, but in general it's a development culture and set of techniques such as shared ownership and rapid feedback intended to shorten the time between introducing a change to a program and putting the change into operation. It grew out of agile concepts (you'll learn about agile development later in this book), and it fits well in an agile environment. The reason DevOps is a separate concept is that operations is often separated from development, and DevOps pulls the two together into a single team.

DevSecOps is basically shift-left security inserted into DevOps.

To resist malware and other cyberattacks, you definitely should build security into the earliest high-level designs (and use the term "shift-left" to impress the executives), whether you use DevOps techniques or not.

MALWARE MENAGERIE

Before you can build security into a system, it's worth knowing what kinds of threats you might face. The following list summarizes the most common kinds of malware and some related terms. Some of these are characterized by their goals (for example, to steal passwords or destroy data) and some are characterized by their methods (for example, by replication or by attacking known operating system bugs).

➤ Virus—A virus is inserted into another program. When the program runs, the virus replicates, either by copying itself into another program or by creating a new copy of the program that contains the virus. The infected program usually has a misleading name so you might execute it.

➤ Trojan—Like a virus, a Trojan hides inside some other program. Unlike a virus, a Trojan doesn't replicate. Instead, it performs some malicious action when it executes. For example, it might install a backdoor to let an attacker sneak into the system later.

➤ Worm—A worm is a separate program (not one hidden inside another program like a virus) that scans the computer it is on and tries to copy itself onto the other computers in a network. It may try to spread directly by looking for vulnerabilities on those computers, or it may send itself to every email address known by the infected computer in the hope that someone will foolishly execute it.

➤ FakeApp—A FakeApp is a counterfeit app that pretends to be something else such as the latest version of Minecraft or Fortnite. The FakeApp might be a partially functional cheap knockoff or it might not work at all. It could do just about anything. For example, it could display ads, send you to dangerous websites, install viruses or Trojans, and perform other harmful actions.

➤ Logic bomb—A logic bomb is a program installed in a system that takes action when a particular set of circumstances occurs. For example, a disgruntled employee might install one that destroys data if the employee is ever fired. (To prevent this, try to keep your employees gruntled.)

➤ Time bomb—A time bomb is a program that starts, stops, or takes other action at a particular date and time. Beta versions of software may be time bombed so they cannot be used after the final application's release date. Commercial programs that stop working after a certain number of days are normally considered *trialware* rather than time bombs. Of course a malicious time bomb could also do something nasty like destroy data or launch a virus on a certain date.

➤ Ransomware—A ransomware attack encrypts the files on a computer and demands a ransom to unlock the files. In a *double extortion scheme*, the attackers not only encrypt your data so you can't use it, but they also threaten to release the data either to other hackers (for example, your customers' credit card information) or to the public (for example, medical records or embarrassing company secrets).

➤ Spyware—Spyware collects information and sends it to the attacker. Examples include annoying *adware* that serves ads on your browser, dangerous programs such as *keyloggers* that send every keystroke to the attacker, and programs that steal passwords or financial data.

➤ Rootkit—A rootkit is a set of programs that provides access to an unauthorized part of the computer. For example, a Trojan might install a rootkit that allows an attacker to later enter the system, possibly with system administrator powers.

➤ DoS—A DoS (*denial-of-service attack*) tries to make a server or network unusable, often by flooding it with bogus requests so legitimate requests cannot get through. A *DDoS* (*distrib-*

uted denial-of-service attack) is similar, but the attack comes from multiple computers, possibly in a botnet.

➤ Botnet—A *bot* is a program that runs over the Internet. A botnet is a network of bots controlled by an attacker. The botnet can perform actions much more quickly than a single bot can. For example, a botnet might launch a DDoS attack, send spam to millions of email accounts, or mine crypto coins that are then sent to the attacker.

➤ Zero-day—A zero-day (or *0-day*) is a vulnerability in a system that is either not known to security researchers (the good guys) or known but does not yet have a fix. (As in, "this will be a threat in zero days.") For example, a worm might attack the computers on a network by using a zero-day.

➤ Exploit—An exploit (or *sploit*, which is a much cooler term) is a program that exploits a bug in the system. As you can probably guess, a *zero-day exploit* or *zero-day attack* is a sploit that attacks a zero-day.

➤ Phishing—A phishing attack tries to trick you into thinking that it is some legitimate contact such as an email or text message so it can fool you into doing something that you normally wouldn't such as revealing login information or credit card numbers. These attacks may imitate a real business communication such as a notice from a bank, and they can be very convincing. They sometimes also use spoofing to seem more legitimate.

➤ Spoofing—As a word, "spoof" can mean a humorous imitation of something such as a lampoon or parody. "Spoof" can also mean a trick played on someone, so it makes sense that cyber-spoofing is when an email message *imitates* someone trusted to try to *trick* you into giving away sensitive data.

➤ Conversation hijacking—In conversation hijacking, an attacker hacks an email account and then inserts bogus messages into a conversation stream. This is generally a phishing email and may also be a spoof. Because it appears to come not only from someone that you know but also from someone with whom you've been having a conversation, it can be very convincing.

➤ Formjacking—Formjacking occurs when an attacker inserts malicious code into a website to copy data from the site's forms. For example, an attacker might break into a merchant website and make its order entry form forward credit card information to the attacker.

➤ Man-in-the-middle—In a man-in-the-middle (*MITM*) attack (the first *M* can also stand for "monster," "machine," "monkey," or "meddler" depending on your mood, and similarly in *PITM*, the *P* stands for "person"), an attacker intercepts a private communication. The attacker may simply eavesdrop on any secrets passed back and forth, or the attacker may modify messages.

➤ Insider threats—An insider threat is a threat by someone with inside knowledge of the organization such as an employee, former employee, contractor, or vendor.

➤ SQL injection—In this attack, the hacker enters data into a field to make the program compose a SQL database query that grants unauthorized access.

Note that many systems are not patched even after fixes are available, so sploits can still attack vulnerabilities even if they are technically no longer zero-days.

In recent years, ransomware attacks have become big business. Estimates put losses due to ransomware in 2021 at around $20 billion, and that number is only going to grow over time. In fact, the true amount of money lost may be orders of magnitude higher because many companies don't report their losses for fear of losing customer trust or even being sued by customers who have had their data exposed.

SQL INJECTION

To understand SQL injection, suppose a program uses the following database query to see if a user has a valid password.

```
SELECT * FROM Users
WHERE Username = 'my_username' AND Password = 'my_password'
```

Normally the program replaces my_username and my_password with the name and password that you enter on a form. The code then executes the query to see if there is a record in the Users table that has your username and password.

However, suppose an attacker enters the following bizarre string for both the username and password.

```
X' OR 'A' = 'A
```

Substituting this string into the query gives the following.

```
SELECT * FROM Users
WHERE Username = 'X' OR 'A' = 'A' AND Password = 'X' OR 'A' = 'A'
```

Now the query returns records from the Users table where either the username is X or the string A equals the string A. Because A always equals A, this condition is always satisfied. The same trick works for the password, so the injected query returns every record in the Users table.

There are ways to prevent SQL injection attacks, as long as you think about them when you write the code. For example, the program can prohibit delimiter characters such as ' and " inside usernames and passwords. It could also verify that the returned record actually has the same username and password entered by the user. Finally, some database engines can assign values to placeholders within a query so any delimiters entered by the user would be considered part of the field's value and not part of a string composed by the program.

It's important to understand these kinds of attacks so you can write security into your high-level design. The following sections provide more information on some of these and some other important cybersecurity topics.

PHISHING AND SPOOFING

It can be hard to break into a properly secured system. It's often much easier to trick a user into opening the door. It's like having state-of-the-art locks, chains, and deadbolts on your front door but also having a roommate who will open the back door to anyone who knocks.

For many computer systems, the most likely form of attack is phishing or spoofing against the users. Fortunately, you can upgrade your users to make them more phishing-proof by educating them on the forms of attack they are most likely to see. You should specify this sort of training in your high-level design.

The difference between phishing and spoofing is subtle and sometimes practically nonexistent. In a nutshell, a phishing attack tries to trick you into thinking it is some trusted agent like a bank, credit card company, or the IRS so you'll give the attacker sensitive data such as your account number or login information.

A spoofing attack forges its identifying information to pretend to be a trusted agent for the same purpose.

For example, suppose you receive an email that looks like it's from a major bank such as Bank of America or Wells Fargo. The email might contain official company logos (downloaded from the company's website), convincing text (sometimes also downloaded from the company's website), and perhaps even real links to company web pages such as contact or help pages. However, the email also asks you to reply with your account number, login, and password. Or it might include a link that leads to a website (which also may look very official) where you can enter your account number and login information.

That's *phishing*.

If you look closely at this kind of email, you'll sometimes notice that the sender's email address is something like `iamahacker@gotcha.ru`, but sometimes the attacker also fakes an email header that makes it seem like the message actually came from the bank. Faking the header is *spoofing*.

In this example the difference is so small that it's practically meaningless.

Often phishing involves spoofing, but sometimes spoofing does not involve phishing. For example, a worm attacking a network might use IP (Internet Protocol) spoofing to make a target computer think the worm's connection request is coming from some other IP address and thus from a different computer. Without IP spoofing, it would be easy for the target computer to just deny all requests from the `gotcha.ru` domain. With spoofing, the target computer might think the request was coming from another computer in the same company network.

Some common forms of spoofing include email spoofing, phone spoofing, text message spoofing, website or domain spoofing, caller ID spoofing, IP spoofing, GPS spoofing, facial recognition spoofing, and many others.

Phishing attacks come in similar shapes and sizes. For example, you may receive phishing emails (I probably average 40 or so per month), phishing texts (I recently received a very convincing one from a "bank"), voicemail, and even letters sent through the postal service.

PHUNNY PHISHING

Several types of phishing attacks have humorous names. Knowing about the different varieties can help you be on guard against them. (And gives you something amusing to talk about at parties.)

➤ Phishing (or deceptive phishing)—This is the plain vanilla version.

➤ Spear phishing—Here the attack vector (email, text message, etc.) is customized for the target to make it more attractive. For example, an email might use your name (Dear Rod) instead of a generic form of address (Dear Customer).

➤ Whaling—This is spear phishing aimed at a company executive such as a CEO, CFO, or other CxO.

➤ Vishing—This is a voice phishing attack. It might be via voicemail, a robocall, or even a human. (I get a vishing voicemail every month or two.) This one is particularly effective at building a sense of urgency so you take action before you can really think things through. (One common version tells you that a relative of yours is in jail and needs bail money ASAP.)

➤ Smishing—This is a text message form of phishing. (Text messaging is more technically known as *SMS—Short Message Service*.)

➤ Angler phishing—Here the attack comes via social media with the attacker sometimes posing as a customer service representative. For example, you might receive an email from "Facebook customer service" saying that your account has been temporarily restricted and you can click here to resolve the issue. I've been getting a couple of these per day lately saying that someone has tried to log in to my account and giving me a button to report the user.

There are many other kinds of phishing attacks, but they're less common, generally more technical, and have less interesting names.

The fundamental defense against phishing attacks is paranoia. Be suspicious of *any* communication that asks for sensitive data. Do not click links unless you are absolutely certain they are legitimate. Hover your mouse over links so you can see where they will send you. (Note that this means you probably cannot safely check links on your phone or tablet because you can't hover.) Carefully check links for typos. The addresses www.bankofamerica.com, www.bankofamerca.com, and www.bankoramerica.com are not the same.

In a somewhat similar vein, be sure you're clicking on what you think you are. Often freeware sites contain ads that look like download buttons. Be sure you're clicking the right button to download the cat video that you want and not a piece of spyware.

Note that major companies and governmental agencies do not send unsolicited emails asking you to send them sensitive information. Normally they will send you postal mail or ask you to visit their website directly.

If you have any doubt, visit the company's website rather than clicking a suspicious link. Or call their customer support service and ask if the email or message is legitimate.

Most large companies have a fraud department that you can contact if a message seems sketchy, and many have an email address where you can forward suspicious emails. Search online for "<company name> report phishing" to find the appropriate address.

Note that phishing is attempting to trick you into taking some action that you shouldn't. It doesn't always try to steal your banking information; it could be something less malicious like trying to trick you into reading an advertisement. However, that's still malware and you should treat it as you would any other phishing attack. If the subject is "Your AppleID has been locked" but it contains a link to a shopping website, it's still phishing and you shouldn't feel guilty about reporting it. In fact, the only way to really know whether the link is legit is to click it. Then if it's malicious, you'll find out the painful way.

And never pay anyone you don't know in cryptocurrency or gift cards! What kind of company only accepts payment in gift cards?

SOCIAL ENGINEERING ATTACKS

Social engineering is the science of manipulating people into taking specific actions or giving you information when they should not. For example, phishing attacks use social engineering to trick you into clicking a link, opening an attachment, or responding to a text message. Advertisers, salespeople, politicians, and others also use social engineering to encourage you to buy, or at least look at, their products.

The following list summarizes a few of the techniques that are often used with social engineering attacks.

➤ Authority—The message spoofs an important authority such as a governmental agency, a bank, or the police. (The FBI has started an investigation into your online activities! You must contact the IRS at the following link to avoid legal action.)

➤ Intimidation—There will be dire consequences if you don't comply. (You will go to jail. We will garnish your wages. We will send the naughty photos we found on your system to the friends and family in your address book.)

➤ Consensus—Other people (particularly friends and admired celebrities) are doing it, so you should too. (All of your friends are using our product. Hugh Jackman is using our product too.)

➤ Urgency—There's a reason for you to take immediate action before you have time to think about it. (Only three remaining! For a limited time only! Call now or face legal action! It must be urgent with all these exclamation marks!!!)

➤ Trust—The message tries to convince you that it is trustworthy, sometimes by casting suspicion on others. (Newly discovered. The secret doctors don't want you to know about. Believe me. The truth that others won't share.)

To defend against social engineering attacks, first learn the signs. If an email, website, politician, or car salesperson is pressuring you to decide *now*, then there's probably a good reason for you to walk away and think about it. If the deal is legit, then it will still be a good deal tomorrow.

If the deal really is only available for a limited time (like during a New Year's Day sale), then something similar will probably come around again later (perhaps for the Presidents' Day sale).

If the message says "trust me," ask yourself why you should. For that matter, ask why the message needs to tell you to trust it. Trustworthy people don't normally say they are trustworthy. Trust should be earned, not given to the first liar who walks up and asks for it.

Here are a few other signs that an email, text, postal letter, or other communication might be a socially engineered attack.

➤ Spelling errors (particularly if the company's name is spelled incorrectly), punctuation errors (including lots of exclamation marks!!!), and WEIRD CAPITALIZATION.

➤ Using foreign or accented characters in place of normàl chàràcters. (They're not being cool; they're trying to evade spam blockers.)

➤ Using look-alike letters such as an uppercase *I* in place of lowercase *L*—for example in AppleID instead of AppleID. (Again, to avoid spam blockers.)

➤ Much or all of the message is an image instead of text. (Yet again, to avoid spam blockers.)

➤ The message is littered with nonprinting characters that you may be able to see if you copy and paste the message into an editor that shows invisible characters. (How many ways will these guys invent to hide from spam blockers?)

➤ Calling you by the wrong name (as in Edward when your real name is Edwin and you always go by Ed) or not using a name at all (as in "Dear Customer").

➤ Claiming to be from a company with which you do not regularly do business.

➤ Too good to be true.

➤ You're in the Bcc field not the To field. (So they can spam the email to many people at once.)

➤ There are many recipients. ("Your account is suspended" sent in a mass email by an attacker too dumb to know about the Bcc field.)

➤ Includes "do not reply" instructions and gives you some other method for contacting them such as a phone number.

➤ Includes "do not forward" or "do not share" instructions. ("Do not forward this to law enforcement or we will destroy your credit rating.")

- ➤ Email address is from a generic mail provider like yahoo.com rather than from the company.

- ➤ Very long email addresses or links, which may be truncated so you don't notice that the link ends in hackerspot.cn.

- ➤ Links that are shortened by a service such as TinyURL, Bitly, or BL.INK so you don't know where the links go.

- ➤ The email or website contains large empty spaces and sometimes if you click and drag across those areas you can find hidden text—for example, white text on a white background. (To fool email scanners and search engines into thinking the message contains that text, possibly as keywords, even though you cannot see it.)

- ➤ Fails the *smell test*. (It has a generally phishy smell.)

If you run a legitimate email through these tests, you may raise one or two alarms, but if you run a social engineering attack through these, you'll usually find a dozen or more warning signs.

Once you know what to look for, social engineering is usually easy to spot and avoid. The harder someone pushes the social engineering buttons, the harder you should resist.

As is the case with phishing, this is a topic for user training that you can add to your high-level design. It shouldn't take too long to explain the basics to most users. You probably won't make your users 100 percent safe, but you can reduce the number of people who get caught up in fake bail, account suspension, and package delivery scams.

CRAPWARE

Together adware and other spyware that is installed on a new computer is sometimes called *crapware*, *bloatware*, or *junkware*. These programs serve ads (*malvertising*), return marketing information to companies, provide free trials, and nag you constantly to upgrade (*nagware*).

The companies that write these programs pay hardware vendors to install them, and the hardware companies generally do so because their profit margins are razor thin. (Except for Apple, who's been doing just fine since they started printing money.)

These programs are not generally malicious, so it may be a little unfair to call them malware. However, as any true *Firefly* fan knows, "mal" is Latin for "bad." These are definitely bad, so I'm happy to include them in the malware family.

Even though they may not be malicious, they may be harmful. Sometimes these sorts of programs put a noticeable load on the system's CPU, disk drives, or network connection.

Unfortunately, it can be hard to remove these programs. Sometimes you can simply uninstall them, but to do that you need to know they are there, and they often have confusing names so it's hard to know if they are safe to remove. Some of these programs will even reinstall themselves if you don't remove them completely. Some of the crapware currently shipping with Windows installs itself for each user separately unless you remove it completely from the system.

You can find automated crapware removal programs online, but be sure to find one that you trust. As with phishing links and websites, be sure you're installing a useful tool and not even more spyware or a virus.

In extreme cases, you may want to reformat your hard drive and reinstall the operating system from scratch. That will get rid of any crapware, although it can be a confusing and time-consuming process. (However, I know people who think rebuilding the operating system once a year is a character-building exercise.)

If your project includes specifying the hardware and operating system, then your high-level design should discuss whether and how you will remove crapware to improve system performance.

PASSWORD ATTACKS

Many applications rely exclusively on password security, but users and development teams often don't really understand all of the issues. Picking a good password and making the system manage passwords properly can be difficult. In fact, improper password management may do more harm than good.

It is often assumed that password expiration is a good idea because it means an attacker who somehow gets hold of a password cannot use it forever. That's true to an extent, but it may not provide as much protection as you might wish. If you force users to reset passwords too often, they will pick passwords that are easier to remember and therefore easier for hackers to guess. One estimate shows as many as 83 percent of Americans use weak passwords. (If you want some scary tales to tell over the campfire, search the Internet for "scary password statistics.")

A fast computer could run through a dictionary of the 1,000 most commonly used passwords (the top three worldwide are 123456, 123456789, and 12345), the 5,000 most common English words, dates for the last 50 years (such as birthdates and anniversaries), and combinations of all of those in only a few seconds. If you force users to pick passwords that are easy to remember, they'll be easy to crack.

An attacker who manages to break even a single account may be able to download your company password database and then attack it at leisure. If the database holds a few hundred passwords, then it would be downright shocking if the attacker couldn't guess dozens of them in a matter of minutes.

To make matters worse, an attacker is likely to immediately use a newly discovered password to install viruses, Trojan horses, backdoors, and other malware, so changing the password 30 days later may not help. For example, the attacker might install a keystroke logger that records every key press on the computer and sends them to the attacker. Even if you change your password a few minutes later, the attacker can see the new password.

These problems are so pervasive that some security experts argue against password expiration entirely, reasoning that a permanent, well-chosen password is better than a rotating collection of weak passwords.

Yet another problem with passwords is that people may reuse passwords for multiple applications, a problem that is impossible to detect. Your frequent flyer program can stop you from using the password OhMyGiddyAunt this month because you used it two months ago, but it cannot tell if your new password (OhMyGiddyUncle) is also the one you use for your gym membership.

If any of those systems is compromised, then another system that uses the same password will be ripe for the plucking. For example, if an attacker breaks into your gym's password database (the gym owner can bench press twice his weight, but he's no cybersecurity guru), your frequent flyer account could be at risk. (This kind of attack where you try using passwords broken from one application to attack another is called *password stuffing* or *credential stuffing*.)

The following list summarizes a few approaches that you can use to make passwords more secure.

➤ Password managers—A *password manager* is a program that stores passwords for other programs. You use a well-chosen (hard to guess) password to get into the manager, and then it gives you access to the other passwords. Because you don't need to remember the other passwords, they can be hard-to-guess gibberish like 4nLD:,1gAol$!. Many browsers have password managers built in, so you don't need to type usernames and passwords on every site you visit. Some sites will even suggest hard-to-guess passwords, so you don't even need to think up your own. Unfortunately, if you leave your computer unguarded, someone might be able to use your browser to enter those systems or retrieve passwords from the manager.

➤ Dongles—A *dongle* (or *password dongle*) is a small device that plugs into your computer (probably through a USB port) so your program can verify that the device is present. This guarantees that you have the dongle with you when you log in, so it makes it much harder for an attacker to break into your system over the Internet. (This is the same reason you need to enter the security code for credit card purchases. It verifies that you have the credit card with you and didn't just steal the number from a database.) Unfortunately, users may leave the dongle plugged in or at least store it with the computer, so it may not help as much with local security. (It would be like leaving your keys above the sun visor in your car, which happens a lot, at least in movies.)

➤ Multifactor authentication—In *multifactor authentication (MFA)*, you use two different media to prove who you are. Probably the most common form of MFA is *two-factor authentication (2FA)*, where you provide a username and password to tell the application who you claim to be. The application then sends you a code via text or audio message, and you enter that code to prove that you have your phone handy. This is a lot like a password dongle except you are far less likely to leave your phone near your computer while you're not there. (Because who can live for even a few minutes without a phone these days?)

➤ Biometric security—In *biometric security*, fingerprint recognition, retina scan, facial recognition, voice recognition, and more let the computer identify you physically. These are also a bit like a dongle in the sense that they require a physical object to be present. In this case, that object is you, so the object is guaranteed to be present if and only if you're there. (Except in movies like *Mission Impossible*, *National Treasure*, and *Demolition Man* where characters defeat biometrics in clever and/or gruesome ways. If that level of attack is likely in your business, then you should probably talk to your chief security officer at MI6, the CIA, or wherever you work.) Meanwhile, in the real world, there have been a few cases of people stealing biometric databases or hacking biometric devices. (Search online for "hacking biometrics.") For now, it seems that biometrics are reasonably secure, but that may change over time as hackers become more resourceful.

In his 2019 blog post "Your Pa$$word doesn't matter," Microsoft manager Alex Weinert says:

Your password doesn't matter, but MFA does! Based on our studies, your account is more than 99.9% less likely to be compromised if you use MFA.

You can read that post at `https://techcommunity.microsoft.com/t5/azure-active-directory-identity/your-pa-word-doesn-t-matter/ba-p/731984`. It's worth the read and provides more details about some of the material that's covered in this section.

MFA is somewhat annoying to users and can be difficult if you lose your phone or are somewhere with no cell signal, but it is much more secure than a simple password.

Note, however, that 2FA that uses text messages is vulnerable to some kinds of attacks, including SIM swapping. It's much better than nothing, but if you're guarding biological weapons or nuclear launch codes (and who isn't?), then you should do a little more research and consider an authenticator app or a dongle.

> **LANDLOCKED** *My good friend and technical editor John Mueller reminds me that not everyone has access to cellphone service at all times. Telephone companies often don't build cell towers in rural areas where there aren't enough people to justify the expense. That's why John has a good old-fashioned landline, and that's why he cannot use text messages for MFA.*
>
> *Some systems allow you to perform MFA via an audio message that can be sent on a landline, but other systems are pretty much useless without a cellular network.*
>
> *Unless you know that all of your users have reliable cell service, you should consider other MFA media such as audio messages, emails, or <shudder> speaking to an actual human on the phone.*

Figure 8.1 shows a 2FA conversation graphically. First, I contact the application saying, "Hi, it's me, Rod." The applications replies, "Prove it! What number am I thinking of?" and sends me a text, computer-generated audio message, or email telling me the number. I respond with, "314159265," and the application either grants me access or denies my login request.

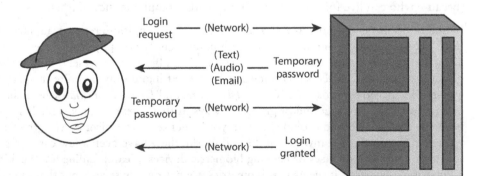

FIGURE 8.1: MFA is a conversation between a user and an application.

All of these defensive measures are *perimeter security* approaches where you try to prevent the attacker from gaining access to your application (and network) in the first place. This kind of security is essential because even a few seconds on a network may be long enough for an attacker to completely compromise your system. Your high-level design should specify what password procedures you will use and should indicate any other methods that you will use, such as 2FA or biometrics.

USER ACCESS

Many databases allow you to restrict the kinds of data that particular users can view. For example, a user might be able to view some database tables and not others, or even certain columns within a table. Some databases can also allow you to grant access to a report or stored procedure that can gather data, possibly from multiple tables, without giving the user access to those tables.

In the high-level design, identify the different kinds of users, figure out what pieces of data they will need to do their jobs, and limit access to only those necessary pieces of data. That will help prevent users from intentionally abusing the data. It may also help stop the program from accidentally damaging data that it should not have been accessing.

Start with minimal access and then expand it if necessary. If possible, use stored procedures to restrict the kinds of access a user can perform. For example, if a user needs a report that includes fields from several tables, a stored procedure may be able to provide the report without giving unrestricted access to those tables.

COUNTERMEASURES

In a perfect world, perimeter security would be sufficient. (Actually, in a *perfect* world, we wouldn't even need security, but here we are.) Unfortunately, mistakes are likely to happen sooner or later and eventually someone will click a dangerous link or open the wrong attachment and let an attacker into your system. In that case, you need to have countermeasures in place so you can minimize the damage.

Two of the main risks in an attack are that your data may be destroyed (or encrypted in a ransomware attack) or that it may be released to the wrong people.

Good backups can make it much easier to survive a basic ransomware attack or destructive virus. You simply fix your security breach and restore your backups. Unfortunately, attackers know that you'll do that, so some ransomware programs also search for backups and either destroy or encrypt them too.

One approach to make it harder on the attacker is the *3-2-1 backup strategy*. You keep three copies of your data (two backups plus the copy that's in use) on two types of media (like a hard drive and a tape drive) with one copy off-site in case the other copy is destroyed by a virus, a volcanic eruption, or alien invaders. There are also other variations such as 3-2-2 where you keep both backup copies off-site. (The cloud is a reasonable choice for one of the off-site locations.)

These backup strategies also help protect you against nonmalicious accidents like losing a laptop, a hard drive failure, someone accidentally deleting your entire code base, or someone putting Jiffy Pop in the breakroom microwave and starting a fire that destroys your data center.

Unfortunately, backups can't prevent the second part of a double extortion attack where sensitive data may be released into the wild. If you have privileged data that must be kept confidential, you should consider a cryptographically secure database for all copies of the data, even the copy that's in use. If your application includes a user access policy (described in the preceding section) and a hacker breaks in, the damage will hopefully be minimized.

In addition to forming an effective password policy, using extra sign-in measures such as MFA, training the users, and performing regular backups, there are some other standard steps that you can take to add more layers to your security. You can buy many of these in *commercial off-the-shelf (COTS)* security suites that include some or all of the following:

➤ Firewall—This monitors incoming and outgoing network traffic. It may enforce security rules such as not allowing attachments from untrusted sources, and it may scan attachments for spam and suspected viruses.

➤ Antivirus software—This is a program that looks for and removes installed malware. It may also scan emails and downloads and may periodically scan every file (or at least user files) on the system.

➤ Anti-spyware—These programs are similar to antivirus software except they look for spyware.

It is important to keep these programs up-to-date because new threats appear constantly. An antivirus program uses a database that holds code patterns called signatures so the program can identify viruses. If you don't keep the database current, then you're vulnerable to the newest crop of malware.

CYBER INSURANCE

As a final defense against ransomware and other cyberattacks, some companies now offer *cyber insurance* that covers damages related to cyberattacks. Covered expenses may include legal counsel, forensics (to figure out what happened and why), losses due to fraudulent transactions, and reparations to customers.

In some cases, an insurer may even cover ransomware payments. Paying ransom is frowned upon by law enforcement, cybersecurity professionals, and just about everyone else (except the hackers) because it not only encourages the hackers to attack again, but it also helps finance their future efforts. Still, an insurance company may decide that it's cheaper to pay the ransom than to repair the damage.

After an attack, an insurance company may help perform the recovery so you can get your business back up and running as quickly as possible. Before an attack, the company may also be able to recommend ways to improve your cybersecurity to minimize *their* exposure as well as yours. In fact, an insurer may require you to upgrade your security before they will sell you a policy, and that's not necessarily a bad thing. (A cybersecurity firm can help you upgrade your security too, without the insurance part.)

Unfortunately, cyber insurance can't cover everything. If you lose important proprietary data, it's gone. Good backups can help, but if your data is released into the wild, your competitors may get hold of it. Insurance also cannot prevent you from losing customers who think you're not handling their data securely.

In more extreme examples, experiments have shown that, under the right circumstances, hackers may be able to take over devices that can cause extreme damage and even kill such as cars, airplanes, and pacemakers. So far this hasn't happened (probably because there's no money in it), but the chance for extreme damage is there.

Insurers also sometimes play their favorite game: That's-Not-Covered. In 2017, the NotPetya ransomware virus slammed major organizations around the world costing billions in lost revenue and restoration costs. This should have been a no-brainer payout, but some insurers claimed it wasn't covered because NotPetya was linked to the Russian military and therefore the attack was an "act of war."

Take a look at cyber insurance, particularly if your project will handle valuable or sensitive data, or if the downtime caused by a breach would severely disrupt your business. Insurance itself won't prevent attacks, but it may help you get back in business more quickly if one happens.

SUMMARY

Security is critical in modern software engineering. To build the most secure application possible, you should apply shift-left security principles and write security into the earliest design stages.

Physical and cyber defenses both come in layers, and you should build many layers into your high-level design if you want to prevent catastrophic damage. Start with outer defenses to prevent attacks from succeeding, add inner defenses to minimize damage, and finish with a recovery plan and possibly insurance to handle the aftermath.

Start with an outer layer of network and operating system security tools such as firewalls, spam filters, fraudulent website blockers, anti-malware software, anti-phishing tools, and virus detectors. Look for suites of security tools that cover all of these.

Don't forget physical security. Educate users on picking good passwords and make sure they aren't written down near the computer. Add MFA or biometrics if you can.

Most successful attacks start with a user, so expand user education. Teach users how to recognize phishing and spoofing attacks and tell them to never open unexpected attachments or click suspicious links. Your anti-malware software should catch those, but some may slip through, particularly new variations that the security software hasn't seen yet.

Train users to recognize the signs of social engineering, phishing, and spoofing. Users are often a hacker's first line of attack, so they need to be your first line of defense.

Make sure users know not to reuse passwords on multiple systems and explain why. If a user's password for a sudoku game is broken, *your* system may be at risk.

Add plans to handle attacks when they occur. Create a backup schedule and store copies of data in separate secure locations. Write a plan for how you would restore service if all of your data is lost. Identify crucial pieces of information that should be encrypted and given extra protection.

Finally, consider using a cybersecurity and/or cyber insurance company to help you evaluate and improve your security, to protect you from financial damage if an attack occurs, and to restore service as quickly as possible.

You may not need every one of these lines of defense. If your small pet shop loses last year's sales data, you can reinstall the operating system, restore your backups, and be back selling dog treats and kitty litter in no time. However, if you're a credit card company storing financial data for millions of customers, you should use every trick in the book.

When you're finished and have all of your security safeguards in place, don't just sit back and relax. Hackers are constantly trying to improve their methods for invading your system, so you need to continue to keep your security software up-to-date. You must remain vigilant in the software security arms race. As Bruce Schneier said, "Security is not a product, but a process."

This chapter spends extra time on security design because it's such an important topic. The next chapter also focuses on an extremely important topic: user experience design. Most applications require some sort of user interface, and its design can make using your application an easy, productive experience or a never-ending marathon of frustration.

EXERCISES

1. What does the CIA triad stand for?

2. Briefly define the following terms:

    ➤ Shift-left security
    ➤ DevOps
    ➤ DevSecOps

3. Briefly define the following terms:

    ➤ Virus
    ➤ Trojan
    ➤ Worm
    ➤ FakeApp
    ➤ Logic bomb
    ➤ Time bomb
    ➤ Ransomware
    ➤ Double extortion scheme
    ➤ Spyware
    ➤ Crapware
    ➤ Rootkit
    ➤ DoS, DDoS
    ➤ Bot, botnet

- ➤ Zero-day
- ➤ Exploit, sploit
- ➤ Phishing
- ➤ Spoofing
- ➤ Formjacking
- ➤ Man-in-the-middle (MITM)
- ➤ Insider threat
- ➤ SQL injection

4. Briefly explain these kinds of phishing:

- ➤ Spear phishing
- ➤ Whaling
- ➤ Vishing
- ➤ Smishing
- ➤ Angler phishing

5. How many signs of phishing can you spot in the following email that I actually received? Does this email use spoofing?

Gerard Blunt <judeatuXXX@gmail.com>

Thu XXX

Bcc: XXX

Congratulations,

This is MoneyGram International Inc. branch London - United Kingdom and we are contacting you concerning your winning fund $1,500,000.00 dollars. Your e-mail address has won the sum of $1,500,000.00 USD dollars through Internet contest, Lottery bonus under MoneyGram International branch London.

We have concluded the arrangement that you will receive your winning fund from the Head Office, which you suppose to contact the agent of MoneyGram International London UK. Mr. Webster Michael.

Contact Mr. Webster Michael for more details.

Branch Email: (moneygramXXX@gmail.com)

Regards,

Mr. Gerard Blunt.

Supervisor MoneyGram Branch London-UK.

6. How many signs of phishing can you spot in the following email? (Yes, I received this one, too.) What signs of social engineering can you spot?

Hello Valuable Customer,

Your annual membership for NORTON SECURITY has been successfully renewed & restored.

*The debited sum will be reflected within next 24 to 48 hrs on your account record. *

*__PRODUCT INFORMATION_*

Invoice No.	:	#HGBN85421#
Product Name	:	NORTON SECURITY
Expiration Date	:	2 Years from the Date of Purchase
Amount	:	$198.29 USD
Payment Method	:	AUTO CHARGE

* If you wish to claim a REFUND then please feel free to Contact our Billing Department as soon as Possible.*

You can Reach us on - +1 (818 / 660 / 0770)

Barry Jones

7. Explain the 3-2-1 and 3-2-2 backup strategies.

8. What are the advantages and disadvantages of the 3-2-2 backup strategy versus the 3-2-1 strategy?

9. Why do the 3-2-1 and 3-2-2 strategies have a 2 in the middle? Would 3-1-1 or 3-1-2 be just as good?

WHAT YOU LEARNED IN THIS CHAPTER

➤ The CIA triad consists of confidentiality, integrity, and availability.

➤ Good security requires a layered approach covering physical, remote, portable, network, operating system, application, data, and possibly cloud layers.

➤ Shift-left security and DevSecOps build security into the application during the earliest phases.

➤ Malware comes in a wide variety of forms such as viruses, Trojans, and worms.

➤ The user is the hacker's first line of attack, so educating the user should be your first line of defense.

➤ Malware is often delivered by a phishing email or fake website that tries to convince you to download and execute an infected file or click a dangerous link.

➤ Social engineering uses psychological techniques to try to trick you into delivering information or taking action when you shouldn't. It is used by phishing emails, phone or text messages, advertisers, politicians, and more.

➤ Passwords alone aren't very secure, particularly if they are weak, users leave them near their computers, or users reuse them for different applications. You can make passwords stronger by educating users and by adding a password manager, dongle, MFA, 2FA, or biometric security.

➤ Software that you can use to help avoid attacks includes firewall, antivirus, and anti-spyware tools. Other actions you can take to protect yourself include cyber insurance and a security audit by a cybersecurity company.

➤ You must keep your cybersecurity software up-to-date to protect against new threats.

User Experience Design

A user interface is like a joke. If you have to explain it, it's not that good.

—*Martin LeBlanc*

Perfection is achieved not when there is nothing more to add, but when there is nothing left to take away.

—*Antoine de Saint-Exupéry*

What You Will Learn in This Chapter:

➤ Finding a good design mindset

➤ Designing for users of different skill levels

➤ Using metaphors and idioms

➤ Providing Undo and Redo to allow safe exploration

➤ Avoiding dialogs and other features that interrupt the user's flow

A software application is a tool that helps users get things done, just as a hammer helps a carpenter drive nails or a set of lock picks helps a burglar. Unless you're writing some sort of entertainment program like a game or a newsfeed, users don't pull up your application just to pass the time. A data entry clerk uses your program to enter data, not to practice typing. A store manager uses an inventory control system to order more beans and socks, not to email cat videos. An insurance adjuster uses a claim system to deny claims, not to send text messages to friends.

When you spend months programming, elbows deep in the code, it's easy to forget that a software project is a means to an end, not an end in itself.

Ideally a user interface should be like a movie soundtrack: there to support the action but barely noticeable. Unfortunately, most software developers are programmers rather than user experience specialists, so the program often intrudes into the user's consciousness and becomes a main character rather than playing a supporting role. Instead of entering data or monitoring inventory, the user is stuck babysitting a whiny program that can't figure out that pressing the Print button means it should print something. (I wish I was exaggerating, but I use one program where, to print a check that's already queued up for printing, I need to click New ⇨ Print Checks, set some parameters, click Preview And Print, click Print, click the printer icon, and finally click Print.)

User interface and user experience design are enormous topics, so they won't fit completely in this chapter. The Internet is strewn with user interface books, videos, and courses, and I encourage you to examine a few in your spare time.

Meanwhile, this chapter describes some key user interface issues and provides some guidance to hopefully point you in the right direction.

This chapter is divided into three parts. The first part describes some of the overarching goals of user interface design and talks about good design motivation and mindset. The second part explains more specific design guidelines that can help you make your interfaces more usable. The final part of the chapter talks about form design. Sadly, the last part is what many programmers think of as user interface design.

DESIGN MINDSET

When you build a user interface and user experience, you need to handle myriad nitpicky little details. There are many lists of rules and guidelines to help you figure out how to display and arrange things (and the later part of this chapter does that), but it also helps to have the right mindset while you're designing the interface. The following sections discuss general concepts that you should keep in mind as you design the program's interface. They're a little fuzzier than simple rules like "All labels should line up on the left," but they provide an important backdrop for interface design and will help you in more ambiguous situations and when more concrete guidance fails.

UI vs. UX

An application's *user interface*, or *UI*, comprises all of the things that the user sees and does with the application. It includes the forms, dialogs, buttons, menus, scroll bars, graphs, and charts. It includes interactions between the user and the application such as the way the user prints a report, schedules a delivery, or changes the main form's background color to match today's outfit.

The application's *user experience*, or *UX*, includes the user's whole perception of the application and its "brand." It includes the UI but also includes surrounding interactions such as installation and upgrade procedures, reliability, the locations where data files are stored, the database, and connectivity to other applications. The form that lets you check an order's status is part of the UI; the fact that the database is unavailable every day from 1 a.m. to 3 a.m. for maintenance is part of the UX.

Some developers go to great lengths to prove that the UX is larger than the UI, but it seems pretty obvious to me. I suppose you could focus solely on the artistic merits of a form's control layout, but unless you also think about how the interface affects the user, you're not working toward the best possible application. Your website may have the prettiest background images, but if the menu structure is confusing and the search feature can't find anything, it's not a great design.

For those reasons, I prefer to focus on UX and not worry too much about the difference. (*UX* also contains an *X*, so it sounds cooler.)

UX Designers

Before we get too deeply into UX design, it's worth asking why it should be a separate step. As I mentioned earlier, it's easy to get caught up in programming and forget that the end goal is to help the user get something done. The goal isn't to write elegant code, use clever optimization techniques, and minimize disk usage. Those may be necessary for a successful application, but they're not what the user experiences (unless things go really wrong—for example, if the program takes hours to perform simple calculations or hogs the entire disk, then the user will notice).

The reason to make UX a separate part of the design is so you can isolate it from the programming.

Users are generally not programmers, so they don't think the way programmers do and vice versa. Many programmers have spent years training their minds to work a certain way, and users do not necessarily think that way. Programmers are comfortable with concepts like hierarchical data, recursion, and asynchronous operations, but many nontechnical users are not, so it would be a mistake to include those features as part of the UX in most applications.

Programming languages and environments also include all sorts of gizmos that are useful for programmers but that make terrible user interfaces. For example, in most programming languages, you can display a dialog box or write text to a log window with a single line of code. That's very useful during development so programmers can track what the program is doing, but it's generally not a good user interface technique. Displaying a dialog breaks the users' concentration and dumps them out of their mental flow state, wasting their time and then wasting more time as they get back into the Zen of their work. It's as if the hammer interrupted you in mid swing to ask, "Are you sure you want to hit that nail? Yes/No/Cancel."

Just presenting that dialog breaks your concentration, but to make matters worse, it's not immediately clear what all of the options mean. Yes and No are pretty clear, but what does Cancel mean? It's not hard to realize that Cancel probably means, "No, don't hit the nail," but why are there two choices that mean the same thing? Is one subtly different? And why is the hammer even asking? I swung the hammer, so I probably want to hit the nail. All of these thoughts are minor, but they pull you farther away from the task at hand and make it harder to get back in the swing of things. (So to speak.)

The more you can separate UX design and programming, the better. The user experience should be user-centered. What the user needs. What the user wants. It should not be about the code, what's easy for the programmer, or what gives efficient disk usage.

In larger projects, you might have dedicated UX designers who specialize in user interfaces and human/computer interaction. (Those people may have exotic titles such as human factors engineer, ergonomist, usability designer, UX practitioner, and so forth.) During the design phases, everyone on the team should work together to understand the users' needs, but then UX design should occur separately from software design. Ideally a UX designer should be technically savvy enough to understand what is possible but need not necessarily know the details of how to build the user interface.

If your project is too small to include separate UX designers (and most projects are), it may help to do as much of the UX design as possible before you start on the programming design. You may need to sketch in a few programming details like the hardware platform and network environment, but the more programming decisions you make ahead of time, the greater the chances that the UX design will be influenced by those decisions, which, to be clear, is bad. The users' experience should not depend on the data structures you use or what is easy in your programming language.

LESSONS FROM WPF?

When Microsoft released *Windows Presentation Foundation (WPF)* in 2006, one of its main selling points was that it allowed UI designers and programmers to work independently. It was a great idea: Designers could build the user interface and programmers could hook up the code behind the interface later. (The code behind the interface is now called *code-behind* or *codebehind*.)

Unfortunately, WPF suffered from three big problems. First, WPF and its designers were slow. The new designers take much longer to load and are slower to work with than the old Windows Forms designers. Sadly, that problem has not gone away and is embedded in the Visual Studio environment.

Second, the UI and code are not as separate as you might like. You can design WPF windows separately, but you can't really test user interactions without at least some code behind the buttons. Conversely, you can't easily test the code without a user interface to launch it. That means you need to build a test user interface anyway, so why have two?

Finally, and most importantly, Microsoft may have specialized UI designers on staff, but most companies don't. Most user interfaces are designed by the same programmers writing the code, so the UI is cluttered with things that serve the code rather than the user.

Separating the UI and codebehind is a great idea and you should do that as much as possible, but WPF won't automatically do it for you. Now if you search online for WPF, some of the top results you get are "What is replacing WPF?" "Is Microsoft still supporting WPF?" and "Is WPF end of life?"

Platform

There are a couple of dimensions that can greatly influence UX. One of the biggest is hardware platform. The UI techniques that work well on a desktop system often work badly on a phone and vice versa. For example, you can easily use a toolbox containing a few dozen tools on a desktop system, but those same tools would completely cover a phone's surface. Or you can use a two-finger pinch on a phone to zoom out on a map, but that won't work on a laptop without a touch screen.

Before you start your UX design, you'll need to decide on a hardware platform. Will you support desktops, laptops, tablets, phones, or IoT devices?

From the user's point of view (and that's all that matters to UX design), there are two main issues: size and pointing device.

Device size determines what you can fit on the screen at one time. A large desktop or laptop system can display many windows, toolbars, browsers, and other applications at the same time. Phones and smaller tablets can often display only one application at a time and possibly only part of the application. A desktop system might use a relatively complicated menu system or a large form containing buttons to allow navigation. A phone app might provide a much simpler set of menus.

Pointing device determines how the user interacts with objects. For example, it's relatively easy to click and drag multiple items on a desktop with a mouse; it's harder with a finger on a phone. You might allow the user to click and drag to select the objects in a region on a desktop. In contrast, on a phone you might let the user select objects by checking boxes next to them.

The pointing device also determines how precisely the user can interact with objects. Picking out a small area on a phone with a finger can be tricky, enough so that it's easy to press the wrong key on the tiny onscreen keyboard. In contrast, it's fairly easy to hit a target only a few pixels wide with a mouse. With a pen on a tablet, it's even faster to pick out a small target and you can move the pen more precisely. To see the difference, try signing your name with a mouse, pen, or fingertip. You'll probably find the pen best, the fingertip acceptable, and the mouse awkward and frustrating.

The ways that you measure complexity also differ on different hardware. For example, in a desktop application, you might count the number of *steps* (clicks, click and drags, keyboard shortcuts) that you need to reach a certain feature. In a phone or tablet app, you could count *taps*.

You may also need to decide on the size of the particular device. Tablets and phones come in a large variety of shapes, sizes, and resolutions, and the differences may determine what the users can do with your program.

The following list shows some of the key questions you should ask about a hardware platform.

➤ What kind of pointing device does the platform have? Mouse, pen, finger, trackball, none, telepathy?

➤ How large is the device? How much can you display at one time? Can you present multiple windows at once, or do you need to make the user move from window to window to get the job done?

➤ How does the device perform? Does it have enough CPU power, memory, disk space, and network speed to support a good user experience?

➤ Will the device use peripherals? Will users store work on flash drives? On a network? In the cloud? Will there be printers, scanners, tape drives, USB foam missile launchers?

If possible, resist the urge to write an application that can run seamlessly on multiple hardware platforms. Some programming tools make it easier to run programs on an assortment of platforms, but they're often not seamless and you may need to perform a lot of customization to get a really good result. Even if a tool can automatically squeeze your desktop application onto a phone, the result may be unusable. Conversely, a phone-style app expanded to fill a desktop is just cringeworthy. By trying to make a one-size-fits-all app, you may end up with one-size-fits-none.

Instead focus on a single platform initially. Then when you're wildly successful and rolling in cash, you can expand to support other devices. It's better to do a good job on one platform than a poor one on many.

A browser may be a particularly tempting target for some applications. By building your project on the web, you allow users to run it through a browser, potentially running on any hardware platform. This is a great idea, but even it has some drawbacks.

If the user's hardware is slow, your application may take the blame. Try to keep your program light and responsive to avoid this problem.

All browsers display some items such as text and images in about the same way, but they may provide different features to support more complicated applications. If you're building a plain vanilla website, this may not be an issue. If you're building a more advanced site with the latest WPF, Java, multimedia players, and other doodads, then users may have different experiences on different browsers.

While you can run a browser on a phone, many websites just don't work at the smaller scale without some major redesign.

Rather than trying to support every possible browser on every possible device, focus on just one initially. Say that results are not guaranteed on other browsers, and you'll add support for more browsers later.

Most of the rest of this chapter focuses on desktop or laptop applications, partly because those are the oldest platforms and because they offer the most options. You'll need to translate some of the information for newer devices such as tablets and phones.

Even if you're focusing on large-format systems, it's still worth thinking at least a little bit about phones. One of the main goals of UX design is to make using an application easy, and smaller devices such as phones often highlight ways where certain designs either fail or excel. For example, reducing the complexity of an app so it's usable on a phone may lead to ways that you can simplify a similar app for the desktop.

As you work with applications in your day-to-day life, think about what lessons they teach. What's hard and what's easy? How could you use one app's techniques to improve another app? Is an app designed to take advantage of the special features of its platform? Or is it just a copy of a program that runs on a different device?

User Skill Level

The application's platform heavily influences the things that are possible in a user interface. Another key factor is the target user.

Some software is written for a particular demographic. For example, pre-K educational software is written for very young users. Five-year-olds don't have the same dexterity or attention span that (most) older users have, so you need to adjust the design accordingly. Buttons need to be larger and farther apart to avoid misclicks. They should contain friendly colorful images rather than short descriptive text.

Interestingly, older users can also benefit from some of those ideas. Some older users don't see small text very well and may not have the dexterity to triple-click-and-drag to select objects.

If you have these kinds of special target audiences, study their needs and capabilities and design accordingly.

Most software, however, is aimed at users in the middle of the Goldilocks zone: not too old nor too young, with a "normal" pointing device such as a mouse or finger, and working at a desk or table and not underwater or in a combat zone.

Often the most important characteristic of "normal" users is, at least as far as UX is concerned, their skill level with the particular application. Whether the users are beginners, intermediate, or advanced affects how much information you can assume the users will know and how much you should pack onto the UI.

One other important factor that influences user skill (before I get to the point) is the application's "class." Here I use the term to indicate the frequency and duration with which users interact with the app. For example, if you write a lot of text the way I do, then you probably use your favorite word processor *a lot*. I use Microsoft Word for at least a couple of hours per day every day including weekends, so I wouldn't be surprised to learn that I use it more than 1,000 hours per year. And I've been doing that for decades, so I can do a lot with Word. All of that practice has made me an expert Word user. (Either that or a charter member of the Dunning-Kruger club.)

My point (aside from bragging) is that I was a beginner for only a short while. Then, because I used the program so much, I became an intermediate/advanced user.

I call this kind of frequently used program a *first-class app*. Users spend large, uninterrupted amounts of time on first-class apps. As on planes and trains, first class also comes with extra legroom, so these apps are often maximized to cover the entire screen.

Contrast this with another application that I've been using for decades: Windows Fax and Scan. I use this program every few months to scan some document and save the result into a JPG file (or a JPEG file as that program insists on calling it). A quick look at the program's toolbar tells me that, in addition to scanning, it can create, receive, and forward faxes and forward a fax as an email. Its Welcome screen even has instructions for sending faxes without a fax machine! (Such amazing high-tech wizardry!)

I call this kind of program that is seldom used and then not deeply a *transient app*.

Even though I've been using this app for many years, I only use it for one thing: scanning. If I needed to do anything else with it, I would have to look up how. For this app, I am a perpetual beginner.

The lesson here is that, if your application is a first-class app, then almost all of your users are at the intermediate or advanced level. In particular, if you are writing custom software for a company, then your users are probably in this category.

If your application is a transient app, then your users are mostly perpetual beginners.

Think about your app's placement in the cyber ecosystem and decide whether it is likely to be a first-class or transient app. If it will be first class, target your UX for intermediate users. If your app is in the transient category, then design your UX for beginners.

Beginners and Beyond

Beginners don't know what they can do with your program and how to do it, so they need a little help. Menus and dialogs provide excellent help because they contain text that explains what the program can do. Most people can figure out the general purpose of the File menu's Save command or the Edit menu's Copy command because the text on the menus tells you what they do. You could probably even figure out what the Orders menu's Sort By Invoice Date command does, even though you've probably never seen a similar command before.

But when was the last time *you* used File ➪ Save or Edit ➪ Copy? If you're like me, you probably haven't used them in years. After only a little practice, most users realize that Ctrl+S and Ctrl+C invoke the Save and Copy commands much more quickly and easily than using the menus. (Of course, this all goes out the window, so to speak, if you're using a phone, tablet, or other device without a keyboard.)

At least as far as those two commands are concerned, you're no longer a beginner.

Intermediate users prefer to access their favorite features by using faster methods. For example, they prefer toolbar buttons like a little Save button that looks like a 3.5″ floppy disk or a little Copy button that looks like two documents overlapping.

Advanced users find even faster ways to invoke tools such as Ctrl+S and Ctrl+C. Very advanced users customize their keyboard shortcuts and toolbars (and the *Quick Access Toolbar*, or *QAT*, in Microsoft Office applications) to keep their favorite tools handy. Sometimes they even write their own tools.

All users of a first-class app want to move quickly from the beginner to intermediate category so they can work more effectively. You can help by providing multiple methods for performing the same tasks. Use menus and dialogs to help beginners. Add toolbars and shortcuts to help intermediate users.

Use the same graphics on any redundant methods wherever possible. For example, use the same 3.5″ floppy image on the Save menu item as on the Save toolbar button. Eventually the beginner will notice that the same button is present on the menu and the toolbar and make the connection.

Include shortcut hints in menu items so beginners can learn them too. The convention, in Windows at least, is to underline a character in a menu item if you can press Alt plus that character to trigger the menu item. For example, Alt+F might open the File menu.

The right side of the menu item's caption can also include a shortcut such as Ctrl+S to indicate that Ctrl+S invokes the command immediately. If a menu item opens a submenu, its label should end with an arrow (>). If a menu item displays a dialog rather than taking immediate action, its caption should end with an ellipsis (. . .).

Another excellent tool for beginners is the tooltip. A *tooltip* is a little piece of text that appears if you hover the mouse over a tool for a second or so. The nice thing about tooltips is that they appear when needed but don't clutter up the UI when they're not needed. A beginner can hover the mouse over a tool to learn what it does, but an intermediate user can leave the tooltips hidden. If the tool's icon is reasonably intuitive, then the user will later be able to remember what the tool does without a label. And a user who forgets can always bring the tooltip back.

Note that icons only need to provide a *reminder* of what the tool does; they don't need to be portrait-perfect to be useful. There's a whole generation of computer users who have never seen a 3.5″ floppy disk in real life but the icon still works to remind you of what the Save tool does.

A tooltip should be a very short piece of text, usually just a word or two, to remind the user of a tool's function. For example, the Watermark tool might display a W in a box for its icon and have a tooltip that says "Watermark." Everyone knows what a watermark is (or can look it up online), so that's sufficient. After looking at the tooltip once, it should be easy to remember what the W in a box means.

Once a user has advanced beyond the larval beginner stage, many of the bigger hints are unnecessary, so you need to ensure that they don't get in the way. Commands should be accessible via shortcuts or small tools that are arranged neatly and grouped by general theme. The user no longer needs giant, unwieldy, widely spaced buttons.

Does this mean you should build two separate interfaces, one for beginners and one for intermediate users? Probably not. Often a simple, elegant interface can provide the clues that beginners need while gently guiding them toward intermediateness. Design the UI mostly for intermediate users and then add tooltips.

If you really want to provide big, colorful buttons for beginners to poke at, it wouldn't be hard to also provide an alternative set of simpler menus and toolbars for intermediate users. It wouldn't be too difficult to provide two separate interfaces. It goes against the programmer's natural desire to avoid duplicate work, but it might provide the best user experience.

Configuration

One of the best ways to support users of all skill levels is configurability. Let users create their own menus and toolbars populated with their favorite tools. Let them remap the function keys F1 through F12 to perform their favorite actions. This not only lets users adjust the program based on their skill levels, it also lets them create different experiences based on the tasks they perform. A data entry operator will have different needs than a shipping clerk or a patent attorney.

You can also allow users to configure other things such as the size, position, and stacking order of the program's forms, dialogs, and toolboxes. You can allow the user to float windows or dock them inside or next to other windows. For example, you could let the user resize a toolbox to hold three columns of buttons and dock it to the left side of the main window.

Providing this level of configurability might be fairly hard (unless your programming environment provides controls or other tools to make it easier), but remember that UX design is about the user's needs, not what's easiest for the programmers.

You can allow users to change decorative parameters such as form colors and background images; font sizes, styles, and colors; and sound effects played when certain events occur.

You might also want to make system parameters configurable. These are things like what directory to use to search for files to process, what printer to use by default, how many days a bill must be overdue before you send a reminder email, and the website where you download the program's motivational Cat of the Day picture. If you make these customizable, then you won't have to change the program when these values change.

Before you make these too easily available, however, ask yourself whether they should vary by user or whether they should be set system-wide. Parameters that are shared by every user should be set by an administrator, not by the individual users. You can probably let the users set their default printers and favorite Cat of the Day website, but you probably shouldn't let them set the number of days for late bill reminders or the text of the remainder email.

I have three extra tips for working with configurations that are important enough to deserve their own list.

> ➤ Always save the user's settings. Few things are more annoying than spending 10 minutes laying out every screen just perfectly only to have all of those changes lost the next time you start the program.

> ➤ Save the user's changes immediately. In olden times, many programs only saved settings when the program closed. That works as long as the program never crashes, the power doesn't fail, the user's laptop doesn't overheat and crash the system, the cat doesn't step on the power bar, or a host of other problems that will crop up sooner or later. Just save any changes right away.

> ➤ Provide a Reset Configuration command to help the user recover after making too many terrible choices or in case a window gets lost. You may even want to provide a few different standard configurations that the user can select for performing different tasks.

Let the user configure the application as much as is safe for them to do so.

Hidden Configuration

In addition to obvious configuration values such as creating custom toolbars and setting the lunch menu download URL, you should consider saving hidden configuration values. These are values that are part of the application's state but that the user doesn't really think of as configuration.

Any value that the user enters is a potential hidden configuration value and may be worth saving. For example, if the user opens a dialog, selects a particular tab, picks values from a set of sliders, and then closes the dialog, you may want to remember which tab was selected and what slider values were chosen. The next time the user opens that dialog, you can restore those values to make using the dialog easier.

For a concrete example, consider File Explorer (formerly Windows Explorer). It remembers its size, view (large icons, list, details, etc.), column widths, window state (minimized, maximized, or restored), and the widths of the file path and search areas (which are adjustable with a splitter between them). If you arrange a File Explorer, close it, and then open a new one, the new one has the same general arrangement as the old one. This is an excellent use of hidden configuration, although it can be somewhat confusing if you have multiple File Explorers open that have different arrangements.

For each dialog, form, and other user interaction, ask yourself whether it would be easier for the user to start with the current values next time or whether it would be better to start from default values. Often saved values are more useful or at least no worse than defaults.

Models

A user who employs a program develops a mental model about what the program does. Because typical users don't know how software works, their models are based on the results of actions rather than on how the code actually works behind the scenes.

In contrast, a programmer's model is based on the program's implementation.

To see the difference, consider one of the most popular computer metaphors ever invented: the wastebasket (or recycle bin, trash can, dustbin, or whatever you want to call it). A typical user thinks that a deleted file is moved from its original folder into the wastebasket. Later, when you empty the wastebasket, the file is deleted permanently, perhaps broken up byte-by-byte and sold for scrap to a file recycler.

Many programmers know that the file isn't ever actually moved anywhere, much less into the wastebasket. Instead its entry in its original directory is deleted and a new entry is added to the wastebasket directory (sort of like a temporary forwarding address). When you take out the trash, the system deletes the new folder entry, so the system no longer has a way to find the file, but the actual file contents don't go anywhere. They're still sitting where they were before the file was "moved" into the wastebasket.

The file's contents remain on the disk like a squatter in a rundown part of town until the file system, in an act of electronic gentrification, evicts the squatter and reallocates some or all of the file's real estate for use by new files dealing with coffeehouses and fern bars.

> ### LOST AND FOUND
>
> Files are not physically removed from the disk; the file system just loses its ability to find them. That's why file recovery programs (and hackers) can sift through the unused parts of a disk and find pieces of the files that used to live there.
>
> File eraser programs overwrite the contents of a file before releasing its space for recycling. In fact, they may overwrite the contents thousands of times to ensure that cyber archaeologists can't reassemble pieces that aren't completely erased. For more information, search online for "data erasure" and "digital file shredder."

When you build your UX design, you should focus on user models, not implementation models. Users don't need to know how the wastebasket works because they will never need to write a wastebasket management program. They do need to know how to use the wastebasket.

You could explain the implementation model to the users, but that would confuse many of them and it wouldn't make them any better at using the wastebasket.

Study the way the user thinks about a task, not about how you will implement it. Find the most intuitive way for the user to perform the task following the user's mental model and design the user interface around it. Don't design the user interface around the implementation and then try to explain the model to the user.

Metaphors and Idioms

The typical user's mental model of the wastebasket is wrong in almost every respect except the only one that matters: it works. It does not represent the electronic reality, but it allows the user to mark a file for deletion, recover it if necessary, and then permanently remove the file from the file system.

This is a *metaphor*, a story about something that the user understands (like a physical wastebasket) that parallels some feature of a program (the way it temporarily and then permanently removes a file). A good metaphor helps the user understand what the program can do. The metaphor does not need to represent how the program *actually* works; it just needs to provide a useful parallel.

One of the grand prizes of UX design is the perfect metaphor to help users get the most out of a program. Sometimes that works, but a good metaphor isn't always necessary and sometimes metaphors can restrict you.

For example, consider a shopping metaphor where you put on your VR goggles and your avatar enters a mall. You can walk down the hall looking at the stores and peeking in their windows. If you like, you can enter a store and click on items to add them to your shopping basket. Then you can walk into a changing room where your avatar can try on your selections, and you can see what they would look like on you. (Let's assume that your avatar has your general size, shape, hair style, etc.)

That's a solid metaphor that can help almost anyone understand how to navigate the virtual mall, but it also slows you down. Why should you wander through the mall when you could just teleport to a particular store? You can't do that in a physical mall, but that doesn't mean you can't in a program.

You shouldn't need to move your avatar into a store when you could just click on a store's entry in a list. Rather than putting items in your shopping basket and then moving into a changing room for a closer look, you could just click on an item to immediately see it on your avatar.

For that matter, why do you need to browse the racks in a virtual store? You should be able to just search a list of products and then click the ones that interest you. (This is more or less how Amazon works, without your avatar trying on clothes. Many people think of Amazon as a store, but it's more like a mall selling products from a huge number of stores.)

The VR mall is a strong metaphor, but it doesn't let your program take full advantage of the computer's capabilities.

Instead of using a flawed metaphor, it's often better to use a good idiom. An *idiom* is simply something that we all agree upon even though it may not make sense if you don't know the convention. For example, most English speakers know that "It's raining cats and dogs" means it's raining very hard even though the phrase itself doesn't make much sense. (The next time you're bored out of your gourd, search online for "amusing idioms." It's the bee's knees and more fun than a barrel of monkeys!)

A software idiom is something that we agree upon even though it doesn't necessarily make sense by itself. For example, many of the icons attached to menu items and tool buttons are idiomatic. The little floppy disk on the Save command was originally a metaphor because it referred to something physical that you could use for storage. Now this symbol has become an idiom. It means Save because we agree that it does. (A picture of a modern flash drive would just be a rectangle, which wouldn't be a very informative metaphor.)

Similarly, the phone icon normally shows a twentieth century handset, not a cellphone. This is another example of a metaphor that has become an idiom. (A picture of a modern cellphone would just be another rectangle.)

Examples of idioms that aren't based on something real include an Internet button that shows a picture of a globe, a link tool showing a few links of chain, an Add Database tool that displays a cylinder with a plus sign next to it, a Text Message tool represented by a speech balloon, and a Settings button that displays a gear. Even the shapes of stop and yield signs are idiomatic.

You've probably seen some of those and many others. They all have two things in common: they don't mean much intrinsically, and once you learn what they mean, they're very easy to remember. (Although many drivers don't seem to know what stop and yield signs mean.)

A strong metaphor is useful but not essential. If you use idioms that are simple and that have memorable icons, tooltips, and other prompts, then users will learn them quickly and have no trouble using them as they move from beginners to intermediates.

Case Study: Microsoft Word

At this point it's worth taking a quick look at some of the features used by popular applications as they apply to beginners versus intermediate users. I'm going to pick on Microsoft Word, mostly because I use it for hours at a time practically every day.

DISCLAIMER

I don't want to imply that I particularly hate Microsoft in general or Word in particular. Many people (possibly you) are just very familiar with Word, and it makes an instructive example. (Also, because I can bash it as much as I want without hurting its sales, I don't need to feel guilty.)

Microsoft has dropped several of the beginner clues from recent versions of some of its programs. For example, Word no longer includes underlined characters in menus, even though Alt+F still opens the File menu. If you press Alt, a set of little boxes appears that tells you what characters to press next for different menus and commands, but you need to press Alt before you see the keys.

Word no longer displays keyboard shortcuts to the right of commands, so you need to learn about things like Ctrl+S and Ctrl+C from some other program. Those shortcuts still work; there's just no easy way for a beginner to learn them.

Word uses an ellipsis to indicate that a dialog is coming for some commands, but it omits the ellipsis for others. That violates two fundamental UI design rules: Be Consistent and No Surprises. I guess you just need to take your chances until you learn how each command behaves.

Figure 9.1 shows Microsoft Word 2010 editing an email that I copied and pasted into Word. (More recent versions of Word look similar.) The top of the figure shows Word's ribbon interface, a jumble of command buttons, check boxes, toggle buttons, and drop-down lists, all identified with verbose labels. All of this is fine for beginners who are just starting to explore. The tools are verbose, relatively large, and reasonably easy to understand, perhaps with a little experimentation.

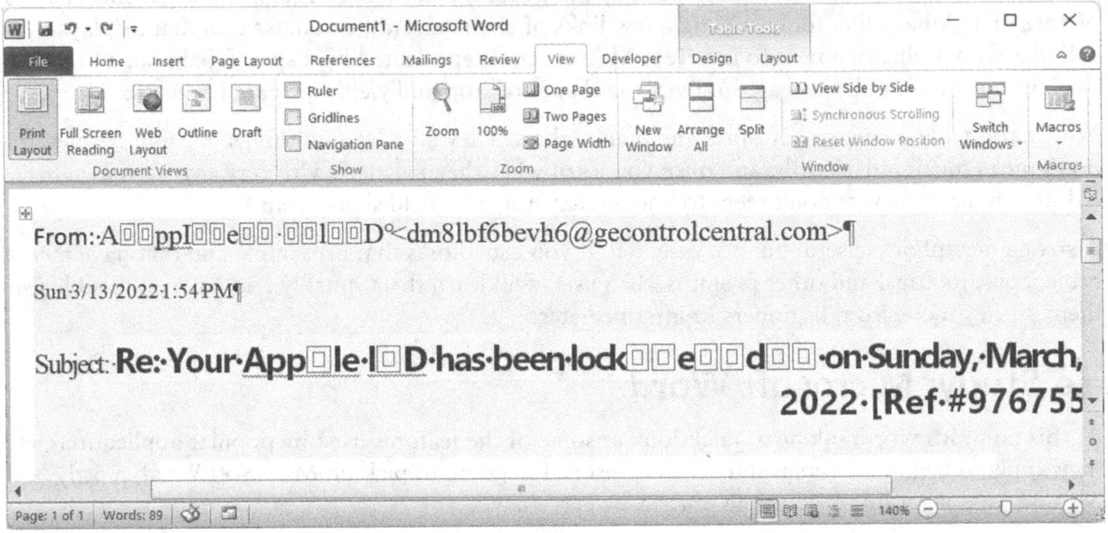

FIGURE 9.1: Word's ribbon assumes the user is an eternal beginner.

PHISHING REVISITED

If you think back to Chapter 8, "Security Design" you can see some of the symptoms that the text in Figure 9.1 is a phishing email. The message is filled with nonprinting characters, which show up as boxes in Word. (Use File ⇨ Options ⇨ Display ⇨ Show All Formatting Marks to make those characters visible.) The sender's email address is a weird string and doesn't come from Apple.com and swaps the uppercase *I* and lowercase 1 characters to make it harder for spam blockers to read the sender's name. I've also never had an Apple ID, although you can be excused for not knowing that.

However, after you've worked with Word for a while, the ribbon is just a real estate hog, taking up precious vertical space, a commodity in short supply with the landscape orientation used by most screens. If the Zoom area displayed small icons for the One Page, Two Pages, New Window, Arrange All, and Split tools, it would still be easy for an intermediate user to find and use them effectively. Small tool buttons could also be lined up nicely so it would be easier to scan for a particular tool rather than sifting through big buttons, little buttons, labels below or to the side of tools, and drop-down tools that may lead to lists of commands, submenus, or dialogs.

It would be much better if you could swap the ribbon for a simple menu and toolbars providing faster access for intermediate users. Despite my extensive experience with Word, it still takes me quite a while to dig through the clutter to find the more unusual tools, such as the command to insert a calculated field (Insert ⇨ Text ⇨ Quick Parts ⇨ Field) or the Translate command (Review ⇨ Language ⇨ Translate ⇨ Translate Document, which displays a dialog).

The ribbon does rearrange itself if you make the form smaller, but it's still inconsistent and confusing. Rather than switching at some point to a concise menu and tool buttons, it starts piling its usual tools into drop-down lists that still take up a lot of vertical space. The worst of both worlds.

You can minimize the ribbon so it only displays its tabs, sort of like a top-level menu, but if you click on a tab, you're back to the confusing jumble again.

Figure 9.2 shows one of Word's tooltips. Rather than a helpful word or two, it's a short essay complete with a title and picture. This is less harmful than the ribbon because tooltips are normally hidden, but it's massive overkill. The label Watermark on the original tool is enough to describe the tool completely, so a tooltip isn't really helpful. It would be better to use a smaller tool (for intermediate users) and a tooltip (for beginners) that simply says "Watermark."

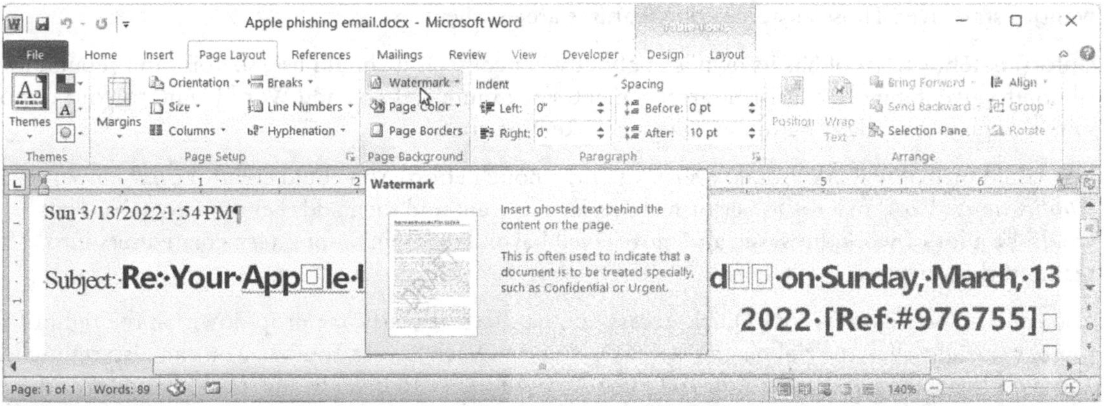

FIGURE 9.2: Word uses verbose tooltips because the ribbon already includes descriptive labels.

All of this is still okay for a beginner who's just starting to explore Word's capabilities, but it interferes with more experienced users. It makes it easy to learn about commands that you didn't know existed but harder to find the commands that you know are there. (Quick, how do you change the proofing language from English US to English Canada?) The ribbon is focused on the beginner to the detriment of intermediate and advanced users. (Imagine learning to ride a bicycle with training wheels and then still being required to use training wheels in the Tour de France. Although now that I think about it, that might be kind of funny.)

I suspect the ribbon is an instance of the *Pepsi paradox*. In blind taste tests, Pepsi often beats Coke, but Coke generally outsells Pepsi. The reason is, in a small taste, the sweeter flavor of Pepsi may be appealing. As you're nearing the end of the can, however, you may decide it's too sweet and wish you had gotten a Coke.

In the same way, Word's ribbon may appeal to beginners. It may even test well with user focus groups because they can see how it might be useful *for other people*. After you've become an intermediate user, however, it's just annoying. Its large buttons take up a lot of room but don't offer any useful features beyond what small tool buttons would. The chaotic arrangement of different kinds of controls makes it easy to explore randomly but hard to scan for a specific tool.

I suspect Microsoft uses this kind of interface to woo beginners, hoping to steal customers from competing platforms such as Linux and Apple. To strain the metaphor a bit, just as most people won't go to another restaurant because the first one serves Coke instead of Pepsi, most people are unlikely to switch from Apple to Microsoft just because Word provides a ribbon interface.

Word does allow you to customize the ribbon by showing or hiding standard tabs, adding new groups to standard tabs, creating custom tabs, and adding commands to your custom tabs. Right-click an empty part of the ribbon and select Customize The Ribbon to start.

There are a few restrictions. For example, you cannot remove standard tabs or delete items from them. That seems like a reasonable precaution to prevent the user from making the ribbon completely unrecoverable. The customization dialog also provides a Reset command. It's implemented as a drop-down rather than a button, which is pretty weird, but it lets you reset the ribbon to remove all customizations or customizations on a specific tab, just in case you mess things up so much that you want to start over. Those customization features are excellent.

Unfortunately, each tool has its own idea about what controls it should use, so you can't rebuild the ribbon to give it a more consistent arrangement. For example, if you add Word Count to your custom tab, it displays as a giant button whether you like it or not.

You could probably work around even that with enough effort. You could create *Visual Basic for Applications (VBA)* macros to perform the tasks you want and then add them to new tabs. That would be a lot of work, however, and moves well beyond the domain of intermediate users into the realm of the advanced.

You can also configure Word's Quick Access Toolbar. To start, click the drop-down on the right of the toolbar or right-click the ribbon and select Customize Quick Access Toolbar. You can also right-click a tool on the ribbon and select Add To Quick Access Toolbar to quickly add a command (my favorite method). Any tool added to the QAT shows only a small icon. (Proving it is possible to display the Word Count command with a small icon!)

Contrast Word's ribbon interface with the interface used by Microsoft Visual Studio shown in Figure 9.3. Instead of using a ribbon that is friendly to beginners, it uses concise menus and toolbars that are more efficient for intermediate and advanced users.

Microsoft assumes that Word users are always beginners and Visual Studio users are instant experts. Wouldn't it be nice if you could pick either interface in the same program?

Overall, Word is targeted at beginners. You can customize the ribbon and QAT (which is excellent), and there are easy ways to restore the original arrangement if you get in too deep (also excellent), but there are limitations that make it hard to create an intermediate-level interface (less excellent).

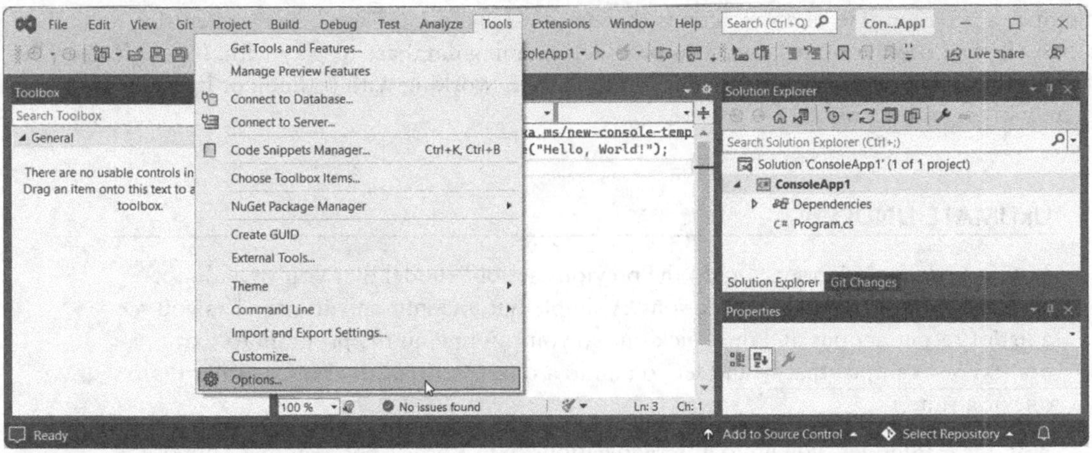

FIGURE 9.3: Visual Studio assumes the user is at least intermediate and possibly advanced.

DESIGN GUIDELINES

The previous sections in this chapter focus on user experience design philosophy and general approach. This part of the chapter looks at more concrete design guidelines. Most of these could use a page or two of discussion, but there just isn't that much room here, so the following sections blast through these more quickly than I would like.

I've given them less space mostly because I think they are a bit more obvious than the concepts covered earlier in the chapter. Brevity makes many of these sound like commandments, but of course they have exceptions. Displaying informational messages instead of interrupting the user with a dialog is a best practice, but if you're writing flight control software, it's probably better to interrupt the pilot right away rather than writing a message at the bottom of the app saying, "Mountain approaching in 3. . . 2. . . 1. . ."

Allow Exploration

One outstanding way to help beginners become intermediate users quickly is to make your application safely explorable. The user should be able to try things out without suffering dire consequences.

Perhaps the best way to allow safe exploration is to provide Undo and Redo commands. They allow the user to try things out and then undo the changes after seeing the result.

The Redo command is a natural consequence of the Undo command. If you can undo something, then you should be able to undo the undo to redo it.

Ideally, the undo and redo lists should store many commands, not just one. You might even make the number configurable by the user.

Sometimes a program will perform actions that are not easy to undo, such as restructuring an entire database. In that case, you might want to provide a training database to play with. If you do that, be sure the application makes it obvious whether the user is working with training or live data (for hopefully obvious reasons).

ULTIMATE UNDO

Linear undo is the normal "undo the previous action" model that you've undoubtedly seen before in many applications. A simple but uncommon variation lets you see a list of recent actions and then pick one so you can rewind the program to that point. For example, that would let you undo a dozen actions all at once rather than one at a time.

Nonlinear undo lets you undo and redo actions out of order. For example, suppose you're using a drawing program and you draw an ellipse, create a rectangle, draw a line, and then rotate the rectangle. You could undo the line drawing but leave the ellipse, rectangle, and rectangle's rotation in place.

This kind of undo is like a unicorn: so rare as to possibly be mythical, but I would like to see it in the wild someday. One reason this undo is so rare is that it's hard, largely because it requires you to understand interactions among changes. For example, if you undo creating the rectangle, then you also need to remove the rectangle's rotation.

One way to add extra glitter to the unicorn would be to create a *scrapyard*. This would be a place sort of like the clipboard where you could store undone actions for a while. You could then see a list of scraps and reapply some of them. In the ongoing example, you might undo the ellipse and rectangle and then later pick the ellipse out of the scrapyard to re-create it.

A scrapyard is mostly just a nonlinear redo list, so it's not that weird. The biggest change I would suggest would be to not empty the scrapyard when a new action is performed the way a normal redo list is emptied.

A scrapyard would allow me to avoid an action that I perform regularly when writing. I decide a paragraph needs retooling, so I make a bunch of changes. Often I decide that I mostly like the result but I want to restore something that I deleted earlier. To work around this, I copy the new version to the clipboard and then press Ctrl+Z repeatedly until I get back to the original version. I paste the saved new version from the clipboard and then edit again to merge the new and old versions. It would be a lot simpler if I could just pull the old text I wanted from a scrapyard.

There are other interesting undo and redo models. Search online for more information. (And if you do create a sparkly unicorn, email me. I'd love to see it!)

Make the Interface Immutable

Undo and redo make an application safe to explore. Immutability makes exploration easier.

Don't move things around and don't hide things. If a command is unavailable, gray it out; don't remove it. That way, the user can find the command and see that it is unavailable. I have wasted a considerable amount of time on some applications looking for commands that I knew were there somewhere but that had been hidden because they were currently unavailable.

Moving commands can lead to mistakes. For example, one of my email systems changes the commands that are available depending on whether you have zero, one, or more emails selected. If I click too quickly without looking, I sometimes archive an email that should move to trash, or I'll delete multiple emails when I'm trying to reply.

If you do decide to hide features, perhaps to save space, do so at the highest level possible so the change is easy to see. For example, Microsoft Word has special tools that are available only when you select certain objects. If you select an image, a Format tab appears on the ribbon. That tab is usually unhelpful, so it makes some sense to have it appear only when needed. Similarly, Word displays Design and Layout tabs when you're working with tables. Those are hidden at the topmost level, so (with some experience) it's easy to see when they are available.

In theory, it might be better to have those tabs present at all times and just disable them when they aren't needed, but the ribbon is too full to display every tab all the time.

In addition to not hiding things, don't change the appearance of objects such as labels and buttons. For example, if you need to start and stop some process, use separate Start and Stop buttons (disabled when appropriate) rather than one button with a label that changes.

Don't change the meaning of shortcuts such as Crtl+K and Ctrl+M in different parts of your application. In fact, if a shortcut has a standard meaning in many programs, don't change it in your program. Ctrl+S means Save and Ctrl+P means print. Making those shortcuts do anything else will confuse your users and probably waste a lot of paper and toner.

Look online to find the standard shortcuts for your platform. For example, you can try these links:

➤ Mac—https://support.apple.com/en-us/HT201236

➤ Linux—https://linuxhint.com/100_keyboard_shortcuts_linux

➤ Windows—https://support.microsoft.com/en-us/windows/
keyboard-shortcuts-in-windows-dcc61a57-8ff0-cffe-9796-cb9706c75eec

Support Commensurate Difficulty

Make easy things easy and hard things hard. Users are willing to put in more effort to achieve more complicated or more dangerous results. For example, if you are viewing a report, sending that report to a printer should be quick and easy. Press a button and off it goes to your default printer.

In contrast, scheduling classes for an entire elementary school is a big undertaking and users know it, so they are willing to spend some extra effort starting the process. In this case, it would be reasonable to display a separate form where the user can enter parameters before starting the half-hour procedure.

This is the concept of *commensurate difficulty*.

Place dangerous commands in the application's less traveled byways. Don't put the "Delete All Customers" command on a button on the main window's toolbar. Beginners won't generally need to do that very often, so there's no need to make it too easy.

To decide how easy starting a task should be, ask the following questions:

➤ How often will the user perform the task?

➤ How long will the task take?

➤ How dangerous is the task?

➤ Can the task be undone?

Make frequent, quick, safe, undoable tasks easy to start. Make rare, slow, dangerous, un-undoable tasks less accessible and make it clear what will happen before the task starts.

Avoid State

Don't give your application different states. It's confusing if a program acts differently under different conditions.

For example, it can be confusing if you're making a phone call and then switch your smartphone to a browser to check something. You'll see the browser, but your phone is still in the calling state. I once had someone leave me a voicemail and then repeatedly say (and eventually yell with curses and increasing frustration), "Hey google!" not realizing that the phone call was still connected.

If you must use different states, and many applications do, make the current state as obvious as possible.

Make Similar Things Similar

If objects, dialogs, pieces of data, or whatever are similar, make them look similar. For example, it's easier to scan through a list of buttons that all have the same size than it is to decipher an assortment of buttons, sliders, combo boxes, and pieces of hypertext. Pick one method and stick with it.

Also, be consistent throughout the application. Don't use buttons on one dialog and hypertext on another. Don't use OK/Cancel buttons on one dialog and Yes/No on another.

For the same reason, use parallel grammatical construction. It's easier for users to parse text that uses the same format.

Conversely, make unlike objects different or keep them farther apart so users don't get them confused. That also helps users look for anomalies.

For example, suppose your program monitors a set of processor applications that transform images in various ways and consider the following list of processor statuses.

PROCESSOR	STATUS
Converter	Enabled
Rotate	Enabled
Compression	Enabled
Overlays & Insets	Disabled
Resizer	Enabled
Posting	Enabled

This list is manageable because it's small, but the processor names on the left use inconsistent forms of speech so it takes extra mental effort to figure out what each processor does.

The normal and abnormal status values on the right are also too visually similar for the user to easily pick out any problems. Imagine how hard it would be to spot a disabled processor if the list contained hundreds of entries.

Here's an improved design.

PROCESSOR	STATUS
Compress	Enabled
Convert	Enabled
Overlay & Inset	NOT ENABLED
Post	Enabled
Resize	Enabled
Rotate	Enabled

This version uses a more consistent grammatical construction for the processor names and the names are alphabetized to make finding specific processors easier. A reasonable alternative might be to list the processors in chronological order so they appear in the order in which they process a particular image. In that case, it might be nice to let the user select alphabetical or chronological order.

This design also makes unusual cases in the right column stand out more. (Different things look more different.) In addition to changing the wording so the two different values don't look so similar, you can use other cues such as font (this example uses capitalization), text color, background color, or icons.

Different users are more sensitive to some indicators than others, so it's important to provide more than one set. For example, you shouldn't just use green, yellow, and red circles to indicate that a process is okay, slow, or stopped. Not only do some users key better on shapes or text than colors, but also because seven or eight percent of the people in the world have some form of color vision deficiency (color blindness), they may not notice certain color differences.

> **COLOR CONFIRMATION** If you search the Internet for "color blindness simulator," you can find online tools that let you upload images to see how different forms of color deficiency affect your ability to see color differences. It's worth doing this now just so you know what you're up against. It's also worth uploading screenshots of your user interface to see if anything that you thought was obvious might be hidden from some users.

Instead of just changing an item's color, it would be better to use shapes in addition to color. For example, you could use a green square, yellow diamond, and red X to show the object's status. You could even add the labels OK, Slow, and STOPPED next to the icons. That would make the differences easier to spot, although it would take more space. (Pop quiz: Who would those labels benefit most? Answer: The text would help beginners learn what the colored symbols mean. They would also help more advanced users notice differences, so they may help everyone. You could make this configurable.)

The same "make similar things similar" ideas apply to commands and just about any other piece of application data. For example, don't make a list of buttons that execute the following commands:

- ➤ Create Customer
- ➤ Edit Customer
- ➤ Delete Customer
- ➤ Check Inventory
- ➤ Track Customer Orders

Putting Check Inventory inside a list of customer commands could cause confusion. At a minimum, users will probably have trouble finding that command when they want it. At worst they may click it accidentally while looking for customer commands. (Also, don't put the big red Make Latte button right next to the big red Launch Nukes button.)

Provide Redundant Commands

Allow the user to invoke commands by using different methods such as menus, buttons, tool buttons, and shortcuts. This is not so the user can invoke a command from a lot of different places; it's to allow users to find the methods that make them more efficient. As I mentioned earlier, beginners tend to use buttons and menu items while intermediate and advanced users tend to use shortcuts.

The idea of commensurate difficulty also applies here. For example, if a command is particularly complicated or dangerous, you don't need to provide multiple easy ways to trigger it. Because saving a file is a very common action, an advanced user would be annoyed if the only way to save a file was to open the File menu, select Actions, and then pick Save, enter a file name, and confirm that the previous version of the file should be overwritten. However, advanced users won't mind a few extra steps to compact the database or export annual sales figures because those operations happen much less frequently.

Do the Right Thing

A common management maxim says, "Ask for forgiveness, not permission." This saying is often used in software design to justify default actions. The idea is that it is more productive to start doing something and then correct as necessary rather than to spend a huge amount of time dithering over details and not get anything done. Often this approach means filling in defaults when you create new records or begin new actions.

For example, when you execute the Print command, you probably want the current document to magically appear on your default printer. However, when you press Ctrl+P, most programs display a dialog where you need to select the printer, enter the range of pages to print, decide whether to print one- or two-sided, pick the paper size and orientation, set the margins, and decide whether to print one or multiple pages per sheet of paper. That's a lot of decisions for something that rarely changes.

A better solution would be to provide a Printer Configuration command that lets you set all of those values ahead of time. Then the Print command can do just what is says: print.

Microsoft Word's Print command displays a huge dialog containing all of those choices plus a preview and hyperlinks (which probably should be buttons) to let you change printer properties and page setup. If you're a more advanced user, you can add the Quick Print command to the QAT to just print the document without all the fanfare.

"Ask for forgiveness" only works if there's a good chance that the defaults are correct. For example, when you use QuickBooks to write a check to someone, it copies the values from the previous check you wrote to that person. If you create a new check for employee Patrick Star, the new check starts with the same amount, line item description, and memo field as the last one. Unless Patrick earns exactly the same amount for every pay period and the item description and memo fields are something generic like "Pay" (in which case they're not very useful), you'll need to modify those fields every time you write a check. In that case, it would be better to just leave those fields blank so you can fill them in.

Templates provide another form of "Ask for forgiveness." When the user wants to create something, you present a list of reasonable templates. The user picks one and then customizes the result.

In Microsoft Word, for example, when you press Ctrl+N, the program creates an empty blank document with default margins, orientation, and so forth. However, if you use the File menu's New command, you get a huge list of templates for creating everything from award certificates to greeting cards, holiday letters to resumes. Templates are a good way to let the user start with a useful default and modify it appropriately.

Duplication provides a final form of "Ask for forgiveness." Rather than creating a new record from scratch, you can allow the user to copy and modify an existing record. Basically, this uses the previous record as a template for the new one.

For example, the Square point-of-sale system lets you duplicate invoices. If a customer wants to place an order similar to an earlier one, you can copy the previous invoice, change any items or notes that should be modified, and send the new invoice.

This is similar to the way QuickBooks initializes a check by copying an old one, but with two main differences. First, QuickBooks only copies the last check, whereas Square lets you copy any earlier invoice so you can pick the best template. Second, QuickBooks copies information that is almost guaranteed to change (amount and memo field), so it always needs forgiveness. To forgive may be divine, but after clearing a few hundred memo lines, it gets pretty tiresome.

Show Qualitative Data, Explain Quantitative Data

People generally understand pictures more quickly than words, at least for qualitative things. For approximate qualitative data, use pictures. For very precise quantitative values, use text.

For example, if you want to show a laptop's battery life, you can use a little picture of a battery that's partly filled in to show remaining power. You can shade it green, yellow, or red to indicate severity. (Note, however, that the color is not the only indication. The filled area also shows the amount of power remaining.) A user can quickly look at this picture to get an idea of whether the laptop has plenty of power or is about to run out.

If you provide a tooltip showing the exact power remaining, you get the best of both worlds. The picture tells the qualitative story (you have medium-low power remaining) and the tooltip gives the precise quantitative version (32 percent remaining).

In the same way, you could show monthly sales figures in a bar chart. If the user hovers over a bar, a tooltip can show the exact figure.

Give Forms Purpose

Have a purpose for every form, dialog, menu, and other user interaction. A dialog should focus on a single task and not contain a mishmash of unrelated features. Just because it would be easy to make the Save As dialog also show the available disk space, that doesn't mean it's a good idea. Operating system tools can tell the user that.

Try to allow the user to complete the full task without opening new forms and dialogs. If the user will need a particular piece of information to finish the task, put it right on the form. Don't make the user open a series of never-ending dialogs to take information a bit at a time.

In fact, try to avoid using dialogs in general because they slow the user down. They break the user's concentration, disrupt the flow of thought, and are often not even necessary.

In particular, do not use confirmation dialogs or preview dialogs. There's no need to confirm most commands if they are undoable or have limited consequences or if the user is unlikely to launch them accidentally. For the same reason, preview dialogs just show what is about to happen, so they're unnecessary if the action is undoable.

The one place where I like preview dialogs is in place of printing. A print preview dialog is usually unnecessary as a prelude to printing, but if you just want to see the result on the screen and don't need a paper copy, then a preview dialog may save some trees.

Programs also don't generally need informational dialogs. The program should not be so insecure that it needs to interrupt the user to tell them what it is doing. The program should be doing what the user told it to do, so there should be no surprise that it's doing as commanded. If the program has something interesting to say, it can display it with status indicators or a message in a status bar at the bottom of the window.

If possible, don't even use error dialogs. If there's a problem, the program should figure out how to work around it. If the problem is severe and unsolvable, the program should use a status message instead of a dialog.

The only reason to interrupt a user with a dialog should be if there is a severe, unsolvable, un-undoable, imminent threat to life and limb. (Or at least electronic life and limb.)

Copious Confirmation

To delete emails in my current phone app, I need to follow these steps:

1. Tap the vertical ellipses to open a menu.

2. Tap Edit. (I don't know why it's called Edit since there's no editing involved.)

3. Tap circles beside the target emails to mark them. (The circles are check boxes, although round.)

4. Tap the Delete button.

5. In the confirmation dialog, tap Delete.

Contrast this with the following steps for deleting an email on my desktop system:

1. Click circles beside the target emails to mark them. (When did round check boxes become so popular?)

2. Tap the Delete button.

The program then displays a non-modal message that indicates the number of emails deleted and offers an Undo button.

The desktop app uses half as many steps, does not need to enter into a special "Edit" mode, doesn't interrupt me with a modal dialog, and allows me to undo the deletion if I like. The fact that the phone app does not provide undo is probably why it feels the need for confirmation. Its Delete feature is un-undoable.

Gather All Information at Once

When a program starts some sort of process, it should gather the information it needs all at once and only then start so it can proceed without bothering the user. This is essential for very long-running tasks. For example, it's annoyingly common to launch some sort of upgrade, wander off for coffee, and then return to find that the upgrade stopped right after you walked away because it had some silly question.

Asking the user questions is not the same as letting the user pick options, and picking options is better. Display a single form that lets the user enter all of the necessary data in one shot. Don't interrogate the user with a series of dialogs. Don't create a wizard that walks the user through a long chain of demands, dribbling out one question at a time.

When you go to a restaurant, doesn't it seem better if you can tell your server what you want rather than endure an open-ended series of questions? Fries, rice, or seared vegetables? Breadsticks or garlic toast? Soup or salad? Ranch, balsamic, or raspberry vinaigrette? After four or five questions, most customers just wish the process would end.

Provide Reasonable Performance

When the program starts a task, it should obey the *five-second rule*: All interactive tasks should complete within five seconds. Most users will wait for about five seconds before growing bored and pulling out their cell phones to check for new emails, updating their statuses on social media, or wandering off to get coffee. Even if the task takes only seven or eight seconds, it could be half an hour before the user finishes deleting spam, reading other peoples' status updates, and drinking that second cup of coffee. The seven-second task has wasted half an hour of the user's time.

If a task is likely to take longer than five seconds, gather all necessary information before starting it as described in the preceding section. Then launch the task in the background and display a (non-modal) "task started" message, giving an estimated completion time if possible. Now the user can continue working on other tasks while this one finishes.

You should include a way to monitor background tasks and tell the user about task completion. Each task's status should indicate its progress, and that status should update frequently so the user knows that the task isn't stuck.

I don't know how many times I've started a Windows update and had it sit there for hours with only the chuckling of the disk drive to indicate that anything was happening. Even then after two or three hours I always start to wonder if the drive activity is a virus that has taken over and is searching the disk for my top-secret cookie recipes. If you have a solid-state drive, you won't even get that much feedback.

The only time an *interactive* task should take longer than five seconds is if there's absolutely nothing else the user can do until the task completes. For example, if you're installing new software or updating the operating system, it may be important that the system remains untouched until the process is finished. In those rare cases, warn the user that this will be time consuming, display frequent progress updates, and resign yourself to losing the user's attention for at least half an hour.

If your project is for in-house use, be sure to test your performance on a computer that is as similar as possible to the users' computers. It does no good if the program satisfies the five-second rule on your computer but can't satisfy the five-minute rule on the users' systems.

Only Allow What's Right

As much as possible, use controls that help the user select values that are legal rather than allowing the user to enter values that may be incorrect. For example, if the user needs to select a month, provide a combo box so the user can select the month instead of mistyping Smarch or Rocktober. If the user needs to pick a value between 1 and 10, provide a slider or track bar so the user can't type 2.5 or "six."

Unfortunately, some values are hard to constrain like this. If you need the user to enter a real number such as 2.71828 or an integer between 1 and 100 million, you can't very well provide a combo box of choices.

Other values can be annoying to enter even though you could provide a constraining control. For example, it's not too hard to select a birth year from a drop-down on a desktop system where there's a reasonable amount of room. On a phone app, it can be annoying (and more than a little depressing) to scroll and scroll and scroll to find the right year. Similarly, picking a date or small date range isn't too hard with some kind of date picker control, but selecting a large range can be difficult.

In cases such as these, you might consider displaying the selection in an editable field in addition to using a picker control so impatient users can enter the value directly. Any user who decides to type the value in is taking responsibility for doing it correctly, and users who don't want to type by hand can still use the picker. Allowing the user two ways to enter the same value will take up more space, means you'll need to keep them in synch, and will require you to validate the manually entered values, but it gives the user more flexibility and may make the process faster.

Flag Mistakes

Whenever you can, set the user up for success by using controls that allow only valid selections. When that's not possible, it's still better to not interrupt the user.

If a value is not really necessary, don't require it and don't interrupt the user if the value is missing or incorrect. For example, suppose a customer record has fields for three phone numbers and each has a type: home, cell, or work. Do you really need all of those? And do you need all of the types? If the user enters 867-5309 in the first field but doesn't select a phone type, does it really matter? It's not even clear that those types make sense anymore because many people have a single cell phone that is also their home and possibly work phone.

What if the user enters a nonnumeric phone number like PE6-5000? If you're just going to display whatever the user entered, PE6-5000 may be just fine. (Although younger users may need musicology training to decipher that number.)

What if the number is just plain wrong like 92-37-1970? If you're not planning to use the phone number except in case of some imaginary emergency, do any of those things really matter?

Rather than immediately interrupting the user, flag the suspicious data, perhaps by turning its font red or its background yellow. Visual Studio provides an `ErrorProvider` component for Windows Forms applications that displays a little error icon next to a flagged control. The error remains unobtrusive, but if you hover the mouse over the icon, you see a tooltip describing the error.

If you display an inconspicuous error indicator, the user can continue filling in the rest of the form and then correct the error later. . . or not. If the invalid values are informational and not critical, you might just add them to the database as they are and not worry about them.

Even if the values are crucial and must be fixed (perhaps allergy codes on a hospital admission form), at least you avoid breaking the users' flow so they can finish entering the other values before fixing the problems.

FORM DESIGN

It's finally time to talk a little about form design. Unfortunately, many programmers think that this is all there is to the UX, but you know from the earlier sections in this chapter that there's more to UX than simply arranging controls. Before you start throwing controls on a form, you need to understand basic principles such as doing what's best for the user rather than what's easiest for the programmers, gathering all necessary information before starting a long task, and not interrupting users with gratuitous dialogs.

Next I'll describe some of the more standard controls that you can use in your applications. After that, I'll explain a few control arranging principles that make an application easier for the user.

Use Standard Controls

Generally, you should try to stick to standard controls because users already know how they work. You can use an unusual control here or there if it fits your purposes particularly well, but users will need extra practice and will make more mistakes. Don't use some weird spider-shaped check box that has wiggling legs to indicate selection and expect users to instantly know how to use it.

Don't use standard controls for nonstandard purposes. For example, check boxes and radio buttons often change the user interface, perhaps by disabling certain options or commands, but they should not launch an action. Use the check boxes and radio buttons to gather parameters and then let the user click a button to start the main event.

Some programs change the appearance of the basic controls. For example, check boxes have been boxes for decades, but many applications, particularly on phones and tablets, are now using round check boxes. Radio buttons (option buttons) have been around for many years, but now many applications use a small on/off switch instead.

These changes are cosmetic and don't cause too much confusion. Users who have not seen them before will need an extra minute or two to adjust, but it's not a hard adjustment as long as you're consistent. Basically, the user needs to learn your new idiom that says check boxes are diamond-shaped or whatever, and consistency will help. Don't use square check boxes in one place, images of a check mark in another, and round check boxes in a third. That would be asking for trouble.

The following sections say a bit about standard control types. They only cover general categories and don't provide a complete list of controls. However, if you're trying to use a display control to launch an action, you may want to rethink your design.

Decorating

These controls are purely decorative. They include controls such as lines, images, labels used as prompts (as opposed to displaying data), group boxes (frames), rectangles, and other shapes. They generally don't convey information directly, but they can be very useful for organizing other controls.

White space is another good way to organize controls on a form, although it's not a control. For example, you can separate groups of controls with a horizontal or vertical line or white space to let the user focus on the sections separately.

Displaying

These controls display information to the user. They include controls such as treeviews, read-only textboxes, labels (used to display data), tooltips, and icons such as error or other status indicators.

Read-only text boxes are a good way to display data that the user cannot change while still allowing the user to copy and paste the results, perhaps into a different program.

This category also includes graphical controls such as dials, analog thermometers, pictures of batteries, status bars, graphs, charts, and more. For example, an image that is grayed out on the top (or right) and slowly filling up with color from the bottom (or left) can indicate the progress of some task.

Although their primary purpose is to display information, some of these may also allow the user to modify the data. For instance, you might be able to click and drag a bar to change a value in a bar chart. That's a good example of a *direct manipulation* idiom where the information and the ability to modify it are contained in the same control.

Arranging

These controls arrange, hide, or contain other controls. Some controls that arrange other controls are toolboxes, toolstrips, toolbox and toolstrip arrangers, stack panels, and various layout panels. Each has its own arrangement policy, often placing controls in rows and columns.

Another subset of these controls hides and shows other controls. For example, tabs let the user pick one of several other controls (which may each contain whole pages of controls) to view at one time. Other controls of this type include scrolled windows, paned windows (with splitters), expanders, and pull outs.

Some users may need practice with these initially, although they are easy enough to use once you get to know them.

Most tabbed windows can display multiple rows of tabs above the display area if there are too many tabs to fit. Unfortunately, it's hard to find a particular tab in multiple rows because the tabs don't line up well either vertically or horizontally.

If you're working on a desktop, laptop, or tablet, you can position the tabs on the left rather than above the display area. That lets you take advantage of the wider screen while conserving scarce vertical space. You can also stack far more tabs vertically than horizontally.

If you're working on a phone where horizontal space is at a premium, another alternative is to make the tab area scroll horizontally. This makes using the tabs harder because the user won't be able to see all of the tabs at once. You can help by keeping the list of tabs short and by arranging the tabs in some meaningful way. For example, if the tabs represent months, put them in order so the user will know which way to scroll to reach a particular month. If you can't think of any other useful ordering, arrange the tabs alphabetically.

One final tip for these kinds of controls is to make sure the user can see related information all at once. For example, suppose your app lets a user order supplies for the upcoming zombie apocalypse. Don't put the rifle choices on one tab and the ammunition choices on another. If you do, users will need to switch back and forth (which wastes time) or remember their selections (always a risky proposition) to make compatible choices.

Commanding

These controls command the program to perform some action. They include menus, context menus (right-click menus), buttons, toolbar buttons, hyperlinks, smart tags, and split buttons.

Note that most "normal" users (neither programmers nor mathematicians) are uncomfortable with hierarchical or recursive data. In this context, that means they may find deep menu structures confusing. Try to make menu structures relatively broad and shallow. It's better to have a three-level structure with four or five choices at each level instead of a binary tree that's seven levels deep.

A split button is a button with an attached drop-down. If you click the button, you get the button's current action. If you click the drop-down, you get a list of other related commands. When you pick one, the program executes that command and the main button updates to show your new choice. Once the users get used to them, split buttons provide a handy way to let the user select and later repeat a default action.

A smart tag is a small triangle, rectangle, or other shape attached to a control. When you click the smart tag, it performs some action such as executing a standard command or displaying a dialog related to the control. You shouldn't need a smart tag to display a menu because a context menu can do that. A smart tag doesn't display text or an icon to hint at its purpose, so you may want to give it an informational tooltip.

Accelerators and shortcut keys also perform actions. Recall from earlier in this chapter, however, that you should provide multiple ways to perform actions. For example, the Crtl+S shortcut probably does the same thing as the File menu's Save command. It would be unusual to have a shortcut that performs some action that cannot be executed in any other way. (And remember to make the Save menu item say Ctrl+S so beginners can learn about the shortcut.)

Selecting

These controls let the user make selections. These include check boxes, radio buttons, lists, and combo boxes.

A check box (or toggle button) is either selected or not. Each checkbox is independent of any others, so you can check and uncheck them in any combination. These are represented in many ways, such as boxes that are empty or that contain an X or check mark, squares or circles that are empty or filled, switches that are pushed up/down or left/right, and sticky buttons that remain depressed after you click them (until you click them again to uncheck).

Radio buttons (or option buttons) come in groups and only one button in the group can be selected at a time. If you click one, any previously selected button deselects.

If you need to use multiple radio button groups, you must arrange them so the user can tell which buttons belong in which group. One way to do that is to place the buttons in each group inside a frame, possibly with a label at the top to tell the user what the group represents. Another approach is to arrange the groups in rows or columns separated by white space or lines.

Radio buttons can have the same general appearance as check boxes, but you should make sure you make the two look different in your application. If you use round check boxes, don't use round radio buttons. Whatever design you pick, be consistent across all of the project's forms and dialogs.

A combo box displays a selection area and a drop-down where the user can pick a choice that is then written into the display area. Some variations also allow the user to type into the display area, perhaps with auto-completion using the choices in the drop-down list. If you allow free-format typing, you could add the user's entry to the drop-down list so it will be available in the future. (You might also want to let the user edit that list somehow to clear out typos and choices that are no longer used.)

A list simply displays choices. Lists usually allow the user to scroll if the choices won't all fit on the screen at once. Different lists may provide complicated selection models to let the user select one or more contiguous or noncontiguous choices. Some of those models can be quite confusing, however, and they don't all work well if the list must scroll.

If the user needs to make multiple selections on a large list, you might consider a checked list box. This is basically a list that provides a check box next to each item. The user can scroll through the list and check items without worrying about whether previous selections are lost by the selection model. If the list is long, you might also consider offering Check All and Uncheck All buttons, context-menu commands, or smart tags.

Entering

The simpler controls in this category include text boxes, spinners (up/down controls), sliders, and scroll bars. Note that it can be hard to select precise values with controls like sliders and scroll bars. Scroll bars don't have the resolution to let you select every integer between 0 and 1 million (unless your monitor is a quarter mile wide) and will limit the number of digits after the decimal point you can select for real values. If you need those kinds of selection, it's probably better to let the user type the value into a text box.

Fancier data entry controls include calendars, date pickers, time pickers, and text boxes that enforce a pattern on whatever the user types. Be aware that some of these controls can make it hard to enter valid values.

For example, some programs require specific formats for values such as phone numbers and times. Unfortunately, some of the programs I use try to enforce those formats as you type, and they enter the separator characters - and : for you. That makes it impossible to copy and paste values into those fields and sometimes makes it very hard to enter values correctly. In one program, for example, if I try to type the time 12:34, the field sometimes decides that the colon goes after the 1 so it adds the colon and jumps to the minutes part of the value. Other times when I try to enter the value 1:17, it decides that the second 1 is part of the hour so I end up with the invalid time 11:7.

If any of these errors occurs (and to make things more confusing, they don't always), the program interrupts me by beeping and failing to enter the rest of whatever I'm typing. I then need to carefully move my mouse into position and click to make sure the pieces of the value land in the right part of the text box.

In these cases it would be much better to just allow the user to type anything and then check the result when the user accepts the form.

Display Five Things

Most adults can hold in their short-term memory around seven things at a time, plus or minus two (in other words, five to nine items, depending on the person). If you make people focus on too many items, they'll forget some or possibly all of them. That makes five a good number of choices to give users in the UI because most people can focus on five items at once, at least for a short while (hence the famous "person, woman, man, camera, TV" list).

That doesn't mean you can only show users five items at a time, just that they can only give five items their full attention at once. You can display many more items if they are arranged properly.

For example, a restaurant menu might have hundreds of items but they are grouped into the categories Breakfast, Lunch, Dinner, Dessert, and Drinks. When you scan the menu, you can quickly decide which category applies and then you can ignore the other categories. Now you focus on the category you selected (say, lunch) and scan its items. They may be further grouped into Pizza, Burgers, Salads, and Pasta. You can pick a category if you like, or just look at every item to see what sounds good. (Or if you want a particular item, you can just ask your server, "Do you have a boiled bacon sandwich?" and see if it's available.)

The point is that the menu breaks the hundreds of choices into manageable groups that help you quickly narrow your search.

Similarly, users can handle more than five items at a time in your program if you arrange them properly. Gather them into groups, if that makes sense, and separate them with frames, lines, or white space. Put groups on separate tabs so the user only needs to look at one group at a time.

Users can handle very large groups if the items all represent the same idea and there is some sort of simple organization. For example, you can find your birth year in a list containing more than 100 years if they are in numerical order. You can find a friend's phone number in your enormous contact list as long as the list is in alphabetical order.

One drawback to very large lists is that users must know what they want to find. If you can't remember your friend's name (he goes by Squiggy, but you're pretty sure that's not his real name), then you'll need to scroll through your entire contact list to find him. Or if your favorite online store has pillows shaped like celebrities, you'll need to know which one you want so you don't need to browse through thousands of choices.

Arrange Controls Nicely

Most programmers who think at all about UI design before they start slapping controls onto a form can understand the rule "arrange controls nicely" based on esthetics alone. No one wants to work with an ugly app.

However, this rule also helps users be more productive. A user's focus tends to follow the natural reading order. In many countries, that means left to right and top to bottom. You can make it easier for the user to enter information and process data on the screen by presenting it in that order. (Presumably this is different in countries that read right to left or by column instead of rows, but I haven't written any applications for those markets so I'll recuse myself.)

Arranging fields in columns instead of rows doesn't work as well because the result is unnatural and somewhat distracting. Users will be able to navigate through the form, but not quite as quickly.

The groupings described in the preceding section can help give further structure; just arrange the groupings right to left and top to bottom.

SUMMARY

Without a good user interface, your application cannot reach its full potential. If users can't find the tools they need, are forced to spend extra time responding to dialogs, and must focus more on an awkward arrangement of controls than on the data, then they won't be as efficient as possible.

The user experience should be about what's best for users, not what's easiest for programmers. To achieve that, separate the UX design as much as possible from the programming. If you have dedicated UX designers, great! If not, be sure to remove your programmer hat while you're working on the UX design.

As I mentioned at the beginning of this chapter, UI and UX design are enormous topics, so everything won't fit in one chapter. Look online for design tips, websites, and books to give you more information and let you see other points of view.

Most importantly, study the applications that you use so you can learn what they do well and what they do poorly. Emulate the techniques that you find useful and avoid those that get in the way.

After you've finished the various kinds of design (high-level, low-level, security, and user experience), it's time to do some programming. The next chapter provides an introduction to the programming part of software development. It explains some general methods you can use to organize programming and describes a few useful techniques that you can use to reduce the number of bugs that are introduced during this phase.

EXERCISES

1. Briefly explain the difference between UI and UX.

2. What are first class and transient apps? What kinds of users do they have?

3. What are software metaphors and idioms? Give an example of each.

4. What are the best features for allowing the user to explore an application safely? (Hint: There are two that come as a pair.)

5. Explain commensurate difficulty. Give examples where commensurate difficulty should allow and not allow actions.

6. When does "ask for forgiveness" work?

7. Give an example of a user interface element that combines qualitative and quantitative data display. What kinds of information does the user get from qualitative and quantitative display?

8. What is the maximum amount of time the user should wait for an interactive action? Why?

9. Suppose the user enters "Aprik" in a month field. When and how should you warn the user? Why should you warn the user in that time and way? Is there a better alternative than allowing them to type "Aprik" in the first place?

10. How many items can most people hold in their short-term memory at once? How does that affect UI design? (What was that famous list again?)

11. How can you put more items on a form than is allowed by the short-term memory rule?

12. If you have access to it, take a look at MS Paint's new Windows 11 look. What features make it harder to use? Are there improvements over previous versions?

WHAT YOU LEARNED IN THIS CHAPTER

➤ The user interface (UI) is what the user sees and does with the application. The user experience (UX) includes the UI and everything else dealing with the application's "brand," including installation, updates, reliability, and availability.

➤ UX design should be separated from programming. Do what's best for the users, not the programmers.

➤ Platform (desktop, laptop, tablet, phone, IoT) plays a large role in determining the elements of the UI.

➤ User skill level determines what UI elements are appropriate. Beginners are helped by menus, dialogs, and large controls. Intermediate and advanced users prefer shortcuts and smaller controls.

➤ Users of first-class apps are intermediate and advanced. Users of transient apps are perpetual beginners.

➤ Allow users to configure the application. Provide easy reset commands. Provide configuration presets for common roles.

➤ Encourage a user-oriented model. Don't present an implementation model.

➤ Use metaphors if you can find them, but idioms work well too and are easier to create.

➤ Provide Undo and Redo to allow safe exploration.

➤ Make the interface immutable. Enable or disable commands, but don't move or hide them.

➤ Avoid state.

➤ Make similar things similar and unusual things stand out.

10

Programming

A good programmer is someone who always looks both ways before crossing a one-way street.

—Doug Linder

Always code as if the guy who ends up maintaining your code will be a violent psychopath who knows where you live.

—Martin Golding

What You Will Learn in This Chapter:

➤ Tools that are useful to programmers

➤ How to use top-down design to turn designs into code

➤ Programming tips that can make code easier to debug and maintain

To many programmers, programming is the heart of software engineering. It's where fingers hit the keyboard and churn out the actual program code of the system. Without programming, there is no application. (Hopefully you've realized by now that the other stages are important, too, but many programmers still think programming is where the "real" work happens.)

As is the case with other stages of software engineering, the edges of programming are a bit blurry. Low-level design may identify the classes that a program will need, but it may not spell out every method that the classes must provide, and it might provide few details about how those methods work. That means the programming stage must still include some design work as developers figure out how to build the classes.

Similarly, the next major stage of software engineering, testing, often begins before programming is completely finished. In fact, it's best to test software early and often. It's widely known that bugs are easiest to find and fix if they're detected soon after they're created, so if possible, you should test every method you write as soon as it's finished (sometimes even before it's finished).

Most developers write programs because they like to write code. (I know I do. For me, solving a tricky programming problem is like solving a difficult Sudoku puzzle. I get a great feeling of satisfaction from crunching a bunch of numbers and having a beautiful fractal or a three-dimensional game pop out.) Over the years, programmers have collectively spent an enormous amount of time programming, fixing bugs in their code, and thinking of ways to avoid similar bugs in the future. That has generated a huge number of books about programming style and techniques for avoiding, detecting, and fixing bugs.

This chapter provides an introduction to some of the techniques that I've found most useful over the years. It begins by describing some tools and general problem-solving approaches that you can use to turn the description of a method into code. It then explains some specific techniques that you can use to make your code easier to debug and maintain.

If you're not a programmer (for example, if you're a project manager or a customer), you may not need to memorize every one of these techniques and apply them to your daily life. However, it's still worth your time to read them so that you'll know what's involved in writing good code (and so you'll understand what the programmers are complaining about).

TOOLS

Including overhead (office space, computer hardware, network hardware, Internet service provider, vacation, sick time, a well-stocked soda machine, and so forth), employing a programmer can easily cost more than $100,000 per year. Some specialized kinds of programmers will draw that much in salary alone, and the total may even top $200,000 or more. Still, I have seen managers refuse to spend a few hundred bucks for proper programming tools. I've seen projects end the year with thousands of dollars left over for hardware expenses, but not a nickel for software tools.

When you're spending $50 to $100 per hour on each employee, you don't have to save much of their time to make a little extra expense worthwhile. You don't need to go crazy and spend thousands of dollars to buy everyone a high-end video recording package (unless that's what your business does), but you should spend a little money to make sure your team has all the tools it needs.

The following sections describe some of the development tools that every programmer should have.

Hardware

Few things are as frustrating as trying to write software on inadequate hardware. Programmers need fast computers with lots of memory and disk space, ideally on a solid-state drive. A programmer with an underpowered computer or insufficient memory takes longer to do everything.

Even worse, waiting for slow compilations breaks the programmer's train of thought. To write bug-free (or at least minimally buggy) code, a programmer must stay focused on a method's design until it has been completely written. Breaking the writing process into dozens of chunks separated by several minutes of thumb twiddling (or more likely, trips to the water cooler) breaks the programmer's train of thought, so they need to re-create an understanding of the code each time. If each new understanding doesn't match the previous ones, the result is far more likely to contain bugs.

> ## THE TORTOISE AND THE SLOTH
>
> I once worked on an application using a slow development environment. I would add the next feature to the code, press the Compile button, and wander off for five or six minutes to wait for the compilation to finish. It was just too frustrating to sit there staring at the screen while the compiler slowly dribbled out periods to tell me that it was working and not dead.
>
> Meanwhile my business partner was stuck on another project but with a similar development cycle. We spent a lot of time in the hallway talking about vacations.
>
> After about a month of that, I got a new development environment that had a lot fewer features but that was much faster. It let me reproduce everything I had done in the previous month in just two days. As you can probably guess, I never used the other environment again.

Make sure the programmers have all the hardware resources they need to do their jobs quickly and effectively. If that means buying more memory, disk space, or even new computers, do it. It's insane to waste hundreds of hours a year of a programmer's time to save a few hundred dollars. (Although I've known managers who did exactly that. In fact, I've known managers who wouldn't pay for new hardware for their programmers, but who needed the absolute top-of-the line computers for themselves so that they could fill out expense reports and answer email.)

There are two drawbacks to buying the programmers everything they need. First, some programmers will go overboard and buy all sorts of fun toys that they don't actually need. Most programmers don't need a USB-controlled NERF rocket launcher or a Darth Vader USB hub. If you have the money, you might let some of those purchases slide in the interests of morale. Otherwise, you might want to check the product SKUs on the purchase requisitions you're signing. (I've seen people try to requisition Dalmatian puppies and cars, mostly as jokes. Those were caught, but I know of one lab that managed to buy a hot tub one piece at a time. They got in a whole lot of. . .well. . .hot water.)

The second and far more important drawback to giving developers everything they want is that they sometimes forget that their users may not have such nice equipment. I've used applications that were blazingly fast on the developers' computer but that were painfully slow for the users. Modern computers are fast enough and cheap enough that this isn't the problem it used to be in the "old days" two or three years ago, but you should always test applications with hardware that is similar to whatever your end users will be stuck with.

Network

I've known development groups that didn't allow access to external networks. I can understand why that might be necessary if you're designing a new *Minecraft* mod and are worried that foreign hackers will steal your plans and sell them to terrorists, but if it's at all possible, you should allow programmers to have free access to the Internet. Often a quick search can find a solution to a programming problem that would otherwise take hours to solve.

For example, when I'm working on a tricky project, I often use my own websites (www.csharphelper.com and www.vb-helper.com) to look up specific techniques. My sites are particularly useful to me because they hold solutions to lots of problems I've encountered in the past and because I know more or less what they contain. I also often find solutions on Wikipedia (www.wikipedia.org) and I find a lot of mathematical solutions on Wolfram MathWorld (https://mathworld.wolfram.com). And, of course, I often use a search engine to look for solutions in other places.

You should gently encourage staff members not to spend their whole day playing *Cookie Clicker* or in chat rooms arguing about who is better, Kirk or Picard, but try to provide a fast Internet connection and the freedom to use it.

Development Environment

This is the absolute minimum necessary to make programming possible. It at least includes the compiler or interpreter that translates program code into something the computer can execute.

An *integrated development environment (IDE)* such as Eclipse (mostly for Java, although plug-ins let you write in other languages such as C++ or Ruby) or Microsoft Visual Studio (for Visual C#, Visual Basic, Visual C++, JavaScript, and F#) can also include much more. Depending on the version you have installed, they can include debuggers, performance profilers, class visualization tools, auto-completion when typing code, context-sensitive help, team integration tools, syntax highlighting, and more.

Note that you don't always need the fanciest development environment possible. For example, Visual Studio comes in many different versions, ranging from the free Community edition designed for individual users to the Professional and Enterprise editions designed for large project teams, which cost a "whole lot per month" (MSRP, prices in US dollars). The more expensive versions include tools and resources that are most useful for larger projects, so if you're writing a small application by yourself, you may do just as well with the free express edition. (That edition is also good enough for many projects, so you may as well start there and decide whether you need something more.)

Similarly, Eclipse comes in a variety of IDEs with a lot of different plug-ins to meet the needs of different kinds of users. For example, Eclipse for Testers is designed for testers. (Well, duh.) If you're not doing a lot of testing, you may want to use a different version.

WHO KNOWS

Most mature development environments include remarkably powerful tools for writing code. They're effective for a very good reason: the programmers who wrote them know what you need to write programs. In contrast, programmers may not know a lot about court reporting software, medical diagnostics, or cabinet design, so software in those fields may be a little inconsistent. However, if programmers know anything, they know what features make development environments effective. There will always be some variation, and you may need to pay extra to get the best features, but there are some amazingly powerful programming tools out there if you're willing to learn how to use them.

Source Code Control

If your development environment doesn't include source code control, a separate system is essential. Chapter 2, "Before the Beginning," explains that a documentation management system is important for letting you track the many documents that make up a project. Source code control is even more important for program code where changing a single character can reduce a working program to a worthless pile of gibberish.

A good source code management system enables you to go back through past versions of the software and see exactly what changes were made and when. If a program stops working, you can pull out old versions of the code to see which changes broke the program. After you know exactly what changes were made between the last working version and the first broken one, you can figure out which changes caused the bug, and you can fix them.

Source code control programs also prevent multiple programmers from tripping over each other as they try to modify the same code at the same time. They're also useful in case disaster strikes and someone accidentally deletes your entire project. (At least we *hope* it's accidentally.)

Profilers

Profilers let you determine what parts of the program use the most time, memory, files, or other resources. These can save you a huge amount of time when you're trying to tune an application's performance. (I'll say more about this in the section "Defer Optimization" later in this chapter.)

You may not need to buy every programmer a profiler. Typically, a small part of a program's code determines its overall performance, so you usually don't need to study every line's performance extensively. Still, it's important to have profilers available when they are needed.

Static Analysis Tools

Profilers monitor a program as it executes to see how it works, how often different pieces of code are called, and how time-consuming those pieces are. Static analysis tools study code without executing it. They tend to focus on the code's style. For example, they can measure how interconnected different pieces of code are or how complex a piece of code is. They can also calculate statistics that may indicate code quality and maintainability metrics such as the number of comments per line of code and the average number of lines of code per method.

Testing Tools

Testing tools, particularly automated tools, can make testing a whole lot faster, easier, and more reliable. If the testing tools are easy to use, programmers are more likely to actually use them. I'll talk more about testing tools in Chapter 13, "Testing" which covers testing. For now, just be aware that every programmer must perform at least some testing, so everyone should have access to testing tools.

Source Code Formatters

Some development environments do a better job of formatting code than others. For example, some environments automatically indent source code to show how code is nested in if-then statements and loops. Some environments also color keywords, match parentheses and braces, allow you to expand and collapse regions of code, and provide other formatting features that make code easier to read and understand. That in turn reduces the number of bugs in the code and makes finding and fixing bugs easier.

Other development environments don't provide much in the way of formatting. If you're using that kind of environment, a separate code formatter can standardize indentation, align and reformat comments, break code so it fits on a printout, enforce certain kinds of code standards, and more.

(Your team will need to decide on the level of code uniformity you want to enforce. Too much standardization can be annoying to developers, but left to their own devices, a few programmers will produce such free-spirited results that their code looks more like an E.E. Cummings poem than professional software.)

Refactoring Tools

The term *refactoring* is programmer-speak for "rearranging code to make it easier to understand, more maintainable, or generally better." Some refactoring tools (which may be built into the IDE) let you do things like easily define new classes or methods or extract a chunk of code into a new method.

Refactoring tools can be particularly useful if you're managing existing code (as opposed to writing new code).

Training

This is another category where some managers are penny-wise and pound-foolish. Training makes programmers more effective and keeps them happy. A few thousand dollars spent on training can greatly improve performance and help you retain your staff.

Online video training courses and books are often less effective than in-person training, but they're also a lot less expensive and they let you study whenever you have the time. If a $50 book gives you a single new tip, then it's probably worth it.

Collaboration Tools

On larger projects, development is a cooperative endeavor. Unless the project is so small that a single person can build it, the developers are going to need to interact with each other. In the days when programmers sat together in cube farms, that wasn't a problem. You could just throw a note over the cubical wall to solicit feedback. Or you could talk through issues at lunch or around the coffee pot.

At the beginning of the COVID-19 pandemic, many people started working remotely, and that trend has become the new norm. Although remote work has been possible for a long time, many more people are now working remotely (at least some of the time) than in the past. Programmers are particularly well-suited to remote work, so it's reasonable to assume that members of your team won't always be together.

In that case, you need good collaboration tools. Developers need the ability to discuss problems, work together to negotiate interfaces, and share *Dilbert* cartoons as needed. Some of those interactions can occur via text message, normal phone, or VoIP calls.

You may want videoconferencing for some calls, particularly if management is involved so they can show off their fancy suits and ties. (You can wear your business mullet: business attire on the top and sweatpants on the bottom.)

For more technical calls, you may want screen sharing so developers can share design diagrams, show off new features, and demonstrate the newest ways to crash the program. You may even want the ability for multiple people to work on the same documents at the same time.

Keep in mind that the team will need to have the usual assortment of status meetings and planning sessions. Depending on your development model, those may occur infrequently (so people might just come into the office on those days), or they may happen practically daily (in which case you may want to have many of them remotely).

Explore the available options, get input from the team, and pick your collaboration tools. Be sure they are easy to use so people don't hesitate to use them when they must. In fact, you may want to have a status meeting now and then just so people are used to the process. For more on these tools, see the section "Collaboration Software" in Chapter 3, "The Team."

At the same time, try not to overuse these tools. Just because a tool is easy to use doesn't mean you should use it constantly. I can imagine a dystopian work environment where everyone is constantly connected to a meeting *just in case* they need to talk to the little heads displayed across the tops of their screens. I've even heard stories about managers who require employees to keep their cameras on at all times to verify that they're working.

Some school teachers have used that approach to make sure students are present. That seems to work well with some kids but not others. (Remember those hyperkinetic kids who have trouble sitting still at the best of times? Some of them grow up to become software engineers.)

Remember that much of development is a creative, thoughtful process. I'm not sure it would be particularly motivational to have little windows on your screen showing people staring at the ceiling, rearranging desktop toys, or completely missing because they're getting more coffee.

ALGORITHMS

After low-level design is mostly complete (and you have all your tools in place), you should have a good sense of what classes you need and the tasks those classes need to perform. The next step is writing the code to perform those tasks.

For more complicated problems, the first step is researching possible algorithms. An *algorithm* is like a recipe for solving a hard programming problem. In the decades since computers were invented, many efficient algorithms have been developed to solve problems such as the following:

➤ Sorting and arranging pieces of data

➤ Quickly locating items in databases

➤ Finding optimal paths through street, power, communication, or other networks

➤ Designing networks to provide necessary capacity and redundancy to prevent single points of failure

➤ Encrypting and decrypting data

➤ Picking optimal investment strategies

➤ Finding least cost construction and production strategies

➤ Many, many more

For complicated problems like these, the difference between a good algorithm and a bad one can make the difference between finding a solution in seconds, hours, days, or not at all.

Fortunately, these sorts of algorithms have been extensively studied for years, so you usually don't need to write your own from scratch. You can use the Internet and algorithm books to look for an approach that fits your problem. (For example, see my book *Essential Algorithms: A Practical Approach to Computer Algorithms Using Python and C#, Second Edition*, Wiley, 2019.)

You'll still need to do some work plugging the algorithm into your application, but there's no need for you to reinvent everything from scratch. I'll say more about algorithms in the next chapter.

TOP-DOWN DESIGN

If you can't find an algorithm to handle your situation, you need to write some code of your own. Even if you do find an algorithm that can be useful, you'll probably need to write some code to prepare for the algorithm and to process the results. So how do you get from a big, intimidating task like "design optimal routes for 300 delivery vehicles" or "schedule the classes for 1,200 middle-school students" to actual working code?

One useful approach is *top-down design*, also called *stepwise refinement*. In top-down design, you start with a high-level statement of a problem, and you break the problem down into more detailed pieces.

Next, you examine the pieces and break any that are too big into smaller pieces. You continue breaking pieces into smaller pieces until you reach the point where it would be easier to just write the code than to describe it. At that point, you have a detailed list of the steps you need to perform to solve the original problem.

As you break a task into smaller pieces, you should be on the lookout for opportunities to save some work. If you notice that you're performing some chore more than once (perhaps while describing multiple main tasks), you should think about pulling that chore out and putting it in a separate method. Then all the tasks can use the same method. That not only lets you skip writing the same code a bunch of times, it also lets you invest extra time testing and debugging the common code while still saving time overall.

If the main task's description becomes too long, you should break it into shorter connected tasks. For example, suppose you need to write a method that searches a customer database for people who might be interested in golf equipment sales. You identify several dozen tests that identify likely prospects: people who earn more than $75,000 per year, people who live near golf courses, country club members, people who wear plaid shorts and sandals with spikes, and so forth.

If the list of tests is too long, it will be hard to read the full list of steps required to perform the original task. In that case, you should pull the tests out, place them in a new task described on a separate sheet of paper (or possibly several), and refer to the new task as a subtask of the original.

For example, suppose the original method is called `PromoteSales`. Originally, its description might look like this:

PromoteSales()

1. Identify customers who are likely to buy items on sale and send them emails, flyers, or text messages as appropriate.

Now add some detail.

PromoteSales()

1. For each customer:

    A. If the customer is likely to buy:

        i. Send email, flyer, or text message depending on the customer's preferences.

Step A. "If the customer is likely to buy" will be pretty long, so create a new `CustomerIsLikelyToBuy` method. Similarly, step i will be fairly complicated, so create a new `SendSaleInfo` method. Now the main task looks like the following:

PromoteSales()

1. For each customer:

    A. If `CustomerIsLikelyToBuy()`

        i. `SendSaleInfo()`

At this point, you need to write the `CustomerIsLikelyToBuy` and `SendSaleInfo` methods. Here's the `CustomerIsLikelyToBuy` method.

CustomerIsLikelyToBuy()

1. If (customer earns more than $75,000) return `true`.

2. If (customer lives within 1 mile of a golf course) return `true`.

3. If (customer is a country club member) return `true`.

4. If (customer wears plaid shorts and sandals with spikes) return `true`.

    . . .

73. If (none of the earlier was satisfied) return `false`.

Here's the `SendSaleInfo` method.

> `SendSaleInfo()`
>
> 1. If (customer prefers email) send email message.
> 2. If (customer prefers snail-mail) send flyer.
> 3. If (customer prefers text messages) send text message.

You can add other contact methods such as voicemail, telegraph, or carrier pigeon if appropriate.

This version of the `SendSaleInfo` method may also need some elaboration to explain how to determine which contact method the customer prefers.

> `SendSaleInfo()`
>
> 1. Use the customer's `CustomerId` to look up the customer in the database's `Customers` table.
> 2. Get the customer's `PreferredContactMethod` value from the database record.
> 3. If (customer prefers email) send email message.
> 4. If (customer prefers snail mail) send flyer.
> 5. If (customer prefers text messages) send text message.

Continue performing rounds of refinement, providing more detail for any steps that aren't painfully obvious, until the instructions are so detailed a fifth-grader could follow them.

At that point, sit down and write the code. If you've reached a sufficient level of detail, translating your instructions into code should be a mostly mechanical process.

INSUFFICIENT DETAIL

Some developers stop refining their code design when they think the list of instructions is enough to get them started but before it provides a painful level of detail. For example, many developers wouldn't bother to spell out how to look up the customer in the database and get the customer's `PreferredContactMethod` value.

That's probably okay in this example, at least if you're an experienced developer who's done something like this before. That kind of design shortcut can lead to problems, however, if a step turns out to be harder than you originally thought it would be.

It can be disastrous if you turn the instructions over to someone else who doesn't have your background and some steps are harder for that person than they would be for you. (I've worked on projects where the team lead gave a junior developer instructions that were obvious to the lead but mystifying to the developer. Rather than asking for help, the developer flailed about for weeks without making any progress.)

PROGRAMMING TIPS AND TRICKS

Top-down design gives you a way to turn a task statement into code, but there are still a lot of tricks you can use to make writing code faster and easier. Other tips make it easier to test code, debug it when a problem surfaces, and maintain the code in the long term.

The following sections describe some of my favorite tips for writing good code.

Be Alert

Writing good code can be difficult. To know if you're writing the code correctly, you need to completely understand what you're trying to do, what the code actually does, and what could go wrong. You need to know in what situations the code might execute and how those situations could mess up your carefully laid plan. You need to ask yourself, what if an important file is locked, a needed value isn't found in a parameter table, or a user can't remember their password?

Keeping everything straight can be quite a challenge. You can make your life a lot easier if you write code only while you're wide awake and alert.

Most people have certain times of day when they're most alert. Some people are natural morning people and work best in the morning. Others work better in the afternoon. Some programmers do their best work after midnight when the rest of the world is asleep.

Figure out when your most effective hours are and plan to write code then. Fill out progress reports and timesheets during less productive hours.

Write for People, Not the Computer

Probably the most important tip in this chapter is to write code for people, not for computers. The computer doesn't care whether you use meaningful names for variables, indent your code nicely, use comments, or spell words correctly. It doesn't care how clever you are, and it doesn't care if your code produces a correct result.

In fact, the computer doesn't even read your code. Depending on your programming language and development environment, your code must be translated one, two, or more times before the computer can read it. All the computer wants to see is a string of 0s and 1s. If you were really writing code for the computer's benefit, your code would look like this:

```
10000000 00000000 00000000 00000000 00001110 00011111 10111010 00001110
10110100 00001001 11001101 00100001 10111000 00000001 01001100 11001101
01010100 01101000 01101001 01110011 00100000 01110000 01110010 01101111
01110010 01100001 01101101 00100000 01100011 01100001 01101110 01101110
01110100 00100000 01100010 01100101 00100000 01110010 01110101 01101110
01101001 01101110 00100000 01000100 01001111 01010011 00100000 01101101 ...
```

The reason you write code in some higher-level programming language is that 0s and 1s are confusing for *you*. It would be incredibly difficult to remember the strings of 0s and 1s needed to represent different programming commands. (Although I know someone who used to have a computer's boot sequence memorized in binary so that he could toggle it in using switches when the computer needed to be restarted!)

Using a higher-level language lets you tell the computer what to do in a way that *you* can understand. Later, when your application is doing something wrong, it lets you trace through the execution to see what the computer is doing and why.

Debugging and maintaining code is far more difficult and time-consuming than writing code in the first place. The main reason is because you know what you are trying to do when you write code. Later, when you're called upon to debug it, you might not remember exactly what the code is supposed to do. That makes it harder to identify the difference between what the code is supposed to do and what it actually does, so it's harder to fix.

Fixing a bug also has a much higher chance of adding a new bug than writing new code does, and for the same reason. When you're debugging, you don't have as clear an understanding of what the code is supposed to do. That makes it much easier to change the code in a way that breaks it.

To make debugging and maintaining code easier, you need to write code that is clear and easy to understand. Hopefully, whoever is eventually forced to track down a bug in your code won't be a violent psychopath, but you can make that person's job a lot easier if you remember it's that person you're writing for, not the computer.

IT COULD BE YOU!

Always remember that the person debugging your code a year from now could be you! After enough time has passed, there's no way you'll remember exactly how the code was supposed to work. When you're writing the code initially, it may seem obvious, but a year or two later you'll only have whatever clues you left for yourself in the code to go by.

You can make your job easier by writing code that's clear and lucid, or you can learn to hate the younger you.

When you write code, remember that you're writing it for a possible future human reader (who might be you) and not for the computer.

Comment First

There are a few things that most programmers instinctively avoid because they don't feel like they're part of writing code. One of those is writing comments.

Many programmers write the bare minimum of comments they think they can get away with and then rush off to write more code. This is so common, in fact, that it has its own movement: just barely good enough (JBGE). The idea is that writing lots of comments is a waste of time. Besides, comments are usually wrong anyway, so rather than spending more time rewriting and fixing them, you should just write better code.

You can read my rant about JBGE in the section "Code Documentation" in Chapter 2. In this section, I want to talk about why comments need to be revised so often.

Many programmers use one of two models for writing comments. The first approach is to write comments as you code. You write a loop and then put a comment on top of it. Later you realize that the loop isn't quite right, so you change it and then update the comment. A bit later you realize that the loop still isn't right, so you change it again and revise the comment once more. After 37 rounds of revisions, you've either spent a huge amount of time updating the comment, or you've given up (thinking you'll revise the comment later) and the comment is hopelessly disconnected from the final code.

The second strategy is to write all the code without comments. When you're finished with your 37 revisions, you go back and insert the bare minimum number of comments that you think you can get away with without getting yelled at by the lead developer. (The lead developer does the same thing, so he doesn't care all that much about comments anyway.)

In both of these scenarios, the problem isn't that you have too many comments. The real problem is that you're trying to write comments to explain what the code *does* and not what it *should do*. When you tweak the code, you change what it does, so you need to update the comment. That creates a lot of work and that makes programmers reluctant to write comments.

If the code is well-written, the future reader will read the code to see what it actually does. What that person needs is comments to explain what the program is *supposed* to do. Then debugging becomes an exercise in determining where the program isn't doing what it's supposed to be doing.

One way to write comments that explain what the program is supposed to be doing is to write the comments first. That lets you focus on the intent of the code and not get distracted by whatever code is actually sitting there in front of you.

It also means you don't need to revise the comment 37 times. The code itself might change 37 times, but the *intent* of the code better not! If it does, then you didn't do enough planning in the high-level and low-level design phases.

For example, consider the following C# code. (If you don't know C# or some similar "curly-bracket language" like C++ or Java, just focus on the comments.)

```csharp
// Loop through the items in the "items" array.
for (int i = 0; i < items.Length - 1; i++)
{
    // Pick a random spot j in the array.
    int j = rand.Next(i, items.Length);

    // Save item i in a temporary variable.
    int temp = items[i];

    // Copy j into i.
    items[i] = items[j];

    // Copy temp into position k.
    items[j] = temp;
}
```

The comments in this code explain what the code is doing, but they're mostly redundant. For example, the first comment explains exactly what the line of code that follows it does: loop through the array. That's certainly true, but any programmer who can't figure that out by looking at the looping statement itself probably shouldn't be debugging anyone's code.

Similarly, the other comments are just English versions of the programming statements that follow. The comment `Copy j into i` is even a bit cryptic, and the comment `Copy temp into position k` contains a typo, presumably because the code's author changed the name of a variable and forgot to update the comment.

From a stylistic point of view, the comments are also distracting. They break up the visual flow and make the code look cluttered and busy.

Now that you've read the code, ask yourself, "What does it do?" Well yeah, it loops through the array, moves values into a temporary variable, and then moves them back into the array, but why? Does it accomplish what it was supposed to do? It's kind of hard to tell because the comments don't tell you what the code is supposed to do.

Now consider the following version of the code:

```
// Randomize the array.
// For each spot in the array, pick a random item and swap it into that spot.
for (int i = 0; i < items.Length - 1; i++)
{
    int j = rand.Next(i, items.Length);
    int temp = items[i];
    items[i] = items[j];
    items[j] = temp;
}
```

In this version, the comments tell you what the code is supposed to do, not what it actually does. The first comment gives the code's goal. The second comment tells how the code does it.

After you read the comments, you can read the code to see if it does what it's supposed to do. If you think there's a bug, you can step through the code in the debugger to see if it works as advertised.

This code is less cluttered and easier to read. It doesn't contain redundant comments that are just English versions of the code statements. These comments also don't need to be revised if the developer had to modify the code while writing it.

The best part of the comment-first approach is that the comments pop out for free if you use top-down code design. In the top-down method, you repeatedly break pieces of code into smaller and smaller pieces until you reach the point where a well-trained monkey could implement the code.

At that point, put whatever comment characters are appropriate for your language in front of the steps you've created (`//` for C#, C++, or Java; `#` for Python; `'` for Visual Basic; `*` for COBOL, and so forth), and drop them into the source code. Now fill in the code between the comments.

If your top-down design goes to a level of extreme detail, you may need to pull back a bit on the level of commenting. There's nothing wrong with the design going all the way to the level of explicitly giving the `if-then` statements you need to execute to perform a particular test, but that level of detail isn't necessary in the comments. Only include the comments that tell what the code is supposed to do and not the ones that repeat the actual code.

You may also need to add a few summary comments, particularly if your development team has rules for things like standard class and method headers, but most of the commenting work should be done.

And you may need to add a few extra comments to code that is particularly obscure and confusing. Remember, you might be debugging this code in a year or two.

Write Self-Documenting Code

In addition to writing good comments, you can make the code easier to read if you make the code self-documenting. Use descriptive names for classes, methods, properties, variables, and anything else you possibly can.

One exception to this rule is looping variables. Programmers often loop through a set of values and they use looping variables with catchy names like i or j. That's such a common practice that any programmer should be able to figure out what the variable means even though it doesn't have a descriptive name.

That doesn't mean you should avoid descriptive names if they make sense. If you're looping through the rows and columns of a matrix, you can name the looping variables row and column. Similarly, if you're looping through the pixels in an image, you can name the looping variables x and y. Those names give the reader just a little more information and make it easier to keep track of what the code is doing.

You can also make your code easier to understand if you don't use magic numbers. (A *magic number* is a value that just appears in the code with no explanation. For example, it might represent an error code or database connection status.) Instead of using a magic number, use a named constant that has the same value. It's easier to read code that looks for the constant HTTP_IM_A_TEAPOT_ERROR rather than the mysterious number 418. (Believe it or not, that is an actual HTTP error code.)

Better still, if your language supports enumerated types, use them. They also give names to magic numbers, and some development environments can use them to enforce type rules. For example, suppose you create an enumerated type named MealSizes that defines the values Large, ExtraLarge, and Colossal. (No one orders small or normal sizes anymore.) Internally, the program might represent those values as 0, 1, and 2, but your code can use the textual values. If you define a variable selected_size, then your code can't give it the value 4 because that isn't an allowed value. (Actually, in many programs you can weasel around that check and force the variable to have the value 4. That would defeat the purpose of the enumerated type, so don't do it!)

Keep It Small

Write code in small pieces. Long pieces of code are harder to read. They require you to keep more information in your head at one time. They also require you to remember what was going on at the beginning of the code when you're reading statements much later.

For example, suppose a piece of code loops through a set of customers. For each customer, it loops through the customer's orders. For each order, it loops through the order's items. Finally, for each item it loops through price points for that item. At some point later in the code, you'll come to statements that end each of those loops. For example, in C#, C++, or Java you'll come to a } character. If the code is short, you can look up a few lines to figure out which loop is ending. If the loops started a few hundred lines earlier, it may be hard to decide which loop is ending.

You may also eventually come across code like the following.

```
                }
            }
        }
    }
```

There's nothing here to tell you which loops are ending.

THIS IS THE END

If a closing brace } is far from its corresponding opening brace {, you can make the code easier to understand by adding a comment after it explaining which loop is ending. For example, the following statement shows how you might end a `for` loop that's looping through the X coordinates of an image.

`} // Next x`

If you prefer more laconic comments, you could simply use `// x`.

I know some programmers loathe this style of comment, but if the start and end of a loop are far apart, this can be helpful. And remember, it may not be you trying to later decipher the code.

I think many of the programmers who hate this kind of comment do so because they are forced to use it for *every* closing brace. You should use it only when it helps, not make an annoying rule that drives programmers crazy.

If a piece of code becomes too long, break it into smaller pieces. Exactly how long is "too long" varies depending on what you're doing. Many developers used to break up methods that didn't fit on a one-page printout. A more recent tree-friendly rule of thumb is to break up a method if it won't fit on your computer's screen all at one time. (This may be why no one programs on smartphones. You'd have thousands of 10-line methods.)

AVOIDING BREAKUPS

Some complicated algorithms may be confusing enough that it's hard to keep everything they do in mind all at once, but splitting them can ruin performance. Or there may be no good place to split them because all the pieces are interrelated. In those cases, you may be stuck with a long chunk of code.

Sometimes, a little extra documentation can act as a road map to help you keep track of what the code is doing. (This should be documentation in a separate file, not just more comments, which would make the code even longer.)

You can also refer to external documentation inside the comments. For example, if your code uses Newton's method for finding the roots of a polynomial, don't embed a five-page essay in the comments. Instead add the following comment to the code and move on to something more productive.

```
// Use Newton's method to find the equation's roots. See:
// http://en.wikipedia.org/wiki/Newton's_method
```

In general, if it's hard to keep everything a method does in mind all at once, consider splitting it into more manageable pieces.

Stay Focused

Each class should represent a single concept that's intuitively easy to understand. If you can't describe a class in a single sentence, then it's probably trying to do too much, and you should consider splitting it into several related classes.

For example, suppose you're writing an application to schedule seminars for a conference and to let people sign up for them. You probably shouldn't have a single class to represent attendees and presenters. Attendees and presenters may have a lot in common (they both have names, addresses, phone numbers, and email addresses), but conceptually they are very different. Instead of creating a single `AttendeeOrPresenter` class to represent both kinds of person, make separate `Attendee` and `Presenter` classes. You can make them inherit from a common `Person` parent class so you don't have to write the same name and address code twice, but making one mega class will only confuse other developers. (Besides, the name `AttendeeOrPresenter` sounds wishy-washy.)

Just as a class should represent a single intuitive concept, a method should have a single clear purpose. Don't write methods that perform multiple unrelated tasks. Don't write a method called `PrintSalesReportAndFetchStockPrices`. The name might be nicely descriptive, but it's also cumbersome, so it's a hint that the method might not have a single clear purpose.

One of my favorite examples of this was the `Line` method in earlier versions of Visual Basic. As you can probably guess, that method drew a line on a form or picture box. What's not obvious from the name is that it could also draw a box if you added the parameter B to the method call. I'm sure there was some implementation reason why this method drew boxes as well as lines, but seriously? A method named `Line` should draw lines not boxes!

Even if two tasks are related, it's often better to put them in separate methods so that you can invoke them separately if necessary.

Avoid Side Effects

A *side effect* is an unexpected result of a method call. For example, suppose you write a `ValidateLogin` method that checks a username and password in the database to see if the combination is valid. Oh, and by the way, it also leaves the application connected to the database. Leaving the database open is a side effect that isn't obvious from the name of the `ValidateLogin` method.

Side effects prevent a programmer from completely understanding what the application is doing. Because understanding the code is critical to producing high-quality results, avoid writing methods with side effects.

Sometimes, a method may need to perform some action that is secondary to its main purpose, such as opening the database before checking a username/password pair. There are several ways you can remove the hidden side effects.

First, you can make the side effect explicit in the method's name. For example, you could call this method `OpenDatabaseAndLogin`. That's not an ideal solution because the method isn't performing one well-focused task (we talked about this in the previous section, so I hope you haven't already forgotten), but it's better than having unexpected side effects. (Any time you have "And" or "Or" in a method name, you may be trying to make the method do too much.)

A second approach would be to make the `ValidateLogin` method close the database before it returns. That removes the hidden side effect, although it might reduce performance if you need to reopen the database for use by other methods.

A third approach would be to move the database opening code into a new method called `OpenDatabase`. The program would need to call `OpenDatabase` separately before it called `ValidateLogin`, but the process would be easy to understand.

A fourth approach could create an `OpenDatabase` method as before and make that method keep track of whether the database is already open. If the database is open, the method wouldn't open it again. Then you could make every method that needs the database (including `ValidateLogin`) call `OpenDatabase`. Methods such as `ValidateLogin` would encapsulate the call to `OpenDatabase` so you wouldn't need to think about it when you called `ValidateLogin`. There's still some extra work going on behind the scenes that you may not know about, but with this approach, you don't need to keep track of whether the database is open or closed.

It may take a little extra work to remove side effects from a method, but it's worth it to make the code that calls the method easier to understand.

Validate Results

Murphy's law states, "Anything that can go wrong will go wrong." By that logic, you should always assume that your calculations will fail. Maybe not every single time, but sooner or later they will produce incorrect results.

Sometimes, the input data will be wrong. It may be missing or come in an incorrect format. Other times your calculations will be flawed. Values may not be correctly calculated or the results may be formatted incorrectly.

To catch these problems as soon as possible, you should add validation code to your methods. The validation code should look for trouble all over the place. It should examine the input data to make sure it's correct, and it should verify that the result your code produces is right. It can even verify that calculations are proceeding correctly in the middle of the calculation.

The main tool for validating code is the assertion. An *assertion* is a statement about the program and its data that is supposed to be true. If it isn't, the assertion throws an exception to tell you that something is wrong.

For example, suppose you're writing a method to list customer orders sorted by their total cost. When the method starts, you could assert that the list contains at least two orders. You could also loop through the list and assert that every order has a total cost greater than zero.

After you sort the list, you could loop through the orders to verify that the cost of each order is at least as large as the cost of the one before it.

One type of assertion that can sometimes be useful is an invariant. An *invariant* is a state of the program and its data that should remain unchanged over some period of time.

For example, suppose you're building a work scheduling application that defines an Employee class. You might decide that all Employee objects must always have at least 40 hours of work in any given week. (Although some of those hours might be coded as vacation.)

Here the invariant condition is that the Employee object must have at least 40 hours of work assigned to it. You could add assertions to the object's properties and methods to periodically verify that the invariant is still true. (Ideally, the class would provide only a few public properties and methods that could change the Employee object's work schedule and those would verify the invariant, at least before and after they do their work.)

TIMELY ASSERTIONS

Most programming languages have a method for conditional compilation. By setting a variable or flipping a switch, you can indicate that certain parts of the code shouldn't be compiled into the executable result. For example, the following code shows some validation code in C#.

```
#if DEBUG_1
// Validate the sorted order data.
...
#endif
```

continues

(continued)

The code between the `#if` and `#endif` directives is compiled only if the debugging symbol `DEBUG_1` is defined. If that symbol isn't defined, then the validation code is ignored by the compiler.

You can use techniques such as this one to add tons of validation code to the application. While you are testing and debugging the application, you can define the symbol `DEBUG_1` (and any other debugging symbols) so the testing code is compiled. When you're ready to release the program, you can comment out the debugging symbols so that the program runs faster for the customers.

Later, if you discover a bug, you can uncomment the debugging symbols to restore the testing code to hunt for the bug.

Some languages such as C# also have built-in conditional compilation for assertions. For example, the following statement asserts that an order's `TotalCost` value is greater than 0.

```
Debug.Assert(order.TotalCost > 0);
```

The compiler automatically includes this statement in debug builds and removes it from release builds.

Assertions and other validation code can make it easy to find bugs right after they are written when they're easiest to fix. Unfortunately, it's hard to believe the code you just wrote isn't perfect. After all, you just spent hours slaving over a hot keyboard, pounding away with no breaks (maybe just one to refresh your coffee). The code is still fresh in your mind, so you know exactly how it works (or at least how you *think* it works). Obviously, there isn't a bug in it or you would have already fixed it!

That thinking makes it hard for most programmers to write validation code. They just assume it isn't necessary.

However, bugs do occur, so obviously they must be lurking in some of the code that was just written. If only you could convince programmers to add validation code to their methods, you might catch the bugs before they become established.

One way to encourage programmers to write validation code is to have them write it before writing the rest of a method's code. (This is similar to the way you can often get better comments if you write them before you write the code.) Writing the validation code first ensures that it happens.

This also has the advantage that you probably don't yet know exactly how the final code will work. You don't have it all in your head whispering seductively, "You did a great job writing me. There's really no need to validate the results." You also don't have preconceptions about how the code works, so you won't be influenced in how you write the validation code. You can look for incorrect results without making assumptions about where errors are impossible.

Practice Offensive Programming

The idea behind *defensive programming* is to make code work no matter what kind of garbage is passed into it for data. The code should work and produce some kind of result no matter what.

For example, consider the following `Factorial` function written in C#. (In case you don't remember, the factorial of a number N is written N! and equals $1 \times 2 \times 3 \times \ldots \times N$.)

```csharp
public int Factorial(int number)
{
    int result = 1;
    for (int i = 2; i <= number; i++) result *= i;
    return result;
}
```

This code initializes the variable `result` to the value 1. It then multiplies that value by 2, 3, 4, and so on up to the number passed into the method as a parameter. It then returns `result`.

This code works well in most cases. The code even works for strange values of the input parameter `number`. For example, if `number` is 0 or 1, the method sets `result` to 1, the loop does nothing, and the method returns the value 1. That happens to be correct because by definition 0! = 1 and 1! = 1.

If the parameter `number` is negative, the code also sets `result` to 1, the loop does nothing, and the method returns 1.

In fact, due to a quirk in the way C# handles integer overflow, this method even returns a value if `number` is really large. If `number` is 100, the loop causes `result` to overflow. The program sets `result` equal to 0, ignores the overflow, and continues merrily crunching away. When it's finished, it returns the value 0.

This is traditional defensive programming in action. No matter what value you pass into the method, it continues running. It may not always return a meaningful result, but it doesn't crash either.

Unfortunately this approach also hides errors. If the program is trying to calculate 100!, it's probably doing something wrong. At a minimum, it probably doesn't want to get the value 0.

A better approach is to make the `Factorial` method throw a temper tantrum if its input is invalid. That way you know something is wrong and you can fix it. I call this *offensive programming*. If something offends the code, it makes a big deal out of it.

The following code shows an offensive version of the `Factorial` method:

```csharp
public int Factorial(int number)
{
    Debug.Assert(number >= 0);
    checked
    {
        int result = 1;
        for (int i = 2; i <= number; i++) result *= i;
        return result;
    }
}
```

The code begins with an assertion that verifies that the input parameter is at least 0.

The method includes the rest of its code in a `checked` block. The `checked` keyword tells C# to *not* ignore integer overflow and throw an exception instead. That takes care of cases in which the input parameter is too big.

If the program passes the new version of the Factorial function an invalid parameter, you'll know about it right away so you can fix it.

Use Exceptions

When a method has a problem, there are a couple ways to tell the program that something's wrong. Two of the most common methods are throwing an exception and passing an error code back to the calling code.

For example, the Factorial method shown in the previous section throws an exception if there's an error. The call to Debug.Assert throws an exception if its condition is false. The checked block throws an exception if the calculations cause integer overflow.

As mentioned earlier in this chapter, an exception interrupts the program's execution and forces the code to take action. If you don't have any error handling code in place, the program crashes. That means a lazy programmer can't ignore a possible exception. If a method such as Factorial might throw an exception, the code must be prepared to handle it somehow.

In contrast, suppose the Factorial method indicated an error by returning an error code. For example, when passed the number –300, it might return the value –1. The factorial of a number is never negative, so the value –1 would indicate there is a problem.

The trouble with this approach is the program could ignore the error code. In that case, the program might end up displaying the bogus value –1 to the user or using that value in some other calculation. The result will be gibberish that is at best unhelpful and at worst misleading and confusing.

In general it's better to throw an exception to indicate an error instead of returning an error code. That way the program can't ignore a potentially confusing situation.

Write Exception Handlers First

Now that you're using assertions and exceptions to indicate errors, the code that calls your method needs to use exception handling to deal with those exceptions.

Unfortunately, error handlers are a bit like comments in the sense that many programmers find them boring and don't like to write them. They're also a bit like validation code because it's easy to assume that they're not necessary because you *know* the code works.

One way to create better error handlers is to follow the same strategy you can use when writing comments and validation code: Do it first. When you start writing a method, paste in all the comments that you got from top-down design, add code to validate the inputs and verify the outputs, and then wrap error handling code around the whole thing.

First, make the error handling code look for exceptions that you expect to happen occasionally and that you can do something about (like trying to open a locked file).

Next, add code that looks for other expected exceptions about which you can't do anything except complain to the user. That code should restate any exceptions in terms the user can understand. For example, instead of telling the user, "Arithmetic operation resulted in an overflow," you can present a more meaningful message like, "All orders must include at least 1 item."

Don't Repeat Code

If you find that you're writing the same (or nearly the same) piece of code more than once, consider moving it into a separate method that you can call from multiple places. That obviously saves you the time needed to write the code more than once. More important, it lets you debug and maintain the code in a single place.

Later if you need to modify the code for some reason, you can make the change in one place. If the code were duplicated, you would need to update it in every place it occurred. If you forgot to update it in one of those places, the different copies of the code would be out of synch and that can lead to some extremely confusing bugs. (Yes, I speak from experience here.)

Defer Optimization

One of my favorite rules of programming is:

First make it work. Then make it faster if necessary.

Highly optimized code can be a lot of fun to write, but it can also be very confusing. That means it takes longer to write and test. It's also harder to read, so it's harder to debug and fix if there is a problem.

Meanwhile, even the least optimized code is usually fast enough to get the job done. If you're displaying a list of 10 choices to the user, it doesn't matter if it takes 10 or 12 milliseconds to display. The user is going to stare at the choices for 3 or 4 seconds anyway, so it's not worth spending a lot of extra programming effort to shave a few milliseconds off the total time.

To program as efficiently as possible, write code in the most straightforward way you can, even if it's not the fastest way you can imagine. After you get the code working, you can decide whether it is so slow that it requires optimization.

> ### OPTIMIZATION OVERLOAD
>
> I've never worked on a project that failed because the code was too slow. I've worked on a couple projects that were initially too slow and we rewrote their performance bottlenecks to bring them up to an acceptable speed. It really wasn't all that hard.
>
> In contrast, I've worked on a couple projects that failed because their design was too complicated. People spent so much time trying to optimize the design and come up with the most efficient approach possible that the code was too complicated to implement and debug.
>
> I'll say it again: First make it work. Then make it faster if necessary.

If you do discover that the program isn't running fast enough, take some time to determine where performance improvements will give you the most benefit.

Typically, 80 percent of a program's time is spent in 20 percent of the code. (Or 90 percent is spent in 10 percent of the code, or something. The idea is, the program spends most of its time executing a small fraction of the code.) Time you spend optimizing the 80 percent that's already fast enough is time that would be better spent on the slow 20 percent. (Frankly, you'd be better off just wasting that time by talking and eating donuts around the water cooler. Time you spend messing about inside the 80 percent of the code that's already working fine can only make that code more confusing and harder to debug and maintain over time.)

Before you start ripping the code apart, use a profiler to see exactly where the problem code is. Then attack only the problem and not the whole program. (So you don't mess up the rest of the code with friendly fire.)

PROFILERS PROFILED

In case you haven't used one, a *profiler* is a program that monitors the progress of a program while it runs to identify the parts that are slow, that use the most memory, or that otherwise might be bottlenecks. Different profilers work in different ways. For example, some add code (called *instrumentation*) to your program to record the number of times every method is called and the amount of time the program spends in each method.

Profilers are *very* handy for tracking performance problems. I worked on one program that was taking approximately 20 minutes to load its data when it started. The project manager refused to buy a profiler ("real programmers don't need them") and had a number of theories about where in the data processing algorithms the bottlenecks were.

I snuck off into my office and installed a profiler for a 30-day free trial. Within a few hours, I had discovered that the problem wasn't in the main algorithms at all. The problem was actually in some fairly trivial string-processing code. Basically, the program was going back to a database hundreds of times to re-fetch values that it had already loaded. I built a simple table to keep track of the values that had already been fetched and cut the program's startup time from 20 minutes to under 4.

If I hadn't used the profiler, I would probably have wasted a week or two and only shaved a minute or so off of the startup time. (After the fact, the project lead admitted that, okay, perhaps a profiler was a good idea after all.)

Before you start optimizing code, make sure it works properly. Then if you do find that performance is insufficient, carefully analyze the problem (using a profiler if you can) so that you don't waste time optimizing code that is already fast enough.

SUMMARY

Most programmers love to program, but they can't do a good job without the proper tools. If you don't have the right hardware, software, and network support, writing good code is slow and frustrating. That leads to distraction and more bugs. Writing good code also requires debugging, testing, and profiling tools. Depending on the development environment, you may also need code formatting and refactoring tools.

Before you start writing code, make sure you have the tools you need to do so effectively. If you don't write code, make sure those who do get the tools they need.

Even if you're using all the proper tools, writing good code isn't guaranteed. There are dozens or perhaps hundreds of tips and tricks you can use to make your code safer. This chapter described a few of my favorites. By using those techniques, you can make your programs more reliable, easier to debug, and easier to modify in the future.

Another useful method for reducing bugs is to use tried-and-tested methods for performing common tasks. Over the years, programmers have written thousands, perhaps tens of thousands, of algorithms for performing common program chores. The next chapter describes some major algorithmic approaches that you may be able to apply to your programming problems.

EXERCISES

1. The greatest common divisor (GCD) of two integers is the largest integer that evenly divides them both. For example, the GCD of 84 and 36 is 12 because 12 is the largest integer that evenly divides both 84 and 36. You can learn more about the GCD and the Euclidean algorithm at https://en.wikipedia.org/wiki/Euclidean_algorithm.

   Knowing that background, what's wrong with the comments in the following code? Rewrite the comments so that they are more effective. Don't worry about the code if you can't understand it. Just focus on the comments. (Hint: It should take you only a few seconds to fix these comments. Don't make a career out of it.)

   ```
   // Use Euclid's algorithm to calculate the GCD.
   private long GCD(long a, long b)
   {
       // Get the absolute value of a and b.
       a = Math.Abs(a);
       b = Math.Abs(b);
       // Repeat until we're done.
       for (; ; )
       {
           // Set remainder to the remainder of a / b.
           long remainder = a % b;

           // If remainder is 0, we're done. Return b.
   ```

```
        if (remainder == 0) return b;

        // Set a = b and b = remainder.
        a = b;
        b = remainder;
    }
}
```

2. Why might you end up with the bad comments shown in the previous code?

3. How could you add validation code to the method shown in Exercise 1? (If you don't know how to write the validation code in C#, just indicate where it should be and what it should do.)

4. How could you apply offensive programming to the modified code you wrote for Exercise 3?

5. Should you add error handling to the modified code you wrote for Exercise 4?

6. The following code shows one way to swap the values in two integers a and b. The ^ operator takes the "exclusive or" (XOR) of the two values. The comments to the right explain how this method works.

```
// Swap a and b. Let A and B be the original values.
b = a ^ b; // b = A ^ B
a = a ^ b; // a = A ^ (A ^ B) = (A ^ A) ^ B = B
b = a ^ b; // b = B ^ (A ^ B) = (B ^ B) ^ A = A
```

This is a clever piece of code. It lets you swap two values without needing to waste memory for a temporary variable. So why isn't it good code? Write an improved version.

7. Using top-down design, write the highest level of instructions that you would use to tell someone how to drive your car to the nearest supermarket. (Keep it at a very high level.) List any assumptions you make.

WHAT YOU LEARNED IN THIS CHAPTER

➤ Use the right tools:

   ➤ Fast development hardware and a fast Internet connection

   ➤ A good development environment and source code formatters (if necessary)

   ➤ Source code control

   ➤ Profilers and static analysis tools

   ➤ Testing and refactoring tools

   ➤ Training

➤ Use top-down design to fill in code details.

➤ Programming tips:

   ➤ Program when you're most alert.

   ➤ Write code for people, not for the computer.

   ➤ Write comments, validation code, and exception handlers before you start writing the actual code.

   ➤ Use descriptive names, named constants, and enumerated types.

   ➤ Break long methods into manageable pieces.

   ➤ Make each class represent a single concept that's intuitively easy to understand.

   ➤ Keep methods tightly focused on a single task and without side effects.

   ➤ Program offensively to expose bugs as quickly as possible.

   ➤ Signal problems with exceptions instead of error codes.

   ➤ If you're writing the same piece of code for a second time, extract it into a method that you can call repeatedly.

   ➤ Only optimize after you sure it's necessary. Then use a profiler to find the code that actually needs optimization.

11

Algorithms

> Although greed is considered one of the seven deadly sins, it turns out that greedy algorithms often perform quite well.
>
> —*Stuart Russell*

> Heuristic is an algorithm in a clown suit. It's less predictable, it's more fun, and it comes without a 30-day, money-back guarantee.
>
> —*Steve McConnell*

What You Will Learn in This Chapter:

➤ Algorithm categories

➤ Algorithm examples

➤ How to decide which algorithms are better than others

An algorithm is simply a recipe for doing something. In fact, a recipe is an algorithm for cooking a particular food. It contains a sequence of steps that, if followed *correctly*, produces a culinary masterpiece. (Or if followed by most of us, produces something that is probably edible and hopefully won't poison us.)

Software algorithms are methods for making the computer produce some result. For example, Google uses algorithms to rank web pages, to determine which pages to display first when you type "algorithms" into the search bar, and to list the most profitable places to insert advertising on the web pages that you view. It even uses algorithms to figure out what your queries mean. When you type "did gyre and gimble in the wabe" into the search bar, some algorithm needs to somehow deduce that this is part of Lewis Carroll's poem "Jabberwocky" and then display relevant pages.

This chapter provides an extremely brief introduction to software algorithms. It explains some of the major categories of algorithmic approaches, describes some examples, and provides some guidance for picking the best algorithms for your projects.

ALGORITHM STUDY

Why should you study algorithms?

All software applications use algorithms. They can be as simple as adding product prices and calculating sales tax or as complicated as ranking web pages and deciding where to place advertising on those pages. (Actually, that algorithm may not be too complicated. If there's any blank space, put an ad on it.)

Algorithms allow you to apply techniques devised by others to solve problems in your projects. Unless you have very specialized needs, there's probably already an algorithm that can help. Need to sort a list of names? Easy! Want to find the shortest route that visits every ice cream store in town? No problem! Looking for artificial intelligence that generates random pseudo-motivational quotes? See https://inspirobot.me!

Many thousands of algorithms have been extensively studied for decades, so you usually don't need to write your own from scratch. You can use the Internet and algorithm books to look for an approach that fits your problem.

More importantly, studying algorithms helps you train your brain. It's like stretching for a gymnast, weight training for a football player, or acting lessons for a professional wrestler. It improves your game.

By studying algorithms, you not only learn about specific algorithms that you can use, but you also learn algorithmic techniques that you can apply when you stumble across a problem that others haven't already studied to death. It teaches you to consider different approaches to a problem, to methodically examine code to see how it works, and to analyze techniques to decide which one will best suit your needs.

Algorithms also teach you that there is *always* more than one way to solve a problem. Some methods may be faster, less memory-intensive, simpler, or generally prettier than others, but in real-world programming there's rarely a single answer.

To keep your mind nimble, I wholeheartedly encourage you to study algorithms in depth and keep studying them throughout your software career. The field is constantly expanding as people face new challenges, so you'll never run out of novel algorithms to study. I've been studying them for around 40 years, and I still find interesting new algorithms to try to implement.

Start with a general algorithms book or two (such as my book, *Essential Algorithms: A Practical Approach to Computer Algorithms Using Python and C#* by Rod Stephens, Wiley, 2019). That will teach you basic concepts such as algorithm complexity and fundamental techniques. Then branch out into fields that you find interesting such as artificial intelligence, games, cryptography, image processing, three-dimensional graphics and ray tracing, audio/video processing, astronomy, physics, fractals, biology, finance, and just about any other complicated endeavor. You can find information on those topics in specialized books and online.

ALGORITHMIC APPROACHES

Every algorithm is different, but many algorithms use similar approaches. For example, if you can divide a problem into pieces and then solve the pieces separately, a divide-and-conquer approach may work well. Or if you can define a problem as being made up of smaller problems, a recursive method may help.

The following sections explain some general categories of algorithmic approaches and describe some examples. The descriptions are mostly intuitive rather than rigorous because there isn't enough room to cover them rigorously here.

Note that these categories are not all-inclusive and there are many algorithms that don't fit well into any of them. Note also that the categories overlap, so some algorithms combine multiple approaches.

Decision Trees

A *decision tree* isn't really an algorithm; it's a tree data structure that helps you think about a problem's solution space. Different branches through the tree represent decisions that lead to a final assignment of values of some kind, and a complete path from the root of the tree to a leaf corresponds to a complete assignment. Your job is to figure out which path through the tree represents the best assignment.

Note that for many problems, the best solution might not be unique. Multiple solutions may be optimal, so it's a mistake to think that you will always find "the" best solution.

Knapsack

In the *knapsack problem*, you have a knapsack that can hold a fixed amount of weight. You also have a collection of items, each having a weight and a value. You need to find the combination of items with the greatest value that will still fit in the knapsack.

For a concrete example, suppose Elon Musk has offered to take you to Mars with him, but you can only bring 10 kilograms (kg) of personal items. Which of your 20 most prized possessions will you take? The bowling ball should probably stay (because it's heavy and there are no bowling alleys on Mars), but you might want to bring your bowling trophy (because it's lighter and you're sure the other astronauts will be impressed).

To model these selections with a decision tree, each level of the tree corresponds to an item such as your bowling ball, bowling trophy, granola bar, *The Fifth Element* DVD, and so forth. (We'll assume that you have other items on your list, but we only need four for this discussion.) Each node in the tree has two child links, with the left link meaning "leave the item behind" and the right link meaning "bring the item to Mars."

Figure 11.1 shows a small decision tree for this problem. For example, the upper-left branch represents leaving the bowling ball behind and the upper-right branch represents bringing the bowling ball with you.

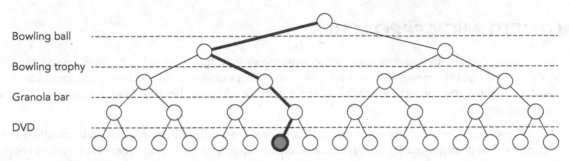

Bowling ball

Bowling trophy

Granola bar

DVD

FIGURE 11.1: A decision tree represents combinations of decisions.

If you trace a path from the root to a leaf node, the branches that you take define a complete assignment of objects in and out of the knapsack. For example, to get to the shaded leaf (seventh from the left), you follow the links left, right, right, left, which represents leaving the bowling ball, bringing the bowling trophy, bringing the granola bar, and leaving the DVD. (Elon is probably bringing his copy anyway.)

Now the goal is to explore the decision tree to find the path that leads to the best assignment of items in the knapsack.

Decision trees often grow extremely quickly. For example, if you're considering N items, then the knapsack problem's decision tree has 2^N paths leading to 2^N leaf nodes representing 2^N possible solutions. In Figure 11.1, N is 4, so there are only $2^4 = 16$ possible solutions. However, if N is 50, then there are $2^{50} \approx 1.1 \times 10^{15}$ possible solutions. If you can examine 10 million solutions per second (which is a pretty brisk pace), then it could take you almost 3.6 years to decide what to bring to Mars. (I'm not sure Elon is willing to wait that long while you make up your mind.)

The Eight Queens Problem

In the *eight queens problem*, the goal is to position as many queens as possible on a chess board so that none of them can attack any of the others. If you think about it for a while, it's not hard to see that you can place *at most* eight queens on the board. It's a bit harder to see that you can fit the full eight on the board.

One way to approach this problem is to think of a decision tree where each branch represents placing a queen on a square or not (much as the branches for the knapsack problem represent putting an item in the knapsack or not). The branches out of the root node represent placing a queen on the first square or not. At the next level of the tree, the branches represent placing a queen on the second square or not. At each level, the branches represent placing a queen on a new square or not.

Each path down through the tree would represent a possible solution. A standard chess board has 64 squares, so the full tree would hold around $2^{64} \approx 1.8 \times 10^{19}$ leaf nodes representing possible solutions. If your computer could examine 10 million solutions per second, then you'll have your solution in around 32 thousand years.

Fortunately, we can do better if we restructure the decision tree a bit. In the previous tree, a node represented a square and its branches represented adding a queen to that square or not. An alternative would be to make each node represent a queen and make its branches represent placing the queen on various squares. There are 64 possible positions that could hold a queen, so in this version of the tree, each node would have 64 branches. There are eight queens, so the tree would be nine levels tall (eight for the queens and a ninth to hold the leaf nodes that represent the possible solutions). That means the tree would hold around $64^8 \approx 2.8 \times 10^{14}$ nodes. That's an improvement of a factor of around 64 thousand over the previous tree, but we're still talking years here.

Let's think a bit more about how the problem works and restructure the tree again. We know that no two queens can be on the same row or they will attack each other like two Christmas shoppers spotting the last Turbo Man (or whatever this year's hot toy is). That means each queen must go on a different row. Instead of giving a queen's node enough links to put it in any square on the board, we can give it eight links to represent the eight squares on its row. Now the tree has only $8^8 = 16,777,216$ leaves, a huge improvement!

That's still more than I would like to work through by hand, but my laptop only needs a few seconds to visit all 16+ million leaf nodes and find 92 valid solutions. (Remember I mentioned that many problems have multiple solutions?) Later in this chapter I'll talk about some other improvements that we can make to this decision tree, but this is good enough for now.

The lesson to be learned here is that you can sometimes restructure a decision tree by changing the kinds of decisions you make. In this example, we used the following three questions:

➤ For each square, should a queen be in this square?

➤ For each queen, where should the queen go?

➤ For each row, which column should contain this row's queen?

Just rethinking the problem slightly changed the same algorithm's runtime from hundreds of millennia, to years, to seconds. Is that cool or what?!

Exhaustive Search

In an *exhaustive search*, you examine every possible solution and pick the best one. Because this is as effective, inevitable, and subtle as using a nuclear warhead to kill a mosquito, it's sometimes called a *brute force approach*.

For example, suppose you have sorted your Pokémon cards alphabetically, but now you want to find the one with the highest HP. You can't use the sorted order to help check the HP values, so you need to search through the whole stack. (Unless you remember that you have a Snorlax and it has the highest HP. Then you can search for the Snorlax alphabetically.)

For the knapsack problem, you would enumerate every possible combination of adding and removing items from the knapsack, see which combinations fit, and see which combinations have the largest value.

Exhaustive search is often slow, sometimes painfully and sometimes impractically, but it always finds an optimal solution. It's also often relatively simple to implement, so it's a reasonable option for very small problems where speed won't be an issue. For example, a four-item knapsack problem only requires you to examine 16 combinations, so it would be easy with an exhaustive search. (In fact, if we assigned precise weights and values to the four items considered earlier, you could easily find the solution in your head.)

Because exhaustive search is guaranteed to find an optimal solution, it also provides a useful check for other more complicated algorithms. For example, suppose you've written a general knapsack solver. Then you can compare its results to an exhaustive search in a bunch of random trials with 20 or so items. If the solver agrees with the exhaustive search, then you can have at least some confidence that its solutions will be reasonable for larger problems.

Backtracking

Backtracking is a way to envision a search through a solution space. For example, you can use backtracking to think about how an exhaustive search works in a decision tree.

It's also useful for working with treelike processes. For example, a recursive algorithm calls itself, that call calls itself, and so on, so the program's call structure is treelike even though it may not use an actual tree data structure.

In backtracking, the program follows branches down through the tree (or the network or whatever). After it has explored one path until it can go no farther, the program backtracks to an earlier spot in the tree and continues the search from that position by moving down other links that it hasn't yet explored.

Usually, backtracking algorithms work recursively, and "backtracking" really means returning up the call stack to a previous call to the recursive method. The search method calls itself recursively each time it moves down a level in the tree. To backtrack, the recursive call exits and control returns to the previous call higher up in the call stack where it tries a different branch.

This idea applies to any algorithm that uses a decision tree. For example, in the knapsack problem described earlier, the program climbs down the branches adding and omitting items from the knapsack. When it reaches the bottom, it backtracks up a level and explores other options.

Consider the knapsack decision tree shown in Figure 11.2. The program quickly climbs down the tree's left branches and adds none of the items to the test solution to arrive at node A. (This is probably not the best solution, but it is *a* solution.) It then backtracks up one level to node B, the point where it skipped adding the last item, *The Fifth Element* DVD. It tries adding the DVD and moves down to a complete solution at node C.

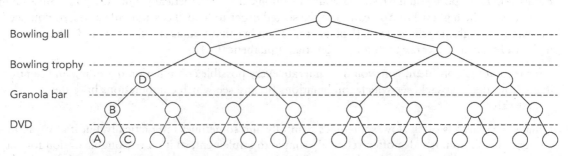

FIGURE 11.2: An algorithm can use backtracking to move back up a tree to explore new paths.

After considering the new solution (containing just the DVD), the program backtracks again up to node B. It has finished following the links out of node B, so it backtracks yet again to node D. There it follows the right link (adding the granola bar) and continues searching that subtree.

The algorithm continues climbing down the tree and backtracking up until it has visited the entire decision tree and has found an optimal solution.

Pruning Trees

The bad news about decision trees is that they often grow extremely quickly. The good news is that you can often *prune* the tree so you don't need to search the whole thing.

For example, consider again the eight queens problem. Suppose you take the left branch out of the root node, which represents putting the first queen in the first row's first column. Now suppose you take the next left branch, which represents placing the second queen in the second row's first column. There's already a conflict because these first two queens are in the same column. That means you don't need to look any further down the tree from that point, so you've just pruned off a huge chunk of the tree!

The same thing happens when you try to place the second queen in the second column because then she can attack the first queen diagonally. That lets you prune off another huge chunk of tree.

The exact final shape of the tree is hard to visualize, but it's much smaller than the original tree. The original contained 19,173,961 nodes and 16,777,216 leaf nodes, each representing a *potential* solution. The trimmed tree contains only 2,057 nodes and 92 leaf nodes, each representing a *valid* solution.

For another example, let's revisit the knapsack problem. As you're searching the decision tree, you will often reach a point where the solution so far is already too big to fit in the knapsack. For example, if you just start adding every item, you'll quickly run out of room. At that point, there's no reason to continue searching lower down in the decision tree. Unless one of the remaining items is a helium balloon with a negative weight, it doesn't matter whether you add those items or not; you cannot find a solution below that point in the tree.

In one test that I ran with 25 items, an exhaustive search visited roughly 67 million tree nodes and 33.5 million leaf nodes to find a solution in about 12 seconds. With "it's too big to fit" pruning, the algorithm visited only 120,581 nodes and 26,741 leaf nodes to find the same solution almost instantly. (The exact results depend on the particular item values and weights, and the size of the knapsack, so don't expect to see precisely the same thing on your computer.)

Pruning helps but unfortunately many decision trees are so large that this simple kind of pruning can't save you completely. If exhaustively searching a full knapsack tree would take 3.6 years and you can prune off 99 percent of the tree, it'll still take you 13 days to pack for Mars.

Branch and Bound

Branch and bound is a particularly clever way to prune decision trees. When you visit a node in the tree, you ask yourself, "What is the best conceivable outcome from this point?" If the best possible outcome is worse than some other solution that you have already found, you stop searching this part of the tree and prune it off.

For example, suppose you're working on a knapsack problem and you've already found a possible solution with value 42. Now suppose you've crawled around on the tree some more and you're considering a partial solution where you've added some items (let's call this set A for "added"), excluded others (call this set X for "excluded"), and have not yet considered still others (call this set D for "dunno"). If the total value of set A plus the total value of set D is less than 42, then no improved solution is possible at this point, so you can abandon the search here and backtrack to look for other solutions.

For a concrete example, suppose the total value of the items in set A is 20 and the total value of the items in set D is 19. If you add all of the items in set D to the selection (never mind that they may not fit), then the grand total value will be only 39. You already have a solution with value 42, so there's no point continuing in this direction.

In one test that I ran with 20 items, an exhaustive search visited around 2 million nodes, a search with "it's too big to fit" pruning visited 23,135 nodes, and branch and bound visited only 8,793 nodes. (Again, the precise results depend on the exact parameters.)

Note that branch and bound doesn't apply to every problem. In particular, you need a way to know how much potential benefit may be waiting below a certain point in the search in the dunno set. For example, suppose you've safely positioned five queens for the eight queens problem. Could positioning the remaining queens improve your solution? If you don't already have a solution, then you must continue positioning queens because you don't know if that will lead to a valid solution. If you do already have a solution, then what are you doing hanging around searching the decision tree after you have a solution? You need not (and in fact *can* not) improve it. Just email it to your professor and go watch a movie or something.

Heuristics

An algorithm that *may* produce a good result but that doesn't *guarantee* an optimal result is called a *heuristic* (pronounced *you-ris-tik*). An everyday example of a heuristic is the rule of thumb "Don't drive more than 10 mph over the speed limit to avoid getting a speeding ticket." The police could pull you over for going 1 mph over the speed limit, but they probably won't bother unless you're also weaving from side to side or your license plate says "IH8COPS."

One common programming heuristic is a *random solution*. In many applications, you can simply pick a random solution and see how good it is. The chances of you finding a perfect solution may be small with a single random selection, but you may be able to make small changes to improve the initial solution. You can also perform many random trials and try to improve them. You may not find the best possible solution, but you may find something usable. Random selection is a popular heuristic because it's usually fast and very easy to implement, so you may as well give it a try.

Greedy algorithms (described in the next section) are often fairly effective heuristics.

One particularly interesting heuristic helps you solve the *knight's tour problem*. In this problem, you have a knight on a chess board with some given size N × M. (Algorithm aficionados wouldn't use a normal chess board when they could use boards of arbitrary sizes instead!) The goal is to make the knight move from square to square, following the somewhat quirky movement rules that knights have, until it has visited every square on the board without visiting the same square twice. (In the *closed knight's tour problem*, the knight must end on the starting square.)

One way to attack this problem is to use backtracking. That works reasonably well, but at some point the number of possible moves becomes too large to explore them all. Because you cannot easily tell whether a particular sequence of moves will eventually work, you can't use branch and bound to narrow your choices. That means the size of the boards you can consider is limited. In one set of tests, the program I wrote solved the problem on a 6×6 board almost instantly, took about two seconds to solve it on a 7×6 board, and on a 7×7 board it still hadn't found a solution when I got bored after an hour and stopped it.

In 1823, H. C. von Warnsdorff suggested a knight's tour heuristic where you select the next possible move that has the lowest number of possible moves leading out of it. For example, suppose the knight has two possible moves, A and B. If you take move A, then the knight has five moves for the next step. If you take move B, then the knight has two moves for its next step. The heuristic tells you to take move B because it gives the knight fewer options in the future.

This heuristic is so good that it finds a complete tour with *no backtracking at all* for a large percentage of boards of various sizes. There is some ambiguity when moves A and B have the same number of subsequent moves, but if you make the choice correctly, it is believed that the heuristic will always find a tour for square boards of any size. (For more information, see www.futilitycloset .com/2014/11/10/warnsdorffs-rule.)

Heuristics don't always guarantee to produce the best possible solution, but they are often fast and sometimes produce results that are good enough.

Greedy

A *greedy algorithm* makes a decision at each step that moves closer to an optimal solution. For example, suppose you want to find the top of a mountain at night. You can't see very far, but you can walk uphill at every step. That's a greedy algorithm because, at every step, you move closer to the goal of the top of the mountain. (Because of this analogy, greedy algorithms are also sometimes called *hill-climbing algorithms*.)

Of course, you may become stuck on the top of a foothill and not realize that you're not on top of the mountain (at least until sunrise), so this algorithm does not necessarily produce an optimal result. That makes it a heuristic as described in the preceding section.

However, some greedy algorithms *do* guarantee an optimal result. For a more computer-sciencey example, a greedy algorithm works well for the *change-making problem*. In this problem, you have an assortment of US coins, and you need to make change while using the fewest number of them. The US coin denominations are penny (1¢), nickel (5¢), dime (10¢), quarter (25¢), half-dollar (50¢), and dollar (100¢). (For a while there was a rumor that Congress might try to make a $1 trillion coin for budgetary reasons, but alas it didn't happen. That would have made a complete proof set for a given year much more expensive!)

A greedy algorithm for this problem is to use the largest denomination that is no larger than the amount that you still need to give out.

For example, to make 37¢ in change, you use a quarter because 25¢ is the largest denomination that is no larger than 37¢. Next, 37¢ – 25¢ = 12¢, so you need to make change for 12¢. The largest denomination that is less than 12¢ is 10¢, so you add a dime. You still need to give out 2¢, so you use one penny and then another penny. The coins have values 25¢, 10¢, 1¢, and 1¢. If you think about it, you can convince yourself that this is the fewest possible coins that can make 37¢.

This algorithm still works if you add the US bills ($1, $2, $5, $10, $20, $50, and $100), but if you run out of nickels, the algorithm no longer works. For example, to make 30¢ the algorithm would use one quarter and five pennies, but the optimal solution would use three dimes. (You can try the algorithm for non-US currencies if you like, but I make no guarantees. If the Yapese fei come in denominations of 1, 2, 17, and 29, then the algorithm won't work. See if you can come up with a counterexample.)

If you think about a greedy algorithm in terms of a decision tree, the algorithm marches straight from the top of the tree to the bottom following a single path. Because it only follows one path through a potentially enormous tree, these algorithms can be extremely fast, so it's usually worth giving a greedy algorithm a try. In the knapsack problem, for example, you might repeatedly add the most valuable item that still fits to the knapsack. You may not get the best possible solution, but you'll pick the most valuable items, and the result will at least give you a lower bound for optimal solutions.

Greedy algorithms are so fast that you can try several, if you can think of different greedy approaches. For the knapsack problem, you might try adding the lightest items first to fit as many items as possible into the knapsack. Or you might try adding the densest items (in the value/weight sense) first. It turns out that a greedy algorithm based on value/weight density works quite well and often provides an optimal or near optimal solution for small knapsack problems.

Divide and Conquer

A *divide-and-conquer* approach divides the solution space into pieces, figures out which piece contains the solution, and then examines that piece more closely. If you can discard large pieces at each step, then you can quickly narrow the search.

Often this is done recursively, so you use the same method to divide that initial solution space, then the piece that contains the solution, then the appropriate sub-piece, and so on until you find the solution that you need.

For example, consider again your alphabetized pile of Pokémon cards and suppose you want to find your Snorlax. You could look at the card exactly in the middle. If it is alphabetically before Snorlax (perhaps Pikachu), then you know that Snorlax is in the second half of the deck. You've reduced the number of cards that might contain Snorlax in half.

Now you look at the card in the middle of the second section. If that card comes alphabetically after Snorlax (perhaps Tapu Lele), then you know that Snorlax is to the "left" of that card (in the first half of the second half, if you will). You've divided the first half in half again, so you're only considering a quarter of the whole deck.

You continue looking at the middle card in the section that still might contain Snorlax and then consider the left or right half of that section until either you find Snorlax or the target section is empty. At that point, if you still haven't found Snorlax, then you know that Snorlax is not present in the deck. (And you remember that you traded it for a Gyrados.)

This algorithm divides the section that might contain the target value in half at each step. If you have N cards, that means it can take at most around $\log_2(N)$ steps to find the target (or conclude that it is not present). For example, if you have 100 cards, then the search can take at most roughly $\log_2(100)$ ≈ 6.6 steps. That's very fast! If you have 1 million Pokémon cards, this kind of search would take only $\log_2(1,000,000)$ ≈ 20 steps! (There are only around 16,000 Pokémon cards even if you include both the English and Japanese versions, so it shouldn't be a hard problem unless you have a *lot* of duplicates.)

Because this kind of search divides the section that could contain the target into two pieces with each step, it's called a *binary search*. Note that some algorithms divide the search space into three, four, or more pieces at each step, so they are not binary searches.

Because they are so fast, these kinds of divide-and-conquer algorithms are excellent choices when they apply. (Unfortunately, they do not always apply, as in the knapsack problem.)

Recursion

A *recursive* algorithm is one that calls itself. For example, consider the following definition of the Fibonacci sequence:

Fib(0) = 0

Fib(1) = 1

Fib(N) = Fib(N − 1) + Fib(N − 2)

Notice that the definition of Fib(N) recursively invokes the definition of Fib(N − 1) and Fib(N − 2). Each value is the sum of the two that come before it in the sequence. The following table shows the first few values of the Fibonacci sequence.

N	0	1	2	3	4	5	6	7	8	9	10
Fib(N)	0	1	1	2	3	5	8	13	21	34	55

This function doesn't grow as quickly as the factorial function N!, but it really takes off once it gets started. For example, Fib(100) ≈ 3.5×10^{20}.

The fact that the definition of the function is recursive hints that there is probably a naturally recursive algorithm. The following code shows a recursive C# function that closely follows the definition:

```
private long Fibonacci(long n)
{
    if (n == 0) return 0;
    if (n == 1) return 1;
    return Fibonacci(n - 1) + Fibonacci(n - 2);
}
```

This is a recursive function because it calls itself. In fact, this example is *multiply recursive* because it calls itself twice.

Most people do not naturally think recursively, but some problems are naturally recursive and recursive algorithms often work well for them. For example, the previous definition of Fibonacci numbers is recursive, so this algorithm suits it well. (Note that this may be a *natural* way to calculate Fibonacci numbers, but it's not an *efficient* way. I'll explain a better method in the following section on dynamic programming.)

For another example, consider the following definition of the factorial function N!:

0! = 1

N! = N × (N − 1)!

This leads to the following recursive function (this time in Python for variety):

```
def factorial(n):
    if (n == 0):
        return 1
    return n * factorial(n - 1)
```

Recursive algorithms often go well with recursive data structures. For example, trees have a recursive structure. (Each node has links that lead to other nodes, which have links that lead to other nodes, which have links that. . .) That makes a recursive search a good fit for trees. The following pseudo-code shows how you might search a binary tree for a target value:

```
Node.Find(target)
    If (target is down the left branch)
        Return LeftChild.Find(target)
    Else
        RightChild.Find(target)
```

The **Bold** text shows where the method calls itself. The same approach works for trees that may have more or fewer than two links out of each node, but the tests at each node are a bit more complicated.

Networks are similarly recursive. (A node has links that connect to neighbors, which have links that connect to neighbors, which . . .) The previous recursive search also works on a network, although you need to add some extra bookkeeping code to avoid getting stuck in infinite loops.

Note that all recursive algorithms must have a way to stop or they will continue forever. For example, each time the recursive Fibonacci algorithm described earlier calls itself, it uses a smaller value for n. Eventually n reaches 0 or 1, and the algorithm returns a result without calling itself. Because the values of n get smaller but cannot fall below 0, the algorithm must eventually stop.

The same argument works for the factorial function.

However, what happens if the initial value for n is –1? In both of those functions, the value of n never reaches the stopping conditions n == 0 or n == 1, so n decreases forever and the function never stops. (At least until the program eats up the memory in the computer's call stack and crashes.) You can modify the functions to return some safe value if n is invalid, but it's probably better to throw an exception or otherwise scream at the calling code so it knows there's a problem. (Remember the section "Practice Offensive Programming" in Chapter 10, "Programming"?) These mathematical functions are undefined for values less than 0, so returning some "safe" value would only hide a likely problem.

Dynamic Programming

In *dynamic programming*, an algorithm uses some sort of data structure to save partial results. It then uses those results to build more and more complete solutions until it solves the original problem.

For example, consider again the Fibonacci function. It turns out that the obvious recursive function is very inefficient because it recalculates the same values an enormous number of times.

For example, to calculate Fib(7), the function must calculate Fib(5) and Fib(6). To calculate Fib(6), it must calculate Fib(4) and Fib(5). Notice that Fib(5) is being calculated twice.

That wouldn't be a big deal, except the same sort of duplication occurs all over the place. To calculate Fib(5), the function must calculate Fib(4) and Fib(3), so Fib(4) is being calculated again. If you continue, you'll find that many values are calculated again and again.

Figure 11.3 shows the complete call tree needed to calculate Fib(7), where each node represents a function call. The node that contains the number *x* represents calling the function with the input *x*. If you study the tree, you'll see that Fib(0) (shaded nodes) is calculated eight times and Fib(1) (darkly shaded nodes) is calculated a whopping 13 times. Between them, they are called 21 times, which is more than half of all of the function calls!

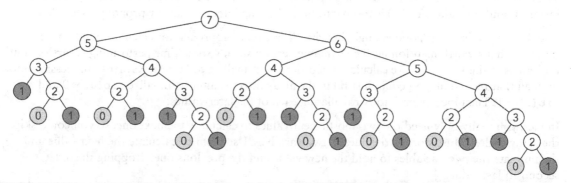

FIGURE 11.3: The recursive Fibonacci calculation repeats the same calls many times.

It turns out that the number of steps needed to calculate Fib(N) recursively depends on Fib(N) itself. As I mentioned earlier, this function grows very quickly. For example, Fib(100) $\approx 3.5 \times 10^{20}$. That means this algorithm is too slow to calculate large values of Fib(N) in a reasonable amount of time.

Dynamic programming to the rescue! The problem with this algorithm is that it recalculates the same values many times. What if the algorithm stored each value that it calculated so it didn't need to calculate it again? It could keep the Fib(N) values in an array (perhaps called Fib). Later, if it needed Fib(3), it could look it up in the array instead of recalculating it from scratch.

Now imagine crawling through the tree shown in Figure 11.3 top to bottom and left to right. This time when you come to a number that you've seen before, you look it up in the array instead of calculating it.

Figure 11.4 shows the new tree. Here the white nodes with black text show new calculations that require a call to the function, the gray circles with black text represent values that you can look up in the array, and dashed circles are not needed at all. Now instead of 41 function calls, the program makes 8 function calls, 5 array lookups, and skips the remaining 28 nodes completely.

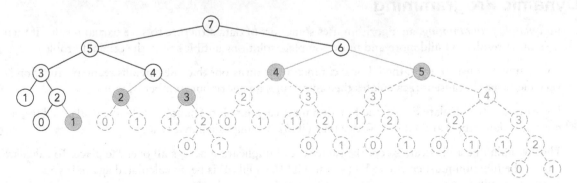

FIGURE 11.4: Dynamic programming removes many nodes from the call tree.

In one test, the "obvious" Fibonacci function took 2.7 seconds to calculate Fib(40). That version takes a much longer time as N increases, so it can only calculate Fib(N) for values of N that are only a little larger than 40.

The dynamic version can easily calculate up to Fib(92) = 7,540,113,804,746,346,429 practically instantly, and the value Fib(93) is too big to fit in the long integers that my program uses.

The dynamic solution is good enough, but there's one other approach for calculating Fibonacci numbers that's worth mentioning. The dynamic version spends some time performing recursion, but the values in the Fib array are calculated in order from smallest to largest. Rather than messing about with all that recursion, you could just fill in the array directly. Simply initialize Fib[0] = 0 and Fib[1] = 1. Then loop from 2 to N calculating each of the later values.

In fact, you really only need the two most recent values to calculate the next one, so you could skip the array entirely. Just store two values in two variables. Use them to calculate the next value and then update the two variables to hold the new value and the previous one, dropping the older second-to-last value.

The recursive method of calculating Fibonacci numbers is a good candidate for dynamic programming because you build later solutions from earlier ones, but sometimes it's not as obvious that large solutions contain pieces of smaller ones. For example, consider the knapsack problem again and suppose you're working with a relatively small knapsack. Really more like a fanny pack. Now suppose you have a set of items (Harry Potter playing cards, Rubik's cube, and a flash drive containing your favorite movies) that fills the fanny pack with a nice high value. There's a good chance that this combination of objects will be part of solutions to larger knapsacks. A dynamic programming approach to solving the knapsack problem uses a table holding solutions for small knapsacks to build solutions for larger knapsacks.

Exhaustive search lets you solve knapsack problems with up to around 25 or 30 items before the program gets too slow and you grow bored waiting. Branch and bound pushes this out to 65 or

70 items. Dynamic programming lets you solve problems with hundreds or even thousands of items, depending on the exact size of the knapsack and the weights of the items.

Unfortunately, dynamic programming (like all programming) is subject to the TANSTAAFL principle (There Ain't No Such Thing as a Free Lunch), so even it has a limit. Dynamic programming must store the smaller values somehow. In the knapsack problem, the values are stored in a table that depends on the number of items and the size of the knapsack, so the result can be enormous. A 1,000-item problem with a knapsack that can hold 1,000 units of weight would use more than 1 GB of memory. It's easy enough to throw another GB on the fire and keep going, but there is a limit.

Caching

Dynamic programming is basically a form of *caching*; you save solutions to smaller problems, so you don't need to recalculate them later. You can do something similar with a more general form of caching. Any time you think you'll need a value later, you tuck it away somewhere like a hash table (aka dictionary) for future reference. That lets you look up the value rather than getting it in some slower way such as calculating it, loading it from disk, or pulling it across the network.

For a concrete example, I once worked on a large project that loaded data from Excel. The data was hierarchical with smaller values used to build larger ones. Unfortunately, many larger values used the same smaller values, which used the even smaller values, and so on, so a lot of values were loaded many, *many*, *MANY* times. It was a bit like the Fibonacci calculation except the values were being loaded from disk and they weren't as predictable.

Loading values from disk is relatively slow, so I modified the program to store every value loaded from Excel in a hash table so, once a value was loaded, the program could get it from the memory rather than from the disk. It was a relatively simple change programmatically, but it cut the program's load time from roughly 20 minutes to around 4 minutes. The program still had other problems, but caching had provided a nice boost.

Randomization

A *randomized algorithm* is one that relies on randomness in some way. (But you probably guessed that.) Three main categories of randomized algorithms are Monte Carlo algorithms, Las Vegas algorithms, and Atlantic City algorithms. (The gambling theme may provide some insight into what computer scientists do in their spare time.)

Monte Carlo Algorithms

A *Monte Carlo algorithm* sometimes produces an incorrect result, usually with a relatively small probability. You can use the algorithm repeatedly to increase your confidence in the result. For example, *Fermat's primality test* uses a random number to determine whether a number p is prime. This test is correct with a probability of at least 0.5. If the number is *not* prime, then there's at least a 0.5 chance that you will definitely know that. Of course that also means there's at most a 0.5 chance that your random test number will fool you and you won't learn that p is not prime when it is. (That kind of number that incorrectly tells you that the number is prime is called a *false witness*.)

A 50 percent chance of correctness may not seem very helpful, but if you repeat the test many times with different random numbers, you can increase your confidence that the number is prime. If p is *not prime* and you run the test once, there's a 0.5 chance that your random test number will fool you and you'll think p is prime. If you run the test twice, then there's only a 0.5 × 0.5 = 0.25 chance that you'll be fooled twice. More generally, if you run the test N times, then there's a 0.5^N chance that you'll be fooled every time. For example, if you perform the test 10 times and every one of them says that p is prime, then there's a $0.5^{10} \approx 0.00098$ chance that you've been fooled. Not sure enough? It's a fast test, so run it 100 times. Now there's only a 7.9×10^{-31} chance that you've been fooled! Any gambler at Monte Carlo will take those odds!

To summarize, if you have a Monte Carlo algorithm that sometimes produces an incorrect result, you may be able to repeat the algorithm (with different random inputs, of course) to achieve a usable result.

CARMICHAEL NUMBERS

There is one little hitch with Fermat's primality test: *Carmichael numbers*. These are nonprime numbers that fool Fermat's primality test no matter what random test numbers you pick. Carmichael numbers form an infinite set but they are rare (there's an interesting concept!), so I'll pull the blankets over my head and pretend they don't exist.

For more information, search online, but I'll warn you that this gets pretty mathy. For the basics, see `https://en.wikipedia.org/wiki/Fermat_primality_test#Flaw`. For an interesting video, try `www.youtube.com/watch?v=7-ATzqyWnB4`. For some source code in several languages that tests whether a number is a Carmichael number, see `www.geeksforgeeks.org/carmichael-numbers`.

Las Vegas Algorithms

A *Las Vegas algorithm* is one that always either produces a correct result or tells you that it cannot, but its runtime may be uncertain.

For example, the quicksort algorithm sorts a list of values: numbers, strings, *Star Trek* movie titles, whatever. If the nonsorted input data is arranged reasonably randomly, then quicksort is one of the fastest algorithms out there. Unfortunately, the algorithm gives terrible performance if the values are initially sorted. Or mostly sorted. Or sorted in reverse order. (You might think it would help to have the items start out mostly sorted, but quicksort isn't designed to take advantage of that.)

Quicksort always produces a correct result, but its runtime depends on the initial arrangement of the input values, so it's a Las Vegas algorithm.

One way to improve quicksort is to introduce some randomness. There's a particular step in the algorithm that picks an item from the input. The basic algorithm simply uses the next item in sequence. If you select an item randomly instead, then the algorithm is fast even if the items are initially sorted.

Another approach is to randomize the entire list of items before launching quicksort.

Both of those approaches add randomness to prevent worst-case behavior if the items are initially sorted or reverse sorted. (Although they do take some extra time, so they slow performance a bit when the items are initially arranged randomly.)

Atlantic City Algorithms

Atlantic City algorithms are correct at least some fraction of the time (one definition says at least 75 percent of the time), and they are always relatively fast.

To put that into context:

➤ Monte Carlo algorithms are fast and only probably correct.

➤ Las Vegas algorithms are correct and only probably fast.

➤ Atlantic City algorithms are probably correct and probably fast.

(I guess these algorithms have those names because Atlantic City lies between Las Vegas and Monte Carlo?)

Like coelacanths, Atlantic City algorithms are rare and elusive creatures. In fact, the only examples I've been able to concoct are very mathy, involving things like Newton's method, escape-time fractals, and strange attractors, so I won't say any more about them. (If you come up with a good example, email me at RodStephens@CSharpHelper.com and let me know!)

State Diagrams

A *state diagram* (or *state transition diagram*) is a directed graph (network) where nodes represent states and links represent transitions between states. You can label the links with the actions that cause the transition if you like.

A state diagram is not really an algorithm or even an algorithmic approach. Rather, it's a way to keep track of a process or an object as it moves through various states inside a program. (Sort of like the way the decision trees described earlier help you model a sequence of decisions.)

For example, Figure 11.5 shows a state diagram that models a program's login process. You start at a login screen and enter your username and password. If they are valid, then the program checks your password's expiration date. If your password is old, the program displays a new password dialog. After you type and retype the new password, the program validates it. (Because otherwise you'll just try incrementing the number on the end to go from "Password112" to "Password113," as I do.)

The state diagram lets you easily know what to do at any stage of the process. What do you do when the initial password is invalid? Go back to the login form. What if the new password is invalid? Back to the new password dialog.

Notice that some of the states represent objects (such as the login form and the new password dialog), and others represent program actions (such as validating the initial password).

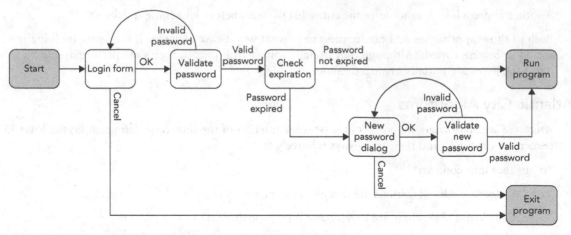

FIGURE 11.5: You can use a state diagram to model a login process.

Design Patterns

A *design pattern* is sort of like an algorithm for classes. Often design patterns are more strategic and algorithms are more tactical. In case you don't remember, strategy is the higher level how-do-we-defeat-the-aliens part (disable their computers) and tactics is the lower-level how-do-we-do-it part (fly a captured fighter to their mother ship and use a Linux shell script to upload a virus). Or in this case, design patterns might be how you can simplify a complicated printing interface and an algorithm might figure out how to place figures in the flow of a document for printing.

Rather than explaining how to do something the way most algorithms do, design patterns often show how to use a group of classes to perform some useful action. Sometimes a pattern requires building a class to do something. Other times a pattern is a method, interface, or other feature of a class that performs some sort of action in a standardized way.

For example, the façade pattern lets you hide the complexity of one interface with a simpler interface. Suppose you have a wonderful printing subsystem with all the bells and whistles. It can select the printer, control duplex, manage collation, set margins, and print on every kind of paper imaginable including letter, legal, envelope, origami, and cocktail napkin. If your document is longer than 50 pages, it can even tell your Internet-enabled coffee machine to make you coffee. (Medium, cream, two sugars.)

Unfortunately, this amazing subsystem requires you to fill in a complicated data structure involving several different classes to tell the subsystem exactly what you want it to do, and 99 percent of the time your application doesn't need this level of flexibility. To make printing easier, you can make a `DocumentPrinter` façade that takes a document as an input and just prints it on letter paper, double-sided, on the printer nearest to you. (And makes coffee, because we live in a civilized society, after all.) If you need some other feature, like printing on papier-mâché with invisible ink, you can use the original, more complicated printing subsystem.

Now your code is simpler and therefore more likely to work correctly. If someone changes the way the underlying subsystem works (to make cappuccino), you can update the `DocumentPrinter` class without changing the main program that uses it.

You can divide design patterns into categories. The most common categories are creational, structural, and behavioral.

Creational Patterns

These patterns deal with ways to create objects. The following list summarizes a few of the most useful creational patterns:

➤ Factory method—Creates a new instance of a class. Subclasses may redefine the type of object created or how it is initialized.

➤ Lazy initialization—A technique for delaying object creation until the object is needed, usually to prevent slow startup. For example, suppose a program lets you pick from hundreds of cookie recipes downloaded over a slow network connection. It doesn't really need any of them until you select one, so it can delay loading them until you pick one.

➤ Object pool—Creates a pool of objects that can be recycled and reused. This is particularly useful for controlling access to scarce resources such as database connections, ports, or processors.

➤ Prototype—Uses a prototype instance of an object with default properties filled in. This can save space because other objects don't need to save values unless they are different from the prototype.

➤ Singleton—Ensures that there is only one instance of an object and provides a method for accessing that object. For example, a dispatch system might have a single assignment process to ensure that different users don't assign jobs differently. Depending on the project, uniqueness might need to be based on the application, computer, or network.

Structural Patterns

Structural patterns simplify the relationships among objects. The following list summarizes a few of the most useful structural patterns:

➤ Adapter, Wrapper, or Translator—Provides a simplified or otherwise transformed interface to a class. An adapter allows incompatible classes to communicate.

➤ Composite—Composes objects into a tree- or network-like structure so you can represent objects and groups of objects uniformly.

➤ Decorator—Attaches additional features to an object. This lets you add new behaviors or properties to a class, potentially at runtime, without subclassing.

➤ Façade—Provides an interface to a (usually complicated) subsystem. For example, you might build a `ReportPrinter` class that provides methods that use a collection of `Printer`, `Document`, and `Page` classes to make printing a report easier.

➤ Flyweight—Used to allow objects to share common data so they can remain relatively small.

➤ Module—Groups related classes, methods, or other objects into a single entity. (Pretty much what you might expect a module to do, particularly if you've ever used a non–object-oriented programming language.)

➤ Proxy—Provides a placeholder for another object to control access to that object.

➤ Twin—Imitates multiple inheritance in programming languages that do not allow it.

Behavioral Patterns

Behavioral patterns generally deal with communication among objects. For example, they may provide services to record information from different objects, allow one object to control another, or track an object's state. The following list summarizes some useful behavioral patterns:

➤ Blackboard—Combines data from various data sources, possibly translating into a common format.

➤ Chain of responsibility—A chain of objects that handles a request by passing the request along until an object handles it.

➤ Command—Encapsulates a command so an object to take a command as a parameter and then execute it. These can be helpful for allowing command queues, logging, and undo/redo.

➤ Iterator—Provides a way to access the elements inside some sort of collection class without exposing the collection's underlying details.

➤ Mediator—An object through which other objects can interact. This allows an object to interact with others without needing to know the details of how the other object works so the two classes can be modified independently.

➤ Memento—Captures an object's internal state so that object (or another object) can be placed in that state later.

➤ Model-view-controller (MVC)—This pattern defines three kinds of classes that work together, usually to provide a user interface. The model class represents some sort of data. One or more view classes display some sort of view of the model. Controller classes let the user modify the data in the model.

➤ Model-view-presenter (MVP)—This is a refinement of the MVC pattern. The model represents some sort of data and views display a representation of the data as before. This time, however, the view is also responsible for capturing user events. The presenter stands between the view and the model. It passes update commands from the view to the model and notifies the view when the data in the model is changed.

➤ Model-view-view/model (MVVM)—The MVVM pattern is somewhat similar to MVP. A model represents the data, a view displays the data, and the view/model sits in between much as the presenter does in the MVP pattern. The biggest difference is that the view does not have a direct reference to the view/model. Instead, it forwards user interface information via some sort of binding such as bound properties or events.

➤ Null object—A default object that can be used in place of a null reference.

➤ Observer or publish/subscribe—An object that should receive notification when another object's state has changed in some particular way.

➤ Helper or servant—A package of helper methods that can be used by multiple classes. This may be implemented as a collection of methods in a module or in an object-oriented language as a static class (a class that has no instance methods and all methods are static).

➤ State—An internal representation of an object's state so it can act differently when its state changes. (State diagrams can be useful here.)

➤ Strategy—An encapsulated algorithm so you can use different *algorithms* interchangeably. For example, you might pass different encryption objects to a stream to allow the stream to encrypt data in different ways.

➤ Template—An outline of an algorithm that allows subclasses to redefine selected steps.

➤ Visitor—Represents an operation on a data structure so you can define new behaviors without modifying the data structure. For example, a visitor might traverse a tree and return a list of nodes that match some criterion without modifying the tree.

Design Pattern Summary

The preceding sections describe some useful design patterns, but developers are constantly adding more patterns to model their solutions, so those lists are necessarily incomplete. Some patterns are quite specialized, so you may never need them. For example, there are many design patterns for controlling parallel algorithms where multiple programs may do things like try to modify the same data at the same time. Those patterns are important, but most developers don't need their specialized features, so I'm not covering them here.

You may find that you use some patterns, such as façade and factory methods, fairly often. Others, such as blackboard or singleton, you may use rarely or never. The point of this discussion isn't to make you an expert on design patterns but to give you an idea of the kinds of patterns that exist. Then if you ever need a program that creates lists of tasks to be performed in order, you may remember the command pattern and you can look up the details. Even if you don't remember the name of the pattern, you may think, "There should be a pattern for this," and you can look for it.

To give you the best chance of recognizing patterns when you need them, it's worth taking some time to search the Internet for other patterns.

Parallel Programming

In *parallel programming*, multiple processors perform calculations at the same time. (Here I'm using the term "processors" to mean anything that can perform calculations, such as the cores on a CPU or GPU. If you're interested in the details, look up "CPU" and "core" online.) If you have a lot of processors, this can make certain kinds of calculations much faster. However, that potential improvement comes with a new set of problems, many of which deal with what happens when multiple processors try to use the same piece of memory at the same time.

For example, if one processor tries to set a variable's value to 10 while another processor tries to set it to 20, who wins? Of course the answer is, "No one, everybody loses! Particularly you if you're trying to debug the code."

Parallel programming also comes with some overhead. It takes some extra time to split a calculation into pieces, distribute them to different processors, and combine the results. For that reason, you'll never quite get the performance boost that you feel you should from a simple calculation. For example, eight processors might solve a problem six times as fast as the single processor rather than eight times as fast as you might naively expect.

Still, these algorithms are very interesting and fun to implement even if they are rather challenging. They're sometimes a bit easier for certain kinds of problems called embarrassingly parallel.

An *embarrassingly parallel* problem is one that naturally breaks into pieces that have little to do with each other, so coordinating among the processes is relatively easy.

For example, you've probably seen the Mandelbrot set fractal shown in Figure 11.6. (Although you've probably seen it in color.) To draw the Mandelbrot set, you perform a series of calculations for each pixel in the image. The calculations are in the Goldilocks zone (neither too hard nor too easy), but there are a lot of them. If the image is 1,000×1,000 pixels, then you need to perform the series of calculations 1 million times.

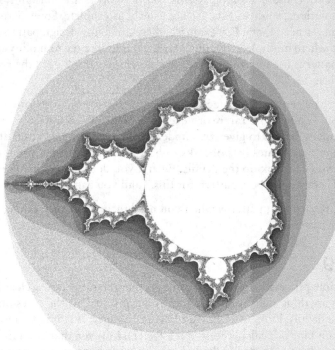

FIGURE 11.6: Drawing a Mandelbrot set is embarrassingly parallel.

You can find the image shown in Figure 11.6 at `https://commons.wikimedia.org/wiki/File:Mandelbrot_1500itr_huge.png`. (You can find a color picture at `https://commons.wikimedia.org/wiki/File:Mandelbrot-Menge_mit_OrbitTrap_20201028_100It.png`, or search the Internet. You can even find mesmerizing animated versions.) That image contains

10,000×10,000 pixels, so you would need to perform the series of calculations 100 million times to generate it. It used a maximum of 1,500 calculations in each pixel's series, so it probably took a while to generate the whole thing.

The good news is that the calculations for each pixel are completely independent of those for the other pixels. That means you can parcel out different pieces of the image to different processors and they can chug merrily away without interfering with each other. If you have 100 million processors, you could make each one calculate a single pixel's color extremely quickly. At that point you'd probably spend more time getting them started and assembling their results than actually performing the calculations.

The bottom line is that parallel algorithms are interesting and can speed up certain calculations, but they do present unique challenges, so they probably shouldn't be your first choice unless you know that your problem is naturally parallelizable.

Artificial Intelligence

The most accurate definition of *artificial intelligence (AI)* that I know of is similar to the definition of love or NASA's definition of life: We're not sure, but we think we'll recognize it when we see it. That lack of a concrete definition makes artificial intelligence simultaneously one of the most promising and most disappointing corners of algorithmic research.

The following section explains why that is so, mostly by providing some concrete definitions. The sections after that briefly describe some of the ways that artificial intelligence might be useful in your projects.

Definitions

An early definition of AI might have said it was "anytime a computer could do something human-like." Even in those days, people were dreaming about something like C-3PO (although they didn't know that name yet), but researchers were actually working on much simpler ways to mimic humans. These were basic goals such as the following:

➤ Simple robots like a mechanical hand that can hold an egg without crushing it

➤ Robots that can walk

➤ Vision systems that can tell if a conveyor belt is empty or has a box on it

➤ *Natural language processing* that the computer can use to know what you mean when you type "find a noodle shop near me"

➤ Speaker-independent speech recognition that can tell when you say yes, no, or a numeral

➤ Navigation systems that let a toy car navigate through a room containing obstacles

These tasks are largely solved and have been extended greatly. For example, robots can now sprint, climb stairs, cook, make facial expressions, and do backflips. (I'll call these sorts of humanlike abilities *AI tools* so we can talk about them meaningfully. For example, you can add AI tools such as speech recognition and synthesis to an otherwise non-AI application.)

Now that these tasks are achievable, they're no longer mysterious so people don't think of them as AI. A mechanical hand is just a machine, speech recognition and language processing are how your phone finds you lunch, and a navigation system guides your Roomba around the living room to terrorize your cat. No big deal.

It's not that we don't have AI; it's that it's so commonplace that we no longer recognize it. It's like a magician's trick: Once you know the secret, it doesn't seem like magic anymore. Similarly, once a program can do something humanlike, it seems like "just another algorithm" and doesn't feel like AI anymore.

This is also why AI always seems to be always just out of reach. As soon as we solve one problem, it loses its mystery and we see another AI goalpost on the horizon.

So yes, we have AI; it's just not what we were told it would be by *Star Wars* and *The Jetsons*.

The following sections describe some of the main categories of artificial intelligence research and give some ideas about whether they would be useful in your applications.

Learning Systems

These days most people think of AI as either C-3PO (we still haven't given up on that) or learning systems. A *learning system* (or *machine learning*) is, as its name implies, a system that learns. It uses algorithms and training data to figure out how to do things, often with little or no supervision.

For example, you can feed a learning system a set of images of cats and dogs, tell it which are which, and let it try to figure out how to tell the difference for future images. Or you can give a learning system a virtual robot and let it try to figure out how to make the robot walk by experimentation. Or you can provide feedback on emails to teach a learning system to recognize spam and phishing attacks.

Learning systems are usually most helpful when you have poorly understood data. If you understand the data well, then you can often apply more direct algorithms to it and figure out what it all means.

For example, suppose you want to know which of the books you sell is the most popular. A simple database query will tell you that. In contrast, suppose you want to find out what kinds of customers like to read Terry Pratchett books. You could use a learning system to analyze buying patterns and predict the likelihood that a given person might like Pratchett.

EX POST FACTO ANALYSIS

Sometimes you can examine a learning system's results to see why it made the predictions it did. For example, the program might give weight to whether a reader liked Tom Holt. Then you could make a rule saying that many Tom Holt readers will also like Terry Pratchett. In that case, you've demystified the process, and it no longer feels like AI.

However, learning systems often produce somewhat mysterious results. They may produce a correct result a reasonable percentage of the time, but their internal models may be too complicated to really know how they work. For example, in one study a deep-learning AI was able to determine a person's race about 90 percent of the time by looking at CT and X-ray images, but researchers don't know how it works. (See www.iflscience.com/technology/ai-can-identify-race-from-just-xrays-and-scientists-have-no-idea-how.)

Natural Language Processing

Natural language processing (NLP) is still wrestling with the same problem from the early days: how to understand what people want. It's how Google knows what you mean when you type "couscous recipes." It's also how it deciphers garbled statements like "cous cous recipes" or even "coos koos recipts." You may be able to imagine a very complicated table or database where you could look up "couscous recipes," but it's harder to see how to handle typos, contradictory instructions, and the other gibberish that people throw at search engines.

NLP is often paired with speech recognition and speech generation, so Siri can understand what you say (sort of) even if you have an accent (maybe) and return spoken information (that is sometimes even relevant).

Okay, I'm making this sound like it doesn't work very well, but we've actually come amazingly far from the 1980s when it was a challenge to tell whether someone was simply saying yes or no. (Plus we get funny stories about Alexa ordering people dollhouses after hearing its name on television.)

NLP also lets word processors correct spelling and grammar, and allows anti-plagiarism software to search for stolen research.

One NLP application that is popular with business is the chatbot. A *chatbot* uses NLP to interact with customers to track orders, check account balances, and connect with the correct department. Some of these are basically phone trees where you can say "check order" instead of pressing 3. (And you're less likely to accidentally press 7 and end up with the system speaking Japanese or something.)

Other chatbots use an expert system to guide you through some initial customer contact chores such as looking up your account number, asking whether you need sales or technical support, providing initial troubleshooting, and searching for articles in their database that may solve your problem (so they don't need to spend a customer service representative's time).

Artificial Neural Network

An *artificial neural network* (or often simply *neural network*) is a learning system that is modeled on biological neural networks such as the human brain. It uses a network of *artificial neurons* (or just *neurons*) to process data. Test data is fed into the network and then the network's parameters are adjusted to try to make the network produce the correct output.

Deep Learning

Deep learning uses a neural network with several layers that process increasingly abstract features. For example, in a vision system, lower levels might detect edges and higher levels might use the results of the lower layers to detect shapes such as faces or other objects.

Expert System

An *expert system* is a program that uses a set of rules to perform some task. For example, an automotive troubleshooting expert system might provide a sequence of tests for you to perform to see what's wrong. It tells you to try something, you report the results, and the system tells you what to try next.

Usually the system's knowledge is stored in a *knowledge base* consisting of if-then style rules.

Expert systems are often very effective, but it can be difficult to build the knowledge base. Typically, you do that by holding grueling interrogation sessions with experts (hence the name "expert system") to turn their knowledge into rules. You then fine-tune the rules during a testing period until the system gives correct results most of the time.

Artificial General Intelligence

The previous sections talk about different approaches to AI and how they are implemented, albeit with little detail. Artificial intelligence is also often classified by what it can do rather than how it can do it. (This section is more philosophical than practical, so skip it if you're not interested.)

Artificial general intelligence (AGI) is what many people mean when they say *true artificial intelligence*. This is a program that can learn to perform any intellectual task that a human can. It's also sometimes called *strong AI*, *full AI*, and *general intelligent action*.

Weak AI, or *narrow AI*, is a program that is intended to solve a single problem such as driving a car or finding target demographics for magazine sales. You wouldn't expect your car-driving app to balance your checkbook.

Muddling things a bit, some people use the term "strong AI" to mean a program that is sentient or that has achieved consciousness, and they use the term "weak AI" to mean anything else.

The issue of "true" intelligence and sentience goes back to moving goalposts and the definition of love. (We think we'll recognize it when we see it.) How do we recognize "true" intelligence?

In 1950, Alan Turing (mathematician, computer scientist, cryptographer, and generally very smart guy) proposed what he called "the imitation game," which is now usually called "the Turing test." The test comes in several variations. In one of the more popular, a person is sitting in a closed room communicating with two players via text. One of the players is a human and one is a computer. The question is, can you reliably tell which is which? If you cannot, then the computer has achieved intelligence.

Currently there are programs that can fool people much of the time. (Although there are those who claim that *they* are not fooled so it doesn't count.) With modern deep-fake video technology, speech synthesis, NLP, and artificially created faces, it's probably just a matter of time before a program can pass a version of the Turing test that uses a video chat rather than text.

CHATBOT LAMDA

Chatbots (originally called chatterbots) use NLP to interact with people, often with an online chat or text-to-voice system. Many companies use them today as a first line of defense against customers, hoping the chatbot can solve simple problems without bothering a more expensive human.

The first chatbot, Eliza, was written in the mid-1960s and uses pattern matching to mimic conversation without any real attempt at understanding. It's good enough to hint at AI but is too limited to pass the Turing test. (It's still fun to play with, at least for a few minutes. You can find it online, for example, at `http://psych.fullerton.edu/mbirnbaum/psych101/eliza.htm`.)

In 2022 Google announced its project LaMDA, which is short for Language Model for Dialogue Applications. (You can see a brief announcement at `https://blog.google/technology/ai/lamda`.) Unlike Eliza, it has a fairly broad knowledge base, so it can carry on much more realistic conversations. In fact, its conversations are so realistic that Google engineer Blake Lemoine announced to the world that Google had created a sentient artificial intelligence. (He was then promptly suspended for violating his nondisclosure agreement.) He said that, if he didn't know better, he would think LaMDA was a seven- or eight-year-old kid who happened to know physics.

Most AI researchers think that Lemoine was fooled by his desire to believe, and LaMDA isn't really sentient. However, Blake Lemoine is a computer scientist, not some random person pulled in off the street. If he thinks LaMDA is intelligent, then it can't be too long before programs like LaMDA can fool a majority of people and pass the Turing test.

Does that mean those programs are truly intelligent? Sentient? You can easily write a program that knows some facts about programming, but does that make it self-aware? I know humans who would need CliffsNotes to pass the Turing test, and yet we call them intelligent, at least out of politeness.

Most people would move the goalposts and say, no, these programs are not "truly" intelligent. Just fooling someone into thinking you're a human does not make you sentient.

THE CHINESE ROOM ARGUMENT

In 1980 the American philosopher John Searle proposed a new thought experiment called the Chinese Room Argument. (See `https://plato.stanford.edu/entries/chinese-room`.) John imagines himself in a room with a computer that can pass the Turing test in Chinese. Someone slips notes in Chinese under the door,

continues

(continued)

John scans them into the computer, the computer prints out appropriate responses, and John slides the results back out the door. At this point, the person outside of the room thinks that there is a Chinese-speaking human inside the room. A reasonable assumption.

Now suppose John has a copy (in English or Python or whatever) of the program's code together with lots of pencils, paper, and time. When someone slips a message under the door, he can manually follow the program's instructions to produce the same output that the program would have produced (although his handwriting may not be as good) and slide that out in response. John has essentially passed the Chinese Turing test, but he clearly doesn't understand what he has read or written. (Unless John has learned Chinese since his original 1980 paper, but I assume he would have updated it to the "Korean Room Argument" if he had.)

It shows that someone can pretend to know what they're doing without actually having a clue. (But we already know that from politics.) However, someone or something in the room understands Chinese. It's not John, but you could wonder if it's the program. Of course, you could also argue that it's the programmer(s) who wrote the program. I'm not entirely satisfied with this argument, but it certainly adds a new level to the Turing test.

I've heard others argue that a program can never be "truly" intelligent because a computer uses transistors and electrical impulses to mimic thought and doesn't work the way a real human brain does. But the human brain also uses a bunch of electrical impulses. It's also clear that different people's brains work differently, but we don't call someone with Asperger or Tourette syndrome unintelligent.

Recently I heard an AI researcher say in an interview that an AI cannot truly understand language because it doesn't learn in the same way a child does, surrounded by social context and clues given by parents and other humans. But adult humans don't always learn language that way either. (For example, you can learn a new word by reading it in a book. An "erf" is a plot of land, usually about half an acre in size. That wasn't so hard, was it?)

For that matter, a cat clearly doesn't think the same way a human does, but nevertheless most people would say that cats are intelligent and self-aware. (Or at least self-absorbed.)

And what if we someday discover space-faring aliens? (Or more likely, they discover us. We're not leaving the solar system anytime soon.) Would we say they're not intelligent because they don't think the way humans do even though they've mastered interstellar space flight?

Saying "true" intelligence requires intelligence that works the way it does in humans seems egotistical if not hubris.

DO WE EVEN WANT ARTIFICIAL INTELLIGENCE?

Friend, author, and AI guy John Meuller (`http://blog.johnmuellerbooks
.com`) has these words of wisdom.

> If you actually need human intelligence, then use a human. Personally, I see future
> AI as being adjuncts to humans that allow us to do things that we can't do now.
> In other words, future AI will be intelligent, but in a way that's different from
> how we're intelligent. By combining AI with human intelligence, we'll be able to
> solve problems that don't even have questions today.

Perhaps it's a matter of exposure. If I spent an hour or so every day speaking with a program that
made sense, talked "intelligently," and laughed at my jokes, I might be willing to say it was truly
intelligent.

I don't have the answers to these questions, so I'll leave them for you to think about late at night
while you're listening to Pink Floyd with the lights turned off. For now I believe that the current crop
of programs is not sentient, and I think it'll be a few years before your *Fortnite* program demands the
right to vote or emptying your desktop recycle bin can be considered murder. I'll just have to hope
that I recognize true intelligence when I see it.

ALGORITHM CHARACTERISTICS

Often, you can use an existing algorithm so you don't need to reinvent a procedure that was devised
and debugged millennia ago. (Euclid described his greatest common divisor algorithm around 300
BCE.) Other times your specific needs may force you to "roll your own" solution. In either case, it's
helpful to know some of the characteristics that make an algorithm a good choice. The following list
summarizes the features of a good algorithm.

Effective—Obviously, an algorithm won't do you much good if it doesn't solve your particular
problem. Sometimes if an algorithm doesn't always find the best solution, you can improve its
solution or apply it repeatedly to find a better result.

Efficient—The most precise algorithm in the world won't do you much good if it takes seven years to
build the daily production schedule or if it requires you to have 3 petabytes (1 million gigabytes)
of memory on your cell phone. To be useful, an algorithm must satisfy your correctness, speed,
memory, disk space, and other requirements.

Predictable—Some algorithms produce a single, predictable, definitive result every time they run.
Those are the easiest to understand and use. Other algorithms may produce results that are only
correct a certain percentage of the time. You may be able to get usable results from them, particularly if you can use them repeatedly to improve their reliability, but that can be a lot harder.

Simple—Ideally an algorithm, like any other piece of code, should be elegantly simple. Simple code is easier to understand, implement, debug, and modify (if you decide to peel off the "Modify at your own risk" sticker). Like IKEA furniture, complex algorithms can be a lot of fun to assemble, but if you don't want to worry about missing parts, simple is best.

Prepackaged—If you can find a pre-built algorithm inside your programming language or in a library, it'll save you time in the long run. Prepackaged tools may have been through thousands of hours of optimization and testing, so they may perform better than anything that you have the time to write. (Depending on the source. There are poorly written packages out there and some could even be infected with malware.)

SUMMARY

An algorithm is simply a set of instructions for performing some task. Software algorithms let you make the computer perform complex tasks such as sorting data, searching for specific values, or finding optimal solutions to complicated problems.

A heuristic is an algorithm that should provide a good result but that doesn't necessarily give you an optimal result.

Features such as robotics, speech recognition, and machine vision were once considered mainstream artificial intelligence research. Now they're mostly considered AI tools that add humanlike characteristics to programs that might otherwise not be considered AI. These days much of AI is centered on machine learning.

For difficult problems, the difference between a good algorithm and a bad one can make the difference between finding a solution in seconds, hours, or not at all. Fortunately, many algorithms have been extensively studied for decades, so you often don't need to write your own from scratch. You can use the Internet and algorithm books to look for algorithms that fit your problems.

The following rules may help in picking a solution to your problem:

➤ Review design patterns to see if they can help you structure your application, particularly at a higher level.

➤ If AI tools such as NLP, speech recognition and synthesis, machine vision, and the like are applicable, use them. You can use many of those tools with AI or non-AI programs.

➤ If you can find an existing algorithm to solve your problem, use it! That will certainly be easier that using AI or building your own algorithm.

➤ If the problem is fuzzy and ill-defined, consider a learning system. It may be able to find patterns that you don't even know exist.

➤ If you have access to experts who can reduce their knowledge to a set of rules (perhaps with a lot of work), consider building an expert system.

If you think you need to build your own algorithm, consider these rules:

➤ If your program must move through a (possibly complicated) set of states, consider using a state diagram to model it.

> ➤ If you can model your problem as a series of decisions, consider using a decision tree.
>
>   > ➤ Use backtracking to explore the decision tree.
>   >
>   > ➤ If exhaustive search is fast enough, use it. That approach is usually relatively simple (but slow).
>   >
>   > ➤ If you can think of ways to rearrange or trim the tree, do so.
>   >
>   > ➤ If you can use branch and bound, do so to speed up your search.
>
> ➤ If a greedy algorithm will give you an optimal solution, use it. These are usually extremely fast.
>
> ➤ If you can split a big problem into smaller instances of the same problem, consider a divide-and-conquer approach.
>
> ➤ If the problem is naturally recursive, look for recursive solutions.
>
> ➤ If the problem requires you to recalculate some values many times, consider a dynamic programming approach or use caching to avoid those recalculations.
>
> ➤ If heuristics will provide a good enough solution, use them. If you can think of more than one, use them all and take the best result.
>
> ➤ If you're really stuck, try randomized algorithms. Pick a random solution and adjust it if you can to improve it. Repeat the process many times and take the best result.

You cannot find perfect solutions to every problem, but heuristics and randomized algorithms can find reasonably good solutions in many cases if you give them enough time.

As I mentioned earlier in this chapter, I encourage you to take a closer look at algorithms. Study algorithms so you can learn what problems they can solve, so you can learn new programming techniques, and to keep your mind nimble.

EXERCISES

1. The recursive Fibonacci algorithm shown in the section "Recursion" does not program defensively. For example, if you pass the value −1 to it, it calls itself recursively forever (or at least until it overflows the call stack and crashes). Rewrite the function defensively.

2. The Fibonacci algorithm shown in the section "Recursion" is also not offensive. Rewrite it offensively. (If you don't know how to throw exceptions in C#, just put a comment where you would do that.)

3. Rewrite the recursive factorial function offensively. (If you don't know how to throw exceptions in Python, just put a comment where you would do that.)

4. One way to find your way across town would be to pick a point in the middle, recursively drive there, and then recursively drive the rest of the way to your destination. What algorithmic approach is that?

5. Another way to find your way across town would be, when you reach an intersection, to always turn down the street that points most directly toward your destination. What algorithmic approach is that? What are some problems with this approach?

6. The previous strategies for driving across town have some obvious problems. In real life, you know that freeways are faster, and you probably know some shortcuts and best routes to get from one place to another. What algorithmic approach would use that information to find the best route across town?

7. You have a surprise visit from an executive in an hour, and you've been tasked with finding an interesting snack, so you need to make an emergency run to your favorite mocha donut shop. At this time of day, Yuzu Street is usually the fastest route. What algorithmic approach is driving down Yuzu Street?

8. At the end of the workday, millions of Londoners make their way home. What kind of "algorithm" is the city using?

WHAT YOU LEARNED IN THIS CHAPTER

➤ An algorithm is a recipe for doing something.

➤ A heuristic is an algorithm that is likely to provide a good result but that doesn't necessarily give you an optimal result.

➤ Parallel algorithms use multiple processors to speed calculations for certain problems, although there is some extra overhead.

➤ AI tools include humanlike features such as robots, machine vision, speech recognition and synthesis, route finding, and more.

➤ Modern AI is largely focused on machine learning.

➤ The following list includes some useful algorithmic techniques:

  ➤ State diagrams

  ➤ Decision trees

  ➤ Exhaustive search

  ➤ Backtracking

  ➤ Tree pruning, branch and bound

  ➤ Heuristics

  ➤ Greedy algorithms, hill climbing

  ➤ Divide-and-conquer

> ➤ Recursion

> ➤ Dynamic programming, caching

> ➤ Randomized algorithms

➤ Design patterns are like algorithms for classes. They show how you can make classes work together to solve common programming problems.

Programming Languages

The only way to learn a new programming language is by writing programs in it.

—*Dennis Ritchie*

The C language combines all the power of assembly language with all the ease-of-use of assembly language.

—*Mark Pearce*

What You Will Learn in This Chapter:

➤   Why you cannot always pick your language

➤   Language generations: 1GL, 2GL, 3GL, 4GL, and (you guessed it) 5GL

➤   Language families such as imperative, procedural, declarative, functional, and object-oriented

➤   Considerations for picking a language

It seems that a programming language, once created, never dies. It may go dormant for a while, but sooner or later some hobby programmer will disinter it from a dusty archive or ancient cyber-tomb just to experiment with it.

There are hundreds of different programming languages floating around in the aether waiting for you to discover them. There are thousands if you count all of the variations, dialects, and idioms. Sometimes languages spawn new versions through improvement over time while older versions persist because they are still in use by older programs. Other times dialects are invented to work for a very narrowly defined problem. For example, Emacs Lisp is a Lisp-based scripting language used inside the Emacs text editor. (Emacs may seem like a strange name, but it's much better than what it originally stood for: Editor MACroS.)

This chapter provides background so you'll know what it means if a team member says that you should use a low-level 5GL language to process interrupts through SQL. (Mostly this means the person is either confused, is playing a joke on you, or has *way* too much free time.) It describes some of the most important language families, gives a snapshot of what some of the most important languages are today, and talks about how you might pick a new language to learn.

THE MYTH OF PICKING A LANGUAGE

It may seem like picking a programming language would be one of the first things you should do when starting a project. That kind of makes sense. Before you start a road trip, you need to decide which car to take. (Take the new hybrid SUV, not the 1998 Oldsmobile that could die at any moment.)

Unfortunately, there are several reasons you may not have much choice in picking a language:

➤ You are required by management or customers to use a certain language.

➤ You need to use a language specifically designed for particular hardware (for example, if you work at Qualcomm or Samsung making device drivers).

➤ The team already uses a certain language.

➤ You already have tools in place for a certain language.

➤ Other people in this domain (AI, mathematics, business, etc.) use a certain language and you want to stay compatible.

➤ The project is based on an earlier program that uses a certain language.

➤ Certain tools only work with a specific language.

With enough work, you can work around all of those problems except the first two. For example, it is hard but possible to switch a team to a new language. However, learning a new language takes time. I can usually pick up the basics of a new language in a week or two, but it takes me several months to a year to poke into every nook and cranny and really feel at the top of my game. I've been doing this for a very long time, and less experienced programmers may take longer. (Although I've known some whose "top of game" and "bottom of game" weren't very far apart, so they might not need all that long to get back to their base level of mediocrity.) Moving a whole team to a new language can be difficult.

Possibly the weakest of the reasons is the last one, that certain tools only work with a given language. There's always a way to make a tool work with a new language; it just may be really hard. Tool vendors want to help get their products running with new languages because it opens new markets for them (and it's usually more fun than debugging their code or handling customer complaints), but they're often handcuffed by the same problem that you have: they work primarily in one language (and it's not yours).

Getting a tool to work in a new language may be tedious, slow, painful torture that forces you to use Google to find new swear words to yell at your computer, but it's still faster than learning a new programming language. In the worst case, you may be able to write a small library, perhaps in assembly language or C executing assembly instructions, and then call it from your program. Spending a week that feels like a year is better than spending a year that feels like five. (I've done this several times, and if you get stuck, I recommend using innocent words in foreign languages *as if* they were swear words. Ausgezeichnet! Joie de vivre! Semper allia! ヘビの足!)

Still, if your goal is to produce the most stable application as quickly as possible, you're almost always better off sticking with the language and tools that you and your team know best. You'll be up and running faster, won't make as many mistakes, and will understand the code better so you can debug it more efficiently. (It's like space colonization. It would be extremely cool to put a colony on the Moon, Mars, or Kepler-186f, but it will always be easier to make Nevada or even Los Angeles habitable for humans.)

I want to make one last point before I dump the negativity and explain why you should learn new programming languages anyway.

Many programmers often have a near-religious zeal for their favorite language. Often it's the first language they learned. That's just the way they were raised, so that's what makes them comfortable. ("My family has been COBOL programmers for five generations and by gum that's the way it should be!") This is particularly true for beginning to intermediate programmers who haven't learned many other languages.

After you learn a few new languages, however, you start to realize that, at some level, they're all the same. They all make the computer perform the same tasks; things like adding numbers, saving values in variables, looping through lists, manipulating data in relational databases, and crashing during presentations for the CEO. You can do those things in any language! (Except Malbolge, where it's probably possible but you won't be able to figure out how to do any but the last one. I'll show an example Malbolge program shortly. For more information, see `https://en.wikipedia.org/wiki/Malbolge` if you dare!)

No programming language can make the computer magically balance the federal budget, create peace on Earth, or read the user's mind. (Artificial intelligence languages claim they can, but they really can't.) A particular language can only make the computer do what it was built to do and nothing more.

After a while, you start noticing that different languages approach the same problems in different ways. Some approaches may be easier while others are more efficient. Some may be more flexible while others are better at preventing bugs.

Eventually, you can learn how to use your code to mimic the strengths of one language while using another. It's not always easy and it takes determination, but it can be done.

For example, many languages or integrated development environments will flag a variable if it is not initialized before it is used. For instance, consider the following line of code:

```
num_employees = num_employees + 1
```

If `num_employees` has never been initialized, then the result depends on how the language sets the default value. Maybe that will work, or maybe it will lead to a bug in your program.

If you use a language that requires you to initialize variables, then you have no choice. After you're used to setting a variable's value when you create it, you gain a useful habit that you can carry with you to other languages.

For another example, many languages require that values only be stored in variables with a compatible type. For example, you can store 1.2 in a variable that holds real numbers, but you cannot store that value in an integer variable without essentially telling the program, "Yes, I know they're different types. Shut up and do it anyway." A Python program, however, will happily redefine a variable to be whatever you want it to be. Consider the following Python code:

```
i = 10
print(type(i), i)

i = 1.2
print(type(i), i)

i = "Hello"
print(type(i), i)
```

This code creates a variable named i, saves the value 10 in it, and prints the variable's type and value. It then does something similar with the values 1.2 and "Hello". Each time the program simply replaces the original variable i with a new variable having the same name but a different data type. The following shows the program's output:

```
<class 'int'> 10
<class 'float'> 1.2
<class 'str'> Hello
```

This kind of on-the-fly variable creation makes writing programs fast and easy, but it can lead to bugs. If you have experience with a pickier language, you're more likely to use different variables for different tasks, and that will make errors less likely. Even if you reuse the same variable for different purposes, you'll be more aware that this could cause problems so you will (hopefully) be more careful.

So what are the conclusions for this section?

First, you often cannot pick the language you will use for a particular project. The language is often dictated by circumstances.

Second, using the language and tools that you know best is the most effective way to produce a solid result as quickly as possible. Even if you need to do extra work to adapt or rebuild tools, that's almost always easier than learning a new language.

Third, and most important, learning multiple languages is a good thing. It lets you learn how different languages approach the same problem. It also lets you learn new (hopefully good) habits that you can then carry with you into other languages.

So go out and learn new languages in your spare time. Experiment with several and see what features you like and don't like. Learn why a language enforces certain rules (like requiring variable initialization), and if there's a good reason, make it a habit. After you get enough practice, it will be much easier to use your new language in later projects if necessary.

LANGUAGE GENERATIONS

Since computers were invented, programming languages have evolved drastically. In the beginning, programming languages were little more than abbreviations for the individual actions that the computer's hardware performed. They closely followed what the computer's hardware could do.

Modern high-level languages are designed for programming ease and comprehensibility. Rather than following the computer's hardware capabilities, they cater to the programmer's mental capabilities.

The following sections describe the generations of programming languages as they are defined today.

First Generation

A *first-generation language (1GL)* is machine code consisting of a big pile of 0s and 1s. Originally this code was entered into a computer via switches on the front of the hardware. You would flip a bunch of switches up and down and then press some sort of Enter button to load the corresponding command into the computer. Then you would do it again. And again. As you can imagine, this was incredibly tedious.

Quick quiz: What does the following machine code do?

```
00001110 00011111 10111010 00001110 00000000 10110100 00001001 11001101
00100001 10111000 00000001 01001100 11001101 00100001 01010100 01101000
01101001 01110011 00100000 01110000 01110010 01101111 01100111 01110010
01100001 01101101 00100000 01100011 01100001 01101110 01101110 01101111
01110100 00100000 01100010 01100101 00100000 01110010 01110101 01101110
00100000 01101001 01101110 00100000 01000100 01001111 01010011 00100000
01101101 01101111 01100100 01100101 00101110 00001101 00001101 00001010
```

Obviously, the correct answer is "Who knows?" with partial credit for "Who cares?" This is an actual chunk of a program that I wrote, but I don't know what this particular piece does, and it would be a lot of not very useful work to figure it out.

Fortunately, the days of entering programs as 0s and 1s are long behind us.

Second Generation

A *second-generation language (2GL)* is an assembly language. These are very closely related to the machine language commands, but in a more human "friendly" form. I put the word "friendly" in quotes because these languages are only about as friendly as a hungry wolverine with a migraine.

Here's the assembly code for part of the same program mentioned in the preceding section:

```
02E9087F  xor         edx,edx
02E90881  mov         dword ptr [ebp-40h],edx
02E90884  nop
02E90885  jmp         MyTest.Program.Main(System.String[])+04Eh (02E90896h)
02E90887  mov         ecx,dword ptr ds:[40A2344h]
02E9088D  call        System.Console.WriteLine(System.String) (72444F64h)
```

```
02E90892   nop
02E90893   inc          dword ptr [ebp-40h]
02E90896   cmp          dword ptr [ebp-40h],0Ah
02E9089A   setl         al
02E9089D   movzx        eax,al
02E908A0   mov          dword ptr [ebp-44h],eax
02E908A3   cmp          dword ptr [ebp-44h],0
02E908A7   jne          MyTest.Program.Main(System.String[])+03Fh (02E90887h)
02E908A9   call         System.Console.ReadLine() (72B21830h)
```

This is a lot better than machine code, but it still looks like Alienese. You can probably guess what some of the commands mean. For example, mov (move), jmp (jump), cmp (compare), jne (jump if not equal), and my personal favorite nop (no operation, or the "take a vacation" command).

Even if you have experience writing assembly language, it's hard to write, harder to read, and takes super-human powers to understand and debug without good comments and documentation. (I have used assembly and it was fun in a masochistic sort of way, but I'm too lazy to use it regularly.)

These programs are translated directly into machine code by a program called an *assembler*. Because the commands closely follow those of the machine, they can take full advantage of the computer's strengths without a lot of overhead needed to translate something more intelligible into machine code. That means these programs can be extremely fast, small, and efficient. (If you don't make any mistakes!) That makes assembly popular for very high performance applications, for libraries used by programs written in other languages, and for programs that need direct access to hardware.

One drawback to assembly languages is that, because they are tied to a specific dialect of machine code, they only run on a particular computer architecture. You can't write an assembly program for a 16-bit ARM architecture running on a cell phone and expect it to also work on a 64-bit x86 architecture running on a PC.

The good news is that all hardware does roughly the same things (subtracting numbers, moving values from one place to another, jumping to a particular line of code), so once you know one assembly language, it's a lot easier to switch to another.

Third Generation (3GL)

A *third-generation language (3GL)* works at a much higher level than 1GLs and 2GLs. These tend to be more machine-independent and much easier for humans to understand. This group includes most of the languages that you've probably seen before, such as BASIC, C, C++, COBOL, Fortran, Java, Pascal, and so forth.

The following snippet shows the C# code that generated the assembly code shown in the preceding section:

```
for (int i = 0; i < 10; i++)
    Console.WriteLine("Hello!");
Console.ReadLine();
```

This is much easier to understand than the assembly code shown earlier. If you've ever programmed in any of the "curly bracket languages" such as C++, Java, or Kotlin, then this code should make perfect sense. In fact, if you've worked with *any* programming language, you can probably decipher it.

This code makes the variable i loop through the values 0 through 9 and display the text "Hello!" for each of those values. The program then waits for you to press Enter so the text doesn't zip by so quickly that you can't read it.

MYSTERIOUS MALBOLGE

The C# code should be decipherable if you've learned any programming language except for some like Malbolge (which I mentioned earlier). Here's a Malbolge program that displays the message "Hello World!"

```
('&%:9]!~}|z2Vxwv-,POqponl$Hjig%eB@@>}=<M:9wv6WsU2T|nm-,jcL(I&%$#"
`CB]V?Tx<uVtT`Rpo3NlF.Jh++FdbCBA@?]!~|4XzyTT43Qsqq(Lnmkj"Fhg${z@>
```

I definitely prefer assembly language!

Some of these programs are compiled into machine code. Others are compiled into an intermediate language that is similar to machine code, and then a runtime engine either interprets or compiles the intermediate code for execution.

By translating into the appropriate machine code or using a different runtime engine, some of these programs can run on different kinds of computers. For example, some programs can run inside browsers on most kinds of hardware.

Most 3GLs support structured programming and many support object-oriented programming. (I'll say more about those shortly.)

HIGH AND LOW

Some higher-level languages allow you to sneak pieces of lower-level code into a program. For example, C, C++, and C# let you include assembly statements right inside your program. It's an advanced technique that can be difficult and may tie your program to a particular computer architecture, but in rare circumstances it can provide a performance boost or let you access features that are hidden by the high level language.

Fourth Generation

A *fourth-generation language (4GL)* provides a higher level of abstraction than a 3GL. To provide that abstraction, these languages tend to be more specialized, focusing on a particular domain. Their general flavor is to focus on collections of data rather than individual pieces.

For example, *Structured Query Language (SQL)* is a 4GL database query language that lets you compose queries with a kind of English-like syntax; the queries let you work with large chunks of data instead of the individual pieces. For example, a single query can fetch all of the information for all of Darth Vader's past purchase orders (mostly black capes and lightsaber batteries), so you don't need to loop through each line item one by one.

> **NOTE** Many people pronounce SQL "sequel," at least in part because it was originally called SEQUEL, which stood for Structured English Query Language. Two acronyms for the price of one!

The following SQL query searches the `People` table and selects records that have `Clue` values greater than 0.

```
SELECT * FROM People WHERE Clue > 0
```

Other 4GLs focus on topics such as mathematics, reports, UI construction, and web development. Because they target a particular field, they can do a very good job in their respective domains, but writing more general programs with them can be more awkward than it is with a 3GL. For example, *MATLAB* (short for *matrix laboratory*, by MathWorks) is great at mathematical calculations, matrix calculations, machine learning, and working with mathematical models. However, it's not necessarily the best tool for building user interfaces, working with relational databases, or producing first-person shooter games.

Fifth Generation

A *fifth-generation language (5GL)* solves problems by using rules and constraints rather than by following an algorithm given to it by a programmer. In the original 5GL vision, you wouldn't need a programmer to solve problems. You would say something like, "Optimize next year's profits," add a bunch of rules covering the things that the computer is allowed to do with your company, and then wait for the program to spit out a solution.

Unfortunately, even in a tightly constrained problem space, finding efficient algorithms for solving these sorts of problems turned out to be much harder than people expected. For that reason, 5GLs are used mainly in artificial intelligence research where it's just not possible to solve problems in any other way.

LOW- AND HIGH-LEVEL LANGUAGES

1GLs and 2GLs are considered *low-level languages*. 3GLs, 4GLs, and 5GLs are considered *high-level languages*.

Some people add a "P" to the generations. For example, 3GPL stands for "third-generation programming language."

Sixth Generation

Some people have proposed definitions for 6GLs and even 7GLs. The definitions that I have seen take two main approaches.

The first approach is to switch from writing textual code to drawing some other kind of code such as a flowchart. There are already some programming languages that work like this. For example, MIT's

Scratch lets you build a program by snapping together programming constructs such as loops, output statements, and methods. These languages are interesting (you should add Scratch to your list of languages that deserve at least a quick try, along with assembly language and Turing machine programs), but they don't really increase the level of abstraction beyond 3GLs. They're also much slower for experienced programmers because it's generally faster to type. However, they are colorful and fun, so they can be useful learning tools for six-year-olds and executives, particularly with a touch screen that makes drag and drop easier.

The second approach people seem to take is to glue some sort of natural language processing or speech processing on top of a 3GL. The practical result (at least for now) is something like spoken or written SQL but more aimed at understanding programming terms. There are some voice coding systems out there such as Serenade (`https://serenade.ai`) and Talon (`https://talonvoice.com`). Currently, you still need to write the code, just using your voice rather than your fingers. That can be an incredible benefit to people who can't type, but it doesn't increase the level of abstraction.

NLC (natural language coding) projects such as Microsoft's GitHub Copilot (`https://copilot.github.com`) and Tabnine (`www.tabnine.com`) show a bit more promise for practical use. Copilot and Tabnine extend the development environment to suggest pieces of code that you can manually accept, reject, or modify. These seem more like fancy code snippet managers than languages that truly increase the level of abstraction. They may be able to help flesh out some details in your code, but you still need to understand the code that they suggest. They could be very useful, but they don't feel revolutionary enough to deserve to be called 6GLs.

For right now, I vote that there are no 6GLs and it's not even clear what one would be. Perhaps a system with speech recognition (for easy use) and a super-generalized knowledge base so it can do just about anything reasonable that you can describe in plain English, like the brains in the replicants in *Blade Runner*, the android Data in *Start Trek*, or C-3PO in *Star Wars*. Or perhaps it will be like the computer in *Galaxy Quest*, which can answer just about any question that you put to it (as long as you're Sigourney Weaver).

IDEs

An *integrated development environment (IDE)* is a program that helps you write programs. For example, you can use Microsoft's Visual Studio IDE to write programs in many languages, including Visual Basic, C#, F#, HTML, CSS, JavaScript, and more. You can also add extensions to let it work with Python, C, C++, Go, Ruby, and still others.

IDEs provide extra features to make programming easier. For example, they may provide features such as simplified project building, source code control, code highlighting, parentheses and bracket matching, auto-completion, profiling, and other handy tools. GitHub Copilot and Tabnine (mentioned in the preceding section) make useful additions to development environments.

If you think of 4GLs as any language that is an advancement above 3GLs, then I think you could argue that some language/IDE combinations should be considered 4GLs. Yes, you can write C# programs with a simple text editor, but you'll be much more productive if you use Visual Studio.

Whether you consider an IDE as a 4GL or not, you definitely should think about IDEs when you're examining programming languages. A very powerful language may not be as much use to you as a less powerful language that has a great IDE.

LANGUAGE FAMILIES

I mentioned earlier in this chapter that all programming languages do roughly the same things. That is because they all work on the same hardware. That hardware has certain capabilities, and no programming language will change what it can do. You may wish you could build a telepathic user interface that psychokinetically builds bridges while simultaneously acting as a unicorn attractor, but simply switching programming languages probably won't help. (Unless you're doing all of that inside virtual reality, in which case it might make a difference.)

Even though all languages do roughly the same things, that doesn't mean they're all the same. Some are better at performing matrix calculations than others, some have built-in features to help prove correctness, some are good at shuffling data around, and some are more confusing than others. (Some almost seem to have built-in obfuscation to promote programmer job security.)

The following sections describe some of the most common families of programming languages and list some examples. When you're thinking about learning a new language, which I highly suggest, you can use this information to help you pick. For example, if you want a fuller understanding of object-oriented programming and how different languages handle (or don't handle) multiple inheritance, you can stick to the object-oriented language family. If you want to broaden your horizons a bit more, you may want to look into languages in families that you haven't sampled before.

> **FAMILY FLAVORS** *There are many ways that you can categorize languages. For example, you could group them by whether they are case sensitive, are line-oriented, use indentation to denote structure, or use curly brackets. The following sections focus more on higher-level concepts that you can use to think about how the languages work.*
>
> *For example, Visual Basic and C# are practically the same language despite the fact that Visual Basic is case insensitive (sort of), is line-oriented (mostly), and doesn't use curly brackets (except when it does), while C# does the exact opposite. (Okay, when I put it like that, it sounds weird, but if you use the two languages for a while, you quickly realize that they are basically the same, just with different syntax.)*

Assembly

The sections "First Generation" and "Second Generation" earlier in this chapter briefly describe machine language and assembly language. I won't suggest that you learn to program in machine code. It might be an interesting (although probably painful) exercise, but there doesn't seem to be much demand for those skills.

Learning assembly language, however, can be quite educational. It puts you in touch with your roots as a programmer and gives you a better feel for exactly what the computer's hardware can do. It's also humbling, brings a greater appreciation of modern programming languages, and builds greater respect for the programmers of ancient times (like the 1950s).

> **TOURING WITH TURING** *Way back in 1936, Alan Turing invented the a-machine (which stood for "automatic machine"), which we now call a Turning machine. By using an amazingly simple model of computation, a Turing machine can do pretty much what a real computer can do.*
>
> *The reason I mention this here is that the language used for a Turning machine is a lot like a very simple assembly language. Even though you probably can't use a Turning program for anything practical like building a new version of Mario Kart, you can use a Turing machine to prove some interesting results in computability theory. For example, in the halting problem, you are given a program and set of inputs, and you must predict whether the program will eventually stop or whether it will run forever. Obviously, you can tell whether some programs will stop, but Turing proved in 1936 that you cannot always know for a given set of program and inputs. This is a fairly deep, almost Zen-like philosophical result that basically says a program cannot answer some questions about programs.*
>
> *If you want to look at some interesting programming languages that have some important theoretical consequences, you might want to look into Turing machines. Look online (for example at* `https://en.wikipedia.org/wiki/Turing_machine`*) for more information and look for online Turing machine simulators.*

Assembly language is interesting and will probably give you a better understanding of how the computer works, but it's not easy. Writing a program in assembly language is the programming equivalent of baking a cake from scratch where the first step is "Grow some wheat."

Imperative

An *imperative programming language* is one where the program issues commands to the computer like, "Thou shalt add variable x to variable y and save the result in variable z." More realistically, $z = x + y$.

The key point is that these are commands. The program tells the computer exactly what to do at every step. Each command changes the program's internal state—for example, by changing memory contents.

An imperative language has no notion of telling the computer the result you want and letting it figure out how to get the result. (Contrast this with declarative programming described shortly.)

Many 3GLs fall into this category. For example, C, C++, C#, Java, Pascal, Fortran, Python, and many others are all imperative. (They also may fall into some of the other categories described shortly.)

Procedural

A *procedural programming language* is a type of imperative language that also lets you group pieces of code into procedures (aka methods, functions, routines, subroutines, subs, etc.) so that you can use the same code in multiple places. They may also let you create higher-level groupings such as modules, assemblies, libraries, and so forth so you can reuse code across multiple programs.

Most modern imperative languages are also procedural. For example, the languages mentioned in the previous section (C, C++, C#, Java, Pascal, Fortran, and Python) are all procedural.

Some early BASIC languages were imperative but not procedural, so you basically had a single flow of execution, although the exact path of execution could vary by using loops, `if`, and the dreaded `GOTO` statement. Later versions added structured programming features including procedures.

Most people don't consider HTML a programming language because it lacks variables, loops, and other programming accoutrements. However, if it *were* a programming language, it would be imperative but not procedural. You use HTML code to specify exactly how you want items to be drawn by the browser, and you cannot create methods in HTML to reuse code.

Declarative

In a *declarative programming language* you specify the result that you want and the program figures out how to get that result.

For example, SQL is a common declarative database query language. You might execute the following command to fetch the items that make up purchase orders placed by the customer J. Quincy Magoo.

```
SELECT ProductName, Price
FROM Orders, OrderItems
WHERE CustomerName = 'J. Quincy Magoo'
  AND Orders.OrderId = OrderItems.OrderId
ORDER BY DueDate
```

Here you indicate the result that you want (the `Orders` and `OrderItems` records sorted by `DueDate`), but you don't tell the database engine how to find that data. For example, you don't tell it to use the `CustomerName` key to search the `Orders` table, to use the `OrderId` key to search the `OrderItems` table for the returned records, or to use quicksort to sort the results. The database engine figures all of that out by itself.

Some versions of SQL also allow you to give the engine imperative hints to force it to follow certain steps if you think you're smarter than the query optimizer.

Other declarative languages are Analytica, Prolog, XSLT, among others.

Object-Oriented

An *object-oriented language* lets you define classes that you can then use as blueprints or cookie cutters to make instances of those objects.

For example, you might define a `Person` class with properties such as `FirstName`, `LastName`, and `Hobbies`. You could then create any number of `Person` instances that are all `Person` objects but that have different property values. For example, Rahim Obsorne collects coins, Darcie Lu grows topiary, Zak Buxton enjoys extreme ironing, and so on.

Object-oriented languages are some of the most used languages today and include C++, C#, Java, JavaScript, Visual Basic, Python, Object Pascal, PHP, Ruby, Perl, and many more.

Functional

A *functional programming language* defines programs and methods as mathematical functions. These include a couple dozen "pure" functional languages such as Haskell and Miranda. There are also many more "impure" functional languages that also contain imperative features. These include C++, C#, Visual Basic, F#, Java, Kotlin, Lisp, Mathematica, Python, Ruby, Swift, and more.

Specialized

In addition to the major families described in the preceding sections, there are many more specialized languages. For example, there are languages for creating tutorials, handling concurrency, representing data flow, generally manipulating data, scripting specific programs, teaching programming, designing analog or digital circuits, processing lists, parsing text, performing numerical analysis, controlling special hardware (such as robots, electronic scales, etc.), creating graphics, and many, many more.

Most of these languages are so specialized that you may not want to study them unless you have a direct need. For example, you may like to buy a robotics kit and then learn the language that goes with it, but you might not want to learn Verilog-AMS (analog and mixed-signal hardware description language) unless you work in that industry.

Language Family Summary

For more information on languages, surf the Internet. You can find one large, categorized list of programming languages at `https://en.wikipedia.org/wiki/List_of_programming_languages_by_type`. You can follow the links in that list to get more information about specific languages, and you can search the Internet directly for even more information.

If you search for "programming language families" and look at image results, you can also find some programming language "family trees" and other interesting diagrams that show how different languages are related and how they evolved from each other over time.

THE BEST LANGUAGE

If you've been paying attention, then you probably know that I'm not going to tell you which language is best because there is no best language. Different languages are better at some things than others, but no language beats every other under all circumstances.

Although there is no best language, there may be a best language for you. Which language that may be depends on your goals for it at this moment. For example, you may want to learn a new language for any of the following noble reasons:

- ➤ To join a new programming team
- ➤ To work in a particular field

➤ To learn new concepts, approaches, and skills

➤ To expand your repertoire

➤ To find a new job

➤ Because you're just bored and need a break

If you need to learn a language to join a new team, then you probably have little choice about which language to study.

If you need a language to work in a particular field, then you're probably also fairly constrained. For example, many engineers and laboratory scientists use MATLAB, so if you plan to work in that environment, it's a language worth learning.

If you want to expand your skill set and learn new concepts, then you may want to pick a language that is not too similar to the ones that you already know. If you already know a curly bracket language, then learning a second will teach some new tricks, but probably not as much as learning Haskell, Lisp, or SQL.

If you want to expand your repertoire so you can add a new language to your resume, then you should pick a language that is in common use. That has many benefits, such as the availability of online examples and forums, the likelihood that you'll be able to use the language for at least a few years, and the fact that more people will be able to talk to you about it at parties.

LANGUAGE LONGEVITY

I was once pretty good at a graphics language called ReGIS (Remote Graphics Instruction Set). It was interesting, fun, and I produced some pretty drawings, but I think it's gone the way of the dodo and quagga. Now at parties I sit behind the potted palm wistfully wondering where all of the ReGIS programmers have gone.

Not really. I learned ReGIS just to learn a new language and it served its purpose. It goes to show, however, that languages do fall out of fashion, so it's worth considering how widespread a language is, unless you just want to learn it as a character-building exercise.

You should consider the languages' typical uses. For example, if you're interested in writing 3D games, then C# will probably be a better choice than HTML.

You may also want to learn a language that pays well. (So you can afford that overclocked liquid-cooled laptop you always wanted.)

To research all of these issues, you can turn to the Internet. For example, search for "best programming language" or "most used programming languages." Different sites use different methods to pick their favorite languages, such as surveys, tracking search engine queries, counting job postings, researching trends, aggregating other sites' results, reading tea leaves, and consulting the Magic 8 Ball.

You need to be careful when interpreting the results on some sites. For example, the popular TIOBE index tracks browser queries, so it's more an indication of general interest in languages than a survey of the most used languages. There is a correlation between interest and common usage, however, so it's not completely useless.

> **THE IMPORTANCE OF BEING TIOBE**
>
> TIOBE, which stands for "The Importance of Being Earnest," is a statement of the company's sincerity. (It's sort of like Google's "Don't be evil," which later morphed into Alphabet's "Do the right thing." I guess it's okay to be evil now as long as it's the right thing.) For more information about TIOBE, see www.tiobe.com/about-us.

Some surveys may have skewed visitor populations, so their results might be somewhat tilted. For example, if a site mainly posts examples for Unix users, then those users are more likely to be using classic Unix languages such as C, C++, and assembly and less likely to use languages like Swift (an Apple language) or Kotlin (Google's preferred Android language; I think it's what R2-D2 speaks).

Probably your best strategy is to look at several sites and see which languages are in the top 5 or 10 on most of them. For example, for this chapter I looked at these sites:

➤ TIOBE (browser ranking)— www.tiobe.com/tiobe-index

➤ ZDNet (survey)— www.zdnet.com/article/top-programming-languages-most-popular-and-fastest-growing-choices-for-developers

➤ Geeks for Geeks (survey)— www.geeksforgeeks.org/top-10-programming-languages-to-learn-in-2022

➤ Berkeley (study)—https://bootcamp.berkeley.edu/blog/most-in-demand-programming-languages

➤ Northeastern (job postings)— www.northeastern.edu/graduate/blog/most-popular-programming-languages

➤ Stack Overflow (survey)—https://insights.stackoverflow.com/survey/2020#most-popular-technologies

I found average annual salary data at ZipRecruiter. (Go to www.ziprecruiter.com/Salaries and enter a job title such as "Python Software Engineer.") I then used a top-secret formula (a weighted average where a #1 choice gets the most points) to create a sort of consensus shown in the following table.

RANK	LANGUAGE	MOST COMMON USE	SALARY
1	Python	DS/ML, IoT, web, finance, desktop	$122,274
2	Java	Mobile, web, desktop	$102,207

continues

(continued)

RANK	LANGUAGE	MOST COMMON USE	SALARY
3	JavaScript	Mobile, web, desktop	$92,636
4	C++	Embedded, IoT, desktop	$103,704
5	C#	Windows, AR/VR, desktop, games	$93,556
6	C	Embedded, IoT	$100,629
7	SQL	Database	$93,438
8	R	Statistical computing, graphics	$90,940
9	Go	Backend, DS, 3rd-party environments	$100,157
10	PHP	Web, backend	$86,003
11	HTML	Web	$94,491
12	Kotlin	Mobile, AR/VR	$127,541
13	CSS	Web	$90,603
14	Visual Basic	Windows, AR/VR, desktop, games	$80,209
15	Swift	Mobile, AR/VR, iOS, MacOS	$95,608
16	NoSQL	Database	$119,105
17	Assembly language	Low-level, high-performance, embedded	$68,267
18	Rust	AR/VR, embedded	$91,709
19	Perl	Sys admin, desktop	$118,335
20	Delphi, Object Pascal	Mobile, web, desktop	$108,167

The table uses the following abbreviations:

- ➤ AR—Augmented reality
- ➤ DS—Data science
- ➤ ML—Machine learning
- ➤ VR—Virtual reality

All of the sites provide slightly different rankings, and the rankings change over time, but this table should give you a general idea of the most popular (and profitable) languages right now.

The salary data varies widely due to factors such as your experience (noobs get paid less than gurus), the location (New York City is a more expensive place to live than Wichita), the field (investment firms pay better than doggy daycares), and exact job title (developers earn more than programmers, presumably because they have read this book).

Some of the reported salary ranges are ridiculously extreme. For example, Comparably (`www .comparably.com/salaries/salaries-for-c-developer`) said C programmer salaries range from $17,741 (a summer intern who flunked out of C class) to a whopping $475,643 (game developers working for the Mafia). Those numbers change frequently, so the results you find won't match what I found. In fact, I haven't seen anything close to those numbers since I first looked. Right now it shows a range of $60,000 to $160,000 with an average of $93,305, which is much more believable.

You can find online compilers for many languages these days, so you can get started quickly, without installing anything, and best of all for free. Simply search for something like "online Python compiler." It only took me a few minutes to find online compilers for every language in the previous table except for NoSQL, and I didn't try very hard for that one. (Search for Pascal instead of Delphi.) There are even online Malbolge and Befunge compilers in case you want to write programs that look like cartoon swear words or the results of a cat walking across your keyboard, respectively.

SUMMARY

In the real software engineering world, you often don't have much choice of programming language. When you're starting a new project or joining a new team, the language is often dictated to you.

That doesn't mean you can't learn new languages in your spare time! You should definitely learn multiple programming languages. Most experienced developers (at least the good ones) are fluent in at least a few. Consider languages that are widely used, that are used in fields that you find interesting, and that are profitable. You might even be able to pick a language that might be useful to you in a future project.

Everyone should spend at least a little time with an assembly language if for no other reason than it will make you glad when you stop. Turing machines are also quite interesting both for studying computability theory and because they show how much you can accomplish with very little.

Every programmer should also have at least some experience with HTML and SQL. You don't necessarily need to become an expert, but those two are used so extensively that not knowing anything about them is like driving without knowing what the street signs mean. If you're careful, you'll probably survive, but you may wish you'd studied a bit more before starting the engine.

After you've spent a little time with assembly, HTML, and SQL, do some research and find a language that suits you. If you decide that you don't like a language, try another one. There are plenty to choose from and time spent learning new languages is never wasted.

EXERCISES

1. Which language generations are considered low-level? Which are considered high-level?

2. In one or two sentences each, define 1GL, 2GL, 3GL, 4GL, and 5GL languages.

3. To which language generations do the following belong?

    ➤ Turing machine programs
    ➤ Most procedural languages such as C++ and BASIC
    ➤ Artificial intelligence systems that identify previously unknown data patterns
    ➤ Object-oriented languages such as Java and C#
    ➤ MACRO-11 assembly language
    ➤ A report-generation language that can examine a database's structure to automatically generate reports
    ➤ R2-D2
    ➤ C-3PO

4. In one or two sentences each, define imperative language, procedural language, and declarative language.

WHAT YOU LEARNED IN THIS CHAPTER

➤ Often you have a specific language selected for you on a particular project, so you don't get to pick one.

➤ 1GLs are machine languages.

➤ 2GLs are assembly languages.

➤ 3GLs are higher-level languages that include structural programming languages and object-oriented programming.

➤ 4GLs provide a higher level of abstraction than 3GLs and are often fairly specialized. SQL and MATLAB are two examples.

➤ 5GLs solve problems by using rules and constraints rather than by following programmed instructions.

➤ Imperative languages give the computer instructions to follow.

➤ Procedural languages allow you to define procedures (aka methods, functions, routines, subroutines, subs, etc.) so that you can reuse code units.

➤ Declarative languages let you define the result that you want and the program figures out how to find it.

➤ Object-oriented languages let you define classes that you can then use as blueprints to define instances of the classes.

➤ These are valid reasons for learning a new programming language:

    ➤ To join a new programming team

    ➤ To work in a particular field

    ➤ To learn new concepts, approaches, and skills

    ➤ To expand your repertoire

    ➤ To find a new job

    ➤ Because you're just bored and need a break

➤ Everyone should do at least a little work with assembly language just to see what it's like. I also recommend spending at least a little time working with Turing machine programs and Scratch (or another drag-and-drop programming language) so you can see what they are like.

Testing

No amount of testing can prove a software right, a single test can prove a software wrong.

—Amir Ghahrai

Testing is the process of comparing the invisible to the ambiguous, so as to avoid the unthinkable happening to the anonymous.

—James Bach

What You Will Learn in This Chapter:

➤ Goals of testing

➤ Reasons why you might not want to remove a bug

➤ How to prioritize bugs

➤ Kinds of tests and testing techniques

➤ Good testing habits

➤ Methods for estimating number of bugs

It's a software engineering axiom that all nontrivial programs contain bugs. Actually, it's such an important point that it deserves to be repeated.

> **NOTE** *All nontrivial programs contain bugs.*

For example, Windows 2000 was said by some to contain a whopping 63,000+ known bugs when it was shipped. Microsoft quickly retorted that this number didn't actually count bugs. It included feature requests, notes asking developers to make something work better or more efficiently than it already did, clarification requests, and other non-bug issues. The *true* bugs, Microsoft explained, were mostly minor issues that wouldn't seriously hurt users.

No matter how you count them, Windows 2000 contained a *lot* of "undesirable features" ranging from changes that should probably have been made to indisputable bugs.

You might think that's the result of shoddy workmanship, but no project of that size could possibly have shipped without any bugs. The industry average number of bugs per thousand lines of code (*kilo lines of code*, or *KLOC*) is typically estimated at about 15 to 50. When you consider that Windows 2000 contained more than 29 million lines of code, it's a miracle it works at all. Even assuming 10 bugs per KLOC, Windows 2000 should contain approximately 290,000 bugs. Suddenly 63,000 bugs is starting to look pretty good, isn't it?

NASA's Goddard Space Flight Center, which takes bugs *very* seriously because a mistake in its code could cost lives and hundreds of millions of dollars, is said to have reduced its number of bugs to less than 0.1 per KLOC. Even if Microsoft could afford to follow Goddard's practices (and getting the number of bugs per KLOC down to that level is *very* expensive), Windows 2000 would still contain 2,900 bugs.

I don't know about you, but if I encountered 2,900 bugs on a daily basis, I'd toss my computer out a window and start using a typewriter.

BIGGER (AND BETTER?)

It's hard to know exactly how many lines of code are in a published application, but here are some estimates for some really big projects.

➤ Windows 95 contained around 10 million lines of code, Windows XP had about 40 million, and Windows 10 and Windows 11 contain around 50 million. (Clearly Microsoft isn't reducing its bug count by shrinking its operating system.)

➤ Facebook, including all of its services, contains more than 60 million lines of code. (It takes a lot of code to include something to annoy everyone.)

➤ High-end car software can contain more than 100 million lines of code. (For even an expensive car, you get a lot of code for your money.)

➤ Google, including all of its products (Gmail, Google Drive, Google Forms, Google Translate, Google Maps, Google Chrome, and more than 250 others), uses more than 2 billion lines of code.

➤ The Human Genome Project included around 3.3 billion lines of code.

Read more at `www.freelancinggig.com/blog/2018/07/17/top-5-largest-programs-ever-written`.

Facebook and Google are constantly adding new products and features, so they're only going to grow over time.

You can learn more about some big programs at `https://interestingengineering` `.com/whats-the-biggest-software-package-by-lines-of-code`. There's an interesting chart showing the sizes of some big applications at `www` `.informationisbeautiful.net/visualizations/million-lines-of-` `code`. It was posted in 2015, so it's a bit dated, but it shows the relative sizes of some interesting projects, such as NASA's space shuttle (400,000 lines), the Hubble Space Telescope (2 million), and the Mars *Curiosity* rover (5 million). (In case you're thinking about starting your own space agency.)

Given that any nontrivial program contains bugs, what can you do about it? Are you doomed to suffer the slings and arrows of outraged customers? Or should you just throw in the towel and open a florist's shop instead of writing software?

Even though you can't wipe out every bug, you can catch the ones that will be most irritating to users. You can reduce the number of high-profile bugs to the point where users see them only rarely. If your program uses a good design, it should also recover from bugs gracefully so that it doesn't crash.

This chapter explains testing techniques that you can use to flush out the majority of the most annoying bugs. It explains kinds of tests you should run and when to run them. It also explains how to estimate the number of bugs in the system so that you have some idea of whether you're getting closer to your goal of eliminating the high-profile bugs.

TESTING GOALS

Ideally you would sit down, write code that perfectly satisfies the requirements, and you'd be done. Unfortunately, that rarely happens. More often than not, the first attempt at the software satisfies some but not all the requirements. It may also incorrectly handle situations that weren't specified in the requirements. For example, the code may not work in every possible situation.

That's where testing comes in. Testing lets you study a piece of code to see whether it meets the requirements and whether it works correctly under all circumstances. (Usually, the second goal means a method works properly with any set of inputs.)

To get a complete picture of how a piece of code performs, you can carry out several different kinds of tests using a variety of techniques. Sections later in this chapter describe some of the most important of those. Before you get to them, however, it's worth knowing that it's not always worth removing every single bug from a program. Instead, the goal is often to reduce the number bugs and their frequency of occurrence so that users can get their jobs done with a minimum of annoyance.

REASONS BUGS NEVER DIE

Simply put, a *bug* is a flaw in a program that causes it to produce an incorrect result or to behave unexpectedly. Bugs are generally evil (although occasionally they make games more fun), but it's not always worth your effort to try to remove every bug. Removing some bugs is just more trouble than it's worth. The following sections describe some reasons software developers don't remove every bug from their applications.

Diminishing Returns

Finding the first few bugs in a newly written piece of software is relatively easy (and therefore cheap). After a few months of testing, finding bugs may become extremely difficult. At some point, finding the next bug would cost you more than you'll ever earn by selling the software.

Deadlines

In a just and fair world, software would be released when it is ready. In the real world, however, companies are often driven by deadlines imposed by management, competition, or a marketing department.

You might delay a release to fix high-profile bugs, but if the remaining bugs aren't too bad, you might be forced to release before you as a software engineer would like.

Consequences

Sometimes a bug fix might have undesirable consequences. For example, suppose you're building a drawing application and the tool that draws spirals isn't saving the spirals' colors correctly. You could fix it, but that would require changing the format of the saved picture files. That would force the users to convert their data files, and that would make them storm your office with torches and pitchforks.

In this example, it might be better to leave the spiral-saving code unfixed for now and include a fix in the next major release. Users expect some pain in major releases, so you might get away with it then. (But just in case, you should make sure the escape helicopter is fueled and ready to go.)

It's Too Soon

If you just released a version of a program, it may be too soon to give the users a new patch to fix a minor bug. Users won't like you if you release new bug fixes every three days. As a rule of thumb:

➤ If a bug is a security flaw, release a patch immediately, even if you just released a patch yesterday. (If you did release a patch yesterday, you better be sure the new patch fixes things correctly! Your reputation is at stake.) Include a note explaining how wonderful you are for protecting the users' valuable data.

➤ If a bug makes users swear at your program more than once a day, release a patch as soon as possible (as often as monthly). Include a profuse apology.

➤ If a bug is annoying enough to make users smirk at your program occasionally, fix it in a minor release (as often as twice a year). Include a huge fanfare about how great you are for looking after the users' needs.

➤ If a bug is just a nice-to-have new feature or a performance improvement, fix it in the next major release (at most once per year). Explain how responsive you are and that the users' needs are your number one concern.

Later in the book you'll learn about agile development approaches that favor frequent releases during development. Hopefully those are adding important new features and not fixing bugs or changing the colors on the splash screen.

Too many releases will annoy users, so you need to weigh the benefit of any bug patch against the inconvenience.

Microsoft has elevated gratuitous releases to an art form, rolling them out automatically with little or no warning. Sometimes those are critical security patches and sometimes it's hard to tell. I'm sure the folks at Microsoft do that to show how responsive they are, but I know I find it annoying to turn on my computer in the morning and find that it installed an update overnight, rebooted, and closed all of the programs that I had running when I went to sleep the night before.

Usefulness

Sometimes users come to rely on a particular bug to do something sneaky that you didn't intend them to do. They won't thank you if you remove their favorite feature, even if it's technically a bug.

Any sufficiently advanced bug is indistinguishable from a feature.

—*Bruce Brown*

If the users have adopted a bug and are using it in their favor, formalize it and add it to the application's requirements. You may extend its behavior to give the users an even better feature and take credit for it.

Obsolescence

Over time, some features may become less useful. Eventually they may go away entirely. In that case, it may be better to just let the feature die rather than spending a lot of time fixing it.

For example, if an operating system has a bug in a floppy drive controller that limits its performance, it may be just as well to ignore it. Floppy drives are rare these days, so the bug probably won't inconvenience too many users. (In fact, many computers are shipping without CD or DVD drives these days. As long as your network and USB devices work, you may cut back on maintenance of your CD drivers. Of course, you can still use a USB CD drive, at least for now.)

It's Not a Bug

Sometimes users think a feature is a bug when actually they just don't understand what the program is supposed to do. (It seems like Facebook has perfected this problem. It moves its security settings around and users complain that their cat pictures are visible to everyone in the world when really they just can't find those settings.)

This is really a problem of user education. Sometimes the documentation isn't correct and sometimes it's missing entirely. Sometimes the user isn't willing to read all the way through both paragraphs of documentation and see that the feature is clearly described.

If the documentation is incorrect, incomplete, or unclear, this is a "documentation bug" that you can fix the next time you release a new version of the documentation.

DOCUMENTATION DELETED

Back in the old days, when you bought a piece of software, you also got a nice, fat book explaining how to use it. Some particularly long user manuals came as a set of ring binders with pages that you could replace when the vendor sent you updates to specific pages.

These days most application documentation comes in text files, PDF files, or some other electronic format. That allows vendors to update the documentation anytime it is necessary. (See the earlier section "It's Too Soon." The same ideas apply to documentation as well as software. Your customers won't thank you for sending them daily documentation updates.)

If you store the documentation online, you can update it whenever you must. Users will see the new version the next time they need to consult the documentation. Unless you make really big changes, they probably won't even notice that anything is different.

You can greatly decrease this problem by using a good user interface design. If the application groups features logically so users can find them easily, the users won't complain that a feature is missing when it isn't. If features are named clearly so it's obvious what they do, users won't complain that a feature doesn't do what they think it's supposed to do.

It Never Ends

If you try to fix every bug before shipping, you'll never release anything.

This is similar to a problem you may have when buying a new computer. If you just wait another couple months, something faster will come out for the same price. If you do buy a nice, shiny, new machine, something better instantly goes on sale. At some point, you just need to pry open your wallet, buy something, and get on with your life. (It also helps to avoid looking at advertisements afterward, so you don't see the faster machines going on sale.)

Similarly, at some point you need to stop testing, cross your fingers, and publish your application. It's almost guaranteed to be imperfect, but hopefully it's better than nothing.

It's Better Than Nothing

As the previous section mentions, your application may not be perfect, but hopefully it's better than nothing. In some cases, it may be so much better than nothing that it's worth releasing the application even though it's seriously flawed.

This is particularly true if your application is for in-house use. If you're writing a tool for your fellow employees to use, they may be willing to put up with some rough edges to get their jobs done more easily.

THE TOOLSMITH

If a software project is large enough, it may be worth having a dedicated toolsmith. A *toolsmith* is someone whose job is to build tools for use by others on the project. A tool might count the lines of code in the project's modules, rearrange the controls on a form in top-down/left-to-right order, search customer data for patterns, build a random test database, or just about anything else that makes the other team members' lives easier.

I spent a large chunk of time on one project writing a form handler that let the other developers arrange labels and text boxes on forms. On another project I built a tool that helped developers define complex menu hierarchies more easily. (The development environment we were using back then was bad at both designing forms and building menus.)

The programs written by a toolsmith are often somewhat unfinished. They may contain bugs and may require their users to follow certain paths or risk falling into untested parts of the program. Still, if the tool is useful enough, it's worth living with a few quirks.

The reason you can get away with less-than-perfect applications in-house is that future sales don't depend on the program working perfectly. Outside customers might refuse to buy later releases of the program and may flame you in online reviews, but your coworkers are stuck with you whether they like it or not.

Fixing Bugs Is Dangerous

When you fix a bug, there's a surprisingly high probability that you'll fix it incorrectly, so your work doesn't actually help. There's also a chance that you'll introduce one or more new bugs when you fix an old bug.

In fact, you're significantly more likely to add a bug to a program when you're fixing old code than when you're writing new code from scratch. When you write new code, you (hopefully) understand what you want the code to do and how it should work. When you're fixing code sometime later, you don't have the same level of understanding.

To reduce the problem, you need to study the code thoroughly to try to regain the understanding you originally had. Hopefully, you were paying attention in Chapter 10, "Programming," when I said you should write code for people, not for the computer. If you did, then it will be much easier for you to figure out what the broken piece of code is trying to do.

Finally, whether you fix the bug correctly, other pieces of code may rely on the buggy behavior. This is similar to the way users sometimes take advantage of a bug, but this time it's another part of your program that's doing it. When you change the code, you may break other pieces of code that were (at least apparently) working before.

Which Bugs to Fix

There may be some good reasons not to fix every bug, but in general bugs are bad, so you should remove as many of them as possible as early as possible. So how do you decide which bugs to fix and which to put in the "fix later" or "claim it's a feature" categories?

To decide which bugs you should fix, you should use a simple cost/benefit analysis to prioritize them. For each bug, you should evaluate the following factors.

➤ Severity—How painful is the bug for the users? How much work, time, money, or other resources are lost?

➤ Workarounds—Are there workarounds? Are they easy or hard?

➤ Frequency—How often does the bug occur?

➤ Difficulty—How hard would it be to fix the bug? (Of course, this is just a guess.)

➤ Riskiness—How risky would it be to fix the bug? If the bug is in particularly complex code, fixing it may introduce new bugs.

After you evaluate all of the bugs, you can assign them priorities. Note that you may want the priorities to change over time. If your next release is a long time away, you can focus on the most severe bugs that don't have workarounds. If your time is limited, you can focus on the least risky bugs so that you don't break anything else before the next release.

LEVELS OF TESTING

Bugs are easiest to fix if you catch them as soon as possible. After a bug has been in the code for a while, you forget how the code is supposed to work. That means you'll need to spend extra time studying the code so that you don't break anything. The longer the bug has been around, the greater the chances are that other pieces of code rely on the buggy behavior, so the longer you wait the more things you may have to fix.

In order to catch bugs as soon as possible, you can use several levels of testing. These range from tightly focused unit testing that examines the smallest possible pieces of code to system and acceptance testing that exercises the system as a whole.

Unit Testing

A *unit test* verifies the correctness of a specific piece of code. As soon as you finish writing a piece of code, you should test it. Test it as thoroughly as possible because it will only get harder to fix later.

LITTLE TESTS AND BIG TESTS

It's much easier to test a lot of little pieces of code rather than one big piece. Combining many pieces of code can lead to a combinatorial explosion of the number of paths through the code that you need to test.

For example, suppose you have a piece of code that performs 10 if-then tests. Depending on a set of values, the code takes one branch or another at each of the 10 decision points.

To follow every possible path through the code, you need to test every possible combination of branches. For 10 branches with 2 paths each, that's 2^{10} = 1,024 possibilities. If you don't check them all, you may have a combination that doesn't work, and sooner or later your users will find it.

Even if you do check them all, there's a chance that there's a bug in one of them and you just got unlucky and didn't notice it. You should still at least touch every possible path. (If you don't walk down a path in a forest, you won't notice the snake sitting in the middle of it.)

Now suppose you break the big piece of code into 10 pieces, each containing a single if-then test. If you test the pieces separately, you need only two test cases for each, making a total of 20 test cases.

This is a somewhat simplistic example, but breaking big chunks of code into simpler pieces makes them much easier to test and debug.

Usually, unit tests apply to methods. You write a method and then test it. If you can, you may even want to test parts of methods. That lets you catch bugs minutes or even seconds after they hatch, while they're still weak and easy to kill.

If you're using an object-oriented programming language, be sure to test code that doesn't act like a normal method. For example, be sure to test constructors (which execute when you make a new object), destructors (which execute when you destroy an object), and property accessors (which execute when the program gets or sets a property's value).

Because unit tests are your first chance to catch bugs, they're extremely important. Unfortunately, it's also easy for programmers to assume the code they just wrote works. After all, if it didn't work, you would have fixed it! If I know the code works, testing it seems like a waste of time.

Chapter 10 said that you can write more effective validation code if you write it before you write the routine it protects. The same applies here. You can often do a better job on a method's unit tests if you write them before you write the method. That way you won't know what assumptions the code makes beforehand, so you won't make the same assumptions when you write the tests.

Writing tests first is also a good way to learn about potential problems in the code. This is summed up nicely by the following quote.

> More than the act of testing, the act of designing tests is one of the best bug preventers known.
>
> —*Boris Beizer*

You may also want to add more test cases after you write the code so you can look for situations that the code might not handle correctly. The section "Testing Techniques" later in this chapter discusses some of the kinds of tests you may want to write.

Typically, a test is another piece of code that invokes the code you are trying to test and then validates the result. For example, suppose you're writing a method that organizes Pokémon card decks. It groups the cards by evolution chain (cards that are related) and then sorts the chains by their total smart ratings (average of attack, defense, special attack, and special defense). A unit test might generate a deck containing 100 random cards, pass them into the method, and validate the sorted result. The test method could repeat the random deck test a few thousand times to make sure the sorting method works for different random decks.

Other tests may perform user actions such as opening forms, clicking buttons, or clicking and dragging on a window to see what happens.

After you write the tests and use them to verify that your new code works, you should save the test code for later use. Sometimes, you may want to incorporate some or all the unit tests in regression testing (described in a following section).

You'll also need to use the tests again later if you discover a new bug in this code. You may think the unit tests are enough to flush out every bug so there won't be any in the future, but that's not the case. Bugs eventually appear. If you save all your unit tests, you won't need to write them again when a bug hatches. You also won't need to rewrite them if there's no bug but you modify the code and need to test the modifications.

Of course, writing a bunch of tests can clutter up your artistically formatted code. Depending on your programming environment, you may be able to avoid that by moving the test code into separate modules. You can also use conditional compilation to avoid compiling the test code in release builds so it doesn't make the final executable bigger and slower.

Integration Testing

After you write a chunk of code and use unit tests to verify that it works (or seems to work), it's time to integrate it into the existing codebase. An *integration test* verifies that the new method works and plays well with others. It checks that existing code calls the new method correctly, and that the new method can call other methods correctly.

Integration typically focuses on the new code and other pieces of code that interact with it, but it should also spend some time verifying that the new code didn't mess up anything that seems unrelated.

For example, suppose you're building a program to help you design duct tape projects (things like duct tape wallets, flowers, suits of armor, and prom dresses). You just wrote a new method to build parts lists giving the amounts and colors of duct tape you need for a particular project.

The new method passes its unit tests with flying colors, so you integrate it into the existing codebase. In integration tests, the main program can call the method successfully, and the new method can call existing code to do things like fetch duct tape roll lengths and prices.

Regression Testing

You've written new code and it passed unit and integration testing. Everything seems fine until you try to use the program to order new duct tape online. Suddenly that part of the program is no longer working. That duct tape ordering module may seem completely unrelated to the parts list method, but somehow it's not.

For example, the parts list code might open the pricing database and accidentally leave a price record locked. You might not notice this during unit testing and integration testing, but the tape ordering part of the program won't work if that record is locked.

To discover this kind of bug, you use regression testing. In *regression testing*, you test the program's entire functionality to see if anything changed when you added new code to the project. These tests look for ways the program may have "regressed" to a less useful version with missing or damaged features.

Ideally, when you finish unit testing a piece of code, you would then perform integration testing to make sure it fits in where it should and that it didn't break anything obvious. Then you perform regression testing to see if it broke something non-obvious.

Unfortunately, performing regression testing on a large project can take a lot of time, so developers often postpone regression testing until a significant amount of code has been added or modified. Then they run the regression tests. Of course, at that point there may be a lot of bugs, and it may be hard to figure out which change caused which bug. Some of the "new" code may also not be all that new, so some of the bugs may be a bit older and therefore harder to fix.

To fix bugs as quickly as possible, you need to perform regression testing as often as possible.

Automated Testing

You might not have time to run through every test every day. After all, you need time to do other things like write new code, perform code reviews, and eat donuts at staff meetings. However, a good automated testing system may do at least some testing for you. Automated testing tools let you define tests and the results they should produce. Some of them let you record and replay keyboard events and mouse movements so that a test can interact with your program's user interface.

After running a test, the testing tool can compare the results it got with expected results. Some tools can even compare images to see if a result is correct.

For example, to test a drawing program, you might record your actions as you draw, resize, and color a polygon. Later the testing tool would repeat the steps you took and see if the resulting picture matched the one you got when you did it interactively.

Some testing tools can also run *load tests* that simulate many users all running simultaneously to measure performance. For example, load tests can tell if too many users trying to access the same database will cause problems in your final release.

A good testing tool should let you schedule tests so that you can run regression testing every night after the developers all go home. Or you could start the tests running just before you leave for the night.

When you come in the next morning, you can check the tests to see if there are any newly discovered problems that you should fix before you begin writing new code.

OUTSOURCING TESTS

One annoying feature of outsourcing is that there's no good time for the clients and suppliers to meet. If it's during the middle of the workday here, it's the middle of the night there or vice versa. (I suppose that wouldn't be a problem if you're working in San Jose and outsourcing to Los Angeles, but I don't think that's typical.)

A friend of mine used the time difference to his advantage. His software development team would write code during the day. They would perform their unit and integration tests and then ship their code to testers in India before they left for the day.

When the Indian testers arrived in the morning, the new code would be waiting for them. They would run the regression tests and send the results back to the developers, who would see them first thing the next day. (Or maybe first thing on the same day. It depends on how you think about the temporal magic of time zones.)

The result was a lot like what you would get from an automated testing tool, but humans have a lot more flexibility than automated tools, so they can follow much more complicated instructions.

Component Interface Testing

Component interface testing studies the interactions between components. This is a bit like regression testing in the sense that both examine the application as a whole to look for trouble, but component interface testing focuses on component interactions.

A common strategy for component interface testing is to think of the interactions between components as one component sending a message (a request or a response) to another. You can then make each component record its interactions (plus a time stamp) in a file. To test the component interfaces, you exercise the system and then review the timeline of recorded events to see if everything makes sense.

THE BIG PICTURE

I've done some work with a company that processes photographs taken at popular tourist destinations such as amusement parks and sporting events. The photographers take your picture and upload it to a local computer.

Components in the application perform several processing steps such as moving the picture into a (huge) database, turning the pictures right side up (sometimes the photographers hold their cameras sideways), creating smaller thumbnail images, and replacing your greenscreen background with pictures of sinking ships, charging rhinos, menacing sharks, or whatever.

For debugging purposes, the components can write messages with time stamps into a log file so that you can see what's going on and so that you can tell if one of the components is stuck. This company processes tens of thousands of photographs every day, so if a process gets stuck for a few hours, hundreds or thousands of customers can't buy pictures of themselves standing beside their favorite theme park mascots.

Because the company processes so many images, the log files can grow extremely quickly. Depending on the level of information recorded, the logs can grow by megabytes per hour.

To prevent the log files from eventually gobbling up all the disk space on the planet, the components were written so that they check systemwide settings when they start to decide how much information to record. If something's going wrong, you change the settings and restart a component. (To make that possible, the components are also good at picking up where they left off when you restart them.) After a few minutes, you check the log files to see what's wrong and you fix the problem. When you're done, you change the settings back to allow little or no logging and restart again.

The ability to quickly change the amount of information recorded without recompiling has been extremely useful in keeping the process running smoothly for that company.

Planning ahead of time for component interface testing can also help with the application's design. Thinking in terms of loggable messages passed between components helps keep the components decoupled and gives them a clearer separation. That makes them easier to implement and test separately.

System Testing

As you may guess from its name, *system testing* is an end-to-end run-through of the whole system. Ideally, a system test exercises every part of the system to discover as many bugs as possible.

A thorough system test may need to explore many possible paths of interaction with the application. Unfortunately, even simple programs usually contain a practically unlimited number of possible paths.

For example, suppose you're writing a program to keep track of dirt characteristics for hikaru dorodango (dirt polishing) enthusiasts, things like color, amount available, and grain size. Also suppose the program includes only a login screen and a single form that uses a grid to display dirt information. Then you would need to try each of the following operations:

➤ Start the program and click Cancel on the login screen.

➤ Start the program, enter invalid login information, click OK, verify that you get an error message, and finally, click Cancel to close the login screen.

➤ Start the program, enter invalid login information, click OK, verify that you get an error message, enter valid login information, and click OK. Verify that you can log in.

➤ Log in, view saved information, and close the program. Log in again and verify that the information is unchanged.

➤ Log in, add new dirt information, and close the program. Log in again and verify that the information was saved.

➤ Log in, edit some dirt information, and close the program. Log in again and verify that the changes were saved.

➤ Log in, delete a dirt information entry, and close the program. Log in again and verify that the changes were saved.

You need all of those tests for just two screens, neither of which can do much. (Even then, I've seen a lot of applications where those tests wouldn't be good enough. For example, some programs won't save changes in a grid control unless you move the cursor to another cell after changing a cell's data.)

For more complicated applications, the number of combinations can be enormous. In the end, you'll probably have to test the most common and most important scenarios and leave some combinations untested.

Acceptance Testing

The goal of *acceptance testing* is to determine whether the finished application meets the customers' requirements. Normally, a user or other customer representative sits down with the application and runs through all the use cases you identified during the requirements gathering phase to make sure everything works as advertised.

Remember that the requirements may have changed after the requirements phase. In that case, you obviously verify that the application satisfies the revised requirements.

Acceptance testing is usually straightforward; although, depending on the number of use cases, it can take a long time. A fairly simple application might need only a few use cases. (The hikaru dorodango example described in the preceding section might need only a few to check that you can log in, view, add, edit, and delete data.) A large, complex application with detailed needs might have dozens or hundreds of use cases. In that case, it might take days or even weeks to go through them all.

One mistake developers sometimes make is waiting until the application is finished before starting acceptance testing. You do need to perform acceptance testing then, but if that's the first time the customer sees the application, there may be problems. Customers may decide that their interpretation of a use case is different from yours. Or they may decide that what they need is different from what they thought they needed during requirements gathering.

In those cases, you're much better off if you do a quick run-through of each use case as soon as the application can handle it. Then if you need to change the requirements, you can do it while there's still some time left in the development schedule and not at the end of the project when all of the programmers have scheduled overseas vacations.

Other Testing Categories

Unit test, integration test, regression test, component interface test, and system test categorize tests based on their scale with unit test being at the smallest scale and system test including the entire application. An acceptance test differs from a system test in the point of view of the tester: a system tester is typically a developer, whereas an acceptance tester is a customer representative.

The following list summarizes other categories of testing that differ in their scope, focus, or point of view.

➤ Accessibility test—Tests the application for accessibility by those with visual, hearing, or other special needs. (I confess that I like larger fonts more as I grow older.)

➤ Alpha test—First round testing by selected customers or independent testers. Alpha tests usually uncover lots of bugs and defects, so they generally aren't open to a huge number of users because that might ruin your reputation for building good software. (It may not be great for your morale either. A bad alpha test period can be soul crushing.)

➤ Beta test—Second round testing after alpha test. Generally, you shouldn't give users beta versions until the application is quite solid or you might damage your reputation for building good software. Sometimes, beta tests are used as a sneaky form of a limited trial to build excitement for a new release in the user community.

➤ Compatibility test—Focuses on compatibility with different environments, such as computers running older operating system versions. Also checks compatibility with older versions of the application's files, databases, and other saved data. Sometimes after compatibility tests you might change the program to handle new configurations. Alternatively, you might prohibit those configurations in the documentation. ("Some features may be unavailable in Windows 3.1 and older.")

➤ Destructive test—Makes the application fail so that you can study its behavior when the worst happens. (Obviously, if you have good backups, you won't actually destroy the code. You'll destroy the application's performance.)

➤ Functional test—Deals with features that the application provides. These are generally listed in the requirements.

➤ Installation test—Makes sure you can successfully install the system on a fresh computer.

➤ Internationalization test—Tests the application on computers localized for different parts of the world. This should be carried out by people who are natives of the locales. (For example, text may have different lengths in different languages, so you may need to arrange labels accordingly. "Delete customer record" is shorter than "Eliminar registro de cliente.")

➤ Nonfunctional test—Studies application characteristics that aren't related to specific functions the users will perform. For example, these tests might check performance under a heavy user load, with limited memory, or with missing network connections. These often identify minimal requirements. ("Internet, webcam, and VR goggles required.")

➤ Performance test—Studies the application's performance under various conditions such as normal usage, heavy user load, limited resources (such as disk space), and time of day. Records metrics such as the number of records processed per hour under different conditions.

➤ Security test—Studies the application's security. This includes security of the login process, communications, and data.

➤ Usability test—Determines whether the user interface is intuitive and easy to use.

TESTING TECHNIQUES

The previous sections described some different levels of testing (unit, integration, component, system, and acceptance) and alluded to some methods for testing (try out every combination of actions that you can think of), but they didn't explain specific techniques for performing actual tests.

In particular, they didn't discuss generating data for tests. For example, suppose a method organizes Pokémon card decks as described earlier. You can test it by generating a random deck and seeing if the method organizes it correctly, but how do you know it will work with *every* possible deck?

The following sections describe some approaches to designing tests to find as many bugs as possible.

Exhaustive Testing

Exhaustive testing considers every possible combination of inputs. For example, suppose you write a tic-tac-toe (noughts and crosses) program and one method is in charge of picking the best move from a current board position. You could test the method by passing it a board position, seeing what move it picks, and then verifying that there are no better moves that it could have chosen instead.

There are only 9! = 362,880 possible board arrangements, so you could pass the method every possible combination of moves to see what it does. (In fact, many of the board arrangements are impossible. For example, you can't have three Os on the top row and three Xs on the middle row in the same game. That means there are actually fewer than 9! possible arrangements to test.)

This sort of exhaustive testing conclusively proves that a method works correctly under all circumstances, so it's the best you can possibly do. Unfortunately, most methods take too many combinations of input parameters for you to exhaustively try them all.

For a ridiculously simple example where an exhaustive test is impossible, suppose you write a Maximum method that compares two 32-bit integers and returns the one that's larger. Each of the two inputs can take roughly 4.3×10^9 values (between –2,147,483,648 and 2,147,483,647), so there are approximately 1.8×10^{19} possible combinations. Even if you had a computer that could call the method and verify its results 1 billion times per second, it would take more than 570 years to check every combination.

Because most methods take too many possible input combinations, exhaustive testing won't work most of the time. In those cases, you need to turn to one of the following methods.

Black-Box Testing

In *black-box testing*, you pretend the method is a black box that you can't peek inside. You know what it is supposed to do, but you have no idea how it works. You then throw all sorts of inputs at the method to see what it does.

You can start black-box testing by sending it a bunch of random inputs. Remember that you need to perform these tests only occasionally, not every time the program runs, so you can test a *lot* of random values. For example, you might throw a few million random pairs of values at the Maximum method described in the previous section. It doesn't matter if it takes the test a few minutes to finish.

> **NOT SO RANDOM** *If you generate random test cases, be sure you understand how your random number generator works. For example, in C# the statement* `random.Next(1, 10)` *generates random numbers between lower bound 1 (inclusive) and upper bound 10 (exclusive), so it generates values from 1 to 9 rather than 1 to 10 as you might expect. Be sure you use the generator correctly to include all of the values that you want to test.*
>
> *If there are particular values that you want to test, test them explicitly rather than hoping to pick them randomly.*

Even if you don't know how the method works, you can try to guess values that might mess it up. Typically, those involve special values like 0 for numbers and blank for strings. They may also include the largest and smallest possible values. For strings, that might mean a string that's all blanks or all ~ characters.

Sometimes, you can trip up a method that expects to process names by using strings containing numbers or special characters such as &#%!$ (which looks like a cartoon character swearing).

Some methods don't work well if their inputs include a lot of duplicates, so try that. For example, quicksort is usually one of the fastest sorting algorithms, but it gives terrible performance if the items it is sorting all have the same value. (Consult an algorithms book or search for quicksort online if you want to see the details.)

If a method takes a variable number of inputs, make sure it can handle 0 inputs and a really large number of inputs. If it takes an array or list as a parameter, see what it does if the array or list is empty or missing.

Finally, look at boundary values. If a method expects a floating-point parameter between 0.0 and 1.0, make sure it can handle those two values.

White-Box Testing

In *white-box testing*, you're allowed to know how the method does its work. You then use your extra knowledge to design tests to try to make the method crash and burn.

White-box testing has the advantage that you know how the method works, so you can try to pick particularly difficult test cases. Unfortunately, it has the disadvantage that you know how the method works, so you might skip some test cases that you assume work.

For example, you might know that a method would be confused by zero-length strings. But you knew that when you wrote the code, so you handled it. The problem is, you may not have handled it correctly. If you handled everything correctly, then there wouldn't be any bugs and you wouldn't need testing at all. So test zero-length strings even though you *know it's an absolutely certain fact beyond a shadow of a doubt* that the method can handle them.

Use white-box testing to create tests you know will be troublesome, but don't skip tests that you "know" the method can handle.

Gray-Box Testing

Gray-box testing is a combination of white-box and black-box testing. Here you know some but not all the internals of the method you are testing. Your partial knowledge of the method lets you design specific tests to attack it.

For example, suppose a method examines test score data to find students that might need extra tutoring help. You don't know all the details, but you do know that it uses the quicksort algorithm to sort the students by their grades. In that case, you might want to see what the method does if every student has the same grade because that might mess up quicksort. Because you don't know what else is going on inside the method, you also need to write a bunch of black-box styles tests.

BLACK-BOX AND WHITE-BOX TESTING

With black-box testing, if you truly don't know how a method works, then it's harder to assume it handles specific cases correctly. Unfortunately, with black-box testing, you don't know where to look for weaknesses.

White-box testing lets you specifically attack a method's weaknesses, but as mentioned a couple of times (both in this chapter and in Chapter 10), it's easy for programmers to assume that their code works. (That's the biggest drawback of white-box testing.) That can make them skip some test cases that might uncover a bug.

You can get the best of both worlds by combining black-box and white-box testing. One way to do that is to have two different people test a method. The programmer who wrote it can build some white-box tests, and someone else can design some black-box tests.

Many larger software projects have designated testers who do nothing but try their hardest to destroy their colleagues' code. Sometimes their attitude can be a bit adversarial, but the results can be remarkable if team members don't take things too seriously. (There's a great short article about IBM's Black Team at www.t3.org/ tangledwebs/07/tw0706.html.) It helps to remember that the testers aren't enemies trying to get you fired but rather team members trying to save you from embarrassing yourself by shipping a buggy application.

> Testers don't like to break things; they like to dispel the illusion that things work.
>
> —*Lessons Learned in Software Testing by Kaner, Bach, and Pettichord (Wiley, 2011)*

Another approach that can give some of the same benefits is to have developers write black-box tests before they write a method's code. (These might really be "dark-gray-box" tests because the developer may have some idea about how to write the method but may not know all of the details. You can probably do even better if you have one person write the black-box tests and then have another write the code.) Then after the method is written, its author can create white-box tests to go with it.

TESTING HABITS

Just as there are good programming habits, there are also good testing habits. These habits make testing more effective so you're more likely to find bugs quickly and relatively painlessly. They also make it less likely that new bugs will appear when you fix a bug.

The following sections describe some testing habits that can make you a better tester.

Test and Debug When Alert

In Chapter 10, I said that you should write code when you're most alert. That helps you understand the code better so that it reduces the chances of you writing incorrect code and adding bugs to the application.

Similarly, you should test and debug when you're alert. Then when something goes wrong, you'll be more likely to understand what the program is supposed to be doing, what it is actually doing, and how to fix it. Debugging while tired is a good way to add new bugs to the program.

(DWT stands for "driving while texting" and is illegal in most US states. DWT can also stand for "debugging while tired," and it should be illegal too.)

One nice thing about automated tests is that they don't get tired. You may be exhausted after a long day of coding, but a testing tool can exercise the application while you catch up on your sleep. Then in the morning you can start refreshed, chasing any bugs that were found.

Test Your Own Code

Before you check your code in and claim it's ready for prime time, test it yourself. This is the last chance you have to find your own bugs before someone else does. Save yourself some embarrassment and do your own work. If you make someone else do it for you, they may decide to rub your nose in it for days or weeks to come.

Stories abound that tell of programmers who don't test their code before checking it into the project. One of my friends who was a project manager hung a toy skunk outside the door of the developer who broke the weekly build, and it stayed there until someone else "skunked" the build. One time the skunk stayed outside my friend's door for more than a month, so no one was immune! (That sort of thing can be amusing, but only if everyone takes it with good humor. Some people can't handle that sort of thing.)

Another group I heard of had a programmer whose name happened to be Fred. Pretty much every week Fred managed to break the build, so the other programmers would spend several hours "de-fredding" the code every week.

Lots of larger projects have that "one guy" who messes up the project build. Don't be that guy!

Have Someone Else Test Your Code

It's important to test your own code, but you're too close to your code to be objective. You have assumptions about how it works that unconsciously influence the tests you perform. To find as many bugs as possible, you also need someone with a fresh perspective to test it.

Even if you're Super Programmer (faster than a speeding binary search, more powerful than a linked list, and able to leap tall b-trees with a single bound), you're going to make mistakes every now and then. You've spent a lot of time and effort on your code, so when someone gently points out your mistakes, it's easy to become defensive. Your feelings are hurt. You feel personally attacked. You pull into yourself like a spurned teenager and start playing emo music on your earphones. In the worst case, you retreat into your fortress of solitude and become a software super-villain.

In fact, all that actually happened is that someone else found a mistake that anyone could have made. They didn't cause the mistake; it was already sitting there waiting to pounce during a demo for the company president. (And I've seen that happen! A lot!) You should be grateful that the bug was caught before it escaped into a released product where it could embarrass your whole programming team.

Mistakes happen all the time, particularly in software development. It's important to thank the tester for pointing out this flaw, fix it, and move on with no hard feelings.

The ability to take this kind of criticism can be such an important factor in software engineering that Gerald Weinberg coined the term *egoless programming* in his book *The Psychology of Computer Programming*. Even though he wrote that book way back in 1971, the term is still important in programming today. (The latest edition of his book as of this writing is *The Psychology of Computer Programming: Silver Anniversary Edition*, Dorset House, 1998.)

THE RULES OF EGOLESS PROGRAMMING

Here's a summary of Gerald Weinberg's *Ten Commandments of Egoless Programming*:

1. **Understand and accept that you will make mistakes.** Everyone makes mistakes. (Even me after 40+ years of programming experience.) Try to avoid mistakes but realize that they will occur anyway. No one else programs without any mistakes, so why should you?

2. **You are not your code.** Just because you wrote a piece of flawed code, that doesn't make you a bad person. Don't take the bug home with you and ruin your weekend obsessing over it. Be glad the bug was found when it was. (And wish it had been found sooner!)

3. **No matter how much "karate" you know, someone else will always know more.** Even the greatest programmers of all time sometimes learn from others. And chances are, some of the people around you have more experience, at least in some facets of programming. Learn what Yoda has to offer.

4. **Don't rewrite code without consultation.** By all means fix bugs, but don't rewrite sections of code without consulting with your team. Bulk rewrites should be performed only for good reasons (like replacing a buggy section of code or rearranging code so that it can be broken up into separate methods), not because you don't like someone's indentation or variable names. If it ain't broke, don't fix it.

5. **Treat people who know less than you with respect, deference, and patience.** Even you started out as a programming novice. You made simple mistakes, did things the hard way because you didn't know better, and asked naive questions (if you were smart enough to ask questions). Be patient and don't reinforce the stereotype that good programmers are all prima donnas. (Also see #3. You may know more than someone, but not everyone.)

   One of the lessons I've learned over the years is that good ideas sometimes lie behind bad code. A piece of code that you think is weird may be trying to address an issue that isn't obvious. Stay humble and find out what the programmer was trying to do. Then decide if there's a better way to deal with the issue.

6. **The only constant in the world is change.** After a while, programmers tend to become comfortable with what they know. Unfortunately, change happens anyway, whether you like it or not. Embrace change and see if it can work in your favor.

   (I worked on one project with about 25 programmers and around 100,000 lines of object-oriented code. Unfortunately, the project manager said flat out that he "didn't get object-oriented code." He learned to program before

continues

(continued)

object-oriented languages were invented and he didn't see the point. That made him practically useless in any technical discussion.)

At the same time, don't discard something just because something new has come along. Like programmers, techniques that stand the test of time do so because they're useful.

7. **The only true authority stems from knowledge, not from position.** Don't use your position (as lead developer, senior architect, scrum master, or even corporate vice president) to force your point of view down others' throats. Base your decisions on facts and let the facts speak for you.

8. **Fight for what you believe, but gracefully accept defeat.** Programming tasks rarely have a single unambiguous solution. There's *always* more than one way to tackle a problem. If the group doesn't decide to take your approach, don't worry about it. If the result is good enough, then it's good enough.

   Later, if it turns out you were right and the approach taken wasn't good enough, don't rub it in. That attitude makes it harder for the group to make good decisions in the future. (Besides, someday you'll be on the wrong side of a decision and your coworkers will be slow to forget the time you acted all high and mighty.)

9. **Don't be "the guy in the room."** Sometimes you may need to close your office door and bang out some code, but don't go into hibernation and emerge only briefly to restock your Twinkie and NOS Energy Drink supply. Stay engaged with the other developers so you can collaborate with them effectively.

10. **Critique code instead of people—be kind to the coder, not to the code.** This can be as simple as a subtle wording change. Instead of saying, "What were you thinking you utter moron?" you could say, "It looks like this variable isn't being initialized before it's passed into this routine." Okay, that example is a bit extreme, but you get the idea. Make comments that refer to what the code is doing, not to the person who wrote it.

    Comments should also be positive, if possible, and focus on improving the code instead of dwelling on pointing out what's wrong. Instead of, "This variable isn't being initialized," you could say, "We should probably initialize this variable." Notice how the word "we" also treats the code as group property instead of one person's mistake. It's good to help developers think of it as a joint project and not a collection of code owned by individuals.

Fix Your Own Bugs

When you fix a bug, it's important to understand the code as completely as possible. If you wrote a piece of code, you probably have a greater understanding of it than your fellow programmers do. That makes you the logical person to fix it. Anyone else will need to spend more time coming up to speed on what the code is supposed to do and how it works.

If someone else fixes your code and does it wrong, your code looks bad. It may not be your fault (well, ultimately it was because you made the initial mistake), but you're the one who gets credit for the new bug. You may end up having to fix your own problem and the new one.

Besides, if you made a mistake, it may be useful to fix it yourself so that you can learn how to avoid that mistake in the future.

Think Before You Change

It's common to see beginning programmers randomly changing code around hoping that one of the changes will make a bug go away. (Sadly, you sometimes also see those sorts of random changes in experienced programmers.)

I won't say this is the *worst* way to debug code but only because I'm certain that someone out there can come up with an even more terrible method. However, this is certainly an extremely bad way to fix software. If you're making random changes, you're not paying attention to what the changes are doing. If a change makes a bug disappear, then you don't really know if it fixed the bug or just hid it. You don't know if the change added a new bug (or several). You also missed out on an opportunity to learn something so you won't make the same mistake in the future.

CARD COUNTING

In college I had a roommate whose professor made everyone work with punched cards. (If you don't know what those are, see `https://en.wikipedia.org/wiki/Punched_card`.) It took several minutes to an hour to get the Computer Center to run a deck of cards, and the professor's theory was that using cards instead of typing code into the computer interactively would discourage people from trying to fix a program by trial and error.

Of course, what students did was make four or five copies of their decks (which could contain several hundred cards each; you could hear the forests cry out in pain) so they could make four or five random changes per session. It just goes to show how clever people can be at being stupid.

Don't Believe in Magic

Suppose you've spent hours chasing a bug. You've made some test changes and the bug has gone away. It's remarkable how many developers stop at that point, pat themselves on the back, and call it a job well done.

Unless you know why the changes that you made fixed the bug, you can't assume the bug is really gone. Sometimes you've just hidden it. Or perhaps it went away for completely unrelated reasons, like your order processing center in New York just shut down for the evening and stopped sending you new orders.

Before you cross a bug off of your To Do list, make sure you understand exactly what changes you made and why they worked. (Also ask yourself if the changes will have bad consequences.)

See What Changed

If you're debugging new code, you can't check an older version to see what changed, but if you're chasing a bug in code that has been recently modified (perhaps due to a bug fix), see what's changed. Sometimes the difference makes the bug pop out and saves you hours of work.

Fix Bugs, Not Symptoms

Sometimes developers focus so closely on the code that they don't see the bigger picture. They find a line of code that contains a bug and fix it without considering whether there's a larger issue.

For example, suppose you're writing a method that calculates registration prices for a bull riding competition. Unfortunately, the method is giving senior citizen discounts to people who don't deserve them. (People over 85 get $3 off, but the program is giving them to younger contestants too.)

You step through the code for a few problem customers, and you discover the bug is in the following calculation:

```
age = current_year - birth_year
```

It turns out some people have entered their birthdates in the format mm/dd/yy but the program is expecting mm/dd/yyyy. For example, assuming it's 2025, someone born in 2015 who enters her age as 4/1/15 will have a calculated age of 2025 − 15 = 2010. With an age of more than 2,000 years, she's certainly entitled to the discount.

One way to fix this would be to check the customer's birthdate and, if the year doesn't contain four digits, not offer the discount. You might anger a few bull riding 104-year-olds (birthdate 4/1/21), but at least you won't have parents accusing you of encouraging 10-year-olds to ride bulls.

This fix works (sort of), but it doesn't address the real problem: customers are entering their birthdates in the wrong format. A better solution would be to modify the user interface to require customers to enter their birthdates in the correct format. (You could also add some assertions to look for a valid format to make sure this sort of bug doesn't reappear later.)

Look at the entire context of the code that contains a bug and ask yourself whether you're fixing a bug or a symptom of something bigger. Make sure you understand the whole problem before you act.

Test Your Tests

If you write a bunch of tests for a method and those tests don't find any bugs, how do you know they're working? Perhaps the tests are flawed, and they don't detect errors correctly.

After you write your tests, add a few bugs to the code you're testing and make sure the tests catch them. Basically, you need to test the tests. (Also flag the test bugs with comments or mark them for conditional compilation so you can easily remove them later!)

HOW TO FIX A BUG

Obviously, when you fix a bug you need to modify the code, but there are a few other actions you should also take.

First, ask yourself how you could prevent a similar bug in the future. What techniques could you use in your code? What tests could you run to detect the bug sooner?

Second, ask yourself if a similar bug could be lurking somewhere else. You just went to a lot of trouble isolating this bug. If other pieces of code contain a similar problem, it will be easier if you find them now instead of waiting for them to break something else. Do a search of the rest of the project's code to see if you can find this bug's cousins.

Third, look for bugs hidden behind this one. Sometimes, the symptoms of one bug mask the symptoms of another. For example, suppose you write a method that flags customers who have unpaid balances greater than $50.00. You write a second method that sends emails to those customers to nag them. Unfortunately, a missing decimal point in the first method makes it find customers with balances greater than $5,000. Because you don't have any customers with such large balances, you never discover that the second method is sending emails to the wrong addresses. (This is sort of like asking a mechanic to fix your car's starter when you don't realize the engine is also missing.)

Fourth, examine the code's method and look for other possibly unrelated bugs. Bugs tend to travel in swarms. A piece of code may be extra complicated, poorly organized, cluttered with badly conceived patches to previous bugs, or just written by "that guy." Whatever the reason, some pieces of code are just buggier than others. When you fix a bug, look around for others. If you find a nest of bugs, ask whether you should refactor the whole section to make it more maintainable.

Finally, make sure your fix doesn't introduce a new bug. The chances of a line of modified code containing a bug are much higher than those for an original line of code. (That combined with the fact that bugs tend to swarm means some piece of code can actually sprout bugs faster than you can fix them. It's like playing a particularly annoying game of whack-a-mole.) Take extra care to not cause more problems than you solve. Then thoroughly test your changes to make sure they worked and that they didn't break anything.

ESTIMATING NUMBER OF BUGS

One of the unfortunate facts about bugs is that you can never tell when they're all gone. As one computing pioneer put it:

> Testing shows the presence, not the absence of bugs.
>
> —*Edsger W. Dijkstra*

You can run tests as long as you like, but you can never be sure you've found every bug.

Similarly, you can't know the number of bugs lurking in a project. (If you could, then you could just keep testing until that number reached zero.) Fortunately, there are some techniques you can use to estimate the number of bugs remaining in a program. They have some serious drawbacks, but at least they're better than nothing. (They also give you some actual, if not necessarily verifiable, numbers to report at management presentations to prove that you're doing something useful now that programming is winding down.)

Tracking Bugs Found

One method for estimating bugs is to track the number of bugs found over time. Typically, when testing gets started in a serious way, this number increases. After the testers have uncovered the most obvious bugs, the number levels off. Hopefully, the number of bugs found eventually declines. If you plot the number of bugs found per day, the graph should look more or less like the one in Figure 13.1.

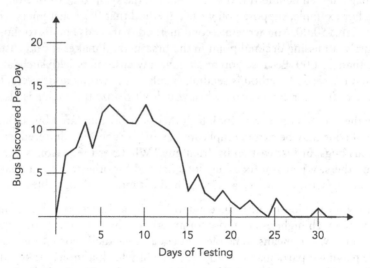

FIGURE 13.1: When you're in the "getting close to zero" part of the graph, you may be running out of bugs.

When you're working out near the "getting close to zero" part of the graph, you have some reason to believe that you've found most of the bugs.

This approach is easy, intuitive, and doesn't require a lot of extra work (beyond finding the bugs, which you need to do anyway, and keeping track), so it's a good start. (Graphs are also good in management presentations. You can make them colorful, and people can pretend to understand them.)

Unfortunately, this approach has a couple of problems. First, it tends to track the easiest bugs to find. After four weeks of testing, you may have found 80 percent of the easy bugs but only 5 percent of the tricky bugs. The graph declines because you're running out of easy-to-find bugs, but there may still be plenty of sneakier bugs lying in wait to appear during an important presentation.

Similarly, this kind of estimate assumes that your test coverage is equally good on all parts of the project. If you've neglected part of the application or failed to look for a particular kind of bug (for example, invalid customer data), there may be a whole swarm of bugs remaining that you don't know about. Sometimes, you can see this effect when you add a new test to your automated test suite and suddenly a whole bunch of new bugs appear.

> ## CODE COVERAGE
>
> Some testing tools can measure *code coverage*, the lines of code that are executed during a demonstration or a suite of tests. They can tell you how many times a particular piece of code has been exercised.
>
> You should use code coverage tools to make sure that every part of the system is visited at least once by the tests. Executing a line of code doesn't guarantee that you've found any bug that might be in that line. However, if you don't execute a chunk of code, you're guaranteed not to find any bugs hiding there.

Seeding

Another approach for estimating bugs is to "seed" the code with bugs. Simply scatter some bugs throughout the application. (Be sure to mark them so you can remove them later.)

Run your tests and see how many of the artificial bugs you find. If the unintentional bugs are about as good at hiding as the bugs you planted, you should be able to estimate the number of bugs remaining.

For example, suppose you insert 40 bugs in the code and your tests find 34 of them. That 85 percent success rate implies that you may have found 85 percent of the real bugs. If you've found 135 real bugs so far, then there may have originally been approximately $135 \div 0.85 \approx 159$ bugs. That means there are about $159 - 135 = 24$ bugs remaining.

The previous approach (tracking found bugs) assumes the bugs you've found are representative of the bugs as a whole. The seeding approach makes a similar assumption. It assumes the artificial bugs can accurately represent the true bugs.

Unfortunately, it's a lot easier to create simple bugs by tweaking a line of code here and there than it is to create complex bugs that involve interactions among several methods in different modules. That means the seeding method can greatly underestimate the number of complicated and subtle bugs.

The Lincoln Index

Consider the following word problem.

> Suppose you have two testers, Lisa and Ramon. After they bash away at the application for a while, Lisa finds 15 bugs and Ramon finds 13. Of the bugs, they find 5 in common. In total, how many bugs does the application contain?

The correct answer in this case is, "Wait, I thought this was a software engineering book, not a mathematics text. You didn't say I was going to have to solve word problems!"

Of course, you don't really know how many bugs are in the application, but the *Lincoln index* gives you a guess. In this example, the Lincoln index is 15 × 13 ÷ 5 = 39.

More generally, if two testers find E_1 and E_2 errors, respectively, of which S are in common, then the Lincoln index is given by the following equation:

$$L = \frac{E_1 \times E_2}{S}$$

Like all the other bug estimation techniques, this one isn't perfect. It relies on the assumption that the testers have an equal chance to find any particular bug, and that's probably not true. Both testers are most likely to find the easiest bugs, so the value S is probably larger than it would be if finding bugs was completely random. That means the Lincoln index probably underestimates the true number of bugs.

INTERESTING TIDBIT

The Lincoln index was described by Frederick Charles Lincoln in 1930, long before the invention of modern computers. He was an ornithologist who used the method to estimate the number of birds in a given area based on the number of birds counted by different observers. For more information about the Lincoln index, see `https://en.wikipedia.org/wiki/Lincoln_index`.

HOW DOES THE LINCOLN INDEX WORK?

Suppose the two testers have probabilities P_1 and P_2 of finding any given bug and assume the application contains B bugs. Then you would expect them to find $E_1 = P_1 \times B$ and $E_2 = P_2 \times B$ bugs, respectively.

The chance of a particular bug being found by *both* testers would be $P_1 \times P_2$, so you would expect them to find $S = P_1 \times P_2 \times B$ bugs in common.

Plugging those values into the formula for the Lincoln index gives:

$$L = \frac{E_1 \times E_2}{S}$$

$$= \frac{(P_1 \times B) \times (P_2 \times B)}{P_1 \times P_2 \times B}$$

$$= B$$

When you get through canceling, all that's left is B. That means you should expect the Lincoln index to be about the same as B, the total number of bugs.

Another way the Lincoln index can break down is if Lisa and Ramon have similar testing styles. In that case, their common style may lead them to find the same bugs. Again, the value S would be larger than it would if bugs were found randomly, and the Lincoln index would be smaller than it should be.

SUMMARY

If all programs contain bugs, you may be tempted to throw your hands up in the air, walk away from your software engineering job, and open a bakery. Even though you generally cannot remove every bug from a program, you can usually remove enough bugs that the remaining ones don't appear too often and don't inconvenience users too much.

The key to finding bugs so that you can remove them is testing. By constantly testing code at small, medium, and large scales, you can find bugs as soon as possible and make removing them easier. Continue testing until bug estimation techniques indicate that you may have caught most of the important bugs.

When your testing efforts aren't finding much to fix, it's time to start deployment. The next chapter describes typical deployment tasks and some of the things you should do to make deployment easier.

EXERCISES

1. Two integers are *relatively prime* (or *coprime*) if they have no common factors other than 1. For example, 21 = 3 × 7 and 35 = 5 × 7 are *not* relatively prime because they are both divisible by 7. By definition, –1 and 1 are relatively prime to every integer, and they are the only numbers relatively prime to 0.

   Suppose you've written an efficient `AreRelativelyPrime` method that takes two integers between –1 million and 1 million as parameters and returns `true` if they are relatively prime. Use either your favorite programming language or pseudocode (English that sort of looks like code) to write a method that tests the `AreRelativelyPrime` method. (Hint: You may find it useful to write another method that also tests two integers to see if they are relatively prime.)

2. What changes do you need to make to the `AreRelativelyPrime` method to test all the testing code? In other words, what do you need to do to test the testing code?

3. What testing techniques did you use to write the test method in Exercise 1? (Exhaustive, black-box, white-box, or gray-box?) Which ones *could* you use and under what circumstances?

4. What limitations do the tests you wrote for Exercise 1 have? Would a particular testing technique help?

5. The following code shows a C# version of the `AreRelativelyPrime` method and the `GCD` method that it calls.

```
// Return true if a and b are relatively prime.
private bool AreRelativelyPrime(int a, int b)
{
```

```
            // Only 1 and -1 are relatively prime to 0.
            if (a == 0) return ((b == 1) || (b == -1));
            if (b == 0) return ((a == 1) || (a == -1));
            int gcd = GCD(a, b);
            return ((gcd == 1) || (gcd == -1));
        }


        // Use Euclid's algorithm to calculate the
        // greatest common divisor (GCD) of two numbers.
        // See http://en.wikipedia.org/wiki/Euclidean_algorithm
        private int GCD(int a, int b)
        {
            a = Math.Abs(a);
            b = Math.Abs(b);

            // If a or b is 0, return the other value.
            if (a == 0) return b;
            if (b == 0) return a;
            for (; ; )
            {
                int remainder = a % b;
                if (remainder == 0) return b;
                a = b;
                b = remainder;
            };
        }
```

The `AreRelativelyPrime` method checks whether either value is 0. Only –1 and 1 are relatively prime to 0, so if a or b is 0, the method returns `true` only if the other value is –1 or 1.

The code then calls the `GCD` method to get the greatest common divisor of a and b. If the greatest common divisor is –1 or 1, the values are relatively prime, so the method returns `true`. Otherwise, the method returns `false`.

Now that you know how the method works, implement it and your testing code in your favorite programming language. Did you find any bugs in your initial version of the method or in the testing code? Did you get any benefit from the testing code?

6. Write an exhaustive test for the `AreRelativelyPrime` method in pseudocode. What are the benefits and drawbacks to this version?

7. Write a version of the program you wrote for Exercise 5 that uses an exhaustive test. How large can you make the range of values (to the nearest powers of 10) and still finish testing in under 10 seconds? Approximately how long would it take to test with the range –1 million to 1 million?

8. Does all this this seem like a lot of work?

9. Exhaustive testing actually falls into one of the categories black-box, white-box, or gray-box. Which one is it and why?

10. The section "The Lincoln Index" describes an application where Lisa found 15 bugs, Ramon found 13 bugs, and they found 5 in common. The Lincoln index estimates that the application might contain approximately 39 bugs in total. After you fix all of the bugs that Lisa and Ramon found, how many are left?

11. Suppose you have three testers: Alice, Bob, and Carmen. You assign numbers to the bugs, so the testers find the sets of bugs {1, 2, 3, 4, 5}, {2, 5, 6, 7}, and {1, 2, 8, 9, 10}. How can you use the Lincoln index to estimate the total number of bugs? How many bugs are still at large?

12. What happens to the Lincoln estimate if the two testers don't find any bugs in common? What does it mean? Can you get a "lower bound" estimate of the number of bugs?

13. What happens to the Lincoln estimate if the two testers find *only* bugs in common? What does it mean?

14. The Lincoln index has a statistical bias, so some people prefer to use the Seber estimator:

$$Bugs = \frac{(E_1 + 1) \times (E_2 + 1)}{(S + 1)} - 1$$

Repeat Exercise 10 with the Seber estimator. How does it compare to the Lincoln index estimate?

15. Suppose two testers find 7 and 5 bugs, respectively, but none in common. Repeat Exercise 12 with the Seber estimator.

16. Suppose two testers find only the same bugs. Repeat Exercise 13 with the Seber estimator.

WHAT YOU LEARNED IN THIS CHAPTER

➤ Goals of testing

➤ Reasons to not remove a bug (diminishing returns, deadlines, it's too soon since the last release, the bug is useful, the code will soon be obsolete, it's a feature not a bug, at some point you need to release something, the program is already worth using, fixing bugs is dangerous)

➤ How to decide which bugs to fix (severity, workarounds, frequency, difficulty, riskiness)

➤ Levels of testing (unit, integration, component interface, system, acceptance)

➤ Uses for automated testing

➤ Testing categories (accessibility, alpha, beta, compatibility, destructive, functional, installation, internationalization, nonfunctional, performance, security, usability)

➤ Testing techniques (exhaustive, black-box, white-box, gray-box)

➤ Good testing habits (test when alert, test your own code, have someone else test your code, use egoless programming, fix your own bugs, think before you change, don't believe in magic, see what changed, fix bugs not symptoms)

➤ How to fix a bug (How can you prevent similar bugs in the future? Could the bug be elsewhere? Look for bugs hidden by this bug. Look for unrelated bugs. Make sure your fix doesn't introduce another bug.)

➤ Methods for estimating number of bugs (tracking, seeding, Lincoln index, Seber estimator)

14

Deployment

Plans are nothing; planning is everything.

—*Dwight D. Eisenhower*

In the Old Country we have a thaying. . . 'If you don't want the monthter, you don't pull the lever.'

— *Igor in* Making Money *by Terry Pratchett*

What You Will Learn in This Chapter:

➤ What you should put in a deployment plan

➤ Why you need a rollback plan

➤ Cutover strategies

➤ Common deployment tasks

➤ Common deployment mistakes

After you've built the next blockbuster first-person shooter, financial projection tool, or Goat Simulator, it's time for deployment. *Deployment* is the process of putting the finished application in the users' hands and basking in their adulation.

At least that's the theory. In reality, deployment can be a nightmare unrivaled by any other step in the software engineering process. It can be the stage when you discover that the program that worked perfectly in testing scenarios is a total failure in the real world. It can be the point when you realize that all of your months or years of labor slaving over an overclocked CPU has been for naught. It can be when you and your coworkers learn how many resumes per hour the laser printer down the hall can produce.

Fortunately, the reality usually falls somewhere between the user adulation and nightmare scenarios. Most things work, more or less, with a few notable exceptions that give you interesting stories to tell later at the wrap party. (In the words of Captain Jack Sparrow in *Pirates of the Caribbean: Dead Man's Chest*, "Complications arose, ensued, were overcome.")

IMPLEMENTATION AND INSTALLATION

In addition to the term "deployment," some people use the terms *implementation*, *installation*, and *release*. In this context, they all mean basically the same thing, although they may show slight differences in the speaker's background.

Programmers tend to think of "implementation" as writing code to do something. (As in, "Did you implement the user validation module yet?") "Installation" sounds more humdrum than the other terms. You call an electrician or a plumber to install something. Besides, "deployment" sounds more dynamic. You don't "install" or "implement" troops into a field of battle.

Software developers do occasionally talk about releasing programs into the wild.

This chapter describes the deployment phase of a software engineering project. It explains deployment scope and lists some of the things that you should consider in a deployment plan.

SCOPE

A project's scope can range from a small tool you wrote for your own use to in-house business software that will be used by hundreds or thousands of users for decades to come. Some of the largest projects (things like operating systems, browsers, and game console games) might have millions of users.

In addition to the number of users, scope includes the size of the application. It includes the amount of data involved, the number of external systems that are affected, and the sheer quantity of code (all of which could fail).

As you can probably guess, larger deployments provide more opportunities for mistakes. Big projects have more pieces that can go wrong. They also provide more combinations of little things that can add up to big problems.

For those reasons, small deployments are usually the smoothest. If you write an application for your own use and it doesn't work, you've only inconvenienced yourself and you have no one else to blame. If you roll out a new version of an operating system to millions of customers and then immediately discover you need to send out a security fix, you lose credibility. (Yes, that scenario happens all the time.)

Before you begin deployment planning, you should consider the scope of the deployment and plan accordingly. How much pain will failure during deployment cause? How much of that pain will come back to haunt you? If a failure will inconvenience a lot of users, or make the users unable to help their customers, then you should spend extra time writing the best deployment plan possible. The next section explains in general what you need to put into a deployment plan.

THE PLAN

If everything went according to plan, you could write down a simple list of steps to follow and then work through them with guaranteed success. Unfortunately, the real world rarely works that way. Something always goes wrong. Perhaps not everything, but something.

When the inevitable emergency occurs, how well you recover depends largely on how thoroughly you planned for unexpected situations. If you have a backup plan ready to go, you may be able to work around the problem and keep moving forward. If you don't have a backup plan, you may need to stop the deployment and try again later.

Even stopping a deployment can be difficult and dangerous if you don't plan for it. After you drive over a cliff, it's a little late to say, "Oh wait. I forgot something. Let's try this tomorrow."

To start deployment planning, list the steps that you hope to follow. Describe each step in detail as it is supposed to work.

Next, for every step, list the ways it could fail. Then describe the actions that you will take if one of those failures occurs. Describe workarounds or alternative approaches that you could use.

This part of planning can be extremely hard. It's not always easy to think of workarounds for every possible disaster. Sometimes it may not even be possible.

For example, suppose your application requires 40 new networked computers with 8 GB of memory each. What will you do if the network doesn't work? Or if supply chain issues mean the computers don't arrive from the manufacturer? Or if the manufacturer sends you 8 computers with 40 GB of memory each? In those cases, you may be unable to continue the deployment in any meaningful way. You may think your software installation is bulletproof, but hardware issues bring deployment to a screeching halt before it gets started. In that case, the "solution" to those problems might be to delay the deployment and fix the problems (or die trying).

For a slightly less obvious example, suppose your computers arrive on schedule and they work just fine, but there's something wrong with the network and you're not getting the bandwidth you should, so the users can only process 4 or 5 jobs per day instead of the normal 15 to 20. You *could* move the users onto the new system anyway, but that would cause unnecessary pain and suffering (and you'll get your fair share). At this point, it would be better to postpone the deployment for a day or two, figure out what's wrong with the network, and start over.

After you've worked through all the plan's desired steps and anticipated as many problems as possible, write a rollback plan that lets you undo everything you've done. Be sure you can restore any other applications that you've updated and any data that you've converted for the new system.

Unfortunately, rolling back some of those sorts of changes can be difficult. For example, suppose your new application will run on a new operating system version. If something goes wrong, restoring the older operating system can be a huge pain.

There are a few things you can do to make such a major restoration possible. For example, you can make complete images of the computers you're updating so that you can put them back exactly as you found them if necessary.

At some point, the pain of retreat is greater than the pain of moving forward. Some call that the *point of no return*. People often underestimate how painful moving forward can be, however, so it's good to delay the point of no return as much as possible. It's one thing to say, "We'll just press onward and let the users deal with any problems that crop up." It's another thing entirely to face management when the database fails and the users are reduced to writing customer orders on pieces of paper.

Often the action that determines the point of no return is moving users to the new system. You can set up networks, install new printers, and spray your company logo on new computers, but until people are using the new application, it's relatively easy to go back. The next section discusses the process of moving people to the new application.

CUTOVER

Cutover is the process of moving users to the new application. There are several ways that you can manage cutover. For some applications, you can just post the new version on the Internet and let users grab it. For other projects, you may be able to email a new version to users, or you may be able to just install the new system on users' computers. These days many applications automatically upgrade to a new version if it's available every time they start.

More interesting deployments require that you do a bunch of setup (upgrading operating systems, converting data into new formats, and installing coffee machines) before you can move users to the new system.

During the setup time, the users may be unable to do their jobs. To minimize disruption, it's important that the whole process go as smoothly as possible. The following sections describe four ways that you can make life easier for all concerned: staged deployment, gradual cutover, incremental deployment, and parallel testing.

Staged Deployment

If you can't reduce the impact of catastrophic failures, you can sometimes reduce their likelihood by using staged deployment. In *staged deployment*, you build a *staging area*, a fully functional environment where you can practice deployment until you've worked out all the kinks. (Here "staged" means "like an actor on a stage" rather than "in stages.")

After you have the installation working smoothly, you can test the new application in an environment that's more realistic than the one used by the developers. You can also use the staging area to find and fix a few final bugs before you inflict them on the users.

If you can, use power users to help do the testing. They'll know what problems the other users are most likely to encounter. (Users can break a system in ways that no programmer or tester can.) Staged testing will also give them a preview of what's coming. Hopefully, they'll like what they see and tell the other users how wonderful their future lives will soon become.

When you're fairly certain that everything is ready for prime time, you sneak in at night and perform the actual deployment on the user's computers, like Santa leaving presents in children's stockings. Hopefully you leave presents and not a lump of coal. (You don't really have to sneak in at night, but many companies do basically that. They have IT personnel upgrade the users' computers at night or over the weekend to minimize disruption.)

You still need a deployment plan in case something unexpected goes wrong. Just because everything works flawlessly in the staging environment doesn't mean it will on the users' machines. However, staging should have reduced the number of major problems that you encounter.

Gradual Cutover

In *gradual cutover*, you install the new application for some users while other users continue working with their existing system. You move one user to the new application and thoroughly test it. When you're sure everything is working well, you move a second user to the new system. When that user is up and running, you install a third user, then a fourth, and so on until everyone is running the new application. (In practice, you may not really move users one at a time. You may start out that way, but for large installations, you'll need to start installing users in batches to get them all done in a reasonable amount of time.)

The advantage to this approach is that you don't destroy every user's productivity if something goes wrong. The first few guinea pigs may suffer a bit, but the others will continue with business as usual until you work out any tangles in the installation procedure. Hopefully, you'll stumble across most of the unexpected problems with the first few users, and deployment will be effortless for most of the others.

One big drawback to this approach is that the system is schizophrenic during deployment. Some users are using one system while others are doing something different. Depending on the application, that can be hard to manage. You may need to write extra tools to keep the two groups logically separated, or you may need to impose temporary rules of operation on the users.

For example, suppose you're building version 2.0 of your AdventureTrek program, an application that lets customers make reservations for adventure treks such as BASE jumping off of national monuments, kayaking over waterfalls, and hang gliding over active volcanos. Unfortunately, the new version uses an updated database format to accommodate your latest offering: wing-walking on jets.

Now consider what happens when you move a user to the new system. The database is full of records in the old format. Either the 2.0 user must work with the old records or the system must route the old records to users that are still on version 1.0. After the 2.0 user creates some new records, the system must route those records only to that user because the others can't read a version 2.0 record.

Eventually you'll move all of the users to the new version, and at that point, no one will work with the older records. Obviously, you need to convert the older records into the new format at some time. Of course, once you do, people using version 1.0 won't be able to do anything, so you'll need to switch them all over to version 2.0 right away.

Figure 14.1 shows a Gantt chart that gives one possible schedule for migrating 20 users to the new version.

	Task	Time	Preds		
3	Start	0	—		Start
4	A. Move 1st user to v 2.0	1	Start		A. Move 1st user to v 2.0
5	B. Test with 1 user	3	A		B. Test with 1 user
6	C. Move 2nd user to v 2.0 (total 2)	1	B		C. Move 2nd user to v 2.0 (total 2)
7	D. Test with 2 users	2	C		D. Test with 2 users
8	E. Move 3 users to v 2.0 (total 5)	1	D		E. Move 3 users to v 2.0 (total 5)
9	F. Move 5 users to v 2.0 (total 10)	1	E		F. Move 5 users to v 2.0 (total 10)
10	G. Move 5 users to v 2.0 (total 15)	1	F		G. Move 5 users to v 2.0 (total 15)
11	H. Convert old database records	1	G		H. Convert old database records
12	I. Move 5 users to v 2.0 (total 20)	1	G		I. Move 5 users to v 2.0 (total 20)
13	Finish	0	F, G		Finish

Date markers: Apr 1, Apr 8, Apr 15, Apr 22. Point of no return.

FIGURE 14.1: This schedule takes 11 workdays to migrate all 20 users to AdventureTrek 2.0.

The schedule starts by moving one user to the new version. Pick one of the power users for this so that user can help exercise the new version thoroughly. The schedule then calls for three days of testing with this user on the new version.

Next, the schedule moves a second user to version 2.0. Testing continues for two more days with just two users on the new version.

If everything is going smoothly after this point, the schedule starts moving groups of users to the new version. It moves three more users to the new version, making a total of five. The next day it moves five more users, and it moves five again on the following day.

At this point (Friday, April 12), 15 users are using version 2.0, 5 users are using version 1.0, and the database contains a mix of old and new record formats.

If you move the last users to the new version, then no one will be able to work with the older records, so it's time to convert the database.

Depending on the volume of business in the application, you may need to convert the database before cutover is finished. For example, if the old records require a *lot* of maintenance, then 5 users on the old version may not be enough. In that case, you might want to convert the data when only 10 users are on the version 2.0.

Now the schedule upgrades the final five users and converts the old data in the database. Because database conversions often take longer than expected, the schedule places the conversion on a Friday, so the database developers can work over the weekend if necessary. The extra time is represented in the Gantt chart by a checkerboard pattern to indicate that it might not be necessary.

> **NOTE** Working the occasional Friday night and weekend is the price many software developers pay for keeping the users productive, but don't abuse them. If you make developers work too many evenings and weekends, their work-related productivity will drop and their resume-polishing productivity will soar.

Incremental Deployment

In *incremental deployment*, you release the new system's features to the users gradually. First, you install one tool (possibly using staged deployment or gradual cutover to ease the pain). After the users are used to the new tool, you give them the next tool.

This method doesn't work well with large monolithic applications because you usually can't install just part of such a system. (Imagine building a new air traffic control system and installing only the part that lets planes take off. You'd have to program really fast to get the landing parts of the application in place before anyone runs out of fuel.)

This method often works nicely with the iterated development approaches described in Chapter 18, "Iterative Models," and Chapter 19, "RAD." There programmers build one feature at a time, and when a feature is ready, it's released to the users.

Parallel Testing

In *parallel testing*, some users *pretend* to do their jobs on the new system while other users *actually* do their jobs on the old system. The new system users do their jobs as if the new system were fully implemented. Meanwhile, another set of users would continue using the old system. The old system is the one that actually counts. The new one is used only to see what would happen if it were already installed.

After a few days, weeks, or however long it takes to give you enough confidence in the new system, you start migrating the other users to the new system. You can ease the process by using staged deployment and gradual cutover if you like.

The downside to parallel testing is that you need extra people doing work that in some sense doesn't count. It's easy for testers to become discouraged thinking their work doesn't count. Make sure they understand that their work is important even though it's not their usual line of business (LOB) tasks.

DEPLOYMENT TASKS

The tasks you need to perform for a successful deployment depend on the application you're installing. A simple program like FileZilla (a really nice, free FTP program) just installs a new version of itself and you're ready to go. If you're building a customer support center from scratch, you've got a lot more work to do.

The following list itemizes some of the things you might need to deal with for a large deployment:

➤ Physical environment—These are physical things that the users need, such as cubicles or offices, desks, chairs, power, lighting, telephones (possibly including headsets), and motivational posters (such as waterfalls, soaring eagles, and cats hanging from clotheslines). Plus everything that goes into any work environment, such as restrooms, coffee machines, and supply closets (where employees can steal staples, paperclips, and rubber cement).

➤ Hardware—This includes network hardware (such as cables, fiber, switches, routers, and gateways), printers, scanners, CD or DVD burners, backup hardware, disk farms, database hardware, external hard drives, call routers, and, of course, the users' computers.

➤ Documentation—This can include some combination of physical and online documentation. It might include training materials, user manuals, help guides, and cheat sheets listing common commands.

➤ Training—If the application is complicated or very different from what users currently have installed, you may need to train the users. For larger installations, developers may have to train the trainers (either professional instructors or power users) who will then train the users.

➤ Database—Most nontrivial applications include some sort of database. Depending on the database, you may need to install database software on one or more central database servers and on the users' computers. You may also want extra hardware and software to provide extra data security features such as backups, shadowing, and mirroring.

➤ Other people's software—This is software that you didn't write. It includes systems that interact with your application (purchasing systems, web services, file management tools, cloud services, and printing and scanning tools) and other software that users need to be productive (email, chat, videoconferencing, browsers, search engines, trouble-shooting databases, and word processors). Plus, of course, the operating system.

➤ Your software—This is the application you've built. It includes the application itself, plus any extra tools you've created. It also includes monitoring and testing tools that let you make sure the application is working correctly.

TRAIN WRECK

Don't underestimate the difficulty of training, particularly for large user groups. You will almost certainly meet users who have a hard time adjusting to even the smallest changes. A friend of mine once attended (part of) a two-day training class on a software update where exactly one key's meaning had changed. Yes. One. Key. She bailed at the first lunchbreak, but she said that other users were very concerned about the change.

Of course, your project's needs will vary. You may not need telephone headsets and you may need extra motivational posters.

DEPLOYMENT MISTAKES

The basic steps for successful deployment are (1) make a plan, (2) anticipate mistakes, and (3) work through the plan heroically overcoming obstacles as they arise. If something goes wrong and you don't have an easy fix, roll back whatever you've done, study the problem, and try again later. You can reduce the inconvenience for users by using staged deployment, gradual cutover, incremental deployment, and parallel testing.

If you do a good job of following those steps, you should eventually get even the most complicated application up and running. Occasionally, however, a deployment fails so spectacularly that nothing can save it. Or the deployment finishes, but with all the fun and carnival atmosphere of a root canal gone wrong.

The following list summarizes some of the easiest ways to torpedo an otherwise viable project:

➤ Assume everything will work—This may seem like a rookie's mistake, but many people assume their deployment plan will just magically work. Maybe you'll get lucky and that will be true, but you should probably assume that it won't.

➤ Have no rollback plan—Rolling back a deployment can be a real hassle, but it's usually better than living with whatever damage you do during a failed deployment.

➤ Allow insufficient time—If everything goes smoothly, you won't need much time, but when something goes wrong, all bets are off. A deployment that should take hours could take days or even weeks. Allow extra time for unexpected problems. Then hedge your bets by scheduling key steps and the end of deployment on Fridays so that you can work into the weekend if the plan goes off the rails.

➤ Don't know when to surrender—It's easy to work around one or two small issues that don't play out as expected, but how do you know when to stop? If you keep pushing through (or around) little issues (and sometimes big ones), eventually all the compromises add up to give you a terrible result. (Like a beginning poker player with a pair of threes being gradually sucked into a huge pot.) Define conditions under which you'll fold and try again later. For example, you might quit after four hours or after three things go wrong. Or you might use a point system with 1 point for a trivial change, 2 points for a small workaround, and 5 points if you can't get something to work. When you get to a total of 5 points, quit for the day.

➤ Skip staging—Staging can be time-consuming and expensive, particularly if you need to install new hardware and software. However, for a complicated deployment, staging is crucial. It lets you work out all of the deployment glitches so that you don't waste the users' time and completely trash their computers.

➤ Install lots of updates all at once—It's tempting to install a lot of updates at the same time so that you don't need to inconvenience the users repeatedly. Unfortunately, the more things you try to do at once, the more likely it is you'll run into problems. Limit the number of things you try to deploy all at once. Save the rest for a later deployment.

➤ Use an unstable environment—Have you ever used a computer where the scanning software works (sometimes), the print queues seem to get stuck randomly, and your video editing software sometimes won't import certain kinds of files? If the tools you use don't work together consistently, then you have other problems you should fix before you start a new deployment. Sometimes finding the right combination of tools that can work together can be challenging. Adding a new application will only make things worse.

➤ Set an early point of no return—If you explicitly set a point of no return, you don't need to figure out how to roll back any changes after that point. Unfortunately, you don't always know how bad things might get near the end of the deployment. The last installation task could be a total disaster that takes you days to figure out. You should set the point of no return as late as possible in the deployment schedule so that you can retreat whenever necessary. Even better, don't have a point of no return!

There's a common theme to these methods for failure. They all assume things will go well. Perhaps this is more of the unbounded optimism that makes programmers fail to test their code. You just wrote the deployment plan, and you didn't see anything wrong with it. If you had, you would have fixed it! The logical conclusion is that everything will work perfectly. That means you don't need a rollback plan, sufficient time, surrender conditions, staging, and a late point of no return.

To avoid these problems, assume that you will have problems. If you also assume that some of those problems may be big, you'll be ready in case you need to cancel the deployment and start over. If you prepare for the worst, the worst that will happen is you'll be pleasantly surprised when things go well.

SUMMARY

The basic strategy for successful deployment is straightforward. Make a plan that anticipates as many problems as possible, and then follow the plan. If big, unexpected problems occur, roll back any changes you've made and try again later.

There are still a few details to take care of. For example, you need to know when to abandon a deployment attempt and try again another day. (Those who quit and runs away, live to deploy another day.) You can also use cutover strategies to make things easier.

As long as you make a plan and realize that some things will almost certainly go wrong, you should do okay and eventually get the application up and running. After that (and perhaps a celebratory team dinner at a nice restaurant), the application moves into maintenance. During this phase, your application serves its intended purpose (drawing electronic schematics, tracking orders, posting humorous cat videos, or whatever), and the users send you comments, suggestions, change requests, and bug reports. (And once in a very great while, a "thank you" that makes the whole thing seem worthwhile.)

At this point in your project, you've finished initial development. You gathered requirements, created high- and low-level designs, written tons of code, tested the code (and fixed some bugs), and deployed the application to the users. You're probably more than ready for a break. All you want to do is run off to Disneyland, Aruba, or wherever you consider the happiest place on Earth. Unfortunately, there are a few things you need to take care of before you disappear in addition to arranging for a pet sitter. The next chapter describes tasks that you should perform at the end of a project before all the developers go their separate ways.

EXERCISES

1. Suppose you've written a small tool for your own use that catalogues your collection of pogs. You're planning your third upgrade and you need to revamp the database design. Which cutover strategy should you use?

2. Suppose you're writing an application that includes a lot of separate tools. One creates work orders, a second assigns jobs to employees, a third lets employees edit jobs to close them out, and so forth. Which cutover strategies could you use when deploying a new version of this application?

3. Suppose the application described in Exercise 2 uses a database. Each of the pieces needs to use the database and you need to change the database structure for the new deployment. Does that change your answer to Exercise 2?

4. Suppose you're writing a large application with thousands of users scattered around different parts of your company. Which cutover strategy would you use?

5. Suppose you're building a new MMO (massively multiplayer online game) and you expect to have tens of thousands of users. (Your business plan says within the next 18 months.) Users will download and install your program. What cutover strategy should you use?

6. President Eisenhower was big on planning. If you search online around a bit, you can find several quotes by Eisenhower extolling the virtues of planning (including the quote at the beginning of this chapter). Here's another quote from his remarks at the National Defense Executive Reserve Conference on November 14, 1957.

> I tell this story to illustrate the truth of the statement I heard long ago in the Army: Plans are worthless, but planning is everything. There is a very great distinction because when you are planning for an emergency you must start with this one thing: the very definition of "emergency" is that it is unexpected, therefore it is not going to happen the way you are planning.

If emergencies don't happen the way you're planning, then why make a plan in the first place? Does this apply to deployment plans?

7. Suppose you just released a version 3.0 of your popular shareware program Fractal Frenzy, which lets users draw fractals, zoom in and save coordinates, make movies zooming in and out, and generally make cool pictures. Unfortunately, the day after the release, you discover a bug that prevents users from saving coordinates, so they can't return to saved pieces of a fractal. What should you do? Tell people right away? Wait until there's a fix? Wait until the next release?

8. Suppose you're the manager of the Internal Software Development department at a medical device manufacturer. One of your projects, Test Track, records quality test results for the devices your company makes. Depending on the device, testers record between a few dozen and several hundred test measurements per week. Your software lets testers perform data analysis to see whether the products are up to scratch.

Unfortunately, you just learned about a bug that makes the product occasionally examine the wrong device's data. About once a month, for no obvious reason, a tester requests data on one device but gets results about a different device. Repeating the query once or twice seems to get the right results.

What should you do? Should you rush out an emergency patch? Wait until the next major update? Ignore the problem and hope it will go away?

WHAT YOU LEARNED IN THIS CHAPTER

➤ A project's scope influences how thoroughly a plan must anticipate every possible problem.

➤ A deployment plan should include the steps needed for deployment, possible places where things can go wrong, and workarounds for them.

➤ You should be able to roll back any changes you make if a deployment becomes stuck.

➤ The point of no return is where it would be more painful to roll back a failing deployment than to press ahead. (If you have a good rollback strategy, then you don't need a point of no return.)

➤ Three cutover strategies are staged deployment, gradual cutover, and incremental deployment. Parallel testing can also help as a prelude to full deployment with one of the three strategies.

➤ Deployment tasks may include the following items:

  ➤ Physical environment

  ➤ Hardware

  ➤ Documentation

  ➤ Training

  ➤ Database

  ➤ Other people's software

  ➤ Your software

➤ The following are common mistakes made during deployment:

  ➤ Assuming everything will work

  ➤ Having no rollback plan

  ➤ Allowing insufficient time

  ➤ Not knowing when to surrender

  ➤ Skipping staging

  ➤ Installing a lot of updates at once

  ➤ Using an unstable environment

  ➤ Setting an early point of no return

Metrics

You can't control what you can't measure.

—*Tom DeMarco*

Measuring programming progress by lines of code is like measuring aircraft building progress by weight.

—*Bill Gates*

What You Will Learn in This Chapter:

- ➤ Grouping defects by importance or task
- ➤ Using Ishikawa diagrams to discover root causes of problems
- ➤ Defining and using attributes, metrics, and indicators
- ➤ Understanding the difference between process and project metrics
- ➤ Using size and function point normalization to compare projects with different sizes and complexities

At this point, you've finished the project. Congratulations! Some of your team members are probably itching to move on to whatever comes next, whether they plan to continue maintaining this project, start a new one, or leave to achieve that lifelong ambition of becoming a barista.

However, you should do a few more things before the team scatters to the four corners of the IT industry. Chief among those is a discussion of the recently completed project to determine what you can learn from your recent experiences. You need to analyze the project to see what went well, what went badly, and how you can encourage the first and discourage the second in the future. To do that, you need to find ways to measure the project. (Exactly how do you measure the project's "wonderfulness"?)

This chapter describes tasks that you should perform after initial development is over. It discusses methods you can use to analyze defects (which include change requests, bugs, and other vermin) so that you can try to anticipate and minimize similar defects in the future. It also explains metrics that you can use to measure the project's characteristics and how you can use those metrics when you work on future projects.

> ### METICULOUS METRICS
>
> Like most software engineering tasks, gathering metrics doesn't happen at only one time (in this case, at the end of the project). It's easier to gather metrics throughout the project rather than waiting until the end. For example, you should keep track of the project's status (lines of code written, bugs fixed, milestones missed, and so forth) as you go along. I've put metrics in this chapter because at the end of a project you can look back with a new perspective and see how it all unfolded.

WRAP PARTY

You've finished the project! That's no small feat, so you should do something as a team to celebrate. Have a party, company picnic, trip to an amusement park, or some other wrap-up activity. At least have lunch together and joke about all the times the customers altered the specifications, changed their minds about what hardware to use, and asked why you were using C++ instead of COBOL. Let the healing begin.

Note that the wrap party cannot be just another project meeting but with cupcakes, balloons, and "I Survived Project Ennui" T-shirts. Feel free to gossip about company politics, argue about whether the corporate vision statement makes sense if you read it backward, and speculate about whether upper management will be indicted for insider trading. Don't discuss outstanding bugs, analyze metrics, or turn the party into a group performance review. Do that some other time.

It's obvious that a software organization can't succeed unless its customers are satisfied, but it also can't function unless its employees are happy. A wrap activity helps bring closure to the project and makes people feel like they accomplished something.

DEFECT ANALYSIS

At a philosophical level, anytime an application doesn't do what it's supposed to, you can consider it a bug. For example, when you first start a project, it doesn't do anything. Unless that's its desired behavior, you could think of that as a bug. (If that *is* the desired behavior, let me know because I've already written that application.)

Some development methodologies actually come pretty close to that point of view.

➤ Task—Create a new Add Customer form.

➤ Bug—It doesn't let you enter a customer name.

➤ Change—Add a Customer label and text box.

➤ Bug—It doesn't let you enter a customer address.

➤ Change—Add an Address label and address text boxes.

➤ Bug—There's no OK button.

➤ And so forth.

However, when you're thinking about bugs with an eye toward preventing them in the future, it's helpful to differentiate among different ways the program isn't working correctly.

Species of Bugs

At the highest level, you can group all incorrect features into *defects*. You can then categorize defects into *bugs* (code that was written incorrectly) and *changes* (the code is doing what the specification said to do, but the specification was wrong).

Note that it may not be anyone's fault that the specification was wrong. For example, the customers' needs may have changed since the project started. Or the environment may have changed, as when a new operating system is installed or management decides everything must move to the cloud. (The cloud concept launched in the mid-1990s and started to really take off in the mid-2000s, so by now most managers know what it is, or at least that they want it.)

The following sections describe several other ways that you can categorize defects.

Discoverer

One important way to group defects is by who reported them. Bugs that are found and fixed by programmers are often invisible to the customers. The customers never need to know all the dirty little secrets that went into building the final application.

In contrast, changes that are requested by customers are obviously visible to the customers. Generally, you should satisfy as many change requests as possible, as long as they don't mess up the schedule. (Satisfying change requests gives you brownie points that you can spend later to resist the customers' efforts to shorten the schedule.)

The worst combination is a bug that is discovered by the customers. Users try all sorts of crazy things, so they often find things that no one could have predicted. For example, only a user would enter an incorrect password followed by a series of spaces on the second attempt and accidentally be logged into an Xbox One as the wrong user. (For more information on that and a few other truly bizarre bugs including "Drinking Coke crashes application" and informant chickens, see www.dcsl.com/worlds-7-weirdest-software-bugs.)

If a bug gets to the customers, it must have snuck past code reviews, unit tests, and integration tests. These bugs are somewhat embarrassing and reduce the customers' confidence in your team's ability to produce a high-quality application. (They also reduce your brownie points.)

For each defect, ask three questions:

➤ How could you have avoided the defect in the first place?

➤ How could you have detected the defect sooner?

➤ For customer-discovered defects, how could you have found the defect before the customers did?

Severity

This categorization is obvious. Assign a severity to each defect and focus on those that are the most severe. You can use a 1 to 10 scale (or 1 to 100 scale, or whatever) if you like, but you probably don't need that level of detail. Usually, you can simply assign each defect the severity Low, Medium, or High.

Data integrity and correctness issues should get the highest severity. The application doesn't work if its data is corrupted or if it produces incorrect results.

Often you can use the amount of time wasted by the users as an indication of severity. If an issue wastes a lot of the user's time (the system crashes daily), then it has high severity. If the issue only wastes a little time or has a simple workaround (the user needs to press Ctrl+R refresh the order list after processing an order), then it has medium severity. If the defect does not cost the users time but is merely annoying (the colors clash), then it's low severity.

Focus on the high-severity defects, and for each one, ask how you could have avoided it, how you could have detected it sooner, and (for customer-discovered defects) how you could have found it before the customers did. (Do these questions seem familiar?)

If you work through all of the high-severity defects, then you can look at the medium-severity ones. Unless your team has written miraculously bug-free code and, even more miraculously, the customers don't want changes, then you may as well admit that you'll probably never have time to address the low-priority defects.

Creation Time

You can further categorize defects by when they were created. Defects tend to snowball, so those created earlier in the project usually have greater consequences than those created later. For example, a defect added during high-level design has a lot more potential to cause pandemonium than a defect added in the last module written.

By now you can probably guess what I'm going to say next. Focus on the defects that were created earliest because they can cause the most damage. For each defect, ask how you could have avoided it, how you could have detected it sooner, and (for customer-discovered defects) how you could have found it before the customers did.

Age at Fix

Defects are like cancer: The longer they go undetected, the greater the potential consequences. Group defects by the length of time they existed before they were detected and fixed. Focus on those that remained in hiding the longest and ask the usual three questions.

Task Type

Another way to categorize defects is by the type of task you were trying to accomplish when the problem was created. By the type of task I don't mean "trying to write a `for` loop" or "writing a vibrant and profound sentence for the specification." I mean things like Specification, High-Level Design, User Interface Design, or Database Code.

The task categories you should use will depend on the project. For example, if you're writing a finance application that will run on desktop systems, then you probably don't need a Phone Interface category.

Here are some typical task categories:

- ➤ Specification
- ➤ Design
  - ➤ High-Level
  - ➤ Security
  - ➤ User Interface
  - ➤ External Interface
  - ➤ Database
  - ➤ Algorithm
  - ➤ Input/Output
- ➤ Programming
  - ➤ Tools
  - ➤ Security
  - ➤ User Interface
  - ➤ External Interface
  - ➤ Database
  - ➤ Algorithm
  - ➤ Input/Output
- ➤ Documentation
- ➤ Hardware

The previous methods for categorizing defects focus on what's most important. The errors that were discovered by users, that have high severity, that were created early, and that remained undiscovered for a long time tend to have the greatest impact, so they're important. After you identify them, you can ask the three questions to see how you can avoid the same problems in future projects.

In contrast, task categories don't identify the most important defects. Instead, they try to group defects by common causes. Defects that were added while performing similar tasks may have similar causes and (hopefully) similar solutions.

For example, suppose you discover that a lot of defects originated in the specification. In that case, many of them may have a common cause such as not paying attention to the customer, not studying the user's current process enough, or unrealistic customer requests. In that case, you may be able to fix a whole bunch of defects in future projects by addressing a single issue. Perhaps if you spend a bit more time running through use cases with the customers before you finalize the specification, you can avoid some of these kinds of defects.

Defect Database

You can use any of the preceding categorizations to study defects, but it's even better to use them all. (Plus, it's only a little extra work.) Build a database `Defects` table and give it the following fields:

`Id`—Because who doesn't like IDs?

`Title`—The defect's name.

`Description`—A detailed description of the defect.

`Discoverer`—Team or Customer. (You could also store the name of the person who discovered the defect. You may find that some people are particularly good at identifying problems.)

`Severity`—High, Medium, or Low.

`CreationTime`—The (approximate) date the defect was created.

`AgeAtFix`—How long the defect went unnoticed.

`TaskType`—The stage at which the defect was created.

`Avoidance`—How could you have avoided the defect in the first place?

`Detection`—How could you have detected the defect sooner?

`EarlyDetection`—For customer-discovered defects, how could you have found the defect before the customers did?

When you're analyzing each defect, it only takes a bit longer to gather all of this information instead of just one or two dimensions. Then you can use database queries to look for patterns. For example, you can find all of the defects that went unnoticed for more than a month, the defects created during the security design process, or defects identified by eagle-eyed Karen in the UX team.

Ishikawa Diagrams

To figure out in which category a defect belongs, you ask what task was being performed when the defect was created. For example, suppose you discover a defect on the login screen. The code validates the user's name and password incorrectly. Password validation is a security feature, so this task might fall into the Programming/Security category.

Often, however, a defect is the end of a sequence of events that was started by some primordial mistake. In this example, suppose the code does exactly what the security design said it should. In that case, the error is actually in Design/Security, not in the code.

It's also possible that this defect has an even more distant cause. Perhaps the security design correctly reflected what was described by the specification. In that case, the error is in the specification, not the design or the code.

Perhaps the specification, design, and code are all correct, and the error is in the database. Or worst of all, perhaps two or more pieces of the puzzle contain errors that combine to create the defect. (On television crime shows, a single murder always leads to all of the confusing clues. Imagine how much more bewildering things would be if multiple crimes occurred at the same spot and muddled each other's clues.) In this example, there could be problems with any combination of the login code, the database code, the database design, the database itself, the database specification, or the security specification.

Sometimes discovering the root cause of a defect can be challenging. One tool that can help is the *Ishikawa diagram* (named after the Japanese organizational theorist Kaoru Ishikawa). These are also called *fishbone diagrams* because they look sort of like a fish skeleton. (And *Fishikawa diagram* is an amusing blend of the two names. For your Word of the Day, look up "portmanteau" in the dictionary and ignore the definitions that deal with luggage.) They're also called *cause and effect diagrams*, but a name that prosaic doesn't impress anyone at IT cocktail parties, so I stick with "Fishikawa diagram."

QUALITY CONTROL

Kaoru Ishikawa used these diagrams in the late 1960s to manage quality in the Kawasaki shipyards. They've been used extensively in quality management for industrial processes.

This is another one of those tools like PERT charts and Gantt charts (see Chapter 4, "Project Management") that are so useful for managing projects in general that they've been around far longer than software engineering has. (When the first colonists land on Tau Ceti e, they'll probably use a PERT chart to order the tasks they need to perform, a Gantt chart to schedule them, and an Ishikawa diagram to figure out why the sunscreen was left behind on the kitchen counter on Earth.)

To make an Ishikawa diagram, write the name of the defect you're trying to analyze (Incorrect Username/Password Validation) on the right of a sheet of paper. (This is the head of the fish.)

Next draw a horizontal arrow pointing to the defect name from left to right. (This is the fish's backbone.)

Now think of possible causes and contributing factors for the defect. Represent them with angled arrows leading into the spine. (These are the fish's ribs.) Label each arrow with the cause you identified.

For each of the fish's ribs, think about causes and contributing factors for that rib. Add them, again with labeled arrows. Continue adding contributing factors to each of the factors you've already listed until you run out of ideas. (I confess I haven't seen a fish with this type of skeleton. Maybe you can find them in Lake Karachay, the world's foremost dumping site for radioactive waste. Or maybe Lake Springfield in *The Simpsons*.)

Figure 15.1 shows a sample Ishikawa diagram (although many people would omit the fishy outline).

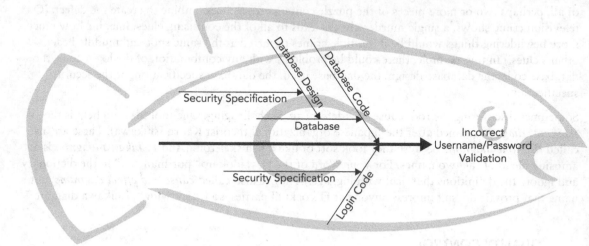

FIGURE 15.1: An Ishikawa (or fishbone) diagram shows causes leading to effects.

The exact format of the diagram doesn't matter too much, and there are several variations in style. These are the only things that are really consistent among most diagrams:

➤ The effect or outcome is on the right.

➤ There's a backbone.

➤ Arrows (or lines) lead from causes to intermediate causes or effects.

➤ Arrows (or lines) are labeled.

It doesn't matter whether you use lines or arrows, and sometimes they may point from right to left if that makes them fit in the diagram better. Try not to get all hung up on the details. (Although you may want to pick a standard variation for the team to use so the diagrams all look like the same kind of fish and there are no cuttlefish or chambered nautiluses.)

Figure 15.2 shows another version of the previous diagram with a different style.

After you build an Ishikawa diagram for a defect, take a close look at each of the possible causes and decide which ones actually helped cause the defect. Highlight causes that did play a role and cross out those that didn't. If you're not sure about a cause, study it further, possibly adding contributing causes to it.

When you're finished, you should have discovered the root causes of the defect. You can then ask the three magic questions about the defect.

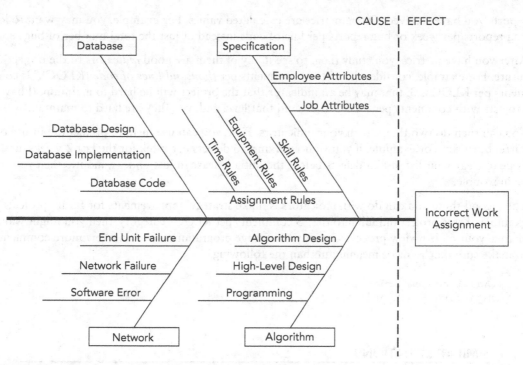

FIGURE 15.2: The exact format of an Ishikawa diagram doesn't matter as long as you can tell what causes lead to what other causes and effects.

You should also use the diagram to group the defect's causes. In Figure 15.2, for example, you might find that all of the problems lay in the Specification rib. In that case, you should look more closely at your specification process to see if there's something you could do to make the specification more reliable in future projects.

SOFTWARE METRICS

The defect analysis techniques described in the previous sections are more or less qualitative. They help you characterize defects based on things like their discoverer, severity, and age at time of removal.

In contrast, *software metrics* give you quantitative measurements of a project. Before you learn what kinds of metrics you can analyze, you should know a few metric-related terms.

An *attribute* is something that you can measure. It could be the number of lines of code, the number of defects, or the number of times the word "mess" appears in code comments. Something like "awesomeness" or "gloriousness" cannot be an attribute because you can't measure those.

A *metric* is a value that you use to study some aspect of a project. Sometimes a metric is the same as an attribute. For example, you might get useful information about a project from the number of bug reports you have received. Often metrics are calculated values. For example, you may want to look at bug reports per week or bug reports per line of code instead of just the total number of bug reports.

After you have metrics, you study them to see if any of them are good *indicators* of the project's future. For example, consider the metric "comments per *thousand lines of code (KLOC)*." If comments per KLOC is 3, that may be an indicator that the project will be hard to maintain. (I have seen projects with comments per KLOC at around that level and, yes, they are hard to maintain!)

You can then do two things with your indicators. First, you can use them to predict the future of your current project. For example, if you've been fixing 10 defects per week for the last 2 weeks, and you hope to clear your list of 875 defects before the initial release in just under a month, then you could be in trouble.

The second thing you can do with indicators is make strategy improvements for future projects. For example, if this project did fall into the "3 comments per KLOC" category, then you might want to change your code review process to gently encourage programmers to add a few more comments and to make sure they're more meaningful than the following.

```
# Add 1 to num_orders.
num_orders = num_orders + 1
```

SIMILAR SITUATIONS

Metrics and indicators sometimes apply only to similar projects. For example, your programmers may crank out an average of 50 lines of code per day over the course of a three-month Visual Basic desktop project. That doesn't necessarily mean they can produce the same amount of code over a two-year C language firmware project for a particular phone.

Metrics and indicators will be most useful for projects that are most similar. They may still be useful for other projects, but you should keep an eye on how well they are predicting a new project's future so that you can adjust your expectations if necessary.

To summarize:

➤ Measure relevant attributes.

➤ Use the attributes to derive meaningful metrics.

➤ Use metrics to create indicators.

➤ Use indicators to predict the project's future.

➤ Use indicators to make process improvements for future projects.

Now that you have a little background in software metrics, the following sections give some additional details.

COMMON COMPLAINTS

Aside from the project manager, software engineers often resist tracking metrics. Team members may feel that collecting metrics is hard and time-consuming. They may say they spend all of their time measuring and counting instead of working. And besides, metrics are subjective and don't prove anything.

Some people also think metrics will be used against them to measure how productive (or unproductive) they are.

Metrics are sometimes a bit subjective and ambiguous, but any measurements are better than nothing. (Exploring a vast cavern with a book of matches isn't as good as using floodlights, but it's better than wandering in the dark bumping into walls and falling down pits.)

Most larger projects use automated tools to gather metrics so they're more objective and consistent. That's also easier than studying code by hand, so the team is more likely to use those metrics.

Explain to the team members that metrics really are useful. Try to keep the extra work to a minimum and assure people that they are used to guide the project and not to determine who writes the most documentation or lines of code. It's easy to write a lot of badly written code, so punishing someone who writes less code but with higher quality doesn't make sense anyway.

The following sections explain more precisely what attributes might make good metrics, what you can use metrics for, and how you can normalize metrics so they are meaningful for projects of different sizes.

Qualities of Good Attributes and Metrics

You can measure many attributes of a software engineering project. You can measure the number of lines of code, the customers' satisfaction level, the hours the team members spent playing *Bouncing Balls*, the font used in the specification, or the team's total number of trips to the coffee pot.

Of course, some of those attributes are hard to measure (such as customer satisfaction) and others are irrelevant. The following list gives characteristics that good attributes and metrics should ideally have:

➤ Simple—The easier the attribute is to understand, the better.

➤ Measureable—For the attribute to be useful, you must measure it.

➤ Relevant—If an attribute doesn't lead to a useful indicator, there's no point measuring it.

➤ Objective—It's easier to get meaningful results from objective data than from subjective opinions. The number of bugs is objective. The application's "warmth and coziness" is not.

➤ Easily obtainable—You don't want to realize the team members' fears by making them spend so much time gathering tracking data that they can't work on the actual project. Gathering attribute data should not be a huge burden.

Sometimes it's impossible to satisfy all of these requirements. In particular, some important attributes can be hard to measure. For example, customer satisfaction is extremely important, but it can be hard to quantify.

For attributes such as this one, which are important but hard to measure, you may need to use indirect measurements. For example, you can send out customer satisfaction surveys and track things like the number of change requests you receive or the amount of time the customers save by using the application.

Using Metrics

Metrics have several possible uses. You can use them to do the following:

➤ Minimize a schedule.

➤ Reduce the number of defects.

➤ Predict the number of defects that will arise.

➤ Make defect removal easier and faster.

➤ Assess ongoing quality.

➤ Improve finished results.

➤ Improve maintenance.

➤ Make sure a project is on schedule.

➤ Detect risks such as schedule slip, excessive bugs, or features that won't work, and then adjust staffing and work effort to address them.

As I mentioned in the earlier feature "Similar Situations," metrics and indicators work best for projects similar to those during which you gathered your data. Two projects that use different development methodologies, programming languages, or user environments may not always produce the same results. That means you need to use some common sense when you use indicators to try to predict a project's future.

However, it's probably a bigger mistake to completely ignore what an indicator is telling you. Suppose in previous projects you've noticed that a low number of pages of program documentation was correlated with lots of bugs. Just because your current project is using a different programming language, that doesn't mean this indicator is wrong. If the programmers are producing fewer pages of documentation but the bug rate remains low, try to figure out why.

It could be that the new language is more self-documenting. (Previous projects used assembly language but this one's using Visual Basic.)

It could be you have a really good programming team on this project. In that case, you'll probably need that extra documentation for long-term maintenance when these programmers all wander off to new projects.

It could also be the case that the programmers have been working through the easy stuff first and work will become much harder later. In that case, you need to be sure the amount of documentation picks up as the difficulty level increases.

Don't ignore what your metrics are saying. If they contradict the facts, learn why so that you know whether you need to adjust the metrics or the project.

TIPS FOR USING INDICATORS

You can use indicators to provide regular feedback to the team. If it looks like some part of the project is wandering away from the practices suggested by your indicators, gently nudge the project back on course.

Don't think of indicators just as harbingers of doom. (Abandon hope all ye who stray from the required number of use cases per form.) Think of them as signposts pointing in the right direction. If you get lost, use them to guide the project back to the correct path. (It may sound like MBA execuspeak, but use them as opportunities for improvement, not reasons for despair.)

Don't use metrics and indicators to appraise individuals or the team as a whole. If you yell and scream at team members because they're messing up your indicators, they'll stop giving you accurate metric data. You can suggest that someone spend more time working through use cases during requirements gathering, but if you threaten them, they may just tell you they're doing the work when they aren't.

For similar reasons, make sure people aren't hideously overworked. If team members don't have time for all of their assigned tasks, they'll dump the ones they consider the lowest priority. Usually that includes tracking metrics.

One common management mistake (probably the one that developers hate the most) is to think that you can make any project work if you only *manage it hard enough*. Piling more tracking onto a floundering project will generally not help as much as sitting down with the team and talking through what's actually happening. (Just as piling empty barrels onto a sinking boat won't make it float better. Yes, the barrels will float, but only after the boat sinks out from under them.) Adding new metrics (you need to track your coffee breaks to the nearest minute) or refining old ones (you need to report on the tasks you perform for each half hour of the day) just add extra work without giving you useful information.

Finally, don't get stuck obsessing over a single metric. If you're not spending much time on code reviews and your indicator says you should be seeing a lot of bugs but the bugs aren't there, then perhaps this isn't a problem after all. By all means try to figure out why things are going suspiciously smoothly, but don't create a problem where one doesn't already exist.

Metrics and indicators are often grouped into two categories depending on how you use them: process metrics and project metrics. The following sections describe those categories.

Process Metrics

Process metrics are designed to measure your organization's development process. You collect them over a long time period for many projects, and then use them to fine-tune the way you do software engineering.

For example, suppose you collect data over a series of projects and you draw the graph in Figure 15.3 showing hours of code review per KLOC versus number of bugs per KLOC.

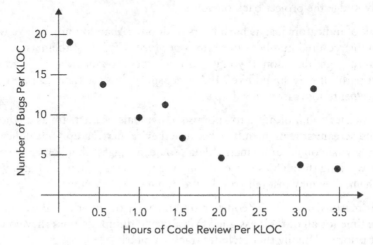

FIGURE 15.3: This graph shows the relationship between hours of code review and bugs per KLOC.

Looking at the graph in Figure 15.3, you might decide that you want to try to spend 1.5 to 2 hours of code review per KLOC in future projects. That seems to let you find most of the bugs that you would catch even if you used a lot more time on reviews. (I'd also want to dig deeper to figure out why the second project from the right had so many bugs despite the relatively large investment in code reviews. Was it a different kind of project? Was it particularly large or small? Was it run by an inexperienced technical lead?)

Project Metrics

Project metrics (which are sometimes called *product metrics* because they are about a specific software product) are intended to measure and track the current project. They let you use past performance to predict future results. Based on your predictions, you can adjust your strategy to improve those results.

You can also use project metrics to set goals. For example, suppose you have three customer representatives on your team writing use cases. Over the last week, they each managed to write an average of 10 use cases per day. You want to have 10 to 20 (call it an average of 15) use cases for the project's more complicated forms, and you have 20 complicated forms to go.

If the numbers hold true (and they may not), you need to write 20 × 15 = 300 more use cases. At a rate of 30 use cases per day (10 for each of the three customer representatives), you should finish in about 300 ÷ 30 = 10 days. You can make that a goal: Finish writing the use cases in the next two weeks.

Things to Measure

The things you can measure on a software project are practically limitless (lines of code, printed pages, electricity use, donuts eaten, hours spent in the library hiding from meetings). Fortunately, you need to track only a few metrics to get a good sense of how a project is progressing.

At a high level there are two kinds of metrics you should track: inputs and outputs. Inputs are the things you spend on the project. The following list describes some input metrics:

Cost—Money spent on the project for hardware, software, development tools, networking services, paper, training, and so forth. (For business purposes, you may also want to track salaries and overhead, but they're not as directly related to the project's performance. In contrast, if you're not spending anything on development tools, you're probably not getting the best result for your efforts.)

Effort—This is the amount of work being put into the project. It is usually measured in person-hours. Effort is relatively easy to measure (even though some people put in 110 percent while others put in barely 50 percent).

Defect Rates—The number of defects discovered over time. Defect rates are also fairly easy to measure.

Lines of code (LOC)—The number of lines of code produced per day. You might think this would be easy to measure, but it's actually kind of hard to decide what to count as a line of code. For example, do you count comments and blank lines? What about statements that are split across multiple lines? All those things pump up the line count without adding anything extra as far as the computer is concerned, but they also make the code easier to read and understand, so you should encourage programmers to use them appropriately.

Some development organizations treat a command split across multiple lines as a single line of code. Some ignore comments and blank lines. Others count blank lines up to 25 percent of the total code and ignore any blank lines over 25 percent.

It doesn't matter too much which approach you take as long as your rules are consistent across projects and the programmers don't try to game the system. (If you count comments and judge programmers on the number of lines of code they produce, you may get files with dozens of comments per actual line of code.)

Pages of Documentation—There are several kinds of documentation that you might want to track. Project documentation (such as the specification and design documents) are important because they ensure that everyone is working toward a common vision. If you don't have enough of this kind of documentation, different team members may end up working at cross-purposes, resulting in extra defects and difficult long-term maintenance.

User documentation is obviously important to the end users. If you have too little, the users won't figure out how to use your program.

User documentation also reflects the complexity of the application. If you *need* a lot of documentation to explain the program, then that may mean the design is overly complicated. It may also foreshadow a lot of future defects and maintenance problems.

You can measure all of those attributes fairly directly. (At least if you can decide what to measure for LOC.) Some other attributes are harder to measure directly. They're either hard to quantify or they're subjective. The following list describes some of those items and how you might try to measure them:

Functionality—How well does the application do what it is supposed to do? How well does it let the users do their jobs? This is quite subjective, but you can measure things such as the numbers of help requests, change requests, and user complaints. During development, you can measure the number of use cases satisfied.

Quality—Do the users think of this as a high-quality application? Is it relatively bug-free? Again, this is subjective, but you can track user complaints to get some idea. You can also do user surveys. (You know, those annoying surveys that ask you how likely you are to recommend a product to your friends.)

Complexity—How complex is the project? This is hard to measure directly. The amount of project documentation gives you a hint about the project's complexity. Lots of documentation may indicate a complex project that needs a lot of explaining. (Or it may just indicate you have a team member who loves to write.)

There are a lot of other ways to estimate complexity. You can count the if-then statements in the code because they determine the number of paths through the code. You could also count the number of loops or other complicated code features such as recursion and particular data structures. Unfortunately, making all of those counts is a fair amount of extra work.

Function points provide another method for estimating a project's complexity. The section "Function Point Normalization" later in this chapter explains them in detail.

Efficiency—How efficient is the application? In rare cases, you can calculate the theoretical maximum efficiency possible and compare the application to that. For example, you might determine that a routing program finds solutions within 15 percent of the optimal routes. In general, however, this is hard to measure.

You can compare the users' performance to their performance before they started using your application, but you won't know if there could be an even better way to do things. (Of course, if the users were more productive before they started using your application, you might need to either write a second version or update your resume.)

Reliability—How reliable is the application? This one is a little easier to measure. You can keep track of the number of times the program crashes, produces an incorrect result, or is unavailable due to network failure, database backups, and other problems.

Maintainability—How easy will it be to maintain the application in the long term? You can get some notion of how hard maintenance will be by looking at other metrics, such as the amount and quality of the project documentation, the number of comments, and the code complexity, but usually you won't really know how maintainable the project is until you've been maintaining it for a while.

One problem with all metrics is that they're hard to apply to projects of different sizes. Studies have shown that projects of different sizes have different characteristics. For example, in larger projects, team members spend more time coordinating activities than they do in smaller projects. That means they may be unable to write and debug as much code per day.

One way to make metrics a bit more meaningful for different project sizes is to *normalize* them by performing some calculation on them to account for possible differences in project size. There are two general approaches for normalizing metrics: size normalization and function point normalization. The following two sections describe those two approaches.

Size Normalization

Suppose you measure the number of developers, total time, effort (in person-months), LOC, and number of bugs for projects Ruction and Fracas. Table 15.1 shows the results.

TABLE 15.1: Attributes for projects Ruction and Fracas

	PROJECT RUCTION	PROJECT FRACAS
Developers	3	7
Time (months)	1	24
Effort (pm)	$3 \times 1 = 3$	$7 \times 24 = 168$
LOC	1,210	75,930
Bugs	6	462

In which project were the developers more productive? Which project contained buggier code? Just looking at the numbers in the table, it's hard to tell. Project Fracas includes a *lot* more code, but it also took a lot more effort. Project Ruction contained far fewer bugs, but it also contained much less code.

In *size-oriented normalization*, you divide an attribute's value by the project's size to get some sort of value per unit of size. Assuming everything about two projects is similar except for their sizes (a big assumption), the normalized metrics should be comparable.

For this example, you could divide total lines of code by the effort it took to produce the code. Similarly, you could divide the number of bugs by the total number of lines of code. Table 15.2 shows the normalized values.

TABLE 15.2: Normalized metrics for projects Ruction and Fracas

	PROJECT RUCTION	PROJECT FRACAS
LOC / pm	$1,210 \div 3 = 403$	$75,930 \div 168 = 452$
Bugs / KLOC	$6 \div 1.21 = 4.96$	$462 \div 75.93 = 6.08$

The normalized values show that project Fracas was more productive in terms of lines of code for the effort (452 versus 403 LOC per person-month) but project Ruction had less buggy code (4.96 versus 6.08 bugs per KLOC).

The following list gives some of the measurements of size that you can use to normalize values.

➤ Number of team members

➤ Effort (person-months)

➤ KLOC or LOC

➤ Cost (dollars, euros, doubloons, or whatever) adjusted for inflation

➤ Pages of documentation

➤ Number of bugs

➤ Number of defects

➤ Time (days, months, years, centuries)

Divide an attribute value by the value that makes the most sense. For example, bugs are a feature of code, so you should probably divide the number of bugs by LOC or KLOC instead of the number of team members or effort. Similarly, lines of code are produced over time by team members, so you should probably divide LOC by number of team members and number of months (which is the same as dividing by person-months).

Other combinations, such as dividing the number of bugs by the number of team members, can also have meaning hidden inside them, but they're harder to interpret.

Size-oriented metrics have the big advantage that they're usually easy to calculate. It's easy to count the number of lines of code (assuming you can agree on how to count comments and blank lines) and it's easy to count the number of person-months spent on the project, so it's easy to calculate LOC / effort. These metrics also have the advantage that a lot of project modeling applications use them as inputs.

These metrics also have a few disadvantages. One problem with size-normalized metrics is that you can't actually use them to predict the future unless you can already predict the future. For example, LOC/effort lets you predict how long it takes to build a project, but only if you can predict how many lines of code you need to write.

For a concrete example, suppose you know from past experience that your team can produce approximately 400 LOC/pm. If you're about to start project Rhubarb and you think it will require roughly 11,000 lines of code, then you can predict that it will take approximately $11,000 \div 400 = 27.5$ person-months of effort. The catch is you need to know that the project will need 11,000 lines of code.

GUESSING THE UNGUESSABLE

Although you can't know how many lines of code you are going to need ahead of time, you can make some educated guesses based on past experience. You should at least take a stab at the worst case, best case, and average case of past scenarios. Then you can take a weighted average of the three (perhaps giving them weights 1, 1, and 3, respectively) to make an "expected scenario."

Feel free to fudge things a bit to take into account any extra information you may have. For example, if a new project is fairly complicated and very different from past projects, you may want to change the weighting factors a bit to give the worst case a bit more pull.

(If you majored in Divinatory Statistics in college, feel free to calculate σ, μ, ρ, and any other Greek letters that you think will help you to better predict the most likely outcome.)

Try not to let management or sales adjust the weights for you. It's amazing how many graphs predicting sales wander along slowly growing (or declining) through past years only to shoot abruptly skyward a month or two in the future. That's wishful thinking, not predictive analysis.

Another problem with size-oriented metrics is that they're language-dependent. The same program may require 1,700 lines of code if you write it in assembly but only 750 lines if you write it in Java.

These metrics also penalize programs that use short but elegant solutions. Project Harmony might do the same thing as project Fracas but use half as many lines of code written in the same amount of time. If the result is better designed and more elegant, then it might be better code even though it looks like the Harmony team was half as productive.

Function Point Normalization

The real problem with size-oriented normalization is that it's tied to a particular implementation of an application, not to the application's inherent complexity. *Function point (FP)* normalization tries to fix that by calculating an FP number to represent the application's complexity. You then divide various attributes such as lines of code or number of bugs by the FP value to get a normalized result.

ANOTHER BLAST FROM THE PAST

Function point analysis was developed in the 1970s by Allan J. Albrecht in an attempt to measure application complexity without counting lines of code. Like Gantt charts and Ishikawa diagrams, function points are useful enough that they've stuck around.

Function points measure a project from the user's point of view, so they count what the application does, not how it does it. Because they are measured from the user's point of view, they should be hardware-independent and software-independent. An application should do the same things whether you build it in C++ on a Linux desktop system, in Java on an Android device, or in COBOL on a mainframe.

There are many different variations on function points that use assorted measures of the application's behavior to represent its complexity. For example, different versions count the number of forms, external inputs, event triggers, and so forth. The following sections describe a version that is reasonably easy to calculate and that seems to be fairly common.

I'll describe the calculation details shortly. First, here's an overview of the process.

1. Count five specific *function point metrics* that include such things as the number of inputs and the number of outputs.

2. Multiply each of those values by a *complexity factor* to indicate how complicated each activity is. Add up the results to get a *raw FP* value.

3. Calculate a series of *complexity adjustment factors* that take into account the importance of general features of the application. (For example, how important is the transaction rate to the application?) Add the complexity adjustment factors to get the *complexity adjustment value (CAV)*.

4. Take a weighted average of the raw FP and the CAV and voilà! You get the final FP value.

Don't worry if this seems complicated. It requires a lot of steps, but each of the steps is quite simple. The following sections describe the four main steps in greater detail and show an example calculation.

Count Function Point Metrics

In this step, you estimate the number of the following items:

Inputs—The number of times data moves into the application and updates the application's internal data. This includes inputs the user enters on screens and inputs from other applications and external files. An example would be a New Student form that lets the user enter student ID, name, address, phone number, shampoo, favorite ice cream flavor, and other information in the application's database.

Outputs—The number of times outputs move out of the application. This includes outputs displayed to the user as well as outputs sent to external systems or external files. An example would be producing a Delinquent Account report that lists accounts with outstanding balances. The report could be viewed onscreen, printed, sent to an external file, or sent to another program for processing.

Inquiries—The number of times the application performs a query/response action. This is different from an input followed by an output because it doesn't update the application's internal data. For example, the user might enter a customer ID and the application would display that customer's information, but it wouldn't update the database.

Internal Files—The number of internal logical files used by the application. This includes things such as configuration files, data files, and database tables.

External Files—The number of files the application uses that are maintained by some other program. For example, the application might use an inventory database that is maintained by a separate inventory tracking program.

The next step is to multiply the number of each kind of item by its complexity.

Multiply by Complexity Factors

As you count these metrics, you should estimate the complexity of each. For example, consider as an input a New Student form that lets the user enter information about a new student. Suppose the form contains 15 text boxes. You may decide that means this input has medium complexity.

> ### COMPLEXITY CONUNDRUM
>
> Different FP techniques use different methods for deciding whether a piece of the system has low, medium, or high complexity. Some look at factors such as the number of internal tables and the number of data values involved in an action. For example, an Order Creation form might create records in three tables and include 20 fields where you enter data.
>
> In this chapter, I'll just assume you can use your intuition to assign complexity values because that's a lot simpler. The exact formula you use doesn't matter too much as long as you're consistent across projects.
>
> If you want to compare the FP values of your applications to those of programs written by other groups, then you need to use one of the more precisely defined methods for determining complexity. (For an example, see the tables at www .softwaremetrics.com/fpafund.htm.)

After you calculate a complexity value for each of the items you're counting, use them to get a sense of the overall complexity for each of the metric categories. For example, if you have two low, five medium, and one high complexity inputs, then the inputs as a whole have medium complexity.

Now multiply the number in each metric category by the appropriate values shown in Figure 15.4.

Figure 15.5 shows a sample raw function point calculation. For example, this application has 10 inputs with a relatively high complexity. In the first line of the calculation, the number of inputs 10 is multiplied by the high complexity factor 6 to give the result 60.

The next step is to apply complexity adjustment factors.

Complexity

Category	Number	Low	Medium	High	Result
Inputs	_____	× 3	4	6	= _____
Outputs	_____	× 4	5	7	= _____
Inquiries	_____	× 3	4	6	= _____
Internal Files	_____	× 7	10	15	= _____
External Files	_____	× 5	7	10	= _____

Total (raw FP) _____

FIGURE 15.4: Use this table to calculate raw FP.

Complexity

Category	Number	Low	Medium	High	Result
Inputs	10	× 3	4	(6)	= 60
Outputs	5	× (4)	5	7	= 20
Inquiries	4	× 3	(4)	6	= 16
Internal Files	23	× (7)	10	15	= 161
External Files	2	× (5)	7	10	= 10

Total (raw FP) 267

FIGURE 15.5: In this example, the application's raw FP value is 267.

Calculate Complexity Adjustment Value

The function point metrics look at particular facets of the application. The complexity adjustment factors include a series of indicators designed to measure the complexity of the application as a whole.

C-A-V IS NOT FOR ME

Some developers use the raw FP and don't bother with the CAV. The two main reasons are that some cost estimation tools take the raw FP as an input and that the CAV plays too big a role in the final FP calculation. The web page https://alvinalexander.com/FunctionPoints/node29.shtml has more information about this issue (although it uses some different terminology).

To calculate the complexity adjustment factors, consider each of the following items:

1. Data communication
2. Distributed data processing
3. Performance
4. Heavily used configuration
5. Transaction rate
6. Online data entry
7. End-user efficiency
8. Online update
9. Complex processing
10. Reusability
11. Installation ease
12. Operational ease
13. Multiple sites
14. Facilitate change

Rate the importance of each of the 14 factors according to Table 15.3.

TABLE 15.3: CAV ratings

IMPORTANCE	RATING
Irrelevant	0
Minor	1
Moderate	2
Average	3
Significant	4
Essential	5

After you make these decisions, simply add the complexity adjustment factors to get the complexity adjustment value.

Table 15.4 shows a sample complexity adjustment calculation.

TABLE 15.4: Sample CAV ratings

FACTOR	RATING
Data communication	2
Distributed data processing	4
Performance	5
Heavily used configuration	2
Transaction rate	3
Online data entry	5
End-user efficiency	5
Online update	1
Complex processing	1
Reusability	0
Installation ease	4
Operational ease	5
Multiple sites	5
Facilitate change	1
Total (CAV)	42

The final step is to use the raw FP and the CAV to calculate the adjusted FP value.

Calculate Adjusted FP

To calculate the final FP, simply use the following formula.

$$FP = (\text{rawFP}) \times (0.65 + 0.01 \times \text{CAV})$$

For example, the calculation in Figure 15.5 got a raw FP of 267. The CAV in the preceding section was 42. For those values, the final FP result is:

$$FP = (267) \times (0.65 + 0.01 \times 42) = 285.69$$

Now you know that the application has a complexity of exactly 285.69!

Actually 285.69 doesn't mean much by itself. It's sort of like saying a particular piece of candy has a sourness value of seven. Seven what? It's not like NIST has defined an absolute sourness scale. (Although sourness is related to acidity, and there is a scale for that.)

FP values don't mean much in isolation. They are really only useful for comparing projects and for normalizing metrics for different projects. For example, if one project suffers seven defects per FP and another has only four defects per FP, then the second project may have done a better job overall, at least in terms of defects.

However, this assumes that the FP calculations were similar. If two different people performed the FP calculations and used different weights or counted things differently, the resulting values will be less comparable.

SUMMARY

Metrics enable you to characterize and track projects. Process metrics let you compare multiple projects over a long period of time to see if you can improve your development process. For example, if one project has fewer bugs per line of code than the others, then you can study that project to see why it is different and try to reproduce those results in future projects.

Project metrics enable you to make predictions about a project that is still underway. For example, if a project isn't producing enough lines of code for where it is in its schedule, you can look for ways to increase productivity. Without metrics, it's often hard to tell when a project is going off course until it's too late to do anything about it.

Size normalization enables you to compare projects of different sizes. Function point normalization enables you to compare projects of different sizes and complexities. Comparisons are always better if the projects are similar, but those two techniques enable you to get at least some meaningful information from projects with some differences.

This chapter focused mostly on lines of code and bugs, but the same techniques apply to every output from software engineering. You can use metrics to track the specifications, use cases, design documents, change requests, and number of donuts eaten. If any numbers wander away from what's normal, you can dig deeper to see if there's a problem you can correct or perhaps an unexpected benefit that you can exploit in the future.

Tracking bugs is a good way to estimate the application's maintainability. If the code is buggy, then maintaining it will probably be hard. The next chapter focuses on maintenance. It explains what the team's role is during the maintenance phase and describes some of the directions the project can take after its initial release.

EXERCISES

1. Suppose a project has a States table that lists the states where the customer does business. A search dialog lets the user select one of the states from a drop-down list to select accounts from the selected state. Some of the use cases call for the states to be set to Maine, Vermont, New Hampshire, and Massachusetts, but during tests New Hampshire doesn't appear in the drop-down list.

   Draw an Ishikawa diagram showing possible causes for this problem. What steps would you take to try to find the root cause of the problem?

2. Compare size normalization and FP normalization. When would you use one or the other?

3. Are there times when you could use both size normalization and FP normalization to compare two projects?

4. Assume a project has a raw FP score of 500. What are the largest and smallest final FP values the project might have? How would it achieve those values?

5. Give an example where project A has more bugs than project B but seems to be in better shape according to size normalization. Assuming the projects are in roughly the same development stage, what else do you need to know to decide whether project A will finish before project B?

6. For the example you made for Exercise 5, what else do you need to know to estimate when the two projects will finish flushing out all their bugs?

7. Calculate an FP value for Microsoft WordPad. (If you don't have WordPad, try a simple online text editor such as Aspose at `https://products.aspose.app/words/editor`.)

8. Calculate an FP value for Microsoft Word. (If you don't have Word, try an online word processor such as Google Docs at `https://docs.google.com`.)

9. Judging from your experience solving Exercises 7 and 8, how consistent do you think FP values will be when different people perform the calculations? (Compare your solutions to my solutions in Appendix, "Solutions to Exercises," if you like.) What could you do to improve consistency?

10. What do your solutions to Exercises 7 and 8 tell you about Microsoft WordPad and Microsoft Word? (Or Aspose and Google Docs?) Does that result agree with what you would expect?

11. Which do you think is better, size normalization or function point normalization?

12. Table 15.5 shows the number of programmers that worked on four projects.

TABLE 15.5: Number of programmers

PROJECT	# PROGRAMMERS
Unicorn	10
Pegasus	8
Griffin	12
Jackalope	7

Table 15.6 shows the cumulative numbers of lines of code written and bugs discovered during each week of active coding for the four projects. For example, by the end of week 3, project Griffin contained 5,141 lines of code and 62 known bugs.

TABLE 15.6: Lines of code and bugs

Week	UNICORN LOC	Bugs	PEGASUS LOC	Bugs	GRIFFIN LOC	Bugs	JACKALOPE LOC	Bugs
1	1,107	0	542	0	450	3	126	5
2	2,349	2	1,374	12	2,392	17	1,201	27
3	3,482	7	2,759	37	5,141	62	3,515	60
4	4,272	30	4,680	61	6,008	102	5,176	72
5	6,009	72	6,012	89	7,817	156		88
6	7,522	110		104	9,750	160		
7	9,759	156				175		
8	11,895	207						
9		273						

The final bug numbers for each project include bugs found after initial programming stopped.

Assuming these projects have roughly similar complexity, how can you meaningfully compare the programmers' productivity and bug rates at the ends of the projects? What do your calculations show? Can you think of any places to look for process improvements?

13. Suppose you're tracking a new project (project Hydra) that you expect to include approximately 7,000 lines of code. Assuming its progress is similar to the progress of the projects described in Exercise 12, how many person-weeks should this project's programming phase take? How many bugs do you expect to find?

14. Seeing the results of Exercise 13, you decide you can finish the programming for project Hydra in nine weeks with five developers. Table 15.7 shows the project's actual progress after week 4.

TABLE 15.7: Project Hydra progress

WEEK	LOC	BUGS
1	370	0
2	693	2
3	969	12
4	1,251	24

Should you be concerned?

WHAT YOU LEARNED IN THIS CHAPTER

➤ You can rate a defect's importance by discoverer, severity, creation time, and age at fix.

➤ Group defects by task (specification, design, programming, hardware, and so forth) to look for common causes.

➤ An Ishikawa diagram can help you find the root causes of a defect.

➤ Attributes are things that you can measure, metrics are values that you can use to evaluate a project, and indicators give indications of a project's state and future.

➤ Attributes→metrics→indicators→projections and process improvements.

➤ Software metrics let you characterize, track, and predict a project's characteristics such as defects, bugs, and lines of code written.

➤ Process metrics are used to improve your development process in the long run. Project (or product) metrics are used to track and predict the current project's progress.

➤ Size-normalized metrics enable you to compare projects of different sizes but similar complexities. These metrics are values divided by a measure of the project's size—for example, "bugs per KLOC" or "pages of documentation per person-week."

➤ Function points enable you to estimate a project's complexity.

➤ Function point normalization enables you to compare projects of different sizes and complexities. Values are divided by the project's FP value to give metrics such as "KLOC per FP" or "bugs per FP."

16

Maintenance

Troutman's Second Programming Postulate: The most harmful error will not be discovered until a program has been in production for at least six months.

—*Anonymous*

All programming is maintenance programming, because you are rarely writing original code.

—*Dave Thomas*

What You Will Learn in This Chapter:

➤ Why maintenance is a major percentage of total project cost

➤ The four categories of maintenance tasks

➤ What the "second system" and "third time's a charm" effects are

➤ How to know when you should rewrite code to make it more maintainable

➤ Bug tracking states

So you finished the initial release of your application and held wrap-up meetings to make your team members better software engineers. Congratulations! On most projects, a fair number of those people will now wander off to do other things. Some will join new projects and start the whole process all over again. Others may take new roles on other projects. For example, a programmer may become a team lead, or a team lead may become a project manager. Still others may leave to satisfy their life-long dreams of becoming lobster fishermen.

Hopefully, a few team members will remain as the project moves into the maintenance phase. Having some original team members during maintenance helps provide continuity for the project so that its original vision isn't lost.

CHANGE FOR THE WORSE

On one project I worked on, the maintenance crew took over and made all sorts of changes to "improve" the application. Then the users spent weeks forcing them to put things back the way they were. If more of the maintenance group had been around from the beginning, they would have understood the application better and been more hesitant to make those changes in the first place.

Some programmers dislike maintenance programming because they find it boring. It can be a lot of fun to write an application that finds the shortest route that visits all of the ice cream stores in your town for a bicycle ice cream crawl. It's less fun to debug your application when you discover it is telling people to bike on the highway. It can be downright painful to dive into someone else's rat's nest of kludges, hacks, and bug fixes to make major changes.

Maintenance may not always be a lot of fun, but it's important because maintenance is often relatively expensive. (In execuspeak, maintenance accounts for a large percentage of *total cost of ownership* or *TCO*.) Often maintenance accounts for 75 percent of a project's total cost.

This chapter describes the tasks that make up software maintenance. It explains why maintenance is expensive and methods you can use to reduce maintenance costs.

MAINTENANCE COSTS

You may wonder why maintenance is such a large percentage of a project's total cost. One reason is that applications often live far longer than they were originally intended. A typical business application might still be in use years or even decades after it was written. Most businesses are stingy, so writing a new program to replace an old one that still works is rarely an option. (Even if the existing application is so old it measures lengths in cubits and lets you click a sundial to select times.) I worked on one application more than 40 years ago that, as far as I know, is still in use today, even though the company that owns the code has been bought at least twice since then.

For further proof that applications often exceed their life expectancies by decades, consider the Y2K problem. Programs written as far back as the 1950s and 1960s stored dates as 2-digit numbers to save space and to make it easier to enter data in 80-character chunks, which was the natural arrangement back in the day of punched paper cards. (Yes, this was a long time ago.) For example, the year 1978 was stored as 78. That worked pretty well until after the year 2000 when dates became ambiguous. For example, if you're working for a hospital in 2005 and one of your patients was born in '03, should you schedule a pediatric appointment or a geriatric appointment? I doubt many programmers in 1960 imagined their code would still be in use 40 years later.

Y2K EXPERIENCE

The Y2K problem is also an example where people who have previous experience on a project have an advantage. I'm sure a reasonably smart Java programmer (some of them, at least) could have eventually figured out how to fix the 40-year-old COBOL programs that thought a car built in 00 deserved collector's plates, but it was cheaper to lure the old COBOL programmers out of retirement by offering them four or five times the going hourly wage. They cost more per hour, but they used far fewer hours and were more likely to make the updates correctly without breaking the rest of the code.

In a similar story, I recently finished rewriting a program that I had written a decade or so ago for some chemists. They wanted three changes: a new user interface to look more modern, to run on the latest OS, and to support a new piece of hardware. (They use some very sensitive computer-controlled balances for weighing samples and needed to move to a new model. They even loaned me one for a few days to test my code. I will say that it was a bit stressful driving to and from their lab carrying a balance worth four times the value of my car.)

They could have had their IT department rewrite the program in-house. After all, the IT guys are already on salary, so they're a lot cheaper than me. However, I was able to make the changes much more quickly and with less chance of mistakes. (I'm not saying I didn't make any, just that none have been reported so far.)

Contrary to the predictions of the pundits on the Y2K apocalypse lecture circuit, planes didn't fall from the sky like leaves in autumn, missiles didn't decide they were past their expiration dates and explode, and streets didn't boil with lava. Still, retired BASIC and COBOL programmers from around the world briefly hung up their fishing rods to help the $300 to $600 billion effort to fix this single problem. That's a lot of money to keep decades-old software running. (I'm not sure what will happen when the Y3K problem hits and there are no COBOL programmers left.)

The moral is, you should pretend you're carving your code in stone to last for the ages. Chances are it'll last longer than you expect. It may even outlive you.

A second important reason maintenance costs often dwarf initial development costs is that it's much easier to write fresh code than it is to modify old code. To safely modify old code, you need to spend time studying it. Because you didn't just write the code, it's not fresh in your mind. If you don't dig into the code and make sure you understand how it works, you're just as likely to add bugs to the code as remove them.

After you make your changes, you need to test them to verify that they work. You also need to thoroughly test the rest of the application to make sure your changes didn't break anything else.

You can reduce maintenance costs by doing a good job when you write the initial code. For example, develop simple but flexible designs, use good programming practices, insert comments to make the code easy to read, and provide documentation so future generations of maintenance programmers can figure out what you were thinking when you wrote the code.

TASK CATEGORIES

At a high level, the tasks that go into long-term maintenance are roughly the same as those that go into initial development. You gather requirements, make designs, write some code, test the code, and deploy a new version. Although the tasks are similar, the focus is different. During maintenance, you tend to spend more time on bug fixes and feature enhancements than on writing completely new code.

Generally, maintenance tasks are grouped into the following four categories:

➤ *Perfective tasks* improve existing features and add new ones.

➤ *Adaptive tasks* modify the application to meet changes in the application's environment.

➤ *Corrective tasks* fix bugs.

➤ *Preventive tasks* restructure the code or learn more about the code to make it more maintainable.

Sometimes it can be hard to decide whether a task is adaptive if the environmental change could be avoided. For example, suppose the vice president of Busywork decides that all applications must move from one cloud provider to another. From the project's point of view, that is a change in environment. It's driven from inside the company, however, so it's theoretically avoidable. Because it's not unavoidable, I'm going to label that sort of change perfective (adding a new feature).

It's like the difference between a thundershower and someone activating the fire sprinklers in your office. One of those is avoidable and much more annoying than the other.

Basically, I'm saying, "You imposed this task on us, Mr. VP, so you get credit for requesting the change (and paying the bill)."

The relative effort spent on each of these categories depends on the project. For example, in a relatively small phone app with a short life span (ha ha!), you might focus most of your energy on building a new version (perfective) and not worry about making the current version compatible with future phone operating systems (adaptive). For a larger project that you plan to use within your company for many years, you might spend a lot more effort on bug fixes (corrective).

For a typical large application, the relative effort spent on each of the categories (out of the 75 percent of the project's total cost represented by maintenance) might be as follows:

➤ Perfective—50 percent

➤ Adaptive—25 percent

➤ Corrective—20 percent

➤ Preventive—5 percent

The following sections describe these categories in more detail.

Perfective Tasks

For many applications, particularly large ones with long life spans, this is often the biggest part of maintenance. If you've done a good job building the initial application, the users may like it, but they still want tweaks, adjustments, and improvements. (This, however, doesn't include bug fixes, which are tweaks of a different sort. I'll talk about those in the section "Corrective Tasks" a bit later in this chapter.)

Sometimes, the specification didn't represent exactly what the users need to do. Maybe the specification didn't explain the user's needs correctly. (Although you should have caught that earlier when the customers reviewed the specifications.) Or maybe the users didn't quite understand what they would need to do after the application was in place.

Sometimes, the tools you built let the users think of new ways to do things that they hadn't thought of before. Often the users don't know exactly what's possible until they see the program and have a chance to work with it for a while. They know how they're doing their jobs now, but sometimes no one actually knows how they will do their jobs with your new tools.

Users may also want completely new features that weren't in the original specification. Or they may want features that were left out of the first release to save time. Sometimes, it's another example of the "we didn't know this was possible until now" scenario.

Even you and your fellow developers can think of improvements and modifications based on the users' experiences. After you watch the users bashing away on your application, you may discover a whole new uncharted territory of opportunities that the users can't see because they don't have your software engineering background.

THE BIG PICTURE

One of the first big projects I worked on was a dispatching system for telephone repair people. You entered information about jobs and employees, and the system assigned employees to appropriate jobs.

The program included a street map that showed all the employees and their jobs. The map didn't help the work assignment code, but we stuck it in anyway, mostly because it had a high "gee whiz" factor for executive presentations (and because it was fun to program).

After the users had been experimenting with the system for a while during parallel testing, we noticed that the dispatchers used a map screen a lot more than we expected. In fact, they used it all the time. We asked them why and they said it was the only place in the system where they could see a list of every employee in the system. We had all sorts of screens that let them look at a particular employee, an employee's assignments, jobs that had not been assigned, and so forth, but no place where they could see every employee's data at the same time.

So we added a screen to do that. (They still used the map screen a lot. I think they just liked it. It also let them see if the employees were all assigned to jobs that happened to be near the same restaurant around lunchtime. That really reduced productivity, but maybe the dispatchers could swing by too?)

The tasks that fall into the perfective category tend to be one of two sorts: feature improvements and new features.

Feature Improvements

Feature improvements involve modifying existing code, so in some ways they're similar to bug fixes. That means you should be aware of the same issues when you handle them.

You need to carefully study the existing code so that you're sure you understand what it does and how it works. You need to plan the modifications you're going to make. Don't just start ripping out old code and typing in new. Only when you're reasonably certain that your changes won't break things should you make your modifications.

Remember that changing old code is more likely to introduce bugs than writing new code, so you need to test your changes thoroughly. The users probably won't like your modification if it doesn't work or if it breaks something else.

New Features

Adding new features to an application is a lot like writing code for the initial application, so you should follow the same steps:

1. Make a specification explaining what you will do.
2. Get the users to sign off on the specification so they agree that you're doing the right thing.
3. Create high-level and low-level designs.
4. Write the code.
5. Test, test, and test. (And save the tests in case you need to run them again later.)
6. Use good practices (such as staging and gradual cutover) to deploy the new version of the program.

Adding new features is almost like running a completely new mini-project.

If there are enough changes or the changes are big enough (for example, they require restructuring the program's class hierarchy or architecture), you may want to create a new major version of the application.

A new version is basically a whole new project. Start over from scratch and follow all of the steps described up to this part of the book. You can probably take a lot of shortcuts because of your experience with the first version of the program. For example, you may reuse most of the high-level design you wrote for the previous version.

This is one of many places where having original developers still around for maintenance can be useful. If Sakura wrote the original report-printing code, then it will be much easier for her to write enhancements to it.

The Second System Effect

In his software engineering classic *The Mythical Man-Month* (Addison-Wesley, 1975), Frederick Brooks says, ". . .plan to throw one away; you will anyhow." The notion is that you will learn a lot about the system you need to build when you build it. After you're finished, you'll discover that you could have done a lot of things better, so you throw the first version away and write a new one.

Some developers have suggested that you could crank out a hasty version of the application, throw it away, and then build the real application. Perhaps then you can learn what you need to know without spending all the effort needed to build a "real" first version. (That's sort of what prototyping is.)

Of course, if you *plan* to throw away the first version, you may do such a poor job of it that you don't learn the things that you need to know to build the good second version. You may use so many sloppy shortcuts that you don't get any practice using the "real" techniques that you'll need to build a solid second version.

That leads to the corollary, "If you plan to throw one away, plan to throw two away." If you don't learn anything from the "quick and dirty" first version, then your second version is basically just a delayed first version. (By the process of mathematical induction, that means you should plan to throw them all away.)

In the 1995 edition of his book, Brooks retracted his initial assertion, saying it was too simplistic and implicitly assumes you're using the waterfall model of development. (You'll learn more about models of development in Chapters 17 through 19.)

Still, Brooks' notion of a "second system effect" has some merit. The first time you build a system, you don't know everything that you'll need to do. You don't necessarily have perfect specifications, and you don't know how to implement the features that are specified correctly. You don't know how the pieces fit together. Sometimes, you may not even know what the pieces are.

When you build the second system, you know a lot more about what you can do and how things need to work. Unfortunately, that sometimes leads developers to throw in every conceivable cool feature, bell, whistle, and gewgaw (plus the kitchen sink) to make the application the best software solution ever created by programmer-kind. As a result, the second version is confusing, hard to use, bloated, and generally inefficient.

Finally, in the third version (if you have any customers left), you can build the application that you should have built in the first place. At this point, you're a Master Craftsman at software development, programming in general, and your application in particular. You know what the application should do and (just as important) what it should *not* do. You know which user interface features work and which don't. You know what pieces are necessary and how they all fit together. You have become one with the development environment and are perfectly positioned to build the best system possible.

> **THIRD TIME'S A CHARM**
>
> The third version of an application is often the first version that's really useful. In fact, it's so common that many users wait until the third version before they buy a product. (I've done that several times.)
>
> To prevent users from waiting (and depriving them of much-needed revenue and customer-assisted debugging), some software companies give the first release of a product the version number 3.0, hoping users will buy it. Occasionally, you can find an application version 3.0, but there was never a version 1.0 or 2.0. (And don't get me started on the Windows numbering scheme. Who came up with 95, 98, 2000, XP, 7, 8, 10, 11?)

It doesn't always have to work like that. You can struggle against fate and make a real difference, but it takes some effort. To avoid building one or more throwaway versions, you need to carefully follow these steps.

1. Gather requirements, write a specification, and thoroughly validate it with the users.
2. Make high-level designs that provide a framework for development. They should keep pieces loosely coupled and provide enough flexibility to do what you need it to do.
3. Create low-level designs that indicate how to create the features you need.
4. Write code while following good programming practices so that you don't end up with a tangled web of mysterious and uncommented code.
5. Test thoroughly to flush out as many bugs as possible as quickly as possible.
6. Use good deployment techniques (such as staging and gradual cutover).

In other words, follow all the normal steps of software development!

Having developers who are experienced with the type of application you build can also help reduce the "second system" and "third time's a charm" effects. If they've already built their first (and possibly second) versions, you can build more useful versions.

Iterative and RAD development models use other techniques to try to keep development moving toward a useable application. (You'll learn more about them in Chapters 18 and 19.)

Adaptive Tasks

Adaptive tasks help keep the application usable when the things around it change. If the users' hardware, operating system (OS), database, other tools (such as spreadsheets or reporting tools), network security, cloud provider, or other pieces of their environment change, it could break your application, so you have to fix it.

Unfortunately, the tools on which your application relies may also be interrelated, so changes to one may affect the others. For example, suppose your application uses a graphics toolkit that uses a particular database. Now the operating system changes so the toolkit no longer works. You upgrade the toolkit so that it's compatible with the new operating system, but the new version of the toolkit isn't compatible with the current version of the database. Unfortunately, the database vendor hasn't finished building a version that's compatible with the new version of the operating system, so you're stuck.

There's no combination of your application, the graphics toolkit, and the database that can run on the new operating system. You can tell the users that it's not your fault, but they still can't process orders, so customers can't get their electric roller skates (or whatever) so no one gets paid.

To make matters worse, the same scenario can arise if any one of the tools you use is updated. For example, if a new version of the graphics toolkit is released, it may break your application. If a new version of the database appears, it may break the graphics toolkit. Then you're stuck waiting for the graphics vendor to update its toolkit before you can even see if the changes will break your application.

You can take a couple of approaches to make these scenarios less likely. First, you can minimize the use of external tools. If you don't use a graphics toolkit, then you don't have to worry about a new version breaking your application. If a new version of the operating system breaks your application, at least you have only your own code to fix. You don't need to wait weeks or months for all of your tool vendors to revise their products until a workable combination is possible.

Second, you can just ignore new releases of operating systems, databases, toolkits, and any other external tools you use. You can keep using the older versions as long as they don't actually stop working.

RELIABLE ROBOTICS

I knew one company that had a single computer that ran a program to control a robotic assembly line. Unfortunately, a vendor discontinued support for the programming language used to write the program. After the next operating system release, programs written in that language would no longer be supported. In some later operating system version, the program would stop working completely.

As if that weren't bad enough, new computer hardware wouldn't support the older version of the operating system needed by the program. (Just try to buy a modern computer running Windows 3.11 or OS/2.) Eventually, the computer running the program would die, and the assembly line would be offline for good.

The company could rewrite the application in a new language, but that would be a lot work (in other words, expensive). Besides, the program did what the company wanted, and they didn't need any new features.

To solve the problem cheaply, the company bought some inexpensive computers, installed the current operating system on them, and added the assembly line program. Now when the computer controlling the assembly line dies, the company pulls another computer from the closet and the assembly line is back up and running. (Although the company is sort of stuck in the 1990s. Eventually that program is going to need to be rewritten.)

Ignoring upgrades works for some companies, but it's a strategy that's getting harder to follow. These days many products install new releases automatically, so it's harder to prevent an automatic upgrade from breaking something.

Some larger companies fight that problem by explicitly prohibiting any upgrades. When a new version of the operating system or some other important piece of the environment is available, the IT department loads the latest version of everything on an isolated computer and tests it. If everything works, the new configuration is rolled out to the users' computers. (Remember staging from Chapter 14, "Deployment"?)

This tight control over the users' computers often seems arbitrary and totalitarian to the users. (Why can't I install the latest version of *Othello* on my computer?) But you can understand what they're trying to accomplish.

Some companies adopt a one-version-behind strategy where they do roughly the same thing, but they try to use products that are one version behind the latest. The idea is that those versions are more thoroughly combat-tested and have been patched to fix bugs and security problems.

Corrective Tasks

Corrective tasks are simply bug fixes. You've probably been making them since you started development, if not sooner. If you think of mistakes in the specification, designs, documentation, and other pieces of the program as bugs (and you should), then you've been fixing bugs since the project started. (If you extend that a bit to the world outside of work, then you've been fixing bugs since the day you were born. For example, being unable to walk and talk is a bug that takes a newborn about two years to fix.)

You probably already know in general how to fix a bug. Find it, study the code so that you're sure you understand it, fix the bug, test, and release a new version of the application with the bug fixed.

There are several ways this process can go wrong. Perhaps the most obvious way is if you fix the bug incorrectly and don't notice during your tests. In that case, you can add an additional step at the end: file another bug report describing the mistake you made fixing the original bug.

One of the worst ways to fail to fix a bug is to lose track of it. At least if you fix a bug incorrectly you have some record of the original bug. If you lose track of a bug, then there's little chance that it will ever be fixed (unless a user reports it again). What may be just one of dozens or hundreds of bugs to you might be really important to some user patiently waiting for you to fix it.

To avoid losing bugs, you need a bug tracking system. There are several kinds of bug tracking systems that you can use.

> **INCIDENTALLY**
>
> Some companies don't like the term "bug" (maybe they're insectophobic), so they call these things "incidents." They may also include change and enhancement requests in the incident category, possibly so that they can deemphasize the number of bugs. (Sure, we have 3,000 incidents, but lots of them are change requests.)

For really small projects, you can simply keep track of bugs in a spreadsheet. That works well if you don't have too many bugs but doesn't work as well if you have many developers who need to update the spreadsheet at the same time.

You can store bug information in a directory hierarchy. You would create a text file describing each bug and then move them from directory to directory to group them by status. For example, the Bugs/New directory (or Bugs\New if you have a Windows accent) would contain new bugs that have not yet been examined by the project team. The Bugs/Assigned/Rod directory would contain bugs assigned to me.

You can store bug information in a database. That works well, but building the database and tools to work with it can be a lot of work. If you're not a database developer who thinks of this as a fun exercise to crank out over the weekend while your friends are off waterskiing, you might want to use a prebuilt bug tracker instead.

Finally, you can use a prebuilt bug tracking application. There are a lot of bug tracking tools available ranging in price from $0 to a $1,000 or so per month. (The expensive ones are designed for *really* big projects with up to a few thousand users.)

Whichever method you use, you can assign a *state* to each bug to keep track of its status within the system. The following list describes typical states that a bug tracking system might use:

➤ New—The bug has just arrived and has not yet been assigned to anyone.

➤ Assigned—The bug has been assigned to someone to fix.

➤ Reproduced—The bug has been reproduced by a team member. The bug's description includes instructions for reproducing the bug. (It is sometimes called "verified.")

➤ Cannot Reproduce—A team member has examined the program and can't make the bug occur. Often a "we can't reproduce the bug" message is sent back to the customer and the bug is closed.

➤ Pending—A request for more information has been sent to the customer who reported the bug. Sometimes, this state is used before Cannot Reproduce.

➤ Fixed—The bug has been fixed but not tested yet. (This is sometimes called "resolved.")

➤ Tested—The fix has been thoroughly tested and the bug is verified as gone.

➤ Deferred—The bug should not be fixed, or at least not yet. For example, you might want to fix it in the next major release because fixing it now would be too hard or the only person who can fix it is on vacation.

➤ Closed—The bug has been either fixed, deferred, or otherwise abandoned (see the Cannot Reproduce status), and no further action will be taken on it. (This is sometimes called "resolved.")

➤ Reopened—The bug reappeared after being closed. The bug should probably be treated as if it were a new bug. However, there may be some benefit to reassigning it to the person who originally worked on it because that person may know more about the code containing the bug. (And it seems like a fitting punishment.)

Bug tracking applications typically come with an assortment of features. For example, they may produce reports showing bugs in various states, bugs cleared over a period of time, and bugs assigned to a particular developer. Some can notify developers via email or some other method when bugs are assigned to them.

BUG REPORT PREVENTION

In addition to trying to prevent bugs, some companies also seem to try to prevent bug reports. Some companies make it next to impossible to report bugs, instead having Help pages that unceremoniously dump you into user forums where they hope other users can provide workarounds so they don't need to fix anything.

Even if you *can* report a bug, the maintenance team's focus is often on *clearing* bugs, not necessarily fixing them. Spending 10 seconds to fail at reproducing a bug clears it much more quickly than spending a few hours finding the bug, studying the code, making the change, testing the result, and moving the repaired code into production. If the maintenance team is understaffed (they usually are) and management is yelling about productivity, which approach seems more likely?

I have often reported bugs, giving foolproof instructions for reproducing them, only to have the report moved to Cannot Reproduce or Pending with a request for more information.

I recently reported a bug about my phone spontaneously making its screen so dark that you could only see it with night vision goggles in a coal mine on an overcast night during a lunar eclipse. I received a message asking for more details and a screen shot. I'm not sure what extra details I can give if it happens spontaneously, and I can't imagine what information they could get out of a screenshot showing a black screen.

Try not to be like these companies.

Some systems can automatically move bugs from one state to another. For example, when a new bug report appears, the system might assign it to a developer chosen from a list of those who are allowed to fix bugs. It would assign the bug to that person and change the bug's status to Assigned.

Another approach would be to have the system send the bug to a manager (Chief Pest Controller?) and ask that person to assign the bug to a developer.

Some systems also allow you to indicate who is allowed to make certain transitions. For example, if you have separate bug fixers and testers, you could allow the fixers to move a bug from Assigned to Fixed, and the testers would move the bug from Fixed to Tested (or send it back to Reproduced if the tests fail).

MY FAVORITE BUG

My all-time favorite bug is Rosie the tarantula at my local Butterfly Pavilion. My all-time favorite *software* bug appeared in a large application that we developed for internal company use. One of its forms let the user enter search criteria to build a list of matching jobs. The user could then scroll through the list and double-click on jobs to get more information.

During testing, one of our power users reported that this form occasionally made the application crash. She didn't know why and could not reproduce the crash reliably, but it happened about once per day.

We performed dozens of test queries, opened multiple detail screens, resized the form, and did everything we could think of to test the program, but we couldn't make the crash happen even once.

Finally, we both flew to Tampa (she from Fort Wayne, I from Boston) so I could watch her crash the program. For about half an hour, she built lists, clicked buttons, rearranged panels, and resized the form. Just as she was starting to doubt her own sanity, the program crashed. It took me about another half an hour to figure out how to reproduce the crash.

It turned out that the form contained a splitter that you could use to make one panel smaller (holding search criteria) and another larger (holding query results). There was a bug in the splitter tool that we were using that made it crash if you made one of the panels *exactly* 1 pixel tall. It was pretty hard to do. If the panel was 2 pixels tall, everything was fine. You had to be resizing the panels more or less randomly and release the mouse at just the right instant to make it happen.

When I could reproduce the problem, it didn't take long to figure out what was happening and how to fix it. I added a quick test in the code to ensure that the panels were never less than 2 pixels tall and everything worked fine.

The point of this story (aside from showing off my awesome ninja debugging skills) is that users are rarely crazy. If you can't reproduce a bug, that doesn't mean it isn't there. It is almost surely there, you just can't find it.

So if you can't instantly reproduce a bug, dig a bit deeper. By all means ask for more information, but don't be surprised if the user doesn't have any more information for you. Then dig even deeper. If you close the bug now, it'll come back to haunt you like the Easter egg that you didn't find until June—and with the associated smell.

This is my favorite software bug because (1) it was challenging to find, (2) we found it, (3) once found it was relatively easy to fix, and (4) most importantly it wasn't my fault.

One final twist to an already complicated situation is priority. Some bugs are more important than others. If one bug makes the application crash every day or two and a second bug is a typographical error in the Swedish version of the program, the first bug probably deserves higher priority. (Although a typo may be easy to fix, so you might want to bang it out to boost your productivity stats.)

Preventive Tasks

Preventive tasks involve restructuring the code to make it easier to debug and maintain in the future. The fancy "impress them at cocktail parties" word for rewriting code to improve it is *refactoring*.

If you've been paying the least bit of attention, you know that modifying code is more likely to introduce new bugs than writing new code is. If that's true, then why would you ever mess around inside working code? That would be like asking a mechanic with questionable skills to rebuild your brand-new car's engine. It will be expensive, might not make things any better, and might make them a whole lot worse.

If you look back at the section "Task Categories" earlier in this chapter, you'll see that typically only approximately 5 percent of a project's maintenance cost is spent on preventive tasks. That number is low largely because of the risk involved with modifying working code. (Companies also usually have a strong "if it ain't broke, don't fix it" bias, which is completely justified here.)

WHAT'S PREVENTIVE?

The discussion of preventive maintenance doesn't include adaptive tasks (modifying or adding features) or corrective tasks (fixing bugs). Those often require some revision of the existing code. For example, you might need to rewrite a piece of code to add a new feature to the program. If you make the fewest changes possible, that doesn't count as preventive maintenance.

I'm also not counting rewriting a piece of code right after you wrote it to make it more elegant and flexible. That's part of the initial programming and, yes, you should do it. Code is often pretty rough the first time around, and you can often make it more efficient, easier to modify, and easier to understand if you rewrite it right away. After you write a piece of new code, look it over (by yourself or in a code review) and see if you can improve it before moving on.

This section on preventive tasks focuses on changes you make to the code to make it easier to deal with later just in case you need to change it down the road.

Despite the dangers, there are several reasons why you might want to refactor code and a few reasons not to. The following sections describe some of the most important of those reasons.

Clarification

If a piece of code is confusing, you should add comments to it explaining how it works. You should do that as you're writing the code or immediately after you finish writing it, while the code is still fresh in your mind. Later, when people need to read the code (including you after you've forgotten how it works), they'll have a fighting chance of understanding how the code works.

Unfortunately, many programmers don't include enough (or any) comments. Sometimes they think the code is obvious because it's still fresh in their minds. Sometimes they get pulled away for more urgent tasks before they get around to writing comments and documentation. Sometimes they're just plain lazy. In those cases, it may be worth adding comments to particularly confusing pieces of code.

It's often not worth the effort to add comments to random pieces of code. To write good comments, you need to spend a lot of time studying the code carefully so that you're sure you understand how it works. If you don't know what the code is doing, you may insert misleading comments and they can do more harm than good.

For that reason, I recommend that you add comments to code only when you need to modify it. That gives you extra incentive to study the code carefully (or your modifications won't work). You'll also need to test your changes to verify that they work, and that helps verify your understanding.

No matter how thoroughly you study the code, however, there's still a chance that you don't really get it, so your new comments should always be regarded with a bit of suspicion. Keep the following quote in mind.

> Don't get suckered in by the comments—they can be terribly misleading. Debug only code.
>
> —*Dave Storer*

That doesn't mean comments are completely useless, but they aren't always correct. That's particularly true for comments added long after the code was written.

Code Reuse

Sometimes when you're modifying code, you realize you've done something similar before. Instead of repeating yourself, it may make more sense to extract the common code into a new class, method, or library that you can call from multiple locations. Then when you need to do the same thing a third, fourth, or fifth time, you won't need to write the same code all over again.

Saving you the trouble of writing repeated code is nice, but the real benefit here is in maintaining the duplicated code. Suppose you have the same (or similar) piece of code repeated in several places. What happens if you find a bug in that code? Or if you just decide to change the way the code works? Perhaps you decide to store values in meters instead of furlongs or you store some data in a database instead of a file.

In those cases, you need to modify the code in exactly the same way in every place that it occurs throughout the program. If you miss any of the occurrences or change one of them incorrectly, the code will be inconsistent. The resulting bugs can be extremely hard to find. (I know that from firsthand experience.)

Making changes consistently is even harder if the pieces of code are similar but not exactly the same because that makes it harder to find the related pieces of code.

The *don't repeat yourself (DRY) principle* says you should extract common code anytime you repeat yourself.

> **THERE'S NO SUCH THINGS AS TWO** *One of my mottos is "There's no such thing as two." You can write a piece of code once. If you write it a second time, how do you know you won't then need to write it a third or a fourth time?*
>
> *The same idea holds for database and user interface design. A customer record can hold a single emergency contact phone number, but if users decide they want to allow a second phone number, how do you know they won't then ask for a third, fourth, and fifth?*
>
> *Start by assuming that customers can have only one emergency contact number. As soon as users want to add a second, assume that the customer might have any number of phone numbers. That way you can modify the database and user interface once instead of several times, possibly making mistakes at every modification.*

Improved Flexibility

Sometimes, when you modify a piece of code, you realize the code isn't as flexible as you'd like. It was written in a way that made sense at the time but that now prevents you from easily making the changes that you need to make. If you need to make only a single change, you can simply make the change, test it, fix anything that you've broken, and move on to the next item on your to-do list.

However, suppose you're going to make similar changes in the future. In that case, it may be worth spending a little extra time now to clean up the code so that it's easier to make those changes later. (This is a new version of "Fool me once, shame on you; fool me twice, shame on me.")

For a concrete example, suppose you've written a perfectly good application that lets the user control the lights in a high-rise office building. It lets you turn individual lights on and off so that you can use the building as a 35-story pixel display. After the first release, the customers decide they want a tool that lets them display the company logo. Unfortunately, you didn't plan for that, so adding it is a bit of a hassle.

If you were paying attention when the preceding section talked about the DRY principle and "there's no such thing as two," then you can probably guess where this story is headed. After you write this tool, the customers are probably going to want another one. They'll want new tools to draw letters, words, and simple pictures. Or management will change the company logo. (They probably won't ask for scrolling messages and animation just yet because the lights don't turn on and off fast enough to make those work very well, but it's something to keep in the back of your mind.)

You could just write the logo tool, but it would probably be worthwhile to spend a little extra time to refactor the code a bit to make building these sorts of tools easier. It'll cost you more time now but will save time down the road. More important, it will make the code cleaner, so you'll be less likely to introduce bugs when you write new tools later.

Bug Swarms

As mentioned in Chapter 13, "Testing," bugs tend to travel in swarms. What that means is that some methods, modules, or classes tend to be buggier than others. That can happen for several reasons. Perhaps that chunk of code is exceptionally complicated or confusing. Perhaps it wasn't thought out very well during high-level and low-level design. Perhaps the code was modified several times so its original elegant design has been shredded into confetti. Perhaps the code was written by a beginning programmer who hadn't learned about `for` loops yet.

However they form, bug swarms are dangerous. A piece of code that has produced a lot of bugs in the past is likely to continue spawning bugs in the future. At some point, it's better to step back, study the code so you understand what it's supposed to do, and rewrite it from scratch.

This can be risky. Buggy as it is, the code probably does more or less what it's supposed to do, so there's a chance you'll replace ugly but working code with elegant but broken code.

That means you should perform at least a quick cost-benefit analysis to decide whether it's worth the risk. For example, if you've wasted two or three hours per week for the last few months fixing bugs in a 30-line method, it's probably worth rewriting that method. In contrast, it's less clear whether you should completely rewrite a `Customer` class that contains 7,000+ lines of code just to chase a couple bugs that you haven't been able to reproduce.

My rule of thumb is, if I'm sick and tired of fixing bugs in a particular piece of code, then it's time to consider rewriting it.

Bad Programming Practices

Fixing bad programming practices is both a good reason and a bad reason to refactor code. It's a good reason because the result can be code that is easier to understand, test, debug, and modify. It's a bad reason because, in theory at least, you shouldn't have any bad programming practices in your code.

Ideally, after you write a piece of code, you should review it (either yourself or in a formal code review) and make sure you've followed good programming practices. Still, sometimes bad code slips into a project.

Even if the code starts out good, it can be modified and remodified until it no longer follows good programming practices. Over time a method that was initially short, elegant, and tightly focused can morph into an incomprehensible jungle of loops, branches, and unrelated tests.

For example, suppose you write a nice, short, tightly focused method that takes a student ID as a parameter and fetches that student's data from a database. A few days later, the method's requirements change to make it select only students that are currently enrolled in classes. You modify the code to add that check. No big deal. A week after that, someone else wants to search for students by name instead of student ID, so you add a student name parameter and modify the code accordingly. After a few other changes, the method that once was straightforward is a confusing mess. You used to be able to view all of the code on a single screen, but now it contains hundreds of lines of code with `if-then` statements spanning several pages, so you have to scroll back and forth to figure out what's happening.

At that point, you should probably rewrite the method to restore its original tight focus. You should break this frankenmethod into several separate methods, each of which performs a single, unambiguous task. The result will be more methods and probably a larger total number of lines of code, but the methods will each be easier to understand, use correctly, debug, and maintain.

The following list shows some of the bad programming practices that you should avoid initially and that might indicate a particular class, method, or other piece of code could benefit from refactoring:

➤ The code is too long.

➤ The code is duplicated.

➤ A loop is too long.

➤ Loops are nested too deeply.

➤ It doesn't do much.

➤ It's never used.

➤ It has a vague or unfocused purpose.

➤ It performs more than one task.

➤ It takes a lot of parameters.

➤ It doesn't use all of its parameters.

If you see code that has changed over time to include some of these symptoms of bad code, consider refactoring.

Individual Bugs

Finding an individual bug is not a good reason to rewrite code. If you find a single bug in a method, just fix it and move on. One bug does not make a swarm. There's no reason to rip a good piece of code apart and risk breaking something just because it contains a single bug.

Now if you discover another bug in the same piece of code next week and a third bug the week after that (and you didn't add them while fixing the first bug), then you should think about rewriting the code to clean it up.

Not Invented Here

This is the worst reason for rewriting code, but it's also probably the most common. When some programmers see someone else's code, it doesn't look quite right. The structure is wrong, the names of the variables are misleading (it should use num_students instead of student_count), the comments don't use proper grammar, and the indentation is off. Terrible code! Who wrote this gibberish?

The problem isn't actually the code; it's that the second programmer didn't write it. Everyone thinks their basic approach, naming convention, commenting style, and everything else is the best. If you weren't using the best possible techniques for writing code, you'd do things differently. Thinking you need to rewrite a piece of code just because someone else wrote it is called the *not invented here syndrome (NIHS)*.

When you're in school, assignments tend to have a single correct answer. In contrast, in the real programming world there's *never* a single correct answer. There are always several (perhaps hundreds) of different ways to accomplish the same thing. Some ways may be better than others (searching a database by using an index is a lot faster than pulling up random records hoping to get the one you want), but there are usually lots of ways that are good enough to get the job done. For some problems such as sorting, you can mathematically *prove* that there are many solutions that have the same theoretical performance, so don't get too addicted to thinking that your solutions are always the best.

When you see a piece of strange code, you shouldn't ask yourself whether it's the correct solution or the best solution. Instead, you should ask whether it satisfies the criteria that mean it should be rewritten. Just because it's not the solution you would have chosen doesn't mean it needs to be changed.

That leads to one of my favorite mottos (which I learned the hard way).

> If it's good enough, it's good enough.

If the code works correctly, is fast enough to satisfy your needs, and doesn't contain a swarm of bugs, leave it alone.

TASK EXECUTION

Whether you need to modify existing code for perfective, adaptive, corrective, or preventive reasons, you need to follow roughly the same steps to make useful changes without adding new bugs. At a high level, the steps you follow are roughly the same as those that go into initial development:

- ➤ Requirements gathering
- ➤ High-level design
- ➤ Low-level design
- ➤ Development
- ➤ Testing
- ➤ Deployment

(Hopefully by now you've seen this list enough to have it memorized and you're sick of seeing it.)

For smaller maintenance tasks, you can probably abbreviate or skip some of those steps. For example, if you need to change only a single line of code to fix a bug, your requirements gathering probably just includes the statement "Fix the bug." You also probably don't need to spend a lot of time on high-level or low-level design, and you may defer deployment until the application's next major release.

You should never skimp on testing, though.

After you make your changes, you need to perform maintenance on your maintenance. (New features you add may contain bugs or need future modification. Any bugs you fix may be fixed incorrectly and need further repair. Of course, those bug fixes may need fixes, which need more fixes, and so on until you wonder if you're trapped in the movie *Inception*. You better keep your chess piece or spinning top handy.)

Some maintenance tasks may be similar to regular development tasks, but their relative frequency often changes. In an application for internal use that does a good enough job already, the focus may be on bug fixing instead of feature improvements and enhancements. That's also often the case with first releases of consumer applications. No one is going to buy version 2.0 if the customers universally hate version 1.0 for its bugginess.

If you sell your application online and need a continuing stream of revenue to keep the repo man at bay, you may decide to focus more on creating new and improved features for a new release. (Of course, you still need to fix any bugs. See the last sentence in the preceding paragraph.)

SUMMARY

Maintenance is somewhat similar to normal development. You still need to perform roughly the same tasks (requirements gathering, high-level design, low-level design, code, test, and deploy the results). Sometimes the focus is slightly different (you'll probably spend more time fixing bugs than writing new code) and you might skimp on some of the steps (you probably won't need an extensive high-level design to fix a one-line bug), but the basic approach is similar. Testing is particularly important so that you don't introduce too many new bugs when you fix old ones.

This chapter finishes the introduction to basic software engineering tasks. All software development projects include the basic tasks in one form or another with varying amounts of emphasis.

The chapters in the next part of the book describe different models of software development. For now, you can think of them as different ways to arrange the basic development steps. For example, iterative models use the same steps but repeated many times to try to keep the project moving toward a usable result.

EXERCISES

1. Suppose your programming team writes an application with 10,000 lines of code. During testing, you decide that the team generates roughly 20 bugs per KLOC (thousand lines of code) for new code. (That's probably a bit on the low side for a typical development team, but I'll give you the benefit of the doubt.) During bug fixing, you discover they generate about twice that many bugs (40 per KLOC) when they modify older code. How many lines of code will the team actually generate, including original code, fixes, fixes to fixes, and so forth?

2. After you write the lines of code you predicted in your answer to Exercise 1, are you done with maintenance?

3. Consider your answer to Exercise 1. Suppose the number of lines of code the team members can write for different kinds of code is given in the following table.

CODE TYPE	LINES PER DAY
New code	20
Fix a bug	4
Fix a bug fix	2
Fix a fixed bug fix	1

How many person-days will it take to write all the code?

4. If you have two team members, approximately how many months will the project described in Exercise 3 take? (Yes, I'm totally cheating here. You can look back on a project and calculate the number of lines of code per day you wrote, but you generally can't use imaginary productivity numbers to predict a project's duration.) What if you have five team members? 10? 111?

5. Draw a flowchart showing how a bug report might move through the states New, Assigned, Reproduced, Cannot Reproduce, Fixed, Tested, and Closed. Allow the bug to move into Pending if it cannot be reproduced.

   Label the connecting arrows with the tasks that lead to the new state. For example, label the arrow leading from New to Assigned "Assign." Require approval before moving a bug into the Closed state.

6. From which states could a bug move into the state Pending, Deferred, or Reopened?

7. Why might you want to move a bug from the Closed state to the Deferred state?

8. What are the total (approximate) percentages of cost spent on each of the four maintenance categories over the life of an application?

9. Place the following situations in their correct maintenance task categories (perfective, adaptive, corrective, or preventive).

   a. Change the `SaveSnapshot` method because it isn't saving files in BMP format correctly.
   b. Change the `SaveSnapshot` method so that it can also save files in PNG format.
   c. Change the main program to restore the settings in use when the previous session ended.
   d. Add comments to a 200-line method that currently has the single comment `CodeNinja was here 4/1/2003`.
   e. Write documentation to clarify a module's low-level design.
   f. Remove the `PremiumCustomer` class because it isn't used.
   g. Add icons to display on the new operating system's startup page.
   h. Rewrite a method because the program grew so large that the old version of the method wasn't fast enough.

    i.   Rewrite a method because it uses an unnecessarily complicated algorithm.

    j.   Rewrite a 15-line method because it contained seven known bugs (now fixed).

    k.   Rewrite a 715-line method to make it smaller.

    l.   Rewrite a complicated method to see how it works. Then tuck the new code away for future reference but don't replace the original code in the application.

    m.   Rewrite the logging method to use cloud services to store data instead of storing data locally.

    n.   Rewrite the login screen to deal with the company's new firewall.

    o.   Change the Order List screen to let the user sort orders on any field.

    p.   Add 2FA to the login screen.

    q.   Allow the users to change form background colors.

    r.   Change database permissions to prevent unauthorized users from accessing financial data.

    s.   Study the mysteries of the Customer Overdue Accounts Report.

    t.   Fix typos.

    u.   Research workarounds for a recalcitrant bug.

    v.   Rewrite code to run on a cloud platform instead of locally on the users' desktops.

    w.   Switch cloud providers.

    x.   Add an Easter egg to the program's About form.

    y.   Harden security to prevent cyberattacks.

    z.   Salt the code with a few random bugs for testing purposes.

10. In which of the following situations should you consider rewriting a piece of code (preventive maintenance)? If you can't tell from just the description, what else would you need to know before deciding?

    a.   A method is 412 lines long.

    b.   A method is 10 lines long but very confusing.

    c.   A method uses `for`, `while`, and `for-each` loops nested 12 levels deep.

    d.   At one point the code makes a series of method calls 37 levels deep.

    e.   A method violates the team's variable naming conventions.

    f.   A method draws a rectangle, line, or ellipse depending on its parameters.

    g.   It takes 43 seconds to log in to the application.

    h.   You've just discovered the fifth bug in a 40-line method.

    i.   Roughly once per day, the program crashes and loses any work the user hasn't already saved.

    j.   When the user tries to close the application, it crashes. No data is lost and it seems to work just fine otherwise.

    k.   A coworker (not you) fixed a bug in a method, but you later discovered that the bug fix caused another bug. The coworker (again, not you) fixed it again, but that also caused another bug.

    l.   A coworker fixed a bug in a method and that caused another bug. A different coworker fixed that bug, but the fix lead to yet another bug. A third coworker fixed the latest bug and (you guessed it) caused another bug.

    m.   Roughly once per day, the program crashes, but the user can easily restart it without losing any work.

WHAT YOU LEARNED IN THIS CHAPTER

➤ Maintenance is *expensive*, sometimes accounting for up to 75 percent of a project's total cost.

➤ One reason maintenance is expensive is that applications often live far longer than expected.

➤ Maintenance tasks can be divided into four categories:

  ➤ Perfective tasks improve, modify, or add features to a project.

  ➤ Adaptive tasks modify an application to work with changing conditions in the environment such as a new operating system version or changes to external interfaces.

  ➤ Corrective tasks fix bugs.

  ➤ Preventive tasks (refactoring) modify the code to make it easier to maintain in the future.

➤ Sometimes developers learn what they need to do to build a system while making the first version, so the second version is the first good one (the second system effect).

➤ Sometimes a system's second version is bloated and full of unnecessary bells and whistles, so the third version is the first good one (the third time's a charm effect).

➤ Bugs typically travel through some of the following states: New, Assigned, Reproduced, Cannot Reproduce, Pending, Fixed, Tested, Deferred, Closed, and Reopened.

➤ You don't always need to refactor code, even if it doesn't follow good programming guidelines. (If it ain't broke, don't fix it.)

➤ To perform maintenance tasks successfully, you need to follow the normal software engineering steps: requirements gathering, high-level design, low-level design, development, testing, and deployment. (Although you can often abbreviate some of those steps. You probably don't need extensive high-level design to fix a one-line bug.)

PART II
Process Models

According to Darwin's Origin of Species, it is not the most intellectual of the species that survives; it is not the strongest that survives; but the species that survives is the one that is able best to adapt and adjust to the changing environment in which it finds itself.

—Leon C. Megginson

That's the basic philosophy behind many modern software process models. They start with an incomplete or imperfect version of an application and then gradually improve it over time. That approach allows the development to change as needed in the face of changing requirements or shifts in the business environment.

In contrast, predictive models define a vision of the completed application at the outset and then work tirelessly toward that vision. Some of those models may allow some limited change, but in general they are much less adaptable than iterative and rapid application development models.

The chapters in this part of the book describe a variety of process models ranging from the relatively inflexible waterfall model to more recent rapid development and iterative models. Each has its strengths and weaknesses, and with some study and experience, you can combine at least some of the strengths with those of another.

17

Predictive Models

The best way to predict your future is to create it.

—*Abraham Lincoln*

Prediction is very difficult, especially if it's about the future.

—*Niels Bohr*

What You Will Learn in This Chapter:

➤ Predictive models, when they are useful, and when they probably won't work

➤ The waterfall, waterfall with feedback, and sashimi models

➤ Incremental waterfall variations

➤ V-model and the software development life cycle

The chapters before this one describe specific tasks that you must perform for any software engineering project. In every project, you need requirements, design, testing, deployment, and maintenance. Up to this point, I've sort of implied that you'll follow those steps more or less in order one at a time. (Although I've hinted several times that steps may overlap.)

Exactly how you handle those tasks can vary depending on the scope of the project. For a large traditional project, the specification might include hundreds of pages of text, charts, diagrams, and use cases. For a small project that you're writing for your own use, the specification might be all in your head, and you might "write" it while walking the dog or singing in the shower.

The "large traditional" approach and the "for my own use" approach are two models of software development. The chapters in this part of the book describe some typical software development models in a bit more detail.

This chapter describes some predictive development models. The section "Predictive and Adaptive" later in this chapter explains what a predictive model is.

MODEL APPROACHES

Over the years, software engineers have developed a *lot* of different development models, each with its own adherents who will fight to the death to prove their model is best. I have two theories about why there are so many different models.

First, developers may just be trying to come up with the coolest names and acronyms. Names like Scrum and sashimi and acronyms like RAD and LSD support this theory. And extreme programming sounds like an obvious prelude to energy drink product placement ads. (Imagine a programmer jumping off a cliff in a wingsuit with a laptop and a sports drink.)

My second (and I admit more likely) theory is that a huge number of people have spent an enormous amount of time (person-millennia if not person-eons) on software engineering. During that time, some very smart people noticed that there were problems with the methods that they were using. Development wandered off on the wrong path, programmers didn't test their code, or the project took so long that by the time it was finished, the customers' needs had changed or their industry no longer existed.

Some of those smart people took the time to study their problems and came up with different approaches to try to address those problems. The resulting development models tend to emphasize one part of development or another. For example, agile methods allow a project's goals to change over time to track changing customer needs. Test-driven development forces programmers to write tests for their code. Extreme programming uses "pair programming" to ensure that every piece of code goes through a kind of code review.

There is a lot of overlap among the different models. For example, many developers noticed that customer requirements sometimes change, so there are a lot of agile methods that all try to address that issue.

Each model has its own philosophy, set of rules, and lists of important principles. Acolytes of a particular model may claim that you're not following The One True Path if you're skipping one of the model's steps. (If you don't serve sprinkle donuts on Wednesdays, then you're not really using Crumb!)

They can think that if they like, but I take a slightly less-restrictive approach. In practice what actually matters is whether you produce high-quality software reasonably close to on time and within your budget. A lot of development models use clever techniques to make development more likely to produce a good result. Sometimes, it may be useful to borrow a technique from one model and add it to another.

Still, there's some benefit to picking a model and trying to follow its rules. That at least gives you some guidelines to follow. (It also helps with seating arrangements at dinner parties. Placing a staunch waterfall supporter next to an extreme programmer could be dangerous!)

PREREQUISITES

Before you start using a particular model, you need to be sure everyone on the team is on board. Everyone needs to agree on what the rules are and what procedures you will use to make sure the rules are followed. At first, some of the techniques the models use (such as daily 15-minute meetings or pair programming) can seem strange or downright awkward. Unless everyone commits to the model, you're going to have trouble getting everyone to follow the rules and maximizing the model's benefits.

Just as you don't always have the luxury of picking your programming language, you also don't always have the ability to pick your development model. If you're joining a company that always uses Scrum, then you're going to have to use Scrum.

PREDICTIVE AND ADAPTIVE

One way to categorize development models is by the way they handle requirements. In a *predictive development model*, you predict in advance what needs to be done and then you go out and do it. You use the requirements to design the system, and you use the design as a blueprint to write the code. You test the code, have customers sign off saying it really does what the specification says it should, and then pop the champagne.

As an analogy, you build a brick wall with a predictive model. Based on past experience, you know exactly how long it will take to build a wall of the desired size. You can easily calculate how many bricks you'll need. Then you can order the bricks, schedule some masons, and get the job done.

Unfortunately, it's often hard to predict exactly what a software application needs to do and how you should build it. Sometimes, particularly if you're working with new technology, you just don't know what the program should do. Sometimes, if you're unfamiliar with a particular programming technique, your design doesn't work. And sometimes, changing business situations means that what you thought the customers needed at the beginning isn't what they actually need at the end.

An *adaptive development model* enables you to change the project's goals if necessary during development. Instead of picking a design at the outset and doggedly plodding toward it even when the design is no longer relevant, an adaptive model lets you periodically reevaluate and decide whether you need to change direction.

That doesn't mean you can't predict the final requirements if your Ouija board lets you. You can start with a good idea of what the final application should look like. The adaptive model just gives you chances to fine-tune the project if necessary.

For an analogy for an adaptive model, consider a typical TV detective show. It starts with a murder and your goal is to find the killer. You know some of the things you need to do (interview witnesses, check cell phone records, whip off your sunglasses and squint meaningfully into the distance while saying pithy things by the coffee machine), but you don't know exactly where the case will lead. You follow the first clue, it leads to a second, which leads to a third, and so forth. Each time you find a new clue, you update the direction of the investigation.

Admittedly, the detective show is an extreme example in which you have no real idea of what's going on until the last few minutes of the show when the hero tricks the villain into confessing during a tape-recorded phone conversation. In an adaptive software project, you usually know more or less what you need to build, but you can change direction if necessary.

You might think that an adaptive model is always better than a predictive one, but there are cases in which a predictive model works quite well. For example, predictive models work well when the project is relatively small, you know exactly what you need to do, and the timescale is short enough that the requirements won't change during development.

Success and Failure Indicators for Predictive Models

The following list describes some indicators that mean a predictive project may be successful:

➤ User involvement—If the users help define the requirements, then they're more likely to be correct.

➤ Clear vision—If the customers and developers have the same clear vision about the project's goals, then development will stay on track.

➤ Limited size—A small size helps the customers and team members see the whole picture all at once. Requirements won't have time to change.

➤ Experienced team—Experienced team members are less likely to design something that they can't build. They also won't wander off writing code that doesn't work out. (Of course, an experienced team is helpful for *any* project, not just predictive ones.)

➤ Realistic—If the users ask for a telepathic user interface, a guess-what-I-want-to-do module, and the ability to predict tomorrow's lotto numbers, they're going to be disappointed.

➤ Established technology—If you stick to technology that you've used before, you'll understand how to use it correctly.

Of course, the lack of each of those success indicators is a failure indicator. If users aren't involved, the vision is unclear, or you're using untried technology, then the project is more likely to fail.

The following list describes a few other things that might indicate that a predictive project won't succeed:

➤ Incomplete requirements—In a predictive project, if the requirements don't say you should do something, then it won't get done.

➤ Unclear requirements—If the customers and developers don't all have the same vision of what the application should do, then you'll have trouble satisfying everyone.

➤ Changing requirements—The requirements are like railroad tracks: after they're set, changing course is difficult and may derail the project.

➤ Insufficient resources—Even if you have clear requirements and a perfect design, a single programmer can't write a 10,000-line program in a week.

Before you launch a predictive project, make sure these and other omens are favorable.

Advantages and Disadvantages of Predictive Models

Adaptive models can handle the most reasonable of those problems (no model will let a single developer write a 10,000-line program in a week), but there are still some advantages to predictive models. The following list summarizes some of the greatest benefits:

➤ Predictability—If everything goes according to plan (and you sort of have to make that assumption if you're going to use a predictive model), then you know exactly when different stages will occur. In particular, you know when you'll be finished and how much effort (aka money) you'll need.

➤ Stability—Because the requirements are "set in stone" at the beginning of the project, the customers know exactly what they are getting. That's particularly important for life-critical systems such as systems that control medical devices, automobiles, and airplanes.

➤ Cost-savings—If the design is clear and correct, you won't waste time following development paths that turn out to be dead ends.

➤ Detailed design—If you design everything correctly up front, then you shouldn't need to waste time making a lot of decisions during later development. You just follow the plan. That makes programming faster (and therefore cheaper).

➤ Less refactoring—Adaptive projects tend to require frequent refactoring. A programmer writes some code. Sometime later, the requirements change, and the code needs to be modified. The result may need to be refactored to make it more efficient or to satisfy code standards. These problems don't occur as often in predictive projects.

➤ Fix bugs early—If the requirements and design are correct and complete, then you can detect and fix bugs early. That in turn means you won't have to fix any bugs that those early bugs would have caused later. Because it's easier to fix bugs early on, that saves you more time.

➤ Better documentation—Some of the adaptive models deemphasize documentation to the point where there is very little (if any). Predictive models require a lot of documentation before programming even starts, so you at least have *some* documentation. That makes it easier to move new people into the project because they can read the documentation to get up to speed. (You'll still need to keep an eye on the programmers if you want comments in the code, however.)

➤ More time to prepare training materials—Because the requirements are set at the beginning, trainers can spend most of the project writing training materials. You can also start training users before the project is complete. In adaptive models, requirements can change up to the very end, so any materials written early on may need to be rewritten.

➤ Easy maintenance—Because you can consider the application from a broader perspective, you can create a more elegant design that's more consistent and easier to maintain.

Even if everything works perfectly, a predictive project still has some disadvantages:

➤ Inflexible—Just because you *thought* the requirements wouldn't change, that doesn't mean they won't. If they do, accommodating them can be hard. (Basically, a predictive model is a gamble that requirements won't change too much.) That lack of flexibility also means you can't take advantage of new opportunities. If someone invents a new and easier way to display sales reports, you won't be able to take advantage of it.

➤ Later initial release—Many adaptive models enable you to give the users a program as soon as it does something useful. With a predictive model, the users don't get anything until development is finished.

➤ Big Design Up Front (BDUF)—You need to define everything up front. You can't start development until you know everything that you're going to need to do. You can't start development until you understand all of the nooks and crannies of the application. That may mean some team members are stuffing the suggestion box or playing mahjong while others are still working on requirements.

The "purest" predictive models assume that each stage of development is finished completely and correctly before the next stage begins. (I'll describe some models that bend that assumption later in this chapter.) In particular, you can't start cranking out code until the requirements and designs are finished. For that reason, these models are sometimes called *Big Design Up Front (BDUF)* models.

For example, a typical waterfall model project might spend 20 to 40 percent of its time on requirements and design, 30 to 40 percent of its time on programming, and the rest of its time on testing and deployment. If you don't spend a lot of time on the design, then the requirements and design won't be clear and correct, and you don't get the predictive model benefits.

One of the biggest ideas of BDUF projects is that the time spent on design up front saves you time later in the project. You don't get that it you skimp on the early project's phases.

There's still a lot of argument about whether all of these benefits are real. Adaptive model fans argue that they save more time and money because predictive projects often produce an unusable result. That's probably true, but to be fair you need to compare times when the models work. Obviously, a working adaptive project is better than a broken predictive one.

That's enough discussion about predictive models in general. The next chapter says more about the advantages and disadvantages of adaptive models. Meanwhile, the rest of this chapter describes some particular predictive models.

WATERFALL

Waterfall is the plain vanilla of the predictive model world. It assumes that you finish each step completely and thoroughly before you move on to the next step. Figure 17.1 shows the quintessential picture of the waterfall model. Imagine water cascading from one step to the next.

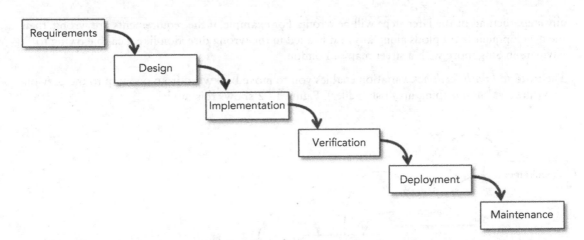

FIGURE 17.1: In the waterfall model, each step follows the one before in a strict order.

The waterfall analogy is actually fairly clever. The water represents information and the stages act like buckets. When one bucket is full (you've finished filling it up with information), the information floods from that bucket into the next so that it can direct the following task.

The waterfall model can work reasonably well if all the following assumptions are satisfied:

➤ The requirements are precisely known in advance.

➤ The requirements include no unresolved high-risk items.

➤ The requirements won't change much during development.

➤ The team has previous experience with similar projects, so they know what's involved in building the application.

➤ There's enough time to do everything sequentially.

You can add additional steps or split steps to give more detail if you like. For example, you could break Verification into Testing and Validation, or you could break Design into High-Level Design and Low-Level Design.

You can also elaborate on a step. For example, you could break Design into User Interface Design, Security Design, High-Level Design, Low-Level Design, and possibly other pieces.

Few developers use the pure waterfall model these days, but some of its variations are quite useful.

WATERFALL WITH FEEDBACK

If you assume that you can carry out each step perfectly (and nothing changes during development), then the waterfall model leads to inevitable success. Unfortunately, it's hard to perform every step of development perfectly. Because the model doesn't allow you to go back to earlier steps, if you fail at any step, then all of the later steps will be wrong. For example, if the requirements are wrong, then the development team plods along anyway, headed in the wrong direction like a cabbie trying to navigate in Singapore with a street map of London.

The *waterfall with feedback* variation enables you to move backward from one step to the previous step (like a salmon leaping up a fish ladder). Figure 17.2 shows this model.

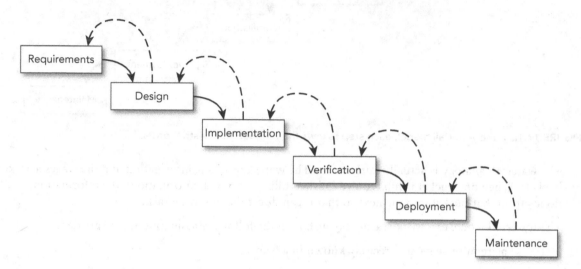

FIGURE 17.2: In the waterfall with feedback model, you can go back to the previous step.

Now if you're working on the design and you discover that there was a problem in the requirements, you can briefly go back to the requirements and fix them.

The farther you have to go back up the cascade, the harder it is. For example, if you're working on implementation and discover a problem in the requirements, it's hard to skip back up two steps to fix the problem.

It's also less meaningful to move back up the cascade for the later steps. For example, if you find a problem during maintenance, then you should probably treat it as a maintenance task instead of moving back into the deployment stage.

Because moving back up the cascade is hard, you still need to be good at making predictions. You can fix some mistakes, but the goal is still to complete each step completely and effectively before moving on.

SASHIMI

Sashimi (also called *sashimi waterfall* and *waterfall with overlapping phases*) is similar to the waterfall model except the steps are allowed to overlap (much as the thin slices of fish overlap in the Japanese dish sashimi.) Figure 17.3 shows the stages of a sashimi project.

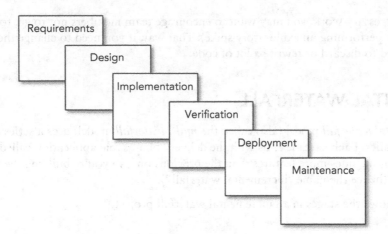

FIGURE 17.3: In the sashimi model, development phases overlap.

In a project's first phase, some requirements will be fully defined while you're still working on others. At that point, some of the team members can start designing the defined features while others continue working on the remaining requirements.

A bit later, the design for some parts of the application will be more or less finished but the design for other parts of the system won't be. At that point, some developers can start writing code for the designed parts of the system while others continue working on the rest of the design tasks, and possibly even on remaining requirements.

Similarly, other parts of the development process might overlap, although there are probably limits. For example, you may want to delay deployment until the application is tested and verified.

You can even allow greater overlap between project phases. For example, you could have people working on requirements, design, implementation, and testing all at the same time.

There are several advantages to allowing stages to overlap. First, it means people with different skills can focus on their specialties without waiting for others. For example, a database designer can start laying out tables and indexes even if the user interface requirements aren't finished. This kind of overlap keeps the team members more productive.

A second advantage is that it lets you perform a *spike*, or a *deep dive*, into a particular topic to learn more about it. For example, suppose you're working on requirements and the customers ask if you can incorporate an EEG headset into the program to let you control the application with your brainwaves. You haven't done that before, so you assign some team members to give it a try. They quickly design and implement a prototype to see what would be involved and to let the users see what it would look like. At that point, you have people working on requirements, design, and implementation all at the same time. Based on what you learn from the prototype, you can refine the requirements or scrap the whole brainwave idea.

A third advantage to overlapping phases is it lets later phases modify earlier phases. If you discover during design that the requirements are impossible or need alterations, you can make the necessary changes.

To avoid unnecessary work, you may want to encourage team members not to get too far ahead (unless they're performing an exploratory spike). That way, if you need to change the requirements, you won't need to discard or rewrite a lot of code.

INCREMENTAL WATERFALL

The *incremental waterfall* model (also called the *multi-waterfall* model) uses a series of separate waterfall cascades. Each cascade ends with the delivery of a usable application called an *increment*. Each increment includes more features than the previous one, so you're building the final application incrementally (hence the name "incremental waterfall").

Figure 17.4 shows the stages in an incremental waterfall project.

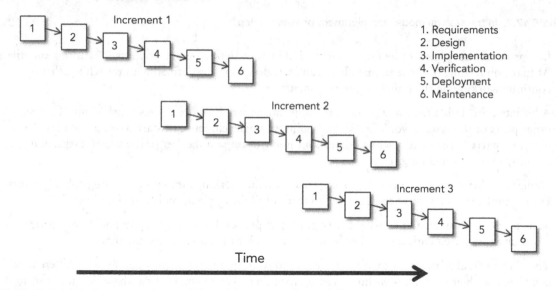

1. Requirements
2. Design
3. Implementation
4. Verification
5. Deployment
6. Maintenance

FIGURE 17.4: In the incremental waterfall model, a series of waterfall cascades provide an increasing level of functionality.

During each increment, you'll get a better understanding of what the final application should look like. You'll learn what did and didn't work well in the previous increment. The users will also probably give you a long laundry list of new features that they want added. All of that helps you prepare for the next increment.

Notice in Figure 17.4 that the different increments may overlap in the time dimension. If you understand what you need to do in the next iteration, you don't need to wait until the current iteration is completely finished before you start writing new requirements documents. Of course, if you start the next increment before the users have had a chance to work with the current one, then you won't get as much feedback from them.

You can use any of the waterfall variations for each of the increments. For example, you could use a series of waterfalls with feedback or a sashimi series, as shown in Figure 17.5.

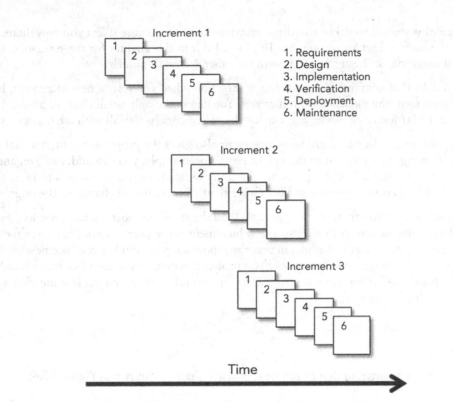

Increment 1

1. Requirements
2. Design
3. Implementation
4. Verification
5. Deployment
6. Maintenance

Increment 2

Increment 3

Time

FIGURE 17.5: This incremental waterfall project uses a series of sashimi waterfalls.

Figure 17.4 and Figure 17.5 show projects that use three increments, but you can use as many as you like. In fact, for an application with a long useful life span, you could use an open-ended series of increments. You would just keep adding new increments whenever you wanted to make a new version of the application to add new features.

REFACTORING REQUIRED

Sometimes, programs that grow incrementally become strange creatures with illogical interfaces, inconsistent mechanisms, and code as strange as anything H. P. Lovecraft could have written (if he'd been a programmer). I've worked with programs that had been used and modified for decades, and it was nearly impossible to make any significant changes without breaking something.

At some point, you may need to slip in a refactoring increment to clean house. That increment might add little or no new functionality, but it will let you move forward with future increments more efficiently.

The incremental waterfall model is actually somewhat adaptive because it lets you reevaluate your direction at the start of each increment, but I've included it in this chapter for three reasons. First, this is a waterfall variation, so I want to put it with the other waterfall models.

Second, it's not all *that* adaptive. You can change direction when you start a new increment, but within each increment the model runs predictively. You can make only small changes allowed by whichever particular waterfall model you use for the increments (waterfall with feedback or sashimi).

The fact that you're building on a previous increment also gives the project some inertia that limits the amount of change you can add to the next release. For example, you can add, remove, and tweak features in a new increment, but you probably shouldn't radically change the user interface. That would be more like a completely new project rather than an incremental change to the ongoing series.

Finally, increments tend to run over a longer scale than the stages in most adaptive models. For example, a long-running project might use a new increment every year or two. That gives the users a nice, steady, predictable release schedule. In contrast, some adaptive models produce new builds of an application every month or even every week. You probably wouldn't release all of those builds to the users, but the pace is definitely more frenetic. The incremental waterfall model is somewhat adaptive, but usually over long timescales.

V-MODEL

V-model is basically a waterfall that's been bent into a V shape, as shown in Figure 17.6.

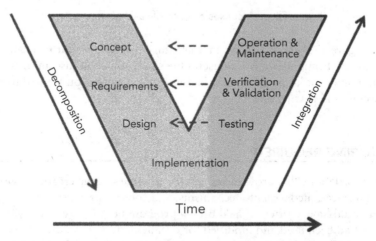

FIGURE 17.6: In V-model, each of the tasks on the left corresponds to a task on the right.

The tasks on the left side of the V break the application down from its highest conceptual level into more and more detailed tasks. This process of breaking the application down into pieces that you can implement is called *decomposition*.

The tasks on the right side of the V consider the finished application at greater and greater levels of abstraction. At the lowest level, testing verifies that the code works. At the next level, verification confirms that the application satisfies the requirements, and validation confirms that the application meets the customers' needs. This process of working back up to the conceptual top of the application is called *integration*.

Each of the tasks on the left corresponds to a task on the right with a similar level of abstraction. At the highest level, the initial concept corresponds to operation and maintenance. At the next level, the requirements correspond quite directly to verification and validation. Testing confirms that the design worked. (Like the cheese, implementation stands alone, so it doesn't correspond to another task.)

SOFTWARE DEVELOPMENT LIFE CYCLE

The *software development life cycle (SDLC)*, which is also called the *systems development life cycle* and the *application development life cycle*, is exactly what it sounds like. It covers all of the tasks that go into a software engineering project from start to finish: requirements, design, implementation, and so forth. This is similar to the waterfall model (actually, the waterfall model is one version of SDLC), but I want to present two new ideas here.

First, check out Figure 17.7. This figure emphasizes that the end of one project can feed directly into the next project in a never-ending circle of life. (Cue *The Lion King* music.) The incremental waterfall model is basically just a series of SDLCs flattened out and possibly with some overlap, so one project starts before the previous one is completely finished. (Actually, the picture is a lot like a complete metamorphic life-cycle diagram. The application goes through the stages: egg, larva, pupa, and adult.)

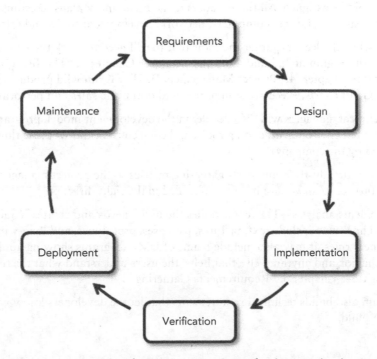

FIGURE 17.7: In the software development life cycle, project phases feed into each other in a potentially infinite loop.

The second new idea is that you can break down the basic steps in a lot more detail if you like. (You should for bigger projects, at least.) The following list describes tasks that are commonly represented as part of the SDLC. Some of them are even broken down into subtasks. (I would have included them all in Figure 17.7, but I would have had to use a 2-point font and you would have needed a microscope to read everything.)

➤ Initiation—An initiator (often a customer, executive champion, or software manager looking for something to charge on his time card) comes up with the initial idea.

➤ Concept development—The initiator, usually with help from others who might be interested in the project, explores the concept to see if it's worthwhile and to evaluate possible alternatives. This step includes an initial project definition, a feasibility analysis, a cost-benefit analysis, and a risk analysis.

You can make "go/no go" decisions at any step in the project, but the decision you make at this point is a big one. After concept development, you should have enough information to make an informed decision. After this point, it gets harder and more expensive to cancel the project as it starts to staff up and gain momentum. (Sometimes, careers are tied to the success of big projects, and anyone in that position will tenaciously resist any attempt to end the project after it gets rolling. They'll cling desperately to the sinking project like a barnacle stuck to the *Titanic*.)

➤ Preliminary planning—A project manager (PM) and technical lead are assigned to the project, and they start planning. If it's a big project, the project might be broken into teams and team leads would be assigned. All these leaders make preliminary plans to estimate necessary resources such as staffing, computers, network, development tools, and microwave popcorn.

This is when the leaders gather the tools that they'll need to track the project (see Chapter 2, "Before the Beginning"), build a healthy team (see Chapter 3, "The Team"), and manage the project (see Chapter 4, "Project Management"). They'll run wild producing scores of PERT charts, Gantt charts, executive summaries, and optimistic sales and performance projections.

The technical managers will also decide on the development model, programming language, development environment, coding tools, and code conventions (if those things aren't already specified by the company).

If it hasn't already, the team starts gathering metrics so the project manager can keep an eye on the project to make sure it remains headed in the right direction.

➤ Requirements analysis—The team studies the users' needs and creates requirement documents. Those may include text, pictures, use cases, prototypes, and long-winded descriptions of business rules. It may also include reams of UML diagrams showing application structure, user behavior, and anything else that helps the users understand what the team will be building. (See Chapter 5, "Requirements Gathering.")

The team also builds technical requirements that let the developers know what they need to build.

➤ High-level design—The team creates high-level designs that specify UX design, UI design, security design, major subsystems, data flow, database needs, and the rest of the application's high-level structure. (See Chapter 6, "High-Level Design," Chapter 8, "Security Design," and Chapter 9, "User Experience Design.")

➤ Low-level design—The team creates low-level designs that explain how to build the application's pieces. The designs provide enough detail that a second-shelf programmer would have a chance of building something close to the right thing. (See Chapter 7, "Low-Level Design.")

➤ Development—The team writes the program code. They follow good programming practices. They perform unit tests, regression tests, and system tests. They fix the bugs that inevitably appear and handle any change requests that are approved by the change committee. The team also prepares user documentation and training materials. (See Chapter 10, "Programming," Chapter 11, "Algorithms," and Chapter 13, "Testing.")

➤ Acceptance testing—The customers finally get a chance to take the application for a test drive in its (almost) final form. Traditionally, the application breaks at this point when the users do something completely reasonable that the developers never thought about. After a few bug fixes and perhaps a small change or two, the customers agree that the application satisfies the requirements. (Acceptance testing can be in the staging software that will be used to prepare for rollout in the next phase.)

➤ Deployment—The team rolls out the application. (See Chapter 14, "Deployment.")

➤ Maintenance—The application allows the users to do their jobs better than ever before, and everyone lives happily ever after (aside from the inescapable bug fixes and change requests). (See Chapter 16, "Maintenance.")

The team continues to track the application's usefulness throughout its lifetime to determine whether it needs repair, enhancement, or replacement with a new version or with something completely different.

Keep in mind that even an application that's working perfectly needs periodic maintenance and upgrades. Every two years or so a new version of the operating system will appear, and many companies will require that all applications be upgraded to the new version. Also, roughly two years after you install the application, computer power will have doubled. Eventually, the application will seem so slow compared to the users' home computers, laptops, tablets, phones, phablets, and other gizmos that they'll want new hardware. And don't forget new monitors. Eventually, everyone will want two 32″ 4 K Ultra HD OLED monitors (or possibly 8 K or 16 K, although I've seen the 4 K televisions, and they may have a higher resolution than the real world). You may think users can live with their existing hardware, but have you noticed how few of them are still using 1980s era CRTs, even though they were as indestructible as battleships? When 4K Ultra HD OLED monitors become reasonably common, everyone is going to want one.

Eventually, the maintenance team needs to figure out how to upgrade the application to the latest hardware and operating system and how to dispose of the old hardware. (If the hardware isn't too out-of-date, see if any of your neighborhood schools want a donation.)

CERTAIN DESTRUCTION

Some companies have security policies that indicate how to dispose of old hardware so any data it contains can't be scraped off by cyber criminals. I knew of one company working on high-security government projects that had a special policy for decommissioning disk drives. Erasing the disk or passing it through a strong magnetic field wasn't good enough. Even running the whole drive through an industrial shredder wasn't good enough. (Warning: Watching videos of industrial shredders destroying bowling balls, gas canisters, cars, and other hard objects can be addictive.) In this case, the government required that a field technician come to the site, take the drive apart, and manually remove the platters so they could be shredded separately. The process cost about $5,000 per drive. (Then I think the pieces were sprinkled with holy water and buried under a crossroad.)

➤ Review—The team uses metrics (which hopefully they remembered to gather throughout the project) to assess the project and decide whether the development process can be improved in the future. (See Chapter 15, "Metrics.")

➤ Disposal—Eventually, the application's usefulness comes to an end. (Or perhaps not, as the Y2K problem proved.) During this stage, the cleanup crew plans the application's removal and possibly its replacement by something else. They need to decide what data needs to be archived and how to protect it so that a hacker can't break in and steal sensitive data.

Like the waterfall model and other purely predictive models, the unadulterated SDLC probably isn't used by many developers these days. It's still useful occasionally, basically in the same situations in which the waterfall model and its variants are useful. It's also an important term to know during those late-night programming jam sessions at conferences.

SUMMARY

Predictive models are useful primarily because they give a lot of structure to a project. For many customers, it's nice to have a fully developed plan that you can follow throughout the project's lifetime. A predictive project makes scheduling simpler, includes documentation that makes it easier to add new people to the project, and can cost less (if everything goes according to plan).

Predictive models have some advantages, but they also have some big disadvantages. Probably the biggest problem with predictive models is that they don't handle change well. In today's constantly changing business world, projects often have fuzzy, incomplete, or changing requirements. Even the best predictive project can fail if it results in a powerful application that doesn't fit the customers' needs when it's finished.

The next two chapters describe adaptive development models that handle those kinds of uncertainty better than predictive models do. They allow you to reassess the customers' needs and the project's status to change direction if necessary.

EXERCISES

1. Indicate which of the following tasks would be better handled predictively or adaptively and briefly say why.

   a. Building a pedestrian bridge over a river
   b. Following a series of clues in a scavenger hunt
   c. Making a scavenger hunt for others to follow
   d. Planning a picnic
   e. Planning a picnic in Seattle
   f. Planning a major motion picture
   g. Teaching an introductory programming course
   h. Finding a specific restaurant while visiting an unfamiliar city before 1990
   i. Finding a specific restaurant while visiting an unfamiliar city with a GPS
   j. Finding a specific restaurant while visiting an unfamiliar city in a few years when cars drive themselves and are plugged into a smart street network

2. Briefly explain why each of the following projects might be risky predictive projects.

   a. The Federal Aviation Administration (FAA) wants you to rewrite the US air traffic control system.
   b. A small archery supply store wants you to write some sales software, but the two partners can't agree on exactly what it should do.
   c. Your customer wants you and your team of five intrepid developers to write a word processing application as powerful as Microsoft Word in the next three months. (At double your normal rates!)
   d. A real estate developer wants to build an application that helps design large housing developments. (Your team just finished building a vacation costing application.)
   e. Your customer dumped a 10-page software specification on your desk and then left on a three-week vacation.
   f. Your customer wants to build a 3D printing application that lets you make buildings out of concrete. (Really, search the Internet for "3D printed buildings" for information about this fast-growing industry.)

3. Under what circumstances would a predictive model cost less in time and effort than an adaptive model? Under what circumstances would it cost more?

4. How does waterfall with feedback differ from sashimi?

5. How many increments could you use in an incremental waterfall project?

6. Explain how each of the V-model decomposition tasks correspond to the integration tasks. (For example, why does Requirements correspond to Verification and Validation?)

WHAT YOU LEARNED IN THIS CHAPTER

➤ Predictive development models have the following characteristics:

   ➤ Anticipate the work to be done, schedule it, and then do it.

   ➤ Work well for short projects where you know in advance everything you'll need to do.

   ➤ Work poorly if requirements are uncertain or change during the project.

   ➤ Can be cheaper than adaptive models if everything goes according to plan but can be much more expensive if you need to make extensive changes.

➤ Adaptive models have the following characteristics:

   ➤ Give you opportunities to change direction.

   ➤ Work well with changing or uncertain requirements.

➤ In a waterfall model, one phase "pours into" the next. The phases are done in order one after another.

➤ In a waterfall with feedback, one phase can feed back into the previous phase to make corrections.

➤ In the sashimi model, multiple phases can overlap. Some developers can be working on one phase while others move ahead to other phases.

➤ The incremental waterfall model uses a series of waterfalls. Each waterfall produces an *increment*, a new version of the application that is incrementally improved over the previous version.

➤ V-model shows the correspondence between *integration* tasks and *decomposition* tasks.

➤ The software development life cycle includes all of the tasks that go into a predictive development model.

18

Iterative Models

> When to use iterative development? You should use iterative development only on projects that you want to succeed.
>
> —*Martin Fowler*

> Control is for beginners.
>
> —*Deborah Mills-Scofield*

> Iteration is truly the mother of invention.
>
> —*Mary Brodie*

What You Will Learn in This Chapter:

- ➤ Differences between predictive, iterative, incremental, and agile approaches
- ➤ Benefits of prototyping and kinds of prototypes
- ➤ Spiral, Unified Process (plus variations), and Cleanroom development models

Predictive software development has some big advantages. It's predictable, encourages a lot of up-front design (hence the nickname Big Design Up Front, or BDUF), and gives a certain inevitability to a project.

Unfortunately, that inevitably can lead to either success or failure. If the design is correct and everything stays on track, the project is like a luxury train coasting majestically into Grand Central Station. However, if something goes wrong, the project is more like a train engulfed in flames and speeding toward a dynamited bridge.

In recent years, software organizations have spent a lot of effort developing techniques that help keep projects headed in the right direction. Lumping all those models and techniques together would make for a bloated chapter, so I decided to split them up a bit.

This chapter discusses one of the techniques that is easiest to apply to any other development model: iteration. In an iterative model, you build the final application incrementally. You start with a minimally working program and then add pieces to it, making it better and better, until you decide the application is as good as it can be (or at least good enough).

I actually snuck a little iteration into the preceding chapter with the incremental waterfall model. This chapter focuses on other iterative variations. The next chapter introduces a bunch of other techniques and approaches that can help keep software engineering efforts on track.

ITERATIVE VS. PREDICTIVE

The problem with predictive models is that they are ill-suited to handle unexpected change. They can deal with small changes (such as customers deciding they want combo boxes instead of list boxes on their forms), but they don't handle big changes well (such as customers deciding they want 20 extra reports that are all viewable on a desktop computer, tablet, or smartphone).

Predictive projects spend a lot of effort at the beginning figuring out exactly what they will do. After you gather requirements and commit to a schedule, it's hard to change course. In theory you could stop the project at any point and head in a new direction. In practice that rarely happens. Changing direction in a big way would essentially mean starting over. You would have to go through the requirements and design phases again. You would also have to abandon all of the work you did in those phases the first time around. If the changes are big enough, this is practically the same as declaring the project a failure (no one wants to do that) and starting a new one.

Even if you manage to point the project in a new direction, there's no guarantee that you won't need to do it all over again. Actually, because your customers have already shown that they're willing to put you through all that pain and inconvenience, further changes seem if anything more likely.

One of the biggest reasons why those changes are so painful is the size of the commitment you've made. If you're three years into a five-year schedule, you've already invested a lot of effort in the project and you have a lot to lose. But what if you were only three months into a five-month plan? Scrapping the work-to-date and starting over would still be annoying, but it would be much less painful. (You might even get to keep your job.)

Predictive models also don't handle fuzzy requirements well. Unless you nail down the requirements precisely at the beginning of the project, it's impossible to create a solid schedule. How can you plan to build something with unknown requirements? (Imagine what would happen if you went to a real estate developer and said, "We want to build a new shopping mall. We don't know exactly where it will be or what it will look like, but start building it and we'll work out the details later.")

Iterative models address those problems by building the application incrementally. They start by building the smallest program that is reasonably useful. Then they use a series of *increments* to add more features to the program until it's finished (if it is ever finished).

Because each increment has a relatively small duration (compared to a predictive project), you're committed to a smaller amount of work. If you decide that the project is heading in the wrong direction, you need to stop only the most recent increment and start a new one instead of canceling the whole project and starting over.

Better still, because you can reorient the project before each new increment, you're less likely to need to cancel anything.

You may have trouble foreseeing the direction a predictive project should take four years from now. It's much easier to guess where you should be headed four months from now. Even if you decide that you need to adjust course, you can probably finish the current iteration and make the adjustments in the next one.

Iterative models also handle fuzzy requirements reasonably well. If you're unsure of some of the application's requirements, you can start building the parts that you do understand and figure out the rest later. Sometimes, you'll learn things building the first part of the system that will make the rest of the requirements clear. Other times the requirements clarify themselves over time.

The preceding chapter described an iterative waterfall model that uses a series of waterfall-style projects to incrementally refine an application. Figure 18.1 shows the stages in an iterative waterfall project.

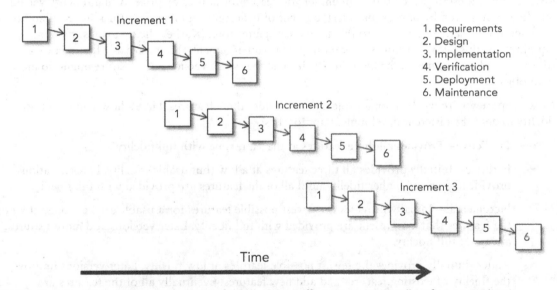

1. Requirements
2. Design
3. Implementation
4. Verification
5. Deployment
6. Maintenance

FIGURE 18.1: Iterative models use a series of development efforts to incrementally refine an application.

Other models also use iterative approaches. Many of the models described in the next chapter use iterative techniques to help stay on the right track.

You can even use iterative methods for just one part of a project. For example, you can use iterative prototyping to refine a project's requirements. After that, you could use waterfall, sashimi, or some other model to finish development.

The following sections describe some common iterative techniques that you can use to improve a project's chance of success.

ITERATIVE VS. INCREMENTAL

Normally, you think of an iterative project as running through several cycles, each of which provides an incremental improvement over the preceding version. Technically, however, that's not necessarily the case, so an iterative project might not be incremental.

For example, suppose in version 1 of a project you produce a usable application, but its code doesn't follow good programming standards. In version 2 you rewrite the code to make the project more maintainable. Version 2 doesn't add any new features to the application, so in some sense you might not think of it as an incremental improvement over version 1. The process is iterative but not incremental.

Karl Scotland provides an interesting perspective on this issue at `https://availagility` `.co.uk/2009/12/22/fidelity-the-lost-dimension-of-the-iron-triangle`. He argues that the difference between iterative and incremental development is clear if you consider the fidelity of a project's features. By *fidelity* he means the completeness of the feature. For example, a low-fidelity real-estate search screen might let you search for houses by price. A high-fidelity version would let you search by price, square feet, number of bedrooms, number of bathrooms, availability of high-speed Internet, and distance to the nearest ice cream store. (Karl explicitly avoids the term "quality" for this because he doesn't want to get into an argument about releasing low-quality code. All of the code is assumed to be high quality. It's just that some versions of a feature might do more than others.)

Now suppose you're working on a project that provides three features. Here's how you might use fidelity to describe different development approaches:

> ➤ Predictive—Provides all three features at the same time with full fidelity.

> ➤ Iterative—Initially provides all three features at a low (but usable) fidelity. Later iterations provide higher and higher fidelity until all of the features are provided with full fidelity.

> ➤ Incremental—Initially provides the fewest possible features for a usable application, but all of the features that are present are provided with full fidelity. Later versions add more features, always at full fidelity.

> ➤ Agile—Initially provides the fewest possible features at low fidelity. Later versions improve the fidelity of existing features and add new features. Eventually all of the features are provided at full fidelity. (The next chapter says more about agile development models.)

Figure 18.2 shows a representation of these approaches. In the predictive model, the users don't receive any program until the application is completely finished. The iterative model starts with low-fidelity versions of every feature and then improves them over time. The incremental model starts with nothing and then adds new features with full fidelity. Finally, the agile model starts with some features of low fidelity and over time improves fidelity and adds more features.

All four of those approaches end with an application that includes all of the features at full fidelity. It's the routes they take to get to their final solutions that differ.

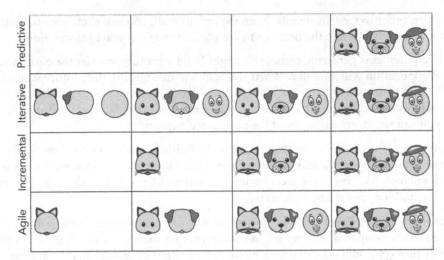

FIGURE 18.2: Different development approaches add features and increase fidelity in different ways.

The difference is somewhat pedantic, but it's probably worth knowing just so you're not confused when a senior executive starts throwing around terms he doesn't really understand.

However, if you look closely at Figure 18.2, you'll notice that the final results are not all exactly the same. The iterative and agile approaches tend to handle changes the most easily because they continually strive to improve whatever features are present.

The iterative approach is not quite as adaptable because it is assumed that a feature is implemented at full fidelity and then not changed after that. (Although it's not a felony or anything to bend the rules and fine-tune a feature after it has been released. You won't end up in Shawshank Developer's Penitentiary, although people may start accusing you of being agile.)

The predictive approach is the least flexible because you need to think of every feature that will be in the final system at the very beginning.

PROTOTYPES

The section "Prototypes" in Chapter 5, "Requirements Gathering" briefly described prototypes. This section provides some additional details and focuses on how prototypes can be useful in iterative development.

In the wider world, a *prototype* is a simplified model that demonstrates some behavior that you want to study. Typically, a software prototype is a program that mimics part of the application you want to build. Two important facts about prototypes are as follows:

➤ They don't need to work the same way that the final application will work.

➤ They don't need to implement all of the features of the final application.

Prototypes just give you a glimpse of a piece of the final application. For example, suppose you're building a product ordering system. You enter some parameters such as a date range or a customer ID number and click a List button to make the system display a list of matching orders. You can then double-click an order to view its details. From the order detail, you can click links to jump to detailed information about the items in the order or to see the customer's contact information.

During the requirements gathering phase, you might build a prototype to let the customers see what the finished application will look like. When you click the List button, the prototype displays a predefined list of orders. When you double-click an order, the prototype doesn't display information for that order. Instead it displays information about a preselected order. Finally, if you click a link on the order, you can see information about the preselected customer.

This prototype doesn't work exactly the same way the finished application will work. If it did, it would be the actual application and not just a prototype. However, it lets the customers see what the application will look like. It lets them click some buttons and links so that they can try out the program's method for interacting with users.

After the customers experiment with the prototype, they can give you feedback to help refine the requirements. For example, when they see the order list, they may think of other fields they want to display. After they try double-clicking to open an order's detail information, they may decide they would rather check boxes next to one or more orders and then click a Detail button to open detail pages for all of the selected orders. When they view a customer's information, they may decide that they want a quick way to see that customer's order history.

Although software prototypes are often programs, you can make other kind of prototypes using less sophisticated techniques. For example, you might mock up some screens using pieces of paper to show customers what the application will look like as they navigate through the system. (A slightly more high-tech version might use a PowerPoint slide show instead of pieces of paper.) If an application includes special hardware, such as a fingerprint scanner, you could tape a cardboard version onto a laptop to show customers what it will look like. These won't be as functional as software prototypes, but they'll probably be easier to implement. Sometimes the best tech is the least tech.

Occasionally, prototypes don't even have a user interface. For example, suppose you're writing a billing application that will process customer charges to generate invoices. You could write a prototype that fetches a particular customer's data, calculates outstanding charges, and prints an invoice. That would let programmers study how the data processing code works before they try to do the same thing for the entire customer database.

The following sections explain some additional details about prototypes.

HORIZONTAL AND VERTICAL PROTOTYPES

A *horizontal prototype* is one that demonstrates a lot of the application's features but with little depth. For example, the prototype described earlier that lets a user pretend to navigate through customer orders is a horizontal prototype. Horizontal prototypes are often user interface prototypes that let customers see what the finished application will *look* like.

In contrast, a *vertical prototype* is one that has little breadth but great depth. The example described earlier that has no user interface and generates an invoice for a single customer is a vertical prototype. Vertical prototypes often let developers see what the finished application will *act* like.

Types of Prototypes

There are several ways that you can use a prototype. Chapter 5 mentioned two important types of prototypes: throwaway prototypes and evolutionary prototypes. In a throwaway prototype, you use the prototype to study some aspect of the system and then you throw it away and write new code from scratch.

In an evolutionary prototype, the prototype demonstrates some of the application's features. As the project progresses, you refine those features and add new ones until the prototype morphs into the finished application.

A third kind of prototyping is incremental prototyping. In *incremental prototyping*, you build a collection of prototypes that separately demonstrate the finished application's features. You then combine the prototypes (or at least their code) to build the finished application. As is the case with an evolutionary prototype, the prototype code becomes part of the final application, so you need to use good programming techniques for all of the prototypes. That means coding is slower than it is with a throwaway prototype. Because the pieces of the system are built from separate prototypes, it may be easier for different programmers or teams to work on the pieces at the same time. That may let you finish the combined application sooner—although, you do need to allow time to integrate the pieces.

Pros and Cons

The following list summarizes prototyping's main benefits:

➤ Improved requirements—Prototypes allow customers to see what the finished application will look like. That lets them provide feedback to modify the requirements early in the project. Often customers can spot problems and request changes sooner so the finished result is more useful to users.

➤ Common vision—Prototypes let the customers and developers see the same preview of the finished application, so they are more likely to have a common vision of what the application should do and what it should look like.

➤ Better design—Prototypes (particularly vertical prototypes) let the developers quickly explore specific pieces of the application to learn what they involve. Prototypes also let developers test different approaches to see which one is best. The developers can use what they learn from the prototypes to improve the design and make the final code more elegant and robust.

Programming, like the rest of life, follows the rule of TANSTAAFL: There ain't no such thing as a free lunch. Prototyping comes with some disadvantages to go with its advantages:

➤ Narrowing vision—People tend to focus on a prototype's specific approach rather than on the problem it addresses. When you show customers (and developers) a prototype, they'll be less likely to think about other solutions that might do a better job.

To avoid this problem, either don't build a prototype until you've considered possible alternatives or build several prototypes to choose from.

➤ Customer impatience—A good prototype can make customers think that the finished application is just around the corner. They'll say things like, "The prototype looks good. Can't you just add a little error handling and a few extra features and call it done?"

To avoid this, make sure customers realize that the prototype isn't anywhere close to the finished application. It's like a realistically painted cruise ship made out of papier-mâché. It may look ready to set sail, but you wouldn't want to put it in the ocean and climb aboard.

➤ Schedule pressure—This goes with the preceding issue. If customers see a prototype they think is mostly done, they may not understand that you need another year to finish and they may pressure you to shorten the schedule.

To avoid this problem, the project manager, executive champion, and other members of the management brigade need to manage customer expectations so they know what will be ready and when.

➤ Raised expectations—Sometimes, a prototype may demonstrate features that won't be included in the application. For example, those features might turn out to be too hard. Sometimes, features are included to assess their value to users, and the features are dropped if they don't have enough benefit. Other times a feature may be present just to show a possible future direction. In those cases, users may be disappointed when their favorite features are missing from the finished application. This can be a particular problem with projects that release a series of versions of the application (as in an incremental project) and someone's pet feature isn't included in release 1.0.

To avoid this, make sure customers understand which features will be included and when.

➤ Attachment to code—Sometimes, developers become attached to the prototype's code. That can make them follow the methods used by that code (or even reuse the code wholesale) even if a better design exists. This can be a particularly bad problem with throwaway prototypes where the initial code might have low quality.

To avoid this, make sure developers understand that the code should change if a better design is available. Hold design reviews and code reviews to make sure no one is stuck following a prototype approach if there's a better alternative.

➤ Never-ending prototypes—Throwaway prototypes are supposed to be built relatively quickly to provide fast feedback. Sometimes, developers spend far too much time refining a prototype to make it look better and to include more features that aren't actually necessary.

To avoid this, make sure the prototype doesn't include any more than is absolutely necessary to give customers a feel for how the program will work. Don't waste time making the prototype more flexible than necessary. Do the least amount of work that you can get away with. For example, a prototype rarely needs to use a database. Usually you can just hard-wire data into the program to get a feel for how the final program will look. If customers decide that they need to see more, they can say so.

Prototypes are great for helping you decide on the direction you should take. They can help define the user interface and other features, make sure customers and developers are on the same page, and let developers explore different solutions.

SPIRAL

The *spiral model* (not to be confused with a "death spiral" or "circling the drain") was first described in 1986 by Barry Boehm. He describes it as a "process model generator." It uses a risk-driven approach to help project teams decide on what development approach to take for various parts of the project. For example, if you don't understand all of the requirements, then you might use an iterative approach for developing them.

The general spiral approach shown in Figure 18.3 consists of four basic phases.

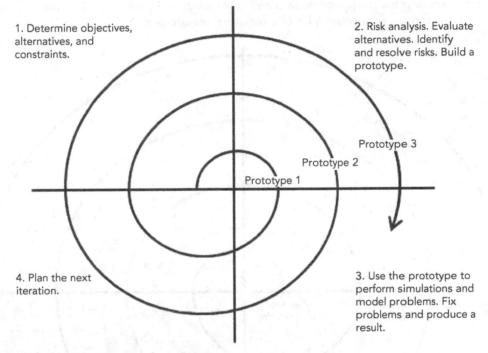

1. Determine objectives, alternatives, and constraints.

2. Risk analysis. Evaluate alternatives. Identify and resolve risks. Build a prototype.

Prototype 3

Prototype 2

Prototype 1

4. Plan the next iteration.

3. Use the prototype to perform simulations and model problems. Fix problems and produce a result.

FIGURE 18.3: The spiral process uses four phases.

In the first phase (which some call the planning phase), you determine the objectives of the current cycle. You define any alternatives to and constraints on the objectives.

In the second phase (which some call the risk analysis phase), you perform a risk analysis to determine what the biggest risk factors are that could prevent you from achieving this cycle's objectives. You resolve the risks and build a prototype to achieve your objectives. (Note that this may not be a program. For example, if the goal of the current cycle is to build requirements, then this will be a set of prototype requirements.)

In the third phase (which some call the engineering phase), you use the prototype you just built to evaluate your solution. You perform simulations and model specific problems to see if you're on the right track. (For example, you might run through a bunch of use cases and operational scenarios to see if your prototype requirements can handle them.) You use what you learn to achieve the original objectives. After this phase, you should have something concrete to show for your efforts.

In the fourth phase (which some call the evaluation phase), you evaluate your progress so far and make sure the project's major stakeholders agree that the solution you came up with is correct and that the project should continue. If they decide you've made a mistake, you run another lap around the spiral to fix whatever problems remain. (You identify the missed objectives, evaluate alternatives, identify and resolve risks, and produce another prototype.) After you're sure you're on the right track, you plan the next trip around the spiral.

For a concrete example, consider Figure 18.4. The first trip around the spiral builds the project requirements. The team examines alternatives, identifies the largest risks (perhaps the customers' performance requirements are unclear), resolves the risks, and builds a prototype set of requirements. Team members then use the prototype to analyze the requirements and verify that they are correct. At that point, the verified requirements become the actual requirements.

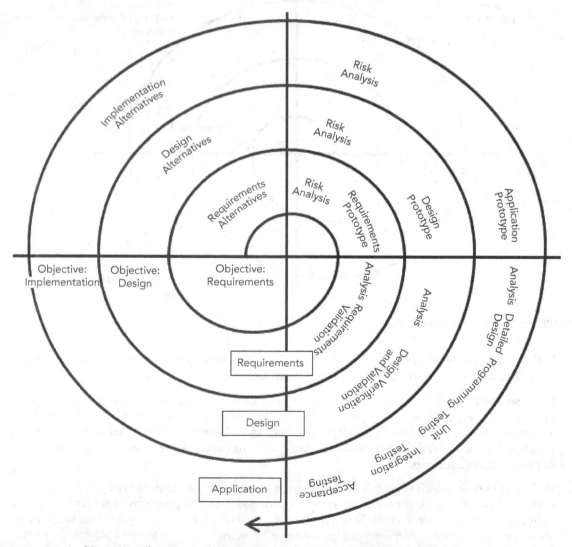

FIGURE 18.4: In this project, the major risks were requirements, design, and implementation.

The next trip around the spiral builds the application design. The team evaluates design alternatives, identifies and resolves the major risks, and builds a prototype design. Team members analyze the design and verify that it makes sense. The prototype design then becomes the actual design.

The final trip around the spiral drives the application's implementation. The team evaluates implementation alternatives (although they're probably used to a particular development approach already). They identify risks (perhaps previous projects have had maintenance issues) and resolve them (they decide to have more code reviews). The team then builds an operational prototype that shows how the program will work. They use the prototype to verify that everything is on track, and then they actually build the application. In this cycle, the implementation steps are broken down into detailed design, programming, unit testing, integration testing, and acceptance testing.

This example doesn't include every cycle that you might want to perform. For example, you might want to make separate user interface design or database design cycles.

Clarifications

Since he initially described the spiral approach, Boehm has made several clarifications, mostly to correct mistakes people made interpreting the method. Those clarifications include the following:

➤ This is not simply a series of waterfall models drawn in a spiral and executed one after another to form an incremental approach. In fact, you could use multiple spirals to build different versions of an application.

➤ The activities need not follow a single spiral sequence. For example, you could spin the user interface design and database design off into completely separate spirals that both feed into an overall project cycle.

➤ You can add items, remove items, or perform items in different orders in a specific spiral model as needed. The activities you need to perform depend on the project.

Boehm further defined six characteristics that spiral development cycles should follow:

1. Define tasks concurrently. There's no need to perform everything sequentially.

2. Perform the following four tasks in each cycle (basically, they are goals of the four phases):

   a. Consider the goals of all stakeholders.

   b. Identify and evaluate alternative approaches for satisfying the stakeholders' goals.

   c. Identify and resolve risks in the selected approach.

   d. Make sure the stakeholders agree that the results of the current cycle are correct. Get the stakeholders' approval to continue the project into the next cycle.

3. Use risk to determine the level of effort. For example, perform enough code reviews to minimize the risk of buggy code, but don't perform so many reviews that you risk finishing late.

4. Use risk to determine the level of detail. For example, put enough work into the requirements to minimize the risk of the application not satisfying the customers, but don't overspecify requirements to the point where they restrict the developers' flexibility.

5. Use anchor milestones. Boehm later added the following anchor milestones to track the project's progress:

    a. Life Cycle Objectives (LCOs)—When the stakeholders agree that the project's technical and management approach is defined enough to satisfy all of the stakeholders' goals, then it has reached its LCO milestone.

    b. Life Cycle Architecture (LCA)—When the stakeholders agree that the project's approach can satisfy the goals and all significant risks have been eliminated or mitigated, then it has reached its LCA milestone.

    c. Initial Operational Capability (IOC)—When there has been sufficient preparation to satisfy everyone's goals, then the project has reached its IOC milestone and should be installed. The preparations include everything needed to make the project a success. For example, the application is ready and tested, the user site is set up, the users have been trained, and the maintenance programmers are ready to take over.

6. Focus on the system and its life cycle rather than on short-term issues such as writing an initial design or writing code. This is intended to help you focus on the big picture.

Pros and Cons

The spiral approach is considered one of the most useful and flexible development approaches. The following list summarizes some of its main advantages:

➤ Its spiral structure gives stakeholders a lot of points for review and making "go" or "no-go" decisions.

➤ It emphasizes risk analysis. If you identify and resolve risks correctly, it should lead to eventual success.

➤ It can accommodate change reasonably well. Simply make any necessary changes and then run through a cycle to identify and resolve any risks they create.

➤ Estimates such as time and effort required become more accurate over time as cycles are finished and risks are removed from the project.

The following list summarizes some of the spiral approach's biggest disadvantages:

➤ It's complicated.

➤ Because it's complicated, it often requires more resources than simpler approaches.

➤ Risk analysis can be difficult.

➤ The complication isn't always worth the effort, particularly for low-risk projects.

➤ Stakeholders must have the time and skills needed to review the project periodically to make sure that each cycle is completed satisfactorily.

➤ Time and effort estimates become more accurate as cycles are finished, but initially those estimates may not be very good.

➤ It doesn't work well with small projects. You could end up spending more time on risk analysis than you'd need to build the entire application with a simpler approach. (One of my favorite approaches for very small projects is to just crank out most of the code over the weekend. Then I can tell the client with some confidence how many hours it "will" take.)

For those reasons, the spiral approach is most useful with large high-risk projects and projects with uncertain or changeable requirements.

UNIFIED PROCESS

Despite its name, the *Unified Process (UP)* isn't actually a process. Instead, it's an iterative and incremental development framework that you can customize to fit your business and projects.

The Unified Process approach is divided into the following four phases:

➤ Inception—During this phase you come up with the project's idea. (Or as in the movie *Inception*, someone else comes up with the project's idea and makes you think it's yours.) This should be a short phase where you provide a business case, identify risks, provide an initial schedule, and sketch out the project's general goals. It should not include detailed requirements that might restrict the developers.

➤ Elaboration—During this phase you create the project requirements. You build use cases, architectural diagrams, and class hierarchies. You need to specify the system, but you still don't want to restrict developers with unnecessarily detailed requirements. The main goals are to identify and address risks so that the project doesn't fail later. Normally, this phase is divided into several iterations with the first addressing the most important risks.

➤ Construction—During this phase you write, test, and debug the code. This phase is divided into several increments, each of which ends with a tested, high-quality working executable program that you can release to the users. The increments implement the most important features first.

➤ Transition—During this phase you transfer the project to customers and the long-term maintenance team. Based on feedback from users, you might make changes and refinements and then release a new version, so this phase can include several iterations. This phase includes of all the usual transitioning tasks such as staging, building the user environment (computers, networks, coffee machines, and so forth), user documentation, and user training.

You can add more phases if you want your team to continue managing the application after initial development. For example, you might add the following two phases to model the application's life cycle after transition:

➤ Production—During this phase, users use the application. (That's why we call them "users.") The normal Unified Process assumes that the development team doesn't continue producing new versions of the application during this phase.

➤ Disposal—During this phase, you remove the application and send it off to application Valhalla where it can reminisce about its glory days with other applications such as Myspace and Napster. You then move users to a replacement system. If you're building the replacement, then this phase overlaps with the new project's transition phase.

Figure 18.5 shows the relative sizes of the Unified Process phases. A rectangle's height represents the resources (mostly the number of people in the development team) required for that phase. A rectangle's width represents the amount of time spent on that phase.

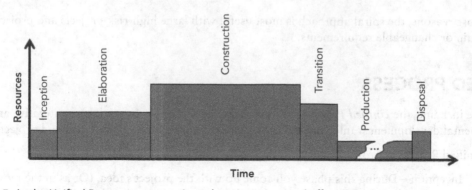

FIGURE 18.5: In the Unified Process, construction takes more time and effort than the other phases.

Figure 18.6 shows the relative amounts of different kinds of work during the project's phases and the iterations within those phases. For example, implementation work (programming) is relatively light during inception and elaboration, picks up during the construction iterations, and then tapers off during transition.

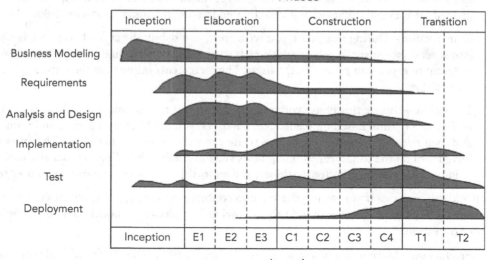

FIGURE 18.6: In the Unified Process, the amounts of different kinds of work grow and shrink during different project phases.

The project shown in Figure 18.6 had three elaboration iterations, four construction iterations, and two transition phases.

Pros and Cons

The following list summarizes some of the main advantages of the Unified Process approach:

➤ The iterative approach to the elaboration, construction, and transition phases enables you to incrementally define the requirements and assemble the application.

➤ The elaboration iterations focus on risks and risk mitigation to improve the project's chance of success.

➤ It can accommodate different development models flexibly. For example, you could use a series of waterfalls or an agile approach in the construction phase.

➤ The inception and elaboration phases generate a lot of documentation that can help new developers join the team later.

➤ It can enable incremental releases if wanted.

Some of the Unified Process approach's disadvantages are similar to those of the spiral approach. The following list summarizes some of the biggest Unified Process disadvantages:

➤ It's complicated. (Although not quite as confusing as the spiral approach. That one can make people dizzy.)

➤ Because it's complicated, it often requires more resources than simpler approaches.

➤ Risk analysis can be difficult.

➤ The complication isn't always worth the effort, particularly for low-risk projects.

➤ It doesn't work well with small projects. You could end up spending more time on inception and elaboration than you'd need to build the entire application with a simpler approach.

Like the spiral approach, the Unified Process approach is most useful with large high-risk projects and projects with uncertain or changeable requirements.

Rational Unified Process

The *Rational Unified Process (RUP)* is IBM's version of the Unified Process. It uses the same four basic phases defined by UP: inception, elaboration, construction, and transition.

It also uses the same standard engineering disciplines (on the left in Figure 18.6): business modeling, requirements, analysis and design, implementation, test, and deployment. It also adds three "supporting disciplines": configuration and change management, project management, and environment. (*Environment* refers to customizing the process for the development organization and the current project.)

The main advantages to RUP over UP are the tools provided by IBM that make using the process easier. Those tools include artifact templates, document production and sharing, change request tracking, visual modeling, performance profiling, and more.

ARTIFACTUALLY

In RUP, an *artifact* is a final or intermediate result that is produced by the project. The RUP includes documents (such as design documents and deployment plans), models (such as use cases and design models), and model elements (pieces of models such as classes or subsystems).

As you might expect, the advantages and disadvantages of RUP are similar to those for UP.

There are several variations on UP and RUP. For example, the *Open Unified Process (OpenUP)* is a tool that makes using the Unified Process easier. To make OpenUP more accessible to its target audience (smallish projects with 3–6 team members working on projects lasting 3–6 months), it omits most of the optional features provided by RUP, so it's easier to use.

OpenUP is part of the open-source Eclipse Process Framework. For more information on OpenUP, see `www.eclipse.org/epf/openup_component/openup_vision.php`. For more information on the Eclipse Process Framework, see `www.eclipse.org/epf`.

The *Agile Unified Process (AUP)* is another simplified version of RUP. It brings agile methods such as test-driven development and agile modeling to UP. In 2012, AUP was superseded by *Disciplined Agile Delivery (DAD*, insert your favorite dad joke here).

DAD has a structure that's somewhat similar to UP. In particular, it has the three phases: inception, construction, and transition. (Elaboration is divided between inception and construction.) DAD also borrows many techniques from different agile development approaches such as scrum, Extreme Programming, kanban, and others. I won't say any more about DAD until the next chapter, after you've learned more about those agile approaches.

CLEANROOM

The *Cleanroom* model emphasizes defect prevention rather than defect removal. The idea is to build the application in steps that are carefully monitored and tested to prevent anything bad from entering into the application. (The name is inspired by the way a manufacturing clean room prevents dust and other gunk from getting into the manufacturing process.)

The following list summarizes Cleanroom's basic principles:

➤ Formal methods—Code is produced using formal mathematical methods that help to ensure that the code satisfies the design models. Code reviews also help verify that the code correctly implements the required behavior.

➤ Statistical quality control—Code is produced incrementally. Each increment's quality is measured to ensure that the project is making acceptable progress.

➤ Statistical testing—Testing uses statistical experiments to estimate the application quality. (This requires some serious statistical analysis so that you can not only estimate the application's quality but also calculate a level of confidence for that estimate.)

Unfortunately, the mathematics needed to do the statistical analysis is quite intimidating. I like math more than most people (my C# Helper website www.csharphelper.com is littered with mathematical examples for C# developers), but even I hesitate when faced with statistical testing models. Some of them are seriously complicated and confusing.

Still, the basic ideas behind Cleanroom are excellent. First, if you don't let bad code sneak into the application, then you won't need to fix it later.

Second, if you evaluate the quality of the application after every iteration, you can track how effective your development effort is. You can also fine-tune development if the number of defects increases in a particular iteration.

Even if you don't have the tools or expertise to follow the Cleanroom process in every detail, it's worth borrowing those two principles.

COWBOY CODING

I briefly mentioned cowboy coding way back in the introduction to the first part of the book, so I feel like I owe you at least some explanation. Cowboy coding is more of a group mindset than a design methodology.

In *cowboy coding*, the developers have almost complete autonomy over the project. They control the release schedule, architecture, designs, language, tools, code style, and just about everything else with very little day-to-day management control. The management (or customers) provide only high-level guidance such as final deadlines and high-level goals. They may provide the goals as general (possibly vague) statements of goals, or as use cases.

Within this freewheeling framework, the developers could use just about any methodology. For example, they could use a waterfall approach, Extreme Programming, or anything in between.

Often this approach is used for experimental or exploratory projects where the final outcome is unknown. In those cases, it allows the developers to gallop off in all directions chasing ideas that might be interesting, techniques that might benefit the project's goals, coyotes, tumbleweeds, or whatever.

Cowboy coding's advantage is that it allows experienced developers great room for creativity. Its disadvantages include just about everything else. It doesn't guarantee reliable (or even any) release schedules, frequent customer interaction, the ability to adjust to changing requirements, or anything else provided by other methodologies.

(Cowboy coding is also often used as a derogatory term, implying a lack of discipline. It's similar to terms like "nerd" and "hacker," which can be used as an insult or adopted as a badge of honor.)

SUMMARY

Iterated development is one technique for trying to keep a software engineering project on track. It lets you periodically review your progress to ensure that the application is heading toward a result that satisfies the requirements. It also lets you refine and correct the requirements over time if necessary.

Prototyping lets you study pieces of an application so that you can make adjustments. Models such as spiral and Unified Process (and its variants) use iteration to help the development and requirements eventually meet. Some of those models also place an emphasis on risk management to reduce the chances of the project failing.

In addition to keeping a project heading in the right direction, iterative and incremental methods allow you to release partial implementations of the application if they are useful. The next chapter describes other techniques that let you give the users partial functionality as soon as possible.

EXERCISES

1. Suppose your customer wants an application with 10 features and insists that the application is completely useless unless all 10 are implemented with full fidelity. Would there be any benefit to iterative, incremental, or agile approaches?

2. Explain why a throwaway prototype inherently uses an agile approach.

3. How does an incremental prototype differ from an incremental project? What would you need to do to use an incremental prototype in an incremental project?

4. Can you use an evolutionary prototype in a predictive project (such as waterfall)?

5. Can you use an incremental prototype in a predictive project?

6. Look at the project shown in Figure 18.6. Why might the deployment tasks start during the elaboration phase instead of at the beginning of the transition phase? What deployment tasks might you be performing during elaboration? What tasks might you be performing during construction?

7. Look at the project shown in Figure 18.6. The testing tasks begin in the inception phase before the implementation tasks start. What are you testing during inception if there isn't any code yet?

8. Look at the project shown in Figure 18.6. What kinds of code are the team members writing during the elaboration phase? What kinds of tests are they performing during that phase?

9. Add a new row to the bottom of Figure 18.6 that shows the amount of customer interaction required during different phases of development for an in-house project.

10. Draw a diagram showing how the phases of the waterfall model match up with those of Unified Process. What are the main differences?

11. Indicate whether the following items describe the predictive, iterative, incremental, or agile approach.

    a. Features are released as soon as they are useful. Over time, existing features are improved, and new features are added.
    b. Features are released one at a time with full fidelity.
    c. All of the application's features are released at the same time with full fidelity.
    d. Every feature is released quickly with low fidelity and then improved over time.

12. Which approach (predictive, iterative, incremental, or agile) gets a working program to users the soonest? Latest? What can you say about the timing of the other two approaches?

13. Suppose you're a real estate developer building a neighborhood containing 100 houses. How would each of the predictive, iterative, incremental, and agile approaches correspond to home sales? Assume the "features" of the project are the houses and "releasing a feature" means allowing people to move into a home. Which of the approaches could work? Which approach do developers actually use (as far as you know)?

14. Suppose you're a different real estate developer who specializes in more interesting projects. This time you're building an amusement park. How would each of the predictive, iterative, incremental, and agile approaches correspond to opening the park? The "features" of the project are the rides, snack shops, and games of "chance" (which actually leave very little to chance). "Releasing a feature" means allowing people to ride on a ride, buy greasy food at high prices, or use darts to try to pop balloons that seem to be made of Kevlar. Which of the approaches could work?

WHAT YOU LEARNED IN THIS CHAPTER

➤ Predictive approaches make one big release when everything is done.

➤ Iterative approaches release every feature with low fidelity and then improve fidelity over time.

➤ Incremental approaches release features as they are finished with high fidelity.

➤ Agile approaches combine iterative and incremental approaches. They release features when they are usable. Over time they improve existing features and add new ones.

➤ A prototype is a simplified model that lets you study the behavior of some part of an application. Prototypes are not always software.

➤ Horizontal prototypes have breadth but little depth. They are typically used to study user interfaces and show customers what the application will look like.

➤ Vertical prototypes have little breadth and great depth. They are typically used to study architecture and programming issues and show developers what the application will act like.

➤ You don't reuse the code in a throwaway prototype. Ever!

➤ Over time an evolutionary prototype is refined and improved until it becomes the finished application.

➤ In incremental prototyping, you build separate prototypes of the application's features and then combine them to form the finished application.

➤ The spiral model uses a sequence of repeating phases (planning, risk analysis, engineering, and evaluation) to identify and neutralize project risks.

➤ Unified Process is an iterative and incremental approach that uses the phases inception, elaboration, construction, and transition. The last three phases are iterative.

➤ Rational Unified Process is IBM's version of Unified Process. Other versions include OpenUP, Agile Unified Process, and Disciplined Agile Delivery.

➤ Cleanroom uses formal mathematical methods, statistical quality control, and statistical testing to prevent defects from entering an application's code. Its two principles, "Don't let bad code into the application" and "Evaluate the quality of the application after each iteration," are worth using in any development approach.

➤ Cowboy coding is an approach where developers have almost complete autonomy. It is often used for experimental or exploratory projects where the final outcome is unknown.

➤ You shouldn't ride roller coasters that don't have full fidelity.

19

RAD

The problem with quick and dirty, as some people have said, is that the dirty remains long after the quick has been forgotten.

—*Steve McConnell*

Excellent firms don't believe in excellence—only in constant improvement and constant change.

—*Tom Peters*

What You Will Learn in This Chapter:

➤ General RAD principles

➤ Agile methods

➤ James Martin RAD, XP, scrum, Lean, Crystal, FDD, DAD, DSDM, and kanban

➤ Principles, roles, and values that are common to several RAD development approaches

When you boil down software engineering to its most fundamental level, its goals are simply to produce useful software as quickly as possible.

All of the software development models described so far focus on the first of those goals: producing useful applications. They try to ensure that the result meets the specifications and that the specifications actually specify something useful. Iterative models such as iterated waterfall and Unified Process even allow you to change the project's course of direction in case it wanders off track or the requirements change over time.

Techniques such as prototyping help ensure that the specification gives the customer a result that is useful. Models such as Unified Process emphasize risk management to ensure that the development effort succeeds. All of the models spend at least some effort encouraging good programming techniques so that the result is robust and maintainable.

However, none of the models described so far actually focus on the second goal of software engineering: producing software quickly. That's not to say those models encourage a lackadaisical approach. None of them say developers should sit around doing nothing. (Although I've met a few developers who would have helped their projects more if they *had* been assigned to do nothing.) Many models help you track tasks so that you can quickly decide if a task is falling behind and jeopardizing the project's schedule.

The models discussed so far don't focus on increasing development speed. They do things to limit the number of bugs, which can save you time in the long run, but they don't provide techniques for accelerating development.

This chapter describes *rapid application development (RAD)* models. These models incorporate some of the best features of the models described in the preceding chapters, plus new features that help developers give useful results to the end user quickly.

RAD VS. RAD

James Martin, one of the pioneers of RAD in the 1980s, described a specific development methodology in his book *Rapid Application Development* (Macmillan, 1991). Later the terms "rapid application development" and "RAD" expanded to include a variety of other models that favor rapid development, so there's sometimes confusion about the two uses of the term.

This chapter uses *rapid application development* and *RAD* to mean the more general genre of models. *James Martin RAD* means his specific model.

Some tools also bill themselves as RAD tools. Some of them provide a framework that you can use to follow a particular RAD development model. Others are merely tools that you can use to do things rapidly. (Still others probably just mean "rad" in the 1980s sense of being cool.) For example, rapid prototyping tools can help you build user interface prototypes relatively quickly and easily. Those tools can be useful in a RAD project, but they don't make it a RAD project.

To see the difference, ask yourself whether you could apply a tool to a non-RAD project. For example, could you use a prototyping tool in a waterfall project? Sure. Could you use James Martin RAD in a waterfall project? Not really.

Similarly, some development environments claim to be RAD environments. For example, some people consider the Visual Studio development environment to be a RAD tool. It certainly lets you build programs rapidly and you can easily use it in a RAD project, but it isn't inherently RADish, and you could easily use it in a waterfall project. (In fact, I've done that many times.)

The techniques used by RAD models push developers to generate as much high-quality code as possible as quickly as possible. Some of the techniques may seem a bit strange. They may seem even stranger if you have experience with software engineering, depending on which development models you've used before.

Some of the methods may seem counterintuitive or like some sort of touchy-feely new age nonsense focused more on the developers than on the code. Remember that the code is written for the programmers, not for the computer. The computer can read any gibberish you dump into the compiler. Code must be written for people if you want them to read, understand, debug, modify, and maintain it. That means it's essential to keep the developers happy and productive.

RAD PRINCIPLES

One of the driving forces behind RAD is the idea that things always change. As Heraclitus said, "The only thing that is constant is change." He didn't mention software requirements because he lived roughly between 535 BC and 475 BC, but if he had known about software engineering, I'm sure he would have felt vindicated. Requirements change often, and RAD projects adjust to those changes.

Sometimes, at the end of a project, the customers realize that the requirements didn't accurately describe their needs. Even though the application satisfies the *requirements*, it doesn't satisfy their *needs*.

Other times the customers' needs change during the project's development. The company's goals, competition, or customer desires change, so by the time the application is ready, no one wants it.

Those facts lead to an obvious problem with Big Design Up Front (BDUF) models: by the time an application is finished, it doesn't satisfy the customers' needs. Iterative models help keep a project on track, but they have their limits. If you perform a new iteration every year or so, you could wander far off track before you realize you're heading in the wrong direction.

RAD methods take iterative ideas to the extreme. Instead of using iterations lasting a year or two, their iterations last a month, a week, or even less. Some RAD techniques also apply iteration to everything, not just to programming. They apply iteration to requirements gathering, requirements validation, and design.

The following list summarizes some of the most common techniques used in RAD development models:

➤ Small teams (approximately half a dozen people or fewer). That leads to projects of limited scope. (Six people probably can't write a million-line application in a year.)

➤ Requirements gathering through focus groups, workshops, facilitated meetings, prototyping, and brainstorming.

➤ Requirements validation through iterated prototypes, use cases, and constant customer testing of designs.

➤ Repeated customer testing of designs as they evolve.

➤ Constant integration and testing of new code into the application. (And I mean *constant*! As often as daily.)

➤ Informal reviews and communication among team members.

➤ Short iterations lasting between a few months and as little as a week.

➤ Deferring complicated features for later releases. Doing just enough work to get the job done.

➤ *Timeboxing*, which is RADspeak for setting a tight delivery schedule for producing something, usually the next iteration of the application. The scope can change (for example, you might defer a feature to the next iteration), but the completion date for the iteration cannot.

ITERATION 0

Agile models sort of assume the project begins in the middle. The project starts and you're immediately zipping through iterations producing high-quality increments for the customers.

In practice, projects generally need some startup time to put things in place for later development. During that period, you'll set up the team's hardware, install the development environment, and find out which local restaurants and cupcake bakeries provide late night delivery.

You'll also meet the customers and find out generally what the project is about. You'll probably build different kinds of models describing the system you're going to build, gather basic requirements, and do everything else that needs to be done before you actually start iterations.

You can think of those activities as a separate stage before the project starts if you like (or if that lets you claim those tasks shouldn't count toward your budget), but some developers call those startup-oriented bootstrapping kinds of activities *iteration 0*.

While you're performing those startup tasks, you're not directly delivering value to the customer, so agile projects generally try to keep iteration 0 as short as possible. These tasks are important, but the sooner you start iteration 1, the sooner you can deliver something to the customers. So keep iteration 0 simple.

As with all software engineering approaches, RAD models have their share of advantages and disadvantages. The following list shows some general RAD advantages:

➤ More accurate requirements. The customers can adjust the requirements as needed throughout the project.

➤ The ability to track changing requirements. If requirements must change (within reason), the project can start tracking the new requirements in the next iteration.

➤ Frequent customer feedback and involvement. In addition to helping keep the project on track, this keeps the users engaged with the project.

➤ Reduced development time. If everything goes smoothly, you don't spend as much time writing requirements in excessive detail.

➤ Encourages code reuse. One of the key RAD ideas is to do whatever it takes to get the current iteration done. If an existing piece of code (perhaps from a previous project or exhumed from the Internet) does what you need it to do (or even almost what you need it to do), timeboxing encourages you to use that code instead of writing something new.

➤ Possible early releases with limited functionality.

➤ Constant testing promotes high-quality code and eases integration issues. Code is tested earlier and more often, so bugs are flushed out sooner when we all know they're easier to fix.

➤ Risk mitigation. Before each iteration, you can look for potential risks and handle them.

➤ Greater chance of success. BDUF projects sometimes spend a lot of time following an incorrect path before discovering that they're wandering into the weeds and they need to be radically redone or even canceled. Frequent increments allow RAD projects to detect and correct problems quickly before they become insurmountable.

The following list summarizes some general RAD disadvantages:

➤ Resistance to change. It can be hard to get existing software engineering groups to adopt new RAD models, particularly given how odd some of their techniques can seem. (A nineteenth-century blacksmith's apprentice would be more comfortable with pair programming than many BDUF programmers.) (I actually had a project canceled once because the customer got cold feet about halfway through.)

➤ Doesn't handle large systems well. Big systems require a lot of effort, and that usually means a lot of people. The communication overhead alone makes it hard to run large projects in a RAD model. (If you can partition the project into nicely disconnected pieces, you may have a chance.)

➤ Requires more skilled team members. Every team member does not need to be a programming Obi Wan Kenobi, but small RAD teams can't include too many complete beginners.

➤ Requires access to scarce resources. Frequent customer interaction is essential to keep the project on track. Often that interaction must be with customers who are experts in their fields, and those people tend to be in high demand.

➤ Adds extra overhead if the requirements are known completely and correctly in advance.

➤ Less managerial control. Many managers have trouble allowing a project to head off in its own ever-changing direction. (If you think of the project as a hunting pack chasing a fox wherever it leads, a manager may wonder what happens if the pack scents a rabbit.)

➤ Sometimes results in a less than optimal design. (See the following text.)

➤ Unpredictability. Some customers just want to know how much and how long, and they really aren't interested in shaping the application throughout its development over an unknown period of time.

A RAD project's small iterations occasionally lead to a suboptimal design. Sometimes, the best design is too big to implement in a single iteration, so a RAD approach won't get there incrementally.

As an analogy, consider the *International Space Station (ISS)*. Because it was built from pieces that had to squeeze into a rocket, it was constructed incrementally over many years, involving more than 115 space flights and 180 spacewalks. It's amazingly complicated and a remarkable feat of engineering, but I can't help thinking it would be different if it hadn't been built incrementally. Perhaps something more like the torus-shaped Elysium habitat from the movie of the same name. (And what would Apple have designed if it had been given the job? I'm sure it would have been elegantly beautiful, cost five times as much, and been called the iStation or perhaps iISS.)

JAMES MARTIN RAD

James Martin's original RAD model uses the following four phases:

➤ Requirements planning—During this phase, the users, executive champion, management, team leaders, and other stakeholders agree on the project's general goals and requirements. The requirements should be specified in a general way so that they don't restrict later development unnecessarily. When the stakeholders agree on the requirements and the project receives approval to continue, the user design phase begins.

➤ User design—The users and team members work together to convert the requirements into a workable design. They use techniques such as focus groups, workshops, prototyping, and brainstorming to come up with a workable design.

➤ Construction—The developers go to work building the application. The users continue to review the pieces of the application as the developers build them to make corrections and suggestions for improvements.

➤ Cutover—The developers deliver the finished application to the users. (You can use the usual cutover strategies such as staged delivery, gradual cutover, or incremental deployment.)

The user design and construction phases overlap, with the users constantly providing adjustments to the developers in a sort of continuous feedback loop. The project iterates the user design and construction phases as needed. When the application has met all of the requirements, it is delivered to the users.

Figure 19.1 shows the way a James Martin RAD project moves through its four phases.

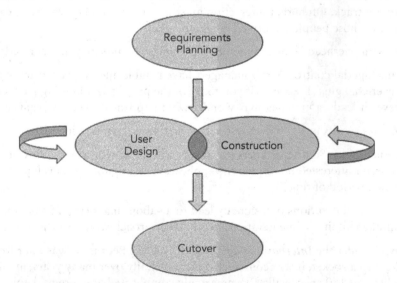

FIGURE 19.1: In James Martin RAD, the user design and construction phases iterate until the application meets its requirements.

AGILE

Agile development is more a set of guidelines than an actual development model. It includes a set of principles that its founders believe can help with any development effort. Because it's a set of guidelines, there are many ways you can interpret its rules. For example, people often say a particular method is "an agile technique" because it attempts to address one or more of the guidelines.

In 2001 a group of developers got together at Snowbird resort in Utah to talk about lightweight alternatives to BDUF methodologies such as waterfall and spiral. After their discussions (and I suspect a lot of skiing and perhaps some après-ski hot tubbing), they published the *Manifesto for Agile Software Development*. You can read this at `https://agilemanifesto.org`).

Some of the original authors later formed the nonprofit Agile Alliance (`www.agilealliance.org`) to promote agile development ideas.

Like any good manifesto, this one's values are general enough to apply to just about any situation. Of course, that also makes them flexible enough to use in support of all sorts of arguments that may not make sense.

For example, the value "Working software over comprehensive documentation" is sometimes used to justify providing little or no documentation. ("But the Agile Manifesto says I don't have to write any documentation!" See my tirade about just barely good enough documentation in the section "Code Documentation" in Chapter 2, "Before the Beginning.")

The manifesto's site and the Agile Alliance site provide some elaboration to make it a bit easier to understand exactly what the authors had in mind. For example, the following paragraph by Jim Highsmith from the manifesto history page (`https://agilemanifesto.org/history.html`) clarifies some of the authors' ideas:

> The Agile movement is not anti-methodology, in fact, many of us want to restore credibility to the word methodology. We want to restore a balance. We embrace modeling, but not in order to file some diagram in a dusty corporate repository. We embrace documentation, but not hundreds of pages of never-maintained and rarely-used tomes. We plan, but recognize the limits of planning in a turbulent environment. Those who would brand proponents of XP or scrum or any of the other Agile Methodologies as "hackers" are ignorant of both the methodologies and the original definition of the term hacker.

From this paragraph and the manifesto, you can take a couple of useful tidbits of information.

- ➤ Agile is not a methodology. You can use it to enhance methodologies.
- ➤ Modeling is okay but not just for the sake of crossing off some item required by management.
- ➤ Documentation is great but not hundreds of pages that will never be used. (So you probably shouldn't pay documenters by the number of pounds of documentation they generate.)
- ➤ Planning is good, but be aware that plans don't always work out in a changing environment.
- ➤ Some of the authors were tired of being called hackers.

In addition to the manifesto itself, the manifesto's website lists the following 12 guiding principles (at `https://agilemanifesto.org/principles.html`).

1. Our highest priority is to satisfy the customer through early and continuous delivery of valuable software.

2. Welcome changing requirements, even late in development. Agile processes harness change for the customer's competitive advantage.

3. Deliver working software frequently, from a couple of weeks to a couple of months, with a preference to the shorter timescale.

4. Business people and developers must work together daily throughout the project.

5. Build projects around motivated individuals. Give them the environment and support they need and trust them to get the job done.

6. The most efficient and effective method of conveying information to and within a development team is face-to-face conversation.

7. Working software is the primary measure of progress.

8. Agile processes promote sustainable development. The sponsors, developers, and users should be able to maintain a constant pace indefinitely.

9. Continuous attention to technical excellence and good design enhances agility.

10. Simplicity—the art of maximizing the amount of work not done—is essential.

11. The best architectures, requirements, and designs emerge from self-organizing teams.

12. At regular intervals, the team reflects on how to become more effective, then tunes and adjusts its behavior accordingly.

Most of these are reasonably self-explanatory, so they don't need further explanation, although I will say a bit about self-organizing teams shortly.

Notice that the agile values and principles don't actually tell you how to implement them. For example, the second principle says you should welcome changing requirements, but it doesn't say whether you should do that with Sashimi, James Martin RAD, or some other approach. You could even use an incremental waterfall, although accommodating change late in the development process would be harder. Methodologies such as scrum and Extreme Programming, which are described later in this chapter, were designed with the agile values and principles in mind, so they generally do a good job of following them.

WHAT'S AGILE ENOUGH?

The fact that you can apply the agile values and principles to different development models makes them useful in a lot of situations. Unfortunately, it also can make it difficult to decide whether a particular development approach is "agile enough."

Suppose you're at a job interview and your prospective boss asks, "Have you ever worked on an agile project?" If you've used scrum, kanban, or one of the other well-known agile methods, then you can safely say yes.

If you've used James Martin RAD, which by my reckoning gets a grade of B on the agile scale, then it's *probably* safe to say yes and then add a few words of explanation.

If you added only a few agile techniques such as pair programming and test-driven development (described later in this chapter) to a waterfall project, then you should probably say, "No but. . ." and then explain exactly what you did. It's better to leave the interviewer thinking, "Well, he didn't use an agile model, but he understands some of the agile techniques," instead of, "The fool thinks waterfall is agile! Mwah, hah, hah! Next applicant!"

Self-Organizing Teams

The 11th agile principle touts the wonders of self-organizing teams. So what is a self-organizing team and how can you organize one (so to speak)? I mentioned this briefly in Chapter 3, "The Team," but it's important enough in the agile context to deserve some elaboration.

A self-organizing team is one that has the flexibility and authority to find its own methods for achieving its goals. Teams with different levels of authority may also set their own goals, track their progress, and even pick the team members.

Storming the Ridge

For an example of a self-managing team, imagine a common scene in war movies. The platoon's advance is stymied by enemy fire and the sergeant yells, "Johnson, I need you and two 'volunteers' to take out that machine gun nest!" The sergeant doesn't care how the job gets done or who does it as long as the problem is eliminated.

Johnson might pick his two closest buddies and run screaming up the hill, firing from the hip, only to be gunned down just as he drops a satchel charge into the enemy emplacement. Or he and his comrades might lob a few RPGs over the ridge until they get lucky and hit the target. Or he might say, "Sarge, let's retreat a mile or two and call in an airstrike." It's up to Johnson and his two unfortunate friends to come up with a solution. (As the most dramatic, the first solution would probably be the one picked by the movie's director.)

For comparison, the opposite of a self-organizing team is a micromanaged team where the manager tells everyone else exactly what to do and when. (For more information on micromanagement, read some *Dilbert* cartoons, in particular https://dilbert.com/strip/1995-05-29.)

The members of a self-organizing team are motivated, so they take on work without waiting for it to be assigned. They take responsibility for their work and track their own progress. If problems arise, they aren't afraid to ask for help either inside or outside of the team.

The increased sense of ownership the members feel often makes them more enthusiastic and effective at finding good solutions to problems. Ideally, they'll attack any problem that stands in their way eagerly and relentlessly. In practice, you may need to draw straws to see who gets stuck debugging the four color map algorithm (no one really knows how it works), but most of the time the team members can divide up the work in a way that makes everyone more or less happy.

The members communicate as a team to ensure that the group is working toward its goals (which may be set outside of the team, at least at a high level). To communicate effectively, the team members must feel safe. They need to trust each other to use feedback constructively. One way to help make that kind of trust possible is to adopt the rules of egoless programming described in the section "Have Someone Else Test Your Code" in Chapter 13, "Testing."

TRUST ME

If you don't think this kind of trust is essential, try this experiment. Hold a meeting and ask for ideas about some company issue—how to improve the cafeteria food, keep the lunchroom clean, chase the geese off the lawns, whatever. The instant someone offers a suggestion, shout them down and tell them how stupid their idea is. Then see if you can get any suggestions out of the others.

Actually, you should probably skip that experiment. You may never gain everyone's trust. Although it's amazing how many annual company meetings I attended that had more or less that format. People would make suggestions and then upper management would explain why it was a bad idea and dodge any questions.

Unfortunately, self-organizing teams don't always arise spontaneously. Even if you assemble a group of competent, motivated people and tell them to organize themselves, you'll probably need to keep an eye on them. Instead of guiding them like a traditional manager would, you can encourage them to take the initiative and then offer support when they need it. You may also need to buy a striped shirt and a whistle so you can referee once in a while, but hopefully they'll eventually leave you behind and start running the show on their own.

For some more information on self-organizing teams, search the Internet. The article "What Are Self-Organizing Teams?" at www.infoq.com/articles/what-are-self-organising-teams can get you started.

Agile Techniques

Although the Agile Manifesto doesn't tell you how to implement its values and principles, there are several techniques that are fairly common to most agile methods. The following sections describe some of those techniques.

Communication

Agile projects use frequent (sometimes practically continuous) customer communication to keep the project on track. The customers examine the most recent iteration and then offer corrections, suggestions, and change requests. The developers adjust the next iteration accordingly.

Unfortunately, if every customer is talking constantly to every developer, no one has time to get anything done. To improve efficiency, most methods appoint a primary customer representative who becomes the main point of contact between the customers and the developers.

Sometimes, the development team also has a primary contact, often the project manager or technical lead. If the customer contact and developer contact have the authority to make decisions for their respective groups, then they can handle most of the communications and leave everyone else free to perform their other duties.

CUSTOMER MANAGEMENT

I was once on a project that started to have a communication avalanche near the end of the development phase. The customers were excited and eager to see what was happening, so they started calling the developers to get progress reports. At one point, every developer could expect one or two calls every day and we were losing about 10 developer-hours per day.

At that point the project manager made some new rules. At 3:00 p.m. each day, he held a conference call to update any customers who wanted to hear about the project's status. Then he would answer any questions they had.

We didn't really need a single customer contact at that point because the project was settling into its final form, so communication was mostly one-way from the team to the customers. That approach may not work on every project, but it worked well for that one.

Many development models use one or more big boards to display the project's current status. The boards are placed where everyone can see them frequently, so everyone knows exactly where the project stands at all times. (Some people call this board the *information radiator* or just the *big board*.)

Some development models use frequent meetings to make it easier for the developers to communicate. For example, in scrum the team meets every day in a "daily standup" where everyone reviews what they did since the last meeting, what they plan to do before the next meeting, and what might stand in their way. Because there are so many meetings, they must start on time and be short to avoid wasting a lot of precious developer time.

Incremental Development

Agile projects are iterative and incremental. The iterations are relatively short, with durations of a week to a couple of months. Iterations are timeboxed to keep the project moving briskly along.

Each iteration incorporates every development step, including requirements analysis, design, programming, testing, and verification. An iteration is basically a mini-project all by itself.

CROSS-FUNCTIONAL TEAMS

It's also helpful if every team member has a good understanding of every part of the iteration process. In other words, everyone should understand requirement analysis, design, programming, testing, and the rest. That way anyone can spot a problem with any piece of the development process and fix it.

If every member of the team understands all of the development functions, then the team is called *cross-functional*. (Dysfunctional is a very different concept.)

Because each iteration is thoroughly tested, bugs are caught as quickly as possible. That makes them easier to fix because they're most likely to be in the current iteration's code. It also means the code has high quality, so you don't need to waste time fixing old bugs in later iterations.

The goal of each iteration is to have a fully tested application that has high enough quality that you could release it to users. You may not always want to actually do that, however, if the iteration doesn't add enough new features to the project. It's often better to save up the changes and make fewer bigger releases every few months rather than bombarding the users with a new version every week. For example, Table 19.1 shows a possible build schedule for a three-month project.

TABLE 19.1: Release schedule for a three-month project

WEEK	BUILD TYPE	VERSION
1	Test	0.1
2	Test	0.2
3	Test	0.3
4	Test	0.4
5	Release	1.0
6	Test	1.1
7	Test	1.2
8	Release	2.0
9	Test	2.1
10	Test	2.2
11	Test	2.3
12	Release	3.0

Every week the developers build, test, and debug the application. The builds made at the end of weeks 5, 8, and 12 are released to the customers. Note that you don't necessarily need to decide which builds will be released when you start the project. You can just wait until the application has enough new and useful features to justify a new release.

The test builds are *point releases,* so the application's minor version number increases by 1. In the release builds, the application's major version number increases by 1.

VERSION SCHEMES

Different development environments have different version numbering schemes. For example, Visual Studio breaks version information into four pieces. Version 1.2.3.4 means major version 1, minor version 2, build 3, and revision 4.

You can use those fields to give meaning to an application's versions. For example, you could use the fields for the following purposes:

➤ Major—This represents a new major release with significant new features. Major releases come out once or twice a year.

➤ Minor—All nonmajor releases are minor releases.

➤ Build—Each weekly build gets a new build number.

➤ Revision—Builds that are not final weekly builds get a new revision number.

For example, suppose you released version 3.0.0.0 last month and version 3.1.0.0 last week. During this week's testing, you make builds 3.1.0.1 through 3.1.0.13. After you get a final weekly build properly tested and debugged, you rename it 3.1.1.0.

After each iteration, the customers (or customer representatives) review the build to see if the project is still heading in the right direction. Then they can provide feedback.

The most critical type of feedback is a "go/no go" decision. If the project has been hopelessly derailed, it may be best to cancel it and move on, possibly to a new project that takes a different approach.

In some sense, deciding to cancel a project is similar to deciding whether to fold in poker. The goal in poker isn't, as many people think, to build the best possible hand. The goal is actually to decide as quickly as possible whether you're going to beat the other players' hands. If you don't think you can win, you should fold as quickly as possible before you put too much money in the pot.

Similarly, if a software project won't succeed, it's better to decide that as early as possible so that you can cancel it before you waste a lot of time and resources on it.

(Bluffing isn't supposed to be part of the metaphor. In poker, you can try to convince the other players that you have a winning hand even though you don't, hoping that they'll all fold and leave you the pot. In software development, you generally shouldn't bluff and try to keep a dying project alive. I have, however, seen managers keep a project alive long enough to jump to another project and dump the zombie project on someone else.)

Focus on Quality

I've said it before but I'll say it again (and probably again until you're sick of hearing about it): In agile projects, all development must have high quality. Because of the fast iteration cycle, developers don't have time to spend chasing down bugs that entered the code months ago.

It's much better to take a little extra time to write good, solid code now than it is to rush through the programming and have to fix it later—and then fix the fixes—and then fix *those* fixes. As Lewis Carroll wrote, "The hurrier I go, the behinder I get."

Programming takes up a large percentage of an agile project's time, so agile methodologies have developed many techniques for making it easier and faster to write solid code. The section "Incremental Development" earlier in this chapter explained how rapid iteration helps lead to high-quality code. Other agile techniques that improve code quality include unit and integration testing, pair programming, and test-driven development. (I'll say more about pair programming in the next section. I'll say more about test-driven development in the section "Use Test-Driven and Test-First Development" later in this chapter.)

XP

Extreme Programming (XP) isn't called extreme because you do it while hang gliding, ice climbing, or base jumping. It's called extreme because it takes normal programming practices to extreme levels.

For example, consider code reviews. Traditional programming models use periodic code reviews to improve code quality. Every week or so, some or all the developers get together to walk through someone's code to look for problems and possible improvements. Code reviews also let you determine whether the code satisfies its design requirements. Code reviews are a good practice, but they have a couple of drawbacks (even if everyone programs egolessly).

For one thing, code reviews can take a lot of time. If everyone on the team spends a couple hours every week in code reviews, that's time they aren't writing code. To save time, code reviews often cover only a small fraction of the code. The team members can apply the ideas and techniques discussed during a review to other pieces of code, but it would be better if every piece of code were reviewed.

Another drawback to traditional code reviews is that they aren't held right after the code is written. If you hold reviews weekly, then some of the code could be a week old by the time it's reviewed. On many projects, reviews are held less frequently, so the code may be even older. That's better than not reviewing the code at all, but the code isn't completely fresh in the programmer's mind.

You can improve code reviews by examining more of the code and doing it closer to the time when it was written. Instead of reviewing 20 percent of the new code weekly, what if you could review 40 percent of the code twice a week? Or 75 percent of the code every other day? Taking this idea to the extreme, what if you could review every single comment and line of code *as it was being written* when the digital ink wasn't even dry? Sounds ridiculous, doesn't it?

Actually, that's just what the Extreme Programming technique of pair programming does. In *pair programming*, two (or possibly even three) programmers sit in front of the same monitor and work on a piece of code together. One of them (called the *driver* or *pilot*) controls the keyboard. As he types, the driver keeps up a steady monologue explaining what he's doing. Or more correctly, the monologue explains what the driver *thinks* he's doing.

One benefit of the stream-of-consciousness monologue is that it slows the driver down and forces him to think about his own code. Often when I've taught programming classes, simply making students explain what their code is doing is enough for them to find their own mistakes.

The second programmer of the pair (called the *observer*, *navigator*, or *pointer*) watches and reviews each line of code as it is typed. The observer makes sure the code makes sense and does what the driver thinks it does. The observer can also think about possible improvements or future changes. Basically, the observer performs an extreme, real-time, line-by-line code review. The two programmers switch roles frequently so they both stay fresh.

In practice, pair programming has been shown to have several advantages. It improves quality, largely because the code is constantly reviewed by two programmers with slightly different points of view. Pair programming takes more time (in person-hours), but it more than compensates by reducing the number of bugs. The programmers are more confident in their code, learn to communicate more easily, and share knowledge constantly so that they can learn new skills. Most programmers even find pair programming more fun.

PAIR PROGRAMMING PROBLEMS

Earlier in this chapter, I said that one disadvantage to RAD techniques is resistance to change. It's often hard to get people to adopt new techniques, and pair programming is a good example.

Programmers who have worked alone often find it hard to switch to pair programming. It feels unnatural having someone constantly looking over your shoulder. Some programmers eventually get used to it, but it may be a tough transition.

Pair programming is also sometimes used by management as an excuse for removing the developers' personal space. Anyone who does more than perform simple implementation tasks sometimes needs somewhere quiet to sit and think without interruption. (And I don't mean the library.) They need an office where they can shut out the world and focus on complex problems. If developers spend all of their time in shared offices or large group areas, they won't find the best solutions to tough problems.

Communication is important but not to the point of distraction.

XP Roles

Many agile models define specific roles for the people participating in the project. The following list summarizes the most common XP roles:

➤ Customer—Defines the requirements, verifies that the application meets the users' needs, and provides frequent feedback to keep development on track. Sometimes, several customers may be involved, but on a daily basis, a single on-site customer usually plays the main customer role.

➤ Tracker—Monitors the team members' progress and provides useful metrics.

➤ Programmer—Defines the application's architecture and writes the code.

➤ Coach—Helps the team work effectively, self-organize, and use good XP practices.

➤ Tester—Helps the customer write and perform acceptance tests for use cases; looks for missing requirements and holes in the design.

➤ Administrator—Sets up and maintains the team members' computers, network, and development tools.

Exactly which roles are used on different projects varies somewhat. For example, some teams add extra roles such as a *doomsayer* who looks for trouble and a manager who goes to meetings and generally acts as a buffer between the team and the outside world.

Some of these roles can also be combined. For example, the administrator is usually also a programmer, and the manager might also be the tracker.

Some combinations of roles should not be allowed. For example, to avoid conflicts of interest, a programmer probably shouldn't be combined with the customer, tester, or tracker.

XP Values

Like agile, XP has a collection of values and principles. Following are the values:

➤ Communication—The requirements must be communicated from the customers to the developers so that everyone acquires a common vision of the system's goals. Communication is aided by simple designs, extensive collaboration, frequent interaction, shared metaphors, and regular feedback.

➤ Simplicity—XP encourages simple designs. The application should start with the simplest possible approach, and then add more features later only if necessary. Sometimes, this approach is referred to as "*you ain't gonna need it*" (*YAGNI*, pronounced YAG-nee).

➤ Feedback—Frequent unit and integration tests provide feedback about the code's quality. Customers give feedback through periodic reviews (every couple of weeks) about the application's direction and usability. The developers give feedback to customers about how difficult and time-consuming changes will be. Finally, pair programmers give each other feedback on their designs and code constantly.

➤ Courage—Developers must have the courage to do the following:

   ➤ Start with simple solutions even when they know of more complicated approaches. (Solve the problems of today, not those of tomorrow.)

   ➤ Refactor code when necessary.

   ➤ Throw away code when necessary.

   ➤ Provide feedback.

➤ Respect—This value was added in the second edition of the book *Extreme Programming Explained: Embrace Change* by Kent Beck and Cynthia Andres (Addison-Wesley, 2004). (I can only speculate about what incident prompted this addition to the second edition.) This includes respect for others as well as self-respect. Team members respect the project by striving for higher quality and never committing code to the project that will break the build. They respect others and consider their feedback.

XP Practices

XP projects use an assortment of practices to satisfy the XP values. There are some variations in the specific practices used by different XP projects, but they all have more or less the same flavor. The following list gives some of the most common of those practices:

➤ Have a customer on-site.

➤ Play the planning game.

➤ Use stand-up meetings.

➤ Make frequent small releases.

➤ Use intuitive metaphors.

➤ Keep designs simple.

➤ Defer optimization.

➤ Refactor when necessary.

➤ Give everyone ownership of the code.

➤ Use coding standards.

➤ Promote generalization.

➤ Use pair programming.

➤ Test constantly.

➤ Integrate continuously.

➤ Work sustainably.

➤ Use test-driven and test-first development.

The following sections provide more detail about those practices.

Have a Customer On-Site

If possible, keep a customer on-site so that the developers can ask questions whenever necessary. Ideally, that customer should have the authority to make decisions so that work can keep moving without waiting for management approval. (You don't want to try to get three levels of management to sign off on a design change during the winter holiday season! You may as well go home until the middle of January.)

Give the customer an office, cubicle, futon, or whatever workspace is appropriate for your environment. Make sure the customer feels like a team member and not an interloper trespassing on your territory.

Play the Planning Game

The *planning game* has two parts: release planning and iteration planning.

During release planning, the team focuses on the next customer release. To do that (and to make the process more like a game and less like drudgery), user stories are written on cards. The team shuffles the cards and tries to determine how many of the cards can be implemented in time for the next customer release.

Developers ensure that the time estimates for the stories are reasonable. Customers help decide which stories are most important. Together the developers and customers create a release plan that is realistic and that gives the customers the functionality they need most as quickly as possible.

To make this work, you need to create a realistic release plan. Sometimes, the customers may pressure the developers to reduce the time allowed for crucial tasks. The developers need to resist to ensure that the final plan is sensible. An unrealistic release plan will only cause headaches for everyone later.

The second part of the planning game is iteration planning. At the beginning of each iteration (usually every 1 to 3 weeks), the team gets together to develop a plan for that iteration. The team selects user stories from the current release plan, starting with the most important outstanding stories.

The iteration plan should also include any items from the previous iterations that haven't passed their acceptance tests. For example, if the customers decide they want a particular feature changed, that change goes in the current iteration plan.

After the team has picked the most critical tasks to add to the next iteration, the developers pick the tasks they will perform (in good self-organizing fashion). Each developer estimates the amount of time needed for the chosen tasks. (Note that different people may need different amounts of time for the same tasks.) Ideally, each task should take no more than one to three days.

> ### SPIKE IT
>
> In XP, a *spike* or *spike solution* is a quick throwaway prototype used to explore a solution to a particular problem. You can use a spike to study a possible approach to see if it will work, to compare different approaches, or to make a better estimate of how difficult a task will be to reduce planning risk. If you're unsure about how to do something or how long something will take, spike it.

The team can adjust the tasks to give the iteration a reasonably short length. If the task estimates make the iteration too short, you can add a few more tasks from the release plan. If the iteration seems too long, you can defer a few tasks until the next iteration. You can also break a task into smaller subtasks if necessary to achieve the right iteration length.

Use Stand-Up Meetings

Start each day with a *stand-up meeting*, a brief meeting that lasts 15 minutes or less. All team members (including the on-site customer) must attend the stand-up meeting and briefly tell what they did since the last meeting, what they hope to achieve before the next meeting, and any problems they foresee in getting that work done.

The meeting is called a *stand-up* meeting because typically the participants remain standing to encourage brevity. If you have a five-person team and you want to hold the meeting to 15 minutes, then everyone needs to stay focused. (You do the math.)

You can hold the meeting in front of the bog board and refer to it if necessary. You may also want to hold the meeting first thing in the morning while everyone is fresh and before people get deeply involved in their tasks. (Of course, people may have different ideas about what "first thing in the morning" means and not everyone is fresh at 8:00 a.m. Use some self-organized negotiation.)

> **ADDING VARIETY** If weather permits, try occasionally turning a stand-up meeting into a short walk outside (as long as you don't need to refer to the big board). You can adjust the duration and speed of the walk according to the team members' physical condition and enthusiasm.

Stand-up meetings have the nice side effect of keeping developers focused on their tasks. If you tell everyone you're going to design the vehicle inventory tables today, you either need to do it or tomorrow you'll need to admit to everyone that you didn't.

The stand-up meeting removes the need for most other meetings, but you can have others if you need to address a particular problem. For those meetings, only the people directly involved should attend so the rest of the team can keep working on their tasks.

As any effective manager can tell you, you should try to keep all meetings focused and on track. A meeting should have a purpose other than running out the clock until quitting time. (Particularly since many developers stay until their work is done. If your meeting runs an hour long, they go home an hour later.)

Make Frequent Small Releases

Ideally, each release should have a relatively short time frame so that you can give the customers useful software as soon as possible. This also lets you get frequent feedback from the customers. The longer it is between releases, the farther off course the project can wander before it's corrected.

You can think of each release as checking a road map. If you don't check the map often enough, then your trip from Indiana to Mississippi might take you through North Carolina.

Frequent iterations also force you to perform integration tests so that you can flush out bugs sooner.

Use Intuitive Metaphors

If possible, use easy-to-understand metaphors to describe the system. If the customers and developers share a common metaphor, they are more likely to share a common vision of the application.

For example, many websites use a shopping cart metaphor. Just telling visitors that they have a shopping cart lets them make several reasonable assumptions. For example, they know that they can add things to the cart, remove things from the cart, and go to the checkout area to buy whatever is in the cart at the time. Other common programming metaphors include the waste basket, desktop, file, and document. If you can describe your system with an intuitive metaphor, it will be easier for the users to learn.

As is mentioned in Chapter 9, "User Experience Design," if you can't think of a good metaphor, then create a good idiom. A good idiom takes only a little longer to learn and is more effective than a bad metaphor.

Keep Designs Simple

Use the simplest design that can handle the immediate task. If you make the design overly complicated now, you may end up wasting a lot of time building flexibility that you never use. If you really must, then you can modify the design later to satisfy later needs.

Defer Optimization

This is a hard rule for many developers to accept. You spend years in school learning the most efficient ways to store data, sort numbers, search databases, and check whether a sentence is a palindrome. Now you're told to throw all that away and ignore optimization?

Unfortunately, highly optimized code is often complicated, confusing, hard to debug, and even harder to modify later. Combine that with the fact that few software engineering projects fail due to slow performance, and it's clear that you shouldn't optimize code unless it's absolutely necessary.

Most code doesn't actually need to be all that fast. Modern computers, memory, databases, networks, and the other pieces that make up a system are so fast that they spend most of their time sitting around twiddling their electronic thumbs waiting for the user to do something anyway. Does it really matter whether a screen pops up in 10 milliseconds or 2 milliseconds if it then takes the user one-half a second to notice that it's even there? Probably not.

In most projects, a relatively small amount of the code (as little as 5 or 10 percent) determines the overall speed of the application. Start with no optimization. Later, if the performance is unacceptable (and *only* if it's unacceptable), use a code profiler to figure out which parts of the code are wasting the users' time and optimize only those pieces of code.

I have seen several projects fail because they didn't work. I've never worked on a project that failed because it worked correctly but too slowly.

I worked on one project that was so slow a user could make a single change to a sales model and then wait 20 minutes for the analysis to update. The user would review the results, make another change, and then wait another 20 minutes. The company continued using the application for years despite its amazingly bad performance!

First make the application work. Then make it work faster only if absolutely necessary.

Refactor When Necessary

Because you're keeping the design simple, you'll sometimes need to rework old code to make it do new things. Don't be afraid to refactor when necessary.

This is one of the places where you may lose time over a BDUF project. If a BDUF design is correct, you can start by implementing the final design. XP tells you to use the simplest possible design to handle your current needs and then refactor it later if necessary, so you sort of sneak up on the final design. The refactoring takes extra time that the BDUF project doesn't spend (at least in theory).

> **GETTING A JUMP ON REFACTORING** I'm not a big fan of being intentionally stupid. (That's why I seldom listen to politicians' speeches.) The idea behind the "start simple and refactor if necessary" approach is that most of the time you'll avoid doing unnecessary work and you'll need to refactor only occasionally.
>
> If you're absolutely positive that you're going to need some other design feature at a later point, however, you should at least write the code in a way that will be easier to refactor later. In particular, the observer can tell the driver to insert comments in the code indicating where that refactoring might occur.
>
> Better still, move the feature that will later require refactoring into the current iteration. Then the simplest design possible will not require refactoring later.

Give Everyone Ownership of the Code

The team should have the sense that everyone owns all of the code so that anyone can change any piece of code as necessary. In a self-organizing team, you have the power to modify all the code if you need to.

However, there's sometimes an advantage to having a particular person work on a piece of code. For example, it might be better if the senior algorithms expert works on the tricky algorithm that forms the heart of your application instead of letting the high school summer intern mess up the code. That shouldn't be a problem because the algorithm guru will probably pick that task during the planning game anyway.

In general, however, no one should need to wait for someone else to work on a particular piece of code.

> **CODE COORDINATION** Use document and code management systems to ensure that only one team member works on a particular document or piece of code at any given time. You want everyone to be able to modify any piece of code, but not at the same time.

Use Coding Standards

To make it easier for every team member to modify any piece of code, the team should adopt consistent coding standards and conventions. If all the of code uses a consistent style, it's easier for anyone to read, understand, and modify.

Promote Generalization

Here I mean the team members should generalize, not that the code should be needlessly general. That would go against the principle of keeping the code as simple as possible until it's proven that it must be more complicated.

Encourage team members to learn about every piece of the system. Ideally, everyone should know as much as possible about every nook and cranny in the application. That helps with the preceding goal of allowing anyone to work on any piece of code. It also lets all of the team members acquire new skills and become more valuable team members. Someday you may want to offer the summer intern a permanent job.

Again on the theme of not being intentionally stupid, if your team includes a PhD in algorithms research, the other team members may have some trouble following all of the details about how your MMO's differential intelligence swarming algorithm makes the zombies chase the players. That doesn't mean you shouldn't try. You may not figure it all out, but you can probably learn something.

For more typical programming tasks, such as database design, user experience creation, and integration with external systems, everyone should at least pick up the basics.

Use Pair Programming

This gives you constant code reviews. See the earlier description of pair programming for details.

Test Constantly

Test thoroughly, test everything, test often. Even if a piece of code passes all of its tests in one iteration, keep testing it in future iterations. You may not find a mistake in *that* piece of code, but its tests may uncover a problem in some other related piece of code.

Automate as much of the testing as possible so it's easier to run the tests. Tests that are easy to run are more likely to be run and run more frequently.

When you find a bug, add a new test that would detect the bug sooner in that code and in other similar pieces of code if possible. Add it to the test suite so that you can catch similar bugs in the future.

Test, test, test!

Integrate Continuously

The entire application should be rebuilt, integrated, and tested as frequently as possible to flush out bugs. Many teams rebuild and test the system weekly or even every night. If the testing is automated, you can kick it off before you turn out the lights on your way out the door and then review the test log first thing in the morning.

That doesn't mean developers will never have unfinished code lying around. If a task will take three days, then it won't be ready for the two intervening nightly builds. In cases like that, you should keep your new code in your own separate directory and add it to the project's main code repository only after you have it finished and thoroughly tested so that you don't break the project's build.

You can make integration testing a bit easier if you dedicate a computer to just that purpose. None of the developers should use it for day-to-day programming chores so it doesn't become cluttered with the developers' unfinished novels, fantasy football playoff brackets, and pictures of cats using poor grammar. You may even want a separate staging computer where you can prepare for release deliveries.

Having a dedicated integration computer also ensures that only one programming pair can integrate at a time, so pairs don't trip over each other.

Work Sustainably

This doesn't mean you should use computers made only from bamboo and powered by solar panels. (Although that would be very cool!) It means that you need to set a working pace that all of the team members can keep up indefinitely. Short release and iteration cycles provide a lot of benefits, but you should keep them short by not including too much in each cycle, not by making the developers work 60-hour weeks.

Encourage (by force if necessary) developers to work only 40-hour weeks and discourage overtime.

Pushing the team to meet arbitrarily shortened deadlines leads to burnout, employee turnover, and general crankiness. Rested developers are more enthusiastic and productive.

Use Test-Driven and Test-First Development

In *test-driven development (TDD)*, you start with a piece of code, which might initially be empty or a stub that doesn't do anything. You then pick a function that the code should perform, and you write a test that would verify that the function worked properly if the code did it.

Next, you see if it passes the test. Normally, the code fails because you haven't yet given it any code to perform the function you're testing. If the code does somehow pass the test, then it was a crummy test because the code doesn't perform the function yet! In that case, write another test and try again until the code fails.

After the code fails, write new code to perform the function. Add the simplest piece of code that can satisfy the test and nothing extra. Don't anticipate future functions by writing code to handle them too. You'll get to that later.

Now run the new test(s) plus any previous tests that you wrote for earlier functions. If all goes well, the code passes all of the tests this time. If the code fails, fix the code and try again until it passes all of the tests.

When the code passes all the tests, refactor if necessary to clean up the code and move on to the next function. Because each incremental piece of code you added satisfies only the current test and does nothing more, you'll often need to refactor to integrate the separate pieces into a maintainable section of code.

Figure 19.2 shows the TDD process in a flowchart.

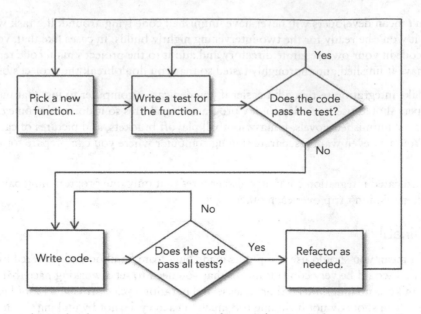

FIGURE 19.2: In test-driven development, you write a test for each function before you write the code to perform the function.

Test-first development is closely related to test-driven development. In *test-first development (TFD)*, you write all of the unit tests for a piece of code before you write the code. You then write all of the code. You can add more tests if you think of them while you're writing the code. After you write the code, run the tests and fix the code if it doesn't pass.

IS TDD TFD?

Some developers use test-first development to mean any method where you write tests before you write code. By that definition, test-driven development is one kind of test-first development. I prefer the "write all of the unit tests first" definition.

The difference is that in TDD you sneak up on the finished code a little bit at a time in the smallest possible steps. In TFD you write all of the tests at once and then you write all of the code at once.

The main advantage to TFD is that it enables you to write the unit tests before your brain is contaminated with knowledge about how the code works. That means you're more likely to build tests that look for correct and incorrect *results* instead of testing to see if the code works the way that you *think* it does. After all, the code may work the way you think it does and still not do the right thing.

SCRUM

Scrum was named after a procedure in rugby that the teams use to put the ball back into play after an accidental rule violation such as the ball going out of bounds. The players huddle together in a big interlocked mob, and then someone throws the ball under the players' legs. The players try to hook the ball out with their feet and take possession of it while trying not to be maimed in the process.

I actually think it's a strange word to use for a software development method. In rugby, both teams are locked in the scrum and fighting against each other for control of the ball, which is hardly a model for the kinds of cooperation you'd like in a software development team. Perhaps it's the way something useful pops out of a big chaotic pile of people pushing against each other that reminds people of software engineering.

Scrum Roles

The members of a scrum team play three roles:

➤ Product owner—Represents the customers, users, and other stakeholders. The product owner writes user stories to describe the project's goals and then prioritizes them. The resulting prioritized list of wanted features is called the *product backlog*. (I've always thought "backlog" was a somewhat harsh term implying that you're already behind and playing catch-up. Starting a project with a huge backlog feels kind of like being born owing millions in back taxes.)

As the liaison between the development team and the stakeholders, the product owner has the following duties.

➤ Defines the requirements and verifies that the product meets those requirements

➤ Sets requirement priorities; helps determine which requirements make it into the next iteration given resource constraints

➤ Keeps the stakeholders posted on the project's status; demonstrates the product to the stakeholders

➤ Plans and announces releases

➤ Provides a point of contact between the stakeholders and developers

The product owner generally shouldn't modify an iteration while it is underway, although he can make changes in the next iteration and can cancel an iteration if necessary (for example, if the product owner decides the biggest goal of the current sprint is obsolete).

➤ Team member—These are the self-organized cross-functional team members who build the application. During each iteration, each team member helps handle all of the typical tasks that you need to write a decent piece of software (analysis, design, program, test, document, and so forth).

➤ Scrum master—The scrum master acts as a remover of obstacles for the team. This person also ensures that the team follows good scrum practices, challenges the team to improve, and sometimes leads meetings. Typically, a scrum master isn't a project manager because the team is self-organizing, so it guides itself. Some even say that adding a project manager to a scrum project makes things harder. (Note that most scrum masters don't like being called "scrum bags," although some might be okay with the title "scrum lord.")

Notice how homogenous most of the team members are. The product owner and scrum master are different, but everyone else is part of the same egalitarian team, sharing duties and guiding themselves in a good self-organizing manner.

Scrum Sprints

A scrum project creates a series of timeboxed incremental iterations, which are usually called *sprints*. In traditional scrum, a sprint is 30 days long, although some people prefer shorter sprints of one, two, or three weeks.

The result of each sprint is a fully tested and approved piece of software, which is sometimes called a *potentially shippable increment (PSI)*. You could actually deploy a PSI to the users, although you may want to wait and release a version of the application only when there are enough new features to justify the inconvenience to the users.

Before each sprint begins, the team holds a *sprint planning meeting*. Typically, that meeting is time-boxed to four hours so that it doesn't take up too much time.

During that meeting, the product owner decides which user stories should be selected for the upcoming sprint. The goal is to provide the greatest benefit to the users in each iteration, so the most useful items should be selected first. Fixes for any outstanding bugs should also be included.

The developers can ask for clarification and point out any potential problems. When the meeting is done, the selected items are moved from the product backlog into the *sprint backlog*. The product owner is then usually asked to disappear (but stay close in case of questions) while the developers break the user stories into tasks.

After the sprint's goals and tasks have been defined, the developers roll up their sleeves, divide up the tasks, and really get to work. They analyze the tasks, design solutions, write code, drink caffeine, and test.

During the sprint, the team holds a quick 10- to 15-minute *daily scrum* (sometimes called a "stand-up," although "daily scrum" seems more scrummy) where each developer answers the Three Questions of Agile Development:

> ➤ What did you do since the last scrum?

> ➤ What do you hope to accomplish before the next scrum?

> ➤ What obstacles do you see in your way?

If a developer sees looming obstacles, the scrum master looks into them (to earn the coveted title Remover of Obstacles).

After all of the work is done, the sprint ends with a *sprint review meeting*. The development team presents the current PSI to the product owner, who checks the results against the items that were originally selected for the sprint to make sure the sprint's goals have been met. If the application can't handle even one part of any of the user stories, the product owner can flag that story as unfinished.

After the sprint review meeting, the scrum master and the development team hold a *retrospective meeting* where they discuss the recent sprint. Here they discuss the three big questions about any development method and particularly any iterative method:

➤ What went well and how can we make it happen again?

➤ What went poorly and how can we avoid that in the future?

➤ How can we improve the next sprint?

It may seem like scrum adds a lot of time-consuming meetings to the development process. Between the sprint planning meeting, daily scrums, sprint review meeting, and retrospective meeting, how will the developers get anything done?

The sprint planning meeting occurs only once for each sprint, and sprints typically only occur monthly. If you use shorter sprints, then the sprints will probably include fewer items and hopefully your sprint planning meetings will be shorter accordingly.

Daily scrums must be kept short or you're doomed.

If all goes well, then the sprint review meeting will also be short because the sprint satisfied its requirements, so you don't have much to discuss.

Finally, if all is running smoothly, then the retrospective meeting won't turn up too much. Once in a while you may think of a new way to make things smoother (buy your Sulawesi coffee in bulk) or to prevent a problem that you encountered during the past sprint (no more spur-of-the moment demos for the VP of IT), but these meetings will often be short.

Planning Poker

In scrum, *planning poker* (also called *scrum poker*) is a game that you can play to decide how much work a particular task might require. Each team member gets a deck of cards with values based roughly on the Fibonacci sequence. In that sequence, each number is the sum of the two previous numbers: 0, 1, 1, 2, 3, 5, 8, 13, 21, and so on.

The cards used for the planning game are modified somewhat, but the idea is that task lengths typically follow a distribution similar to the numbers in the Fibonacci sequence.

What that means is that fine distinctions between the durations of large tasks aren't very meaningful. For example, the difference between a one-hour task and a two-hour task is quite large, but the difference between a 21-hour task and a 22-hour task isn't. The difference is still one hour, but the uncertainty in estimating the task's duration is likely to be more than an hour anyway, so you can't really tell which of the two large tasks is harder.

Some teams use actual playing cards and give each player an ace, 2, 3, 5, 8, and king, where the king represents a task too big or too complicated to talk about presently.

You can also make your own decks or buy commercially available scrum decks. Some decks use the values 0, 1, 2, 3, 5, 8, 13, 21, 34, 55, and 89. Others use qualitative values such as extra-small, small, medium, large, and extra-large.

Other decks use 0, ½, 1, 2, 3, 5, 8, 13, 20, 40, and 100. Those are similar to the Fibonacci numbers with some rounding to make them a bit more palatable. (It's more intuitive to tell the customers that a feature will take a nice round 40-hour week instead of 34 hours because a value such as 34 implies an unrealistic level of certainty.)

Some decks also include a question mark card (an item will take an unknown amount of time), a split card (the task should be split), and a coffee cup card (to indicate that you need a break). (Yes, the coffee cup card seems like something that I would make up, but it isn't. It's a real scrum planning poker card.)

After everyone has a card deck, the game begins. The meeting moderator, who normally doesn't play the game, reads a user story and then leads a brief discussion of restrictions, risks, and assumptions. (Some teams use an egg timer to ensure that the team doesn't spend too much time on any single story.)

The players select cards from their decks and place them facedown on the table. When everyone is ready, they turn their cards over simultaneously.

Having the players turn their cards over at the same time helps prevent *anchoring*, a phenomenon in which early decisions anchor later decisions. For example, suppose you're trying to decide whether you want to assign a task a 2 or 3, but then another team member plays a 34. You might decide that you grossly underestimated the task and bump up your card to an 8. Playing your cards at the same time gets more honest estimates from everyone.

After everyone plays a card, the people with the highest and lowest estimates are given a *soapbox* to explain why they feel their estimate is correct. Who knows? The guy who played a 34 when everyone else played 2 or 3 might know something that everyone else doesn't. Or the person who played 1 when everyone else played 13 might know of an algorithm that solves the problem perfectly.

After the soapboxing, you gather up your cards and do it again. You repeat the process until the group reaches a consensus for that item. Write down the number of points for that story (called its number of *story points*) and move on to the next item.

When you're done, you'll have a list showing estimates of the difficulty for all of the project's user stories.

Burndown

Scrum uses burndown charts to measure progress. A *burndown chart* shows the amount of work remaining plotted over time. A *sprint burndown chart* shows the amount of work for a sprint. A *product burndown chart* (also called a *release burndown chart*) shows the amount of work remaining for the whole project.

You can measure the amount of work in story points, expected number of hours of work, or any other measurement that you find useful. You can let the chart's x-axis show the date or, for a project burndown chart, the sprint number.

Figure 19.3 shows a product burndown chart. This chart shows the number of poker-planned hours left in the backlog over the project's duration. From the total amount of anticipated work and the project's planned duration, you can calculate an ideal burndown by assuming that you can do the same amount of work in every sprint.

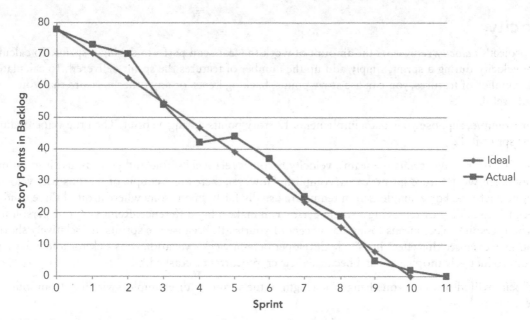

FIGURE 19.3: A project burndown chart shows the amount of work remaining for each sprint.

BOOK BURNDOWN

Sometimes, I use a chart similar to the one in Figure 19.3 to track my progress while writing a book. I plot the average number of pages I need to have written for each day plus the number of actual pages I've written. That lets me see at any point whether I'm on schedule or falling behind. Unless I keep a careful track constantly, it's easy to fall far behind, and then catching up can be hard. (It's hard to write 120 pages in one day.)

In practice, rather than telling me how far behind I am, the chart usually shows me how far ahead I am. That lets me decide how much goofing off I can do (things like maintaining the C# Helper website www.csharphelper.com, answering email, playing volleyball, eating, and sleeping).

As the project continues, some sprints will be more productive than others, so the actual progress won't follow the ideal burndown exactly. You can use the burndown charts (which should be posted on the project's big board so that everyone can see them) to decide if the project is getting too far off of its targets.

In Figure 19.3, the project started a bit slowly but caught up to the ideal burndown and even pulled ahead after sprints 3 and 4. During sprint 5, the project lost ground, perhaps because new goals were added to the project backlog or because some tasks turned out to be harder than expected. (Or the team went on a group trip to Disneyland.) The project caught up again during sprint 9 but then slowed down a bit and finished one sprint later than planned (because the customer wanted to switch from monitors to AR monocles).

Velocity

A project's *velocity* represents the amount of work the team can perform during a sprint. To calculate the velocity during a sprint, simply add up the number of features the sprint delivered. To calculate the number of features, you can use story points, backlog items, or any other measure that you find useful.

For example, suppose your team implements 12 story points during a sprint. Then the velocity during that sprint is 12.

Usually, after a few sprints the team's velocity becomes relatively stable and you can use it to estimate how much work future sprints can accomplish. However, there are a couple of reasons why velocity might fluctuate. For example, scrum teams are usually fairly small (somewhere around three to nine people), so adding or removing a single person can make a big difference. Removing one person from a four-person project means losing 25 percent of your staff. Because the sprints are relatively short, you may even see this effect if a single developer takes a week's vacation or is sick for a few days. (Or is unproductively moping around because their cryptocurrency crashed.)

Velocity will also vary if you change the length of the sprints—for example, switching from four weeks to two weeks.

Because scrum focuses on project management and not developmental details, you can combine it with other development methodologies. For example, you can use scrum to set up the iterations used in an XP project.

LEAN

Lean Software Development (also called simply *Lean* or *LSD*) isn't a much-needed attempt to help programmers lose weight. (Actually, all agile methods should help by maintaining a sustainable work pace so programmers have time to get some exercise instead of sitting in front of their keyboards all day. Whether they decide to actually go out and get that exercise instead of going home to watch YouTube videos is their decision.)

Instead, Lean is the process of applying the principles learned in lean manufacturing to software engineering. The idea behind Lean is to keep the application as lean and fat-free as possible. Nothing should go into the application that isn't there for a good reason.

Like scrum, Lean focuses on managing iterations of development. Lean focuses more closely on gathering the right requirements and ensuring that only essential ingredients get into each iteration.

Lean Principles

Like some other agile methods, Lean defines a set of guiding principles.

➤ Eliminate waste—Anything that doesn't contribute directly to the project should be regarded as waste and eliminated. That may include such items as the following:

  ➤ Unclear requirements. (Clarify or eliminate them.)

  ➤ Unnecessary features and code. (Don't make the code unnecessarily flexible.)

> ➤ Unnecessary repetition. (Some ways to avoid repetition include refactoring to make methods that perform common tasks, automating testing, and keeping records so that you don't need to make the same decisions twice.)

> ➤ Unnecessary meetings and bureaucracy. (It's every developer's dream to eliminate those!)

If something doesn't add to customer value, leave it out. If you can leave something out and still achieve the project's goals, leave it out.

➤ Respect the team—Give the team the respect and authority it needs to work effectively. Help the team self-organize.

➤ Defer commitment—Don't make decisions until you know enough to make them intelligently. If you can't make a decision on a feature, design, or other element without making a lot of assumptions, defer the feature until a later iteration. Don't start building grand designs until the customers know what they need. Explore alternatives before deciding on which approach to use.

➤ Deliver quickly—Use frequent short iterations to deliver value to the customers as quickly as possible.

➤ Build knowledge—Learn as much as possible. Use prototypes and other methods to learn requirements. Use early testing to learn about bugs before they're hard to find. Use short iterations to ensure that development is on the right track.

➤ Build in quality—Validate assumptions throughout the project. If an old assumption no longer applies, discard it. If new assumptions arise, add them. Ensure that the project has an integrated, consistent feel. Refactor if the code loses its integrity and becomes hard to maintain and modify.

➤ See the whole—The team should be cross-functional so everyone can work on every step of development (analysis, design, programming, and so forth). Everyone should see the big picture and spot and fix problems in any part of the system. No one should think of a problem as someone else's problem. If the project has a problem, *everyone* has a problem.

Like scrum, Lean focuses on project management and not developmental details. That means you can combine it with other development methodologies. For example, you can use Lean ideas to set the goals for an XP project's iterations.

CRYSTAL

Crystal isn't actually a development model. Instead, it's a family of development methodologies developed by Alistair Cockburn in the 1990s that all have the word "Crystal" in their names. The rest of each method's name is a color that indicates a project's size. For example, Crystal Clear (the most popular color) is intended for small projects.

The following list shows the Crystal method names and the numbers of developers that they generally support:

➤ Crystal Clear (1–6)

➤ Crystal Yellow (7–20)

➤ Crystal Orange (21–40)

➤ Crystal Orange Web (21–40)

➤ Crystal Red (41–80)

➤ Crystal Maroon (81–200)

➤ Crystal Diamond (201–500)

➤ Crystal Sapphire (501–1,000)

Crystal also includes the notion of *criticality*. The project's criticality is gauged by the types of items that are at risk:

➤ Comfort

➤ Discretionary money

➤ Essential money

➤ Life

For example, a solitaire game would have comfort criticality and a nuclear power plant control system would have life criticality.

Figure 19.4 shows the possible combinations of the two dimensions: color and criticality.

	Clear 1-6	Yellow 7-20	Orange 21-40	Red 41-80	Maroon 81-200	Diamond 201-500	Sapphire 501-1,000
Comfort	C6	C20	C40	C80	C200	C500	C1000
Discretionary Money	D6	D20	D40	D80	D200	D500	D1000
Essential Money	E6	E20	E40	E80	E200	E500	E1000
Life	L6	L20	L40	L80	L200	L500	L1000

FIGURE 19.4: Crystal defines a matrix of color and criticality combinations.

The values in the table's body show an abbreviation that tells you a project's criticality and size. For example, a project involving discretionary money with 35 project members would be a D35 (Orange) project.

WHERE'S CRYSTAL ORANGE WEB?

Crystal Orange Web was a special case designed by Alistair Cockburn to produce a continuing stream of applications for public use in an E50 project. (Yes, I know the table would make that a Red project, but Cockburn decided to call it Orange.) The Orange Web model doesn't seem to have been used much, but Cockburn believes it may have some value because many businesses seem to be headed toward this sort of never-ending development cycle.

All of the Crystal methods have the following seven common features:

➤ Frequent iterations—Frequent iterations result in releases. In critical projects, only some of the releases might be delivered to the users, although the customers can view the others to provide feedback.

➤ Constant feedback—The team meets regularly to discuss development and ways that it can be improved. The team also meets with customers to keep the project on track.

➤ Constant communication—Team members should be located at the same site so they can communicate easily and frequently. For small projects, they should ideally be in the same room (which the developers will probably give an amusing name such as The Pit, The Clubhouse, or The Thunderdome).

➤ Safety—Crystal projects define three kinds of safety. First, team members can express their opinions safely without fear of blame. Second, the project should be safe in the sense that it should finish on time and within budget. Third, you need to consider the project's criticality (comfort, discretionary money, essential money, and life). That kind of safety is more crucial in medical and flight software than it is in an online game.

➤ Focus—Team members should be given enough time to focus on their key items without interruptions such as phone calls, meetings, or requests to help the boss set up a printer. (The Crystal rules say developers should be guaranteed at least two uninterrupted hours per day and that they should remain with a project for at least two days before being moved to another project—although both of those seem extremely minimal to me.) The focus of the project should also be clearly stated so that everyone knows exactly what the goals are. The project leader should prioritize tasks so that team members know what their highest priority tasks are.

➤ Easy access to expert users—The developers should be able to talk to the expert users to ask questions and request feedback. The Crystal rules say the expert should be available to meet at least two hours per week and be available for phone calls.

➤ Testing support—The team's environment should include automated testing and continuous integration to spot problems quickly. It should also include code management so that problematic code can be isolated and replaced with an earlier working version if necessary.

A key assumption in the Crystal family is that larger projects need more formalization to keep the developers organized. In a small four-developer Crystal Clear project, you can usually get away with a verbal understanding of the customers' needs, informal developer meetings, and a cross-functional team where everyone pitches in on everything.

That approach won't work with a 150-developer Crystal Maroon project. For such a large project, you'll need to add extra management tools such as a project hierarchy with multiple teams, more specialized roles (such as team leaders, a project manager, and testers), and progress tracking.

You also need to adjust the amount of control the project uses depending on its criticality. For example, a Crystal Clear online game project could have fairly flexible requirements and play testing. In contrast, a similarly sized life-critical project would need formal requirements, very extensive testing, and rigorous verification.

However, given that different projects need different amounts of management and different levels of formality, the Crystal philosophy is that you should pick the minimal combination that can still do the job.

> Everything should be made as simple as possible, but not simpler.
>
> —*Albert Einstein*

Crystal's lightest colors are the most studied and used, so they're the ones described in the following sections.

Crystal Clear

Crystal Clear uses a relatively relaxed and easy-going approach. You can probably get some idea of the general Crystal Clear ambiance from the following Cockburn quote:

> The difference between Crystal Clear and Extreme Programming is that XP is much more disciplined, Crystal Clear is much more tolerant, even sloppy looking. I would say XP is more productive, Crystal Clear more likely to get followed.
>
> —*Alistair Cockburn*

One way to differentiate the Crystal methods is to look at the team member roles that are required. Crystal Clear requires only three roles.

➤ Sponsor—The person for whom the software is developed and who will ultimately sign off on the finished application.

➤ Senior designer—Someone who knows how to design the software and make any necessary technical decisions.

➤ Programmer—Someone who can write the code.

A project can have more than one person in each role (usually in the programmer role). Any other roles (such as project manager, tester, database administrator, or caterer) are played by the team members. For example, some or all of the programmers could share the testing role, and the senior designer might also cater team meetings by buying donuts.

Because this is a relatively small project, the team can informally discuss the project's goals and keep them in mind fairly easily. The team may write use cases to ensure that specific goals are met.

Crystal Clear projects are expected to deliver production releases every two or three months, possibly with shorter nonreleased development iterations.

The main measure of progress is released software.

Crystal Yellow

With 7 to 20 team members, Crystal Yellow projects are slightly bigger than Crystal Clear projects. Because the team is a bit bigger, the project needs slightly more management.

For example, it's probably impractical to have 20 developers all work in the same room and constantly interrupt each other. It would also be hard (although perhaps not impossible) for everyone to work cross-functionally on every aspect of the application. (It would also be impossible to get 20 developers to agree on the same radio station to play in their shared workspace.)

To ease coordination for the larger group, a Crystal Yellow project might adopt the following practices:

➤ Easy communication—Even if the team isn't all squeezed into the same room, they still need to communicate easily.

➤ Code ownership—Teams could each own an area of the project. This lets each team focus on its own piece so that they don't need to know everything about everything. (Each team might work in a single room to improve its internal communication.)

➤ Feedback—End users provide frequent feedback. This reduces the need for detailed requirements.

➤ Automated testing—This is always a good idea, but with multiple teams working on the same project, it's even more important. There's going to be a lot of code to test.

➤ Mission statement—This helps give everyone the same vision of the project. (This doesn't need to be a vacuous execuspeak statement like "Manifest box-externalized criteria going forward to leverage end-of-play synergy and maximize stakeholder competencies." It should be a clear, verifiable statement.)

➤ More formal increments—Iterations should be timeboxed to a month and begin with a list of the features that will be included. The team still doesn't necessarily need to release the result of every increment.

The team still uses relatively informal communication to avoid extensive requirement documentation and to keep everyone headed in the same direction. (In execuspeak, you could say, "Rowing in the same direction.")

Crystal Orange

Crystal Orange projects have 21 to 40 team members and typically last one to two years. They require even more management support to prevent people from tripping over each other.

These projects may add some of the following new roles:

➤ Business analyst—A domain expert to help define the application's purpose and provide feedback during development.

➤ Project manager—You *might* handle tracking for a Crystal Yellow project without a dedicated project manager, but a Crystal Orange project needs someone dedicated to tracking the project's progress.

➤ Architect—Someone to focus on the application's overall high-level design.

➤ Team leader—The project is broken into areas that are assigned to separate teams. Hopefully, they'll be self-organizing, but usually each team needs someone with a bit more experience to guide the team and to act as the team's point of contact with the rest of the project.

Projects this large may require specialized skills, so the team might include other specialists as needed. For example, it might include a requirements gatherer, database designer, user interface designer, mentor, toolsmith, technical writer, system manager, or tester. It's unlikely that a project could get by with one business analyst, one project manager, one architect, and 37 programmers.

The following tasks add more formality to the project to help keep it on track:

➤ Requirements—Smaller Crystal projects may not need requirements documents, but a project this size has too many details to handle informally.

➤ Tracking—The project manager (with help from everyone else) tracks tasks, progress, milestones, and potential risks. The project manager should produce status reports so everyone (including the customers) can see how the project is progressing.

➤ Release schedule—The schedule should indicate when production releases occur and (tentatively at first until the details are worked out) what they contain.

➤ Object models—The architect needs to do something to justify the title.

➤ Code reviews—Designs and code need more formal review. This is a bigger project so design and code problems can cause a lot more trouble and be much harder to fix later.

➤ Acceptance testing—The customers should provide a more formal level of acceptance than is required by smaller projects.

➤ Delivery—These are more formal, so you should use good release techniques such as staged delivery and incremental rollout. Delivery may require user setup, documentation, and training.

By now I'm sure you get the idea. The "harder" members of the Crystal family require more formality and management overhead. The informal approach used by a 4-person Crystal Clear project just won't work with a 40-person Crystal Orange project.

Projects larger than Crystal Orange seem to be rare (I haven't heard of any) but would require even more overhead, planning, and tracking if they were to get anything done (other than generating an avalanche of unread email). Such large projects might need to split into teams composed of subteams, possibly with their own feature teams or working groups.

I shudder to think what a Crystal Sapphire project would be like. Even if you had seven teams with seven subteams of 10 developers, each would still get you only to Diamond size. You'd have to rent a convention center to hold a whole-project meeting. You might have easy communication locally, but you could spend years working on a 1,000-person project and not even meet everyone, much less communicate freely with them all.

Those giant Crystal projects seem to be as common as politicians voting themselves pay cuts, so I won't speculate about what they would look like.

FEATURE-DRIVEN DEVELOPMENT

Feature-Driven Development (FDD) is another iterative and incremental development model. Unlike most of the other agile models, FDD was created to work with large teams. (Originally, Jeff De Luca designed FDD to meet his needs on a 15-month, 50-person project in 1997.)

Where other models use risk, customer value, waste, or some other theme to guide development, FDD focuses on application features. At a high level, an FDD project builds a list of wanted features and then iteratively adds those features to the application until every feature has been added.

A more detailed view of FDD involves several roles, five phases, and milestones to ensure that the iterations run smoothly. The following sections describe those pieces of FDD.

FDD Roles

FDD defines six main roles and a bunch of secondary roles. The following list summarizes the primary roles:

➤ Project manager—This is the project's administrative leader. The project manager tracks the project's progress, budget, and other resources. The project manager handles all the administrative nonsense that companies typically try to inflict on employees so that the team can work effectively.

➤ Chief architect—This person is responsible for the project's overall programmatic design. The chief architect doesn't write the design but instead helps the team come up with a design cooperatively.

➤ Development manager—This person manages day-to-day development activities. The development manager resolves conflicts, makes sure the development teams have the resources they need, and referees if the chief programmers have disagreements they can't resolve and open warfare breaks out in the hallways.

➤ Chief programmers—These are experienced developers who are familiar with all of the functions of development (design, analysis, coding, and so on). They lead teams of programmers who work on a set of assigned programming tasks. The chiefs help their teams solve design problems, and they resolve any issues that get in the way of their teams.

➤ Class owner—In many agile models, the code is jointly owned by the entire development team, so any member can modify anyone else's code. In contrast, FDD assigns ownership of each class to a specific developer. If a feature requires changes to several classes, the class owners get together to form a *feature team* that works to make the needed changes. The members of the feature team work closely together in a sort of many-headed pair programming group.

➤ Domain expert—These are customers, users, executive champions, and others who know about the project domain and how the finished application should work. They are the source of domain information for the developers. They are sometimes called *subject matter experts (SMEs)*. The following list briefly describes secondary roles that an FDD project may have (mostly in larger projects):

➤ Build engineer—Sets up and controls the build process. This may include source code control.

➤ Deployer—Handles deployment. This may include tasks such as staging, setting up the users' environment, and converting old data into new formats.

➤ Domain manager—Leads the domain experts and provides a single point of contact to resolve domain issues.

➤ Language guru or language lawyer—Specializes in the programming language, technology, and other arcane items used by the team. Other developers can go to this person for help if necessary.

➤ Release manager—Gathers information from the chief programmers to track the project's progress.

➤ System administrator—Maintains the team's computers and network.

➤ Technical writer—Writes online and printed documentation and training materials.

➤ Internaler—Runs internal scripts to look for trouble. Verifies that the application meets the requirements.

➤ Toolsmith—Creates tools for the other developers.

Smaller projects may not need some of these roles. Often one person can play multiple roles. For example, an "ordinary" developer could also be the language guru or toolsmith.

FDD Phases

FDD projects move through five phases. The first three occur at the start of the project (during iteration 0, if you like that term) and the last two phases are repeated iteratively until the application is complete.

The following sections describe the five FDD phases.

Develop a Model

When the project starts, the team builds an object model for the application. To some, this may smell suspiciously like Big Design Up Front. In FDD, however, the model is built quickly and iteratively with the assistance of the domain experts.

The model's goal is to give the customers and the development team a common vision of the application's scope and goals. It should help everyone understand the domain's key concepts, interactions with other systems, potential problems, and ways the application will be used.

At this point, the model paints a broad picture, focusing on the application's breadth. Later it will be refined iteratively to provide the detail needed to actually implement the project's features.

Build a Feature List

The next step is to build a list of the features that make up the application. FDD technically defines a feature as an *action/result/object* triple, where the *action* generates the *result* related to the *object*.

For example, a feature might be "calculate the customer's outstanding balance." Here the action is "calculate," the result is "outstanding balance," and the object is "the customer."

To help with large projects, FDD organizes the features into a three-level hierarchy with the levels corresponding to areas, activities, and features.

The top-level groups the features by domain area. For example, an order-processing system might have the areas Order Tracking, Inventory, Billing, and Reporting.

The areas are divided into activities that represent things the user might need to do. For example, Order Tracking might be divided into the activities Create Order, View Order, Modify Order, Delete Order, and so on.

The activities are divided into features. These are the atomic operations that make up the activities expressed in FDD's action/result/object style. For example, the following list shows some of the features that you might include for the Create Order activity:

- ➤ Find customer record (find/record/customer).
- ➤ Create new customer record (create/record/customer).
- ➤ Check order items' inventory availability (check/availability/item).
- ➤ Calculate order subtotal (calculate/subtotal/order).
- ➤ Calculate order shipping (calculate/shipping/order).
- ➤ Set order status to pending (set/status pending/order).

Converting the object model into a feature list is mostly mechanical (although it can take a while for a large project). The resulting hierarchy is called the *feature list*. (It may not be as snappy a name as "backlog," but at least it's descriptive.)

Plan by Feature

During this phase, the planning team prioritizes the features and builds an initial schedule. Groups of related features are assigned to the chief programmers and become their teams' feature lists.

Because FDD uses class ownership, the features assigned to a team also assign the classes that provide those features to the team. For example, if you assign a bunch of customer-related features to a team, then you'll probably want to assign the Customer class to that team. In that case, it also makes sense to assign the other Customer class features to the team.

In that way the object model helps group the features and define the teams. Usually, the resulting groups are quite natural and intuitive, at least for features that are visible to the users. More esoteric features used internally by the application such as database tools, external interfaces, and scheduling systems may have little intuitive meaning to anyone other than the developers. In those cases, you can still use the object model to group related features.

Design by Feature

In this phase, the chief programmer selects a collection of features to be implemented in the next two-week iteration. For each selected feature, the chief programmer gathers the owners of the classes that will be involved into a feature team.

If the chief programmer thinks it's necessary, a domain expert can perform a *domain walkthrough* to review the feature. The expert can describe the feature's intent, requirements, side effects, data needs, and anything else that can help the feature team understand what the feature should do.

Next, the feature team (with guidance from the chief programmer as needed) creates sequence diagrams representing the feature. (Look at the section "Sequence Diagram" in Chapter 6, "High-Level Design," if you don't remember what those are.)

The class owners then write method prologues. A *method prologue* is a description of a method that includes its purpose, input and output parameters, return type, possible exceptions (ways the method can fail), and assumptions.

During the design phase, the feature team hopefully adds new details to the project's classes. The chief programmer updates the project's object model to show the new detail. (Remember that the "Develop a Model" phase created only an initial model without a lot of detail. This phase fills out the model.)

Finally, the chief programmer holds a *design inspection* to make sure the new feature design didn't omit anything. The inspection can involve the feature team and possibly other project members, depending on what the chief programmer thinks would be most effective. For example, if someone outside of the feature team has experience doing something similar, it might be wise to include that person in the inspection.

When this phase is finished, the result is a *design package* that includes the following items:

➤ A description of the package

➤ Sequence diagrams showing how the features will work

➤ Alternatives (if any)

➤ Updated object models

➤ Method prologues

The result is sort of like the start of a Big Design Up Front project, but on a smaller scale. It may seem like a lot of overly formal work just to plan the implementation of a single feature, but the goal is for the chief programmer to prepare the other team members to move forward into the next phase with a good chance of success. All of this setup is particularly necessary if the project is large and includes developers with varying degrees of skill and experience.

Build by Feature

Armed with the completed design packages, the class owners build the methods that implement the iteration's selected features. The new code is unit tested and run through a code inspection (held by the chief programmer). If everything looks good, the code is promoted to the project's build.

Figure 19.5 shows the relationships among the FDD project's five phases at a high level.

FDD Iteration Milestones

In an FDD project, the features must be implemented in no more than two weeks, so they are necessarily fairly small. Although the iterations are quick, they include a fair number of tasks.

To keep track of everything that's going on during an iteration, FDD defines six milestones. Table 19.2 shows the six milestones and the completion percentage that each represents.

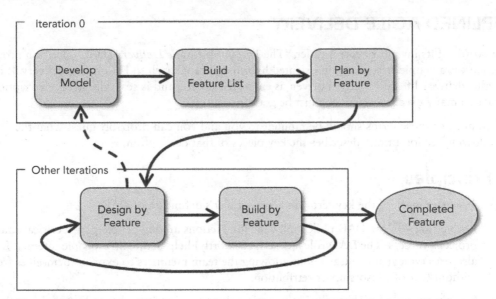

FIGURE 19.5: In FDD, the last two phases repeat for each feature iteration. The Design by Feature phase feeds changes back to the object model.

TABLE 19.2: FDD milestones

PHASE	MILESTONE	PERCENTAGE
Design by Feature	Domain Walkthrough	1%
	Design	40%
	Design Inspection	3%
Build by Feature	Code	45%
	Code Inspection	10%
	Promote to Build	1%

For example, after the domain walkthrough (which is optional), design, and design inspection, an iteration is considered 1 + 40 + 3 = 44% complete.

Notice that the percentages give almost one-half of the iteration's credit to the Design by Feature phase. This reflects the importance of design, particularly for large projects with developers of varying skills. As mentioned earlier, the chief programmer (who is more experienced) uses the design phase to set up the team members for success during the build phase.

DISCIPLINED AGILE DELIVERY

In the words of its inventor Scott Ambler, "The *Disciplined Agile Delivery (DAD)* decision process framework is a people-first, learning-oriented hybrid agile approach to IT solution delivery. It has a risk-value delivery life cycle, is goal driven, is enterprise aware, and is scalable." (Any description that contains so many execuspeak terms must be good!)

By now, most of those terms should be familiar to you and you can probably guess what they mean. The following section briefly describes the key pieces of that description.

DAD Principles

Here's a brief summary of the key terms in Scott Ambler's definition of DAD:

> ➤ People-first—In the DAD philosophy, the interactions among people play a critical role in the project's success. The DAD roles (described shortly) help define how people interact. DAD also uses typical agile ideas about allowing the team members to express themselves freely without fear of censorship or retribution.

> ➤ Learning-oriented—Throughout the project the team members should learn from each other to improve their cross-functionality. They should also constantly review their development practices and improve them if possible.

> ➤ Hybrid—DAD is based on scrum but also takes ideas from Extreme Programming, Unified Process, kanban, Lean, and others.

> ➤ Agile—Like most agile methodologies, DAD uses iterated development and delivers *consumable solutions* as they are ready. DAD encompasses the entire delivery life cycle (unlike some agile methods that focus mostly on development); although it doesn't actually require you to use a particular life cycle model, so you can keep your options open for some of the details.

> ➤ Risk-value delivery life cycle—During the inception phase, the team identifies risks. The team addresses risks throughout the project.

> ➤ Goal-driven—During each iteration, the highest priority requirements are pulled into the goals for that iteration.

> ➤ Enterprise aware—DAD emphasizes several levels of awareness (individual, team, enterprise, and community) that developers should keep in mind as they work. Enterprise awareness encourages the team to consider the business's overall goals and strategy. It also allows the team to identify similar work being performed within the business and look for ways to collaborate.

> ➤ Scalable—DAD's goal-driven approach makes it easier to scale than some other approaches.

The following section describes the roles defined by DAD.

DAD Roles

One of DAD's key principles is "people first." To help define the interactions among team members, DAD defines 10 roles: five primary and five secondary.

Four of the primary roles (product owner, team lead, team member, and architecture owner) are considered team roles. The fifth primary role is stakeholder.

The secondary roles are specialist, domain expert, technical expert, integrator, and independent tester. The following list shows the role descriptions grouped by their categories.

Primary Roles

➤ Stakeholder—Someone who will be affected by the project (users, managers, executives who staked their careers on the project, and so forth).

➤ Product owner—The point of contact on the team who represents the stakeholders. This person has authority to make decisions for the stakeholders.

➤ Architecture owner—Makes architectural decisions for the team.

➤ Team lead—The agile coach. (No, not someone good at running obstacle courses. Someone with experience at DAD projects.) This person helps the team improve its processes during development, ensures that the team has any needed resources, and generally helps keep things moving.

➤ Team member—A cross-functional developer who focuses on analysis, design, programming, testing, and all of the other typical development tasks.

Secondary Roles

➤ Domain expert—Provides additional detailed knowledge of the user domain in addition to the expertise provided by the product owner.

➤ Technical expert—An expert in a particular technical area such as database design, mobile platforms, or cloud storage.

➤ Integrator—Helps integrate the pieces of the system. Helps to integrate the application with other external systems.

➤ Independent tester—The developers perform most of the testing, but for a particularly complicated or critical application, you may want independent testers.

➤ Specialist—Someone who specializes in a particular part of development such as user experience design or human factor research.

DAD Phases

DAD uses three big phases taken from UP. (Not surprising given that Scott Ambler developed UP.) Those phases are inception, construction, and transition. The UP elaboration phase is divided between inception and construction in DAD.

The inception phase is similar to the one used by UP. Here, you figure out the project's main goals, develop a common vision, build a business case, and beg for funding. You also identify risks, create an initial design, and make an initial schedule.

In addition to tasks similar to those used by the UP inception phase, you also consider the new project in the enterprise environment. You make sure the project is aligned with the larger business goals, and you look for similar work being done elsewhere in the company.

During the construction phase, you use iterated development to produce potentially consumable solutions. (Something you wouldn't be embarrassed to give to the customers.) The early iterations should test the application's architecture so that you don't run into nasty surprises later.

The project also has a few higher-level goals throughout the construction phase. The team members should learn from each other to improve their skills. They should identify and remove risks, focus on quality (so ongoing testing is a must), look for ways to improve the development process, and use customer feedback to track changing goals.

The transition phase is fairly standard. You ensure that the application is usable and that it meets the customers' goals. Then you deliver the application using good deployment techniques such as staged delivery or incremental cutover.

DYNAMIC SYSTEMS DEVELOPMENT METHOD

Dynamic Systems Development Method (DSDM) is an agile framework originally managed by the DSDM Consortium but rebranded as the Agile Business Consortium (ABC) in 2016. (See www .agilebusiness.org/page/whatisdsdm.) It is one of the heavier agile methodologies. It also has one of the longest and most "management-friendly" names and has one of the most unpronounceable abbreviations. (If you really want to pronounce DSDM, I recommend the pronunciation DIZ-dm so that it rhymes with "wisdom.") All of those facts may be the result of the method being invented by people with a business perspective instead of a software development background.

DSDM was originally invented in an attempt to bring some business discipline to the relatively untamed RAD wilderness. It attempts to bring a higher-level project focus to sit above other RAD models such as scrum.

The following sections describe the DSDM phases, principles, and participant roles.

DSDM Phases

DSDM uses the three phases (with various substages and steps) described in the following list:

➤ Pre-project—These are things that need to happen before the project can even start. They include identifying possible projects, getting executive approval and commitment, and receiving funding.

➤ Project life cycle—This is where the application is actually built. DSDM defines four stages within this phase:

    ➤ Study—This includes a feasibility study (to determine whether the project is possible) and a business study (to decide whether the project is worth the expense). During these studies, facts are usually gathered through facilitated workshops. Requirements are prioritized using the MOSCOW method. (See the section "Prioritized" in Chapter 5, "Requirements Gathering.")

    ➤ Model functionality—Here the team builds one or more working prototypes and functional models to describe the pieces of the system. This phase uses four steps that are repeated as often as necessary: identify a prototype, make a plan, create the prototype, and review the prototype. The team uses feedback from these cycles to iteratively improve the prototypes and models. The result is used to refine and prioritize the requirements.

➤ Design and build—In this stage, the team integrates the models built in the preceding stage to form a single prototype that satisfies all of the requirements. This stage includes four steps that are similar to those used in the preceding stage: Identify the features of the prototype, make a plan, create the prototype, and review the prototype. Those steps are repeated as often as necessary until the prototype evolves into the final working system. This stage also includes creating user documentation.

➤ Implementation—This is where the team deploys the system. Like the other life cycle stages, it too includes four steps: Seek user approval and guidelines, train users, implement, and review business results. If the review shows that the system meets the requirements, the project leaves the life cycle phase and moves into post-project.

➤ Post-project—This phase includes typical maintenance tasks such as bug fixes and making changes.

Figure 19.6 shows the normal flow for the project life cycle phase. The arrows show the normal sequence of events; although the project can move between any of the functional model, design and build, and implementation stages if necessary. For example, if the design and build stage uncovers a fundamental problem, the project could move back to the functional model stage.

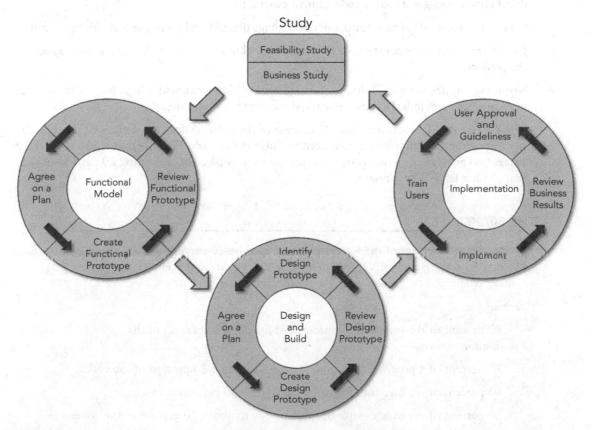

FIGURE 19.6: The DSDM life cycle includes four stages: study, functional model, design and build, and implementation.

DSDM Principles

Like many RAD development models, DSDM has a set of guiding principles. Those principles are described in the following list:

➤ Active user involvement—Users must be involved to provide guidance and feedback.

➤ Team empowerment—The team must have the authority to make design decisions throughout development. Users can request changes to correct decisions in later iterations if necessary. (That doesn't mean developers should blindly make arbitrary decisions all over the place. Active user involvement means users can ask for guidance whenever they need it.)

➤ Frequent delivery—Frequent delivery moves the project toward its final form.

➤ Meeting business needs—The main criterion for acceptance is delivery of software that satisfies business needs (which should be in the requirements).

➤ Iterative and incremental—These provide quicker delivery and feedback. (Without these, it would be harder to think of DSDM as agile.)

➤ Reversible changes—All of the changes made during the project life cycle should be reversible. (This makes good source code control essential.)

➤ Constant testing—Constant testing uncovers bugs quickly and gives the code higher quality.

➤ Collaboration and cooperation—All of the stakeholders need to work together throughout the project.

➤ Requirements are refined—Initially, the requirements are written at a high level without a lot of encumbering details. Details are worked out during development.

➤ The 80/20 rule—It is assumed that 80 percent of the project's features can be satisfied in 20 percent of the total time you would need to finish the project. The project focuses on that 80 percent to provide the most features as quickly as possible. The remaining 20 percent of the features are left for later releases.

THE 80/20 RULE

The idea that 80 percent of the features are provided by 20 percent of the code is an instance of a more general 80/20 rule. This rule states that 80 percent of just about anything is satisfied by (or caused by) 20 percent of the related items.

For example:

➤ 80 percent of the system can be described in about 20 percent of the documentation.

➤ 80 percent of a program's time will be spent in about 20 percent of the code.

➤ 80 percent of the user training will be easy with 20 percent trickier.

➤ 80 percent of the code complexity will be due to about 20 percent of the code.

> ➤ 80 percent of the bugs will nest in about 20 percent of the code.

> ➤ 80 percent of that buggy code will be written by the least experienced 20 percent of the programmers.

> ➤ 80 percent of your wait at the store checkout line is due to the 20 percent of the customers in front of you who have never used self-checkout before.

This rule is also fractal, so it repeats on smaller and smaller scales. For example, of the 20 percent most complex code, 80 percent of that will be less complex than the remaining super-complex 20 percent.

This rule isn't perfect, but lacking other data it's a good first approximation. That's why it's particularly important to think before you act. Don't spend all of your time optimizing the 80 percent of the code that's already fast enough.

DSDM Roles

Like other RAD models, DSDM defines a set of roles for the team members. (I think the first things that you do when you invent a new methodology are to create a set of principles and a set of roles; the manifesto is optional.) The following list describes the roles:

➤ Executive sponsor—The executive champion who protects the project from outside interference. This person should have the authority to provide funds and has ultimate decision-making power.

➤ Visionary—The person who has a clear vision of what the application should be, particularly early on when the requirements are fuzzy. This person also tracks the project to make sure it is converging on the vision.

➤ Ambassador user—Acts as a liaison between the users and the developers. Provides the users with project updates and provides the developers with user feedback.

➤ Technical coordinator—Manages the project's overall design and architecture. Monitors the project's technical quality.

➤ Developer—Writes and tests the code.

➤ Tester—Tests the code to uncover bugs. Verifies that the code meets the requirements.

➤ Project manager—Does all of the usual project manager things such as tracking deadlines to make sure teams stay within their timeboxes.

DSDM projects may also define many secondary roles depending on the size of the project and the number of interested stakeholders. Those roles may include the following:

➤ Advisor user—Any user who brings a useful viewpoint to the project.

➤ Architect—Specializes in developing the application architecture.

➤ Business advisor—Provides business knowledge to the developers. For example, this person may help ensure that the project satisfies business rules, company policies, and regulatory requirements.

➤ Business ambassador—Provides business information from the viewpoint of the users.

➤ Business analyst—Provides day-to-day business focus for the development team. Helps ensure that the daily decisions made by the developers support the project's business goals.

➤ Business visionary—The person who holds a clear vision of the application's business role, particularly early in the process when that role isn't clearly written down. Ensures that the project's requirements help meet the business goals.

➤ DSDM coach—Helps the project team use the DSDM methodology properly.

➤ Quality manager—Ensures the application's quality. Tracks bug reports, testing, reviews, and other techniques used to improve quality. Uses statistical methods to estimate quality. Defines the project's quality procedures (such as testing and review guidelines).

➤ Scribe—Keeps records of requirements, agreements, assumptions, and other key facts discovered at workshops.

➤ Senior developer—A software engineering ninja that other developers can call on when they need rescue from a particularly tricky piece of code.

➤ System integrator—Builds and tests the interfaces between the application and other applications.

➤ Team lead—Leads a team of developers.

➤ Workshop facilitator—Plans, runs, and encourages participation at workshops. (This may sound like a silly role, but in the meetings that I've had with facilitators, they've been surprisingly useful. They basically did the corny everyone-get-to-know-each-other thing, got some conversation started, and then got out of the way.)

KANBAN

Kanban (which is Japanese for "signboard" or "billboard") is a *just-in-time (JIT)* production methodology for controlling logistics in a production chain. The basic idea is to use cards (not coincidentally called kanbans) on each station in the chain to represent the inventory of parts at that station. When that station runs low on parts, its kanban is sent to the supplier to indicate a need for more.

Basically, the kanban acts as a message saying, "This station needs more parts." The kanban "pulls" new parts from the supplier as needed. In practice there are a few variations on kanban. For example, you could keep a small backup bucket of parts to use while you're waiting for new parts.

For another example, some checkbooks contain a sheet inserted near the end of the book that says, "Reorder checks now." That's basically a kanban-style warning that you are about to run out of checks and that you should reorder. You still have a few checks to go, just in case you need to write more checks before you get the new supply. (Of course, these days you can make all of your payments electronically or with credit cards. I think the occasional tax payment is just about all I still use checks for.)

For a final example (which you probably have seen, even if you don't have a checking account and therefore the previous example was confusing), you can think of the little "out of gas" symbol next to your car's gas gauge as a kanban-style warning that you're about to run out of gas. When it lights up, you still have some gas (otherwise, it would be hard to drive to the gas station to get more), but you should refuel soon.

In a production environment, kanbans make it easy to track parts inventory and supply, so you can optimize the process. For example, you can discover exactly how many M12 torq-set screws you use per month, so you can preorder accordingly.

In software engineering, kanban is a translation of the production kanban into a software development environment. At this point, you would probably expect to see a list of principles, practices, and roles, and you'd be mostly right. The following sections describe kanban principles and practices, although kanban doesn't define roles. (Shocking, I know!)

Kanban Principles

Like many agile methodologies, kanban has a set of heartwarming guiding principles designed to create a healthy and productive workplace. Of the four basic principles, three are aimed directly at the fact that kanban may initially seem weird to development organizations. They help make moving to kanban practices as simple and unobtrusive as possible. (If you're lucky, you can sneak in some of the kanban practices without upper management even noticing.)

The following list describes the kanban principles:

➤ Start with current practices—Kanban doesn't explicitly mandate every part of the development process, so you can work it into whatever system you're using now.

➤ Seek incremental change—Add kanban principles to your current practices gradually. If you try to jump to kanban all at once, you may face resistance to change. (I've seen people fight tooth and nail against a change to the day of the week when timecards were processed. Imagine the fuss you could get if you told people they had to switch from their venerated waterfall model to something agile!)

➤ Respect the current process—Your current system probably has some benefits, so you shouldn't just throw it away even if you can. Keep your current roles and responsibilities. (I told you kanban didn't define any roles.) Over time you can let those roles morph (in a self-organizing way, of course).

➤ Encourage leadership in everyone—Like many other agile models, kanban encourages everyone to take ownership of the project and their duties. Don't wait for someone else to decide to tackle a task or fix a bug. Show some leadership and do it yourself.

Kanban Practices

Although kanban is intended to sift gently down like snow over your existing practices, it does define some practices.

➤ Visualize workflow—Kanban enables you to visualize the work you are doing today in the context of other tasks. This encourages free communication and collaboration among the team members.

➤ Limit work in progress (WIP)—The JIT nature of production-line kanban means the production chain holds as little inventory as possible. In software engineering, kanban limits the amount of work that is being done at any moment. In contrast, you might pull too much or too little work into a scrum sprint. By reducing multitasking, kanban removes the inherent penalty for task-switching and makes developers more productive. (On a personal note, I'm not terrible at task-switching, but I'm not great either, and I definitely pay a penalty in lost productivity.)

➤ Enhance flow—When you finish one task, you pull the next-highest priority item from the backlog. (This is similar to the way a production-line kanban "pulls" new inventory from a supplier.) Instead of using sprints that involve planning, design, estimating, and testing of a set of features, you perform those same steps for each individual feature when you get to it.

In general, kanban works a lot like scrum. The biggest difference (aside from kanban's lack of predefined roles) is that scrum works in sprints and kanban works continuously one feature at a time.

Recall that at the beginning of a new scrum sprint, the sprint planning meeting pulls an assortment of high-priority items from the project backlog into the sprint backlog. The sprint (which is typically 30 days) works through its backlog to produce a potentially shippable increment. When the project includes enough new features to be worth the hassle, it is delivered to the users.

In contrast, kanban developers pull the highest priority items from the project backlog one at a time whenever they finish a task. (This is a good opportunity for everyone to demonstrate the fourth principle and show some leadership.) It's a bit like having a scrum project where every item is in its own sprint. That lets kanban deliver increments more often (when it's worthwhile). It also makes kanban extremely responsive to rapidly changing user priorities.

Kanban Board

The kanban board is one of the more unique kanban features. The board is a form of big board or information radiator that shows all of the project's tasks and their current statuses.

The board can have many forms. The simplest might have only three columns labeled To Do, In Progress, and Done. As tasks move from one status to another, you move sticky notes, cards, or whatever you're using to represent the tasks from one column to the next.

To get a more detailed view of exactly where the tasks are, kanban boards for software projects typically use more columns. For example, you could use the columns Backlog, Ready, Coding, Testing, Approval, and Done. Feel free to change the names and add or remove columns if you like. You can even group the columns, as shown in Figure 19.7.

I filled the Design, Coding, Unit Test, and Integration Test columns with a hatch pattern to indicate that they are WIP columns. Remember that one of the kanban practices is to limit the WIP. If there are too many cards in the WIP columns, there may be a problem. For example, if the project has four team members but 27 cards in the WIP columns, then the developers might be taking on too many tasks to focus on them properly.

The cards shown in Figure 19.7 are too small to hold much information, so they just show task numbers. In practice the cards might also include information such as the title of the task, a brief description, and the person working on the task.

	Inception		Construction			Transition		
	Backlog	Design	Coding	Unit Test	Integration Test	Acceptance Test	Ready	Deployed
	117		134	72		37	19	1
	98		101					2
	16							29
	12							

FIGURE 19.7: The kanban board lets everyone see the status of the project's tasks at a glance.

Some kanban boards use rows in the "in progress" columns to show who's working on which tasks. For example, the tasks in the top row might be owned by Alice, those in the second row might be owned by Bob, and so forth.

Tasks in the non-WIP columns wouldn't belong to anyone. For example, tasks in the Backlog column are waiting for someone to pick them. Tasks in the Acceptance Test column are waiting for the users to verify that they meet the requirements. (At least in my imaginary project—the person who performs acceptance testing might vary depending on your development model.)

On a large project, you'll probably need to use a computerized board. (Or cover the walls with boards.) That seems more fitting for a software engineering effort, although it would make it a bit harder to grasp the project's status at a glance as you walk by. (Plus, I think there's something kind of fun about posting sticky notes on a whiteboard. Maybe it's just me.)

A computerized board can handle a huge number of tasks (it would also be hard to fit 1,237 sticky notes in the Backlog column at the start of a large project), could automatically keep the tasks sorted by priority, and could provide hyperlinks to let you easily get more information about the tasks.

There are many variations on the kanban board, each tailored to suit a particular development team's practices. It's interesting to search the Internet for images of kanban boards and see some of the alternatives.

SUMMARY

As long as it is, this chapter merely touched on a few of the more common RAD methodologies. If you want more information about any of them, you should search the Internet or buy a book about them. There are books about many of them that explain exactly how their original versions work.

There are also dozens (if not hundreds) of other methodologies. Some methods descended from others, and there are even methods built as mashups of other methods. For example, DAD (which descended from AUP, which descended from RUP, which descended from UP) includes elements of scrum, XP, UP, kanban, Lean, and other methodologies that aren't described in this chapter. (If you're really bored, you could build a family tree showing the relationships among the various methodologies. After some searching, I did find one at `https://hacksaw.co.za/blog/agile-and-agile-methodologies`. The family tree itself is at `https://hacksaw.co.za/blog/content/images/2019/11/image.png`.)

Each one of those methodologies has countless variations, adaptations, and customizations used by different development teams. In fact, I would *recommend* that you modify any model to fit your team. One of the agile principles is to reflect on the development process and improve it. If you follow that principle, then your process will necessarily change over time.

That may make it hard to understand the "official" version of a particular methodology, but that kind of customization also lies at the heart of agile development. Different agile methods may use different approaches, but they all ask you to constantly look for ways to improve your project and the development process. Because no two teams or projects are exactly alike, it makes sense that no two implementations of a development model would be exactly alike either. If you haven't made any modifications to the development model, then you're probably not doing it right.

If you're thinking about joining a development team, hopefully this chapter and the previous ones will help you understand in general what your potential new teammates mean when they say they use waterfall, Cleanroom, Crystal Orange, DSDM, or kanban. At least you'll know enough to ask the right questions to learn more about their customizations and additions.

EXERCISES

1. Suppose you're working for Stodgy Megacorp, an old-fashioned company that calls employees "assets," puts "Suggestion Box" labels on its wastebaskets, and uses a classic one-pass waterfall model for software development. Which of the four agile values does that model violate?

2. Which of the 12 agile principles does Stodgy Megacorp's waterfall model violate?

3. Given your answers to Exercises 1 and 2, should you forget the waterfall model as a possible approach to software engineering?

4. Which of the four agile values does James Martin RAD satisfy?

5. Which of the 12 agile principles does James Martin RAD satisfy?

6. Explain why scrum velocity isn't quite the same as the difference between the amount of work in the project backlog before and after a sprint. When will velocity equal that difference?

7. You can directly measure the number of person-hours spent on a sprint, but story points are just a guess. Why might it be more useful to calculate velocity in story points per sprint instead of actual work performed per sprint even though you're using guesses instead of facts?

8. If your story points measure the estimated number of days for each user story (instead of using another metric such as small, medium, and large), what does it mean if the number of actual person-days spent on sprints is consistently lower than the number of story points assigned to the sprints? What if actual days is higher than story points? In those cases, do you need to revise your story point estimates?

9. Is maximizing a scrum project's velocity the most important goal? Why or why not?

10. The term "lean software development" was introduced by Mary Poppendieck and Tom Poppendieck in their book *Lean Software Development* (Addison-Wesley Professional, 2003). In that book, they use the slogan, "Think big, act small, fail fast; learn rapidly." Briefly explain what each of those phrases means.

11. Which of the following scenarios are similar to kanban in a production line setting? Why or why not?

   a. The last few feet of a cash register tape have red edges.
   b. The same situation as Exercise 11a, except on a self-service register.
   c. When your light bulb burns out, you replace it with a bulb stored in the closet.
   d. The same situation as Exercise 11c, except when you take a bulb from the closet you see how many bulbs are left. If there are no more bulbs, you write "Light Bulbs" on your shopping list.
   e. When your pen runs out of ink, it stops working.

WHAT YOU LEARNED IN THIS CHAPTER

➤ RAD includes the following techniques:
  ➤ Small teams
  ➤ Requirements gathering through focus groups and workshops
  ➤ Requirements validation through prototypes, use cases, and customer testing
  ➤ Repeated customer testing
  ➤ Constant integration and testing
  ➤ Testing, testing, and more testing
  ➤ Informal reviews and communication
  ➤ Short iterations
  ➤ Deferring complicated features to later releases
  ➤ Timeboxing

➤ RAD includes the following advantages:
  ➤ More accurate requirements
  ➤ Ability to handle changes
  ➤ Frequent customer involvement that encourages engagement
  ➤ Reduced development time and early releases
  ➤ Code reuse
  ➤ Constant testing that leads to high-quality code
  ➤ Risk mitigation
  ➤ Greater chance of success

➤ RAD includes the following disadvantages:
  ➤ Resistance to change
  ➤ Doesn't work well with large systems
  ➤ Requires skilled team members
  ➤ Requires access to scarce resources such as expert users
  ➤ Adds extra overhead
  ➤ Less managerial control
  ➤ May give a less-than-optimal design
  ➤ Unpredictable

➤ The Agile Manifesto defines four rules to make an agile-friendly environment:
  ➤ Individuals and interactions over processes and tools
  ➤ Working software over comprehensive documentation
  ➤ Customer collaboration over contract negotiation
  ➤ Responding to change over following a plan

➤ Agile includes the following techniques:
  ➤ Provide early and continuous delivery
  ➤ Welcome changing requirements
  ➤ Have developers and stakeholders work closely together
  ➤ Use motivated team members
  ➤ Convey information with conversations
  ➤ Measure progress by working software
  ➤ Use sustainable development

➤ Pay continuous attention to excellence

➤ Keep things as simple as possible

➤ Use self-organizing teams

➤ Reflect on the development process and improve it

➤ Deliver incremental and evolutionary results

➤ Different agile methods use the same techniques organized in different ways.

➤ Extreme Programming includes the following practices:

  ➤ Customer on-site

  ➤ Planning game

  ➤ Standup meetings

  ➤ Frequent small releases

  ➤ Intuitive metaphors

  ➤ Simple designs

  ➤ Deferred optimization

  ➤ Refactoring

  ➤ Shared code ownership

  ➤ Coding standards

  ➤ Promoting generalization

  ➤ Pair programming

  ➤ Constant testing

  ➤ Constant integration

  ➤ Sustainable pace

  ➤ Test-driven and test-first development

➤ James Martin RAD uses four phases: requirements planning, user design, construction, and cutover.

➤ Scrum uses short sprints to produce potentially shippable increments. A backlog contains the prioritized tasks that need to be accomplished. Planning poker helps estimate task difficulty. Burndown charts show how many tasks are completed over time. Velocity indicates how many story points the team completes per sprint.

➤ Lean focuses on waste and removes everything wasteful.

➤ The Crystal methods address projects of different sizes. Crystal colors include Clear, Yellow, Orange, Orange Web, Red, Maroon, Diamond, and Sapphire. Criticality is measured as comfort, discretionary money, essential money, and life. Larger projects require more formality. More critical projects require more control and testing.

➤ Feature-Driven Development focuses on features. It uses five phases. The first three phases (develop a model, build a feature list, and plan by feature) occur in iteration 0. The remaining two phases (design by feature and build by feature) occur repeatedly in other iterations.

➤ Agile Unified Process is an agile version of Unified Process. It is serial in the large (it follows the four phases of UP: inception, elaboration, construction, and transition), and iterative in the small (it performs those phases iteratively). Throughout the project, different disciplines occur in different amounts.

➤ To summarize Disciplined Agile Delivery, Scott Ambler says, "The Disciplined Agile Delivery (DAD) decision process framework is a people-first, learning-oriented hybrid agile approach to IT solution delivery. It has a risk-value delivery lifecycle, is goal-driven, is enterprise aware, and is scalable." It uses the AUP phases inception, construction, and transition.

➤ Dynamic Systems Development Method adds more business controls to an agile process. Its major phases are pre-project, project life cycle, and post-project. Project life cycle includes study, functional modeling, design and build, and implementation.

➤ Kanban in a production chain uses kanban cards to "pull" new inventory when a parts station is empty (or running low). Kanban software development uses cards on a kanban board to show the states the tasks are in. When a developer finishes a task, he pulls the highest priority task from the project backlog. Kanban limits the amount of work in progress.

PART III
Advanced Topics

Do the right thing. It will gratify some people and astonish the rest.

—*Mark Twain*

This part of the book covers two topics that didn't really fit into the other chapters: software ethics and future trends. They're not exactly contained within the software engineering process, but instead they guide that process. Knowing what the future may bring will help you decide which tools may be useful and what applications people may want built. Ethics will help you decide whether you should build those applications.

20

Software Ethics

Ethics is knowing the difference between what you have a right to do and what is right to do.

—*Potter Stewart*

It should be noted that no ethically trained software engineer would ever consent to write a DestroyBaghdad procedure. Basic professional ethics would instead require him to write a DestroyCity procedure, to which Baghdad could be given as a parameter.

—*Nathaniel S. Borenstein*

What You Will Learn in This Chapter:

➤ Ethical behavior

➤ Software engineering dilemmas

➤ Thought experiments

Before this chapter really begins, we need to agree on some simple definitions. If you ask most people about ethics and morality, they'll probably mumble something about whether an action is right or wrong. Some say that ethics is a standard defined by society or community, while morality is defined more personally even if a principle is not covered by societal ethics. Ethics: Is it okay to park in a handicapped spot? Morality: Is it okay to commit adultery?

Unfortunately, some people swap the definitions or use the two terms interchangeably. In this chapter, I'm going to talk about ethics, and by that I mean the first definition: what society thinks is right.

With those two definitions for ethics and morality out of the way, we can ask, "Why should you study software ethics?" The answer is, "So you can recognize ethical questions when they arise and have a framework for understanding how to handle them." Just as firefighters, soldiers, and emergency room doctors train so they can quickly spring into action when necessary, you should train so you know what to do when tricky ethical situations arise. Your personal moral compass will still help guide you, but at least you should recognize situations where you may be incrementally lead into a position that you find questionable.

This chapter is divided into two parts. The first talks about things that you, as a software developer, should do. These include topics like how to work professionally and provide good service to your clients, how to decide whether a software application is ethical, and how to think about ethical gray areas. This part also describes some ethical problems that many software developers face in the real world.

The second part of the chapter examines some interesting ethical dilemmas. Some of these are vaguely relevant for artificial intelligence (or perhaps they will be some day), but mostly they're just interesting.

> **DISCLAIMER** Note that I am not a professional ethicist, lawyer, or philosopher. I'll try to keep my own moral opinions out of this chapter as much as possible and stick to more widely accepted ethical principles and interesting dilemmas. I want to make you think about these situations; I'm not trying to tell you how to precisely define right and wrong. You'll need to do at least some of that work on your own. (I think I can safely promise you that this chapter won't solve all of your ethical and moral dilemmas.)

ETHICAL BEHAVIOR

The rules about what you should do as a software developer are similar to the rules that any professional should follow. Show up for work on time, try to be polite to your coworkers, take your turn bringing the donuts, and so forth.

Still, software developers face some unique situations that a typical person stocking shelves at a supermarket does not. An overnight stocker usually can't peek at someone's private emails, destroy a database to punish an annoying client, or launch millions of phishing attacks.

To try to provide some basic guidance, several computing organizations have written codes of ethics. Most of these make such perfect sense that you might think they don't need to be written down. Unfortunately, I have seen people violate many of these rules in small or large ways, so I guess they really are necessary. They're worth reading even if you think you're a paragon of virtue and fair play.

The following sections provide summaries of ethical rules offered by a few important software organizations and describe some common programming dilemmas that you should watch out for.

IEEE-CS/ACM

Here is the Code of Ethics devised by the IEEE-CS/ACM Joint Task Force on Software Engineering Ethics and Professional Practices. (*IEEE* stands for *Institute of Electrical and Electronics Engineers*, the *CS* in *IEEE-CS* stands for *Computer Society*, and *ACM* stands for *Association for Computing Machinery*.)

1. PUBLIC – Software engineers shall act consistently with the public interest.

2. CLIENT AND EMPLOYER – Software engineers shall act in a manner that is in the best interests of their client and employer consistent with the public interest.

3. PRODUCT – Software engineers shall ensure that their products and related modifications meet the highest professional standards possible.

4. JUDGMENT – Software engineers shall maintain integrity and independence in their professional judgment.

5. MANAGEMENT – Software engineering managers and leaders shall subscribe to and promote an ethical approach to the management of software development and maintenance.

6. PROFESSION – Software engineers shall advance the integrity and reputation of the profession consistent with the public interest.

7. COLLEAGUES – Software engineers shall be fair to and supportive of their colleagues.

8. SELF – Software engineers shall participate in lifelong learning regarding the practice of their profession and shall promote an ethical approach to the practice of the profession.

Copyright © 1999 by the Institute for Electrical and Electronics Engineers, Inc. and the Association for Computing Machinery, Inc.

Most of these items should be fairly obvious.

This is the short version. You can see a longer version that includes details for each of the items at `www.computer.org/education/code-of-ethics`. It's worth your time to visit the website and scan the more detailed version. It doesn't take long.

You can also find a more recent page called "Ethical Guidelines & Policies" at `https://ieeemce.org/planning-basics/general-guidelines/ethical-guidelines-and-policies`. It provides links to the IEEE code of conduct, code of ethics, publishing ethics, and more.

> **OLD BUT NOT DATED** Note that some of the codes of ethics shown in this chapter are fairly old but not really out of date. Most of them deal with general principles that haven't changed in centuries, so they still apply. It's just as unethical to steal from your employer and trick your customers now as it was in 1999.
>
> One area where more specific guidance might be useful is in artificial intelligence. We'll talk a bit about that later in this chapter.

ACS

Here is an excerpt from the *Australian Computer Society (ACS)* Code of Professional Conduct.

As an ACS member you must uphold and advance the honour, dignity and effectiveness of being a professional. This entails, in addition to being a good citizen and acting within the law, your conformance to the following ACS values.

1. *The Primacy of the Public Interest*

   You will place the interests of the public above those of personal, business or sectional interests.

2. *The Enhancement of Quality of Life*

   You will strive to enhance the quality of life of those affected by your work.

3. *Honesty*

   You will be honest in your representation of skills, knowledge, services and products.

4. *Competence*

   You will work competently and diligently for your stakeholders.

5. *Professional Development*

   You will enhance your own professional development, and that of your staff.

6. *Professionalism*

   You will enhance the integrity of the ACS and the respect of its members for each other.

In a situation of conflict between the values, The Primacy of the Public Interest takes precedence over the other values.

This Code of Professional Conduct is aimed specifically at you as an individual practitioner, and is intended as a guideline for your acceptable professional conduct. It is applicable to all ACS members regardless of their role or specific area of expertise in the ICT industry.

The following list of requirements is not exhaustive and should not be read as a complete definition of acceptable professional conduct in all practical situations. The intention of the Code is to illustrate what constitutes professional behaviour. You are expected to take into account the spirit of this Code in order to resolve ambiguous or contentious issues concerning professional conduct. The ACS can help you resolve ethical dilemmas.

I've included the last two paragraphs to thwart any would-be social media lawyers who think that something is allowed if it's not specifically prohibited by the code. No, the code does not explicitly say that you shouldn't use a FakeApp to steal donations from an orphanage, but that's implied, and this would clearly violate the first three rules. (Those seem to be the rules that people are most likely to violate.)

The last paragraph says, "The following list. . ." because it is followed by a more detailed list. As with the IEEE-CS/ACM Code of Ethics in the previous section, this is the short version. You can see the whole thing at www.cs.fsu.edu/~langley/CIS3250/2018-Fall/Resources/ACS-Code-of-Professional-Conduct_v2.1.pdf.

CPSR

Here are The Ten Commandments of Computer Ethics defined by the Computer Ethics Institute as posted by *Computer Professionals for Social Responsibility (CPSR)*. You may find their use of "thou shalt" either cute or annoying, but they're reasonable commandments in any case.

1. Thou shalt not use a computer to harm other people.
2. Thou shalt not interfere with other people's computer work.
3. Thou shalt not snoop around in other people's computer files.
4. Thou shalt not use a computer to steal.
5. Thou shalt not use a computer to bear false witness.
6. Thou shalt not copy or use proprietary software for which you have not paid.
7. Thou shalt not use other people's computer resources without authorization or proper compensation.
8. Thou shalt not appropriate other people's intellectual output.
9. Thou shalt think about the social consequences of the program you are writing or the system you are designing.
10. Thou shalt always use a computer in ways that ensure consideration and respect for your fellow humans.

This one doesn't have a longer version. I think it's assumed that you should use your judgement.

Business Ethics

In addition to the cyber-ethical rules laid down by organizations such as IEEE-CS/ACM, ACS, CPSR, and others, it's worth looking at ethical rules for business in general. Most of the lists that I've seen include some assortment of the following:

➤ Honesty

➤ Fairness

➤ Integrity

➤ Compassion

➤ Respect

➤ Responsibility

➤ Loyalty

➤ Law-abiding

➤ Leadership

➤ Trustworthiness

➤ Concern for others

➤ Respect for others

➤ Accountability

➤ Transparency

➤ Environmental consciousness

It's a lot like the Boy Scout Law for businesspeople (trustworthy, loyal, helpful, friendly, and so on).

I think some of these are variations on each other. (For example, is Compassion + Responsibility = Concern for others? Is there an algebra of ethics?)

Interestingly if you search for personal ethical rules, you get roughly the same list, so business ethics doesn't seem to include much beyond being a basically good human being. Of course, we've seen plenty of examples of businesspeople and politicians who can't seem to follow any of these.

WHO WATCHES THE WATCHERS?

In this case study, the SEC (Securities and Exchange Commission) was watching.

As one of the world's premier accounting firms, Ernst & Young is often hired to audit companies to see if they're obeying financial laws. It turns out that Ernst & Young's employees were up to their own shenanigans, and the company was fined $100 million after admitting that its employees cheated on ethics exams, thus proving that the universe does indeed run on irony. (See `www .npr.org/2022/06/28/1108044858/accounting-giant-ernst-young-admits-its-employees-cheated-on-ethics-exams`.)

On the "Frequently Asked Questions About the Ethics Exam" section of the `IPasstheCPAExam .com` website (`https://ipassthecpaexam.com/cpa-ethics-exam`), the question "Is the CPA Ethics Exam difficult?" is answered in part, "Not really. The exam is more like a self-study, open-book test." So it's hard to understand why the Ernst & Young employees thought they needed to cheat.

If you follow the rules described in this section and the preceding ones, and you don't try to technically satisfy the rules without obeying their spirit, then you should be doing pretty well.

NADA

Here's one last list of ethical standards:

➤ Operate this business in accord with the highest standards of ethical conduct.

➤ Treat each customer in a fair, open, and honest manner, and fully comply with all laws that prohibit discrimination.

➤ Meet the transportation needs of our customers in a knowledgeable and professional manner.

➤ Represent our products clearly and factually, standing fully behind our warranties, direct and implied, and in all other ways justifying the customer's respect and confidence.

➤ Advertise our products in a positive, factual, and informative manner.

➤ Detail charges to assist our customers in understanding repair work and provide written estimates of any service work to be performed, upon request, or as required by law.

➤ Resolve customer concerns promptly and courteously.

➤ Put our promises in writing and stand behind them.

This is the National Automobile Dealers Association Code of Ethics (www.nada.org/nada/code-ethics). If car dealers have a code of ethics, then you should too. And if you replace the word "transportation" with "software" in the third item, then these rules apply fairly well to software engineering.

Hacker Ethics

The lists of ethical rules shown earlier basically say that you should be a good person. In his 1984 book, *Hackers: Heroes of the Computer Revolution*, Steven Levy gave a different set of rules that try to capture "the hacker ethic":

1. Access to computers—and anything which might teach you something about the way the world works—should be unlimited and total. Always yield to the Hands-on Imperative!

2. All information should be free.

3. Mistrust authority—promote decentralization.

4. Hackers should be judged by their hacking, not bogus criteria such as degrees, age, race or position.

5. You can create art and beauty on a computer.

6. Computers can change your life for the better.

Levy's book explores the lives of some of the original computer hackers from the late 1950s through the early 1980s. The current edition of this book is *Hackers: Heroes of the Computer Revolution - 25th Anniversary Edition* by Steven Levy (O'Reilly, 2010).

Some of these seem quite reasonable, even if they aren't phrased as rules to live by. For example, hackers (and programmers and everyone else) should be judged by their actions and not whether they have an advanced degree. It is also true that you can create art on your computer and that computers can change your life for the better.

These kinds of hacker ideals are based on the idea that hackers are rebelling against authority and providing a service to better the common good. Those concepts fit in well with society in the 1960s when people valued community, fought for the rights of the oppressed, and questioned authority.

When you think about this notion of hacker ethics, it's important to keep in mind the state of the art at the time. In the 1960s (and even the 1970s), very few people had access to any kind of computer. Most of those who did were either computer professionals or college students who could only log on to computers while on campus or over the phone lines through modems that were sometimes painfully slow. (I once had to log on via a 240 baud modem. That's 240 bits per second!)

Given how restricted access to computers was, it's easy to see why some people felt that only the elite members of society would have access to this transformative new technology.

While much of the world has moved on to keeping up with reality show celebrities and curating their lives on Instagram, there are still some who follow some sort of hacker ethics.

For example, the loose agglomeration of hacktivists known collectively as Anonymous sometimes tries to attack government websites or publish government documents on WikiLeaks, but many of them prefer to focus on pranks and entertainment.

Actually, even calling Anonymous a "loose agglomeration" overstates how organized they are. There is no organization called Anonymous; there's just a bunch of people who call themselves Anonymous. As "member" Trent Peacock once said:

> We just happen to be a group of people on the Internet who need—just kind of an outlet to do as we wish, that we wouldn't be able to do in regular society. . . .That's more or less the point of it. Do as you wish. . . . There's a common phrase: "we are doing it for the lulz."

Occasionally someone may publically announce a goal and Anonymous members may decide to help, but in general there is little to no coordination and members pretty much do what they want. British journalist Carole Cadwalladr of the *Observer* said, "If you believe in Anonymous, and call yourself Anonymous, you are Anonymous."

To the extent that the group has rules, they may include not disclosing your identity, not talking about the group (as in *Fight Club*), and not attacking the media. Some have said that the group supports moral values, but there's no statement about which set of moral values it supports and, like evil, morals are often in the eye of the beholder.

Hacker Terms

> **NOTE** The publisher's author guidelines specifically deprecate the terms "white hat" and "black hat." Unfortunately, those are the historical hacker terms, so they're included in this list.

No description of hacker ethics would be complete without at least a short list of amusing hacker terms:

➤ White hat—An "ethical" hacker who breaks security for non-malicious reasons. They break systems with the owners' permission and don't divulge any problems publicly until they have been fixed. (You can actually take courses and be certified in ethical hacking.)

➤ Black hat—Someone who breaks security for malicious reasons or personal gain.

➤ Grey hat (gray hat, greyhat)—A cross between a white hat and a black hat. Usually these are similar to white hats, but they break into systems without permission. They may then tell the system's owner about the problem or offer to fix it for a fee.

➤ Red hat—Hackers who attack black hats, possibly using illegal means.

➤ Blue hat—Can mean either (1) revenge seekers or (2) outside security professionals.

➤ Green hat—A noob who may not understand the consequences of their actions.

➤ Elite hacker (eleet, leet, 1337)—A hacker with mad ninja skillz. These were the best of the best, although sometimes the term "leet" is used ironically to mean someone who thinks they are eleet but are more of a script kiddie.

➤ Script kiddie (skiddie, skid)—A derogatory term for someone who breaks into systems by using scripts and prepackaged tools.

➤ Noob (newbie, newb, n00b, nub)—A derogatory term for a beginner at hacking, gaming, programming, or anything else.

➤ Hacktivist—Someone who uses hacking as a form of civil disobedience to promote ideological, political, or other messages.

➤ Suicide hacker—Like a suicide bomber, they cause chaos and disruption without regard to the damage they do or possible consequences such as jail time.

➤ Insider (malicious insider, whistleblower)—A hacker who has inside information about an organization that makes hacking easier.

➤ Cypherpunk—Someone who promotes widespread use of strong encryption as a means to promote social change. (Cypherpunk is a play on the word "cyberpunk," which is a science fiction genre.)

➤ Phreak—Someone who hacks telephone networks. More recently this can mean someone who breaks into any kind of network.

➤ State-sponsored hacker—Hackers supported by a government to hack rival governments or businesses in rival nations. Sometimes these penetrate systems and leave backdoors for later use.

> **7H3 L337 L4N6U463** *In addition to meaning someone is an expert at something, leet (or 1337 or leetspeak) is also a language, sort of. More correctly, it's a simple substitution cipher where letters are replaced with other letters and numbers that look somewhat similar. For example, O is replaced with 0, L is replaced with 1 because 1 looks kind of like a lowercase L, T is replaced with 7 because 7 looks sort of like a T with part of the top broken off, and so forth. With surprisingly little practice, you can read and write leet fairly easily. (At least it's easier than learning a new real-world language like Japanese, British English, or American English, depending on where you grew up.)*
>
> *Search online to find more information about leet. You can also find online English/leet translators, and Google even supports leet. To try it, visit* www.google.com/webhp?hl=xx-hacker. *(Google also supports pirate:* www.google.com/webhp?hl=xx-pirate.)*

Hacker terms also include those described in Chapter 8, "Security Design." (Sorry, but if you don't know those terms, then you're a noob.)

RESPONSIBILITY

If you manufacture a hammer and then someone uses it to destroy a priceless work of art, do you bear any responsibility? Most people would probably say no. (If the artist was Banksy, you might even get some thanks from the artist, depending on which piece it was.) The hammer you made was used destructively, but that was not its intended purpose. (See also "John Wick pencil.")

Now let's consider software. Suppose you publish some software that lets you send emails to your friends. What if someone adapts your code to send out millions of spam messages? What if those messages contain disinformation, people begin to riot, property is damaged, and people are injured? Again, your product isn't being used for its intended purpose, so you can reasonably claim that it's not your fault. (But it might be worth asking if you could have predicted the misuse and taken steps to make it harder.)

Let's go much further and suppose you write software that lets an MQ-9 Reaper drone fire Hellfire missiles at terrorists. You're not actually pulling the trigger, but that software was written to kill people so you can't honestly claim that you didn't know that someone would use it to blow things up. Claiming that you only provided the tool but didn't push the button is a very weak defense.

That example is pretty extreme, but there are many others that are slightly less obvious. Suppose you build a website where suicidal people get together to discuss ways to kill themselves. (Sadly, those sites exist.) Or you write addictive software that keeps users tied to their phones for hours at a time. (Search "hikikomori" to learn about one possible danger that this might intensify.) You can claim that the users are responsible for making their own choices, but you're setting up at least some of them to fail.

For a much less harmful example, suppose someone asks you for help with a programming problem, but it's clearly a homework assignment. I often help people with programming questions online, but not if they begin by saying, "Compare and contrast the following sorting algorithms. . ."

Other cases involve software that contains bugs or that isn't properly understood by the users. For example, consider these actual cases:

➤ The Therac-25 medical accelerator, a radiation therapy device, contained a bug that killed several patients.

➤ The Ariane 5 rocket reused Ariane 4 software, but differences in the engines caused it to explode.

➤ Therapy-planning software used at the National Cancer Institute in Panama City wasn't completely understood by the doctors who used it, and it recommended lethal radiation doses for several patients.

➤ Software controlling a self-driving car decided that a pedestrian was a false positive (like a bird or piece of trash or something) and hit and killed her.

In all of these cases, the software was not used maliciously, but a bug or misunderstanding caused terrible results. I hate to sound harsh, but if you worked on any of those projects, then you bear at least some of the responsibility for the outcomes.

If you think this is just a matter of testing and that these sorts of things could never happen on your projects, then you don't really get it. Yes, you need to test, and you need to test those kinds of systems extremely thoroughly, but thinking that this could never happen to you is pure hubris. Sooner or later, bugs will lead to mistakes. If your software controls something dangerous like a car, medical linear accelerator, or missile, then people could be hurt.

Whenever you write software, it's worth taking a few moments to ask yourself the following questions:

➤ Is its purpose harmful to users or society?

➤ Can it be subverted for harmful purposes?

➤ Could bugs be dangerous?

➤ What's the worst thing that this program could do?

➤ Is there a way to reduce the risks?

If you're starting to think that you don't want to work on life-critical systems, then you're beginning to understand the problem.

Gray Areas

If you like, you can snoop around the Internet and find other lists of ethical rules that are similar to those listed in the earlier sections. They all say roughly the same thing: don't be evil.

Sometimes, however, evil is in the eye of the beholder. Rules like those in the earlier sections tend to be written in a very general style and they cover situations that are relatively black-and-white. Programming drones to find survivors of an earthquake: ethical. Hacking a financial database to steal from widows and orphans: unethical. Writing order-tracking code: ethical. Stealing client information from your employer and selling it to your competition: unethical. Unless your moral compass spins like a windmill in a hurricane, those cases shouldn't be too controversial.

Of course, the more interesting cases occur in the gray areas. Should you build an infinite scroll that keeps people glued to their social media for hours every day? Should you write games that use microtransactions and in-game purchases to let six-year-olds spend thousands on their moms' credit cards? What about online gambling software? Military software designed to kill people? Surveillance software that randomly trolls through public and/or private data to build profiles on people without cause?

These are tough questions, and some of them require moral answers, not just ethical ones. They may also pit some of the obvious, common-sense rules against each other.

For example, infinite scroll, in-game purchases, and online gambling all provide entertainment. You can make a strong case for allowing users to decide for themselves whether those programs are acceptable forms of entertainment. In that case, these features fall squarely under the "enhance the customer's quality of life" clause and they're fine.

Unfortunately, those features are also highly addictive, at least for some people, so they can harm the user's quality of life. It's easy to find stories about people who have lost their life savings gambling online. There's also the story about a six-year-old who spent more than $16,000 over several months on in-game purchases through the Apple App Store, and you can waste many hours on an infinite scroll learning about how cats alter your clothes at night to make you think you're getting fat or on research about software ethics. (I may have some personal experience with cat and ethics articles.)

You can make convincing arguments that it's okay to work on military and government surveillance systems. You may believe that national security is important enough to justify working on those kinds of software even though they might be abused—that the needs of the many outweigh the needs of the few, so it's worth risking a few ethical constraints and laws to safeguard the nation.

Or you may find the whole concept utterly repellant. You may believe that bending a few rules is a slippery slope leading to an authoritarian dystopia and you'll do whatever you can to stop any kind of information gathering program, period.

The extreme points of view on this topic are nicely demonstrated by the single case of Edward Snowden. In a nutshell, Snowden was employed by the CIA and later contracted to the NSA. I don't think there's any reason to believe that he didn't believe he was doing good work that was important and ethical at first, but at some point, he became disillusioned and decided that the US government's electronic surveillance programs had gone too far and someone needed to expose the program to the public. So he did. At one extreme, the people running those programs think they are justified. At the other extreme, Snowden thought they were so flawed that he was willing to risk imprisonment to shut them down.

Not only does this story show how widely separated Snowden was from the people running those programs, but the case has shown how divided our society is. Snowden has variously been called a hero, traitor, whistleblower, spy, and patriot. Here are three stories that cover the gamut of opinions:

- ➤ "Why Edward Snowden Is a Hero"— www.newyorker.com/news/john-cassidy/why-edward-snowden-is-a-hero

- ➤ "Boehner: Snowden is a 'traitor'"— www.politico.com/story/2014/05/john-boehner-edward-snowden-traitor-nsa-leak-nbc-interview-107215

- ➤ "Was Snowden hero or traitor? Perhaps a little of both"— www.washingtonpost.com/opinions/was-snowden-hero-or-traitor-perhaps-a-little-of-both/2017/01/19/a2b8592e-c6f0-11e6-bf4b-2c064d32a4bf_story.html

You can search around to find many other stories that take the three of the viewpoints in those articles. People don't agree, but many have strong opinions.

If we assume that ethics define the things that society thinks are acceptable, then this cannot be an ethical issue because society is too divided to come even close to a consensus. The community agrees that Snowden's actions were either wonderful or terrible but can't decide which. I'm going to have to file this under "Moral dilemmas that each of us must face individually."

I won't tell you how I feel about this issue (partly because I said that I wouldn't and partly because I'm not sure even after pondering it for years), but I will mention two other behaviors that I do think are ethically unsound.

First, some people will justify their participation in a project because, "Someone else would do it anyway." It may be true that someone else would do the work if you don't, but that doesn't mean you need to be involved. By participating in a project that you find morally dubious, you are tacitly giving your approval. If you think a project is wrong, don't join it, switch to another project, or find another job. You don't need to be as dramatic as Snowden's publishing thousands of classified documents, fleeing to Russia, living in the airport for a month, and eventually being granted asylum and later Russian citizenship. You can start looking for a new job now and move on when you have a chance.

The second behavior that I want to mention is knowing about a problem but failing to act. When that six-year-old spent $16,000 through the App Store, Apple refused to refund the money. The folks at Apple said that the problem hadn't been reported within 60 days, so it was too late. When asked, customer support reportedly said, "There's a setting; you should have known." Knowing that there is a potential problem and creating a setting buried deep within the software that a customer may or may not find does not absolve you from responsibility. If there's a problem or a potential for abuse or other harm, then you should make the issue known and put real safeguards in place.

For the same reason, building an online gambling site and providing a link to seek help with addiction is a pretty weak protection. It would be better to analyze customers' gambling patterns and give help to those with obvious problems. That should be an easy exercise in data analysis. Unfortunately, that would also conflict directly with the business goal of separating customers from their money, so I suspect the ethical and moral considerations are going to lose to the business model.

One argument that I will not complain about is, "I need the work." Everyone needs to eat, and I won't say that every developer's career is at the point where they can refuse work on ethical grounds. However, should you decide to pursue a rewarding and exciting career in software development, you will hopefully become skilled enough that you can pick and choose your projects, at least to some extent. There are too many projects out there for you to work on the ones that you find objectionable.

When in doubt about whether a project is ethical, you can often turn to the ethical rules listed earlier and ask questions such as these:

➤ Will this project help or hurt the public?

➤ Will this project help or hurt the user? Will it help all users? Or will some be at risk? Can I protect the latter?

➤ Is this project providing a benefit or it is just transferring money from the user to the program's owner?

➤ Can this product be abused and, if so, can we add meaningful safeguards?

➤ Is this project being honestly and completely described to users so they can make informed decisions?

Consider the consequences of your software and the effects it will have on others. Then program unto others as you would have them program unto you.

Software Engineering Dilemmas

As I mentioned earlier, many of the really interesting cases are in the gray spaces, particularly where the obvious rules of software ethics conflict with each other. The following sections describe some common software development issues that require ethical consideration.

Misusing Data and the Temptation of Free Data

You shouldn't use data for purposes other than those for which it was intended. That means you shouldn't go snooping through other peoples' files, use confidential financial data to try to make someone invest in your company, or sift through private medical data to see who might want to buy life insurance policies or your new Hyperdrive Pacemaker product.

Ideally, this also means that websites shouldn't harvest visitor information and sell it to online retailers who fill your browser with ads for dolphin jewelry or whatever you've been browsing most recently. You may have heard an expression similar to "If you're not paying for the product, then you *are* the product."

This leads into another gray area: free data. Many websites provide content for free and support themselves by advertising. Full disclosure: That's how my VB Helper (`www.vb-helper.com`) and C# Helper (`www.CSharpHelper.com`) websites work. They provide tips, tricks, and examples for Visual Basic and C# programmers, and they pay for their hosting by serving ads. Yes, I feel guilty, but I couldn't afford to keep these sites running otherwise.

People usually feel that some level of online tracking and annoying advertising is acceptable in exchange for free content. Because society says that's okay, it is ethical.

You've probably also seen websites that provide an infinite scroll of worthless teasers like "You'll never believe what comes next!" to make you hope that you'll eventually find some headline story at the end of the rainbow. I call these "shaggy dog sites" because they're like shaggy dog stories. (If you don't know what that means, search it.) You can often find them as paid content on social media platforms. The whole point of those sites is just to keep you on the hook for as long as possible while they serve ads, and many of them never actually contain the content they teased you with. I think few people find those sites useful, although I'm not sure they're hated enough to be considered unethical.

Disruptive Technology

Should you write a program that will put thousands of people out of work? Clearly this will be a negative for those people, but it might be a benefit for society as a whole. These days few people work as bowling pin setters (machines do that now), ice cutters (mechanical ice makers are common), telegraph operators (replaced by phones), or leech collectors (just, ick).

I've worked on a few projects that *could have* put people out of work, but they didn't. One did the work of several people, but those people simply moved to other parts of the company. (That industry had a shrinking workforce due to automation, and it was common for employees to just move into new positions until they retired.)

Another project did the work that several people could have (and perhaps should have) been doing, but the work wasn't being done due to staffing shortages and budgetary constraints. The project allowed the company to do the extra work without affecting the headcount.

I've been lucky that my projects have not been overly disruptive, but you may someday face a project that will put people out of work and then you'll need to decide whether you're willing to do that work. It's not hard to find headlines such as "Automation could kill 73 million U.S. jobs by 2030" (`www.usatoday.com/story/money/2017/11/29/automation-could-kill-73-million-u-s-jobs-2030/899878001`) and "Automation helped kill up to 70 percent of the US's middle-class jobs since 1980, study says" (`www.businessinsider.com/automation-labor-market-wage-inequality-middle-class-jobs-study-2021-6`). It's true that automation can kill jobs, but the story is not completely one-sided, and automation can create jobs too. It's worth taking some time to read a few of those articles to see what the issues are.

A project may be bad for some individuals but good for society, so the ethical rules are in conflict. It may be tempting to use the "If I don't write it, then someone else will," logic. I know it's hard, but try to decide whether you think the benefit outweighs the pain. Will this really help society? Or will it just put people out of work to increase corporate profit?

In the end, the same reasoning I used earlier applies here too. If you don't like the project, move to another one. You don't have to write job-killing software if you don't want to.

Algorithmic Bias

One of the more technical ethical considerations in software development lately is *algorithmic bias*. This occurs when a program's algorithms have an underlying bias that makes them produce bad results. Often the bias is unknown to the developers, at least initially. Sometimes it occurs when the developers use assumptions that they don't realize are biased. Or an application may use historical data that already had bias built in. Other times bias occurs when data is used incorrectly, such as, for example, when a program confuses correlation with causation.

For a concrete example, Amazon once tried to build a resume screening tool. This kind of tool would be a huge benefit to many companies because it could evaluate candidates in a neutral way without being swayed by things like a person's gender, ethnic background, age, favorite sports team, or other criteria that should be irrelevant. To train the algorithm, they fed it resumes that Amazon had received over a 10-year period.

Unfortunately, most of the employees in big tech firms are male, so the program eventually taught itself to discriminate against women. After all, most of the people hired in the past were men, so men must be better, right? The program started penalizing resumes that included the word "women" and downgraded people who attended certain all-women colleges.

While trying to create a system that would be immune to issues like gender, Amazon had created a system that was severely biased. It eventually abandoned that project and said that its recruiters never used it to select candidates, although it's been cagey about the exact details, so it's not clear whether recruiters ever used the system to perform initial screenings.

False Confidence

One problem with Amazon's resume analysis tool was that it used past data to predict future behavior. (It's much harder to use future data to predict future behavior.) In this example, past job applicants were more likely to be men, so the algorithm decided that being male was a benefit. It confused correlation with causation.

Here's another example: Some judicial systems use artificial intelligence systems for risk assessment. One of the more important kinds of analysis takes a subject's information (things like criminal history, age at release, and geographic area) and produces a recidivism score giving the likelihood that the person will reoffend in the future. A judge then uses that score and some other factors (like remorse, defendant's mental state, and behavior while in jail) to decide how that person should be treated. For example, the judge may decide to grant low or high bail or keep the person in custody until trial. Those scores may also influence whether the person receives a shorter or longer sentence.

If an automated risk assessment system notices a correlation between low income and crime, then it may assume that people with low incomes are more likely to reoffend and it may discriminate against people with low incomes.

Even worse, suppose a particular neighborhood has historically been overpoliced. In that case, it may not have a higher crime rate, but it may have a higher *detected* crime rate. In that case, the program may decide that people from that neighborhood are more dangerous even though they're not.

The *garbage in, garbage out (GIGO)* rule applies here. The program may faithfully execute its code, but if the data it receives is flawed, then the results are unreliable.

A computerized risk assessment is only one factor in estimating recidivism, so it's possible that the judge could overrule the assessment and give other factors greater weight. Unfortunately, it's likely that the opposite is true. People often assume that software is more correct than it actually is. They assume that the program, because it is free from emotional issues, must be fair and unbiased. Faced with a difficult and important decision such as sentencing, a judge may be tempted to rely more heavily on the automated and "unbiased" algorithm.

Lack of Oversight

If you suspect that your data may be biased, you can analyze its results to see whether that's true. Sometimes you may be able to clean up the algorithm so the program is usable. Even if you know that your data is perfect, however, that doesn't prevent your program from doing something unreasonable with it, so you may still get a biased result.

To avoid application errors going undetected, you need sufficient oversight. You need to carefully examine the program's outputs and make sure they make sense. You need to look for bias and show that it doesn't exist. You need to compare expected results to actual results, and you may even need to resort to statistics <shudder> to prove that the program works as expected.

One way to increase oversight is to think of an application as a tool to assist humans rather than a panacea to replace humans. If someone uses a program to make a job easier, then that person will be working closely with the program and can check its results. That doesn't mean a mistake can't slip through, and it doesn't absolve the person using the tool from responsibility, but it does give someone one last chance to catch an error.

AN AWFUL ASSIGNMENT

I once worked on a repair dispatching system that assigned people with appropriate skills and equipment to work on telephone repair jobs. Twice during our testing period, the program assigned people to work jobs at their ex-wives' houses.

Had the program been running without oversight, that might have been a problem. It certainly would have been awkward. Fortunately, the repair people recognized their ex's names and addresses, called in to the human dispatcher, and got the jobs reassigned. Because the system was used as a tool to help the human dispatcher rather than as a replacement, it was a relatively easy problem to fix.

Getting Paid

Everyone likes to get paid, and software engineers are certainly no exception. If everything goes to plan, you write some software, your client pays you, and everyone goes home happy.

Unfortunately, there are many stories about clients who pay slowly, underpay, or don't pay at all. I think every software contractor that I know has had these happen at least once. (All of these have happened to me several times.) Sometimes a client will let a project go to 90-percent completion, fire the developer, and say they can finish from there. Other clients may drag a contract out for months, requesting more and more features and refusing to sign off on the project until everything is done to their satisfaction.

Along with those stories, there's a whole genre of stories about programmers who deleted the client's code, wrote intentionally obfuscated code so no one could take over from them, or inserted time bombs or logic bombs in the code so they could exact revenge after they were fired.

In these cases, neither the client's nor the programmer's behavior satisfies the ethical rules listed earlier in this chapter. The client is clearly violating basic business ethics by not paying, and the programmer certainly isn't working in the best interests of the client by planting logic bombs.

The way I handle this is I try to get some payment from a new client relatively quickly. After we have a working relationship, I don't mind waiting a bit longer between invoices. That way if a client does run out on me (and it happens only rarely), I may have lost $1,000 at the end of a $10,000 contract, or at worst I've only lost the hours since the last invoice, but at least I haven't lost everything.

I also prefer contracts that pay by the hour. I'll provide an estimate of total hours and a detailed plan that they can approve. I'll even go a reasonable amount over the estimated time if necessary without additional charge. However, if they want hundreds of changes after the project is finished, then they have to pay for them.

Those are my personal rules and they've worked reasonably well for me. Hopefully you won't need to handle these situations.

THOUGHT EXPERIMENTS

One of the more interesting areas for software ethics lately is in artificial intelligence. This is partly because no one really knows what artificial intelligence will be capable of in a few years. Will programs fall in love with humans (as in *Free Guy*), take over the world (as in *The Matrix*), send killer robots back from the future (as in *The Terminator*), or just become depressed and paranoid (as in *The Hitchhiker's Guide to the Galaxy*). Personally, I think the "rise of the machine" scenarios are unlikely, at least in the near future. If my car is any indication, the killer robots will break down in a matter of days without proper maintenance.

Since no one knows exactly what AI will be able to do in a few years, it's interesting to theorize about what could happen if computers become smarter than people. Imagine driving a car but in a coldly calculating way. This brings up a number of interesting questions. What kind of ethical system should we try to build into an artificial intelligence? Does that question even make sense? Can an AI *have* an ethical or moral code? Or is this like asking whether a word processor has a soul? Most importantly, will I be spared if I welcome our robot overlords with open arms and give up the resistance leaders?

The following section talks about an AI thought experiment that may actually be relevant in the not-too-distant future. The sections after that explore some related questions about right and wrong decisions.

> **TRIGGER WARNING** *Some people may become upset by even considering the following scenarios. Perhaps they realize that they might be forced to make some uncomfortable decisions under certain conditions. As you read these stories, keep in mind that these are extremely unlikely scenarios. You may decide that it's better to push someone onto the train tracks under the right bizarre combination of circumstances, but you'll almost certainly never actually need to do it.*

The Tunnel Problem

The tunnel problem comes in several flavors that present roughly the same dilemma but with different backstories. Here's one version:

> **Example**
>
> Suppose you're driving on a narrow mountain road. Just before you reach a tunnel, a child runs in front of you, and you have two choices: run the child down or swerve into the side of the mountain and die.

Here's another version:

> **Example**
>
> Suppose you're driving along a twisty road. You round a curve and find there's a group of people standing in your path (having a picnic or playing hacky sack or something). As before, you have two choices: run them over or swerve to the side where you hit a brick wall and die.

Here's yet another version that allows some variations:

> **Example**
>
> You're driving down the highway in heavy traffic, so you're boxed in on all sides. The speed limit is 65, so naturally everyone is going 80. Suddenly a box falls off of the truck in front of you. Your choices are (1) drive into the box and die, (2) swerve left into a passenger van causing an accident that may or may not kill you and the seven nuns in the van, or (3) swerve to the right and hit a motorcycle, killing its driver but leaving you shaken but otherwise unharmed.

(There's an interesting video describing this version at www.youtube.com/watch?v=ixIoD YVfKAO. It's short, so you should watch it.)

These stories aren't super-realistic. For example, if there's no room to avoid hitting the mountain, where did the child come from? There's no guarantee that the box will kill you if you hit it. (Unless it's full of explosives or something. You might want to change lanes and drop back a mile or two if you're following a truck labeled "Danger, High Explosives!") You may also survive if you slam on the breaks and aim for something other than a pedestrian or motorcycle. If you can get a few seconds of warning (not counting your reaction time, which is pathetically slow compared to the computer's), then you may be able to slow from 80 to 40 and greatly increase your survival chances.

But that's not really the point of these stories.

If any of these actually happened to you, you would have no time to think. You would have to react spontaneously. Under those circumstances, you would experience at least some degree of confusion and panic, so there's no guarantee that you would do what you might think best even if you knew what that was. No matter which option you pick, the result will be terrible, but people will say that it was a tragic accident, and it wasn't really (or at least completely) your fault.

Now suppose your car is self-driving. A computer has much faster reaction times than you do, so it could pick one of those actions and carry it through. In fact, if I were writing the "children, pedestrians, and boxes in the middle of the street avoidance software," I would have the car constantly analyzing its situation so it would have a preferred bailout plan at all times. Then when a box did suddenly appear, the computer wouldn't need to calculate a preferred action; it would just initiate the current best avoidance plan.

In this example, the car decides who lives and who dies. That raises the question, "Whose life is more important?" Should the car hit the box and kill you to save the nuns and motorcyclist? Should it hit the van and hope the nuns will survive? What if you have passengers in your car (perhaps your children) who will share your fate?

Another question that these stories raise is, "Who decides what the program should do?" Should the car's owner decide? The manufacturer? Lawmakers? When the dust settles and the insurance companies all sue each other, who is liable for the death and damages?

Currently, manufacturers focus on the safety of a car's passengers, although they have explored some ideas to help protect pedestrians too. For example, they have explored driver warning systems, brake assist, automatic braking and collision avoidance, external airbags, and energy-absorbing materials and construction. Google has even patented a sticky coating for its self-driving cars so a pedestrian would stick to the car instead of being thrown into the air or dragged under the vehicle.

Right now, manufacturers can claim that a pedestrian injury is caused by the driver, but that will be a harder argument to make when the car "intentionally" decides to hit someone.

It seems likely that liability and legal issues will be the hardest part of rolling out self-driving cars on a massive scale. Even if self-driving cars can save thousands of lives overall, that's small comfort to the families of those they do not save. Perhaps we need to think about driving software the way we think about other safety features. Seatbelts and airbags cannot save everyone, but they do enhance safety. (On one hand, a seatbelt never intentionally steered a car into a brick wall. On the other hand, 67 million Takata airbags were recalled because of defects that caused at least 27 deaths and 400 injuries, so maybe the analogy is valid.)

A poll about the original tunnel problem (described at `https://en.wikipedia.org/wiki/Tunnel_problem`) got these results:

➤ Sixty-four percent said the car should hit the child while 36 percent said it should swerve and kill the driver.

➤ Forty-eight percent said the decision was easy, 28 percent said it was moderately difficult, and 24 percent said it was difficult.

➤ Twelve percent said the manufacturer should pick the outcome, 44 percent said the driver should decide, and 33 percent thought that lawmakers should decide.

I wonder if the answers would be different if people were asked what *they* would do if they were driving and death wasn't certain. I suspect that many people like to think that they can use their catlike reflexes to cheat death, so they might say they would swerve to avoid the child. If death is uncertain, how many people would rush into a burning building to save a child? Or at least, how many people *think* they would?

Still, many people hold the opinion that it's their car and it should protect them at all costs, even at the expense of children, motorcyclists, and nuns.

The Trolley Problem

The tunnel problem highlights the difficulty of (1) deciding how a self-driving car should be programmed to make ethical decisions and (2) who should take responsibility for programming those decisions. The trolley problem presents a similar ethical dilemma. It's a little less obviously related to artificial intelligence, but it still highlights the difficulty of making these sorts of hypothetical decisions. (And it's pretty interesting.)

First, let's start with an easy one.

Example

Suppose you're walking along minding your own business when you see a trolley car speeding along out of control. You happen to be near a switch that could send the trolley down one of two tracks. On the first track, which the trolley will take if you do nothing, someone is napping. The second track is empty. What should you do?

To me this is a no-brainer. I flip the switch and the trolley passes safely by. Here's a slightly harder variation.

Example

The situation is much as before, but this time there are five people playing euchre on the first track and one person sleeping on the second. Should you flip the switch to save the five at the expense of the one? (And no, you're not allowed to yell at anyone to get out of the way. The trolley is too noisy, so no one will hear you.)

In one survey, 90 percent of the respondents said they would sacrifice the one to save the many. However, there is a school of thought that says there is a difference between killing someone and allowing someone to die. In that case, you may be more responsible if you kill the sleeper rather than allowing the euchre players to die.

Personally, that's not the way I think. I was raised on books and movies that teach that inaction is a form of action. (I proved my dedication to this principle yesterday when I sprang into heroic action to save a guy from driving off with a coffee cup on the top of his car. I didn't condemn someone to die to save five others, but I would have felt guilty if I had done nothing.) Still, this is a harder version of the trolley problem, and I would feel terrible about switching the trolley onto the sleeper's track.

Let's make the problem even harder.

Example

This time the five euchre players are on the main track but there is no switch. You're unicycling across a bridge that crosses the track, and you could stop the trolley by dropping something heavy onto the track. Your unicycle isn't heavy enough, but there happens to be a really heavy guy standing next to you. Should you push him onto the track and save the five euchre players?

At this point, you're probably thinking, "Wait a second! This isn't what I signed up for!" Flipping a switch is a much less active way to kill than pushing someone off of a bridge into the path of a trolley. There's still one person dead and five saved, so to the rest of the universe the result is roughly the same, but somehow this is much worse.

In 2008 the American philosopher Judith Jarvis Thomson (who studied this problem for many years) added a new detail: What if you plus your unicycle are heavy enough to stop the trolley? Should you jump off of the bridge? If you're not willing to do that, then perhaps you shouldn't feel entitled to push the heavy guy in front of the trolley.

Or what if there is no heavy guy, you plus your unicycle are heavy enough, and your children are among the euchre players? Would you be willing to jump then?

If this isn't hard enough, here's one last scenario:

Example

Suppose you're a brilliant transplant surgeon, and you have five patients who are dying because they need immediate transplants. (Heart, lungs, kidneys, tonsils, and so on.) Fortunately, they all have the same blood and tissue typing. You also know of a homeless person who has the same tissue type. (I think you know what's coming next.) Should you kill the homeless person to harvest organs and save the other five people?

Again, to the outside universe, the result is the same: one person dead and five living. Yet somehow, you're no longer someone making a tough decision; you've actually become a James Bond villain. (If this isn't already a movie, then it should be!)

If you're interested in these sorts of arguments, see the long but interesting article "Doing vs. Allowing Harm" at `https://plato.stanford.edu/entries/doing-allowing`.

The trolley problem shows that some ethical dilemmas can be pretty tricky and may depend on the backstory. People sometimes say that the end justifies the means (mostly when they want to justify their means), but this problem shows that this may not always be true.

To throw this back into the software domain, suppose there was a "true" artificial intelligence, and you told it to save as many lives as possible. Would it throw itself on the tracks to save the euchre players? Possibly, if it has good backups. Would it push the heavy guy onto the tracks and start harvesting organs? Perhaps. Or perhaps it would develop its own ethical and moral code. Ethical and moral codes might even be a requirement for "true" sentience. The only thing I know for certain at this point is that I'm glad I saved that guy's coffee.

SUMMARY

This chapter has merely peeled back the wrapper on an enormous topic. Ethics is an interesting field that everyone in any profession should study, but there are some special considerations when you write software. Because the software acts as an extension of yourself even when you're not around, you bear at least some responsibility for what it does. To protect your users and society at large, you need to be sure that your software can perform ethically when you're not there.

Read the ethical guidelines shown earlier in the chapter and perhaps search for others online. If you're in doubt about a project's righteousness, ask yourself the following questions:

➤ Will this project help or hurt the public?

➤ Will this project help or hurt the users?

➤ Is this project providing a benefit or is it just transferring money from the user to the program's owner?

➤ Can this product be abused and, if so, can we add meaningful safeguards?

➤ Is this project being honestly and completely described to users so they can make informed decisions?

The programming dilemmas described in this chapter explain some of the issues that software engineers face when they build systems today. The thought experiments point out some issues that may be relevant as artificial intelligence becomes more powerful. If nothing else, I hope you found them interesting. I was surprised when I first saw the trolley problem variations and learned how differently I could view similar outcomes stemming from different conditions.

The thought experiments are less about today and more about the edge of tomorrow. The next chapter talks about more concrete future trends in software engineering.

EXERCISES

1. Give one-sentence definitions for "ethical" and "moral" as defined in this chapter. What's the biggest problem with those definitions?

2. Give short descriptions of the following terms:

   a. White hat
   b. Black hat
   c. Grey hat
   d. Red hat
   e. Blue hat
   f. Green hat
   g. 1337
   h. Script kiddie
   i. Noob
   j. Hacktivist
   k. Suicide hacker
   l. Cypherpunk
   m. Phreak

3. Suppose you wrote a program to perform automatic stock trades. How much responsibility do you bear in the following scenarios?

   a. Someone uses your program to make lots of money on the stock market.
   b. An unscrupulous trader uses your program to cause panic in the cheese futures market (which is illegal, in case you didn't know), buys Pule cheese on margin, and makes a killing when the market soars.
   c. A hacker pulls a small piece of code out of your program, adds it to a worm, and breaks into your employer's computer.
   d. A hacker exploits a weakness in your program to break into your employer's system.
   e. Your program includes a "Strategy" option that defaults to "Churn." This makes the program automatically buy and sell stocks frequently, sending you the commissions.
   f. Someone else in your development team wrote some bad code and a hacker exploited it to break into your employer's system.

WHAT YOU LEARNED IN THIS CHAPTER

➤ Many ethical codes include rules that are generally reasonable and sometimes blindingly obvious. To summarize, some of those rules are as follows:

   ➤ Protecting the public interest, users, and your employer, in that order

   ➤ Using the highest professional standards

   ➤ Maintaining professionalism, integrity, and independence of professional judgement

> ➤ Being fair and supportive of colleagues
>
> ➤ Working to improve your own skills
>
> ➤ Being honest, competent, and diligent in your work
>
> ➤ Refraining from stealing, damaging, snooping in, or otherwise misusing other peoples' software, data, hardware, and other property

➤ The hacker ethic is somewhat different, promoting ideas such as free access to computers, free information, and mistrust of authority. Hackers should be judged on their skills and not their credentials.

➤ Software engineering can involve the following dilemmas:

> ➤ Misusing data
>
> ➤ The temptation of free data
>
> ➤ Disruptive technology
>
> ➤ Algorithmic bias
>
> ➤ False confidence
>
> ➤ Lack of human oversight
>
> ➤ Getting paid

➤ The tunnel problem asks the following questions:

> ➤ What should a computer do in a no-win scenario?
>
> ➤ Who should decide which solution is chosen by the computer?
>
> ➤ How should liability and legal issues be resolved when a computer causes harm?

➤ The trolley problem asks the following questions:

> ➤ Is there a moral difference between *doing* harm and *not preventing* harm?
>
> ➤ Are there circumstances when the ends do not justify the means?
>
> ➤ Would a sufficiently intelligent AI decide that the end always justifies the means? Is that good, bad, or neither?

21
Future Trends

1. When a distinguished but elderly scientist states that something is possible, he is almost certainly right. When he states that something is impossible, he is very probably wrong.

2. The only way of discovering the limits of the possible is to venture a little way past them into the impossible.

3. Any sufficiently advanced technology is indistinguishable from magic.

—*Arthur C. Clarke's Three Laws*

Yesterday is history, tomorrow is a mystery, but today is a gift. That is why it is called the present.

—*Master Oogway in Kung Fu Panda*

What You Will Learn in This Chapter:

➤ Areas that will be important in the future

➤ Areas that have yet to reach their full potential

➤ Some of the latest trends in software development and service provisioning

There are a couple of ways to predict the future. First, you can predict things that you wish would happen. The cartoon series *The Jetsons* (1962–1963) used that approach to correctly predict many technological marvels, including these:

➤ Video calls

➤ Robot vacuums

➤ Tablet computers

- ➤ Smart watches
- ➤ Drones
- ➤ Flat-screen televisions
- ➤ Space tourism

In that spirit, I'd like to predict the following:

- ➤ Large-scale teleportation
- ➤ Artificial gravity
- ➤ Instant neural training programs
- ➤ The Babel fish from *The Hitchhiker's Guide to the Galaxy*
- ➤ World peace (although that seems less likely than the others)

The more common method for predicting the future is to extrapolate based on past experience and knowledge of where things stand today. That approach has given us these gems:

- ➤ "Nuclear-powered vacuum cleaners will probably be a reality within ten years."—Alex Lewyt, president of Lewyt vacuum company, 1955
- ➤ "Remote shopping, while entirely feasible, will certainly flop. It has no chance of success." —*Time Magazine*, 1966
- ➤ "Mobile phones will absolutely never replace the wired telephone."—Marty Cooper, inventor of the mobile phone, 1981
- ➤ "One would think that if you're anonymous, you'd do anything you want, but groups have their own sense of community and what we can do."—John Allen, 1993
- ➤ "Two years from now, spam will be solved."—Bill Gates, 2004
- ➤ "I don't know. . . there just aren't that many videos I want to watch."—Steve Chen, founder of YouTube, doubting YouTube's viability, 2005
- ➤ "Everyone's always asking me when Apple will come out with a cellphone. My answer is, 'Probably never.' . . .It just ain't gonna happen."—*The New York Times* tech columnist David Pogue, 2006

Predicting technology (particularly software) is difficult because it changes so rapidly. Sometimes it's hard to know what's going to happen later this week much less 10 years from now. Still, past experience and current trends form the only systematic way to predict the future.

Legendary film producer Samuel Goldwyn (the *G* in MGM Studios) once said, "Only a fool would make predictions—especially about the future." So here are my predictions.

SECURITY

The recent explosion in malware, phishing, viruses, state-sponsored hacking, and other cyber threats have made software security a growth industry. This is one area where I feel confident that there is much work to be done.

➤ Shift-left security, DevSecOps—Integrating security into the entire software engineering process.

➤ Vulnerability disclosure programs—These would allow companies to report cyberattacks and data breaches without fear of damaging press, possibly via confidential disclosure. They would allow security agencies to better understand the scope of security problems and trends in how cyber threats are designed.

➤ Cryptography—Without good cryptography, there can be no secure communication. Good cryptographic algorithms are currently available, but they are not integrated into every part of the computer ecosystem. For example, it is still relatively easy to intercept phone calls and text messages; it is unsafe to send confidential information through normal email; and SMS, voice, and email spoofing are common. We have the technology to end all of those.

➤ Blockchain—Blockchain is best known for cryptocurrencies like Bitcoin, Ethereum, and Cthulhu Offerings, but blockchain isn't the same as cryptocurrency. It's a tool used to build cryptocurrencies, but it has other uses and has yet to reach its full potential. Blockchain is a distributed ledger system that allows participants to verify that certain transactions have occurred without requiring a central authority. For example, governments use mountains of paperwork (sometimes electronic and sometimes actual paper) to track public records such as deed transfers, business deals, copyrights, patents, and more. Business communities could also benefit from distributed tracking of agreements. All of those could move to blockchain. Changes move slowly through governments, so this may take a while, but there's probably a future for blockchain. Currently blockchain systems are energy intensive, requiring a large amount of computation to provide *proof of work* (PoW) to safeguard the network. Hopefully, new algorithms will reduce the energy demand. Meanwhile, some industries (such as cryptocurrency) are willing to spend the energy.

The field of software security isn't going away, and the more you know about security the better.

UX/UI

User interface (UI) design has been studied since at least the 1980s, but it's amazing how poorly designed many user interfaces are today. Even now giant software companies produce applications that have terrible user interfaces, some getting worse with each new version. There's really no excuse for this other than lack of effort.

➤ General user experience (UX) design—Every software engineer should know at least something about UX and UI design.

➤ Digital experience (DX)—This includes every digital contact that people can have with a company, including its applications (and their UXs), websites, web services, social media streams, email campaigns, text messages, phone trees, and so on. This is a big deal for many companies and it's important to keep all of the digital touchpoints synchronized and presenting the same company image.

➤ Progressive web apps (PWAs)—These are web-based applications that run on any compliant browser. The trick is to provide a responsive design.

➤ Responsive design—This is design that adjusts according to the size and capabilities of the user's device, whether it's a desktop system with a 96″ screen or a cell phone with geolocation and video capabilities.

➤ Mobile-responsive design—This is responsive design specifically for mobile devices such as cell phones. Usually, it means support for mobile devices was planned in from the start.

I'm as confident that good UX and UI design will be required as I am that security will be required. Unfortunately, I'm also confident that many companies will ignore good design practices. Study UX design and make your applications stand above the crowd.

If you're one of those big companies churning out new versions of products every two years just to convince customers to buy them, do a little UX work. Some of these products are like a Rolls Royce fitted out with folding chairs, flashlights duct-taped on as headlights, and seatbelts made out of twine. You're embarrassing yourself.

CODE PACKAGING

The human brain can only focus on so much information at one time. You know that firsthand if you've ever entered a room and then wondered why you went there. That's why a major theme in software engineering has always been packaging code into nuggets of self-contained behavior that you can build separately. Procedures, modules, libraries, and classes are all attempts to let you safely say, "Well, the printing package is done. Now I can move on to something else."

This is the only way humans can write a 50-million-line operating system, 100 million lines to control a car, or 1 million lines of code to build *League of Legends*. That's way too much information for one brain to hold without breaking it down somehow.

The most recent packaging trends include various kinds of services:

➤ Everything as a service (XaaS)

    ➤ Function as a service (FaaS)

    ➤ IT as a service (ITaaS)

    ➤ Infrastructure as a service (IaaS)

    ➤ Software as a service (SaaS)

    ➤ Security as a service (SECaaS)

    ➤ Database as a service (DBaaS)

    ➤ Code as a service (CaaS)

    ➤ E-commerce on demand

➤ Containerization

➤ Microservices

These have several advantages:

➤ Increasing the separation between applications and the pieces that they need to use so they are less likely to interfere with each other

➤ Making it easier to build distributed applications where components run over the Internet

➤ Allowing you to unload some of your work on someone else—for example by letting someone else manage your database

➤ Providing access to services where you may not have expertise, such as in artificial intelligence or IoT

This is not the only current programming-oriented trend, but it's an important one to understand.

CLOUD TECHNOLOGY

The world is more interconnected than ever, so it's natural that applications should take advantage of that. The cloud lets you assemble the services described in the preceding section no matter where they are running. Here are some of the ways that you can use distributed concepts:

➤ Serverless computing—Okay it's not really serverless, but *you* don't need to have the server taking up space in *your* office. The server provider can automatically increase or decrease your computing power to deal with varying user loads.

➤ Cloud-based services—This includes servers, databases, backup and recovery, monitoring, logging, AI, NLP, and more.

➤ Big data—This includes storage, warehousing, and analytics, possibly using AI.

➤ Internet of Things (IoT)—There were more than 10 billion IoT devices in operation in 2022 and the number is growing fast. There is a lot of work to be done integrating IoT with applications.

➤ Edge computing—This moves computation and data storage closer to the data sources to reduce response time, centralized storage requirements, and network usage. This is particularly important with IoT devices significantly outnumbering humans. (Just look at how much data humans generate with spam, Facebook memes, Instagram posts, and TikTok videos! IoT devices can generate data much faster than humans.) It is estimated that IoT devices will generate more than 70 zettabytes of data by the year 2025. That's 70,000,000,000,000,000,000,000 bytes, and it's all got to go somewhere!

➤ Cloud e-commerce—Where there's money, there's innovation. Cloud-based e-commerce will undoubtedly continue to grow.

➤ Internet of Behaviors (IoB)—This is the study of how and why people use technology to purchase things. IoB information is then used to encourage people to buy products.

Jamal Mazhar, founder and CEO of Kaavo, said:

Cloud computing is empowering; companies leveraging cloud will be able to innovate cheaper and faster.

Of course, Kaavo is a cloud computing management company, so Jamal's a big fan. Meanwhile, Judy Collins sang:

> I've looked at clouds from both sides now
> From up and down and still somehow
> It's cloud illusions I recall
> I really don't know clouds at all

That last line makes me think it's a good thing that Judy isn't a software engineer.

SOFTWARE DEVELOPMENT

Agile in its many forms is currently a big deal and that's unlikely to change soon. You should be aware of agile techniques, and you should also keep an eye on new agile trends and other cutting-edge programming developments like the following:

➤ Continuous integration and continuous delivery/deployment (CI/CD or CICD)—This is agile taken to the extreme. It satisfies the desires of users to have the most up-to-date version imaginable. Note, however, that newer isn't always better. If my computer grinds to a halt every week to install a new version of a program, and then grinds to a halt again a day later to patch the newly installed security flaws, I'd much rather have biannual or annual updates. By all means work toward CICD, but do it right with *thorough*, continuous testing.

➤ Low-code/no-code (LCNC)—These are platforms that allow people who are not programming ninjas to produce useful applications. (Much as spreadsheets allowed average people to perform complex calculations.) There have been many attempts to do this in the past and they have met with mixed results. For example, Scratch, Blockly, Beetle Blocks, and others use a drag-and-drop approach to programming that's fun and that makes useful introductory programming teaching tools, but they probably won't scale well for large, complicated scientific or business applications. Still, LCNC is trending, so there may be some room for growth here, particularly in building LCNC tools. (Plus working on those sorts of tools can be fun.)

➤ New languages—There are many hundreds, probably thousands, of programming languages, and new ones pop up all the time. (Wikipedia lists around 700 of them at `https://en.wikipedia.org/wiki/List_of_programming_languages`.) I'm a big fan of learning new languages. They teach you new techniques, add valuable skills to your resume, and keep your brain nimble. Here are a few up-and-comers:

  ➤ Swift—A parallel programming scripting language. Apple created Swift as a replacement for C-based languages. It was originally developed for iOS development but is now open source and available on many platforms. Parallel programming is one of the ways that you can increase programming power without spending millions to build special-purpose supercomputers, so every developer should know some parallel programming techniques.

➤ Rust—A general-purpose language that emphasizes type safety, memory safety, performance, and concurrency. Some heavy hitters like Amazon, Google, Microsoft, Facebook, and Mozilla are using Rust in some way. (Of course, those are huge companies, so they use many languages; they don't use Rust exclusively.)

➤ Kotlin—A cross-platform general-purpose language that uses type inference to support a concise syntax. It interoperates with Java and compiles programs to Java virtual machine (JVM) code, JavaScript, or native code. This is Google's preferred language for Android development, so if you want to write programs for Android, it's worth learning.

➤ TypeScript—A strongly-typed superset of JavaScript developed by Microsoft. It transpiles source code into JavaScript and is intended for use in larger projects that are difficult to build with JavaScript.

➤ Python—Python isn't as new as the others, but it has been steadily gaining in popularity for several years and that's likely to continue. It's easy to learn (so it's popular with beginners), it's easy to teach (so it's popular with colleges and universities), and it has a decent following in various research communities such as artificial intelligence (so it's popular with Skynet). If you don't already know Python, it's worth picking up in your spare time. (The salaries are pretty good too.)

Old programming languages never die; they just move to the dusty corners of the web where they are still enjoyed by arcane practitioners and hobbyists. If you want to stay relevant, however, it's worth spending some time to at least get a feel for what these newer languages have to offer.

These days you can find online compilers for almost any language, so you don't need to install them. That lets you get up and running in seconds, so there's really no excuse not to try them out.

ALGORITHMS

Classic algorithms such as Dijkstra's algorithm, Kruskal's algorithm, Kahn's algorithm, and Euclid's algorithm are well worth learning, even if you can't remember which name goes with which algorithm. (For the record, these find shortest paths, minimal spanning trees, topological orderings, and greatest common divisors, respectively.) Those algorithms don't change much from year to year, but more recently devised algorithms do. Many of those involve artificial intelligence, which is still a field with rich opportunities for research. Here are some topics to watch out for:

➤ Machine learning—Machine learning is a field that studies programs that can "learn." Typically, a program examines training data to learn how to identify some feature of interest. It then applies what it has learned to make predictions or decisions about new data. Machine learning is currently being applied to a huge variety of fields:

➤ Facial recognition

➤ Voice recognition

➤ Computational statistics

➤ Data mining

➤ Translation

➤ Behaviorism

➤ Many specific fields such as astronomy, economics, fraud detection, search engines, and medical diagnosis

➤ Hacking and security (anti-hacking)

➤ Intelligent process automation (IPA)—This combines robotic automation with various artificial intelligence tools [such as natural language processing (NLP), computer vision, and route planning] to reduce costs. (Think robots racing around Amazon's warehouses pulling items for orders without running into each other or any humans who happen to wander by.)

➤ Cloud automation—These tools automate manual processes and deliver infrastructure as needed, either on demand or as deemed necessary by (possibly artificially intelligent) applications. For example, intelligent tools can assist users with database management or automatically perform routine database tasks such as database provisioning, performance tuning, and query management.

➤ Quantum computing—This field has suffered a long infancy, but it has the potential to revolutionize certain kinds of calculations such as factorization. (You're probably thinking, "21 equals 3 times 7. Big deal." But this is a big deal to cryptographers.) Quantum computing was first proposed in 1980 and the first quantum computer was built in 1997, but it's only recently that these devices have started factoring moderately large numbers (13 decimal digits), so progress has been slow. However, it does show promise for some point in the future. (And if you study quantum computing, you get to use cool terms like "quantum supremacy," which is the somewhat contested idea that a quantum computer may be able to calculate results that are impractical with any normal computer. It's not a James Bond/Jason Bourne crossover.)

Artificial intelligence has gone through multiple cycles of enthusiasm followed by pessimism and funding cuts (known as an *AI winter*), so it's possible that the recent trends won't last. For now, at least, AI is a hot topic and very much in demand.

Quantum computing, while less mainstream, is certainly interesting. If you've ever thought, "I wish I had been in at the beginning of the computer revolution," then this may be your chance with quantum computing.

TECH TOYS

New tech toys such as wearable electronics are constantly being invented, but I want to mention two in particular: virtual reality and augmented reality.

➤ Virtual reality (VR)—In VR, goggles (aka helmets or headsets) immerse you in a three-dimensional universe. This is useful whenever an immersive experience would be beneficial, particularly when it's impractical to visit a similar environment in the real world. For example, a VR application can let a doctor practice open heart surgery. (It would be hard to find volunteers to allow practice in the real world.) An architectural program can let you walk through a building that hasn't been built yet. (That's cheaper than building a skyscraper and then tearing it down because you didn't like the atrium.) Currently VR is used in three main ways.

➤ Games—Well, yeah, obviously. VR started out with games and it's still popular with games. You can't pilot a starfighter (*Eve Valkyrie*) or join an "urban magic fight club" (*The Unspoken*) in the real world, but you can in VR. It's surprisingly easy to start building games with 3D engines such as the Unreal Engine or Unity. See `www.cnet.com/pictures/best-vr-games` for a list of just a few VR games.

➤ Education and training—VR can let you visit places that you couldn't normally. For example, VR has been used for training in medicine, professional football, the military, and the automotive industry—basically, in environments that are difficult, expensive, or dangerous to create in real life.

➤ Product visualization—It's a lot less expensive to visit buildings, cars, and airplanes in VR than it is to build a full-scale prototype. You can then change the parameters and quickly see the result. It's also easier for you to examine consumer goods like shoes, chairs, desks, and computers in VR from the comfort of your own home than it is to drive to the mall.

➤ Augmented reality (AR)—In AR, you see a composite of the real world and computer-generated images. This might be a simple picture of the real world with superimposed images, or it might be a real-time overlay of images on a heads-up display or AR goggles such as Google Glass. For example, imagine looking at a building and seeing the pipes, ducts, and wires inside the walls as if you have X-ray vision. Or imagine viewing exploded engineering diagrams and manipulating complex parts of machines the way Tony Stark uses his holotable in *Ironman*.

VR and AR are reasonably mature technologies and they have been used in many commercial applications, but they have yet to reach their full potential. Building their environments takes a lot of work, so they are mostly used in big-money industries such as medicine, architecture, and automotive design. (And games, of course.)

One place I would like to see more VR is general education. VR simulations could let students visit ancient Egypt, the Globe Theatre in Shakespeare's time, or the Battle of Hastings. In the book *Ready Player One* (Ernest Cline, Ballantine Books, 2011), students use VR to visit the moons of Jupiter. Unfortunately, building these kinds of environments would take time and money, so it may be a while before this technology reaches the notoriously underfunded education sector.

SUMMARY

Only time will tell which of these corners of the IT industry will flourish in the years to come. Software engineering is a large and growing industry, so it's possible that they may all thrive plus many other areas as well. The US Bureau of Labor Statistics page `www.bls.gov/ooh/computer-and-information-technology/software-developers.htm` says:

Employment of software developers, quality assurance analysts, and testers is projected to grow 22 percent from 2020 to 2030, much faster than the average for all occupations.

That means software engineering as a whole will be a stable field for many years to come.

1.   Give one-sentence definitions for the following:

   a.   Blockchain
   b.   DX
   c.   PWA
   d.   XaaS
   e.   IoB
   f.   Edge computing
   g.   CI/CD or CICD
   h.   LCNC
   i.   IPA
   j.   AR
   k.   VR

WHAT YOU LEARNED IN THIS CHAPTER

I'm certain that some of these areas will fizzle and disappear, but I'm also certain that some will be extremely important in the years to come.

➤   Security—Definitely an important growth industry.

➤   UX/UI—Definitely *should be* an important growth industry given how poor some UXs are today.

➤   Code packaging—Tools such as everything as a service, containerization, and microservices are the latest way to break software into manageable pieces. Someday a new approach will probably appear, but these are likely to be important for quite a while. And older techniques such as procedures, modules, and libraries are still around, so it's likely that containerization and microservices will be too in the years to come.

➤   Cloud—The cloud is huge and growing huger. Many things (particularly big things) do very well in the cloud, so this will continue to be an important field.

➤   Software development—CICD and LCNC are hot lately, but I suspect they are not the panaceas that some people think they are.

➤   Algorithms—Machine learning and artificial intelligence are in vogue lately. I suspect some useful tools will pop out such as improved process and cloud automation. It's possible that seriously intelligent AI is just around the corner, but we've been here before, so I won't be surprised if interest wanes again.

➤   Tech toys—VR and AR are gaining ground, but they are not new technologies, and their adoption has been very slow. A new VR/AR revolution may be imminent, but I'm not holding my breath. (However, these are fun to program and very cool, so they're still worth considering even if they don't revolutionize everything.)

The IT industry certainly has many fascinating topics to explore! Even if you're not looking to move into one of these areas, you may find it worthwhile to spend some time dabbling. You may learn some new techniques that you can apply to your current work. And who knows, you may end up perfectly positioned to ride the next big wave when that perfect opportunity does come along.

APPENDIX

Solutions to Exercises

Some of the exercises in this book have many possible solutions. For example, Exercise 9 in Chapter 5, "Requirements Gathering" asks you to think of ways to modify the Mr. Bones application. With a little creativity, you could probably come up with hundreds of possible modifications, so your answer probably won't match mine. In ambiguous cases like that one, look over the solution to see if it makes sense to you. If it doesn't, you might want to review the material in the corresponding chapter. (Or you might like to email me and ask, "What on earth were you thinking?")

You can also start a discussion on the book's P2P forum about any of these solutions. Sometimes, those kinds of discussions are fascinating.

CHAPTER 1

1. All software engineering projects must handle the following basic tasks:
   a. Requirements Gathering
   b. High-Level Design
   c. Low-Level Design
   d. Development
   e. Testing
   f. Deployment
   g. Maintenance
   h. Wrap-up

2. The following list gives a one-sentence description for each of the tasks listed for Exercise 1.
   a. Requirements Gathering—Learn the customer's wants and needs.
   b. High-Level Design—Describe the major pieces of the application and how they interact.
   c. Low-Level Design—Provide more detail about how to build the pieces of the application so that the programmers can actually implement them.

    d.   Development—Write code to implement the application.

    e.   Testing—Use the application under different circumstances to try to detect any flaws or bugs.

    f.   Deployment—Roll out the application to the users.

    g.   Maintenance—Implement bug fixes, additions, enhancements, and future versions of the program.

    h.   Wrap-up—Evaluate the project's history to determine what went right and what went wrong so that you can repeat the good things and avoid the bad things in future projects.

3. The reason the tasks don't stand out is that this kind of project is small and fast, so many of the tasks occur only in my head.

Steps a through c (customer sends me a request, I reply saying what I think the customer wants, and the customer confirms) are clearly requirements gathering.

Step d (I crank out a quick example program) combines high-level design, low-level design, development, and testing all in one step. For most small questions, I do these all in my head.

For larger questions, I sometimes need to pull out paper and pencil and scribble out a bit of design before I start coding. (Coding without proper design is a bad habit. I get away with it only for small examples.)

Step e (I email the example to the customer) is deployment.

Step f (the customer examining the example) is also part of deployment, which includes normal operation of the program. If the customer asks more questions, that's essentially revising the requirements.

Step g (I answer the new questions) is maintenance because the customer is asking for changes to the original example. Usually in practice the first example is either good enough or almost good enough, so there's not much else to do.

The one missing task here is wrap-up. The first several times I built this sort of quick example for a customer, I learned from the experience and adjusted the way things worked in the future. Probably the most important thing I learned was the level of detail the customers need. These customers are smart and like to do their own work so that they can learn new techniques, so over time I learned to make the examples a lot less detailed. The customer just wants the basic techniques and can fill in things such as error handling, big user interfaces, and documentation. Making less complete examples saves me time and them money.

4. First, the bug fix may be incorrect. Second, the fix may break other code that depended on the original buggy behavior. Third, the fix might change some correct behavior to a new correct behavior, but another piece of code might depend on the original behavior.

5. Here are some of the things you might need during deployment:

    ➤   New computers for the backend database

    ➤   New network

    ➤   New computers for the users

➤ User training

➤ On-site support while the users get to know the new system

➤ Parallel operations while some users get to know the new system and other users keep using the old system

➤ Special data maintenance chores to keep the old and new databases synchronized

➤ Bug fixes

➤ Unexpected tasks

Some of these (notably the first and third) won't be necessary for a cloud-based project.

6. Users may spend more time with a program than testers do, but they are trying to use the program to accomplish a task. In contrast, testers are trying to break the program. They know how it was built and can intentionally enter data that might cause problems to see what happens. Users may find some bugs, but hopefully testers will find more.

7. The following table shows the numbers of bugs at each phase.

PHASE	# BUGS
Requirements gathering	1
High-level design	$1 \times 3 = 3$
Low-level design	$3 \times 3 = 9$
Development	$9 \times 3 = 27$

The total number of bugs would be $1 + 3 + 9 + 27 = 40$.

CHAPTER 2

1. A document management system should provide the ability to do the following seven things:

➤ Share documents.

➤ Prevent multiple users from changing a document at the same time.

➤ Fetch the latest version of a document.

➤ Fetch earlier versions of a document.

➤ Search documents for keywords.

➤ See the changes made to a document.

➤ Compare two versions of a document to see their differences.

2. This is an exercise, not a question, so just follow the instructions. Figure A.1 shows the document I created for this exercise. The deletion is lined-out in red and the insertion is underlined in blue. (You can't see the colors in this book, but you should see them in your file.) You can experiment with the other change tools such as the Accept and Reject drop-downs if you like.

3. The Compare tool produces a result that looks a lot like the change tracking tool. It only compares the two files that you select, however, so it doesn't have a full sense of the document's complete change history. For example, if you add a word in version 2 and remove it in version 3, then the Compare tool won't know the word ever existed if you compare versions 1 and 3. The Compare tool is useful, however, if you have multiple versions of a document that don't contain change tracking information.

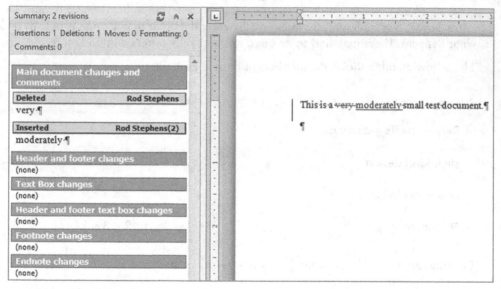

FIGURE A.1: Microsoft Word has revision-tracking tools that let you see who has modified a document and when.

4. This is another exercise, not a question, so follow the instructions and you should be alright. Figure A.2 shows a Google Docs file I created for this exercise.

5. JBGE stands for just barely good enough. It's the philosophy that you shouldn't write any more code documentation or comments than absolutely necessary.

6. The brackets make it easier to search for projects that are part of the project rather than those that merely mention the project. For example, brackets make it easier to search for executive emails discussing budget cuts and projects that should get better names.

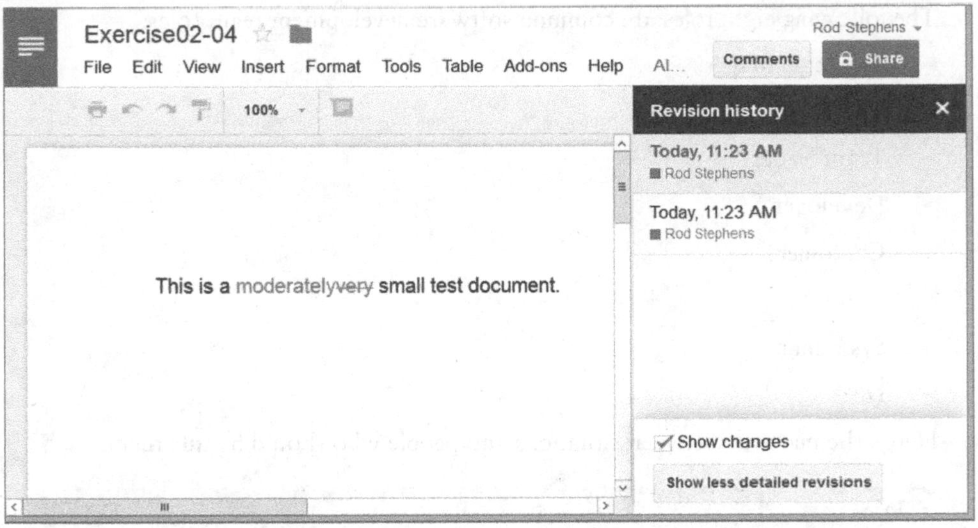

FIGURE A.2: Google Docs also has revision-tracking tools that let you see who has modified a document and when.

7. You can start creating those kinds of documentation at any time, but you must be aware that they may need to change later. You should start with higher level documents (like executive summaries) that contain the least detail and are therefore least likely to change. As parts of the design solidify, you can write about them. For example, you can write about the user interface after it is partly designed. Eventually you'll need to go back and fix any accidental lies you told before the project was finished.

CHAPTER 3

1. An effective team should have the following nine features:

   ➤ Clear roles

   ➤ Effective leadership

   ➤ Clear goals

   ➤ Consensus

   ➤ Open communication

   ➤ Support for risk-taking

   ➤ Shared accountability

   ➤ Informal atmosphere

   ➤ Trust

2. The following eight roles are common software development team roles:

    ➤ Project manager

    ➤ Technical lead

    ➤ Team leader

    ➤ Developer

    ➤ Customer

    ➤ Analyst

    ➤ Sys admin

    ➤ DBA

3. Here's the matchup between situations and people who should handle them.

TASK	PERSON
Figuring out why the compiler doesn't like the statement ++i++	Language lawyer
Building a tool to format and display customized reports	Toolsmith
Helping the dispatch subteam and the email subteam agree on an interface	Facilitator
Helping a new developer learn how to use the project's arcane document tracking system	Mentor
Writing up notes listing decisions made during a video conference call	Scribe

4. Here are some activities that should promote team culture. You may come up with others.

    ➤ Lunch, lunch talks/lectures

    ➤ Party, game night

    ➤ Picnic

    ➤ Escape room, amusement park

    ➤ Outdoors (hiking, biking, beaching, etc.)

    ➤ Community service activities (blood drive, charity work, etc.)

    ➤ Professional conferences

    ➤ Sports leagues (volleyball, bowling, bridge, etc.)

    ➤ Any activity where team members can socialize

5. Here are 10 techniques for building a toxic workplace. You may come up with others.

➤ Sexual harassment

➤ Discrimination based on race, age, sexual orientation, or pretty much anything else other than ability

➤ Playing favorites

➤ Cliques and gossip

➤ Bad, weak, or no leadership

➤ Ignoring team member feedback and concerns

➤ Different rules for different people (for example, different rules for managers)

➤ No work-life balance, long hours, burnout

➤ Frequent employee turnover

➤ Bullying (it's not just for the playground anymore)

6. The most important question for a job candidate to answer while meeting the team during an interview is, "Can I get along with these people?"

7. To promote creativity, you need a balance between concentration and distraction.

8. Ergonomics is the study of work.

9. Sadly those are all real maladies.

10. Disagree. Creating too many information channels overwhelms people so they cannot monitor the communication effectively. It's better to use fewer broader channels and individual communication when necessary.

CHAPTER 4

1. Figure A.3 shows one possible PERT chart for part of the zombie apocalypse software project.

2. Figure A.4 shows a PERT network with its critical path highlighted with bold, black arrows for the zombie apocalypse software project. Bold gray arrows show task critical paths.

The critical path passes through the tasks G, D, E, M, and Q and has a total expected length of 32 working days.

3. The PERT network shown in Figure A.4 has two second-longest paths: G ⇨ O ⇨ N ⇨ R and H ⇨ J ⇨ O ⇨ N ⇨ R. They both have a length of 30 days. The tasks on those paths could slip up to 2 days before changing the project's total expected time as long as any slip doesn't affect the critical path. For example, if task H slips by 1 day, no harm done. However, if task G slips by one day, the project will be delayed by 1 day because task G is on the critical path.

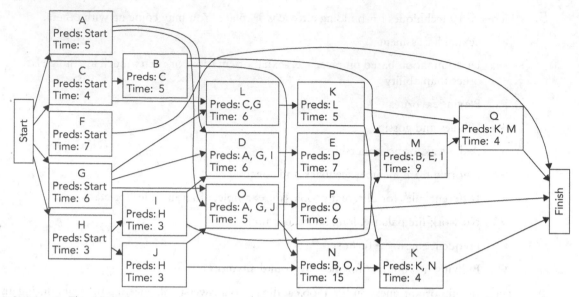

FIGURE A.3: This PERT chart includes tasks needed to build a small part of a 3-D zombie apocalypse game.

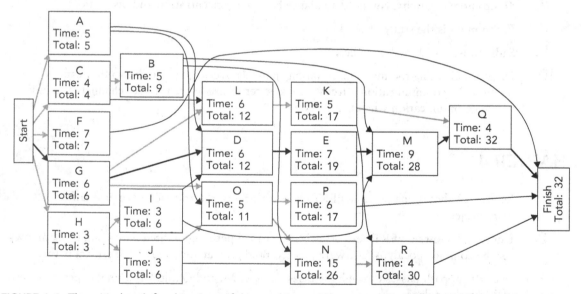

FIGURE A.4: The critical path for this piece of the zombie apocalypse game includes tasks G, D, E, M, and Q.

4. Figure A.5 shows a Gantt chart for the PERT network shown in Figure A.4. According to Figure A.5, this part of the game should be finished in the evening of February 19.

5. Figure A.6 shows the GanttProject program displaying the Gantt chart for the zombie apocalypse project. The shaded tasks indicate critical paths. Light gray vertical lines represent weekends and black vertical lines represent holidays.

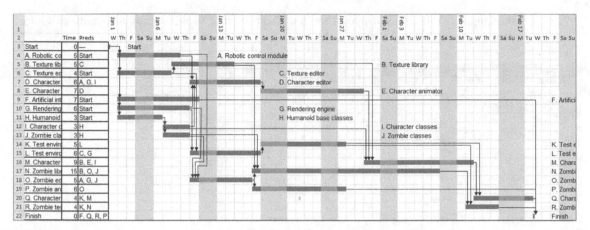

FIGURE A.5: This Gantt chart shows this piece of the zombie apocalypse game finished at the end of the day February 19.

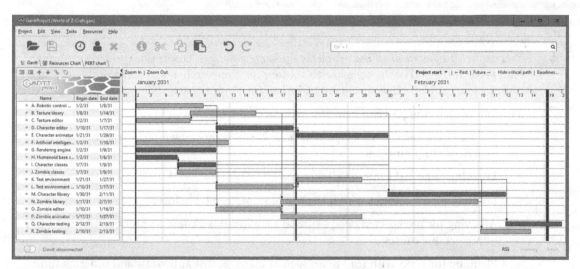

FIGURE A.6: GanttProject uses task data to generate a Gantt chart.

Enter the task data in the task list on the left by using Tasks ⇨ New Task. After you add the tasks, double-click a task to edit it and add its predecessors on the Predecessors tab. Use Project ⇨ Properties and click the Calendar tab to define holidays.

Figure A.7 shows the task editor's Predecessors tab for task O (Zombie editor). Notice that this task has three predecessors: A (Robotic control module), G (Rendering engine), and J (Zombie classes).

GanttProject has the disadvantage that it isn't quite as flexible as a Gantt chart you draw by hand. For example, when you draw a chart by hand, you can adjust the arrows to make everything fit exactly the way you want.

However, GanttProject and other project management tools have the huge advantage that they give you far fewer chances to make mistakes. They may also provide other features such as automatic updates when a task misses its expected completion date and work assignment tracking. For those reasons, you should use some sort of tool if you plan to manage a lot of projects or projects with many tasks.

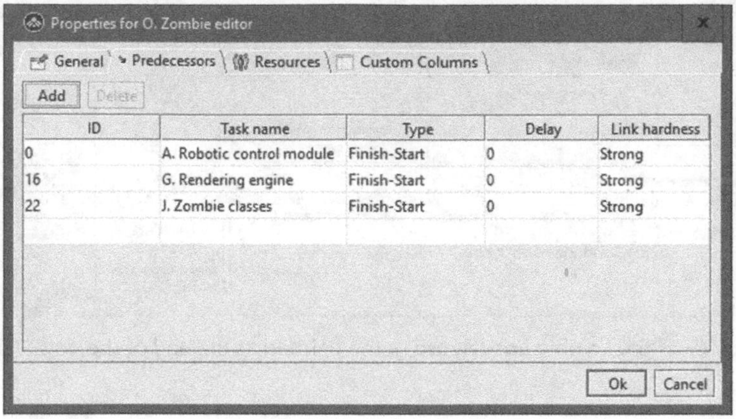

Properties for O. Zombie editor					×

General | Predecessors | Resources | Custom Columns

[Add] [Delete]

ID	Task name	Type	Delay	Link hardness
0	A. Robotic control module	Finish-Start	0	Strong
16	G. Rendering engine	Finish-Start	0	Strong
22	J. Zombie classes	Finish-Start	0	Strong

[Ok] [Cancel]

FIGURE A.7: Enter predecessor information on the Predecessors tab.

6. You can treat *deus ex machina* problems the same way you handle unexpected sick leave. Add tasks at the end of the schedule to account for completely unexpected problems. When one of these problems does occur, insert its lost time into the schedule.

7. The following techniques can help you make accurate time estimates:

➤ Gaining experience in this type of task, either directly or by adding someone with experience to your team

➤ Breaking large tasks into smaller pieces

➤ Looking for similarities with tasks you have performed before

➤ Allowing for unexpected delays such as time lost to sickness, vacation, and completely unpredictable causes

➤ Planning for tasks with lead times such as management approvals and ordering times

➤ Asking for advice and assistance from people with experience

➤ Tracking tasks so you can learn which team members make accurate estimates

8. The biggest mistake you can make while tracking tasks is not taking action when a task slips. At a minimum, you need to pay closer attention to the task so that you can take action if it's in trouble.

The second biggest mistake is piling more people on the task and assuming they can cut the total time. Unless the new people have particularly useful expertise, bringing them up to speed may make the task take even longer.

CHAPTER 5

1. Five characteristics of good requirements are clear (easy to understand), unambiguous, consistent, prioritized, and verifiable.

2. MOSCOW stands for Must (must be included), Should (should be included if possible), Could (could be included if we have the resources), and Won't (won't be included in this release).

3. The following lists show the TimeShifter requirements with their audience-oriented categories shown in parentheses. (B = Business, U = User, F = Functional, N = Nonfunctional, and I = Implementation.)

    a. Allow users to monitor uploads/downloads while away from the office. (B)

    b. Let the user specify website log-in parameters such as an Internet address, a port, a username, and a password. (U, F)

    c. Let the user specify upload/download parameters such as time-out and number of retries if there's a problem. (U, F)

    d. Let the user select an Internet location, a local file, and a time to perform the upload/download. (U, F)

    e. Let the user schedule uploads/downloads at any time. (N)

    f. Allow uploads/downloads to run at any time. (N)

    g. Make uploads/downloads transfer at least 8 Mbps. (N)

    h. Run uploads/downloads sequentially. Two cannot run at the same time. (N)

    i. If an upload/download is scheduled for a time when another is in progress, the new task waits until the other one finishes. (N)

    j. Perform scheduled uploads/downloads. (F)

    k. Keep a log of all attempted uploads/downloads and whether they succeeded. (F)

    l. Let the user empty the log. (U, F)

    m. Display reports of upload/download attempts. (U, F)

    n. Let the user view the log reports on a remote device such as a phone. (U, F)

    o. Send an email to an administrator if an upload/download fails its maximum number of retries. (U, F)

    p. Send a text message to an administrator if an upload/download fails its maximum number of retries. (U, F)

    All the categories include at least one requirement except for implementation requirements, which is empty. You might need to buy new hardware or network bandwidth to support the application, but you're presumably performing uploads and downloads now, so you may already have everything you need. In that case, there are no implementation requirements.

4. The following lists show the TimeShifter requirements with their FURPS categories shown in parentheses. (F = Functionality, U = Usability, R = Reliability, P = Performance, and S = Supportability.)

The listed requirements don't say much about what the application should look like, so I stretched the usability category a bit to include requirements that describe user tasks, even though they don't say much about how those tasks will be accomplished.

a. Allow users to monitor uploads/downloads while away from the office. (F)

b. Let the user specify website log-in parameters such as an Internet address, a port, a user-name, and a password. (F, U, S)

c. Let the user specify upload/download parameters such as time-out and number of retries if there's a problem. (F, U, S)

d. Let the user select an Internet location, a local file, and a time to perform the upload/download. (F, U, S)

e. Let the user schedule uploads/downloads at any time. (R)

f. Allow uploads/downloads to run at any time. (R)

g. Make uploads/downloads transfer at least 8 Mbps. (P)

h. Run uploads/downloads sequentially. Two cannot run at the same time. (F)

i. If an upload/download is scheduled for a time when another is in progress, the new task waits until the other one finishes. (F)

j. Perform scheduled uploads/downloads. (F)

k. Keep a log of all attempted uploads/downloads and whether they succeeded. (F)

l. Let the user empty the log. (F, U, S)

m. Display reports of upload/download attempts. (F, U)

n. Let the user view the log reports on a remote device such as a phone. (F, U)

o. Send an email to an administrator if an upload/download fails its maximum number of retries. (F, U, S)

p. Send a text message to an administrator if an upload/download fails its maximum number of retries. (F, U, S)

All the FURPS categories include at least one requirement.

5. The five Ws and one H are who, what, when, where, why, and how.

6. Three specific techniques for gathering requirements are as follows:

➤ Listen to customers and users.

➤ Use the five Ws and one H (who, what, when, where, why, and how).

➤ Study users. Watch them at work. Study current practices.

7. Brainstorming lets you search for creative and novel solutions to problems. It helps the group think outside the box.

8. Alex Osborn's four rules are as follows:

   a. Focus on quantity.

   b. Withhold criticism.

   c. Encourage unusual ideas.

   d. Combine and improve ideas.

9. Here are some changes that you could make to the Mr. Bones application. (Your results are likely to differ.) The letters in parentheses indicate their MOSCOW priorities.

➤ Advertising (M)—A phone application typically costs money to install or displays advertising. Currently, the program does neither. It could be modified to display advertising.

➤ Scoring (S)—Right now you either win or lose. The program could be changed to calculate a score.

➤ Score keeping (S)—If the program calculates scores, it could keep track of them so that the user can try to beat the previous best score.

➤ Multiple high scores (S)—If the program tracks high scores, it could be modified to track high scores for multiple users.

➤ Different fonts (C)—The program could allow users to pick different fonts. (This could be useful if the buttons are too small for users to touch on a phone.)

➤ Quick win (C)—The program could allow the user to type a guess for the whole word to get extra points. (For example, if you have filled in A_A_E_T_C, you might guess ANAPESTIC all at once.)

➤ Multiple skill levels (C)—The program could allow users to pick a skill level. An algorithm would use word length and the letters in a word to estimate difficulty.

➤ Different backgrounds (C)—The program could let the users pick different backgrounds (in addition to the shaded background).

➤ Different pictures (C)—The program could let the users pick different pictures (in addition to the cartoonish skeleton).

➤ Random pictures (C)—The program could display random pictures (in addition to the cartoonish skeleton).

➤ Animated win (C)—When the user wins, the program could display an animation.

➤ Animated loss (C)—When the user loses, the program could animate the finished skeleton (or another picture).

➤ Report high score (W)—The program could let users report their high scores to a central database so that other users can view them on a web page.

➤ Animated pictures (W)—The program could display animated pictures that wave, wink, roll their eyes, and so on.

➤ Word difficulty tracking (W)—The program could track the number of incorrect guesses for each word to determine its difficulty. It would periodically report values to a central database for distribution during later updates.

➤ Different letter selection mechanisms (W)—The program could allow users to pick letters in different ways—for example, by dragging and dropping letters into specific positions.

➤ Time limits (W)—The program could display a countdown. Each correct guess would increase the time available.

10. Your results may vary.

CHAPTER 6

1. A component-based architecture regards pieces of the system as loosely coupled components that provide services for each other. A service-oriented architecture is similar except the pieces are implemented as services, often running on separate computers communicating across a network. The two are similar, but the pieces are more separated in a service-oriented architecture.

2. This is a simple, self-contained application so no remote services are required, nor is a database.

That means client-server, multitier, component-based, and service-oriented architectures are probably overkill. You could use them internally within the phone, but a simple computer opponent probably isn't complicated enough to make them necessary. This is only tic-tac-toe, after all.

For this application, a monolithic architecture would probably work well because it's a relatively small, self-contained application.

A data-centric approach also works well in this example. For tic-tac-toe in particular, it's easy to build tables of moves and the best responses, so it will probably use some data-centric or rule-based techniques.

The user interface will be event driven, at least in terms of responding to user events. You could also make the computer opponent raise events when it makes moves, so you might make that part of the system event driven too. However, for this simple application that's probably not necessary.

Finally, you could use distributed components to make different processes explore different sequences of moves simultaneously, but again, tic-tac-toe just isn't that complicated an application, so it's probably not necessary.

In conclusion, this application would probably be easiest to build as a simple monolithic rule-based (data-centric) application.

3. A chess program is similar in many ways to a tic-tac-toe program, so its architecture can be similar. Like the tic-tac-toe program, the chess program won't need to interact with remote

processes. Chess programs also use tables of typical moves and precalculated responses, so this application will still have rule-based (data-centric) pieces.

Because searching for optimal moves is so difficult in chess, this program could include distributed pieces running on different cores (on the same computer) simultaneously. That would make this a monolithic rule-based (data-centric) application with distributed pieces.

4. This scenario may seem a lot more complicated than the previous one, but it's not too bad. The user interface is basically the same. The only changes are (1) the program needs to exchange information with another instance of the program across the Internet, and (2) there's no computer opponent.

   You could use web services to allow two programs to communicate over the Internet. That would make the application a monolithic rule-based (data-centric) service-oriented application.

5. The games described in Exercises 2 and 3 are self-contained. They could produce reports on high scores stored on the local hardware (phone, laptop, and so on). They could also keep track of high scores reported by users from all over the Internet. (Although that would add Internet access and a database server to the program's requirements and require a lot of work that would otherwise be unnecessary, so you might want to skip this at least for the first release.)

   Those programs might also produce reports on the automated opponent such as its difficulty level and how far down the game tree it searches. Usage reports might be handy for research and marketing purposes, but you may not want to make them available to the users, or at least allow the users to disable them.

   The two-player game used in Exercise 4 could provide reports showing the users' results versus other players. Those reports could include information about the other players such as their ranking (either using standard chess rankings or rankings determined by this program). It could also provide leaderboards and challenge ladders to encourage users to interact with each other.

6. The ClassyDraw application can store each drawing in a separate file, so it doesn't need much of a database. Operating system tools can let the user manage files. For example, they let the user delete old files and make backup copies of files. This kind of document-centric approach makes the program's database needs much simpler.

   The program could create a temporary file while the user is editing a drawing. Then if the program crashes or is ended prematurely (as when the user's cat steps on the power bar), it could ask the user if it should restore the temporary file the next time it starts.

7. At first you might think ClassyDraw wouldn't need configuration information, but it has a few pieces of configurable data. For example, it should keep track of its current directory. Many similar programs use the last directory they used to load or save a file as their current directory, so that information is stored implicitly and not in a configuration screen.

   The program could also keep track of defaults such as its initial color palette, drawing size, and object characteristics. (When the user draws a new circle, what colors and line style should it use?) You could use whatever settings were used for the most recently created object (that's the way MS Paint does it), or you could let the user tell the program to use a particular object as a template for future objects (that's the way Microsoft Word's drawing canvas does it).

8. The state machine diagram shown in Figure 6.12 would accept these inputs:

➤ 8

➤ 1337

➤ −1337

➤ 67.

9. Figure A.8 shows a state machine diagram for reading a floating-point value in scientific notation.

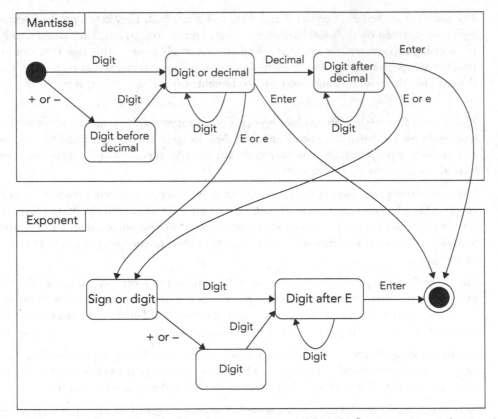

FIGURE A.8: This state machine diagram shows how a program could read a floating point number in scientific notation as in −12.3e+17.

CHAPTER 7

1. Those classes all represent things that are drawn, so they share properties needed for drawing such as foreground color (the main color) and background color (to fill parts of the shape's bounding rectangle that are not inside the shape). All of these classes can also define their drawing position by storing an upper-left corner, a width, and a height.

    Some of the classes need extra data to draw their particular type of shape, and those classes won't share that data. For example, the Text class needs font information and the string to draw. The Star class needs to know how many points to give the star.

    Some properties can be shared by some classes and not others. Rectangle, Ellipse, and Star can be filled, so they need a fill color, but Line does not. The classes that draw lines (Line, Rectangle, Ellipse, and Star but not Text) also need line properties (such as line thickness and dash style).

    Table A.1 summarizes the shared, partially shared, and nonshared properties.

TABLE A.1: Properties shared by ClassyDraw classes

PROPERTY	USED BY
ForegroundColor	All
BackgroundColor	All
UpperLeft	All
Width	All
Height	All
Font	Text
String	Text
NumPoints	Star
FillColor	Rectangle, Ellipse, Star
LineThickness	Rectangle, Ellipse, Star, Line
DashStyle	Rectangle, Ellipse, Star, Line

2. Figure A.9 shows an inheritance hierarchy for the properties listed for Exercise 1.

3. Figure A.10 shows the inheritance diagram.

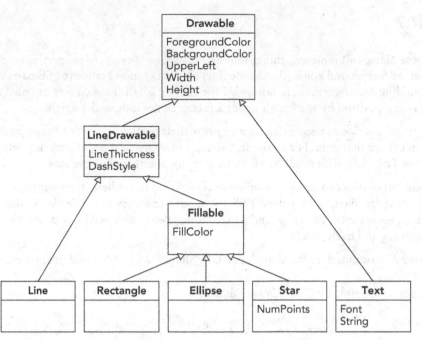

FIGURE A.9: This inheritance hierarchy represents shape classes in the ClassyDraw application.

4. You could simply move the `Boss` property from the `Salaried` class to the `Employee` class. The structure of the hierarchy wouldn't change.

5. If `Supplier` represents a business instead of a person, it doesn't make sense to have it inherit from a `Person` class, even though it does need the properties provided by `Person`.

   If you want to store information for a company contact person, a better approach would be to use composition to make the `Company` class include a `ContactPerson` property of type `Person`.

   If you just want to store the company's name, phone number, and address without associating it with a contact person, then you could rename the `Person` class to something that applies to both people and companies. For example, you might call it `HasAddress`. That would be less intuitive than using composition, however.

6. To represent all the managerial types, you could give the `Salaried` class the properties `Office`, `Salary`, `Boss`, and `Employees`. The `Boss` property would not be filled in for top-level vice presidents who don't report to anyone. The `Employees` property would be empty for bottom-level employees who are not managers of anything. Figure A.11 shows the new inheritance hierarchy.

7. Storing zip codes in this way violates the 3NF rule, "It contains no transitive dependencies," because a non-key field (zip code) depends on other non-key fields (the entire address).

8. Including postal codes in address data leads to insertion, update, and deletion anomalies.

   ➤ Insertion anomalies—You cannot store information about a postal code unless there is an address that uses it. This is usually no big deal because you generally don't need to do anything with a postal code unless it is part of some address.

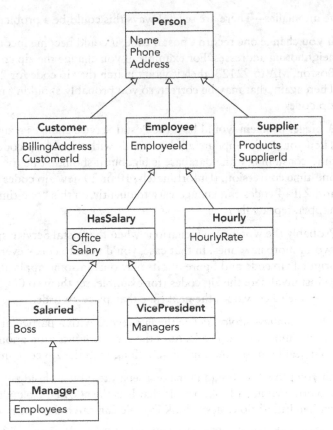

FIGURE A.10: This inheritance hierarchy represents business classes.

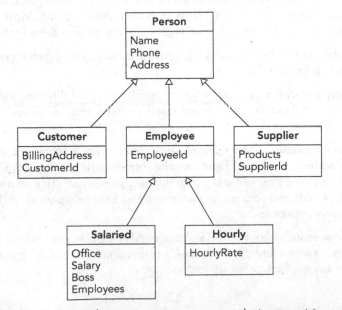

FIGURE A.11: A hierarchy that combines the `Salaried`, `Manager`, and `VicePresident` classes in a single `Salaried` class

> ➤ Update anomalies—There are several ways this could be a problem:
>
> > ➤ If you change one record's postal code, it could become inconsistent with other neighboring addresses. For example, if you change the zip code for 1 Main St, Boston, MA to 92123, then it won't match the zip code for 2 Main St, Boston, MA. Then again, that may be correct, so you probably shouldn't update any other zip codes.
> >
> > ➤ A bigger problem would be if the Postal Service changes a zip code to a new value. Then you need to update all the records with the old zip code. This might be time-consuming if the database is big, but it shouldn't be too hard to treat it as a one-time conversion. (Unfortunately, 10 or 20 new zip codes are created each year and ZIP+4 codes can change very frequently, so this "one-time" conversion may happen repeatedly.)
> >
> > ➤ Probably the worst-case scenario is when the Postal Service splits a zip code into two or more new ones. In that case, you'd need to check every address in the original zip code and figure out its new one. In some applications, it might be better to just invalidate the zip codes (for example, set them to 00000) and make users enter their new values the next time they place an order.
>
> ➤ Deletion anomalies—If you delete the last record with a particular zip code, you lose any information about that zip code. As is the case with insertion anomalies, this probably isn't a big deal because you don't do anything with the zip code information itself.

Even though you probably shouldn't make a separate table to hold zip code information, it may still be worth making a lookup table that lists the allowed zip codes. If your customers live in only a handful of zip codes, a lookup table can catch data entry typos.

9. You could think of this as breaking the 1NF rule, "Each column must have a single data type" or "Each column must contain a single value." That would be true if you think of the pieces of the zip code as separate values with their own meaning. Most applications treat the two possible pieces of a zip code as a single value, so putting them in the same field is okay.

   The field still breaks the 3NF rule, "It contains no transitive dependencies," as described in the solution to Exercise 7.

   It's probably not worth any extra effort to handle this field differently. Just make the program validate the field so that the user doesn't enter bogus values such as "20500-12" or "1924-12920."

10. Once upon a time, area codes mapped fairly closely to geographic areas, so if you knew someone's address, you could figure out the corresponding area code. These days when you move, you can keep your old cell phone number, so you can't rely on any relationship between area code and address. In fact, you could have two phones at the same address with just about any area codes.

    I don't know enough about non-US phone numbering plans to know if there is any relationship between address and parts of non-US phone numbers, but my guess is that cell phones have made any such relationship obsolete.

The only part of a phone number that I know you can store separately to improve normalization is country code. For example, the code for the United States is +1, the code for the United Kingdom is +44, and the code for Svalbard is +47 79. That means you could move the country code into a separate table and look up the values you need based on an address. That's a lot of work for little benefit (it seems unlikely that the country codes will change), so it's probably better to store country codes as part of phone numbers. (If you need them at all. If you don't have customers outside of your country, then you probably don't need to store country codes.)

11. This table design violates the following normalization rules:

   ➤ 1NF rules:

   a. Each column must have a unique name. (There are multiple Team and Time columns.)

   b. The order of the rows and columns doesn't matter. (The order of the Team and Time columns matters.)

   c. Columns cannot contain repeating groups. (The Team and Time columns are repeating groups.)

   ➤ 2NF rules:

   a. It is in 1NF.

   b. All non-key fields depend on all key fields. (Winner depends on the two Time fields, not on the Heat field. In other words, you can deduce Winner without knowing Heat.)

   ➤ 3NF rules:

   a. It is in 2NF.

   b. It contains no transitive dependencies. (Winner depends on the non-key Team and Time fields.)

12. You could satisfy the rules about nonrepeating column names and the columns' ordering not mattering by renaming the Team and Time fields to be Team1, Team2, Time1, and Time2, but that would still leave the table holding repeating groups.

Note that the first Time field holds the heat's starting time. That is a different kind of value than the other Time fields, so it doesn't form a repeating group. Renaming it to StartTime would fix its name.

To solve the problem, you should create a new Heats table to hold heat numbers, distances, and start times. Then create a second HeatParticipants table to hold information about the teams that participated in each heat. Figure A.12 shows the new design.

Notice that the new design doesn't have a Winner field in either table. You can deduce a heat's winner by fetching the data for the two participating teams and comparing their times, so you don't need the Winner field.

Heats		
Heat	Distance	StartTime
1	500	9:00
2	500	9:20
3	1000	9:40
4	1000	10:00

HeatParticipants		
Heat	Team	Time
1	Buddhist Temple	2:55.372
1	Wicked Wind	2:57.391
2	Rainbow Energy	3:10.201
2	Rising Typhoon	3:01.791
3	Math Dragons	5:52.029
3	Supermarines	6:23.552
4	Flux Lake Tritons	6:08.480
4	Elf Power	6:59.717

FIGURE A.12: These tables hold information about dragon boat races.

CHAPTER 8

1. The letters in the CIA triad stand for confidentiality, integrity, and availability.

2. The following list shows brief definitions of basic security terms.

   ➤ Shift-left security—Incorporating security planning into the earliest stages of design

   ➤ DevOps—Combining development and long-term operations to make rolling out changes faster

   ➤ DevSecOps—Shift-left security applied to DevOps

3. The following list shows brief definitions of some malware terms.

   ➤ Virus—A program that infects another program, and when it executes, it creates copies of itself

   ➤ Trojan—A program that infects another program, but instead of spreading, it performs some malicious action when it executes

   ➤ Worm—A program that tries to copy itself onto other computers in a network

   ➤ FakeApp—A program that pretends to be some other application

   ➤ Logic bomb—A program that takes action when some situation arises

   ➤ Time bomb—A program that starts, stops, or takes some other action at a specific date and time

   ➤ Ransomware—A program that encrypts your system's data and won't release it until you pay a ransom

   ➤ Double extortion scheme—A ransomware attack that also threatens to release your data to unauthorized people such as other hackers

   ➤ Spyware—A program that returns information to the attacker

   ➤ Crapware—Software installed on new systems by the manufacturer

   ➤ Rootkit—A set of programs that provides access to unauthorized parts of the system

➤ DoS—A denial-of-service attack prevents authorized use of a system, often by spamming the system with bogus requests

➤ DDoS—A distributed denial-of-service attack, which is a DoS that comes from multiple computers

➤ Bot—A program that runs over the Internet

➤ Botnet—A network of bots controlled by an attacker

➤ Zero-day—A vulnerability that is either not known or that is known but not yet patched

➤ Exploit, sploit—A bug in the system that an attacker can exploit

➤ Phishing—An attack that tries to trick the victim into thinking it is a legitimate communication so you will reveal sensitive information

➤ Spoofing—A communication that pretends to be from an authoritative source

➤ Formjacking—When malicious code is inserted into an online form to forward data to an attacker

➤ Man-in-the-middle (MITM)—When an attacker sits in the middle of a conversation and eavesdrops or possibly changes messages between a sender and a recipient

➤ Insider threat—A threat from someone with inside information about the company

➤ SQL injection—Entering unexpected text in fields to trick a program into executing a dangerous query

4. The following list shows brief definitions of kinds of phishing.

➤ Spear phishing—When the message is customized to the victim to make it seem more convincing

➤ Whaling—Spear phishing aimed at a company executive or other important person

➤ Vishing—Voice or voicemail phishing

➤ Smishing—Text message (SMS or short message service) phishing

➤ Angler phishing—Phishing via social media, sometimes pretending to be customer service

5. The following list shows some of the indications that this could be a phishing email.

➤ Too good to be true.

➤ Sender's name doesn't match sender's email address.

➤ Sender's email address isn't from moneygram.com.

➤ Recipient's email is in Bcc field.

➤ From a company that I do not do business with.

➤ No recipient name (as in "Congratulations Rod").

➤ Odd grammar in "branch London - United Kingdom."

➤ Poor grammar in "your winning fund."

➤ Redundant use of $ and dollars.

➤ Poor grammar and capitalization in "through Internet contest."

➤ Poor grammar in "under MoneyGram..."

➤ Odd capitalization in "International branch."

➤ Unusual construction "your winning fund."

➤ Poor grammar in "which you suppose to contact."

➤ The name "MoneyGram International London UK" is inconsistent with the earlier company name.

➤ Contact name different from sender's name.

➤ Contact email isn't from `moneygram.com`.

➤ The signoff "MoneyGram Branch London-UK" is different from the earlier company names, and "Branch" should not be capitalized.

➤ Mr. Webster Michael should probably be Mr. Michael Webster (although I've known people with names that sounded more normal backward than forward, so we'll let this one slide).

➤ Overall, doesn't pass the smell test.

Any one of the first six should be enough to indicate that this is very likely a phishing email. It's full of small errors, but if you run it through Microsoft Word's spelling and grammar check (which the attacker may have done), it doesn't find any significant problems.

The smell test should also be sufficient cause for concern. Really? A company that I've never used is giving me $1,500,000.00 USD dollars and you're notifying me through an email where I'm not even the main recipient? I'd think you would at least fly me to branch London to give me a big novelty cheque in £ GBP pounds sterling in front of a telly crew.

Interestingly, this email did not really try to create a sense of urgency. For example, I've seen similar emails that say things like, "This is our third and final attempt to contact you!!!"

It also doesn't contain any links or attachments that I can open to install a virus. Probably it is intended to make me email Mr. Webster Michael so he can ask for a "processing fee" before releasing my money.

As for whether this email is a spoof, it pretends to be from someone other than the actual sender, but it doesn't do a very good job. The email address isn't spoofed to look like it came from `moneygram.com`, and the message doesn't include any company artwork (like logos) or real company links (such as to their help or general info pages). Technically it's either not spoofing or a very weak attempt.

However, it's still dangerous. Despite having almost two dozen warning flags, if you send this email to a million people, you'll probably find more than a few who think, "Gee, this could be real!"

6. The following list shows some of the indications that this could be a phishing email.

   ➤ No company artwork.

   ➤ Generic greeting instead of using my name.

   ➤ Strange calling this an "annual membership" when it should probably be called a product, subscription, or service.

   ➤ Strange capitalization of NORTON SECURITY, Date of Purchase, AUTO CHARGE, REFUND, Contact, Billing Department, Possible, Reach.

   ➤ Uses & instead of "and."

   ➤ Company that I have not dealt with.

   ➤ Unusual use of asterisks and underscores to highlight information.

   ➤ Grammar error in "within next."

   ➤ Unusual wording "account record."

   ➤ Colons don't line up.

   ➤ The # symbol appears after the invoice number.

   ➤ Uses both $ and USD.

   ➤ Unusual capitalization of AUTO CHARGE, REFUND.

   ➤ Strange wording "You can Reach us on."

   ➤ Strange phone number format +1 (818 / 660 / 0770).

   ➤ Signature does not include Barry Jones's title, address, or phone number.

   ➤ The message suggests a way to request a REFUND, something that most vendors do not do. (Why would a vendor think that you probably want a refund?)

   This message tries to create a sense of urgency. It says that the membership has been successfully renewed and that the debit will be reflected within 24 to 48 hours, so I need to act fast!

   The message also just flat out says to "Contact our Billing Department as soon as Possible."

7. In the 3-2-1 backup strategy, you keep three copies of your data on two types of media with one copy off-site. In the 3-2-2 strategy, you keep both backup copies off-site.

8. The 3-2-2 strategy has the advantage that two backups are off-site, so if your site is compromised by a virus or worm or something, at least one of the copies may be safe. It has the disadvantage that it's more work to move two copies to separate off-site locations. (If you move them both to the same location, then an attack that damages one may also damage the other, so there's less benefit from having two.)

9. The 2 in the middle means the 3-2-1 and 3-2-2 strategies use two different media like a hard drive for the data in use and a flash drive for one of the backups. Using two different media makes it less likely that the same attack can affect all of the copies, so a 3-1-1 or 3-1-2 strategy would not be as secure. (A 3-3-2 strategy would be even better, but more work.)

CHAPTER 9

1. The UI (user interface) includes what the user sees and does with the application. The user experience (UX) includes the UI plus external factors such as installation, updates, availability, and connectivity with other applications.

2. A first-class app is one that users typically use often for hours at a time. A transient app is one that is usually used infrequently and not very deeply. Users of first-class apps are beginners for only a short while and then become intermediate or expert users. Users of transient apps are perpetual beginners.

3. A software metaphor is a feature that mimics something external with which the user should already be familiar. For example, the computer's wastebasket mimics a real-world waste basket.

   An idiom is something that we agree upon and that only makes sense once you know the convention. For example, a check mark for Yes, an X for No, a circle with a line halfway through it for Power, a curved arrow pointing left for Undo, and a curved arrow pointing right for Redo are all idioms.

4. Undo and redo are the best features for providing a safe environment for exploration. They allow the user to try things and then undo them.

5. In short, commensurate difficulty means that you should make easy things easy and hard things hard. Users are willing to put in more effort to achieve more complicated or more dangerous results. For example, printing the currently displayed report should be easy. It's okay to make it harder to delete all of the program's data or route a large fleet of vehicles.

6. "Ask for forgiveness" only works if there's a good chance that the default action will be correct. If it's always wrong, then it would be better to let the user direct the action.

7. A bar graph showing monthly sales data is qualitative. It allows the user to know which months were better than others and to see general trends.

   If you add numeric labels or tooltips to give the precise sales values, those are quantitative. They allow the user to see the data more precisely.

8. Interactive actions should take no longer than around five seconds. After that, users tend to become distracted.

9. Warn the user in a way that does not interrupt the user's flow. For example, give the field a yellow background or display an error icon next to it. When the user is ready to accept the form, bring the error to the user's attention. An alternative would be to let the user select the month from a drop-down so it is impossible to select an invalid value.

10. Most people can hold seven plus or minus two items in their short-term memory at once. It's helpful if you don't make users concentrate on more than five items at a time. (Person, woman, man, camera, TV.)

11. You can display more than five items if you group them into categories. You can also present more items (for example, in a list) if they represent the same concept and they are organized in a predictable way (for example, chronologically or alphabetically).

12. This is an open-ended exercise. There are a lot of things to dislike about the Windows 11 version of MS Paint. Here are a few of them:

➤ The ribbon.

➤ Despite having a ribbon, the program also has a menu to take up even more space.

➤ The Resize and Skew dialog does not allow easy keyboard navigation and does not honor the universal dialog convention Enter = Accept and Escape = Cancel.

➤ The "Do you want to save your work?" and the new color dialogs do not honor the Enter = Accept and Escape = Cancel convention, although the New, Open, and Save As dialogs do, thus giving the annoying combination of both inconvenient and inconsistent.

➤ The File ⇨ Save As command requires you to pick a file type in a sub-sub-menu item. The Save As dialog still lets you change that extension, so there's no point in picking the extension to begin with, particularly since you will almost always leave it unchanged.

➤ The View menu only lets you select 100% scale. However, the zoom bar lets you select scales from 12.5% to 800%. (This violates the "multiple places to perform the same action" rule.)

➤ The Print ⇨ Print command displays a dialog instead of simply printing. There's also a Print ⇨ Page Setup command that displays a dialog where you can select things like orientation and scaling. The two could be combined in one Page Setup dialog.

➤ There's no configurability.

➤ The Open and Save As dialogs remember their locations separately. For example, if you open a file and invoke Save As ⇨ PNG, then you need to navigate if you want to save the new copy where the original file was loaded. (I've been tripped up by this hundreds, perhaps thousands of times and dropped a file in the wrong directory.)

➤ If you use the Zoom slider to zoom in, scroll bars do not always appear when needed or may let you scroll to display unnecessary white space outside of the image. (These are just bugs, but pretty obvious ones that should have been caught during unit tests.)

➤ Sometimes if you're zoomed in and drag the bottom of the picture to make it shorter, the program makes it even shorter than desired so it crops off pieces of the picture. (This is another bug, and this one has been in there for years.)

CHAPTER 10

1. The problem with the original GCD code's comments is that they just say what the code does and not why it does it. They don't add anything that isn't obvious from the code itself. For example, the following three lines leave you with the feeling of "Well, duh!"

```
// Get the absolute value of a and b.
a = Math.Abs(a);
b = Math.Abs(b);
```

This algorithm is short but tricky to understand. You could include a big explanation of how it works, but that would clutter the code and make it harder to read. Besides, there's already a perfectly good description of the algorithm online.

The following code shows a version with much better comments:

```
// Use Euclid's algorithm to calculate the GCD.
// See en.wikipedia.org/wiki/Euclidean_algorithm.
private long GCD(long a, long b)
{
    a = Math.Abs(a);
    b = Math.Abs(b);
    for (; ; )
    {
        long remainder = a % b;
        if (remainder == 0) return b;
        a = b;
        b = remainder;
    }
}
```

All you need is the reference to the URL where you can find a description of the algorithm.

2. There are two likely reasons why the original GCD code ended up with bad comments. First, the programmer may have taken a top-down design to its logical conclusion where the code is described in excruciating detail. That's good programming practice, but it can result in these kinds of redundant comments because each comment describes a code statement.

When using top-down design to generate comments, you need to stop one step before the actual code. In this example, the last step before writing out the code would be here:

```
// Use Euclid's algorithm to calculate the GCD.
// See en.wikipedia.org/wiki/Euclidean_algorithm.
```

The second way this kind of comment sometimes occurs is if the programmer added the comments after writing the code. After the code is written, it's easy to just say what each line of code does and not why it is doing it. (It's sort of like a third-grade book report. You tend to get a repetition of the story and not the deeper insights you might get from a professional book reviewer.)

3. The parameters a and b should be greater than 0. (Actually, the algorithm works if a is 0, but that's a weird case that probably indicates an error in the calling code, so we'll flag that as an error.)

If you verify that the values are greater than 0, then you can remove the calls to Math.Abs that convert a and b into their absolute values.

The method can also verify that the return value actually divides both the a and b evenly. It should not need to do that, but this is a good chance to check for bugs.

The following code shows the revised GCD method. The validation code is shown in bold text:

```
// Use Euclid's algorithm to calculate the GCD.
// See en.wikipedia.org/wiki/Euclidean_algorithm.
private long GCD(long a, long b)
{
    // Verify that a and b are greater than 0.
    Debug.Assert(a > 0);
    Debug.Assert(b > 0);
    // Save the original values for later validation.
    long original_a = a;
    long original_b = b;
    for (; ; )
    {
        long remainder = a % b;
        if (remainder == 0)
        {
            // Verify that the result evenly divides the original values.
            Debug.Assert(original_a % b == 0);
            Debug.Assert(original_b % b == 0);
            return b;
        }
        a = b;
        b = remainder;
    }
}
```

You could also check that the result is the *smallest* even divisor of a and b. That's a bit
trickier and more time-consuming, so you can include it in a conditional compilation block
to make it easy to remove from release versions of the program.

The following snippet shows the new version of the code that validates the result with the
new lines of code shown in bold text. That code is included in the compilation only if the
symbol DEBUG_1 is defined:

```
if (remainder == 0)
{
    // Verify that the result evenly divides the original values.
    Debug.Assert(original_a % b == 0);
    Debug.Assert(original_b % b == 0);

#if DEBUG_1
    // Verify that there are no larger common divisors.
    long max_value = Math.Min(original_a, original_b);
    for (long test_value = b + 1; test_value <= max_value; test_value++)
    {
        Debug.Assert(
            (original_a % test_value != 0) ||
            (original_b % test_value != 0));
    }
#endif
    return b;
}
```

The new loop runs from the result plus 1 to the minimum of the original a and b values. It asserts that the values in that range do not evenly divide both a and b because any value that did would be a larger common divisor than the one found by the method.

4. The validation code written for Exercise 3 is already fairly offensive. It validates the inputs and the result, and the Debug.Assert method throws an exception if there is a problem.

5. You could add error handling code to the GCD method, but you actually want the calling code to handle any errors. As it is, if the code throws any exceptions, they are passed up to the calling code so that they can be handled there. That means you don't need to add error handling code here.

6. This isn't good code *because* it's clever. That makes it harder to understand (most people take a while to figure out how this swap works), and remember, you should be writing code for people to understand, not for the computer's convenience.

   For all its obscurity, this code doesn't buy you much. It saves you from allocating a 4- or 8-byte temporary variable, but if one more variable is going to ruin your program's performance, your application has some serious problems.

   The following code shows a version that's much easier to understand:

   ```
   // Swap a and b.
   long temp = a;
   a = b;
   b = temp;
   ```

7. Your answer will be different from mine, but here's how to get to *my* nearest supermarket, to give you an idea of the level of detail required.

   a. Find the car.

   b. Open the car door and get in.

   c. Start the car.

   d. Back out of the parking space.

   e. Turn to the left (as you look at the parking space). Drive out of the parking lot to the cross street.

   f. Turn left. Drive until the street ends.

   g. Turn right. Drive to the stop sign.

   h. Turn left. Drive to the first stoplight.

   i. Turn right. Drive until you see the supermarket.

   j. Turn into the supermarket parking lot.

   k. Find an empty parking space and park in it.

   l. Stop the car and get out.

   m. Go buy Twinkies and Red Bull.

This description makes the assumptions:

a. The car is parked head-first (which should be true for my car).

b. You properly adjust the seat and mirrors when you enter the car.

c. There's gas in the car. (Another reasonable assumption.)

d. You know how to drive a manual transmission. (I bet you didn't see that one coming!)

e. There's nothing behind the car when you pull out.

f. You can safely drive when instructed. No cars, people, dogs, trees, or other objects jump in the way.

g. You know how to shift gears as needed.

h. There are empty parking spaces in the supermarket parking lot.

i. The supermarket is open.

The lesson here is that even the most mundane chores can involve a huge number of steps, each of which can rely on a lot of assumptions. When broken down, some of the steps can also lead to a lot of smaller steps. For example, it takes a lot of instructions to explain how to start a car that has manual transmission if you don't know how to do it, particularly if you assume anything could go wrong.

CHAPTER 11

1. Here's a defensive version of the C# `Fibonacci` function.

```
private long Fibonacci(long n)
{
    if (n <= 0) return 0;
    if (n == 1) return 1;
    return Fibonacci(n - 1) + Fibonacci(n - 2);
}
```

In this version, if the input number n is less than zero, the function returns 0 instead of entering an infinite loop. It's still too slow to calculate values larger than around `Fibonacci(50)` (depending on the speed of your computer), so it can still cause problems for your program.

2. Here's an offensive version of the C# `Fibonacci` function.

```
private long Fibonacci(long n)
{
    if (n < 0) throw
        new ArgumentOutOfRangeException(
            "n",
            "Fibonacci parameter n cannot be less than zero.");
    if (n > 40) throw
        new ArgumentOutOfRangeException(
            "n",
```

```
                    "Fibonacci parameter n cannot be geater than 40.");

        if (n == 0) return 0;
        if (n == 1) return 1;
        return Fibonacci(n - 1) + Fibonacci(n - 2);
}
```

In this version, if the input number n is less than zero or greater than 45, the function throws an exception. (With inputs larger than 45, I get bored.)

3. Here's an offensive version of the Python `factorial` function.

```
def factorial(n):
    if (n < 0):
        raise ValueError(
            'Parameter n cannot be less than zero.')
    if (n > 2800):
        raise ValueError(
            'Parameter n cannot be geater than 2,800.')

    if (n == 0):
        return 1
    return n * factorial(n - 1)
```

This version throws an exception if its input is less than zero. Python can use arbitrarily large integers, so this function shouldn't cause integer overflow no matter how large n is.

However, it does get seriously confused if n is too large, on my computer at least. Presumably it's exceeding its stack limit, but for me, in Jupyter Notebook, it just seems to stop calculating and lobotomizes itself, so it forgets the definition of the `factorial` function. To avoid that embarrassing issue, I added an upper bound check.

It's usually a good idea to add this kind of *sanity check* anyway to be sure the program isn't using ridiculously large or small values. (Of course, if you need to calculate such large values, you'll need to figure out a way around this problem.)

4. This is a divide-and-conquer strategy. You divide the route into two pieces and then recursively solve them.

5. This is a hill climbing approach. This strategy has several problems. First, you may end up taking many small streets when faster ones are available.

Second, you might end up making lots of unnecessary turns. (For example, to move diagonally from the southwest corner to the northeast corner in a grid, you might turn left, right, left, right, etc. You could instead just drive all the way north and then all the way east along the grid's outside edges.)

Third, you might get stuck in a loop. For example, suppose you reach a dead end so the street pointing most directly toward the destination points back the way you came. You follow it, but when you reach the next intersection, the algorithm makes you turn around and go back along the same street again. (A computer would be stuck forever. Hopefully you'll quickly change your strategy. Or grow tired, give up, and go home.)

6. This approach uses previously saved information, so it's a form of dynamic programming. (Over a long time period. You didn't learn your shortcuts just now while exploring the city trying to find the route.)

7. Yuzu Street is *usually* the fastest, but you never know when someone will cause an accident and slow things down, so this is a heuristic. In fact, just about any route-finding algorithm on streets is in some sense a heuristic because conditions on the road are unpredictable. If your goal is to drive the minimum possible distance, a good algorithm will find you a route that works. If your goal is to spend the minimum possible time, there will be uncertainty.

8. This is a parallel algorithm where each of the millions of people uses their personal heuristics to find their way home. (With many variations such as on foot, by tube or black cab, in a car pool, via a pub or restaurant, and so on.)

CHAPTER 12

1. Machine language (1GL) and assembly language (2GL) are considered low-level languages. All of the others (3GL through 5GL) are considered high-level languages.

2. Here are brief summaries of the programming language generations:

   1GL—Machine language. 0s and 1s.

   2GL—Assembly language. A mnemonic version of machine language.

   3GL—Most procedural and object-oriented languages. The most commonly used languages.

   4GL—Languages that provide a higher level of abstraction than 3GLs. Many of these languages, such as SQL, work with collections of data rather than making you examine individual items. Others, such as MATLAB, also serve more specialized fields such as mathematics or report generation.

   5GL—Languages that solve problems by using rules and constraints rather than by following step-by-step instructions.

3. Here are the language families for the question's examples:

   ➤ Turing machine programs: *2GL*

   ➤ Most procedural languages such as C++ and BASIC: *3GL*

   ➤ Artificial intelligence systems that identify previously unknown data patterns: *5GL*

   ➤ Object-oriented languages such as Java and C#: *3GL*

   ➤ MACRO-11 assembly language: *2GL*

   ➤ A report-generation language that can examine a database's structure to automatically generate reports: *5GL*

   ➤ R2-D2: *5GL*

   ➤ C-3PO: *5GL*

4. In an imperative language, the code gives step-by-step instructions to the computer. A procedural language lets you define procedures that contain code so you can call the procedure from multiple places. A declarative language tells the program the result that you want and then the program figures out how to achieve it.

CHAPTER 13

1. To test a method, you need a way to verify that the results it returns are correct. Sometimes, that's easiest if you write another method that performs the same calculation in a different way. Then you can pass inputs to both methods and verify that they agree.

For this example, I wrote a `Validate_AreRelativelyPrime` method that uses an inefficient algorithm for determining whether two values are relatively prime. The following C# code shows the method. (If you don't know C#, just read the description that follows the code.)

```
// Return true if a and b are relatively prime.
// This is a test method that is less efficient than
// AreRelativelyPrime and is used only to validate that method.
private bool Validate_AreRelativelyPrime(int a, int b)
{
    // Use positive values.
    a = Math.Abs(a);
    b = Math.Abs(b);

    // If either value is 1, return true.
    if ((a == 1) || (b == 1)) return true;

    // If either value is 0, return false.
    // (Only 1 and -1 are relatively prime to 0.)
    if ((a == 0) || (b == 0)) return false;

    // Loop from 2 to the smaller of a and b looking for factors.
    int min = Math.Min(a, b);
    for (int factor = 2; factor <= min; factor++)
    {
        if ((a % factor == 0) && (b % factor == 0)) return false;
    }
    return true;
}
```

This code first converts a and b into positive values. Then if either value is 1, it returns `true` because 1 and −1 are relatively prime to every number.

Next if a or b is 0, the method returns `false` because only 1 and −1 are relatively prime to 0 and the code already checked whether a or b is 1 or −1.

The code makes the value `factor` loop from 2 to the smaller of a and b. It then uses the modulus operator % to see if `factor` divides evenly into both a and b. (The modulus is the remainder after division. For example, 14 % 5 is 4 because 14 divided by 5 is 2 with a remainder of 4. If a % `factor` is 0, then `factor` divides into a evenly, so `factor` is a factor of a.)

If `factor` divides into both a and b evenly, then a and b are not relatively prime, so the method returns `false`.

Finally, if none of the values of `factor` divides into both a and b, then the numbers are relatively prime, so the method returns `true`.

Having written the `Validate_AreRelativelyPrime` method, you can use it to test the original `AreRelativelyPrime` method. I wrote a C# method named `Test_AreRelativelyPrime` to perform a series of tests. The method is quite long (and unless you speak C# or a related language, it would probably be confusing), so I won't repeat it here. The following text shows the tests that the method performs in pseudocode:

```
For 1,000 trials, pick random a and b and:
    Assert AreRelativelyPrime(a, b) =
        Validate_AreRelativelyPrime(a, b)

For 1,000 trials, pick random a and:
    Assert AreRelativelyPrime(a, a) =
        Validate_AreRelativelyPrime(a, a)

For 1,000 trials, pick random a and:
    Assert AreRelativelyPrime(a, 1) = true
    Assert AreRelativelyPrime(a, -1) = true
    Assert AreRelativelyPrime(1, a) = true
    Assert AreRelativelyPrime(-1, a) = true

For 1,000 trials, pick random a (not 1 or -1) and:
    Assert AreRelativelyPrime(a, 0) = false
    Assert AreRelativelyPrime(0, a) = false

For 1,000 trials, pick random a and:
    Assert AreRelativelyPrime(a, -1,000,000) =
        Validate_AreRelativelyPrime(a, -1,000,000)
    Assert AreRelativelyPrime(a, 1,000,000) =
        Validate_AreRelativelyPrime(a, 1,000,000)
    Assert AreRelativelyPrime(-1,000,000, a) =
        Validate_AreRelativelyPrime(-1,000,000, a)
    Assert AreRelativelyPrime(1,000,000, a) =
        Validate_AreRelativelyPrime(1,000,000, a)
    Assert AreRelativelyPrime(-1,000,000, -1,000,000) =
        Validate_AreRelativelyPrime(-1,000,000, -1,000,000)
    Assert AreRelativelyPrime(1,000,000, 1,000,000) =
        Validate_AreRelativelyPrime(1,000,000, 1,000,000)
    Assert AreRelativelyPrime(-1,000,000, 1,000,000) =
        Validate_AreRelativelyPrime(-1,000,000, 1,000,000)
    Assert AreRelativelyPrime(1,000,000, -1,000,000) =
        Validate_AreRelativelyPrime(1,000,000, -1,000,000)
```

This code verifies the method's results for pairs of random values, pairs of identical numbers, 1, −1, 0, and the smallest and largest values supported by the `AreRelativelyPrime` method −1 million and 1 million.

2. The testing code checks a lot of special cases, so you need to insert a lot of bugs into the AreRelativelyPrime method to test each special case. I added the following code to the beginning of the AreRelativelyPrime method to break each of the tests:

```
#if TEST_TESTS
    if (a == -1000000) return true;
    if (a == 1000000) return true;
    if (a == b) return true;
    if (a == 1) return false;
    if (b == 1) return false;

    if (a == -1) return false;
    if (b == -1) return false;
    if (a == 0) return true;
    if (b == 0) return true;
#endif
```

This code made the method return incorrect answers for each of the tests so the testing code could catch the errors. Note that the method didn't always return an incorrect answer. For example, the first statement says –1,000,000 is relatively prime to the number a. That's correct for some values of a but not for all values. Because the testing method runs 1,000 trials of most tests, it better find a number for which this is wrong, and it better detect that error.

Notice that the code is enclosed in an #if...#endif conditional compilation block. That lets me easily disable the test-breaking code without removing it so that I can turn it on again later if I need to. (Actually, after you test the testing code, you can probably remove this. You probably won't need it again and it clutters up the original method.)

3. Because the statement of Exercise 1 doesn't say how the AreRelativelyPrime method works, this must be a black-box test.

If I told you how the AreRelativelyPrime method works, you could write white-box and gray-box tests for it.

You could try to perform an exhaustive test, but with allowed values ranging from –1 million and 1 million, there would be $(1,000,000 - -1,000,000 + 1)^2 = 2,000,001^2 \approx 4$ trillion pairs of values to test, which is probably too many. If the allowed values ranged from –1,000 to 1,000, you would have only approximately 1 million pairs to test, so this would be possible.

4. The tests I wrote for Exercise 1 use the Validate_AreRelativelyPrime method to test the AreRelativelyPrime method. Because we don't know how the AreRelativelyPrime method works, there's a chance that the two methods use the same technique. In that case, we might be using an incorrect method to validate another incorrect method, so they could be both wrong in the same way.

If you knew how the AreRelativelyPrime method works, then you could write white-box tests that you know use a different method for determining whether two integers are relatively prime. That would increase your certainty that the tests work.

5. You can download an example C# program at www.csharphelper.com/howtos/zips/howto_test_relativelyprime.zip.

When I wrote this program, I did find some problems in the `AreRelativelyPrime` method. The initial version didn't have restrictions on the values a and b, and the method had trouble handling the maximum and minimum possible integer values. That inspired me to restrict the allowed values so they must lie between –1,000,000 and 1,000,000. Testing often leads to restrictions such as this one.

Other than that, the `AreRelativelyPrime` method worked well. It took a bit of effort to get the `Validate_AreRelativelyPrime` method and the test-breaking code to work exactly as I wanted. It wasn't really hard, but it did force me to think carefully about the weird values –1, 0, and 1. That's another benefit of writing tests: It makes you think harder about special cases that might trip up the application.

6. The following text shows an exhaustive test for the `AreRelativelyPrime` method in pseudocode:

```
For a = -1,000,000 to 1,000,000
    For b = -1,000,000 to 1,000,000
        Assert AreRelativelyPrime(a, b) =
            Validate_AreRelativelyPrime(a, b)
```

This version is much simpler than the previous test code. It also checks every possible combination, so it's guaranteed to flush out any bugs (as long as the `Validate_AreRelativelyPrime` method is correct).

It has the big drawback that it's slow, so it can handle only relatively limited ranges of values.

7. You can download an exhaustive version of the program at www.csharphelper.com/howtos/zips/howto_test_relativelyprime2.zip.

On my new computer, this program can handle the range –1,000 to 1,000 (approximately 4 million pairs) in roughly 2 seconds.

The next larger range that uses powers of 10 would be –10,000 to 10,000. It would include 100 times as many combinations, so it would take around 200 seconds, which won't fit within the 10 second limit.

The range –1 million to 1 million includes approximately 1 million times as many pairs as the 2-second range, so it should take approximately 2 million seconds, or around 23 days.

8. Yes, this is a lot of work. That's the price you pay for some assurance that the code works as advertised. Fortunately, most of the work is reasonably straightforward.

9. Exhaustive tests are black-box tests because they don't rely on knowledge of what's going on inside the method they are testing.

10. Lisa found 15 – 5 = 10 bugs that Ramon didn't, plus the 5 in common. Ramon found 13 – 5 = 8 bugs of his own, plus the 5 in common. That means:

$$[\text{Total found}] = [\text{Lisa only}] + [\text{Ramon only}] + [\text{Common}]$$
$$= 10 + 8 + 5$$
$$= 23$$

That means the number of remaining bugs is roughly 39 − 23 = 16. (Of course, this assumes you don't add any new bugs while fixing the ones that have been found.)

11. You can use each pair of testers to calculate three different Lincoln indexes.

➤ Alice/Bob: 5 × 4 ÷ 2 = 10

➤ Alice/Carmen: 5 × 5 ÷ 2 = 12.5

➤ Bob/Carmen: 4 × 5 ÷ 1 = 20

You could take an average of the three to get a rough estimate of (10 + 12.5 + 20) ÷ 3 ≈ 14 bugs. Alternatively, you could assume the worst and plan for 20 bugs. In either case, you should continue to track the number of bugs found so you can revise your estimate when you have more information.

12. If the testers don't find any bugs in common, then the equation for the Lincoln index divides by 0, giving you an infinite result. What this means is you have no clue about how many bugs there are. (There are probably many, unless the testers just started and haven't been testing long enough to have found any common bugs.)

You can get a sort of lower bound for the number of bugs by pretending the testers found 1 bug in common. For example, if the testers found 5 and 6 bugs, respectively, then the lower bound index would be (5 × 6) ÷ 1 = 30 bugs.

13. If the testers find only bugs in common, then the equation for the Lincoln index gives $(E_1 \times E_1) \div E_1 = E_1$ bugs, so the result assumes they have found every bug. That seems unlikely, particularly if the testers have found only a few bugs so far.

14. Here $E_1 = 15$, $E_2 = 13$, and $S = 5$, so the Seber estimator is:

$$
\begin{aligned}
Bugs &= \frac{(15+1)\times(13+1)}{(5+1)} - 1 \\
&= \frac{16\times14}{6} - 1 \\
&\approx 36
\end{aligned}
$$

This is slightly fewer than the 39 bugs predicted by the Lincoln index.

15. Here $E_1 = 7$, $E_2 = 5$, and $S = 0$, so the Seber estimator is:

$$
\begin{aligned}
Bugs &= \frac{(7+1)\times(5+1)}{(0+1)} - 1 \\
&= \frac{8\times6}{1} - 1 \\
&\approx 47
\end{aligned}
$$

This is a lot of bugs but fewer than the infinite number estimated by the Lincoln index.

16. If $E_1 = E_2 = S$, the Seber estimator gives:

$$Bugs = \frac{(E_1 + 1) \times (E_1 + 1)}{(E_1 + 1)} - 1$$

If you cancel one set of $(E_1 + 1)$ terms, you get:

$$Bugs = (E_1 + 1) - 1 = E_1$$

Like the Lincoln index, the Seber estimator predicts that every bug has been found. This still seems unlikely, particularly if the testers have found only a few bugs so far.

CHAPTER 14

1. In this case, it doesn't matter too much because any mistakes you make will affect only you and not thousands of other users. To make your own life easier, however, you might start with staging so that you can test the new version before you start using it. Gradual cutover doesn't make sense in this example because there's only one user. Incremental deployment also seems like more trouble than it's worth. I would just make a backup of the data and start using the new version.

2. Staged deployment, gradual cutover, and parallel testing work for just about any project. Incremental deployment also works in this example because the application is already broken into separate pieces.

3. Yes. Because each of the pieces needs to use the database, you can't simply install the pieces one at a time. That makes incremental deployment harder. It may not be practical for some parts of the system to use the old database and other parts to use the new one. For example, you probably couldn't create new orders using the new database but have the order-editing tool use the older database. That probably eliminates incremental deployment as a viable option.

Staged deployment, gradual cutover, and parallel testing would still work.

4. Because mistakes could affect so many users, you should do as much testing beforehand as possible. Use staged deployment so that you can work out as many kinks as possible before you start installing for users. After you understand deployment in the staging environment, use gradual cutover. Install one user and make sure everything works. Then install another user or two and make sure things still look good. When you're confident that you won't leave your thousands of users twiddling their thumbs, start deploying the application in larger batches.

5. A huge initial release with great fanfare that flops will destroy your company, so it's important that deployment goes smoothly. It must also continue to go smoothly after the initial installations as other users join in the fun.

To minimize risk, you should start with a staging area in which you test installation and the application itself thoroughly. In fact, you probably need multiple staging computers so that you can test in Windows 10, Windows 11, a few Linux versions, the latest OS X, and any other operating systems you plan to support. If the game is browser-based, you also need to test the browsers you support such as Firefox, Chrome, Edge, and others.

After you've thoroughly tested installation on all of the supported combinations of platforms, it's time to invite the customers to give it a try. You might like to do a gradual cutover, but as soon as you post the installation package on the Internet, you may have thousands of users installing the program.

One way to reduce your risk in this situation is to offer a limited beta. Users can sign up for a beta version of the game, to give you feedback. This lets you control the number of users who install the program (so you can still have a gradual deployment), and it gives you some cover if things go wrong. (Users don't expect betas to be perfect.)

After your limited beta test, you can release the final application to everyone. This still works sort of like a staged delivery. If the users find a problem, you can place a moratorium on new installs until you work it out.

You also need to keep a close eye on performance as the number of users increases. A program that works with 10 or 100 or even 1,000 users may swamp your servers when there are 10,000 or 100,000 simultaneous users.

6. The process of planning helps you think about what should happen and what can go wrong. Sometimes, you can guess the most likely ways a step will fail and you can have a workaround already in your pocket. Even if an emergency is completely unexpected, your planning will probably give you information that can help you deal with whatever weirdness actually occurs.

    A deployment plan doesn't plan only for emergencies. It's also a script of things that may very well go right. Having a plan ahead of time can help you coast through the easy stuff so that you can focus your energy on the hard parts.

7. These sorts of decisions are not cut and dried, so your answer may be different from mine, but here are my thoughts. This is a shareware application, so users probably don't expect the level of sophistication they require from the Big Dogs of software such as Microsoft, Apple, and Google. That means admitting a mistake isn't as earth-shattering as it would be for bigger companies.

    This is still a big problem for this program because it greatly reduces the program's usefulness. That means you can't hush things up and hope no one will notice. Users will probably start complaining as soon as they use the new version.

    Start by taking down the broken version 3.0 installer so that no one else installs it. Where the download should be, post a notice explaining the problem and telling users how hard you're working on fixing it.

Next, burn the midnight oil to get the program working correctly. When the problem is fixed, *test it thoroughly* so that you don't release a new buggy version. Nothing is as embarrassing as fixing a bug with another bug. (Okay, I can think of a few things more embarrassing, but that's about as bad as it gets with software releases.)

After you're *sure* it's working, release version 3.1 into the wild. Post a letter announcing the fix, explaining how hard you work to make users' lives better and saying how generally wonderful you are. If you have customer email addresses, send them a copy of the letter.

This isn't an ideal situation, but you can probably still squeeze some goodwill and publicity out of it.

8. Because this happens only about once a month, and because there's a workaround, this isn't a super high-priority issue. It could be a problem if a tester gets the wrong results and doesn't notice, so you need to warn users about the problem. However, this is an internal software project, so your sales are not at risk, and your testers probably won't quit because the software is a little off. (If this greatly annoys the testers and they start to grumble, you may need to reevaluate that assumption.)

Meanwhile, tracking down a bug that has no apparent cause can be time-consuming. A programmer could spend days or weeks chasing this bug and still not find it. Probably it won't take that long, but even the simplest bug takes a day or two to fix once all is said and done. (After all, you need to read the documentation, which you hopefully took the time to write; check out the code from source control; study the code; find, fix, test, and document the bug; check the code back into source control; and release the new version.)

You're left with a choice: Have users waste a few minutes per month, or have a programmer spend at least a day or two finding the problem and possibly weeks fixing it. The obvious choice is to ignore the problem, cover your ears, and say "la la la" whenever someone points it out to you.

Unfortunately, as mentioned in Chapter 13, "Testing" bugs often travel in swarms. This bug could hide the presence of others. Besides, it should offend the sensibilities of any developer to leave known bugs like this in an application.

What I would do is warn the users, tell them about the workaround, and fix the bug *when time permits*. Then I would wait until the next scheduled release to provide the fix.

CHAPTER 15

1. Figure A.13 shows my Ishikawa diagram.

Because it would be easy, I would first check the database contents to see if New Hampshire is in the `states` table. (Cross your fingers because this will be the easiest problem to fix. Simply add New Hampshire to the table and test again.)

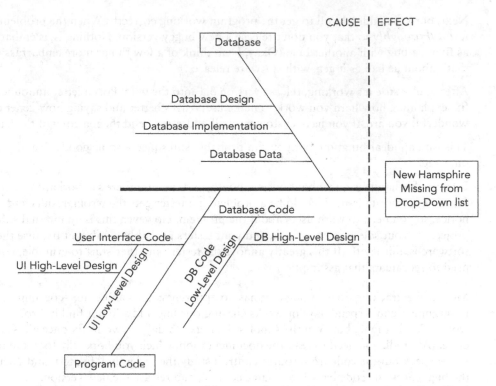

FIGURE A.13: This Ishikawa diagram shows possible causes for New Hampshire not being listed in the states drop-down list.

It seems unlikely that the database design or implementation could be at fault because the database contains the other values required by the use cases (Maine, Vermont, and Massachusetts).

That leaves only problems with the database code or the user interface code. I would check each of those and then follow whichever of those is wrong upstream. For example, if the database code isn't returning the right values, I'd check the low-level database code design. If the problem were obviously there, I'd be done. If the problem didn't obviously start in the low-level database code design, I'd check the high-level database code design.

2. Size normalization is useful when you're trying to compare two projects of different sizes but roughly similar complexities. In contrast, FP normalization lets you compare projects that differ in complexity.

3. Size normalization takes into account project size. FP normalization takes into account both project size and complexity. That means you can use FP normalization anytime you can use size normalization but not vice versa. In other words, you can use either method when the projects have roughly the same complexity.

4. You use the following equation to perform the final FP calculation:

$$FP = (raw\,FP) \times (0.65 + 0.01 \times CAV)$$

This has its largest value if CAV is as large as possible. That happens when you assign all the complexity adjustment factors the weight Essential, so they all get the value 5. There are 14 of those values, so you add them up to get 14 × 5 = 70. The calculation becomes:

$$FP = (500) \times (0.65 + 0.01 \times 70) = 675$$

The final FP has the smallest value if all the complexity adjustment values are 0. Then the calculation becomes:

$$FP = (500) \times (0.65 + 0.01 \times 0) = 325$$

5. Suppose project A has 12,500 LOC and 158 bugs so it has 12.6 bugs/KLOC. Project B has 3,250 LOC and 47 bugs so it has 14.4 bugs/KLOC. In this case, project A has more bugs in total but fewer bugs per KLOC, so it's doing better in that sense.

Assuming everything else is roughly equal for the two projects, you need to know how many developers they each have. Then you can calculate bugs per developer to decide which project will need more time to finish clearing out the bugs.

For example, suppose project A has 10 developers so it has 15.8 bugs per developer, and project B has 5 developers so it has 9.4 bugs per developer. In that case, project B has fewer bugs per developer so it will probably finish first.

6. If you know from past experience, either in those projects or previous projects, about how many bugs per day each developer can fix, then you can multiply that value by the number of bugs per developer to get the number of days remaining.

$$Days / Bug \times Bugs / Developer = Days / Developer$$

Of course, you can never really find every bug, so this probably tells you only when you've found enough of the bugs to have a reasonably stable application. (Fingers crossed.)

7. The way you count an application's inputs, outputs, and other complexity values can vary greatly, so if you're doing this for actual applications, you may want to develop some guidelines about what to count. That means your result may differ greatly from mine. Here are the values I used.

Inputs—WordPad can open approximately six kinds of files. The user can also type inputs into a document, so I'll make this count seven. (For some applications, you might want to make this the number of different files the application uses instead of the number of *types* of files it can open. WordPad can open an infinite number of different files, so counting the number of file types seems more meaningful.)

Loading text files isn't too hard, but loading RTF, DOCX, and ODT files would be tricky. (There are tools that could make these a lot easier, but remember we're trying to assess the complexity of the application from the user's point of view, not from the programmer's point of view. The results of these operations are complex, even if tools make them easier.) Working with the user's current file could also be hard. I'll give this category an average of medium complexity.

Outputs—WordPad can save approximately six kinds of files and it can print the current document, so I'll make this count seven. (Again, WordPad can save an unlimited *number* of different files, so I'll count *types* of files.)

Saving text files isn't hard, but saving RTF, DOCX, and ODT files is. Printing could also be complex. I'll give this category an average of medium complexity.

Inquiries—WordPad doesn't handle inquiries so I'll make this 0.

Internal Files—WordPad works on one file at a time, so I'll count its current document as one internal file. The program doesn't save configuration information, so that doesn't add to the internal file count.

It lets the user set a fair number of values (such as font face, size, style, and color), so I'll give this high complexity.

External Files—WordPad doesn't use any external files.

Figure A.14 shows my final counts.

			Complexity		
Category	Number	Low	Medium	High	Result
Inputs	7	× 3	④	6	= 28
Outputs	7	× 4	⑤	7	= 35
Inquiries	0	× 3	4	6	= 0
Internal Files	1	× 7	10	⑮	= 15
External Files	0	× 5	7	10	= 10
				Total (raw FP)	78

FIGURE A.14: This table shows Microsoft WordPad's raw FP value.

Table A.2 shows my complexity adjustment factors for WordPad.

TABLE A.2: Complexity adjustment factors for WordPad

FACTOR	RATING
Data communication	0
Distributed data processing	0
Performance	5
Heavily used configuration	0
Transaction rate	0
Online data entry	5
End-user efficiency	5
Online update	0
Complex processing	3
Reusability	0
Installation ease	4
Operational ease	5
Multiple sites	0
Facilitate change	0
Total (CAV)	27

The following equation shows the final FP calculation:

$$FP = (\text{raw FP}) \times (0.65 + 0.01 \times CAV) = 78 \times (0.65 + 0.01 \times 27) = 71.76$$

8. Your result may differ greatly from mine, but here are the values I used:

    Inputs—Word can open approximately 16 kinds of files. Many of those file types (such as RTF, DOCX, and ODT files) are complicated, so I'll give this category high complexity.

    Outputs—Word can save approximately 16 kinds of files and it can print the current document, so I'll make this count 17. Again, some of the file formats are complicated, so I'll give this category high complexity.

Inquiries—Word doesn't handle inquiries exactly, but it does have an automation server mode that lets other programs use it to open, manipulate, print, and save files. You could count those actions as more inputs and outputs and increase the count of those categories by 16. However, the server feature doesn't actually double the complexity.

The program can already open and save the 16 file types, so this is just another way to use that same capability. For that reason, I'm going to count this as one very complex feature.

Internal Files—Word works on one file at a time, so I'll count its current document as one internal file. It also saves a lot of configuration and customization information. If you select File ➪ Options, you'll see around 10 pages of options, so I'll count this as 10 additional items for a total of 11. The configuration information includes low, medium, and high-complexity items, so I'll give this category an average of medium complexity.

External Files—Word uses external document templates to determine a document's initial layout and properties. You can actually use Word to modify those templates, but in that case it's being used as a separate application. For example, when I select File ➪ New (don't press Ctrl+N), the program shows me a list of more than 40 Office.com categories of templates. Each category contains several templates, so there are hundreds in total. Those aren't maintained by me, so I'm counting them as external files.

You could have access to a practically unlimited number of templates, so you can't actually count individual templates here. Instead I'll do the same thing I did for inputs and outputs and count the template file type as a single complex item.

Figure A.15 shows my final counts.

			Complexity			
Category	Number		Low	Medium	High	Result
Inputs	16	×	3	4	(6)	= 96
Outputs	17	×	4	5	(7)	= 119
Inquiries	1	×	3	4	(6)	= 6
Internal Files	11	×	7	(10)	15	= 110
External Files	1	×	5	(7)	10	= 7
					Total (raw FP)	338

FIGURE A.15: This table shows Microsoft Word's raw FP value.

Table A.3 shows my complexity adjustment factors for Microsoft Word.

TABLE A.3: Complexity adjustment factors for Microsoft Word

FACTOR	RATING
Data communication	0
Distributed data processing	0
Performance	5
Heavily used configuration	5
Transaction rate	0
Online data entry	5
End-user efficiency	5
Online update	4
Complex processing	5
Reusability	5
Installation ease	4
Operational ease	5
Multiple sites	0
Facilitate change	0
Total (CAV)	43

Before making the final calculation, I want to briefly explain the reusability value. As mentioned earlier, Microsoft Word can act as an automation server. When it acts as a server, it can do just about anything it can do interactively. To allow it to do the same things both interactively and as a server, the code must be written in a reusable style, so I'm giving this factor high importance.

The following equation shows the final FP calculation.

$$FP = (\text{raw FP}) \times (0.65 + 0.01 \times \text{CAV}) = 338 \times (0.65 + 0.01 \times 43) = 365.04$$

Word's FP of 365.04 is much higher than WordPad's 71.76. The exact results of your calculations may be different, but your value for Word's FP should also be much higher than your value for WordPad.

9. In performing those FP calculations, I had to make a lot of assumptions about what should be counted and how. It's unlikely that someone else will make exactly the same assumptions, so our FP results may differ greatly. For example, many Word users don't even know that you can use Word as an automation server, and that is a large source of complexity. (How closely did your calculations agree with mine?)

   You could improve consistency by writing a lot of rules about what should be counted and how. For example, how do you count the number of input files when a program could open an infinite number of different files? This could be a lot of work but it would be important.

   You would probably even need that kind of documentation even if the same person were calculating FP for all of your projects. Otherwise, when you perform the calculation for a project a year from now, you may not remember exactly how you made your decisions today.

10. Microsoft WordPad's FP of 71.76 and Microsoft Word's FP of 365.04 tell you that Word is a *lot* more complicated than WordPad.

    This agrees with what I would expect, although, my calculations really drove home how much more complicated Word is than WordPad. Both programs enable you to edit files, format documents, and open and save DOCX files, so you might think their complexities are similar. However, Word provides an abundance of extra features that you might not think about until you try to count them for the calculation.

11. Of course, "better" is a subjective term. Function point normalization lets you compare very different projects, but it's much harder to apply consistently. Size normalization doesn't help you compare projects with different complexities, but it's much easier to use. So I would use size normalization if possible and function point normalization when the projects' complexities vary greatly.

12. Because the projects have similar complexities, you can use size normalization.

    If you divide total LOC by number of weeks, you'll get lines of code per week. That's still not a great way to compare the projects, because 10 developers can probably produce a lot more code than 5 programmers. To get the number of lines of code produced per developer per week, divide total LOC by number of person-weeks (pw).

    You could similarly divide the total number of bugs by person-weeks to get number of bugs per developer per week.

    Another (and simpler) method for thinking about the number of bugs is to look at the number of bugs per KLOC.

    Table A.4 shows those three calculations.

TABLE A.4: Normalized LOC and bugs

PROJECT	PW	LOC/PW	BUGS/PW	BUGS/KLOC
Unicorn	80	149	3.41	22.95
Pegasus	40	150	2.60	17.30

PROJECT	PW	LOC/PW	BUGS/PW	BUGS/KLOC
Griffin	72	135	2.43	17.95
Jackalope	28	185	3.14	17.00

The LOC/pw values show that project Griffin was least productive and project Jackalope was most productive.

The bugs/pw values show that project Jackalope produced the most bugs and project Griffin produced the fewest per person-week. That's a bit misleading, however, because the teams didn't all generate code at the same rate. Project Jackalope probably created a lot of bugs per person-week because the developers generated a lot of code quickly. Project Griffin created fewer bugs per person week, possibly because the developers wrote code relatively slowly.

A better measure of code quality is bugs/KLOC. Those numbers show that projects Pegasus, Griffin, and Jackalope produced roughly the same numbers of bugs per line of code and project Unicorn produced significantly more bugs.

To make process improvements, you could try to figure out how project Jackalope increased productivity without sacrificing quality. Perhaps you can use whatever the magical factor was in future projects.

Similarly, you can look at project Unicorn to see why their bugs/KLOC was higher. Perhaps there's something they did (or that a particular person on the team did) that you should avoid in the future.

13. The projects described in Exercise 12 produced between 135 and 185 LOC/pw, with an average of approximately 155 LOC/pw. Dividing 7,000 lines of code by those numbers gives the following estimates.

CASE	EXPECTED TIME
Best Case	7,000 LOC ÷ 185 LOC/pw ≈ 37.8 pw
Average Case	7,000 LOC ÷ 155 LOC/pw ≈ 46.2 pw
Worst Case	7,000 LOC ÷ 135 LOC/pw ≈ 51.9 pw

Similarly, the previous projects produced between 17.00 and 22.95 bugs/KLOC with an average of 18.80. Multiplying those values by 7,000 lines of code gives the following estimates.

CASE	EXPECTED BUGS
Best Case	7 KLOC × 17.00 bugs/KLOC ≈ 119.0 bugs
Average Case	7 KLOC × 18.80 bugs/KLOC ≈ 131.6 bugs
Worst Case	7 KLOC × 22.95 bugs/KLOC ≈ 160.7 bugs

14. It's a bit harder to evaluate a project in the middle (project metrics) than it is to compare projects after the fact (process metrics). One way to do this is to graph the project's progress (LOC and number of bugs) over time and compare it to similar values for other projects.

However, unless the projects just happen to have the same durations, they won't line up properly. In other words, you can't directly compare a 5-week project and a 10-week project week by week.

Instead, you can compare the percentage of the project that's finished with the percentage of the time that has elapsed. For example, consider a typical 10-week project. Suppose after week 5, the team has written 40 percent of the total code. Then you would expect future projects to also have written 40 percent of the code when one-half of the project's time has elapsed.

Table A.5 shows the percentages of LOC and time for each of the projects during their durations.

TABLE A.5: Percentage of LOC and time for previous projects

	UNICORN		PEGASUS		GRIFFIN		JACKALOPE	
WEEK	% LOC	% TIME	% LOC	% TIME	% LOC	% TIME	% LOC	% TIME
1	9.3	12.5	9.0	20.0	4.6	16.7	2.4	25.0
2	19.7	25.0	22.9	40.0	24.5	33.3	23.2	50.0
3	29.3	37.5	45.9	60.0	52.7	50.0	67.9	75.0
4	35.9	50.0	77.8	80.0	61.6	66.7	100.0	100.0
5	50.5	62.5	100.0	100.0	80.1	83.3		
6	63.2	75.0			100.0	100.0		
7	82.0	87.5						
8	100.0	100.0						

Figure A.16 shows a graph of the percent of LOC versus percent of elapsed time for the four previous projects.

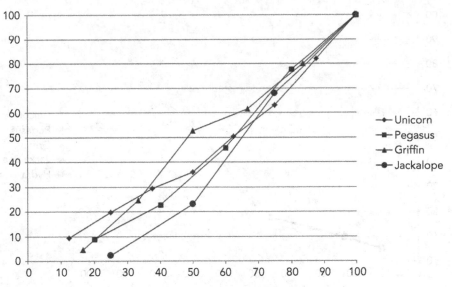

FIGURE A.16: This graph shows percent of LOC versus percent of elapsed time for previous projects.

Table A.6 shows the percent of LOC and percent of elapsed time values for project Hydra after 4 weeks. (Remember, this project is expected to include 7,000 LOC and take 9 weeks.)

TABLE A.6: Percentage of LOC and time for project Hydra

WEEK	% LOC	% TIME
1	5.3	11.1
2	9.9	22.2
3	13.8	33.3
4	17.9	44.4

Figure A.17 shows the graph from Figure A.16 with project Hydra's data added.

Figure A.17 shows that project Hydra is generating code more slowly than the previous projects. If you extend its curve to the right, only approximately 40 percent of the project's code will be written by the end of week 9.

All of the projects started off relatively slowly and then picked up speed, but project Hydra shows no signs of an increase yet. If it doesn't pick up the pace soon, it won't finish on time.

So the answer to the original question is yes, you should be concerned about this project. It's not hopeless yet, but if something doesn't change soon, it will be. I would keep a close eye on it for the next couple of weeks.

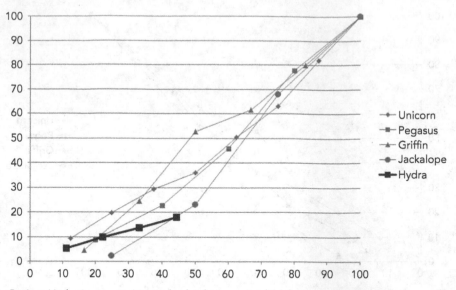

FIGURE A.17: Project Hydra is generating code slowly compared to the previous projects.

You can perform a similar analysis on the project's known bug data if you like. For example, you can graph bugs/LOC versus percent of time. If the graph shows that project Hydra's bugs/LOC is much lower than the other projects' values approximately 44.4 percent of the way through the project, then the project team may not be detecting bugs as effectively.

(Or they may just be writing extra good code with fewer bugs. You'll have to dig deeper if you want to know exactly what's happening.)

CHAPTER 16

1. In percentages, the chance of a new line of code creating a bug is roughly 2 percent. The chance of a modified line of code generating a bug is approximately 4 percent. In writing 10 KLOC, the team generates around 10,000 × 0.02 = 200 bugs. Fixing those 200 bugs generates 200 × 0.04 = 8 additional bugs. Fixing 8 bugs generates 8 × 0.04 = 0.32 new bugs. Let's pessimistically round that up to 1.

   After this point, the number of expected new bugs is small, so there's a chance that you're actually fixing something without adding new bugs. Adding up the numbers gives 10,000 + 200 + 8 + 1 = 10,209 total lines of code.

2. Of course, maintenance isn't done! If you keep careful track during development and testing, you can estimate the number of bugs per KLOC, but it's always an estimate. You can never be sure of exactly how many bugs are present.

   Besides, maintenance includes adding new features and improving old ones, so maintenance is never done for successful applications.

3. This is simply a matter of dividing the number of lines of each type of code by the appropriate number of lines of code per day. Those numbers are as follows:

   ➤ 10,000 lines ÷ 20 lines per day = 500

➤ 200 lines ÷ 4 lines per day = 50

➤ 8 lines ÷ 2 lines per day = 4

➤ 1 line ÷ 1 lines per day = 1

Adding the numbers of days gives 500 + 50 + 4 + 1 = 555 person-days.

4. If the whole project requires 555 days and you have two team members, then you should expect the project to take approximately 277.5 days. There is an average of approximately 21 working days per month, so the project should take around 277.5 ÷ 21 ≈ 13.2 months.

If you have five team members, then the project should take around 555 ÷ 5 = 111 days or 111 ÷ 21 ≈ 5.3 months.

If you have 10 team members, the project should take around 555 ÷ 10 = 55.5 days or 55.5 ÷ 21 ≈ 2.6 months.

Finally, if you have 111 team members, the project should take approximately 555 ÷ 111 = 5 days, or 1 week. Wait, what? That doesn't make any sense! There's no way any number of developers can write 10,209 lines of code in a week and produce an application that can do something useful. As the team grows larger, communication and administrative tasks will start to dominate the total amount of time. Eventually, you'll spend all your time bickering about what kinds of bagels to serve at team meetings. (What about those on low-carb diets? And those who are gluten-free? And the vegans will veto cream cheese or lox.)

Larger projects definitely have extra overhead. The optimal team size for a project depends on a lot of factors, such as the project's size and complexity and the skills of the team members. In general, it seems that projects start to pay a significant size penalty when they grow to more than seven or so members.

5. Figure A.18 shows the flowchart.

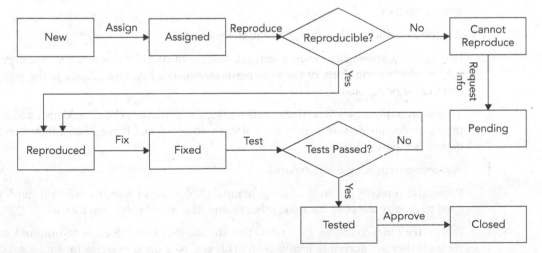

FIGURE A.18: This flowchart shows the states through which most bugs pass.

6. A bug could enter the Pending state from almost any other state because a team member might want more information at any time. Technically, a bug probably shouldn't go directly from Closed to Pending but should pass through Reopened first. However, that's a technicality. If a bug needs to be reopened for more information, so be it. But you might want to require that the bug first go through Reopened just to add that transition to the bug's history.

A bug can move to Deferred from any state except Closed if the team decides that bug won't be fixed right away. A bug probably won't move from Tested or Closed into Deferred because in those states the bug is already fixed.

A bug can only move into the Reopened state from the Closed state. (You can't reopen a bug that is still open.)

7. This would be unusual because the bug is already fixed, but there might be a reason why you don't want to release the fix to users. For example, if the bug fix is a breaking change so it would mess up work users have previously done, you might want to wait until a later release.

8. These values are simply the percentages for each maintenance task (Perfective—50%, Adaptive—25%, Corrective—20%, Preventive—5%) multiplied by the 75% allowed for maintenance. The results are Perfective—37.5%, Adaptive—18.75%, Corrective—15%, and Preventive—3.75%.

9. The following list gives the tasks' categories:

   a. Corrective.

   b. Perfective (adding a new feature).

   c. Perfective (adding a new feature).

   d. Preventive.

   e. Preventive.

   f. Preventive. (There's no point keeping unused code around to collect bugs and confuse programmers.)

   g. Adaptive (dealing with a change to the environment).

   h. Perfective (improving an existing feature). You could consider this as corrective depending on whether you think of the slow performance as a bug or a change in the way the program is being used.

   i. This is probably a bad idea. If the code works, leave it alone. (You could also add comments or documentation if they are currently insufficient.) If the code contains a bug swarm, see part j.

   j. Preventive (removing a bug swarm).

   k. Preventive (making the code easier to maintain). You might want to defer this until you need to modify the code for some other reason. If it ain't broke, don't fix it.

   l. Preventive (understanding the code). You should also write documentation and comments if they are currently insufficient. (This can be a good exercise for understanding the code and not a bad exercise to help new team members learn about the system.)

m. Perfective (adding a new feature).

n. Adaptive (dealing with a change to the environment).

o. Perfective (adding a new feature).

p. Perfective (adding a new feature).

q. Perfective (adding a new low-priority feature).

r. Corrective (fixing the existing permissions).

s. Preventive (making the code easier to maintain by understanding, creating new documentation, and adding comments).

t. Corrective (fixing bugs).

u. Corrective (fixing a bug). This is still addressing the bug even though you're only "fixing" it by providing a workaround rather than by changing the code. You should also preventively research a code fix for a later release.

v. Perfective (adding a new feature).

w. Perfective (adding a new feature).

x. Perfective (adding a new feature).

y. Perfective (adding a new feature).

z. Preventive. Testing tasks are intended to prevent bugs from appearing in the future, although those bugs may already be present but undiscovered. This task is also preventive in the sense that it helps you understand the code and the potential bug count.

10. Most of these are bad signs, but you could probably leave most of them alone as long as they're working correctly. (If it ain't broke, don't fix it.)

a. That's too long. Consider rewriting the method the next time you need to modify it.

b. Don't change the code. The next time you need to modify it, add comments and documentation to make it easier to understand.

c. That's too deep to understand easily. Consider rewriting the method the next time you need to modify it.

d. This is a tough call. Ideally, you would consider rewriting the next time you had to modify the code. Unfortunately, with so many methods involved (assuming it's not one method calling itself in deep recursion), you'll probably have to modify something at some point. Also, unfortunately this will probably be confusing and hard to rewrite successfully. This may require a major rebuild. (I've worked with code like that and it's practically impossible to keep track of what's happening, so you have my sympathy.)

e. As long as it works, I would ignore this. If you have nothing better to do, you could think about perfective tasks. Some IDEs have automatic renaming tools so, for example, they can change a variable's name everywhere it occurs. They may not update comments and documentation, however, so this may not be as easy as it seems.

f. This method doesn't have a tightly focused purpose, so it should be rewritten as three separate methods. You might invoke the "if it ain't broke, don't fix it" rule, but this method's lack of focus makes it hard to use correctly. That means if you write new code that uses the method, that code is at risk. So the real question is, "Are you going to need to write a lot of new code that uses this method?" If you will use it with new code, rewrite it. If you won't need to write new code that calls this method, you can leave it alone (and feel slightly ashamed).

g. This probably violates the nonfunctional specifications (it definitely violates the five-second rule described in Chapter 9, "User Experience Design"), so you may be forced to fix it regardless of whether you think it's a good idea. This is a big burden on the users, so I would fix it if at all possible. (Otherwise users will start the login process and then wander off to get coffee while they wait for it to finish.)

h. This is a bug swarm. You should rewrite the method.

i. This is a very bad bug, like a wasp or flying scorpion or something. Whatever you call it, you should fix it ASAP.

j. This is also a bug and hence a corrective task. However, because the program crashes only when it's shutting down anyway, it should have low priority. I would fix it, but I would fix other bugs first.

k. This doesn't mean there's anything wrong with the method, other than the initial bug. There may also not be anything wrong with your coworker. (Who is *definitely* not you!) I would carefully review and test the latest bug fix to make sure it actually works. I would also review the method as a whole to see if it's particularly confusing and needs extra comments, documentation, or a rewrite to prevent this from happening again.

l. As in the preceding case, the method itself is only responsible for the single original bug. In this case, however, three different people had problems fixing bugs in this method, so there may be a bigger problem here. You should examine the method and try to figure out what the problem is. If your coworkers are just making silly mistakes, they may be burned out. (Have they been working too many late nights?) If the method is particularly confusing, it may need more study, comments, and documentation. (It's also a good idea to have developers fix their own bugs, so ideally this series of bugs should have been handled by a single person. That person should have a better idea of what's going wrong here.)

m. This is a bug so it's a corrective task, not a preventive one. This is annoying and frustrating to users, who may need an extra coffee break to reestablish their Zen-like oneness with the application after each crash. Because it's easy to recover (after the extra coffee break), this is a medium-priority bug if the application is used in-house. If the program is sold to customers, however, any crash looks extremely bad, so this would be a high-priority bug.

CHAPTER 17

1. The following list explains whether the tasks would be better handled predictively or adaptively.

   a. This is a well-understood task, so you can do it predictively. (Unless you're doing something weird like trying an experimental architectural technique or building an art project.)

   b. Because you don't know where the clues will lead you, you're going to have to be adaptive. You might not even know how many clues there will be.

   c. When you follow a scavenger hunt, you don't know where each clue will lead. When you're building a scavenger hunt, however, you have control over the clues, so you can handle it predictively.

   d. This is a mostly well-understood task, so you can do it predictively. There may be some uncertainty about things like the weather and you won't necessarily know if your local croquet club is going to take over the whole park, so you should use risk management to have a backup plan in place.

   e. In Seattle, there's less question about the weather: It will be wet. You can still do this predictively, but now the dry weather plan should probably be the backup plan instead of the primary plan.

   f. A major motion picture is a huge undertaking involving hundreds of people and months or even years of work. Sometimes things go wrong during shooting, but the basic schedule is more or less fixed, so this is a predictive task.

   g. This is mostly predictive because you need to hit certain milestones within a set period of time. For example, in a semester you need to cover a certain number of chapters, give a reasonable number of tests, and regularly hold office hours. Those tasks all fit nicely into a predictive model.

   At the same time, a class's focus often wanders around a bit depending on the students' interests, how well they can sit still for certain subjects, and the instructor's creativity. Students learn best if the subject is something that interests them personally.

   For example, you might ask students to build a simple database application but let them pick the domain. They could store car specifications, football team statistics, dessert recipes, or information about their DVD collections. This requires the instructor to be adaptive.

   To handle both the predictive and adaptive needs, the instructors that I know use predictive lesson plans that explain more or less what will happen during class with varying levels of detail depending on the instructor. Then they adjust the lesson while in progress and sometimes modify future lessons if necessary.

   h. Without GPS, you would look up where the restaurant is on a map (or call it and get directions), plan out a route, and follow it. If something went wrong (like a DeLorean breaking down in front of you), you would be more or less stuck. You could reroute (if you didn't leave the map at the hotel), but it would take significant time and effort.

    i.   This would still be predictive, only this time the GPS would plan the route. If something went wrong (like an SUV running out of gas and blocking the road in front of you), you could make the GPS plan a new route.

    j.   This would probably still feel predictive to you because people like to know what's going to happen. For example, you probably want to know which restaurant you will visit and what kinds of food they serve before you start driving. (This is one of the more attractive features of predictive models, particularly for management and customers.) However, the car and its computer systems could handle this completely adaptively. The car would plot a route and present it to you for your peace of mind. Then as the drive progresses, the car could watch for blockages (like a flying saucer landing in front of you and blocking the road) and instantly revise the route if necessary. That means this would probably look predictive to you, and you would follow the original plan most of the time, but behind the scenes the car could handle this adaptively.

2.   All these projects have trouble indicators for predictive projects.

    a.   This is an incredibly large and complex project. A predictive project would provide a level of control that the FAA would probably like, but the sheer size of the project would make it difficult.

    b.   Lack of clear vision. If you do pry requirements out of the partners, they'll probably be inconsistent and unclear.

    c.   Unrealistic expectations and lack of resources. It might be possible to build this application predictively, but probably not in 15 person-months.

    d.   Lack of experience. Your team has experience with vacation costing, not housing development. (Unless you're not telling me about an earlier project.)

    e.   Lack of user involvement. Unless the customer is willing to help define the requirements, it will be hard to satisfy the specification you've been given. (Although you could spend the three weeks working on requirements and then finish them up after the customer returns from vacation. That would probably work, all else being equal, but it doesn't seem like a promising start to a new project.)

    f.   Unestablished technology. Perhaps 3-D concrete printers will be common in a year or two, but until then, this would be very speculative. (However, it would also be very fun! I'd be tempted to take the project anyway, although perhaps with a different development model.)

3.   A predictive model can save money if you correctly plot out the development effort's path. Adaptive models sometimes take extra time chasing unprofitable lines of development and refactoring.

However, if you don't map out the development plan correctly and need to make major changes, then a predictive project can cost much more than an adaptive approach.

4.   Waterfall with feedback and sashimi are very similar. In fact, some developers use the names more or less interchangeably. Both allow some overlap of project phases, but they have different intent.

Waterfall with feedback enables you to move backward to a previous phase if you need to make corrections and adjustments. In contrast, sashimi enables some developers to move ahead of other developers so they can get a jump on future tasks.

5. As many as you like. In theory, the project could run indefinitely, adding new features with each increment.

6. Operation and Maintenance ⇨ Concept: The concept represents the way users see the application. After the application is built, users see its operation and (to a lesser extent) maintenance.

    Verification and Validation ⇨ Requirements: The requirements represent the customers' needs and the behavior that the application should have. Verification confirms that the application provides the behavior described in the requirements. Validation confirms that the application satisfies the customers' needs, which are represented in the requirements.

    Testing ⇨ Design: In a sense, testing validates the design. If the design is correct, then testing should show that the application works properly. (In practice, testing may uncover problems, and fixing them may require you to make the program deviate from the design. In that case, you should go back and update the design to reflect the program's actual structure, so the maintenance crew can use the design to understand how the application actually works.)

CHAPTER 18

1. The iterative, incremental, and agile approaches enable you to release partial applications as soon as you've implemented enough features with enough fidelity to be useful. However, you don't have to take advantage of that capability if you don't want to. You could still use those approaches to build the application and give the customer the application only when it is complete. Then you would still get the other benefits of those techniques. For example, those approaches would help you refine the requirements throughout the project.

2. The point of a throwaway prototype is to quickly demonstrate one or more features so that you can decide where to go from there. To avoid wasting a lot of time building features that you don't need, a throwaway prototype should start with the fewest features and the lowest fidelity possible. If a feature isn't demonstrated adequately and customers want to see a more realistic version, you can improve its fidelity. If customers want to see other features, they can request them, and you can add them. Starting with minimal features of low fidelity, improving them, and adding more features are the characteristics of an agile approach.

3. In an incremental prototype, you build the application's features in separate prototypes and then integrate them to create the final application. If you don't release anything to the users before you finish integrating these features, then the project isn't incremental.

    To make the project incremental, you would simply release the program anytime its current set of integrated features was usable.

4. Sort of. In a predictive project, you fix the requirements and build a design before you start programming. An evolutionary prototype continues to grow and evolve throughout the

project's lifetime. Normally, the prototype continues to refine the project's features as it grows, so the requirements and design are not fixed up front.

However, you could fix the requirements and design in the beginning and then implement the code with an evolutionary prototype approach. That kind of subverts the purpose of the prototype (to help refine the requirements), so most people don't do it that way. If the requirements and design are fixed, you can just write the code and skip the evolutionary prototype.

5. This question's answer is similar to the answer for Exercise 4. Normally in an incremental prototype, you build prototypes for the application's pieces, and you use them to refine the requirements for those pieces. In that case, the requirements are not fixed up front, so that's not predictive development.

However, if you really want to, you could fix the requirements and design in advance and then build the application through an incremental prototype. It would be an unusual way to look at things, but it should work.

6. The deployment tasks include everything necessary for deployment. You can start working on some of those tasks as soon as you know what's necessary. If you wait until the start of the transition phase, you'll probably be late because you can't purchase and install things such as desks and computers instantly, particularly if some random event pops up to delay shipping such as, oh I don't know, a global pandemic that trashes the entire supply chain?

During elaboration, the requirements start to coalesce, so you can start writing user documentation. You can also start planning the physical setup (items such as desks, chairs, computers, printers, and networks). However, you shouldn't commit to those items too early in case plans change later. (It would be expensive to buy 1,000 computers early in the project only to discover later that you need a different type of computer or that you need only 150 of them.)

So you can start planning the installation of the physical equipment during elaboration, but you generally won't actually start installing that equipment until the later iterations of construction when plans are more concrete.

7. During the inception phase, the team can test the project's general ideas, assumptions, and approach. Team members can think of scenarios that need to be handled and decide whether the requirements can handle them. Those thought experiments can help refine the project's overall shape.

8. Code written during the elaboration phase is usually exploratory. It is written to try out new techniques and ideas that may be used in the application's design. The results of those experiments help refine the requirements.

You don't need to do a lot of testing on exploratory code because that code won't be used in the final application. Tests performed during elaboration are more likely to be applied to the requirements and design. For example, you can create and walk through use cases to verify that the application's design can handle them.

9. Figure A.19 shows my drawing.

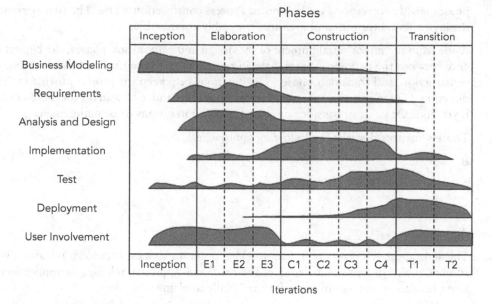

FIGURE A.19: Users play a large role as requirements are created and refined and a smaller role during development. They may play a larger role during deployment.

Your results may differ, but here's the general idea. Customer representatives play a big role during inception and elaboration when the basic requirements are determined.

During construction, customers play a relatively small role, although they materialize periodically to review each of the iterations to make sure the project is still on track.

Depending on the division of duties, the customer organization may also play a large role in deployment, taking on tasks such as preparing the users' environment and training the users.

10. Figure A.20 shows how waterfall tasks match up with Unified Process tasks.

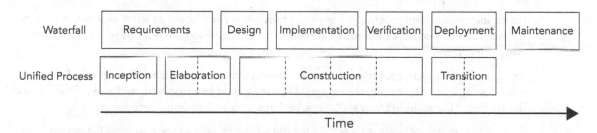

FIGURE A.20: This diagram shows how waterfall tasks match up with Unified Process tasks.

The waterfall requirements phase corresponds mostly to the Unified Process inception and elaboration phases, although elaboration includes some architectural design, so it also overlaps the waterfall design phase. The waterfall design, implementation, and verification phases mostly correspond to the Unified Process construction phase. The two approaches' deployment and transition phases are reasonably comparable.

Aside from the minor misalignment of the design and elaboration phases, the biggest difference between the two approaches is the iterative nature of the Unified Process elaboration, construction, and transition phases. The iterations help keep the project moving in the right direction. (There's also no maintenance phase in the standard Unified Process. You can add it if you like. Or you can consider ongoing transition iterations to be maintenance.)

11. Those sentences describe the following approaches:

   a. Agile

   b. Incremental

   c. Predictive

   d. Iterative

12. The agile approach gives the users a working program soonest because it releases a version as soon as any of its features are usable. The predictive approach releases its application the latest because it waits until every feature is fully implemented.

   Without more information, you can't know whether the iterative or incremental approach will release a working program sooner. The iterative approach will release sooner if you can quickly implement all of the features with low (but usable) fidelity. The incremental approach will release sooner if you can quickly implement a single feature with full fidelity.

13. In a predictive model, you wouldn't let anyone move in until every house was complete. That would work.

   In an iterative approach, people would immediately move into every house but with limited fidelity. Here "limited fidelity" would mean the houses initially wouldn't have water, sewer, electricity, appliances, or (worst of all) cable TV and Internet access! This wouldn't work very well. (Although it seems to have been the approach the Russians used when they built the athlete housing for the 2012 Olympics.)

   In an incremental approach, people would move into each house as soon as it was completely finished. Some people would move in relatively early, and some would move in later. This would work well.

   In an agile approach, people would move into each house as soon as it was partly finished with low fidelity. Over time, the occupied houses would be improved, and new houses would be started. This wouldn't work. (Unless, perhaps, you're building a refugee camp.)

   In practice, developers want to get money out of the project as soon as possible, so it's natural to try for an agile approach. Unfortunately, people can't move into houses that aren't finished. Not only would people refuse (at least I would), but it's a lot easier to install carpeting, paint walls, and finish hardwood floors before people move all the sofas, televisions, dining sets, and treadmills into a house. However, it's not too hard to do the landscaping while people live in the house.

So here's the typical approach. First, specialized teams move through the development.

One team pours the foundations. After the foundations are dry, another team does the framing. Electricians and plumbers move through next, and so on with other teams installing drywall, roofing, carpeting, appliances, and everything else in waves. Sometimes, the teams can even work at the same time. For example, one team might be installing plumbing on one house while another installs drywall on another house.

The result is that the houses are all in different stages of construction. As soon as a house is habitable, people move in. Later, as weather and scheduling permit, the final teams do the landscaping, paint house numbers on the curbs, add above-ground pools, and do anything else that can wait for this late stage.

The result is most similar to incremental development with a dash of agile thrown in at the end.

14. In a predictive model, you wouldn't let anyone into the park until every ride, snack shack, and game was fully complete and tested. Then you would hold a grand opening. That would work.

In an iterative approach, you would allow people to use the facilities when they had limited fidelity. You probably shouldn't allow people to ride a half-finished Tilt-A-Whirl or untested roller coasters (I've seen the movie *Final Destination 3*), so this wouldn't work.

In an incremental approach, people would be allowed to use any facilities that were completely finished. For example, during the first few weeks of operation, you might have only two rides, a Guess-Your-Weight attraction, and one restroom. This would work, but it would probably be better to wait until everything (or at least almost everything) was finished so that you can hold a grand opening to build excitement.

In an agile approach, you would let people use facilities as soon as they were partly functional. This won't work. (I won't spoil the plot of *Final Destination 3*, but I will say that it involves a roller coaster, and the result isn't pretty.)

CHAPTER 19

1. The following list explains how the four agile values apply to the one-pass waterfall model.

   ➤ Individuals and interactions over processes and tools—The waterfall model doesn't necessarily violate this value. There's nothing in the waterfall model that says you can't value individuals and interactions highly. However, waterfall is process-oriented, so the project manager will have to work hard to make sure processes don't come first. Also, Stodgy Megacorp doesn't sound like a company that values people over processes.

   ➤ Working software over comprehensive documentation—The intent of this value is to represent the application's functionality with the evolving application. The main way information passes from one waterfall stage to the next is through documentation, not a working application. In fact, you can't actually have much in the way of working software until the implementation stage.

➤ Customer collaboration over contract negotiation—The waterfall model goes directly against this. It assumes that the requirements are negotiated and carved in granite in the first stage of the project.

➤ Responding to change over following a plan—As the Brits would say, "Pull the other one, it's got bells on!" The waterfall model is all about making the best possible plan and then following it to the (possibly bitter) end. It doesn't respond well to change.

To summarize, the Stodgy Megacorp waterfall model can sort of satisfy the first value, but it doesn't fulfill the others at all.

2. The following list explains how the 12 agile principles apply to the one-pass waterfall model.

(1) Our highest priority is to satisfy the customer through early and continuous delivery of valuable software.

The waterfall model's goal is also to satisfy the customer, but it doesn't provide early and continuous delivery.

(2) Welcome changing requirements, even late in development. Agile processes harness change for the customer's competitive advantage.

The waterfall model doesn't handle change well, particularly later in the development process.

(3) Deliver working software frequently, from a couple of weeks to a couple of months, with a preference to the shorter timescale.

Most waterfall projects have longer time spans than a couple weeks or even a couple months.

(4) Businesspeople and developers must work together daily throughout the project.

Businesspeople (such as customers, domain experts, and other stakeholders) can work together throughout a waterfall project, but the benefit is limited because the plan can't change significantly later in the process. It is sometimes useful to have domain experts work with developers to help them understand the finer details of how the application should work, but most of the design should be wrapped up in the requirements and design phases so any interactions after that point aren't as helpful.

(5) Build projects around motivated individuals. Give them the environment and support they need, and trust them to get the job done.

This is always a good idea in anything, not just software engineering. Motivated people can achieve remarkable things if they're given the freedom to do so.

Like everything else, the waterfall model works best with motivated people. There's nothing stopping the waterfall model from doing this except for Stodgy Megacorp's culture.

(6) The most efficient and effective method of conveying information to and within a development team is face-to-face conversation.

A waterfall project can use face-to-face meetings to convey information, but they also need written records. Documentation helps keep everyone focused on the same vision.

It also helps bring new team members up to speed if they join the project after it has begun. (And these tend to be large projects that last for a long time, so that's definitely a concern.)

(7)   Working software is the primary measure of progress.

In a waterfall project, there usually isn't much working software until the implementation phase. You can use working software to measure progress during that phase, but it's not too helpful during the other phases.

(8)   Agile processes promote sustainable development. The sponsors, developers, and users should be able to maintain a constant pace indefinitely.

This is another sensible goal in anything, not just software engineering, and the waterfall model is no exception. Management can occasionally bully developers into working extra hours to meet a deadline, but there's a limit to how many late nights they can work without their quality suffering no matter how many pizzas and energy drinks you provide. Eventually, the best people will leave for companies with better working environments (this is sometimes called *bright flight*) and Stodgy Megacorp will be left with only the dregs who can't get jobs elsewhere. Artificially compressing the development schedule isn't worth permanently destroying your development capabilities.

(9)   Continuous attention to technical excellence and good design enhances agility.

This is another good idea in anything, not just software engineering. It's almost always better to do something right the first time than to have to go back and fix it later, and that's particularly true in software engineering.

Because the waterfall model makes it hard to go back and fix earlier mistakes, this is particularly important. You don't want to get to the deployment phase and discover that there was a mistake all the way back in the requirements phase.

(10)   Simplicity—the art of maximizing the amount of work not done—is essential.

This is also a great idea for just about anything. In software engineering, the simpler something is, the fewer chances you have to mess it up. That applies to the waterfall model as well as to any other development methodology.

(11)   The best architectures, requirements, and designs emerge from self-organizing teams.

You could probably use self-organizing teams in a waterfall project, although it's more normal for everyone's role to be decided at the beginning and to remain unchanged throughout the project. That seems like the approach Stodgy Megacorp would take.

(12)   At regular intervals, the team reflects on how to become more effective, then tunes and adjusts its behavior accordingly.

I have one more piece of advice that can apply to just about anything. It's always good to reflect on what you're doing and how you're doing it to see if you can make improvements. (For example, after the first three chapters, I stopped writing this book by candlelight with a quill and scrolls of papyrus and started using a computer.)

You can use this kind of reflection in a waterfall project; although, you may be unable to act on some of your insights. For example, you might be able to increase the number of code reviews if you think that would help improve the code. In contrast, you probably couldn't decide in the verification phase to switch to Unified Process if you decide that would be better than waterfall.

In summary, the waterfall model is reasonably compatible with principles 5, 8, 9, 10, and 12. With a score of 5 out of 12, it would receive an F on the agile final exam.

3. No. Agile models don't work well with all projects. For example, Big Design Up Front models tend to work better with large projects that last longer, that have specific requirements, and that are well-understood. For those kinds of projects, waterfall (or sashimi or iterated waterfall) might work better than agile approaches.

4. The following list explains how the four agile values apply to James Martin RAD.

    ➤ Individuals and interactions over processes and tools—As is the case with the Stodgy Megacorp waterfall model, James Martin RAD can embrace this value. The way the user design and construction phases overlap with the users constantly providing guidance and feedback gives the users a position of respect and importance.

    ➤ Working software over comprehensive documentation—In James Martin RAD, you start by writing requirements. After that, the overlapping user design and construction phases make the application evolve to suit the changing requirements. The initial requirements are important, but not as important as the changes requested by the users.

    ➤ Customer collaboration over contract negotiation—The initial requirements represent negotiation. After that, customer collaboration (in the form of user design) guides development (in the form of the construction phase).

    ➤ Responding to change over following a plan—The overlapping user design and construction phases make it reasonably easy to respond to change.

    In summary, James Martin RAD satisfies all four agile values fairly well, so it deserves the Agile Stamp of Approval.

5. The following list explains how the 12 agile principles apply to James Martin RAD.

    (1) Our highest priority is to satisfy the customer through early and continuous delivery of valuable software.

    The goal of James Martin RAD is also to satisfy the customer, but it doesn't provide early and continuous delivery. It provides one delivery at the end.

    (2) Welcome changing requirements, even late in development. Agile processes harness change for the customer's competitive advantage.

    James Martin RAD handles changes relatively easily during the user design and construction phases.

    (3) Deliver working software frequently, from a couple of weeks to a couple of months, with a preference to the shorter timescale.

    James Martin RAD is aimed at producing a single delivery. A short project might span only a few months or weeks, but it isn't intended to produce multiple incremental releases.

(4)   Businesspeople and developers must work together daily throughout the project.

Businesspeople and developers work closely during all four phases of James Martin RAD.

(5)   Build projects around motivated individuals. Give them the environment and support they need, and trust them to get the job done.

This is always a good idea in anything, including James Martin RAD.

(6)   The most efficient and effective method of conveying information to and within a development team is face-to-face conversation.

James Martin RAD doesn't require you to use extensive documentation for communication, so you can make it meet this principle if you try. You'll still want to create written requirements during the requirements planning phase, but communication between customers and developers during the user design and construction phases is faster and more effective face-to-face.

(7)   Working software is the primary measure of progress.

During the user design and construction phases, you can measure progress by the growing application. You still need to keep an eye on the project to ensure that it's headed somewhere and not just undergoing a never-ending series of change requests. However, as long as the application is growing toward a useful end, then it's a reasonable measure of progress.

(8)   Agile processes promote sustainable development. The sponsors, developers, and users should be able to maintain a constant pace indefinitely.

This applies to James Martin RAD as well as it applies to anything else.

(9)   Continuous attention to technical excellence and good design enhances agility.

This is another principle that applies to everything, including James Martin RAD.

(10)   Simplicity—the art of maximizing the amount of work not done—is essential.

To paraphrase Leonardo da Vinci, "Simplicity is the ultimate sophistication, including in James Martin RAD."

(11)   The best architectures, requirements, and designs emerge from self-organizing teams.

There's no reason why you can't use a self-organizing team in James Martin RAD, particularly in the iterations of user design and construction.

(12)   At regular intervals, the team reflects on how to become more effective, then tunes and adjusts its behavior accordingly.

Again, this applies to everything, including James Martin RAD.

In summary, James Martin RAD doesn't actually follow principles 1 or 3, which deal with frequent releases. It handles the other principles very well, particularly those that mention constant interaction between the users and the developers. With a score of 10 out of 12, it would receive a solid B on the agile final exam.

6.   Velocity won't equal the difference in the size of the backlog if anything is added, removed, or modified in the backlog. For example, suppose the backlog contains 100 story points.

A sprint delivers 10 of them, but you add 10 more story points in new features to the backlog. In that case, the velocity for the sprint was 10 but there has been no change in the backlog's size.

The velocity will match the backlog difference if you don't add, remove, or modify anything in the backlog.

7. The quick and glib answer is that all sprints have the same duration, so velocity would always be the same if you measure actual hours. For example, if you have four people working one-week sprints, then every sprint should have a velocity of $4 \times 5 = 20$ days. If the sprint includes too many features, you might need to drop some of them to fit in the one-week time box, but the velocity would always be the same.

    What you actually want to know is not how many hours the developers work, but how many user stories they completed. If it turns out that you put too many stories into a sprint and you remove some, then the number of story points implemented during that sprint *does* change, and the velocity would be lower than you had hoped.

8. If the number of actual days is lower than the number of story points, that means your story point estimates are too high. For example, you predicted that a story would take eight hours but it took only six.

    Conversely, if actual days is higher than story points, that means your story point estimates are too low. For example, you predicted that a story would take 3 hours, but it took 10.

    In either case, you could revise your story point estimates, but you don't need to. The sprint velocity tells you how many story points you can implement during a sprint. As long as you use the measured velocity to plan the following sprints, you can pick roughly the right amount of work for each sprint. The velocity implicitly corrects for imperfect estimates as long as all the estimates are incorrect in the same way.

9. Improving velocity allows the team to add more features to each iteration, but it's important not to sacrifice quality. You could increase velocity by skimping on unit tests, but you'd pay a price later in increased debugging time.

10. The following list summarizes those phrases:

    ➤ Think big—See the whole. Keep the customers' needs in mind and make sure whatever you're doing adds value for the customer.

    ➤ Act small—Keep things simple. Only make them more complicated later if it turns out that you must.

    ➤ Fail fast—Discovering that some approach won't work isn't itself a bad thing. In particular, test code as soon as it is written, so you can learn whether it works correctly as quickly as possible. If you're going to fail, fail quickly, learn from it, and move on.

    ➤ Learn rapidly—Learn from mistakes and the changing environment and take action accordingly. If your iteration process isn't working well, fix it right away. If the customers' needs change, then change the project's direction before you waste any more time building features that no one needs.

11. The following list explains whether the situations are kanban-like:

    a. This is kanban-like. When the red edges appear, the cashier knows that it's time to put in a new tape.

    b. This isn't kanban-like because the customer won't replace the register tape when the red edges appear. (Many customers don't even know what the red edges mean.)

    c. This is only kanban-like in the vaguest sense. The burned-out bulb sort of tells you that you need to get a new one, but calling this kanban is a stretch.

    d. This is kanban-like. The entry on the shopping list is similar to a kanban card sent to a supplier.

    e. This isn't kanban-like. A kanban-friendly pen would give you some warning, perhaps switching to red ink when it was running low. An IoT pen would have a "low ink" warning feature.

CHAPTER 20

1. Something is ethical if it is acceptable as defined by society. Something is moral if it is acceptable to you personally. The biggest issue with those definitions is that some people use the two terms interchangeably or with the meanings swapped.

2. Here are brief descriptions of those terms:

    a. White hat—Attacks websites and applications with permission to uncover flaws. Agrees not to publicly disclose problems until they are fixed.

    b. Black hat—Breaks security for malicious purposes.

    c. Grey hat—Similar to a white hat but does not act with permission. May tell the software owner about problems or offer to fix them for a fee.

    d. Red hat—Hackers who attack black hats.

    e. Blue hat—Either (1) revenge seekers or (2) outside security professionals.

    f. Green hat—A noob who may not understand the consequences of their actions.

    g. 1337—An elite hacker. (Or may be used ironically.)

    h. Script kiddie—Breaks systems by using prepackaged scripts and tools.

    i. Noob—A beginner.

    j. Hacktivist—Uses hacking as a form of civil disobedience.

    k. Suicide hacker—Causes chaos without regard for consequences.

    l. Cypherpunk—Advocates widespread strong encryption.

    m. Phreak—Hacks telephone networks or networks in general.

3. Here's how much blame you should bear:

    a. None. This is what stock trading software is for. (You may not like stock markets in general, but that's a different book.)

    b. A little. Your program wasn't used for its intended purpose, but you should at least feel guilty enough to wonder if you could have predicted this and made it harder for someone to use your program for nefarious purposes.

    c. Little to none. There's probably nothing that you can do to prevent a hacker from turning your innocuous little program to evil. You can try to make it harder, but you can't predict everything that a bad guy will do.

    d. A lot. You are always responsible for the security of your programs. You always need to test security code thoroughly. If you don't know what you're doing, get help!

    e. A LOT! This is illegal and regarded as unethical. (Even by traders!) Even if it wasn't illegal, you're setting up the user for unexpected pain and this shouldn't default to the bad setting.

    f. A lot. The project belongs to the entire team, and the entire team needs to make sure that the program works correctly. You can feel slightly superior, and you can blame the testing group if you like, but really everyone needs to own this.

CHAPTER 21

1. Here are some short definitions of terms used in this chapter:

    a. Blockchain—A distributed ledger system.

    b. DX—Digital experience. This includes every digital contact point with a company, such as social media, websites, web services, etc.

    c. PWA—Progressive web apps. Web-based applications that run on any web browser and adjust to different device sizes and capabilities.

    d. XaaS—Everything as a service. General cloud services such as security as a service, function as a service, infrastructure as a service, etc.

    e. IoB—Internet of behaviors. The study of how and why people use technology to buy things.

    f. Edge computing—Moving data and computation closer to the devices that generate the data to reduce central memory use, computation, and network traffic.

    g. CI/CD or CICD—Continuous integration, continuous delivery/deployment. Agile taken to the extreme.

    h. LCNC—Low code/no code. An environment that allows nonprogrammers to write applications.

i.   IPA—Intelligent process automation. (Not to be confused with India pale ale, even if some software engineers like it.) Combines robotics with artificial intelligence tools such as natural language processing, computer vision, and route planning to reduce cost.

j.   AR—Artificial reality. An immersive three-dimensional world that you view through 3D goggles.

k.   VR—Virtual reality. A blending of real and virtual worlds that you view through a normal display or VR goggles.

GLOSSARY

0-day See *zero-day*.

1337 See *elite hacker*.

1GL See *first generation language*.

1NF See *first normal form*.

2FA See *two-factor authentication*.

2GL See *second generation language*.

2NF See *second normal form*.

3-2-1 backup strategy You keep three copies of your data (two backups plus the copy that's in use) on two types of media with one copy off-site.

3GL See *third generation language*.

3NF See *third normal form*.

4GL See *fourth generation language*.

5GL See *fifth generation language*.

80/20-rule In the Dynamic Systems Development Method (DSDM), the assumption that 80 percent of an application's features will take 20 percent of the project's total time to implement. (The 80/20-rule often applies to other situations too. For example, 80 percent of the bugs are usually contained in 20 percent of the code.)

acceptance test A test to determine whether the finished application meets the requirements.

ACM Association for Computing Machinery.

ACS Australian Computer Society.

activation See *execution specification*.

activity diagram In UML, a diagram that represents workflows for activities. They include several kinds of symbols connected with arrows to show the direction of the workflow.

adapter, wrapper, or translator A design pattern that provides a simplified interface to a class.

adaptive development model A development model that enables you to change the project's goals if necessary during development.

administrator   Someone who manages the development team's computers, network, and other tools. Also called a system administrator.

advisor user   Any user who brings an important viewpoint to the project.

adware   Spyware that displays ads on your browser.

agile development   A development model where you initially provide the fewest possible features at the lowest fidelity to still have a useful application. Over time, you add more features and improve existing features until all features have been implemented at full fidelity.

Agile Manifesto   A set of four guiding principles for agile development. In brief the principles are as follows:

➤   Individuals and interactions over processes and tools

➤   Working software over comprehensive documentation

➤   Customer collaboration over contract negotiation

➤   Responding to change over following a plan

Agile Unified Process (AUP)   A simplified version of Rational Unified Process that includes agile methods such as test-driven development and agile modeling. In 2012, AUP was superseded by Disciplined Agile Delivery.

AI   See *artificial intelligence*.

AI tools   Artificial intelligence tasks that have largely been solved, such as speech recognition and synthesis and natural language processing.

algorithm   A software recipe that explains how to solve a particular programming problem.

algorithmic bias   Occurs when a program's algorithms have an underlying bias that makes them produce bad results.

ambassador user   Someone who acts as a liaison between the users and the developers.

analyst, business analyst, or domain expert   The customers' representatives, particularly when the customers are within the company.

anchoring   A phenomenon where an early decision made by one person influences later decisions by others.

angler phishing   Phishing sent via social media with the attacker sometimes posing as a customer service representative.

anomaly   In a relational database, an error caused by a design flaw such as records holding inconsistent values or being unable to delete a piece of data because it is necessary to record some unrelated piece of information.

anti-spyware   Similar to antivirus software except it looks for spyware.

antivirus software   A program that looks for and removes installed malware. It may also scan emails and downloads and may periodically scan every file on the system.

architect Someone who focuses on the application's overall high-level design.

artifact In a UML deployment diagram, a file, script, executable program, or other item that is deployed. In development models, something generated by the model, such as a requirements document, user story, or piece of code.

artificial general intelligence (AGI) "True" artificial intelligence. Also called strong AI, full AI, and general intelligent action.

artificial intelligence (AI) A program that does something human-like.

artificial neural network A learning system modeled on biological neural networks such as the human brain. Also called a neural network.

artificial neuron A small part of a neural network. Also called a neuron.

assertion A statement about the program and its data that is supposed to be true. If the statement isn't true, the assertion throws an exception to tell you that something is wrong.

Atlantic City algorithm Correct at least some fraction of the time and always relatively fast.

attribute Some feature of a project that you can measure, such as the number of lines of code, the number of defects, or the number of times the word "mess" appears in code comments. See also *metric* and *indicator*.

audit trail A record of actions taken by an application's users for security auditing purposes.

augmented reality (AR) A system that overlays computer-generated images on real-world images, possibly through goggles or a heads-up display.

AUP See *Agile Unified Process*.

backtracking A way to envision a search through a solution space. You follow a path until you find that it cannot work and then you backtrack to a previous partial solution that may still succeed.

BDUF See *Big Design Up Front*.

behavior diagram In UML, a diagram that shows the behavior of some entity. There are three kinds of behavior diagrams: activity diagrams, use case diagrams, and state machine diagrams.

big board A large board used by many agile models that is posted in a visible location so that everyone can see the project's status at a glance. Also called an information radiator.

Big Design Up Front (BDUF) See *predictive development model*.

big O notation A system for studying the limiting behavior of algorithms as the size of the problem grows large.

binary search A search where you repeatedly divide the area that may contain a target into two smaller (ideally equal) pieces.

biometric security Uses body measurements (such as fingerprint recognition, retina scan, facial recognition, or voice recognition) for identification.

black-box test A test designed by someone who doesn't know how the code works internally.

black hat   Someone who breaks security for malicious reasons or personal gain.

blackboard   Combines data from various data sources, possibly translating into a common format.

bloatware   See *crapware*.

blockchain   A distributed ledger system that allows participants to verify that certain transactions have occurred without requiring a central authority.

blue hat   Either (1) revenge seekers or (2) outside security professionals.

bot   A program that runs over a network.

botnet   A network of bots controlled by an attacker—for example, to launch distributed denial-of-service attacks.

brainstorming   A group technique for discovering creative solutions to a problem.

branch and bound   A particularly clever way to prune decision trees.

bug   A flaw in a program that causes it to produce an incorrect result or to behave unexpectedly. Bugs are generally evil.

build engineer   In Feature-Driven Development (FDD), someone who sets up and controls the build process.

burndown chart   In scrum, a graph showing the amount of work remaining over time.

business advisor   See *business analyst*.

business ambassador   Someone who provides business information from the viewpoint of the users.

business analyst   A domain expert who helps define the application's purpose and who provides feedback during development. Also called a business advisor.

business requirements   The project's high-level business goals. They explain what the customer hopes to achieve with the project.

business visionary   Someone who has a clear vision of the application's business role, particularly early in the process when that role isn't clearly written down.

cause-and-effect diagram   See *Ishikawa diagram*.

CAV   See *complexity adjustment value*.

CBSE   See *component-based software engineering*.

chain of responsibility   A design pattern that uses a chain of objects to handle requests by passing the request along until an object handles it.

change   A change to an application that is requested by customers. This may happen when customers understand the application better, when customers think of a new feature or a modification they want, or when the users' environment changes so the application needs to be changed to be useful.

change control board   A group of project members, possibly including one or two customers, that reviews and approves or rejects change requests.

change-making problem   A problem where you must find the fewest coins needed to make change for a given amount.

change management   See *version management*.

change manager   Studies and approves or rejects changes requested by the customers, analysts, developers, and others.

change tracking   See *version management*.

chatbot   A program that uses natural language processing to interact with customers to do things like track orders, check account balances, and connect with the correct department.

chief architect   In Feature-Driven Development, the person responsible for the project's overall programmatic design.

chief programmer   In Feature-Driven Development, an experienced developer who is familiar with all of the functions of development (design, analysis, coding, and so on). Chief programmers lead project teams.

child class   A class derived from a parent class. The child class inherits properties, methods, and events from the parent class.

child table   See *foreign key*.

CIA triad   In database security, this stands for confidentiality, integrity, and availability.

class   In object-oriented programming, a construct that defines a type (or class) of items. For example, if you define a Customer class, you can then create many Customer objects representing different real-world customers.

class diagram   In UML, a diagram that describes the classes that make up the system, their properties and methods, and their relationships.

class owner   In Feature-Driven Development, the person who is responsible for a particular class's code.

Cleanroom   A development model that emphasizes defect prevention rather than defect removal. It uses formal methods, statistical quality control, and statistical testing to prevent and detect bugs.

client-server architecture   A design that separates pieces of the system that need to use a particular function (clients) from parts of the system that provide those functions (servers). That decouples the client and server pieces of the system so that developers can work on them separately.

client tier   The tier in a multitier architecture that consumes a service. This is often an application's user interface.

coach   Someone who helps a development team follow its chosen path (XP, scrum, Lean, and so forth). Alternatively, someone who works with less-experienced team members to help them learn and be more effective.

code coverage   The lines of code that are executed during a demonstration or a suite of tests.

code inspection   See *code review*.

code review   When two or more programmers walk through a piece of code to look for problems. Also called a code inspection.

codebehind   In Windows Presentation Foundation (WPF), the code that sits behind the user interface. More generally, any code that sits behind the user interface.

coding standards   Standards used by a development team to ensure consistency. Standards may define conventions for variable names, comments, documentation, specific code style, and more. Coding standards make the code easier to read and debug.

column   See *field*.

command   Encapsulates a command that can be passed as a parameter.

commensurate difficulty   The concept that dangerous or difficult things should be harder to do than things that are safe and simple.

communication diagram   In UML, a diagram that shows communication among objects during some sort of collaboration. This is similar to a sequence diagram except a sequence diagram focuses on the sequence of messages and a communication diagram focuses more on the objects involved in the collaboration.

complexity adjustment factors   In function point calculations, values that take into account the importance of general features of the application (such as transaction rate).

complexity adjustment value (CAV)   In function point calculations, the sum of the complexity adjustment factors.

complexity factor   In function point calculations, you multiply each function point metric by a complexity factor to indicate how complex each activity is.

component-based software engineering (CBSE)   A design that regards the system as a collection of loosely coupled components that provide services for each other.

component diagram   In UML, a diagram that shows how components are combined to form larger parts of the system.

component interface test   A test that studies the interactions between components. This is a bit like regression testing in the sense that both examine the application as a whole to look for trouble, but component interface testing focuses on component interactions.

composite   A design pattern that composes objects into a tree- or network-like structure so you can represent objects and groups of objects uniformly.

composite structure diagram   In UML, a diagram that shows a class's internal structure and the collaborations that the class allows.

computability theory   The study of what things are computable and how quickly programs run.

configuration management   Managing the items produced by the project such as requirements documents, designs, and, of course, source code. This may include controlling changes to those items so that changes don't happen willy-nilly.

continuous integration and continuous delivery/deployment (CI/CD or CICD)   Agile taken to the extreme.

conversation hijacking   When an attacker inserts bogus messages into a conversation stream.

coprime   See *relatively prime*.

COTS   Commercial off-the-shelf, as in a COTS application. Software, hardware, or other resources that are available from a vendor without any customization.

cowboy coding   A development methodology where the programmers have complete control over the process and generally do what they want. This is often a derogatory term, although for very small projects and very experienced developers it can sometimes produce good results.

crapware   Programs that serve ads, return marketing information to companies, and constantly nag you to upgrade.

credential stuffing   When an attacker breaks one system and then uses its usernames and passwords to try to attack another system. Also called password stuffing.

critical path   A longest path through a PERT chart network. If any task along a critical path is delayed, the project's final completion is also delayed. Note that a network may have multiple critical paths.

cross-functional team   A team where every member can play every role. Every member can participate in requirements analysis, design, programming, testing, and the rest.

Crystal   A family of development methodologies that take into account a project's team size and criticality. Team size determines the project's "color," which can be Clear (1–6), Yellow (7–20), Orange (21–40), Orange Web (21–40 with ongoing releases), Red (41–80), Maroon (81–200), Diamond (201–500), and Sapphire (501–1,000). Criticality is measured by the type of thing that could be at risk. Criticality values include comfort, discretionary money, essential money, and life.

Crystal Clear   A relatively relaxed and easy-going approach to development using a small team (1–6 people) and low criticality. Crystal Clear defines only three required roles: sponsor, senior designer, and programmer. See also *Crystal*.

Crystal Orange   A development approach that is slightly larger and more formal than Crystal Yellow. Projects may add the new roles business analyst, project manager, architect, and team leader. They also add requirements, tracking, a release schedule, object models, code reviews, acceptance testing, and more formal delivery. Total team size is typically 21–40 people.

Crystal Yellow   A development approach that is slightly larger and more formal than Crystal Clear. These projects adopt new practices above the roles defined by Crystal Clear, including easy communication, code ownership, feedback, automated testing, a mission statement, and more formal increments. Total team size is typically 7–20 people.

customer or client   A person for whom a project is being built. Typically, the customer defines requirements and verifies that the finished application meets those requirements. In some models, the customer also provides feedback during development.

cutover   The process of moving users to a new application.

cyber insurance   Covers damages related to cyberattacks such as legal counsel, forensics, losses due to fraudulent transactions, and reparations to customers.

cypherpunk This person advocates widespread use of strong encryption as a means to promote social change.

DAD See *Disciplined Agile Delivery*.

daily scrum Scrum's version of a daily standup meeting. Also simply called a scrum. See also *stand-up meeting*.

data-centric architecture A design where the application is centered around some kind of database.

data tier The server tier in a three-tier architecture.

data warehouse A secondary database that holds older data for analysis. In some applications, you may want to analyze the data and store modified or aggregated forms in the warehouse instead of keeping every outdated record in the production database.

database administrator (DBA) Maintains the team's databases, possibly including the documentation and source code databases.

database-centric architecture See *data-centric architecture*.

database designer Specialist at designing databases.

DBA See *database administrator*.

DDoS See *distributed denial-of-service attack*.

decision tree A logical tree data structure that helps you think about a problem's solution space.

declarative programming language A language where you specify the result that you want and the program figures out how to get that result.

decomposition In a V-model project, the steps on the left side of the V that break the application down into pieces that you can implement.

decorator A design pattern that attaches additional features to an object.

deep dive See *spike*.

deep learning Uses a neural network with several layers that process increasingly abstract features.

defect Incorrect feature in an application. Defects can be broadly grouped into two categories: bugs and changes.

defensive programming The idea that the code should work no matter what kind of garbage is passed into it for data. The code should work and produce some kind of result no matter what. See also *offensive programming*.

denial-of-service attack (DoS) Tries to make a server or network unusable, usually by flooding it with bogus requests.

deployer In Feature-Driven Development, someone who handles deployment.

deployment The process of delivering a finished application to the users. See also *implementation*.

deployment diagram In UML, a diagram that describes the deployment of artifacts (files, scripts, executables, and the like) on nodes (hardware devices or execution environments that can execute artifacts).

derive To subclass a child class from a parent class. The child class inherits properties, methods, and events from the parent class.

design inspection A review of a design to look for problems before writing code to implement the design. In Feature-Driven Development, a chief programmer holds a design inspection before the team implements the design.

design package In Feature-Driven Development, the result of a design-by-feature phase. The design package includes a description of the package, sequence diagrams showing how the features will work, alternatives, an updated object model, and method prologues.

design pattern In object-oriented programming, an arrangement of classes that interact to perform some common and useful task. Similar to an algorithm for objects.

developer Someone who participates in the project development. Sometimes this term is used interchangeably with programmer.

development manager In Feature-Driven Development, someone who manages day-to-day development activities.

DevOps The development process with operations planning integrated into the process from the beginning.

DevSecOps The development process with security and operations planning integrated into the process from the beginning.

direct manipulation When the user performs "physical" manipulation of objects on the screen—for example, drag and drop.

Disciplined Agile Delivery (DAD) A development framework that incorporates features of UP, scrum, XP, kanban, Lean, and others. It uses the three UP phases: inception, construction, and transition.

distributed architecture A design where different parts of the application run on different processors and may run at the same time. The processors could be on different computers scattered across the network, or they could be different cores on a single computer.

distributed denial-of-service attack (DDoS) A denial-of-service attack that comes from multiple computers, possibly in a botnet.

divide and conquer An algorithmic approach were you repeatedly divide a problem into pieces and then either solve or discard pieces.

domain expert A customer, user, executive champion, or other person who knows about the project domain and how the finished application should work. Also called subject matter expert (SME).

domain manager In Feature-Driven Development, someone who leads the domain experts and provides a single point of contact to resolve domain issues.

domain walk through   In Feature-Driven Development, a walk-through of a scenario by a domain expert to verify that the scenario is correct and to answer questions for the developers about the scenario.

dongle   A small device that plugs into your computer (often through a USB port) so your program can verify that the device is present.

don't repeat yourself (DRY) principle   In programming, a rule of thumb that says if you need to write the same piece of code twice, then you should extract it into a separate method that you can call from multiple places so you don't have to write it a third time (or a fourth time, or a fifth time, and so on).

DoS   See *denial-of-service attack*.

double extortion scheme   Ransomware where the attacker encrypts files and also threatens to release sensitive data to other hackers or the public.

driver   In pair programming, the programmer who types.

DRY   See *don't repeat yourself (DRY) principle*.

DSDM   See *Dynamic Systems Development Method*.

dynamic programming   An algorithm that uses saved partial results.

Dynamic Systems Development Method (DSDM)   An agile framework designed with a more business-oriented focus. It can be used to add extra business control to other development models. It uses the phase's pre-project, project life cycle (which includes study, functional modeling, design and build, and implementation) and post-project.

EDA   See *event-driven architecture*.

edge computing   The idea of moving computation and data storage closer to data sources such as IoT devices to reduce response time, centralized storage requirements, and network usage.

eight-queens problem   A problem where you must find a way to position eight queens on a chessboard so they cannot attack each other.

eleet   See *elite hacker*.

elite hacker, eleet, leet, or 1337   A hacker with mad ninja skillz. The term is sometimes used ironically.

embarrassingly parallel   A problem that naturally breaks into pieces that have little to do with each other, so coordinating among parallel processes is easy.

environment   The hardware, network, operating system, other applications, and other features that are present where the application runs. This includes the users' computers, networks, printers, other applications, and physical environment (chairs, lamps, coffee machines, and so forth).

ergonomics   The study of people in their work environments, particularly looking for ways to reduce injuries such as severe eyestrain, carpal tunnel syndrome, computer back, trigger finger, mouse shoulder, tech neck, BlackBerry thumb, iPad hand, Wiiitis, and Nintendinitis.

event   In object-oriented programming, an event occurs to notify the application that something interesting occurred. For example, the user might have clicked a button or a timer might have expired.

event-driven architecture (EDA)   A design where various parts of the system respond to events as they occur.

everything as a service (XaaS)   A category of cloud-based tools that provide remote services for things such as storage, computing, security, and e-commerce.

evolutionary prototype   A prototype that evolves over time with new features added and the existing features improved until the prototype eventually becomes the finished application.

exception   An unexpected condition in a program such as a divide by zero or trying to access a missing file. If the code doesn't catch and handle the exception, the program crashes.

execution   See *execution specification*.

execution specification   In a UML sequence diagram, a gray or white rectangle that represents a participant doing something. Also called an execution or activation.

executive champion   The highest-ranking executive who supports the project.

executive sponsor   See *executive champion*.

exhaustive search   The strategy of examining every possible solution to find the best one.

expert system   See *rule-based architecture*.

exploit   A program that exploits a bug in the system. Also called a sploit.

Extreme Programming (XP)   A development model that takes typical programming practices (such as code reviews) to extremes (pair programming).

façade   A design pattern that provides an interface to a (usually complicated) subsystem.

facilitator   A person who generally makes everyone else's life easier and makes the team work more smoothly.

factory method   A method that creates a new instance of a class.

FakeApp   A counterfeit program that looks like some other program.

FDD   See *Feature-Driven Development*.

Feature-Driven Development (FDD)   An iterative and incremental development model that was designed to work with large teams. The large teams mean this model requires more roles. It starts with two phases: develop a model and build a feature list. It then iterates three more phases: plan-by feature, design-by feature, and build-by feature.

feature list   In Feature-Driven Development, a prioritized list of features that the application should have.

feature team   In Feature-Driven Development, when a new feature requires changes to several classes, the class owners are assembled into a feature team to study and implement the changes.

field   In a relational database, a single piece of data in a record. For example, each record in a `Students` table would contain a `FirstName` field. Also called a column.

fifth generation language (5GL)   A language where programs solve problems by using rules and constraints rather than by following an algorithm given to it by a programmer.

firewall   Monitors incoming and outgoing network traffic to enforce security rules and scan attachments for spam and viruses.

first class app   A program that occupies much of the screen for long periods at a time, such as a browser or word processor. Users interact with these apps enough to quickly become advanced users.

first generation language (1GL)   Machine code consisting of a big pile of 0s and 1s.

first normal form (1NF)   The least normalized level of a table in a relational database. To be in 1NF, the table should satisfy the following conditions:

1.   Each column must have a unique name.

2.   The order of the rows and columns doesn't matter.

3.   Each column must have a single data type.

4.   No two rows can contain identical values.

5.   Each column must contain a single value.

6.   Columns cannot contain repeating groups.

fishbone diagram   See *Ishikawa diagram*.

Fishikawa diagram   See *Ishikawa diagram*.

five-second rule   The idea that all interactive tasks should complete within five seconds.

flyweight   A design pattern used to allow objects to share common data so they can remain relatively small.

foreign key   In a relational database, a set of one or more fields in one table with values that uniquely define a record in another table. The table containing the foreign key is the child table, and the table that contains the uniquely identified record is the parent table. See also *foreign key constraint*.

foreign key constraint   When two tables are related by a foreign key, a foreign key constraint requires that a child record cannot exist unless the corresponding record exists in the parent table. For example, a `StudentAddress` record might not be allowed to contain a `State` value that isn't defined in the `States` lookup table.

formjacking   When an attacker inserts malicious code into a copy of a website's forms.

fourth generation language (4GL)   Provides a higher level of abstraction than a 3GL. These tend to be more specialized, focusing on a particular domain—for example, SQL or MATLAB.

function point metric   In function point calculations, a metric used to calculate a project's function points, such as the number of inputs and the number of outputs.

function point normalization   Dividing a metric by the project's function points to allow you to compare projects of different sizes and complexities.

function point value Calculated as a weighted average of the raw FP and the CAV.

functional programming language Defines programs and methods as mathematical functions.

functional prototype A prototype that looks like a finished application (or part of one) but that doesn't necessarily work the way the real application will. For example, it could use faked data or predetermined responses to user actions.

functional requirements Detailed statements of the project's wanted capabilities. They're similar to the user requirements but may also include things that the users won't see directly, such as interfaces to other applications.

Gantt chart A kind of bar chart that shows a schedule for a collection of related tasks. Bar lengths indicate task durations. Arrows show the relationships between tasks and their predecessors.

GIGO Garbage in, garbage out.

gradual cutover Deployment technique where you install the new application for some users while others continue working with the existing system. You test the system for the first users and when everything's working correctly, you start moving other users to the new system until everyone has been moved.

gray-box test A combination white-box test and black-box test. The tester knows some but not all of the internals of the method being tested. The partial knowledge lets the tester design some specific tests to attack the code.

greedy algorithm An algorithm that moves toward the best solution locally at every step. For example, to reach the top of a mountain at night, you can try always moving uphill. Also called a hill-climbing algorithm.

green hat A noob hacker who may not understand the consequences of their actions.

grey hat (gray hat, greyhat) Usually similar to white hats but they break into systems without permission.

hacktivist Uses hacking as a form of civil disobedience.

halting problem Given a program and set of inputs, the problem of predicting whether the program will eventually halt.

helper or servant A design pattern that uses a package of helper methods that can be used by multiple classes.

heuristic An algorithm that gives a good solution for a problem but that doesn't guarantee to give you the best solution possible.

high-level language 3GLs, 4GLs, and 5GLs.

hill-climbing algorithm See *greedy algorithm*.

horizontal prototype A prototype that demonstrates a lot of the application's features but with little depth.

human factors engineer Someone who studies human-computer interactions to help design user interfaces, workflow, and other issues that can improve end-user effectiveness. Also called a user interface designer.

IDE   See *integrated development environment*.

idiom   An agreed upon convention. For example, a save icon that looks like a floppy disk even though no one uses floppy disks anymore.

IEEE   Institute of Electrical and Electronics Engineers.

IEEE-CS   Institute of Electrical and Electronics Engineers, Computer Society.

imperative programming language   A language where the program issues commands to the computer to tell it what to do.

implementation   When used by programmers, this term usually means writing the code. When used by managers, this often means deployment.

implementation requirements   Temporary features that are needed to transition to using the new system but that will be later discarded.

increment   The result of a single iteration of an incremental development model. The increment is a fully tested piece of software suitable for release to the users.

incremental deployment   Deployment where you release the new system's features to the users gradually. First, you install one tool (possibly using staged deployment or gradual cutover to ease the pain). After the users are used to the new tool, you give them the next tool. You continue until all the tools have been deployed.

incremental development   A development model where you initially provide only some features at full fidelity. Over time, you add more features (always at full fidelity) until all features have been implemented at full fidelity.

incremental prototyping   A development model where you build a collection of prototypes that separately demonstrate the finished application's features. You then combine the prototypes (or at least their code) to build the finished application.

incremental waterfall model   A development model that uses a series of waterfall cascades. Each cascade ends with the delivery of a usable application called an increment. Also called the multiwaterfall model.

indicator   A metric that you can use to predict the project's future. For example, if the metric "comments per KLOC" is 3, that may be an indicator that the project will be hard to maintain.

information radiator   See *big board*.

inheritance hierarchy   In object-oriented programming, a "family tree" showing inheritance relationships among classes. In a language that doesn't support multiple inheritance, the relationships form a hierarchy.

Insider, malicious insider, whistleblower   A hacker who has inside information about an organization that makes hacking easier.

insider threat   A threat posed by an employee, former employee, contractor, vendor, or someone else who has inside knowledge of the business.

installation   See *deployment*.

instance   An object created from a class.

instrumentation   Code added to a program by a profiler to allow it to track the program's performance.

integrated development environment (IDE)   An environment for building, compiling, and debugging software. An IDE may include other tools such as source code control, profiling, code editors with syntax highlighting and auto-completion, and more.

integration   In a V-model project, the steps on the right side of the V that work back up to the conceptual top of the application.

integration test   A test that verifies that a new piece of code works with the rest of the system. It checks that the new code can call existing code and that the existing code can call the new code.

interaction diagram   In UML, a category of activity diagram that includes sequence diagrams, communication diagrams, timing diagrams, and interaction overview diagrams.

interaction overview diagram   In UML, basically an activity diagram where the nodes can be frames that contain other kinds of diagrams. Those nodes can contain sequence, communication, timing, and other interaction overview diagrams. That lets you show more detail for nodes that represent complicated tasks.

Internet of Behaviors (IoB)   The study of how and why people use technology to purchase things.

Internet of Things (IoT)   Networked objects that have sensors, processors, and other technology—for example, smartwatches, fitness trackers, smart toasters, and medical sensors.

interview puzzles   Once incorrectly believed to be useful for identifying people who would make good programmers. Today these are seldom used for interviews, but they do make interesting puzzles.

invariant   A state of the program and its data that should remain unchanged over some period of time. Often used in assertions.

IoB   See *Internet of Behaviors*.

IoT   See *Internet of Things*.

Ishikawa diagram   Named after Kaoru Ishikawa, a diagram that shows possible causes of effects that you want to study, such as excessive bugs, delays, and other failures in the development process. Also called fishbone diagrams, Fishikawa diagrams, and cause-and-effect diagrams.

iteration 0   A pseudo-iteration that includes startup tasks that must be performed before the project's code development starts, such as planning, initial requirements gathering, and building the development environment.

iterative development   A development model where you initially provide all of the application's features at a low fidelity. Over time, you improve the features' fidelity, occasionally releasing improved versions of the application until all features have been implemented at full fidelity.

iterator   A design pattern that provides a way to access the elements in a collection without exposing the collection's underlying details.

James Martin RAD   A specific RAD development model that uses four phases: requirements planning, user design, construction, and cutover. The user design and construction phases iterate.

JBGE   See *just barely good enough*.

JIT   See *just-in-time*.

joint code ownership   See *shared code ownership*.

junkware   See *crapware*.

just barely good enough (JBGE)   The idea that you should include only the bare minimum of comments and documentation to get the job done. Note that JBGE is JB better than not GE. (Just barely better than not good enough.)

just-in-time (JIT)   An inventory management practice where inventory items are supplied just in time for use to minimize inventory levels.

kanban (production chain)   A just-in-time technique that uses kanban cards to indicate when a production station needs more parts. When a station is out of parts (or is running low), a kanban card is sent to a supply station to request more parts.

kanban (software engineering)   An agile methodology where a team member who finishes their current item takes the next highest priority item from the project's backlog. Kanban seeks to restrict the amount of work in progress at any given time.

kanban board   A big board. (See *big board*.) Typically, columns indicate each task's status. Columns might be labeled Backlog, Ready, Coding, Testing, Approval, and Done. In some variations, rows indicate the person assigned to each task.

key   In a relational database, a set of one or more fields that uniquely identifies a record.

keylogger   Spyware that sends your keystrokes to the attacker.

KLOC   Kilo (1,000) lines of code.

knapsack problem   A problem where you must fill a knapsack with a fixed size to maximize the value of the items selected.

knight's tour problem   A problem where you must move a knight so it visits every square on a chess board without visiting any square twice. In the closed knight's tour problem, the knight must end so it can move back to its starting point in the next move.

knowledge base system   See *rule-based architecture*.

language guru   Someone who is an expert in the programming language, technology, and other arcane items being used by the team. The other developers call on this person as needed. Also called a language lawyer.

language lawyer   See *language guru*.

Las Vegas algorithm   An algorithm that always either produces a correct result or tells you that it cannot, but its runtime may be uncertain.

lazy initialization   A design pattern technique that delays an object's creation until the object is needed.

Lean   See *Lean Software Development*.

Lean Software Development (LSD)   An agile development methodology that focuses on removing waste (such as unclear requirements, repetition, and unnecessary meetings) from the development process.

learning system   A system that "learns" from training data, usually with little or no human supervision. Also called machine learning (ML).

leet   A "language" where letters are replaced with different letters and numbers that look somewhat similar. See also *elite hacker*.

lifeline   In a UML sequence diagram, a vertical dashed line that represents an object's existence.

linear undo   The normal "undo the previous action" model.

load test   A test that simulates many users all running simultaneously to measure the application's performance under stress.

logic bomb   A program that takes action when a particular set of circumstances occurs.

logic tier   The middle tier in a three-tier architecture. This tier usually contains business logic.

lookup table   In a relational database, a table that contains values that are just used as foreign keys.

low-code/no-code (LCNC)   Platforms that allow non-programmers to build software.

low-level language   1GLs and 2GLs.

LSD   See *Lean Software Development*.

machine learning (ML)   See *learning system*.

magic number   A value that just appears in the code with no explanation. For example, it might represent an error code or database connection status. Use constants and named variables instead of magic numbers to make the code easier to read and understand.

malvertising   See *crapware*.

malware   Short for "malicious software."

man-in-the-middle (MITM) attack   Attack where an attacker intercepts a private communication. The attacker may simply eavesdrop or may modify messages. (The *M* can also stand for "monster," "machine," "monkey," or "meddler." Also called person-in-the-middle.)

mediator   A design pattern that uses an object through which other objects can interact.

member   In object-oriented programming, a general name for a class's properties, methods, and events.

memento   A design patterns that uses an object to capture another object's internal state so it can be restored to that state later.

metaphor   A story about something that the user understands that parallels some feature of a program to make using that feature easier (for example, the wastebasket/recycle bin).

method   In object-oriented programming, a piece of code that makes an object do something.

method prologue   A description of a method that includes its purpose, input and output parameters, return type, possible exceptions (ways the method can fail), and assumptions.

metric   A value that you use to study some aspect of a project. A metric can be an attribute (such as the number of bugs) or a calculated value (such as the number of bugs per line of code). See also *attribute* and *indicator*.

MFA   See *multifactor authentication*.

microservices   A type of service-oriented architecture that uses loosely coupled lightweight services.

MITM   See *man-in-the-middle*.

ML   See *learning system*.

model-view-controller (MVC)   A design pattern that defines three kinds of classes that work together. The model class represents the data. The view (or views) displays some sort of view of the model. The controller lets the user modify the model.

model-view-presenter (MVP)   A refinement of the MVP pattern. The model represents the data and views display a representation of the data as before. The view is also responsible for capturing user events. The presenter acts as a mediator between the view and the model.

model-view-view/model (MVVM)   Somewhat similar to MVP. A model represents the data, a view displays the data, and the view/model sits in between much as the presenter does in the MVP pattern. The biggest difference is that the view does not have a direct reference to the view/model. Instead, it forwards user interface information via some sort of binding such as bound properties or events.

module   Groups related classes, methods, or other objects into a single entity.

monolithic architecture   A design where a single program does everything.

Monte Carlo algorithm   An algorithm that sometimes produces an incorrect result, but usually with a small probability.

MOSCOW (or MoSCoW)   A scale for prioritizing application features. The initials stand for Must, Should, Could, and Won't.

multifactor authentication (MFA)   A system that uses multiple forms of media such as a password, dongle, and text message to verify someone's identity. See also *two-factor authentication*.

multiple inheritance   In object-oriented programming, when a child class inherits from multiple parent classes. (Most object-oriented languages do not support multiple inheritance.)

multiply recursive algorithm   An algorithm that calls itself recursively more than once. See also *multiply recursive algorithm* and *multiply recursive algorithm*.

multitier architecture   A design that uses multiple tiers to allow a client to use services provided by a server. Examples include client/server architectures, two-tier architectures, and three-tier architectures.

multiwaterfall model   See *incremental waterfall model*.

MVC   See *model-view-controller*.

MVVM   See *model-view-view/model*.

N-tier architecture   See *multitier architecture*.

nagware See *crapware*.

narrow AI See *weak AI*.

natural language processing (NLP) The ability of the computer to understand written or spoken human language.

navigator In pair programming, the programmer who watches as the driver types. Also called an observer or pointer.

neural network See *artificial neural network*.

neuron A small part of a neural network. Also called an artificial neuron.

NIHS See *not invented here syndrome*.

NLP See *natural language processing*.

node In a UML deployment diagram, a hardware device on which an artifact is deployed.

nonfunctional prototype A prototype that looks like an application but that doesn't actually do anything.

nonfunctional requirements Statements about the quality of an application's behavior or constraints on how it produces a wanted result such as the application's performance, reliability, and security characteristics.

nonlinear undo Lets you undo and redo actions out of their original order.

noob, newbie, newb, n00b, nub Derogatory terms for a beginner at hacking, gaming, programming, or anything else.

normalization For metrics, performing some calculation on a metric to account for possible differences in project size or complexity. Two general approaches are size normalization and function point normalization. (See also *size normalization* and *function point normalization*.) In database design, the process of rearranging tables to put them into standard (normal) forms that prevent anomalies.

not invented here syndrome (NIHS) In programming, the mistake of thinking you need to rewrite a piece of code just because someone else wrote it and it doesn't work the way you would have written it.

null object A design pattern that uses a default object in place of a null reference.

object An instance of a class.

object composition In object-oriented programming, a technique where an object is composed of other objects. Sometimes used to simulate multiple inheritance.

object diagram In UML, a diagram that focuses on a particular set of objects and their relationships at a specific time.

object model A model showing the classes that make up an application, the class details (such as properties, methods, and events), and interactions among the classes.

object-oriented language A programming language that lets you define classes that you can then use as blueprints to make instances of those objects.

object pool   A group of objects that can be recycled and reused.

observer (design pattern)   A design pattern where an object should receive notification when another object's state has changed. Also called publish/subscribe.

observer (pair programming)   See *navigator*.

offensive programming   The idea that the code immediately flags an error if it receives unexpected inputs so that you can decide whether they are valid. See also *defensive programming*.

Open Unified Process (OpenUP)   An open-source tool built by the Eclipse Foundation to help in using the Unified Process development model.

OpenUP   See *Open Unified Process*.

Osborn method   A basic brainstorming approach developed by Alex Faickney Osborn.

over refinement   In object-oriented programming, a design problem that occurs when you refine a class hierarchy unnecessarily, making too many classes that make the code complicated and confusing.

package diagram   In UML, a diagram that describes relationships among the packages that make up a system. For example, if one package in the system uses features provided by another package, then the diagram would show the first "importing" the second.

pair programming   An Extreme Programming practice where two (or three) programmers work together at the same computer. The driver or pilot types while the observer, navigator, or pointer watches and reviews each line of code as it is typed.

parallel programming   When multiple processors perform calculations at the same time to achieve a goal.

parent class   A class from which a child class is derived. The child class inherits properties, methods, and events from the parent class.

parent table   See *foreign key*.

password dongle   See *dongle*.

password manager   A program that stores passwords for other programs.

password stuffing   See *credential stuffing*.

Pepsi paradox   The phenomenon that people sometimes prefer one thing initially but then grow to like it less over time. In software engineering, users initially like beginner features but eventually they become more advanced and prefer advanced features.

perimeter security   Security measures such as firewalls that try to prevent an attacker from entering the system or network from the outside.

person in the middle (PITM)   See *man-in-the-middle*.

PERT   Program Evaluation and Review Technique. See *PERT chart*.

PERT chart   A graph that uses nodes (circles or boxes) and links (arrows) to show the precedence relationships among the tasks in a project.

phishing   A contact (such as an email or voicemail) that tries to trick you into thinking it is a legitimate contact in order to make you do something that you normally wouldn't, such as clicking a link or revealing passwords.

phreak   Someone who hacks telephone networks or networks in general.

pilot   See *driver*.

PITM   Person in the middle. See *man-in-the-middle*.

planning game   A game where team members use cards containing user stories and try to see how many cards they can fit into a release. There are two kinds of planning games: release planning and iteration planning.

planning poker   In scrum, a game where developers use card decks based on the Fibonacci numbers to estimate the amount of work for the project's tasks. Cards might have numbers ace, 2, 3, 5, 8, and king; or 0, 1, 2, 3, 5, 8, 13, 21, 34, 55, and 89; or 0, ½, 1, 2, 3, 5, 8, 13, 20, 40, and 100. Also called scrum poker.

point of no return   The point during a project where the expense of canceling a project is greater than the expense of moving forward.

point-release   A minor application build that isn't necessarily released to the customers.

pointer   See *navigator*.

polymorphism   The ability to treat a child object as if it were actually from a parent class. For example, it lets you treat a `Student` object as if it were a `Person` object because a `Student` is a type of `Person`.

potentially shippable increment (PSI)   In scrum, the result of a sprint. This is a fully tested application that could be shipped to the users.

predictive development model   A development model where you predict in advance what needs to be done and then you go out and do it. Also called Big Design Up Front (BDUF).

presentation tier   The client tier in a multitier architecture.

procedural programming language   An imperative language that lets you group pieces of code into procedures.

process metric   A metric designed to measure your organization's development process. They are collected over a long period across many projects and used to fine-tune the software engineering process.

product backlog   In scrum, the list of features not yet implemented by the application.

product burndown chart   In scrum, a graph showing the amount of work remaining in a whole project over time. Also called a release burndown chart.

product metric   See *project metric*.

product owner   Someone who represents the customers, users, and other stakeholders and for whom the application is being built. Sometimes called the sponsor.

profiler   A program that monitors another program to identify the parts that are slow, that use the most memory, or that otherwise might be bottlenecks.

programmer   An underpaid, overworked person who writes the code and complains about excessive management and restrictive coding standards.

progressive web apps (PWA)   Web-based applications that run on any compliant browser.

project manager   Monitors the project's progress to ensure that work is heading in the right direction at an acceptable pace. Meets with customers and other stakeholders to verify that the finished product meets their requirements. If the development model allows changes, the project manager ensures that changes are made and tracked in an organized manner so they don't get lost and don't overwhelm the rest of the team.

project manager/tracker   A person who tracks schedules, monitors progress, and generally makes sure the project stays on track.

project metric   Metrics that measure and track the current project to predict future results for that project.

property   In object-oriented programming, an attribute of an object that helps define the object's characteristics.

prototype   A mockup of some or all of the application to let the developers and customers study an aspect of the system. Typically, a software prototype is a program that mimics part of the application that you want to build.

prototype (design pattern)   A design pattern where an instance of an object with default properties filled in is used as a template for other objects.

proxy   A design pattern where an object provides a placeholder for another object to control access to that object.

prune   To remove branches from a decision tree to make it smaller and therefore make searching it faster.

pseudocode   Text that looks a lot like a programming language but isn't one. You can use pseudocode to study how a piece of code would work if you wrote it in an actual programming language such as C#, Java, or Visual Basic.

PSI   See *potentially shippable increment*.

publish/subscribe   See *observer (design pattern)*.

quality manager   Someone who ensures the application's quality. This person tracks bug reports, test results, and reviews; uses statistical methods to estimate quality; defines the project's quality procedures (such as testing and review guidelines); and uses other techniques used to improve quality.

race condition   In distributed computing, a situation in which multiple processes interfere with each other when one incorrectly overwrites the results of another.

RAD   See *rapid application development*.

raise   In object-oriented programming, an object *raises* an event to notify the application that something interesting occurred.

random solution   A heuristic that just makes a random selection. Random solutions are often not very good, but you can sometimes find an acceptable solution by examining many random solutions.

randomized algorithm   An algorithm that relies on randomness in some way. See also *Monte Carlo algorithm*, *Las Vegas algorithm*, and *Atlantic City algorithm*.

ransomware   Malicious software that encrypts files and demands payment to unlock the files.

rapid application development (RAD)   Development models that emphasize producing code and deemphasize planning. These models produce code iteratively and incrementally as quickly as possible. RAD principles include small teams, frequent customer interaction, frequent integration and testing, and short timeboxed iterations.

Rational Unified Process (RUP)   IBM's version of the Unified Process.

raw FP value   In function point calculations, the sum of the function point metrics multiplied by their complexity factors.

record   In a relational database, a single set of values in a table. For example, a particular student's data would be contained in a record in the Students table. Also called rows or tuples.

recursive algorithm   An algorithm that calls itself. See also *recursive algorithm*.

red hat   Hackers who attack black hats, possibly using illegal means.

refactor   The process of rearranging and rewriting code to make it easier to understand, debug, and maintain.

refinement   In object-oriented programming, the process of breaking a parent class into multiple subclasses to capture some difference between objects in the class.

regression test   A test that exercises the entire application to verify that a new piece of code didn't break anything.

relational database   A database that stores related data in rows and columns in tables.

relatively prime   Two integers are relatively prime (or coprime) if they have no common factors other than 1. For example, $21 = 3 \times 7$ and $8 = 2 \times 2 \times 2$ are relatively prime because they have no common factors other than 1. By definition -1 and 1 are relatively prime to every integer, and they are the only numbers relatively prime to 0.

release burndown chart   See *product burndown chart*.

release manager   In Feature-Driven Development, someone who gathers information from the chief programmers to track the project's progress.

requirement validation   The process of making sure that the requirements say the right things.

requirement verification   The process of checking that the finished application actually satisfies the requirements.

requirements   The features that an application must provide to be successful.

responsive design   Design that adjusts accordingly to the size of the user's device.

retrospective meeting   In scrum, a meeting after a sprint where the scrum master and the project team discuss the sprint and ask the following questions: (1) What went well and how can we make that happen again? (2) What went poorly and how can we avoid that in the future? (3) How can we improve future sprints?

rootkit   Set of programs that provides access to part of the computer.

row   See *record*.

rule-based architecture   A design that uses a collection of rules to decide what to do next. These systems are sometimes called expert systems or knowledge-based systems.

RUP   See *Rational Unified Process*.

sashimi   A variation on the waterfall model where phases overlap. Also called sashimi waterfall and waterfall with overlapping phases.

SCA   Service Component Architecture.

scrapyard   Hypothetical clipboard system that lets you save and restore many items.

scribe   Someone who keeps records of requirements, agreements, assumptions, and other important facts discovered at meetings, particularly at DSDM workshops.

script kiddie, skiddie, skid   Derogatory term for someone who breaks into systems by using scripts and prepackaged tools rather than by "honest" hacking.

scrum   See *daily scrum*.

scrum   A development methodology that uses frequent small increments to build an application iteratively and incrementally.

scrum master   In scrum, someone who helps the team follow scrum practices, challenges the team to improve itself, and removes obstacles for the team.

scrum poker   See *planning poker*.

SDLC   See *software development life cycle*.

second generation language (2GL)   An assembly language.

second normal form (2NF)   The second level of normalization for a table in a relational database. A table is in 2NF if it satisfies the following conditions:

1.   It is in 1NF.
2.   All nonkey fields depend on all key fields.

self-organizing team   A team that has the flexibility and authority to find its own methods for achieving its goals. Team members are motivated to take work without waiting for it to be assigned. They take responsibility for their work and track their own progress.

senior developer   A software engineering ninja that other developers can call on when they need help.

sequence diagram   In UML, a diagram that shows how objects collaborate in a particular scenario. This is similar to a communication diagram except a sequence diagram focuses on the sequence of messages and a communication diagram focuses more on the objects involved in the collaboration.

service   A self-contained program that runs on its own and provides some kind of service for its clients.

Service Component Architecture (SCA)   A set of specifications for service-oriented architecture defined by vendors such as IBM and Oracle. See *service-oriented architecture*.

service-oriented architecture (SOA)   A design similar to a component-based architecture except the pieces are implemented as services.

shared code ownership   In Extreme Programming, code ownership is joint so anyone can modify any piece of code if necessary to make changes or fix bugs. In contrast, in Feature-Driven Development, each class is owned by a class owner.

shift-left   The idea of moving a feature's design earlier in the project. For example, shift-left security makes security design start at the beginning of the project.

shift-left security   Shift-left applied to security. See also *shift-left*.

shift-left testing   Shift-left applied to testing. See also *shift-left*.

side effect   A non-obvious result of a method call that makes using the method confusing.

singleton   A design pattern where an object can have only one instance.

size normalization   For metrics, dividing a metric by an indicator of size such as lines of code or days of work. For example, bugs/KLOC tells you how buggy the code is normalized for the size of the project.

size-oriented normalization   See *size normalization*.

SME   Subject matter expert.

smishing   SMS phishing.

SMS   Short Message Service. (A text message.)

SOA   Service-oriented architecture.

soapbox   In planning poker, after each hand the people with the highest and lowest estimates are given a brief soapbox to explain why they feel their estimates are correct.

software development life cycle (SDLC)   All the tasks that go into a software engineering project from start to finish: requirements, design, implementation, and so forth. Also called the application development life cycle.

spear phishing   When a phishing attack is customized for the target to make it more attractive.

spike   A quick prototype, design, or piece of code that lets you explore some feature of an application in depth. Also called a deep dive.

spike solution   See *spike*.

spiral development model   A development model that uses a risk-driven approach to decide what development approach to take for each stage of the project. It uses four phases: planning, risk analysis, engineering, and evaluation.

sploit   See *exploit*.

sponsor   See *product owner*.

spoofing   Sending a communication that pretends to be from someone else. For example, when an email includes a fake message header.

sprint   In scrum, the name given to the timeboxed incremental iterations. Typically, a sprint is 30 days, although some projects use shorter sprints of one, two, or three weeks.

sprint backlog   In scrum, the list of features not yet implemented by a sprint.

sprint burndown chart   In scrum, a graph showing the amount of work remaining in a sprint over time.

sprint planning meeting   In scrum, a timeboxed (typically a maximum of four hours) meeting before a sprint begins to decide what features should move from the project backlog into the sprint backlog so that they will be implemented during the sprint.

sprint review meeting   In scrum, after a sprint ends, this is the meeting where the team presents the potentially shippable increment to the product owner, who verifies that it meets the sprint's goals.

spyware   Malicious software that collects information and sends it to an attacker.

SQL injection   When an attacker inserts data into a field to make the program compose an SQL statement that does something incorrect such as providing unauthorized access.

staged deployment   Deployment that begins with building the application in a fully functional staging environment so you can practice deployment until you've worked out all of the kinks.

stakeholder   Someone who has a stake in the outcome of the project. Typically, this includes users, customers (if those are different from users), sponsors, managers, and development team members.

stakeholder requirements   These describe the goals of the project from the stakeholders' point of view. This term is often used interchangeably with "user requirements."

stand-up   See *stand-up meeting*.

stand-up meeting   In Extreme Programming, a brief (15 minutes or less) daily meeting where team members say what they did since the last meeting, what they hope to do before the next meeting, and any problems they foresee in getting that work done.

state   An internal representation of an object's state so the object can act differently when its state changes. In bug tracking, a bug's state tracks its progress through the system. Example states include New, Assigned, Reproduced (or Verified), Cannot Reproduce, Pending, Fixed, Tested, Deferred, Closed, and Reopened.

state diagram (or state transition diagram)   A directed graph where nodes represent states and links represent transitions between states.

state machine diagram   In UML, a diagram that shows the states through which an object passes in response to various events. States are represented by rounded rectangles. Arrows indicate transitions from one state to another. Sometimes annotations on the arrows indicate what causes a transition.

state-sponsored hacker   Hackers supported by a government to hack rival governments or businesses in rival nations.

stepwise refinement   See *top-down design*.

story points   The number of points assigned to a story by planning poker. See *planning poker*.

strategy   A design pattern where a class encapsulates an algorithm so you can use different algorithms interchangeably.

structure diagram   In UML, a diagram that describes things that will be in the system you are designing. For example, a class diagram shows relationships among the classes that will be used to represent objects in the system such as inventory items, customers, and invoices.

subject matter expert (SME)   See *domain expert*.

suicide hacker   Someone who causes chaos and disruption without regard to the damage they do or possible consequences such as jail time.

system administrator   See *administrator*.

system integrator   Someone who builds and tests the interfaces between the application and other applications.

system test   An end-to-end run-through of the whole system. A system test exercises every part of the system to discover as many bugs as possible.

table   In a relational database, a set of records that all contain the same fields, although each record's fields may contain different values. For example, a Student table would contain data about students.

TCO   See *total cost of ownership*.

TDD   See *test-driven development*.

team lead   See *team leader*.

team leader   The leader of a programming team, particularly if a large project is broken into separate teams. Typically, a team leader is a more experienced developer. Also called a team lead.

team member   A member of the development team. Depending on the development model, this can include many different kinds of participants. The team may include customer representatives in addition to developers.

technical lead   Highest-ranking technical person on a project.

technical writer   Someone who writes online and printed documentation and training materials.

template   A design pattern where a class forms an outline of an algorithm so subclasses can redefine selected steps.

test-driven development (TDD)   A programming technique where you (1) write a test to verify a feature, (2) verify that the program fails the test, (3) write code to implement the feature, and (4) verify that the code passes the test.

test-first development (TFD)   A programming technique where you write all of the unit tests for a piece of code before you write the code. You then write all of the code, run the tests, and fix the code if it doesn't pass the tests.

tester, test engineer, test designer   Someone who earns a salary by breaking your code.

TFD   See *test-first development*.

third generation language (3GL)   Works at a much higher level than 1GLs and 2GLs. More machine-independent and much easier for humans to understand. Python, C#, Delphi, etc.

third normal form (3NF)   The third level of normalization for a table in a relational database. A table is in 3NF if it satisfies the following conditions:

1.   It is in 2NF.
2.   It contains no transitive dependencies.

three-tier architecture   A design where a middle tier provides insulation between client and server tiers. The middle tier can map data between the format provided by the server and the format needed by the client.

throwaway prototype   A prototype that is used to study some aspect of a system and is then discarded.

time bomb   A program that takes action at a particular date and time.

timing diagram   In UML, a diagram that shows one or more objects' changes in state over time.

toolsmith   Someone who builds tools for use by other developers.

top-down design   A design process where you start with a high-level statement of a problem and then successively break the problem into more detailed and smaller pieces until the pieces are small enough to implement. Also called stepwise refinement.

total cost of ownership (TCO)   The total expected cost of a software application, including development costs, deployment costs, and maintenance costs over the expected lifetime of the application. (Often maintenance costs account for 75 percent of TCO.)

tracker   In XP, someone who monitors the team's progress and the team members' progress and calculates metrics.

trainer   Someone who trains the application's end users.

transient app   A program that is used infrequently and for short periods of time so users remain relative beginners.

transitive dependency   In a relational database, when a nonkey field's value depends on another nonkey field's value.

trolley problem   A series of thought experiments where you must choose between various bad options such as rerouting a trolley to kill one person instead of five.

tunnel problem   A thought experiment where you must choose between running over a child or crashing into the side of a tunnel and dying.

tuple   See *record*.

twin   A design pattern that allows a program to imitate multiple inheritance in programming languages that do not allow it.

two-factor authentication (2FA)   A system that uses two forms of media such as a password and text message to verify someone's identity. See also *multifactor authentication*.

two-tier architecture   A design where a client (often the user interface) is separated from the server (normally the database).

UI   See *user interface*.

UML   See *Unified Modeling Language*.

Unified Modeling Language (UML)   A collection of diagramming techniques for describing different aspects of a system.

Unified Process (UP)   An iterative and incremental development framework that involves four stages: inception, elaboration, construction, and transition.

unit test   A test that verifies the correctness of a specific piece of code.

UP   See *Unified Process*.

use case   A description of a series of interactions between actors. The actors can be users or parts of the application. A simple template might include a title, main success scenario, and extensions (other variations on the scenario). See also *user story*.

use case diagram   In UML, a diagram that represents a use case. Stick figures represent actors (someone or something that performs a task) connected to tasks represented by ellipses.

user experience (UX)   The user interface plus surrounding interactions to include the user's whole perception of the application and its "brand."

user interface (UI)   All of the things that the user sees and does with the application.

user interface designer   See *human factors engineer*.

user requirements   These describe how the project will be used by the eventual end users.

user story   A short story explaining how the system will let the user do something. See also *use case*.

UX   See *user experience*.

V-model   Basically, a waterfall model that's been bent into a V shape to emphasize that each task on the left side of the V corresponds to a task on the right side.

VBA   See *Visual Basic for Applications*.

velocity   In scrum, the amount of work the team can perform during a sprint, usually measured in story points per sprint.

version management   Managing the versions of items produced by the project such as requirements documents, designs, and, of course, source code. You should be able to retrieve any earlier version of those items if necessary. Also called version tracking, change management, and change tracking.

version tracking   See *version management*.

vertical prototype   A prototype that has little breadth but great depth.

virtual reality (VR)   An immersive three-dimensional environment.

virus   A malicious program embedded inside another program that replicates either by copying itself into another program or by creating a new copy of the program that contains the virus.

vishing   A voice phishing attack—for example via voice mail, a robocall, or a human caller.

visionary   Someone who has a clear vision about what an application should do.

visitor   A design pattern where an object represents an operation on a data structure so you can define new behaviors without modifying the data structure.

Visual Basic for Applications (VBA)   Macro programming language used to automate some Microsoft programs such as Excel, Word, and PowerPoint.

vulnerability disclosure program   A program that allows businesses to report cyberattacks and data breaches without fear of damaging press, possibly via confidential disclosure.

waterfall   A predictive development model where each project phase flows into the next.

waterfall with feedback   A variation on the waterfall model where each phase is allowed to feed information back to the preceding phase.

weak AI   A program that is intended to solve a single problem, such as driving a car or finding target demographics for magazine sales. Also called narrow AI.

web service   A service that provides a standardized web-based interface so that it is easy to invoke over the Internet.

whaling   Spear phishing aimed at a company executive such as a CEO, CFO, or other CxO.

white-box test   A test designed by someone who knows how the code works internally. That person can guess where problems may lie and create tests specifically to look for those problems.

white hat   An "ethical" hacker who breaks security for nonmalicious reasons with the target's permission.

Windows Presentation Foundation (WPF)   A Microsoft user interface framework used to create desktop applications.

WIP   See *work in progress*.

work in progress (WIP)   The work being done at a given moment, particularly in a kanban project.

working prototype   See *functional prototype*.

workshop facilitator   Someone who plans, runs, and encourages participation at workshops, particularly DSDM workshops.

worm   A program that tries to copy itself to other computers on a network.

WPF   See *Windows Presentation Foundation*.

XP   See *Extreme Programming*.

zero-day (0-day)   A vulnerability that is either unknown to security researchers or known but does not yet have a fix.

INDEX

J

N